LAW FOR
SOCIAL WORKERS

15TH EDITION

Helen Carr & David Goosey

OXFORD
UNIVERSITY PRESS

OXFORD
UNIVERSITY PRESS

Great Clarendon Street, Oxford, OX2 6DP,
United Kingdom

Oxford University Press is a department of the University of Oxford.
It furthers the University's objective of excellence in research, scholarship,
and education by publishing worldwide. Oxford is a registered trade mark of
Oxford University Press in the UK and in certain other countries

Twelfth edition 2013
Thirteenth edition 2015
Fourteenth edition 2017

Impression: 1

Published in the United States of America by Oxford University Press
198 Madison Avenue, New York, NY 10016, United States of America

British Library Cataloguing in Publication Data

Data available

Library of Congress Control Number: 2019937820

ISBN 978–0–19–882598–2

Printed in Great Britain by
Bell & Bain Ltd., Glasgow

LAW FOR
SOCIAL WORKERS

15TH EDITION

Helen Carr & David Goosey

OXFORD
UNIVERSITY PRESS

OXFORD
UNIVERSITY PRESS

Great Clarendon Street, Oxford, OX2 6DP,
United Kingdom

Oxford University Press is a department of the University of Oxford.
It furthers the University's objective of excellence in research, scholarship,
and education by publishing worldwide. Oxford is a registered trade mark of
Oxford University Press in the UK and in certain other countries

Twelfth edition 2013
Thirteenth edition 2015
Fourteenth edition 2017
Impression: 1

Published in the United States of America by Oxford University Press
198 Madison Avenue, New York, NY 10016, United States of America

British Library Cataloguing in Publication Data
Data available

Library of Congress Control Number: 2019937820

ISBN 978–0–19–882598–2

Printed in Great Britain by
Bell & Bain Ltd., Glasgow

As always, this edition contains details of new legislation, although the changes in law have slowed slightly as a result of the Parliamentary deadlock caused by Brexit. At the time of writing there appears to be no agreed way forward about how the UK should leave the European Union, or indeed whether it should leave at all. It is impossible for us to judge the full implications for social work law which would result from the UK's exit or otherwise. Only time will tell. Instead, we have steadfastly concentrated on the changes that we do know about. The Children and Social Work Act 2017 is now incorporated into Part 2 of the book, as are the changes to the law relating to information sharing and confidentiality which resulted from EU regulatory changes, the General Data Protection Regulations (GDPR), and the Data Protection Act 2018, in Part 1. In Part 3, references to the statutory guidance to the Care Act have been updated to reflect the latest version of the guidance. We have also provided an outline of the changes to the Deprivation of Liberty Safeguards (DoLS) proposed in the Mental Capacity (Amendment) Bill 2018. We have continued to expand the Toolkit, which we hope provides a useful resource for those beginning their social work careers. The online resources will have updates in due course.

As usual the edition has been a team effort. We want to thank in particular Leanne Taylor, a social worker with a law degree who sits on mental health tribunals, who has provided useful guidance on the law relating to mental health.

We are also very grateful to the production team at OUP, who have ensured that we have continued to make progress with this edition despite broken elbows and computer glitches and the inevitable competing demands on our time. Most importantly, they have done so in the most professional and congenial way.

We persist in our hope that the book will provide useful, clear, and comprehensive information and analysis for those of you studying Social Work Law, and that possibly, for some of you at least, the process of reading about the law will be an enjoyable, albeit challenging task.

Helen Carr
David Goosey
December 2018

Law for Social Workers is full of features designed to help you to continuously develop and improve your legal skills, from the first stages of your degree through to placements, your first job, and beyond. This guide to the book shows you how to fully utilize its key features, whether you're a student new to the subject or a qualified professional.

OVERVIEW AND OBJECTIVES

The aim of this chapter is to explore th
Children Act 1989 and some common d
law. It also describes the inter-agency con
in some detail the agencies which share y
dren and other vulnerable people and expl
range of problems which vulnerable peop
sector agencies which provide advice and

Overview and objectives

Key learning objectives are set out at the beginning of each chapter to enable you to draw out the main themes. They provide a helpful signpost to what you can expect to learn from the chapter and offer a recap of the key issues discussed, making them ideal for revision.

CASE STUDY

A and another v Essex County Council (2003)

Why are we asking you to read this case?

Social services departments and social workers
lustrates how some of those duties should be ap
are expected to act reasonably within the law an
Court of Appeal held that professional decisions

Case study

Each chapter opens with a discussion of a significant case or inquiry, helping you to learn the facts of key cases and demonstrating how the law applies in practice. Each case study is followed by an explanation of its key themes and relevance to your studies and career.

Private family law	176	Role
Marriage, civil partnership, and other couple relationships	176	Lc
Parental responsibility	179	Du
Private disputes involving		Th
children—s. 8 orders	180	Ec
Changing the safeguarding and		He
inter-agency system	183	Da
The Munro Review of		Th
		N

Chapter content lists

These quick-reference lists at the beginning of each chapter allow you to find information easily—perfect for quick advice and fact finding on practice placements and in the workplace.

SUMMARY

In this chapter we have considered:

* the meaning and scope of adult soci
* the role of local authorities and the l
* the principles underpinning the Car
* overarching legal principles includir

Summary

Chapters end with concise summaries to allow you to check your understanding and return to any areas that are not completely clear.

EXERCISES

1 Read the whole of this chapter carefully and c
will need to consider before recommending t
respect of an individual child.

2 Locate and read one of the articles listed in Ar
100–150 words.

3 Try to construct a time line of events following

Exercises

Chapter exercises help you to consider how to approach real-life issues and give you the opportunity to practise advising the service user. Guidance on how to approach these scenarios can be found in the online resources, allowing you to check your ideas and prepare for exams.

Where do we go from here?

These sections provide a useful review of what has been covered in each chapter and demonstrate how topics link together, ideal for planning essays and revision as well as considering how the law relates to your role as a social worker.

WHERE DO WE GO FROM HERE?

In this chapter, we have considered a number o
particular its philosophy, structure, overarching
decision making by the courts. This serves as a
your responsibilities to children. However, it is
purposes and the principles upon which the Act
tion to understand your role within the Act. In a
where social services fit into the organizational

Annotated further reading and web links

Further reading suggestions and useful websites are provided at the end of each chapter, with author advice to help you to direct your research and find more detailed information.

ANNOTATED FURTHER READING

Mental capacity

There are a number of useful books covering th
of Practice is an excellent starting point. These
(3rd edn, Sweet & Maxwell, 2008) (targeted at l
The Mental Capacity Act 2005: A Guide for Practi
Learning Matters, 2015).

Extracts and key point boxes

Essential information and extracts from significant judgments or inquiries are reproduced in coloured boxes to help to provide useful context for key issues and recap important information.

BOX 3.4 Key differences between the Dis
Equality Act 2010

The Disability Discrimination Act 1995 provided prote
crimination in employment and related areas only.
people against direct discrimination in a broader rang
facilities, and services.
    The Equality Act 2010 introduced improved pro

Figures and tables

Useful information and key processes are distilled into easy-to-follow figures and flowcharts, while essential points are summarized in tables for quick reference and exam preparation.

Stage 1—Local resolu

Complainant brings concerns to the attention of the pe
local authority should consider mediation and conflict
stages. The local authority should make an initial attem
days (unless an extension

If not resolved—or if there is
for investigation

GUIDE TO THE SOCIAL WORKER'S TOOLKIT

This book includes a Social Worker's Toolkit designed to help support and reinforce your learning as you move from the classroom to placements and employment. Common questions that you will come across are addressed and explained with practical advice given on how to tackle each scenario.

- When and how can you be personally liable for mistakes? What happens if you do make a professional misjudgement?
- What rights do you have as an employee?
- What should you do should you wish to raise any concerns about malpractice?
- How should you deal with personal information?
- How should you perform risk analyses?
- How do you write a report? A fully worked practical example is included.
- How do you make decisions about what kind of care is appropriate?
- How will you interact and work with lawyers?
- What happens when you go to court? Will you be cross-examined? What evidence will you need to present?
- How do you decide if someone needs to be sectioned?

The online resources which accompany this book provide extra resources which are free to use and designed to help support your legal learning and development as a social work student and professional.

 www.oup.com/uk/carr-goosey15e

For students:

Guidance on answering exercises in the book

Ideal for checking your knowledge on a particular subject or preparing for exams, this online guidance provides the extra support needed to give you confidence when applying the law to real-life situations.

Multiple-choice questions

A selection of multiple-choice questions, arranged by chapter, allows you to quickly assess your knowledge of the various topics in social work law.

Video tutorials

Author David Goosey offers succinct video tutorials on a range of practical topics including: information sharing, risk analysis and assessment, writing a report, child care plans, working with lawyers, and going to court.

Further reading

Suggested sources for more information on the topics covered in each chapter help you to prepare for assessments and continue your studies once qualified.

Glossary

An online glossary allows you to check your understanding of key terms and provides clear explanations of the legal jargon you may encounter as a social work student or professional.

Updates

Regular updates on new cases, legislation, and proposals affecting social workers allow you to keep up to date with developments in this fast-moving area.

For lecturers:

Test bank of multiple-choice questions

This fully customizable resource, containing 200 interactive multiple-choice questions accompanied by answers and feedback with which to test your students, offers versatile testing tailored to the contents of the book.

Lecture outlines

PowerPoint® slides for each chapter of the book are provided, which can be downloaded and adapted for your own use in class notes and lecture materials.

Lecture notes

Each set of slides is accompanied by a short discussion on issues which you might like to consider when teaching this area of law.

- General Data Protection Regulations.
- Children and Social Work Act 2017.
- Expansion of coverage in the *Social Worker's Toolkit*, including new accompanying video tutorials.

CONTENTS

DETAILED CONTENTS

ABBREVIATIONS

AMHP	Approved Mental Health Practitioner
ANH	artificial nutrition and hydration
ASBO	anti-social behaviour order
ASW	approved social worker
BASW	British Association of Social Workers
Cafcass	Children and Family Court Advisory and Support Service
CCG	clinical commissioning group
CCTV	closed-circuit television
CDA	Crime and Disorder Act 1998
CJA	Criminal Justice Act 2003
CP plan	child protection plan
CPS	Crown Prosecution Service
CQC	Care Quality Commission
C(RS)A	Carers (Recognition and Services) Act 1995
CSA 2000	Care Standards Act 2000
CTO	community treatment order
CYPA	Children and Young Persons Act
CYPP	Children and Young People's Plans
DASS	Director of Adult Social Services
DoH	Department of Health
DoLS	Deprivation of Liberty Safeguards
DST	decision support tool
DWP	Department for Work and Pensions
ECHR	European Convention on Human Rights
ECM	Every Child Matters
ECtHR	European Court of Human Rights
EHRC	Equality and Human Rights Commission
EIA	equality impact assessment
EINA	equality impact needs assessment
EPA	enduring power of attorney
ERRA	Enterprise and Regulatory Reform Act 2013
EU	European Union
FCWO	Family Court Welfare Service
FTT	First-tier Tribunal
GBH	grievous bodily harm
HCPC	Health and Care Professions Council
HRA	Human Rights Act

HSCA	Health and Social Care Act
IB	individual budget
ILF	Independent Living Fund
IMCA	independent mental capacity advocate
IMHA	independent mental health advocate
IRO	independent reviewing officer
ISA	Independent Safeguarding Authority
ISS	intensive supervision and surveillance
LA	local authority
LAC	local authority circular
LADO	local authority designated officer
LASPO	Legal Aid, Sentencing and Punishment of Offenders Act 2012
LASSA	Local Authority Social Services Act 1970
LPA	lasting power of attorney
LSCB	Local Safeguarding Children Board
MAPPA	multi-agency public protection arrangements
MCA	Mental Capacity Act 2005
MDT	multidisciplinary team
MHA	Mental Health Act 1983
MHRT	Mental Health Review Tribunal
MIAM	family mediation, information, and assessment meeting
MP	Member of Parliament
NAA 1948	National Assistance Act 1948
NACRO	National Association for the Care and Resettlement of Offenders
NAM	new asylum model
NASS	National Asylum Support Service
NCB	National Children's Bureau
NHS	National Health Service
NIAA 2002	Nationality, Immigration and Asylum Act 2002
NSPCC	National Society for the Prevention of Cruelty to Children
Ofsted	Office for Standards in Education, Children's Services and Skills
ONS	Office for National Statistics
PACE	Police and Criminal Evidence Act 1984
PCCSA	Powers of Criminal Courts (Sentencing) Act 2000
PCT	primary care trust
PEP	personal education plan
PIDA	Public Interest Disclosure Act 1998
PSED	public sector equality duty
PVS	permanent vegetative state
RAS	research allocation system

RC	responsible clinician
SAB	Safeguarding Adults Board
SAQ	self-assessment questionnaire
SCB	Safeguarding Children Board
SCIE	Social Care Institute for Excellence
STC	secure training centre
SVGA	Safeguarding Vulnerable Groups Act 2006
TWOC	taking without owner's consent
UBC	upper banding calculator
UNCRC	United Nations Convention on the Rights of the Child
YDA	youth detention accommodation
YJB	Youth Justice Board
YOT	youth offending teams
YRO	youth rehabilitation order

TABLE OF LEGISLATION

Part 1

The legal context of social work

Part 1 The legal context of social work

You have chosen a career assisting vulnerable or socially excluded members of society. Your motivation probably includes both altruism and idealism. Social workers want to do their best for the people who use their services.

For a person wanting to make a difference, it can be tempting to see law, with its complexity, its language, its procedures, its institutions, as bit of an irrelevance, or worse, an obstacle to achieving these ideals. But you must not underestimate its importance. It is integral to your chosen career.

Law is the product of Parliament, judges, international agreements, and ancient legal tradition. In the area of social services, it defines what services should be provided and the rights and responsibilities of providers and users of those services. Legislation establishes what agencies (e.g. social work departments of local authorities) will provide the services, which services will be obligatory and which discretionary (a matter of whether a local authority wishes to or can afford to provide them), and sets out procedures for delivering those services. If you are a social worker, the law establishes rules for when it is appropriate or when it is necessary for action to be taken. The law sets out your obligations—requiring you to act—but also sets out the restraints on your actions when you try to fulfil those obligations. Laws provide a framework for holding you, the social worker, to account.

This book aims to be about law rather than about social work. The context you work in is the English/Welsh legal system.

Chapter 1 describes where law comes from and examines the institutions you will encounter or which make and apply the law you will use. **Chapter 2** describes the regulation of social work and the relationship between the law and different roles of the social worker. It also looks at important issues such as consent and capacity. **Chapter 3** looks at the European Convention on Human Rights and the Human Rights Act 1998, as well as considering anti-discrimination law. **Chapter 4** focuses on the legal framework which governs when you can and when you cannot share confidential information about service users.

The legal system in England and Wales

1

OVERVIEW AND OBJECTIVES

Lawyers talk of the Rule of Law. This is the principle that we are all equal before the law and all should have access to the courts to enforce our rights. In *R (on the application of UNISON) (Appellant) v Lord Chancellor* [2017], a case about whether the high levels of fees for employment tribunals unjustifiably limited access to justice and discriminated unlawfully against women and other protected groups, the Supreme Court said this:

> At the heart of the concept of the rule of law is the idea that society is governed by law. Parliament exists primarily in order to make laws for society in this country. Democratic procedures exist primarily in order to ensure that the Parliament which makes those laws includes Members of Parliament who are chosen by the people of this country and are accountable to them. Courts exist in order to ensure that the laws made by Parliament, and the common law created by the courts themselves, are applied and enforced. That role includes ensuring that the executive branch of government carries out its functions in accordance with the law. In order for the courts to perform that role, people must in principle have unimpeded access to them. Without such access, laws are liable to become a dead letter, the work done by Parliament may be rendered nugatory, and the democratic election of Members of Parliament may become a meaningless charade.

None of us are above the law, particularly not the government or those who work for the government, whether police, civil servants, Inland Revenue staff, or social workers. So even when these people are doing the work required of them by law or under the orders of government, they must do that work within the law—the parliamentary legislation as interpreted by the courts and the common law; traditional principles of English law (applied in Wales and Northern Ireland as well as in England, but not Scotland) established and reinterpreted by judges down the centuries.

Courts are required to administer the law without bias towards the government, the powerful, or anyone else. In our democracy, law-makers in Parliament are expected (in theory) to make laws balancing the wishes of the electorate, the good of the country, and the need to protect the vulnerable. These laws are then interpreted by judges on the basis of the real-world cases that come before them. Neither Parliament nor the courts and tribunals always get things right, but you are required to follow the law even if you think they have got it wrong.

The state establishes public institutions or makes use of private bodies to act on its policies, delivering services that the law says must or may be made available to people. They include the police, education authorities, health authorities under the National Health Service (NHS), and, of course, social services departments within local authorities.

Social workers derive their powers and have duties imposed on them primarily through parliamentary legislation (statutes) but against a background of international human rights legislation (such as the European Convention on Human Rights (ECHR) or the United Nations Convention on the Rights of the Child) and common law (e.g. on confidentiality or damages claims in tort). It is important to note that social workers are governed by the general law of the land as well as specific statutes. They cannot break the law by restraining people or breaching their confidentiality or their privacy, for example, even if it is to achieve the duties placed on them by Parliament, unless Parliament has given them specific powers to do so. And even then, the legislation will be interpreted in court according to wider human rights obligations that the UK is signed up to, particularly the ECHR. Social workers are not above the law any more than police officers or government ministers.

This book is designed to make the law familiar to you. We use extracts from statutes and case studies to illustrate our points. Every professional person needs to know the core elements of the law that dictate how they carry out their profession, and then, through their own research or knowing who to ask, to know how to find out more when the need arises. As a social worker you need to know enough about the law to ensure that your decisions are lawful. When decisions are particularly complex you need to know that you should consult lawyers to help you to make those decisions.

In order to practise successfully you must go beyond what we provide in this book. We provide further reading suggestions at the end of each chapter. We remind you at all stages that the principles we are dealing with derive, above all, from statute and from court and tribunal cases, so we quote from the important statutory materials and we mention important or illustrative court cases throughout. We refer to other materials, such as the findings of inquiries, where useful.

We also, after this chapter, give you a case study as your route into each topic at the beginning of the chapter. If you have to think about a real-life issue, and how the law dealt with it, you then have a context for the issues you will be looking at yourself. We hope to expose you to the full range of materials that are relevant to law for social workers, so even if you do not always agree with our interpretation, you will know where we got our information.

Our own thinking can be summarized as follows:

- Law must be obeyed, by individuals and professionals, including law you may consider to be wrong.

- Law indicates what social workers must do (duties) and what they *may* do (areas of work where they have powers to act but the actions are discretionary and may depend on the policies of your local authority).

- Law tells social workers how they should go about their work, including what powers they have. You should know this part of the law, not just be able to look it up.

- Other laws affect the lives of service users including their rights in relation to social workers. It is essential at least to know the broad principles of these laws.

- Lawyers, particularly those employed by the authority for which you work, are paid to know the rest of the law in full (or to find it), so know your limits and use the lawyers when you reach that limit.

Sources of law in England and Wales

Common law

Common law has been established in England and Wales by the law courts over centuries to solve the problems brought before them. Principles are developed by looking at previous decisions by judges, known as precedents, and trying to arrive at new decisions that are consistent with the precedents, or at least with the principles that appear to underpin them. Common law cannot create entirely new rights or obligations.

Much criminal law, such as the law against murder, is derived from the common law. Common law is also the foundation of civil law, non-criminal law in which monetary claims are made against individuals, companies, or state agencies. Social workers could face negligence cases under common law tort, for example where a person or organization is sued for compensation because they failed to act with sufficient care.

Equity

This developed centuries ago as a branch of law in which judges could use discretion, within certain limits and according to certain long-standing rules, to remedy unfairness in the rigidity of the common law, particularly in financial disputes. Equity is still important in family law work. Principles derived from equity, for instance, decide how the family home of an unmarried couple is divided when the house is in the man's name but both partners have contributed to it. The principles of equity are used in certain legal remedies, such as injunctions—a temporary ban at the judge's discretion on one person acting to the detriment of another prior to a court hearing on the issue—thus freezing the status quo until one side or the other wins a subsequent court case. For example, if a tenant alleges harassment against a landlord, a judge might, at his or her discretion, grant an injunction to prevent further acts of harassment. That would be temporary pending a full court case at which the claims against the landlord are heard and dealt with. Breach of the court order can give rise to financial penalties or imprisonment for up to two years at the judge's discretion.

Equitable principles also underlie domestic violence injunctions (non-molestation orders), though judges have statutory powers to issue these under the Family Law Act 1996 and Domestic Violence, Crime and Victims Act 2004—which made breach of such an order a criminal offence, with a maximum imprisonment of five years. If an allegation of assault or some form of harassment is made, an order might be issued against, say, the accused husband (or cohabiting partner—the law calls spouses of cohabitees in this context 'associated persons'). But it is at the discretion of the judge, and it is temporary (though renewable).

Statute law

This is law that has been passed by Parliament. Almost every aspect of child protection, assisting children in need, and community care is based on detailed statutory provisions. According to legal theory, statute law is supreme. Parliament is able to create any new laws or amend or repeal previous statutes—however modern or ancient they may be. It can also enshrine in statute legal principles established by judges under the common law system—and also change, redefine, or abolish those principles. It does so by passing statutes, or Acts of Parliament. These set out mandatory legal provisions, which must be followed by everyone, including the judges. The judges' role is to work out what the words in a statute actually mean (or what the intention of Parliament was) and how the statutes apply in particular cases. Often judges disagree. Lawyers may appeal against a judgment to a higher court such as the Court of Appeal or the Supreme Court. These appeals are taken on issues of law that the original judge may have got wrong rather than reruns of the whole case. Often, they may be remitted (sent back) to the original court for reconsideration in the light of the legal clarification provided by the appeal judge. The judgment of the higher courts trumps the lower courts and is taken as the correct interpretation of the statute or any legal principle involved.

It is therefore often necessary to look at court case decisions to establish the meaning of a law. If Parliament does not like the way judges are interpreting the law or Members of Parliament (MPs) decide the law is wrong after all, they can change it through new statutes.

Note that the UK Supreme Court used to be known as the House of Lords (strictly, the Judicial Committee of the House of Lords, containing judges, not politically appointed peers). You are likely to see cases dating back to the period when the House of Lords was the highest court—before October 2009. The Supreme Court is supreme in the United Kingdom (apart from criminal matters in Scotland, which cannot be appealed to the UK Supreme Court).

International law

Rulers (including governments) have always made agreements with other rulers. This system of agreements, or treaties, between different states has evolved into what is known as international law, some of which, as noted in **Overview and objectives**, is directly relevant to social workers, who are doing the work of the state under statute. Most significantly, Parliament decided that the ECHR would have legal force in Britain. It gives people in the many nations signing up to it (all of the European Union (EU), but other European and non-European nations as well) rights against their governments—and hence against 'agents' of government doing its work.

The ECHR was established in 1952. It starts by asserting that 'everyone's right to life shall be protected by law', then lists many rights—against torture, slavery, and illegitimate deprivation of liberty, in favour of privacy, freedom of expression, and a right to a family life, for example. Although the intention was to try to avoid a renewed rise in totalitarian states after the Second World War, many of these rights have a day-to-day application in quite ordinary circumstances. Social workers, for example, since they are 'agents' of the state (set up by the state and given powers and direction by the state to do its work) have to abide by the Convention. One can imagine cases in which social workers or those setting policy in a social work department might seek to restrict people's liberty, or intervene in family life, or put someone's privacy at risk. They may be able to—but only if they have powers under law and with reference to the ECHR.

The major ECHR court cases are heard by judges in Strasbourg who are drawn from all the signatory nations. For years it was a complex and costly process to pursue rights in Strasbourg. The Human Rights Act 1998 embeds all ECHR rights in UK law by requiring UK judges to take account of ECHR law and Strasbourg judgments when considering cases in the UK. This allows people to use UK courts to pursue those rights. The law also required all parliamentary legislation to be 'Convention-compliant'—always adhering to the ECHR's principles. In this way, European human rights law has become part of UK law. The Strasbourg court may be a final recourse for those who consider that the UK law as interpreted by British judges remains contrary to one or more of the ECHR principles. The court will not overturn UK judgments but is able to declare the UK non-compliant with the ECHR and award relatively modest damages. It is expected that the government will then pass legislation to put the matter right.

(Note that the ECHR and the Strasbourg court are not European Union entities; the EU has its own Court of Justice in Luxembourg regulating legal relations, in particular on trading issues, between the EU nations.)

Procedural rules

These are rules that cover court and tribunal processes—how cases are dealt with, the documentation required, and what must happen at each stage before, during, and after the hearing. For example, if a local authority intends to take a child into care, this requires a court order that must be applied for. Certain requirements will have to be met before the court will issue the order. Procedural rules are derived from the principles underpinning natural justice and due process.

Is 'good practice' a form of law?

Good practice describes the ideal way that social work principles should be put into day-to-day practice. It is not law, and much of what amounts to good practice is not issued in the form of either regulations ('secondary' legislation issued by ministers usually setting out practical details of the statute) or statutory guidance (which expands on the legalistic words of statutes, explaining how, for example, particular powers or responsibilities given to social workers should be acted on in practice). Therefore, good practice must always give way to the requirements of statute, regulations, guidance, and case law on the rare occasions when the requirements conflict. Quite often judges in their judgments can set out rules of good practice covering the sort of issues that have arisen in the cases. This guidance should be followed.

We have now completed our overview of the sources of law. See **Table 1.1** for a summary, and some additional terms you may come across.

TABLE 1.1 Overview of sources of law

Law	Sources	Comment
Common law	Legal precedents set by judges hearing court cases	The advantage of flexibility and expertise but uncertain and lacks the democratic authority of Parliament
Procedural law	The Rule Committee (the judiciary) and in statute, for instance, the Supreme Courts Act 1981	Often overlooked, but critical to the effective implementation of the law
Statutes	UK Parliament, National Assembly of Wales	Has democratic authority but may be slow to enact. The government may be reluctant to legislate on controversial matters. The courts have a role in interpreting statutes.
Secondary legislation	Government ministers (in both Westminster and Cardiff) given powers in particular statutes to fill out details of the legislation after it is passed	Contains the critical detail of legislation. Can be changed relatively easily, but is not extensively scrutinized by Parliament.
Statutory guidance	Parliament or government departments, or the National Assembly of Wales	Not binding, but authoritative
International law	Treaty obligations, judgments in international court cases	Binding on the state and hence agents of the state, including social workers

Some conceptual issues relevant to law for social workers

All law, to be valid in England and Wales, will derive from one of the sources listed in **Table 1.1**. Now we need to explore some legal concepts that do not depend on where the law comes from. The exploration will provide a framework for understanding the areas of law relevant to social workers.

The distinction between private and public law

Private law cases involve private disputes between individuals or between organizations or between individuals and organizations. Private law, perhaps through a civil case in the County Court, might assist in a dispute between a car owner and a garage over the quality of a repair.

Public law regulates the actions of bodies exercising public functions—government, government agencies, local authorities, but also many private organizations tasked with duties by the government such as privately run prisons or care homes.

Because public authorities or their private agents (organizations, sometimes private companies, which the authorities use to do their work) often intervene in people's lives, they are required to conform to certain standards. Care proceedings, for example, are an area of public law. The state must ensure that it has powers to remove children from their parents; establish the circumstances in which it can remove those children; ensure that its agents (those working for the state) follow proper procedures in doing so; and that when it interferes in liberty and family life in this way, it can offer legal justification for doing so if challenged on human rights grounds.

Individuals with a grievance against such bodies may bring a civil law case, perhaps through a specialist tribunal or the High Court.

The particular area of the law that performs this function of ensuring public bodies act according to those standards is administrative law. Sometimes both public law and private law proceedings will arise from a particular situation that has reached the courts. For example, divorce proceedings are private law. However, under the provisions of the Children Act 1989 there are powers during divorce proceedings to require the local authority to carry out an investigation if the court is concerned about the welfare of the children. One outcome of this investigation can be the local authority commencing care proceedings, which as we have stated, are public law.

Administrative law

The state is very powerful and well resourced in comparison with any individual. Administrative law, in principle, attempts to ensure that justice is done between the state and the individual. It seeks to apply principles that operate to restrain arbitrary or wrong or corrupt decision making by the state. It can also be seen as restraining well-meaning state agents (e.g. social workers) with power over individuals' lives who might overstep the limits of their lawful powers or threaten an individual's rights or liberties. Administrative law can also be seen as enabling beneficial intervention by the state. For example, if there had been no legislation about rights and protections for children, then there would have been no role for social workers in child protection. So, the Children Act 1948 identified the duties of local authorities over children and in providing for orphans. The Local Authority Social Services Act 1970 makes provision for 'the organisation, management and administration of local authority social services'.

The principles underlying administrative law have developed in common law cases. They are:

- openness (often described as transparency);
- fairness;
- rationality (including giving reasons for decisions);
- lawfulness (meaning the state and its agents are not above the law);
- impartiality (which means that decision makers should be independent);
- accountability;
- the control of discretion;
- consistency;

- participation;
- efficiency;
- equity; and
- equal treatment.

These principles can be collectively described as the requirements necessary for fairness, and are often referred to as the requirements of 'natural justice'. Sometimes they conflict with one another, and then the decision maker must weigh up the various principles and make the best decision he or she can in the circumstances. Your understanding of professional ethics may help you at this point. We shall explore some of the guiding principles that exist when decisions under administrative law have to be made.

Natural justice

Natural justice embodies a set of principles that courts will apply. It is law because courts have consistently described it as governing their decisions, and therefore it forms part of the common law. It means that whatever the law is, citizens are entitled to have the law applied fairly, in accordance with law, and that the courts will uphold that right. These principles informed the work of the British lawyers who did most of the work drafting the ECHR after the Second World War. Many actions of the state have clearly defined avenues for challenging that action in a court: to contest care proceedings, for example.

The mechanism available for people who believe that they have not been treated fairly by the state and who have no right of appeal is to apply for judicial review—the process by which the courts oversee decisions made by public officials to ensure they have been made fairly and lawfully. You will come across several cases of judicial review in the case studies in this book.

In general, judges will not substitute their decision for the public officials' decisions. The judges' task is to ensure that the state agents applied the principles of natural justice when making the decisions. What they will scrutinize, therefore, is the process of decision making.

For example, a social worker may fail properly to assess whether someone is potentially eligible for community care services, perhaps because of personal antagonism. The person could seek a judicial review of the decision by stating that natural justice had been infringed since the law was not fairly applied. Facts relevant to the decision had not been considered. Facts that were not relevant *were* considered. The court could overturn the decision of the local authority and make a new one, or tell the local authority to make a fresh decision, this time properly. The doctrine of natural justice means that the decision must be arrived at through the correct procedures and be reasonable in the light of facts that the decision maker has.

The '*Wednesbury* principles'

In establishing what is reasonable, judges will use what are often described by lawyers as 'principles', which were articulated by the judges sitting in a case called *Associated*

Provincial Picture Houses v Wednesbury Corporation [1948] 1 KB 223. The corporation (local council) had the power to permit Sunday cinema opening and impose conditions. In this case it banned the cinema from allowing in children aged under 15. The cinema challenged the ban as unreasonable, but lost. The judge, Lord Greene MR (Master of the Rolls, head of the Court of Appeal), set out the principle that a judge should only find unreasonableness if an administrative decision 'was so unreasonable that no reasonable authority could ever have come to it'. So, as long as the council was not acting *'ultra vires'*—beyond its powers (which it was not)—what those conditions should be was a matter of its own judgement, as long as they were not wholly unreasonable. The fact that you or I or even the judge might think letting children in to see the Sunday pictures would be perfectly reasonable or even *more* reasonable is irrelevant. This is the 'test of reasonableness'.

This test protects local authorities more on issues of policy than day-to-day decisions about individual social work cases—as the next section, **Proportionality**, will show.

Proportionality

Decisions made by public authorities are constrained by the Human Rights Act 1998. One particular requirement is the need for decisions to be proportionate to the outcome that is sought. So, for instance, in *Re C and B (Children) (Care Order: Future Harm)* [2000] 2 FCR 614, the Court of Appeal allowed a mother's appeal against the making of a care order in respect of two of her children with a view to placement for adoption. Two older children had been taken into care on the basis of actual harm. The court accepted that there were reasons for concern about the younger children, one ten months and the other newborn, and that there was evidence to suggest there was a real possibility of future harm. However, there were no long-standing problems preventing the mother caring for her children. Intervention, which inevitably impacts on the European Convention right to respect for family life, had to be proportionate to the degree of risk. Here the court considered that a care order was not justified. Other options should have been looked at to help the mother, and the court decided a supervision order would be the proportionate response instead.

What do administrative law principles mean for a social worker making a decision?

When you make a decision about a family or a vulnerable person, if your decision is to be lawful then it must follow these principles:

- You will ensure that you have followed the requirements of natural justice, so you will have found out all the information that is relevant, you will have considered the relevant information carefully, and excluded from your consideration irrelevant matters.

- You will ensure that evidence that goes against the interests of, for example, the parents of the child about whom you are making a decision has been put to the parents, and they have had an opportunity to consider it and respond.

- You will carefully document your decision-making process, so that if there is a dispute in the future you can demonstrate that your decision making was within the bounds of the law.

Law and devolution

Traditionally we talk about English law and the English legal system. However, the National Assembly for Wales was set up in May 1999 with powers and functions determined by the Government of Wales Act 1998. The Government of Wales Act 2006 subsequently empowered the National Assembly for Wales to make its own legislation on devolved matters such as health, education, social services, and local government. Following a 'yes' vote in a referendum in 2011 there is no need for the National Assembly to get permission from Westminster before passing legislation known as Assembly Acts.

Further details of the powers given to the Assembly by various Acts of Parliament can be found on the Assembly website www.assemblywales.org. Inevitably, the National Assembly for Wales will have different priorities from the Westminster Parliament and be interested in different solutions to problems. There will be interesting opportunities to see how different projects proceed and develop best practice. The most up-to-date information on legislation relating to children in Wales can be found on www.childreninwales.org.uk. We will not describe provisions separately for England and Wales unless the laws do actually differ.

Our book does not cover Scotland, which has always had a separate legal system and separate law (despite sharing much law and legislative institutions).

Sources of law—more detail

Statute law

Social workers have 'statutory powers'. This means that their powers and their authority derive from statute—laws made in Parliament. This is not to say that the courts do not have a role. They interpret the meaning of statutes in particular factual situations and their decisions provide authoritative guidance for future decision makers and courts. As time passes, the role of common law diminishes; more and more statutes are passed dealing with more and more areas of behaviour within society.

Primary legislation

Statutes—Acts of Parliament—start life as bills. These may be bills sponsored by government ministers, or private members' bills sponsored by backbench MPs. Most bills are government bills, but within the field of social care there have been some significant Acts that started life as private members' bills, for instance the Homeless Persons Act 1977 and the Disabled Persons (Services, Consultation and Representation) Act 1986.

Often the subject matter of a bill is discussed and consulted upon extensively before it gets to Parliament. The government may publish a Green Paper (originally with green covers) that sets out a number of proposals to change the law and ask for comments. Following this consultation, the government may set out its revised policy objectives in a White Paper. A relatively recent innovation is the draft bill procedure whereby the government publishes a bill in draft form before it is introduced in Parliament as a formal bill. This enables consultation and pre-legislative scrutiny before it is issued formally. This procedure was used during the reforms to the law on adult social care. A draft bill, the Care and Support Bill, was published in July 2012, at the same time as the government's White Paper *Caring for our Future: Reforming Care and Support*. The government held a public consultation from July to October 2012. It attracted about 1,000 written responses through a variety of channels, including an online comments platform created for clause-by-clause comments. The government also held a number of engagement events with stakeholders, those who use social care services, and their carers. A summary of the responses was published in December 2012. Following consultation, a Joint Committee of Parliament was established to conduct pre-legislative scrutiny. Over three months, the Joint Committee received further written evidence and held ten oral sessions with a range of stakeholders. The Joint Committee's work concluded on 7 March 2013, and their final report was published on 19 March 2013. When the Care Bill was presented to Parliament on 19 May 2013, it reflected the government's responses to the consultation and the pre-legislative scrutiny.

The presentation of a bill, generally by the minister responsible for it, marks the beginning of the normal parliamentary process. A bill may commence in either the House of Commons, or the House of Lords. The Care Bill started in the Lords and was presented by Lord Howe, the Parliamentary Under-Secretary of State for Health. There are a series of 'readings' when the bill is first presented in the Commons and the Lords and later debated, with time in between for scrutiny of the bill in committee. Eventually the bill reaches its final form, when it is presented to the monarch for signature. Once it receives Royal Assent it becomes an Act of Parliament. Acts of Parliament are also described as primary legislation.

Even when the Act receives the Royal Assent there may be a delay before particular sections are brought into effect, either on a date stated in the statute or by a commencement order issued by a minister under delegated powers (i.e. Parliament gives the minister the power to bring the Act into effect). If you would like to learn more about the legislative process, the Parliament website on www.parliament.uk contains user-friendly guidance.

Delegated legislation

Most Acts of Parliament contain only the essentials of the new law. The details may be brought in later, usually by a minister or another body authorized by the Act to do so. This is delegated legislation or secondary legislation. It is generally done by issuing statutory instruments in the form of regulations or orders. It is not important to distinguish between these. For the delegated legislation to come into force, normally it must be 'laid before Parliament'. This requires a copy of the proposed delegated legislation to be placed (or laid) in the House of Commons and the House of Lords for a specified number of days. It may then require a vote without a debate or, alternatively, it may come into effect by 'negative resolution'. This means that it will come into force after 40 days unless sufficient MPs or members of the House of Lords vote to annul it. A small number of statutory instruments have to be accepted by positive votes in Parliament—'affirmative resolution'.

A good deal of the law that concerns social workers will be found in statutory instruments, which can contain more of the practical details of how the law should be followed than is possible in primary legislation. Such statutory instruments can be updated more quickly than a new statute.

Guidance, directions, and intervention issued under statutory powers

We include this source of law (or authority, since we shall see that guidance is not law) under the section dealing with statutes, because in social work law the power of government to issue guidance or directions is created by statute.

Local authority social services functions are defined by the Local Authority Social Services Act 1970 (LASSA). We cover this in more detail in **chapter 2**. Under s. 7, these functions must be exercised under the general guidance of the Secretary of State. Where guidance is issued to local authorities under s. 7, it is not, in law, mandatory. Such guidance, nevertheless, must be followed unless there are justifiable reasons for not doing so. An explanation of the role of such guidance is to be found in the following quotation, where Sedley J (the 'J' means a High Court judge: in this case Mr Justice Sedley) stated that local authorities have:

> to follow the path charted by the Secretary of State's guidance, with liberty to deviate from it where the local authority judges on admissible grounds that there is good reason to do so, but without freedom to take a substantially different course.
>
> (*R v Islington LBC, ex p Rixon* (1997))

It is also worth noting that although local authorities have to follow guidance, it cannot be guaranteed that by doing so they will be acting within the law. It remains the function of the court actually to decide what the legislation means. As the foreword to *An Introduction to the Children Act 1989* (Department of Health, 1989) says, 'The Government is not entitled to give an authoritative interpretation of the law and ultimately any interpretation is a matter for the courts.'

Examples of guidance issued under statutory powers

Although guidance can be linked to a particular Act (e.g. the Children Act 1989), sometimes it can stand alone. One example is the 2010 *IRO Handbook: Statutory Guidance for Independent Reviewing Officers and Local Authorities on their Functions in Relation to Case Management and Review for Looked-after Children*, which seeks to improve outcomes for looked-after children by providing guidance to independent reviewing officers about how they should discharge their distinct responsibilities to looked-after children. It can be downloaded from www.gov.uk/government/publications/independent-reviewing-officers-handbook.

Directions may be published in the form of circulars and other documents issued under s. 7B of LASSA. If a local authority does not follow a non-statutory direction, it is in breach of the law because s. 7B says it must be followed. The social worker should always check whether the document they are using is issued under s. 7B of LASSA. If it is, this is indicated clearly in the preface to the document.

In extreme circumstances, a Secretary of State (the chief minister of the main government departments) has powers to intervene to direct a local authority to take a particular course of action. This form of direction is what happened when the Secretary of State for Children, Schools and Families, Ed Balls, intervened to have Sharon Shoesmith, Director of Education and Social Services at Haringey Council, London, sacked following the high-profile death of 'Baby Peter' in 2007. In the event, Balls was later found by a judge to have overstepped the mark. Ms Shoesmith took the government to court, alleging proper procedures were not followed in her sacking. The judicial review in 2011 found in her favour.

The Children Act 1989—an example of statute law and law derived from it

Later in the book we consider the effect of the Children Act 1989. The Act sets out in detail how the courts, local authorities, and others are to deal with the care and welfare of children. There are 108 sections in this particular Act and 15 schedules (additional material appended to the Act), and the bill that became the Act spent almost a year being debated in the House of Lords and the House of Commons. Despite all this it has had to be amended many times since it was first enacted. Moreover, about 30 sets of regulations have been issued under the Act. Together with these go ten books of guidance. Merely looking at the Act will not give the full picture of what it is about. So detailed are the regulations and guidance that there is even a separate index published. We refer to these books of regulations and guidance throughout the relevant chapters. To help you to understand these books, the government has issued a book of guidance on *The Care of Children: Principles and Practice in Regulations and Guidance*. What the Act means in practice is also the subject of numerous reported court decisions (meaning reported in professional law reports), which will crop up throughout the first three parts of the book.

Finding statutes

You may need to read appropriate statutory provisions. Statutes are available in law libraries and on the internet, and are summarized and commented on in secondary sources (such as this book). It is important that you read the up-to-date version of any statute. This is not easy without the resources of a full law library or access to a commercial database, since versions published by the government on the internet are not necessarily up to date with amendments. Our best advice is for you to talk to your legal department to find out what resources it has available for you to use.

Reading statutes

We think it is important that you feel confident enough to read some statutory materials for yourself and not rely solely on lawyers to do that for you. This book aims to provide you with a great deal of support in doing just that. If you find a particular word or phrase difficult, then ask your lawyer what he or she thinks it means. The chances are that it is genuinely a difficult word that could be interpreted in several different ways. Often, we do not know what a word or phrase means in law until it has been interpreted by the courts. Once a court of record (one of the more important courts such as the Court of Appeal or Supreme Court) declares what a word or phrase means in a statute, that is in law what it means, unless and until a higher court explains why that was the wrong approach—either by considering the same case appealed from the lower court or a later case that involved similar facts and the same principles. In exceptional circumstances, a court of the same level considering a later similar case may also retrospectively declare a previous interpretation of the statutory phrase incorrect—in effect the court overrules itself. Normally, though, the earlier case remains the precedent that is followed. The courts use a variety of techniques to enable them to interpret statutes in a manner that is intended to be rational, objective, and consistent. These are the rules of statutory interpretation. Before we go on to discuss these, we provide some general guidance on reading a statute.

The Adoption and Children Act 2002 as an example

The date 2002 is the year that the Act received Royal Assent. It is not necessarily the year when the statute comes into force. Many statutes contain complex provisions that need to be prepared for. The delegated legislation is published after the Act.

In the case of a complex piece of legislation such as the Adoption and Children Act different parts of the Act will have different commencement dates.

The front cover of the hard copy of the statute has the Royal Coat of Arms, the name of the statute, and the words 'Chapter 38'—it is the thirty-eighth statute of this parliamentary session. You can ignore the chapter number. There is also a note to say that explanatory notes have been produced to assist in the understanding of this Act and are available separately (on a tab for the web version). This is a relatively recent innovation. If an Act is one you frequently use, the explanatory notes provide a useful source of information about its provisions.

The contents of the statute

Turning the page, you will see the contents of the statute (the first tab on the web). This particular Act is divided into three Parts and then each Part has a number of chapters. Part 1, 'Adoption', is the largest part. It has seven chapters. Each chapter is subdivided. Chapter 2 is subdivided into sections on the adoption service, regulations, and supplemental provisions. In each of the subdivisions there are numbers. These relate to the section numbers of the Act. The contents page therefore provides you with a very useful navigation tool for the whole of the statute. If you are looking to find out how adoption orders are made under the legislation you can very quickly find out which are the relevant sections. A subdivision of Chapter 3 of Part 1 is headed 'The making of adoption orders', and we can see that the relevant section numbers are ss 46–51.

Sections and subsections

If we look at one of those sections, say s. 47, we can see the typical layout for a section of an Act. The section has a heading, in this case 'Conditions for making adoption orders'. It is then divided into subsections, which are numbered in brackets. If you want to refer to a particular subsection then you would say 'section forty-seven, subsection one'. In writing you would refer to s. 47(1). There may be further subdivisions indicated by letters and Roman numerals as here: s. 47(4)(b)(i). There is generally no need to refer to Parts or to chapters when directing someone to a section of an Act.

Schedules

Not everything is contained in the body of the statute. Most Acts have schedules containing further material, usually of a more detailed kind. The Adoption and Children Act 2002 has six schedules. They are listed after the contents of the Act. Schedules are set out slightly differently from the main body of the Act. If you turn to Schedule 1 you will see its title, 'Registration of Adoptions'. In small script to the right of the title there is a section number, s. 77(6). This is the section in the Act giving legal effect to the schedule. The schedule is then set out in paragraphs and subparagraphs (rather than sections and subsections). If you wish to refer to a paragraph within a schedule then you refer to it as paragraph 1(2) of Schedule 1 to the Act. We say 'to' the Act rather than 'of' the Act because the schedule is attached to the Act.

Amendments

Frequently statutes contain provisions that amend earlier statutes. The Adoption and Children Act 2002 is no exception. So, for instance, s. 113 of the Act provides:

> In section 9 of the 1989 Act (restrictions on making section 8 orders)—
>
> > (a) in subsection (3)(c), for 'three years' there is substituted 'one year', and
> >
> > (b) subsection (4) is omitted.

What this means is that from the commencement date of this provision of the 2002 Act, that particular section of the Children Act 1989 has to be read in the new way. Note that online versions of the Act on the government's website cannot always be trusted to have up-to-date amendments.

Acts can do more than amend particular sections. They can introduce whole new sections into other Acts. In the Adoption and Children Act 2002 new provisions are introduced to the Children Act 1989 to provide for special guardianship. The new sections are introduced by s. 115 of the Adoption and Children Act but they have become ss 14A–14G of the Children Act 1989. You will always recognize sections of legislation that have been introduced by subsequent legislation because of the use of the capital letter.

Acts are also amended by subsequent legislation. The Adoption and Children Act 2002 has been amended by the Children and Families Act 2014. For instance, that Act (at s. 4) has added a new section—s. 3A—to the Adoption and Children Act 2002. The section concerns the recruitment, assessment, and approval of prospective adopters. A reference to another new section, s. 51A headed 'Post-adoption contact'—also inserted by the Children and Families Act 2014—is inserted into s. 1 of the Adoption and Children Act 2002. (At the time of writing these amendments had not appeared on the web version of the 2002 Act—indicating the dangers of relying on it. Additionally, many sections are described as 'prospective' as if they are not in force—even when they are. Students should use Westlaw or Lexis and social workers should check with their legal teams.)

Reading statutes—principles of statutory interpretation

Because the words of statutes are not necessarily clear and unambiguous, judges have developed a series of so-called 'rules' to guide the courts. Traditionally, there are said to be three main 'rules':

- the 'literal rule', which says that the words in a statute are taken to have their literal meaning;
- the 'golden rule', which says that if the literal meaning produces an absurd result, then you look at it in the overall context of the statute;
- the 'mischief rule', which is applied when the first two rules do not help. This rule states that you interpret the meaning of the words in the light of what the problem or 'mischief' was that the statute was supposed to deal with.

For centuries no judge would deign to look at what ministers or parliamentarians may have said about the purpose of the Act under consideration. Now they may take such a 'purposive' approach by looking at White Papers, statements to Parliament reported in Hansard, Law Commission reports, and any other documentation giving clues to the intention of the legislators. Individual judges may use any of the 'rules' or all of them, perhaps combining them into what is called a 'unified common approach'. This would say: use the literal meaning of the Act unless the words are unclear or a manifest absurdity would result; in which case look at the purpose of the Act—using official material to do so if necessary.

The Human Rights Act 1998 has an impact on statutory interpretation, in that it requires courts to interpret legislation in a way that is compatible with the ECHR (see **chapter 3**). Where it is not possible to interpret the legislation in this way, the courts may strike down delegated (secondary) legislation. If they find primary legislation to be incompatible, they cannot strike it down, but they may make a declaration of incompatibility, which should prompt government action to change the law. This can be done by a special form of secondary legislation—a remedial order—which must be laid before Parliament for 60 days and approved by both Houses of Parliament.

Reading statutes—powers and duties

Something else that you will need to check when you read statutes concerning social services is whether the statute provides you with a duty to act or a power to act. The distinction is relatively straightforward. Where a statute imposes a duty on a person or a body, then they have to carry out that duty if the situation described in the statute occurs. There is no choice, however hard the carrying out of the duty may be. Lack of finance, for instance, is not an acceptable reason for not carrying out the duty. Where a statute gives a person or a body a power to do something, the person or the body may exercise that power but they are not obliged to do so.

The distinction is important for a number of reasons. First, it sets your priorities as a social worker. If Parliament has considered that carrying out a particular action is so significant that it should be a duty upon a social services department, then it is a course of action that must be given priority. Second, it is significant when a person is unhappy with the behaviour of a statutory person or body. If there is a duty, then in general the person will be able to take court action to enforce that duty. If there is only a power, then it is unlikely that there will be any legal redress—though, if the person can show that the way in which the decision to exercise or not exercise the power was made was unreasonable, that could be challenged by a judicial review.

It is important to read the scope of the duty in the statute carefully. The law has distinguished between general or target duties and personal or particular duties. General or target duties are expressed in broad terms, leaving the public authority with a wide measure of discretion over the steps to be taken to perform the duty owed to the relevant section of the public. Personal or particular duties are specific and precise and are owed to each individual member of a relevant section of the public. Target duties must be performed, notwithstanding their general nature, in accordance with the principles of public law and they can be enforced like powers through judicial review. However, the public authority has discretion on how it delivers services under the duty, and individuals have no personal right of action. One particular general duty we will discuss in **chapter 6** is s. 17 of the Children Act 1989—the duty to safeguard and promote the welfare of children in need. The local authority must decide what services it thinks are appropriate to meet this duty. Personal duties provide no discretion to the public authority and are actionable (i.e. court proceedings can be taken) by the individual, who can sue for breach of statutory duty.

Whatever you are doing as a social worker, you should be clear in your own mind whether you are acting under a personal duty, a general duty, or a power, and regulate your actions accordingly.

Case law

When we want to know what the law in a statute is, we first read the relevant part of that statute. As we explained earlier (**Reading statutes—powers and duties**, p 19), this is not always the whole solution. Often it is necessary for the courts to interpret what the words of the statute mean. Similarly, judges will interpret common law, where there is no statute, according to the circumstances of each case—and each new case becomes part of the common law. Whether we are concerned with statutory interpretation or the common law, to find out what the courts have declared the law to be we need to look at the law reports.

Reading and finding cases

Cases, like statutes, follow a standard format. They are referred to by their name (usually of the main people or organizations involved on each side) and a reference to a law report. You will notice that when we tell you about a case, we provide the name of the case and a date. The full citation to the case is found in the table of cases at the beginning of the book. Take *F v Lambeth LBC, also known as F (Children: Care Planning), Re* as an example. If you want to find that case yourself you will first need to check the full reference. It is [2002] 2 FR 512, Fam Div.

The law reports

These are produced by private firms using specialist legal reporters. They are taken as accurate reflections of what went on in court and are referred to by judges when making their decisions in later cases, since they contain legal precedents and the reasoning of judges in the earlier cases. They also contain references to previous related cases so the decisions on a particular issue of law can be tracked all the way back. Frequently used series of general law reports are:

Appeal Cases (AC)

Chancery Division (Ch)

Queen's Bench (QB)

Family Division (Fam)

The Weekly Law Reports (WLR)

The All England Law Reports (abbreviated to All ER)

Family Law Reports (FLR).

Summaries of recent cases can be found in *The Times* and the *Financial Times*, and in professional journals such as the *Solicitors Journal*, the *New Law Journal*, *Family Law*, and the *Law Society Gazette*.

Note that some citations use round brackets instead of square brackets around the date of the report. Round brackets indicate that it is the volume number, and not the date of the report, which is essential if you are to locate it on the shelves. The use of round and square brackets can be summarized as:

[2010] Date is essential. The volumes are arranged on the shelves by year, and the volume number is used only to distinguish between different volumes published in the same year, for example [1999] 1 FLR 40.

(1989) Date is not essential, but volume number is essential; that is, the arrangement on the shelves is by volume number, not by date, for example (1980) 70 Cr App R 193.

Cases can also be found online, particularly on the Bailii website at www.bailii.org, a non-profit organization. If you look at a recent example such as *Re N (Children)*, you will notice it has a Weekly Law Report citation—[2016] 2 WLR 1103—(and an invitation to buy it) but also what is known as a 'neutral' citation, designed for the internet age: [2016] UKSC 15. The traditional WLR citation tells you where to find the case in printed copies of the Weekly Law Reports: 2 for second volume of the 2016 edition, then page 1103. The neutral citation tells you it was the fifteenth judgment issued by the UK Supreme Court in 2016.

Here is another example: *Re O (Supervision Order)* [2001] 1 FLR 923 is a Court of Appeal decision published in the Family Law Reports. It should be cited as: [2001] EWCA Civ 16; [2001] 1 FLR 923. The '16' means that it was the sixteenth case heard in the Court of Appeal Civil Division in 2001. 'EW' stands for England and Wales.

The neutral forms of citation are shown in **Table 1.2.**

TABLE 1.2 Forms of neutral citations

Supreme Court	[2010] UKSC 1, 2, 3, etc.
House of Lords (functions taken over in October 2009 by the Supreme Court)	[2008] UKHL 1, 2, 3, etc.
Court of Appeal (Civil Division)	[2005] EWCA Civ 1, 2, 3, etc.
Court of Appeal (Criminal Division)	[2004] EWCA Crim 1, 2, 3, etc.
Administrative Court	[2010] EWHC Admin 1, 2, 3, etc.

Note that a version of a law report downloaded from a site such as Lexis or Westlaw may have in apparently random places an asterisk and number that indicates the page of the case in the print version. These page references are used when quoting from the case. Internet reports, such as Bailii's or official transcripts, are split into paragraphs that can be used for quoting from the case.

Legal databases and non-subscription web sources

Cases are available from legal electronic databases. Lawyers subscribe to services such as Lexis Library and Westlaw and can search for and find cases and up-to-date versions of statutes relevant to the area of law they are researching extremely quickly. The databases may not offer all the cases you want, but official transcripts produced by the courts are often available on the internet and are offered by the legal services too.

The best free website for accessing judgments (including tribunals such as the Asylum and Immigration Tribunal, and including European Court cases) is www.bailii.org. Reports of decisions of the House of Lords are also available on the Parliament website (www.publications.parliament.uk/pa/ld/ldjudgmt.htm); and those of the Supreme Court on www.supremecourt.uk.

Courts and tribunals

We will now move from the law itself to look at the legal system that administers the law.

When a dispute cannot be resolved by agreement between the people involved, the legal system provides for decisions to be made at a judicial hearing. Sometimes there is a need for a judicial hearing even if there is total agreement between the persons involved; for example, if a couple agree to get divorced, they must get a decree of divorce at a judicial hearing. At some time, every social worker is going to have to attend some form of judicial hearing.

We use the term 'judicial hearing' since it is somewhat wider than just 'court'. For example, apart from courts there are tribunals dealing with mental health detentions that a social worker may be required to attend. From now on, where we use the term 'court', it is intended to include these other forms of judicial hearing. What we mean by the term 'court' in this chapter is 'court and tribunal hearings in England and Wales'.

The difference between criminal and civil courts

Criminal courts are required where the state prosecutes offences and courts impose penalties on those convicted. (In rare circumstances private individuals can take criminal proceedings themselves.) People can be convicted only where the evidence points to guilt 'beyond reasonable doubt'. This requirement, for almost a 100 per cent certainty, is known as the criminal standard of proof. The parties to proceedings are the prosecution and the accused or defendant.

Civil courts are used where people can gain remedies for injustices 'proved on the balance of probabilities'. This civil standard of proof means more likely than not, or more than 50 per cent likely. The remedies are normally financial—in the form of damages that compensate someone for loss—or restitutional—putting right the wrong complained of. The courts have a full range of orders that they can issue and the parties are obliged to follow, including orders that someone should do or not do a particular act. The parties to proceedings are described in most cases as the claimant (or plaintiff in cases before 1999), the person or organization asking for a court order, and the defendant, the person who is resisting the order. If a case is appealed to a higher court, the side that appeals is the appellant and the other side becomes the respondent. Social workers are more likely to come across cases where the parties are described as applicant and respondent. In tribunals, parties are called the applicant (rather than claimant) or the appellant (or in mental health cases, 'the patient'), and the government department whose decision is disputed is referred to as the respondent.

Sometimes the same facts can give rise to both a criminal and a civil case. If a person driving hits another car, then the person may have committed a criminal offence, for example careless driving, and also be liable to be sued in civil law for damages. The civil case (known as the 'claim') for damages would be separate, unconnected with the careless driving charge. A person may be successfully sued for damages arising out of a road accident, without there being any proceedings for driving offences, or vice versa. Because of the different standard of proof, it is also possible for a case to be unsuccessful in the criminal courts but give rise to successful proceedings in the civil courts.

The court structure

Figure 1.1 gives an overview of the court system. It reflects the fact that courts are arranged in a hierarchical structure. A lower court must follow decisions of any court higher than itself in the judicial 'ladder'; there is also a system of appeals against the decision of one court from one level to another. Cases begun in the lower courts can, normally, work their way up to the highest court by way of appeal. We will return to the question of appeals at a later stage.

What happens in the criminal courts?

Social workers, in their official capacity, will mostly appear in these courts when presenting pre-sentence reports on someone who has been convicted of an offence to assist the court in deciding upon appropriate punishment. They may, of course, be

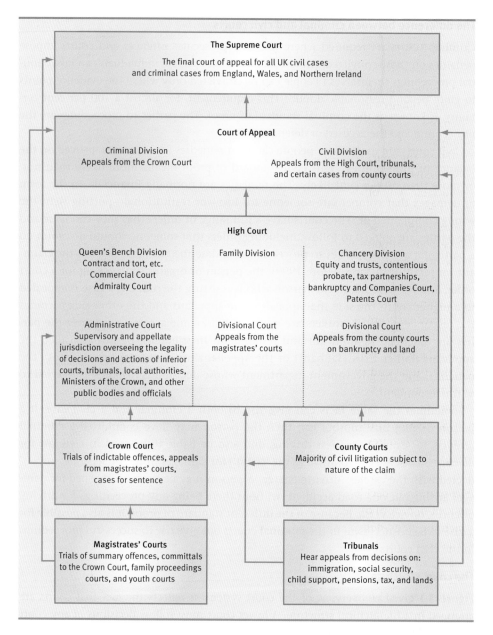

FIGURE 1.1 Overview of the court system
Source: judiciary.gov.uk.

called as a witness to an alleged offence, for example if he or she has been assaulted by a service user or the service user's carer, or is able to give evidence in prosecution for abuse of a child. Social workers may also accompany children to provide support in criminal trials: see **chapter 10**.

All criminal cases start in the magistrates' court. There are three types of offences:

(a) summary offences;

(b) indictable-only offences; and

(c) either-way offences.

Summary offences are the most numerous. Examples include common assault, less serious criminal damage, and taking a motor vehicle without consent (known by the acronym 'TWOC'). They can normally be dealt with only in the magistrates' court. Therefore, the court has the limited powers of sentence described later (**Magistrates' courts' powers of sentencing adults**, p 26).

Indictable-only offences are processed by the magistrates' court to ensure they are ready for trial, but cannot be tried or sentenced there. They are serious offences such as serious burglaries, serious assaults, murder, rape, and arson that, for an adult (over 18), can be dealt with only by the Crown Court. Cases triable either way may be dealt with in the magistrates' court or sent up to the Crown Court if considered serious enough.

Criminal proceedings in the magistrates' court

All criminal cases begin in the magistrates' court. The vast majority (95 per cent) stay there. Cases are heard either by three lay (non-lawyer) magistrates or one district judge. The lay magistrates—or 'Justices of the Peace', as they are also known—are local people who volunteer their services. They lack formal legal qualifications, but are given legal and procedural advice by qualified clerks. District judges are legally qualified, and salaried.

Cases do not go straight to the Crown Court for historical and practical reasons. The practical reason is that where a person is accused of serious burglaries or murder, for example, it requires a great deal of time for the prosecution and defence lawyers to prepare their cases before the trial can take place in the Crown Court. Meanwhile, the question of what is going to happen to the accused person has to be dealt with. The magistrates will decide whether the accused should be remanded into custody (meaning kept in prison) or be granted bail (which would be rare in serious cases or those in which the accused might reoffend, abscond, or interfere with witnesses).

The youth court is part of the magistrates' court and is dealt with in **chapter 10**. Usually, an indictable-only offence is dealt with in the youth court if the accused is under 18—see **chapter 10**.

'Either-way' offences are hybrid offences that can be dealt with by the magistrates' court or by the Crown Court (before a judge and jury). An example of such an offence is theft. What may appear to be the theft of a small amount may be regarded by many as trivial, but for the defendant the consequences of being convicted of such an offence may be extremely serious. Therefore, Parliament has decided that the person accused of such an offence can insist on the case being tried before a judge and jury in the Crown Court.

However, if the magistrates consider the case to be not too serious, they can offer the defendant a 'summary' trial. This has the advantage of being dealt with more quickly and sometimes, if the person pleads guilty, on the spot. In an 'either-way' case the defendant or the court can insist on a Crown Court trial. A defendant's solicitor might consider that a trial before a jury may give the accused a better chance of being found not guilty; a magistrate or district judge might feel that only a Crown Court can offer a punishment fitting the seriousness of the crime. The defence can require the magistrates' court to consider the written prosecution evidence before committing the case for trial, to see whether there is a case to answer (which is not difficult to prove and most defence solicitors do not spend time contesting this).

The different hats worn by the magistrates' court

The magistrates' court is divided into different parts. Youth courts deal with most juveniles accused of crime. For fuller details see **chapter 10**. The magistrates also have some civil functions. Until April 2014, all family proceedings commenced in the family proceedings court, part of the magistrates' court system. However, the Children and Family Act 2014 abolished family proceedings courts, so family proceedings, including care proceedings, now take place within a unified family court, as outlined later (**The Family Court**, p 27).

Magistrates' courts' powers of sentencing adults

Magistrates have restricted powers in relation to the sentences that they can impose, including a maximum six months' imprisonment for any one offence committed by an adult. Many of the offences dealt with by the magistrates' court carry no power of imprisonment so the heaviest penalty is a fine or perhaps a community rehabilitation order. The courts are obliged by law to follow sentencing guidelines depending on the seriousness of the case, previous convictions, and whether a guilty plea was entered. If a person has committed more than one offence, each of which is an either-way offence and each of which could have a six-month sentence imposed for it, the total maximum sentence the magistrates could impose is 12 months' imprisonment (i.e. two six-month sentences to run consecutively). If they do not feel their powers of punishment are sufficient for either-way offences, they can commit the offender to the Crown Court for potentially tougher sentencing. (The youth court does not have this power, though its maximum sentencing powers can be two years' custody. If a charge is particularly serious, the youth court may send the case to the Crown Court for trial—see **chapter 10**.)

Crown Court

By tradition there is deemed to be one Crown Court, which sits (i.e. is convened) in cities around England. (The Old Bailey in London, where the court is known as the Central Criminal Court, hears the most serious criminal cases from central London and sometimes elsewhere.) The Crown Court is where more serious criminal cases are heard before a judge and jury. Whereas the magistrates, in their court, decide on the facts of the case (deciding what happened on the basis of the evidence) and also decide the law (whether a law has been broken—after being advised by their clerk), in the Crown Court there is a separation of these functions. The jury, composed of randomly selected people on the electoral roll, decides the facts based on the evidence and hence whether the accused is guilty. The judge, being a professional lawyer (barrister or, less often, solicitor), is the authority on the law and also decides on sentences for those found guilty.

When sentencing an adult, the powers of sentence of the Crown Court are limited only by the lengths of sentence that are set out in the statute governing the crime or by common law. Courts have less discretion in sentencing a person under 18—see **chapter 10**. The Crown Court hears some criminal appeals from the magistrates' court.

The civil courts

This section will look at the following courts:

(a) magistrates' courts;

(b) the County Court (this has capital letters because there is a single County Court, although hearings are heard in county court centres throughout England and Wales);

(c) High Court (this has capital letters because, again, there is one single High Court which sits in London, but may sit in other places).

Civil functions cover such areas as:

(a) matrimonial cases;

(b) contact with children cases;

(c) child care cases;

(d) contract cases;

(e) personal injuries cases;

(f) administrative law cases.

You are most likely as a social worker to appear in these courts in family matters as:

(a) an applicant and/or witness in applications for an order under the Children Act 1989 or the Adoption and Children Act 2002 (details of the relevant law are dealt with in Part 3);

(b) a 'welfare officer' presenting a report to the court to assist it in deciding what, if any, type of order should be made.

Rules of court

The procedures of the courts are governed by rules of court. Those issued under the Children Act 1989 will be the ones the social worker will come across most often. They are a form of delegated legislation (issued by the government rather than passed directly by Parliament), as the powers to make these rules come from statute.

The Family Court

In England and Wales, the Family Court deals with most family proceedings including:

- divorce;
- dissolution of civil partnerships;
- child arrangements orders;

- care and supervision orders;
- adoption;
- non-molestation and occupation orders.

The Family Court is made up of High Court judges, circuit judges, recorders, district judges, magistrates, and legal advisers.

Social workers in the Family Court

The majority of the social worker's dealings with the courts will be in the Family Court. The Crime and Courts Act 2013 set up a single Family Court for England and Wales, replacing the three separate tiers of court that used to deal with family proceedings. It came into force on 22 April 2014, at the same time as provisions of the Children and Families Act 2014 designed to ensure a more effective and speedy system for dealing with cases involving children.

You may appear in the Family Court:

(a) on behalf of your authority when it is applying for a care or supervision order—your role is as an applicant and a witness;

(b) at the request of the court, where it appears during family proceedings that it may be appropriate for a care or supervision application to be made by the local authority (Children Act 1989, s. 37); or

(c) the most frequent, where the court requires a welfare report to assist it to decide what order should be made in family proceedings (Children Act 1989, s. 7).

We look at the work of the social worker in the Family Court more closely in **chapter 8**. We look at the range of tools—such as how to write a court report, how to give evidence, and to survive cross-examination—that social workers need to succeed in the Family Court in the **Social Worker's Toolkit**, given in the **Appendix**. The introduction of a single Family Court means that judges of different levels will sit in the same building. This means that cases can be allocated to a judge of appropriate seniority quickly, and it will reduce the delays in the old system caused by cases being transferred between different courts. The intention is that care proceedings should be dealt with within 26 weeks to avoid the damaging effect of delays on vulnerable children.

County Court divorce proceedings

The County Court is the court where most divorces are processed, and it follows that it is the court in which s. 8 Orders under the Children Act 1989 (see **chapter 5**) will be made ancillary to those divorce proceedings. Ancillary relief refers to the powers of the court to make orders related to divorce or other matrimonial proceedings. Section 7 of the Children Act gives the court, in any divorce proceedings, the power to ask either the local authority or the probation service to prepare a report in the course of divorce proceedings.

Civil hearings other than family matters

The magistrates' courts, the County Court, and the High Court exercise a civil jurisdiction other than in family matters. These cover such matters as contract disputes, alcohol licensing, claims for compensation arising from accidents, etc. The High Court hears applications for judicial review—a court examination of the actions and decisions of the state and its agents (including social services). Normally social workers will not deal with these cases in the course of their work.

Appeal hearings

There are normally provisions for a party unhappy with a decision of a lower court to appeal to a higher court. A dissatisfied party may want to appeal because:

(a) they think the court got the facts of the case wrong;

(b) they think that the court got the law wrong;

(c) they think that the court, in exercising its discretion in the case, came to the wrong decision.

Most appeal hearings do not involve hearing the case again with the same witnesses. An exception is an appeal to the Crown Court against a criminal conviction in the magistrates' court. Normally the court hearing the appeal will look at the reasons the lower court gave for arriving at its decision. In some courts the reasons (the judgment) are available in writing. Having heard representations from the parties and having looked at the judgment, the court hearing the appeal will give its own judgment. Accordingly, it will be difficult to succeed in an appeal on ground (a) regarding facts—only in exceptional circumstances would a lower court be held to have got the facts wrong, since that court has heard the evidence directly.

Most decisions are on ground (b): that the lower court misstated or misunderstood the law. The clarification of the law is an important function of the appeal system. In the field of family matters it is ground (c) that presents the greatest difficulty. When dealing with such family proceedings there can rarely be only one correct decision. The appeal courts, generally, will not interfere in such a case provided that the exercise of that discretion was not unreasonable. Thus, an appeal court may say that it would have arrived at a different decision, but if the original decision was within the area of the lower court's discretion, then it will not interfere. The case of *MA, SA and HA* set out in **Box 1.1** illustrates that different judges faced with the same facts may come to different views (just as Wilson and Hedley did), but also the reluctance of appeal courts to substitute their views for those of the judge hearing the original case who was presented with the evidence, the testimony of witnesses, and the cross-examination of those involved.

So, if the original judge has his or her law right, ground (b) for an appeal fails; and if the judge came to a judgment that is not unreasonable on the evidence before the court, ground (c) for an appeal fails. The judgment is then likely to stand, since it is difficult to sustain an appeal on ground (a) that the judge got the facts wrong.

If a court decides that there has been an error of law or failure to exercise discretion properly, it will either replace the decision with the correct decision or, if it cannot do this because the evidence must be looked at again, it will send the case back to a different judge or bench in the court below with instructions as to what matters need to be looked at again.

BOX 1.1 *MA, SA and HA (Children by Their Children's Guardian) v MA and HA and the City and Council of Swansea* (2009)

The parents of three children had been found to have physically and sexually abused another child, known as X, living with them. There was also a claim the child had been trafficked illegally from Pakistan. The three siblings were taken into care but a judge found that even though there had also been some physical abuse of one of the children, MA, there was no likelihood of significant harm coming to the three children if they were returned home. The parents were likely to act in a different way towards their own children than to X, who was no longer with them. The 'threshold criteria' between harm and significant harm (see the Children Act 1989, s. 31(2)) had not been crossed, so the judge, Hedley J, dismissed the care proceedings, saying 'society must be willing to tolerate very diverse standards of parenting, including the eccentric, the barely adequate and the inconsistent . . . It will mean that some children will experience disadvantage and harm, while others flourish in atmospheres of loving security and emotional stability.' The children should be returned to their parents.

The children's guardian (an official figure appointed to protect the interests of the children; see **chapter 5**) took the matter to the Court of Appeal, claiming the judge's decision was irrational. The court refused to overturn the original judgment, with Ward LJ saying: 'Although [the father's] treatment of X was to be deplored, the judge had been best placed to decide on the primary facts and was plainly not wrong in declining to find that the threshold of significant harm had been crossed.' He added that it was a 'paradigm case where this court has to respect the findings and conclusions of an experienced judge and uphold his decision'. By 'paradigm case' he means one that fits the standard pattern of cases in which the original trial judge's view of the facts must be accepted.

In this case, however, one of the Court of Appeal judges, Wilson LJ, gave a minority dissenting judgment declaring that the facts before the original trial judge must have given rise to a likelihood that all three of the children were at significant risk of harm if returned to their parents.

If you look at the diagram of the court structure (**Figure 1.1**) you will see that the two highest courts are the Court of Appeal (which has separate branches—criminal and civil) and the Supreme Court. The Supreme Court is the court of final appeal. The UK's membership of the EU has meant that courts, including the Supreme Court, have had to defer to decisions of the European Court of Justice (the European Union court) and 'take account' of the rulings of the European Court of Human Rights (the Council of Europe court). This position will undoubtedly change when the UK exits the EU, although at the time of writing it is not clear what the changes will be.

The actual practicalities of appeals are beyond the scope of this book. If you do find yourself in a situation that you think should be the subject of an appeal, you should consult your lawyer immediately. You will need to know about appeal cases, however, because the appeal courts generate the reported cases vital to your understanding of the law, as they tell you how the law should be understood. By definition, what an appeal court says is treated as correct, both on the facts of the particular case and in respect of the legal principles it sets out, unless a higher court declares it to have been wrong.

Tribunals

A great deal of dispute resolution within the English legal system is carried out by tribunals. Most disputes are between the citizen and the state, such as social security disputes; but they can also hear disputes between tenant and landlord, or employer and employee. Tribunal numbers have dramatically increased over the past 50 years. Currently, there are over 80 types. Their purpose is to provide a quicker and less formal forum than the courts and to allow cases to be adjudicated on by judges sitting where appropriate with people with an expertise in the particular jurisdiction. For instance, psychiatrists sit on mental health cases and surveyors on property cases. Tribunals tend to be of particular importance to social work service users as their lives are likely to be more dependent on decisions made by state bodies, such as benefit decisions made by the Department for Work and Pensions.

Tribunals grew up in response to the need to settle particular disputes, and used to be managed by the same government department whose decisions were challenged. This is not now considered to be in accordance with the right to a fair determination, under Article 6 ECHR. Tribunals now are managed within the HM Courts and Tribunals Service under the Ministry of Justice, and legal members are judges. First-tier Tribunals (FTT) are divided into six chambers on the basis of their specialisms. So, for instance, the asylum support tribunal sits within the social entitlement chamber. Appeals from FTTs go to the Upper Tribunal, which is similarly divided into four chambers.

New jurisdictions for tribunals are created relatively frequently, partly in response to the increasing complexity of society and also stimulated by Article 6 of the ECHR, which requires the existence of courts or tribunals to determine a person's civil rights. One example relevant to social work practice is the Care Standards Tribunal. This is an FTT within the health education and social care chamber. It considers appeals against a decision made by the Secretary of State to restrict or bar an individual from working with children or vulnerable adults and decisions to cancel, vary, or refuse registration of certain health, child care, and social care provision. Appeals from the Care Standards Tribunal go to the Administrative Appeals Chamber of the Upper Tribunal.

Inquiries

Here we are using the term 'inquiries' to refer to a whole range of investigations/hearings that take place outside the court system. Local authorities may initiate, participate in, or contribute to many types of inquiries. Some are more formal than others. They are a useful mechanism for dealing with complaints or investigating failure and may prove more helpful in finding out facts than the adversarial system used in the courts. We set out here some of those you may come across.

Inquiries ordered by a minister

These are the type of inquiry with which you are probably most familiar. They arise when a Secretary of State, acting under powers conferred upon him or her by statute, orders the local authority to conduct an inquiry or appoints an external person to conduct an inquiry.

For example, the death of 'Baby P' (Peter Connelly) in 2007 gave rise to a number of inquiries into social services in Haringey, north London and into the health authorities and police. A wider review of child protection issues arising from the case was chaired by Lord Laming. He had also been in charge of a statutory public inquiry (in reality three inquiries covering social services, NHS, and police actions) into the murder of Victoria Climbié in 2000, also known to Haringey social services. Inquiries established by statute normally have power to order witness attendance and compel disclosure to the inquiry. The reports of ministerial inquiries are essential learning documents. We will refer to several of them throughout this book.

Inquiries established by the local authority

Local authorities are empowered to carry out inquiries by the Local Government Act 2000. These can cover a variety of different procedures depending upon the reason for the inquiry, and their remit will vary according to time and expense constraints, and whether criminal proceedings are pending. For instance, they can be chaired by an independent chair or by a member of the local authority, such as the chief executive. They can be public or private, though owing to the sensitive nature of many of these inquiries, they tend to be private. Clwyd Council carried out a series of inquiries into allegations of child abuse in its children's homes before the Waterhouse Inquiry ordered by Parliament (launched in 1996 and published in 2000). Clwyd had failed to publish its inquiry for fear of legal action by victims.

Inter-agency inquiries

These can be undertaken by one or more statutory bodies. They may involve local authorities, health authorities, police, or other interested parties. They may be ad hoc in nature or subject to standing procedures. The type of inter-agency inquiry which you are most likely to come across is the serious case review coordinated by the Local Safeguarding Children Board (LSCB). A serious case review is appropriate when a child has sustained a potentially life-threatening injury through abuse or neglect, serious sexual abuse, or sustained serious and permanent impairment of health or development through abuse or neglect, and the case gives rise to concerns about the way in which local professionals and services work together to safeguard and promote the welfare of children. Any professional may refer a case to the LSCB if it is believed that there are important lessons for inter-agency working to be learned from the case. In addition, the Secretary of State for Education has powers to demand an inquiry be held under the Inquiries Act 2005.

Ombudsman schemes

Public ombudsman schemes originated in Scandinavia and were imported into the UK in the 1960s. Ombudsman schemes are designed to provide a possible source of redress where private individuals believe they have suffered through the poor administration—maladministration—of a public body, such as a local authority. What the ombudsman looks at is not the failure of the public body to obey the law, but its failure to implement the law in a competent way. Ombudsmen are not able to investigate complaints where legal proceedings are possible.

The Parliamentary Ombudsman

The first ombudsman created was the Parliamentary Commissioner for Administration, who deals with allegations of administrative failings by government departments. The public does not have direct access to the ombudsman. Complaints must go first of all to MPs. MPs are not obliged to refer the complaints they receive to the Parliamentary Ombudsman if they consider that they can deal with the matter themselves. This filter was introduced to preserve the primary responsibility of Parliament to call the administration to account.

The Local Government Ombudsman

The Local Government Ombudsman (technically called the Parliamentary Commissioner for Local Government) is the officer you are most likely to have dealings with. Typically, in any year there are 15,000 complaints to the Local Government Ombudsman, six per cent of which relate to social services (37 per cent, in contrast, relate to housing departments—mainly the administration of housing benefit). The objective of the Local Government Ombudsman is to provide, where appropriate, satisfactory redress for complainants and assist in the improvement of administration by local government. The Local Government Ombudsman has the power to issue general advice on good local administration.

A complainant must satisfy the ombudsman that all other procedures of internal complaint to the local authority have been tried and exhausted without giving the complainant redress. (While many complaints will be covered by the local authority complaints procedures, the ombudsman can investigate delays in hearing complaints or allegations that councils are trying to exclude people from using the complaints process.) The complainant has to approach the ombudsman through a local councillor. If the complainant cannot find a councillor willing to make the application, the complainant may approach the ombudsman direct. The ombudsman then has wide powers of investigation and the ability to look at files and compel people to give information.

More information is available on the Local Government Ombudsman's website www.lgo.org.uk. The site also contains reports of the Local Government Ombudsman's decisions and details on how to make a complaint.

Other ombudsmen

There are several other examples of ombudsmen who may provide useful redress for your clients. The Health Service Commissioner investigates complaints about the failures of NHS hospitals or community health services and other NHS provision. Any member of the public may refer a complaint direct, though normally only if a full investigation within the NHS complaints system has been carried out first. More recently a range of specialist ombudsmen has been created. For instance, the Housing Ombudsman Service deals with complaints against housing associations. An Office for Legal Complaints deals with complaints about lawyers.

▣ Complaints

Complaints are an important driver for improvement in services. Complaints may be generally defined as expressions of dissatisfaction or disquiet that require a response. They should not be taken personally. It is important not to define complaints too narrowly since this may prevent service users from having a legitimate outlet for their concerns. We look at complaints about adult social care provision in greater detail in **chapter 13.**

The Children Act 1989 complaints procedure

The procedure is that required by s. 26(3) of the Children Act 1989. Every local authority must establish a procedure for considering representations (complaints) about the exercise of its functions under Part III of the Act, made by or on behalf of any children looked after or in need—we explain these phrases fully in **chapter 6.** The requirements are set out in the Children Act 1989 Representations Procedure (England) Regulations 2006. Local authorities have to give complainants information about the representations procedure when they first make representations and they must also give information about advocacy services where relevant; that is, where the complainant is a looked-after child or a child in need and so is entitled to an advocate under s. 26A of the Act.

Important points to note about the complaints procedure are that it:

- imposes a one-year time limit on the making of representations so that local authorities and voluntary organizations do not have to consider representations that arise from incidents several years ago;
- imposes tight time scales for the handling of representations, including a local resolution phase upfront so that issues may be resolved quickly and efficiently;
- requires the involvement of independent persons in the consideration of representations so that the process is fair and transparent for the complainant; and
- requires monitoring of the procedure and the outcome of each representation so that local authorities can learn and improve services as a result.

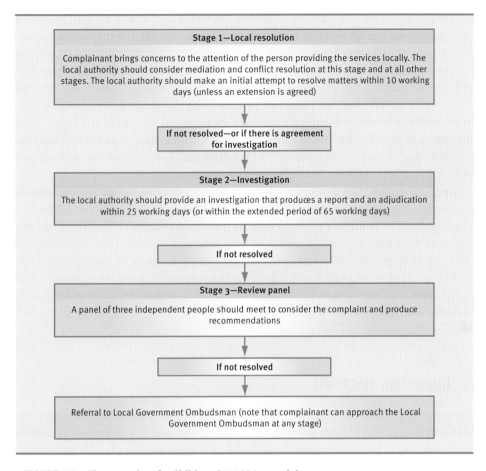

Stage 1—Local resolution

Complainant brings concerns to the attention of the person providing the services locally. The local authority should consider mediation and conflict resolution at this stage and at all other stages. The local authority should make an initial attempt to resolve matters within 10 working days (unless an extension is agreed)

If not resolved—or if there is agreement for investigation

Stage 2—Investigation

The local authority should provide an investigation that produces a report and an adjudication within 25 working days (or within the extended period of 65 working days)

If not resolved

Stage 3—Review panel

A panel of three independent people should meet to consider the complaint and produce recommendations

If not resolved

Referral to Local Government Ombudsman (note that complainant can approach the Local Government Ombudsman at any stage)

FIGURE 1.2 The procedure for Children Act 1989 complaints

Figure 1.2 sets out the complaints procedure laid down by the Department for Children, Schools and Families (now the Department for Education) for complaints relating to children's services.

Children's Commissioners

The Children's Commissioner for Wales is an independent body with the role of ensuring that the rights of children and young people are upheld. It was set up following a recommendation in the report of the Waterhouse Tribunal which looked into the abuse of children in care in the former county council areas of Gwynedd and Clwyd (see **Inquiries established by the local authority**, p 32). The office of the Children's Commissioner for Wales was established under the Care Standards Act 2000. The Commissioner's functions include reviewing and monitoring the arrangements for complaints made by service providers, whistle-blowing (meaning 'protected disclosures' by staff reporting failings of their management or employer to someone outside the immediate organization such as to a lawyer, the police, or a politician and possibly to the media under certain circumstances), advocacy, the provision of advice and information, the power to examine particular cases, providing other assistance, and making reports. In 2001 the Children's Commissioner for Wales Act extended the Commissioner's role to all children. It also gave him or her the power to review proposed legislation and policy from the National Assembly for Wales, considering the potential effect that it might have on children, and to make representations to the National Assembly for Wales about any matter that affects children. The website is www.childcom.org.uk.

The Children Act 2004 established the Children's Commissioner for England to promote and safeguard the rights and interests of children in England. The Children's Commissioner is required to have regard to the United Nations Convention on the Rights of the Child. The role is similar to the Children's Commissioner for Wales but does not include power to review proposed legislation to assess its impact upon children. The Children and Families Act 2014 further strengthened the remit, powers, and independence of the Commissioner, giving her special responsibility for the rights of children who are in or leaving care, living away from home, or receiving social care services. The website is www.childrenscommissioner.gov.uk.

◼ Inspection and audit

The government says it is committed to improving the performance of public services. One way it does this is by inspection and audit. In the health and social care system there are a number of organizations described as regulatory. arm's-length bodies that hold services to account. They operate independently of government.

Care Quality Commission

This body registers and monitors the care services of adult health and social care providers in England and protects the interests of people whose rights are restricted under the Mental Health Act. Its responsibilities were set out in the Health and Social Care Act 2008, broadly 'to protect and promote the health, safety and welfare of people who use health and social care services'. We look at the work of the Care Quality Commission more carefully in **chapter 14**.

Children's services and Ofsted

From April 2007 children's social care services have been regulated by the Office for Standards in Education, Children's Services and Skills—Ofsted.

Achieving public accountability

It is clear that there is a multitude of mechanisms to achieve public accountability. In **Table 1.3** we list them and provide a summary of the advantages and disadvantages they bring.

TABLE 1.3 A summary of the different forums for public accountability

Forum	Advantages	Disadvantages	Comment
The courts	Prestigious	Expensive and time consuming	Very few cases that you are involved in will get reported in the law reports. Decisions which are reported tend to arise from very complex factual circumstances that you may feel have little relevance to your day-to-day practice
	Extensive expertise and specialist knowledge	Can be very alienating to people unfamiliar with its operations	
Tribunals	Less formal hearings, with greater accessibility and speed	Different tribunals run on different procedural rules. Sometimes the informality can work to the disadvantage of the vulnerable person	
		Generally, no funded legal help available	
Inquiries	Public inquiries are very influential on subsequent practice	Public inquiries are expensive and time consuming. Other inquiries may be held in private and provide very little public accountability	
Complaints	These provide a speedy informal system of addressing issues of concern to ordinary people	Children and vulnerable people may find it very difficult to complain	
Local Government Ombudsman	Inexpensive and can have repercussions beyond an individual complaint, leading to reforms	Limited compensation	

Forum	Advantages	Disadvantages	Comment
Children's Commissioner	Provides a service which children need, since they find it difficult to complain or influence policy and the law It will also provide a useful coordinating role	England's Commissioner has limited role	
Regulators	Can concentrate on improving the quality of services and respond to systemic problems	Do not respond to individual complaints, although service users' views are taken into account	

SUMMARY

In this chapter we have introduced you to the English legal system. We have discussed:

- sources of law;
- important legal concepts such as reasonableness and proportionality;
- devolution;
- statutes and case law, including assistance in locating relevant law and suggestions on how to read the law;
- courts and tribunals;
- inquiries, ombudsmen, and inspection and audit regimes.

EXERCISES

1 Explain the differences between courts and tribunals.

2 Accountability

   A service user is dissatisfied with a decision you have made. Outline the various options open to her and indicate under what circumstances which option is likely to be most appropriate.

3 The ombudsman

   Find the Local Government Ombudsman's site on the web. Find the decisions on complaints about social services. What types of complaint are most common?

4 Reading statutes

   Find the Care Standards Act 2000 on the internet (or find a paper copy). Now answer the following questions:

(a) How many parts are there to the Act?

(b) What is the title of Part IX and how many chapters does it have?

(c) How many schedules are there to the Act?

(d) Find s. 11 of the Act. Does this impose criminal or civil liability on the person who fails to register?

(e) Find s. 16 of the Act. What is the legal status of regulations made under this section?

(f) Look at s. 23. What powers does the minister have? What statutory duties are imposed upon him?

(g) What section of the Act deals with the title 'social worker'? Write, in your own words, what it provides.

(h) How does the Act define 'vulnerable adults'?

(i) Has s. 81 of the Act come into force?

(j) Is your version of the Act up to date? How do you know?

5 Reading cases

Find *Gillick v West Norfolk and Wisbech Area Health Authority* [1985] UKHL 7 and answer the following questions:

(a) In which court was the case heard?

(b) Name the judges.

(c) When was the case heard? On what date was the judgment handed down?

(d) Who were the parties to the case?

(e) Set out briefly the legal history of the case.

(f) Is the case one of statutory interpretation, or is it about the common law?

(g) Was the decision of the court unanimous?

(h) Who were the barristers in the case? Who were the solicitors?

(i) Find Lord Scarman's judgment and copy it. If you have time, read it. It is a good decision to read as it has been extremely influential, as you will find out in **chapter 2**.

ONLINE RESOURCES

For guidance on how to answer these exercises, visit the online resources at www.oup.com/uk/carr-goosey15e.

WHERE DO WE GO FROM HERE?

This chapter makes it clear that you are operating in a legal arena and provides a very important foundation to your legal studies. The most important message to draw from this chapter is that the law determines what you do. Social workers must be able to account for their decisions. In addition, any correct answer that a social worker can give, when asked why he or she took a particular course of action, must include the statement 'I took the step because that was what appropriate social work practice demanded within the framework of the law.' Without the ability to say that, the professional social worker will have failed themselves and, more importantly, the service user. We now move to **chapter 2**, where we look more closely at the regulation of the professional social worker.

 ANNOTATED FURTHER READING

The legal system

If you would like to read more about the English and Welsh legal system there is any number of books available. Martin Partington's *Introduction to the English Legal System* (Oxford University Press) is concise, updated annually, and takes a critical as well as a descriptive approach.

Websites of (some of) the bodies mentioned in this chapter are:

    www.parliament.uk

    www.assemblywales.org

    www.justice.gov.uk

    www.ombudsman.org.uk (covers Parliament and the NHS)

    www.lgo.org.uk (Local Government Ombudsman)

    www.childrenscommissioner.gov.uk (Children's Commissioner for England)

    www.cqc.org.uk (Care Quality Commission)

Lawyering and judging

There are a number of books which you may find interesting on the practice of law. Here are two you might enjoy.

The Secret Barrister—Stories of Law and How It is Broken (Macmillan 2018) is an anonymous, unrestrained, and damning critique of the legal system in England and Wales. Everyone who works in the courts should read it. You can also read the secret barrister's blog—https://thesecretbarrister.com.

Quite different, but equally revealing is Sir Mark Hedley's *Modern Judge: Power, Responsibility and Society's Expectations* published by Family Law in 2016. The publisher's description says:

> As society becomes more complex, so does the law. However, law cannot provide for every circumstance and so its application often involves the exercise of discretion. Criminal sentencing, child welfare, the protection of those who lack mental capacity and disputes about medical treatment are obvious examples. How do judges go about that? How far are judges influenced or affected by their backgrounds, beliefs and own life experiences? And, if consistency is an aspect of public justice, can that be achieved? And what about the conflict between public justice and personal privacy? Many see these as pressing questions in a society where judges have perhaps greater effective power than ever before.

The BBC Radio 4 programme Law in Action covers current legal debates some of which are very relevant to your work. The episodes are listed here www.bbc.co.uk/programmes/b006tgy1/episodes/guide.

The roles and responsibilities of the social worker

2

OVERVIEW AND OBJECTIVES

This chapter focuses on the roles and responsibilities of the social worker. In particular it considers the role of the social worker as an ethical professional, a statutory creation, and an employee. It also considers the nature and extent of the redress that the law provides to those who are damaged in some way by the actions of social workers. The chapter concludes by providing some guidance on the thorny legal, ethical, and professional issue of consent.

CASE STUDY

A and another v Essex County Council (2003)

Why are we asking you to read this case?

Social services departments and social workers have a range of duties and this case illustrates how some of those duties should be applied in practice. Ultimately, professionals are expected to act reasonably within the law and within their context. As will be shown, the Court of Appeal held that professional decisions should be judged by what would be regarded as acceptable to a responsible body of opinion within that profession at that time.

What is at stake for the parties and beyond?

The adoptive parents wanted recognition of the difficulty they faced in caring for their adopted son and payment for the damage he had caused. Ultimately, they said that they would not have agreed to adopt him had they known all of his background history. The local authority argued that they had fulfilled their duty of care to the adoptive parents. Adoption practice today is very concerned to ensure that prospective adoptive parents have all the information pertaining to the child that is known to the local authority. Sometimes, however, expert reports provided to the court for care proceedings are not automatically given to prospective adopters. A request for their release to adoptive parents is normally required.

Background information

A and B were married in 1985. Both had been married before and A had two children from his first marriage. They had no children together and, in 1990, applied to be approved as prospective adoptive parents. Their local authority, Essex, was the relevant adoption agency as defined under the Act then in force, the Adoption Act 1976. A and B were interviewed by a social worker and adoption adviser, employed by Essex, who recommended that they were suitable adoptive parents. In June 1991, A and B were approved by the adoption panel.

In June 1994 the adoption panel recommended two young children, a brother and sister, for adoption. The boy was born in 1990 and his sister was born in 1993. The children had had a very difficult start in life, witnessing and being at risk of physical and emotional abuse. By 1994 they were in the care of Essex. In October 1995 the adoption panel recommended linking A and B with the children. In February 1996 the children were formally placed with A and B, and finally on 1 May 1997, the court made adoption orders, when the children were 7 and 4, respectively.

Following the adoption, the boy proved impossible to control, to such an extent that he had damaged A and B's home, health, and family life. The judge referred to evidence of the boy's behaviour as follows:

> B described his behaviour as 'spiralling out of control'. She has suffered black eyes, split lips, and bruises on various occasions and ended up in hospital as a result of being attacked by him while pregnant. He smashed their greenhouse with a spade, damaged their conservatory, poured gloss paint on the walls and carpets of the hall and their bedroom, and generally behaved violently including attacking other children. On one occasion at a party he attacked A's father and bit him, he attempted to attack his sister, took a carving knife and threatened to kill A, and attempted to electrocute himself with bare wires from his bedside lamp which he had destroyed.

In October 1997 he was diagnosed as suffering from Attention Deficit Hyperactivity Disorder and medicated with Ritalin. A and B wanted compensation—damages—from Essex. They alleged that Essex local authority was negligent in particular in failing to inform A and B of the extent of the boy's difficulties of which it knew; had A and B been properly informed, they would not have agreed to the placement. Essex denied negligence, in the sense of carelessness, but also denied that it owed A and B a duty of care and that it was responsible for the problem. Its argument was that a fair and sufficient amount of information was conveyed, and it did not accept that A and B would have rejected the children in any event. The question before the court was whether Essex owed a common law duty of care to A and B when it was acting in a statutory context.

High Court decision

The judge in the High Court found that Essex had been negligent for failing to provide A and B with all the relevant information about the two children whom they were to adopt. This decision represented a considerable extension of the previous law on responsibility for decisions. However, he also found that Essex was only liable for injury, loss, and damage sustained between the time when the children were placed with A and B as prospective adopters and the date of the adoption orders. Both Essex and A and B appealed against the decision.

The Court of Appeal decision

The Court of Appeal, whilst still finding that Essex had some responsibility for the inadequate information that A and B received, came to a narrower view of Essex's responsibility.

- It saw no difficulty in agreeing a duty of care to communicate to the prospective adopters that information which the agency had decided that they should have.

- The Court also held that the primary duty of social workers, doctors, and others who complete forms on behalf of an agency was to that agency. The reports were required by the agency so that it could fulfil its statutory obligations. Could the compilers of reports simultaneously owe duties towards the people who were the subject matter of those reports and towards the people who may read and rely upon them? The court was reluctant to impose such a duty because there was a statutory framework for adoption which was closely regulated 'with a view to ensuring best contemporary practice in this difficult and sensitive exercise in social engineering'.

- The court further held that even if there were a duty of care, as long as the professional judgement made in the report was one which would be acceptable to a responsible body of opinion within that profession at that time, then there would be no breach of duty. In this particular case it decided that the social worker was not in breach of her duty in compiling the form.

- It also decided that there was in general no duty of care owed by an adoption agency or the staff whom it employed in deciding what information was to be conveyed to prospective adopters. Only if they took a decision which no reasonable agency could take could there be liability.

- However, once the agency had decided what information should be given, then there was a duty to take reasonable care to ensure that that information was both given and received.

- The Court of Appeal decided that A and B did not need to have all the relevant information; they should receive the information which a reasonable and competent agency would provide. (This principle was used on a very recent case involving the sharing of information with a foster carer; see *Kunnenkeril v London Borough of Enfield* [2017] EWHC 1779.)

The court was clear that Essex had breached a duty of care in that Essex had not provided A and B with the information that it had decided they should be provided with. As a result, they were liable for all of the harm that resulted from that failure, but only to the point of the adoption order. 'The adoption order changes everything for ever. From that point on the adopters became as much like birth parents as it is possible for them to be.'

WHAT DOES THIS CASE TELL YOU ABOUT SOCIAL CARE LAW AND PRACTICE?

In each chapter from now on we start with real legal cases, designed to highlight the issues which that chapter will examine.

In the judgment discussed above, there is stress on social workers' professional responsibilities to the people who are affected by their decisions. It makes it clear that 'doing your best in difficult circumstances' is not always good enough. As you read through the case, ask yourself the following:

- Why did the social workers not tell the whole truth to A and B?
- Can you understand the pressures on them?

- Put yourself in the position of the prospective adopters—what pressures were upon them?
- Think about the children involved in this case—how have their lives been damaged by this?
- Do you agree with the barrister representing Essex who argued that the law must be careful not to impose burdens on social workers which get in the way of the interests of children and their statutory responsibilities?
- Or do you agree with the High Court judge when he said that the possibility of an award of damages should lead to an improvement in the practice of social work?
- What do you think the Court of Appeal meant when it did not rule out a duty of care to a child in these circumstances?
- What are the implications of the decision for your practice of social work?
- Does the case tell you anything about the extent of your professional responsibilities?

The case study illustrates how social service departments can be taken to court by those who are unhappy with the way social workers carried out their work. So, one of the subjects we look at in this chapter is the accountability of social workers.

The case also highlights some of the problems which social workers face: a hugely demanding role where there is pressure to achieve particular outcomes and where time to complete paperwork properly and consider the full implications of the course of action that you have embarked upon is in short supply. A similar case emerged in a Welsh authority. This time the subject matter was not adoption but sexual abuse. If you are interested in extending your understanding of professional responsibilities and duties, you may wish to read the official transcript of *Merthyr Tydfil CBC v C* (2010).

The relevance of law to good social work practice

The relationship between law and social work is complex. Although social workers first emerged with the Charity Organization Society in the nineteenth century, they are now largely authorized by government; government is therefore accountable to the public for their work and obliged to regulate their activities. Social workers are also professionals and are required to account for their actions and inactions to the government and the public within a framework of law. For social workers employed in public authorities, the law lays down their tasks, the scope of their work, their discretions, and their powers.

It is our task to emphasize the relevance and importance of law to social work practice. Law alone is not enough for good social work practice. But failure to practise according to the requirements of the law leaves you open to criticism. Failure to understand and act within the legal framework will usually let service users down.

Criticism of the law is valid and useful; but working outside the law is unacceptable. The rule of law requires the state—which you as a social worker in a public authority represent—to use its formidable powers according to the law and in an accountable way. It is an illusion to think you can protect the interests of vulnerable people better outside the legal framework than within it. At the very least it will destroy your credibility in court and your chance of obtaining appropriate court orders; at its worst, there may be a disaster, and you will be the first in line for any criticism. That is not to say that values are not important to your work. It would be impossible for you to do your job without a strong set of values. Part of our purpose in this chapter is to demonstrate the link between value-driven, ethical practice, and legally informed practice.

We have already suggested that social workers are both social care professionals and creations of statute working within the law. In what follows we will identify the range of social work roles and responsibilities.

An ethical professional

One way of understanding what it means to be a social worker is through the Professional Capabilities Framework developed initially by the Social Work Reform Board, then the College of Social Work, and now by the British Association of Social Workers. **Box 2.1** identifies the following capabilities:

BOX 2.1 Capabilities of a social worker—extract from British Association of Social Workers' Professional Capabilities Framework

- *professionalism*—identify and behave as a professional social worker, committed to professional development;

- *values and ethics*—apply social work ethical principles and values to guide professional practice;

- *diversity*—recognize diversity and apply anti-discriminatory and anti-oppressive principles in practice;

- *rights, justice, and economic well-being*—advance human rights and promote social justice and economic well-being;

- *knowledge*—develop and apply relevant knowledge from social work practice and research, social sciences, law, other professional and relevant fields, and from the experience of people who use services;

- *critical reflection and analysis*—apply critical reflection and analysis to inform and provide a rationale for professional decision making;

- *intervention and skills*—use judgement, knowledge and authority to intervene with individuals, families and communities to promote independence, provide support, prevent harm and enable progress;

- *contexts and organizations*—engage with, inform, and adapt to changing organizational contexts, and the social and policy environments that shape practice. Operate effectively within and contribute to the development of organisations and services, including multi-agency and inter-professional settings;

- *professional leadership*—promote the profession and good social work practice. Take responsibility for the professional learning and development of others. Develop personal influence and be part of the collective leadership and impact of the profession.

Professionals have a particular type of relationship with the people who use their services because of the level of expertise and authority that being a professional implies. The law recognizes the particular nature of the relationship and imposes responsibilities to act with care, and also intervenes to ensure that the professional has the appropriate qualifications. In this section of the chapter, we will look at both of these aspects of your professional identity, but we will start with the most fundamental aspect of professional identity—integrity.

All professionals are bound by ethical codes, and their actions are underpinned by agreed values. At the time of writing the current regulator is the Health and Care Professions Council (HCPC) and it sets out its Standards of Conduct, Performance and Ethics (2016) at www.hcpc-uk.org/standards/standards-of-conduct-performance-and-ethics. **Box 2.2** gives the 10 points:

 BOX 2.2 Standards of Conduct, Performance and Ethics—Health and Care Professions Council (2016)

promote and protect the interests of service users and carers;

communicate appropriately and effectively;

work within the limits of their knowledge and skills;

delegate appropriately;

respect confidentiality;

manage risk;

report concerns about safety;

be open when things go wrong;

be honest and trustworthy; and

keep records of their work.

The Children and Social Work Act 2017 removed the Health and Care Professions Council as the regulator of social workers. Social Work England is a new, non-departmental public body which was set up to act as the profession's regulator from the spring of 2019. The new regulator will cover both child and family social work and adult social work and will focus on raising the quality of social work education, training, and practice with children young people, families, and adults. The over-arching objective of the regulator in exercising its functions is the protection of the public (s. 37(1)). **Box 2.3** sets out the objectives of Social Work England.

 BOX 2.3 Objectives of Social Work England—s. 37(2) of the Children and Social Work Act 2017

The pursuit by the regulator of its over-arching objective involves the pursuit of the following objectives—

(a) to protect, promote and maintain the health, safety and well-being of the public;

(b) to promote and maintain public confidence in social workers in England;

(c) to promote and maintain proper professional standards for social workers in England.

The British Association of Social Workers (BASW), after widespread consultation from several sources, also published a Code of Ethics for Social Work. The latest Code was launched in January 2012 and updated in October 2014 (see www.basw.co.uk/about-basw/code-ethics).

Box 2.4 summarizes the values and ethical principles underpinning social work as expressed in the Code:

 BOX 2.4 Values and ethical principles of social work—BASW Code of Ethics for Social Work (updated October 2014)

Human Rights

Social work is based on respect for the inherent worth and dignity of all people as expressed in the United Nations Universal Declaration of Human Rights (1948) and other related UN declarations on rights and the conventions derived from those declarations.

Social Justice

Social workers have a responsibility to promote social justice, in relation to society generally, and in relation to the people with whom they work.

Professional Integrity

Social workers have a responsibility to respect and uphold the values and principles of the profession and act in a reliable, honest and trustworthy manner.

These three values and ethical principles are further expanded into seventeen applications for practice. These are worth considering and having to hand during practice. Social work is inherently fraught with a number of ethical and moral dilemmas. The right thing to do is not always obvious. A careful analysis using the BASW Code of Ethics is recommended in those instances.

One particular aspect of your role as an ethical professional requires further consideration—your role as a champion of equality and diversity.

A champion of equality and diversity

The British Association of Social Workers' Professional Capabilities Framework is clear that recognizing diversity and challenging discrimination are fundamental parts of the social work role. It states that:

> Social workers understand that diversity characterises and shapes human experience and is critical to the formation of identity. Diversity is multi-dimensional and includes race, disability, class, economic status, age, sexuality, gender (including transgender), faith and belief, and the intersection of these and other characteristics. We understand that because of difference, and perception of difference, a person's life experience may include oppression, marginalisation and alienation as well as privilege, power and acclaim. We identify this and promote equality.

A competent professional

The next aspect of professional identity we must consider is competence. Professional competence is a key legal and ethical requirement. The British Association of Social Workers' Professional Capabilities Framework states that:

> Social workers are members of an internationally recognised profession. Our title is protected in UK law. We demonstrate professional commitment by taking responsibility for our conduct, practice, self-care and development. We seek and use supervision and other professional support. We promote excellent practice, and challenge circumstances that compromise this. As representatives of the profession, we safeguard its reputation. We are accountable to people using services, the public, employers and the regulator. We take ethical decisions in the context of multiple accountabilities. The state translates this ethical requirement to a legal one by insisting on a rigorous qualification system. Under the Care Standards Act 2000 (CSA) a social worker falls within the general category of 'social care worker'. Section 55 of the CSA defines a social worker as someone who engages in social work (s. 55(2)(a))—the definition does not really help to define what social work is, but there is no doubt that if you act as, or call yourself, a social worker, you must be qualified and registered. In fact, it is a criminal offence for anyone else to use the title 'social worker' (s. 61).

A qualified professional

The HCPC is currently responsible for the Standards of Education and Training in the professions it registers. Under the Health and Social Care Act 2012 it is the statutory responsibility of the HCPC (or Welsh Assembly) to approve training courses on behalf of the Secretary of State and to recognize, where appropriate, foreign qualifications. Social Work England will take over the responsibility for regulating social work training, including post-qualifying courses, from the Spring of 2019.

▓ Professional responsibilities

The person you are responsible for used to be called your client. We used that term in early editions. That word was inaccurate in capturing the nature of your responsibilities, because the word 'client' somehow suggests a person who has chosen and instructed a professional. Nowadays the word is service user. The relationship is defined by the service, and there is no instruction by the service user. The service is made available by statute, so the social worker who provides it or arranges for it to be provided is not instructed, as a lawyer or accountant would be, by a client. Sometimes, as we shall see later in this chapter, it is provided without the service user consenting because they may be too young or otherwise incapacitated to do so.

You do not decide who is a service user. This is defined in the Local Authority Social Services Act 1970 (LASSA). We will come to that very important statutory list later in the chapter. The service user will either be a child in need or an adult in need of some form of community care service.

In any case involving children, each individual child on your caseload is the service user, the person to whom you have statutory responsibilities. You need to build up an individual relationship with each child, distinct from the relationship you may have with the child's parents or guardians. The Report of the Inquiry into Victoria Climbié—the Laming Report (see **chapter 5**) was just one in the long series of reports which make it clear what happens when social workers lose sight of the core statutory responsibility to the child.

This point about service users is not just applicable to children. For example, if you are responsible for the well-being of an older person it is easy to overlook that that person is your service user and that his or her needs are the starting point for assessing what should be done. The pressures of the family can lead you to concentrate on what the family may want, which often may not be what the older person wants or what your statutory duty requires.

Responsibilities other than to service users

The dropping of the word 'client' is helpful. When that word was used, it was common to see the parent of a child as 'the client'. This is wrong. You do not have a client, and any responsibility is owed to the person who uses the services—which is not to minimize the vital importance of working with others, especially parents.

As the case study at the beginning of this chapter demonstrates, you do, of course, have responsibilities to others, such as prospective adopters, foster parents, and carers. You have duties to society at large, for instance in your responsibility to diminish offending by young people. These responsibilities may arise from your common law duty of care or from other statutory responsibilities, for instance those arising under the Carers (Recognition and Services) Act 1995 (C(RS)A)—see **chapter 13**. There will be legal consequences if you fail in your professional responsibilities to such people. Nonetheless, it is critical that your prime focus is the person to whom you have statutory responsibilities.

The nature of the responsibility to the service user

There is a conflict at the heart of the social work role. You have two clear relationships with the service user:

(a) an adviser/friend to the service user, or to those involved with the service user, such as their carers or parents. Such a role is often talked of as 'being an agent of social change'. That is to say, that you will be seeking to make life better for the service user. This is often the motivation behind the decision to become a social worker; and

(b) a statutory relationship in relation to the service user. This is more commonly referred to as being 'an agent of statutory control'. This is where you are sometimes required to use statutory powers to protect the service user.

This second function may well involve you in investigations of the conduct of a service user or of those who are close to that service user. The conflict is clear. A friend does not investigate you or monitor your behaviour. You may be required to make risk assessments of the future behaviour of the service user or those caring for them. A friend does not work out the likelihood of you behaving badly in the future. The tensions are even more apparent with the increased emphasis on partnership working with other agencies, such as the police—see **chapter 7**. Friends do not collude with others against our interests.

Is there a duty to act in the best interests of the service user?

Perhaps this gives us an insight into what went wrong in the case study at the beginning of this chapter. The children's social worker very much wanted the children to have this opportunity of a family life. She forgot that her statutory responsibilities were to act in the best interests of the children. Their best interests would have been served by full disclosure of the information about the difficulties of the boy to the prospective adopters. The social worker's wishes for the children overrode her professional judgement. However, best interests cannot override the legal rights of others. Even if the children's best interests had been served by achieving an adoption placement by concealing from the adopters the history of the children, the decision interfered with the legal duty of care to the adopters. You will come across the word 'paramount' when dealing with court cases such as care orders and contact orders concerning children. In those cases, s. 1 of the Children Act dictates that the court decision is driven by the interests of the child, which are paramount. What this means is that they override any other competing interests with which the court might have the power to interfere, not that they override the legal rights of all and sundry.

It is clear that your prime role has to be within the statutory framework that has created social workers. A social worker who fails to bear this in mind will ultimately fail him- or herself and the service user. This does not mean that your role as friend and adviser is or should be diminished. Nevertheless, you need to build up your relationship with the service user with your statutory role as your first consideration. This is to be honest with that person, which is the best basis for a relationship. The idea of honesty raises questions, however, about the extent to which information is for sharing. The issues are so complex that they require a full chapter to analyse—see **chapter 4**.

Duty of ethical practice in relation to the service user

Box 2.5 sets out the ethics and value of the second domain in the British Association of Social Workers' Professional Capabilities Framework:

BOX 2.5 Ethics and values—BASW Code of Ethics for Social Work (updated October 2014)

Social workers have an obligation to conduct themselves and make decisions in accordance with our Code of Ethics. This includes working in partnership with people who use our services. We promote human rights and social justice. We develop and maintain our understanding of the value base of our profession throughout our career, its ethical standards and relevant law. Experienced social workers will be expected to:

- demonstrate confident and critical application of professional ethical principles (using the Code of Ethics) to decision-making and practice, supporting others to do so using a legal and human rights framework
- model and support others to reflect on and manage the influence and impact of own values on professional practice and the skilled use of self
- provide guidance and support to analyse, reflect on and work with ethical dilemmas
- ensure . . . practice is underpinned by commitment to working in partnership with people who use services, carers, families, communities and networks, wherever possible . . . negotiate and establish boundaries to underpin such partnership, using transparency and honesty
- promote service user and carer participation in developing service delivery
- promote and advance wherever possible individual's rights to autonomy and self-determination, providing support, guidance and challenge to others to promote human and citizenship rights and entitlements
- demonstrate skills in the sensitive exploration of issues of confidentiality, privacy and information-sharing in complex or risky situations, offering support and guidance to colleagues in managing such dilemmas.

These are professional guidelines that will inform the assessment of social workers' capabilities throughout their professional career, and must be respected.

Duty to respect autonomy of the service user

The ethical principle that every person has a right to self-determination and is entitled to their autonomy is set out clearly in the BASW Code of Ethics. In para. 2.1.2 of the Code the following is set out:

> Social workers should respect, promote and support people's dignity and right to make their own choices and decisions, irrespective of their values and life choices, provided this does not threaten the rights, safety and legitimate interests of others.

These principles are also enshrined in law, through the requirement for consent and the duty of confidentiality. Actions taken without consent are unlawful, and in some circumstances, criminal. We provide an overview of this difficult area of legal and ethical practice later in this chapter.

Professional accountability through the courts

Traditionally, local authorities have been protected by the courts from being sued for policy reasons—local authorities should be able to carry out the difficult task of child protection without the risk of being sued. For these reasons, the House of Lords, in *X (Minors) v Bedfordshire County Council* (1995), dismissed claims by children trying to sue for failures by local authorities. There was a shift away from this absolute legal immunity. Local authorities can be sued for negligence as long as the three criteria for the imposition of a duty of care are present. The three criteria were explained by the House of Lords in *Caparo Industries plc v Dickman* (1990) as foreseeability of damage (to what extent was the loss or damage predictable), proximity of relationship (how close was the relationship between the person causing the damage and the victim), and the reasonableness or otherwise of imposing a duty. For social workers, the relationship with the service user is clearly sufficiently proximate, and the damage to the victim is generally predictable. The stumbling block in the past has been whether it was reasonable to impose a duty.

There has been a range of cases demonstrating that negligence by local authorities is now actionable. Among these are *S v Gloucestershire County Council* (2000), where the child was sexually abused by foster parents and *Barrett v Enfield LBC* (1999), where a social worker was careless in implementing decisions made about a child in care. In *W and others v Essex County Council* (2000), the foster parents successfully sued where they had not been told by the social worker that the foster child had come into care for abusing his sister—a case similar to our case study in this chapter. Much more recently, in *Armes v Nottinghamshire County Council* [2017] UKSC 60, [2017], the Supreme Court found the local authority to be vicariously liable to the claimant for damages. The claimant was placed by the authority with foster carers who had systematically abused her. Previously, the local authority could only be liable if it or its employees were negligent. In this case, the Supreme Court agreed that the local authority's relationship with foster carers is sufficient to establish liability where abuse is proved. These cases are distinguished from *X v Bedfordshire* on the basis that the facts in that case concerned the failure of the local authority to take children into care, which was a statutory responsibility which could not be ignored, and not the failure to carry out responsibilities in a particular way.

The House of Lords considered the extent of the duty of care of local authorities and the professionals it employs to carry out its statutory responsibilities in *Phelps v London Borough of Hillingdon* (2000). This case was the legal authority for the judge's decision in the case study at the beginning of this chapter. In *Phelps*, their Lordships make it clear that local authorities are liable for professional misjudgements by their staff; and where a duty of care arises between a professional and a particular child the professional can be sued if there is a breach of that duty.

You may be wondering about time limits for suing a local authority, given that a child who seeks to sue because social services are alleged not to have protected him or her probably will not be able to take action until adulthood. There is a normal three-year limitation period for personal (which includes psychological) injuries under the

Limitation Act 1975, though time does not run until a person reaches adulthood. After that, time only starts to run when a person has actual knowledge of the injury caused, which may be years later in the case of suppressed memories of events in early childhood. Even after that, a court must exercise discretion: *A v Hoare* (2008).

Claims against social workers or agencies under the European Convention

We will be devoting half of **chapter 3** to human rights questions, including the role of the European Court of Human Rights (ECtHR). For now, all you need to know is that individuals have the right to complain against the UK government at the ECtHR if they claim that their rights have been overridden within the UK. The judgment of the ECtHR in *Z and others v UK* (2001) (the name under which the *X v Bedfordshire County Council* case was taken to Europe) was that the English law on negligence was valid. However, the children's human rights had been breached and the law of negligence had not provided them with a way of getting a judgment in court; on that basis the court awarded the children substantial damages against the local authority. The authority's failure to remove the children from the home over a period of four-and-a-half years, during which the children suffered emotional and physical abuse, meant that the authority had breached Article 3 of the Convention— 'No one shall be subjected to torture or to inhuman or degrading treatment or punishment.' The failure of English law to allow the children to sue for breach of Article 3 was a breach of Article 13—'Everyone whose rights and freedoms as set forth in this Convention are violated shall have an effective remedy before a national authority notwithstanding that the violation has been committed by persons acting in an official capacity.'

What this means is that children can sue for breach of their Convention rights where there has been a failure to take appropriate preventive action and can sue in negligence where local authorities have failed to act properly once the child is in care. This does not mean that social workers owe a duty of care to everyone who may be affected by their actions. The duty is only owed where, on the basis of the particular facts of a case, it is fair, just, and reasonable that such a duty should exist. This was made clear by the House of Lords in *JD v East Berkshire Community NHS Trust* (2005). Here the parents sued health professionals for psychiatric harm caused by false allegations of child abuse committed by the parents against the children. The House of Lords decided that their complaint was non-actionable (they had no right to compensation). Health professionals responsible for investigating suspected child abuse did not owe the person suspected of having committed the abuse a duty if they carried out that investigation in good faith but carelessly. The court believed there were cogent public policy reasons for concluding that no common law duty of care should be owed to the parents, since the child's interests were paramount and in potential conflict with those of the parents. It would be inappropriate to have the important work of child protection hamstrung by the fear of litigation. In *Lawrence v Pembrokeshire County Council* (2007) the appellant attempted to extend the ambit of negligence. She appealed against a decision striking out her claim in negligence against the local authority. It had placed L's children on the child protection register for about 14 months. The ombudsman upheld a number of complaints by L of maladministration by Pembrokeshire County Council and recommended that it should pay her compensation. L then issued proceedings in negligence against Pembrokeshire. L sought to challenge the reasoning of *JD v East Berkshire*, claiming that Article 8 called for an evolutionary change to the law of negligence where it overlapped with a parent's right to respect for family life. Her claim that the court should take a small incremental step beyond the East Berkshire decision was rejected. The Court of Appeal said that a 'small incremental step' was a step too far. The public interest in effective and fair investigation and the prevention of criminal behaviour had fashioned the common law to protect those suspected of it from malice or bad faith, but not from a well-intentioned but negligent mistake. There was a need to provide protection to those who had a duty to enforce the law in good faith from the imposition of a duty in negligence that could or might inhibit them in the effective fulfilment of that duty. However, in *CN vs Poole Borough Council* in December 2017, the Court of Appeal held that the judgment in *JD vs East Berkshire* should no longer be followed. Effectively, this means that local authorities owe no duty of care in exercising child protection functions to prevent significant harm. In this instance, the local housing authority was implicated in the maladministration of the case, as were the police. To single out the local authority would be unjust. This case is now before the Supreme Court, the outcome of which is eagerly awaited, since the implications of the Court of Appeal decision is far reaching and seems to run contrary to a trend in negligence cases (see *Armes v Nottinghamshire County Council* [2017] above).

◼ The social worker as statutory creation

Having considered what it means to be a professional social worker, we turn to the second identity of the social worker which we recognized at the beginning of the chapter, the social worker as a statutory creation.

Local Authority Social Services Act 1970

The principal Act imposing the social services function on local authorities (metropolitan boroughs and county authorities) is the Local Authority Social Services Act 1970 (LASSA). Social workers employed in local government, as we know them today, were effectively created by this Act. It is not an easy Act to understand. What it does is to establish the framework for local authority social work, and then refer you to all the other statutes that set out social work responsibilities (statutes dated both before and after 1970, since it is amended continuously). The modern social work professional role did not exist before this statute, and it is to this statute that you look to signpost your statutory powers and duties. Although there is plenty of room for good intentions, these do not define your role; the statute does. The statutes tell you who you have responsibilities towards, and to some extent define how those responsibilities shall be exercised.

Whatever the social services department does is supervised by the relevant Secretary of State. This is because s. 7 of LASSA provides:

> Local authorities shall, in the exercise of their social services functions, . . . act under the general guidance of the Secretary of State.

Section 7 also provides two other mechanisms to ensure that social services committees are accountable to their users and to the government. Section 7C provides for the Secretary of State to set up inquiries into performance of functions and s. 7D provides for the Secretary of State to take over the running of the authority's functions.

You may remember that we discussed the complexity of devolution in **chapter 1**. Here is an example of the sort of differences which result. Section 7B which provided for complaints procedures was repealed *in England only* by the Health and Social Care (Community Health and Standards) Act 2003. Section 7B remains in force for Wales. While LASSA sets out the framework for the provision by the local authority of social care, it is not very specific about the particular way this is to be organized. For instance, it may or may not be of comfort to you to know that the only people within the social services department who actually warrant a specific mention in the Act are the directors of adult social services and directors of children's social services.

LASSA establishes the overall framework. Detailed specific duties, responsibilities, and powers are to be found in other relevant Acts such as the Children Act 1989, the Children Act 2004, or the Mental Health Act 1983. By and large, duties are placed by the legislation not on individual social workers but on the employing local authority. Children's guardians (formerly guardians *ad litem*) and independent reviewing officers (IROs) in child care work and approved mental health practitioners in mental health work, however, have duties imposed on them as individuals.

The social worker as professional who complies with LASSA professional duties

In many ways this is the easiest identity to grasp. You are a professional social worker because of what you do. What you can (and the authority overall must) do is set out in the 1970 statute we mentioned above: LASSA. Schedule 1 sets out every statutory duty which a local authority must carry out. Although it does not specify that individual social workers carry out these duties, or even mention the social work profession, any local authority of necessity carries out these duties by employing social workers.

The 1970 legislation suffers from two major defects. First, it does not systematically organize and define social care services using any coherent framework or philosophy, or, in fact, any framework at all. It merely lists all the bits of all the existing statutes directing what local authorities do for children or for adults and states that this is what must be done. Second, as this list has been added to or amended over four decades, the collection of duties has become less and less coherent. The actual list covers enactments dating from 1933, which specify certain duties to assist children facing criminal proceedings. It sets out the most important sources of duties to adults which date back to 1948 and the beginnings of the welfare state. The 1989 legislation on children is, by comparison, recent. The list is constantly being tweaked, with duties frequently amended and occasionally added.

Table 2.1 gives a quick summary of some key areas of LASSA duties. Those duties which can be grouped under providing services to children in need, or protecting

TABLE 2.1 Key statutory duties of the social worker

The Acts	Nature of the duties of local authority social services committees
Children and Young Persons Acts 1933 and 1963	Support for children involved in criminal prosecution
Children Act 1989	Support for children in need and to protect children at risk of significant harm
Adoption and Children Act 2002	Providing adoption services
National Assistance Act 1948	Providing care services in the community or residential care for those who cannot cope without such services
Children Act 2004 (CA 2004)	Establishing a children's commissioner; reorganizing aspects of child protection work
Mental Capacity Act 2005	Appointment of independent advocates for patients
Children and Young Persons Act 2008	Strengthening the role of the independent reviewing officer
Care Act 2014	General responsibilities in relation to care and support services
	Assessing and meeting needs for care and support, and carers' needs
	Direct payments, deferred payment agreements, and loans
	Continuity of care and ordinary residence
	Safeguarding adults
	Provider failure
	Children in transition to adult care and support
	Independent advocacy support
	Recovery of charges
	Appeals against local authority decisions
	Discharge of hospital patients
	Registers
	Delegation of functions

children, are considered in detail in **Part 2** of this book. Those relating to adults are dealt with in **Part 3**. However, whilst these statutory functions are important, there is, as you are already becoming aware, far more law with which you have to be familiar.

The LASSA duties identify the service user, as well as providing the link to the statute which sets out in more detail how the needs for the service are to be assessed and provided. It would be nice, at this stage, to say that if a duty is not on this list, it does not exist. But there is a grey area where social service authorities have been given explicit duties without these creating a duty to provide a service to a service user. These mainly fall within the area of youth justice (**chapter 10**). It falls on social services to organize youth offending teams, to send social workers to police stations when a child or vulnerable adult is being interviewed, to provide assistance to the court in deciding on sentence of children, and to assist in administering community sentences handed down by the courts. However, it is reasonably clear—though the link is not made explicit—that you can find a service user whose needs would otherwise fall into the LASSA list each time one of these responsibilities arises, either a child in need or a vulnerable adult.

The social worker as an employee with rights and duties

You have obligations, as does any employee, to do the best you can for your employer. This may produce conflicts arising in individual cases. As an employee you are legally required to follow the instructions of your employer. However, your employer has hired you because you are a professional, and the exercise of professional judgement is part—a major part—of your duties to the employer. We hope conflict occurs rarely, but it remains a real possibility.

In the event of irreconcilable conflict, you must do what the employer tells you to do (so long as the request is legal), but this does not mean keeping quiet about your professional opinion. In fact, to express as your opinion a belief that you actually do not hold is itself a breach of your professional duty. If expressed in court it would be close to perjury (false testimony). It is, of course, rare that opinions differ in an irreconcilable way.

Accountability to your employer

Many social workers are concerned that they may be personally liable if they make mistakes. There is no doubt that if things go wrong you will have to explain your decisions. If you have taken reasonable care, kept your written records properly, and acted within an acceptable level of professional competence, then you will be able to do this. If you do make a professional misjudgement there may be several consequences. First, the case may become the subject of an inquiry and you may be personally blamed in the report. Many feel that such an emphasis on individual social workers is unfair. The Laming Report on the death of Victoria Climbié made this point:

> It is not to the handful of hapless, if sometimes inexperienced, front line staff that I direct most criticism for the events leading up to Victoria's death. Whilst the standard of work done by those with direct contact with her was generally of very poor quality, the greatest failure rests with the managers and senior members of the authorities whose task it was to ensure that services for children like Victoria were properly financed, staffed, and able to deliver good quality support to children and families.

(para. 1.23)

Despite this statement, the social worker for Victoria was sacked, as was the social worker for Peter Connelly some years later. Second, you are subject to the risk that you will be disciplined, and even dismissed, because of your mistake. The incompetent social worker will always take this risk. As Laming points out, the risk to you is almost always greater than the risk to senior managers.

Finally, as we saw earlier (**Professional accountability through the courts**, p 53), the person who suffers may be able to sue for compensation for the effects of your mistake. He or she is far more likely to sue the local authority than you, and even if you are sued, you will be indemnified by your employer.

Confidentiality as an employee

We discuss in **chapter 4** the duty of confidentiality you have to service users and others. Social workers will also have duties of confidentiality which arise from their employment. If you breach a term of your contract then you may be disciplined, or even dismissed. Your trade union, professional association, or a lawyer experienced in employment law will have to advise you on procedure.

There may, however, be occasions when you would feel justified in breaching the requirement of confidentiality between you and your employer. For instance, a social worker may wish to disclose that the social services department is chronically understaffed or that a colleague is professionally incompetent. The BASW Code of Ethics may be of some assistance here. Paragraph 9 of the Ethical Practice Principles states:

> Social workers should be prepared to report bad practice using all available channels including complaints procedures and if necessary use public interest disclosure legislation and whistleblowing guidelines.

The responsibility is on the social worker to know the internal complaints procedures. Where these do not produce satisfactory results, social workers should consult their trade union or professional association for advice. In the last resort, the Public Interest Disclosure Act 1998 may provide some assistance.

'Whistle-blowing' under the Public Interest Disclosure Act 1998 (as amended by the Enterprise and Regulatory Reform Act 2013)

The Public Interest Disclosure Act 1998 (PIDA) is designed to encourage people to raise genuine concerns about malpractice in the workplace by providing legal protection against dismissal or victimization. The motivation for the legislation is that workers are often aware of poor or dangerous work practices but are too scared to sound the alarm or do not know how to raise an issue. Examples of a reluctance to 'blow the whistle' can be found in social work inquiries. Since the implementation of the legislation, if a social worker makes a disclosure in good faith to a manager or an employer, he or she will be protected as a whistle-blower if he or she has a reasonable suspicion that the malpractice has occurred, is occurring, or is likely to occur. The Enterprise and Regulatory Reform Act 2013 (ERRA) amended the scope of the protection slightly by making it clear that any disclosure must be in the public interest. The Act also protects disclosures made in good faith to prescribed regulatory bodies where the whistle-blower reasonably believes that the information and any allegation in it are substantially true. Wider disclosures (e.g. to the police, the media, Members of Parliament (MPs), and non-prescribed regulators) are protected if, in addition to the test for regulatory disclosure, they are reasonable in all the circumstances and:

- they are not made for personal gain;
- the whistle-blower must have reasonably believed he or she would be victimized if he or she raised the matter internally or with a prescribed regulator; and
- the whistle-blower reasonably believed a cover-up was likely and there was not a prescribed regulator, or had already raised the matter internally or with a prescribed regulator.

If the concern is exceptionally serious, a disclosure will be protected if it meets the test for regulatory disclosures and is not made for personal gain. The disclosure must also be reasonable, having particular regard to the identity of the person it was made to.

Where the whistle-blower is victimized in breach of the Act, he or she can bring a claim to an employment tribunal for compensation. The ERRA has amended the protection by enabling a tribunal to reduce any compensation awarded by 25 per cent if the disclosure was not made in good faith.

Your employer's responsibilities to you

Local authorities have responsibilities and duties towards you as their employee. The nature and volume of your work, with its associated risks of violence and abuse, place you under a great deal of stress. You must balance individuals' needs with limited resources, and you are responsible for decisions which have significant implications for people's lives. In *Walker v Northumberland County Council* (1995), where a social worker suffered a nervous breakdown as a result of stress, the court made it clear that all employers have a duty of care and a duty in contract to ensure that the employee is kept safe from psychiatric as well as physical harm. Local authorities which breach this duty may be liable to pay substantial compensation to social workers. In September 2001, headline news was made by a former social worker who received £140,000 damages in settlement of her claim against Worcestershire County Council for a stress-related illness developed through work. In *Gogay v Hertfordshire County Council* (2001), a worker in a care home was suspended when concerns were raised about allegations of abuse made by a vulnerable child. The facts on which those concerns were raised were not clear. The court found that the local authority could suspend the worker only if it was 'reasonable and proper' to do so. So, the law should protect you from excessive work pressure and being treated in an arbitrary manner, although having to go to court to settle disputes is not straightforward or easy. The Social Work Reform Board established a set of Standards for Employers and Supervision Framework in 2011 following criticism explored in the Munro Report about social workers' excessive workloads. However, there was no regulatory body to oversee those Standards and they appear to have fallen by the wayside. Assistance can be provided by membership of a Trade Union or through membership of BASW.

We now move to consider one important aspect of a social worker's relationship with service users—the need for consent or legal authority before acting.

Lawful authority

Interference with another person's physical integrity, property, or affairs without their consent will be unlawful unless explicit legal authority is given. Examples of lawful authority in the absence of consent would be:

- a court order, for example a care or specific issue order under the Children Act 1989, a compulsory detention order under the Mental Health Act 1983, removal to residential accommodation under s. 47 of the National Assistance Act 1948, or a common law declaration of the lawfulness of carrying out medical treatment;
- an explicit police power, for example of arrest under the Police and Criminal Evidence Act 1984, a power to remove to a place of safety under the Mental Health Act 1983, or the Children Act 1989;
- powers to act for the benefit of an incapacitated person under the Mental Capacity Act 2005;
- power under s. 3(5) of the Children Act 1989, which provides that 'A person who (a) does not have parental responsibility for a particular child; but (b) has care of the child, may (subject to the provisions of this Act) do what is reasonable in all the circumstances of the case for the purpose of safeguarding or promoting the child's welfare';
- the power of the Department for Work and Pensions under social security legislation to appoint someone to apply for and receive benefits on another person's behalf, where this is in the interests of the claimant.

Alternatively, interference without consent would require implicit authority under previous court rulings, or explicit court authorization, for example:

- intervening as a matter of necessity to save life or prevent serious harm (permissible for medical treatment under the common law);
- other medical interventions including cessation of treatment and pain relief, for example if it is in the best interests of a terminally ill patient.

These two examples do not apply if the person has given advance directives or is presently able to give, or refuse, consent as to whether or not to be treated. If action is taken without consent or legal authority, the consequences could be criminal prosecution or civil liability for damages. Therefore, in *Re B (Consent to Treatment: Capacity)* (2002) the Court of Appeal upheld the refusal of a woman with a deteriorating physical condition who made a deliberate choice to refuse artificial ventilation should her breathing deteriorate further. It was up to her to decide. The circumstances may not be so clear-cut. In *HE v A Hospital NHS Trust* (2003) the patient had given an advance directive that she did not wish to have a blood transfusion, but on admission to hospital it became clear that she was no longer a Jehovah's Witness and had not communicated any such desire prior to treatment. It was decided that she could be treated without consent as it was not proven that her wishes were, now, clearly opposed to such a transfusion.

▨ Social work ethics and consent

If there is no lawful authority enabling you to intervene, then you must get consent for your actions. The ethical principle that every person has a right to self-determination and is entitled to their autonomy is set out clearly in the BASW Code of Ethics. In para. 3.2 of the Code, headed 'Assessing and Managing Risk', the Code sets out the following:

> Social workers should recognise that people using social work services have the right to take risks and should enable them to identify and manage potential and actual risk, while seeking to ensure that their behaviour does not harm themselves or other people. Social workers should support people to reach informed decisions about their lives and promote their autonomy and independence, provided this does not conflict with their safety or with the rights of others. Social workers should only take actions which diminish peoples' civil or legal rights if it is ethically, professionally and legally justifiable.

The principle is also enshrined in law, through the notion of consent. Actions taken without consent are unlawful, and in some circumstances, criminal. They also breach the right to respect for private life under Article 8 of the European Convention on Human Rights (see **chapter 3**).

We provide here a very brief outline of this difficult area of law. Most of the case law relates to health professionals, but the principles will be relevant to decisions which have to be made by social workers in relation to provision of services to children and adults. It is particularly important when you are asking a service user to consent to the sharing of confidential information.

Forms of consent

Consent may be express or implied. It is expressed when someone explicitly agrees to the action being taken. When a person signs a consent form in connection with the Data Protection Act, they are consenting to the holding and using of personal information.

Implied consent is a more difficult concept. The person making the decision may, from the circumstances, deduce from a person's conduct their state of mind. An example is that when you participate in team sports you implicitly consent to the bodily contact, and risk of injury, that will almost inevitably arise. But if you are assaulted deliberately in the course of the game, you did not consent to that (unless the game is a form of fighting, such as boxing, where even severe injury will have been consented to).

Reliance on implicit consent, particularly to the sort of interventions in personal autonomy which arise in the course of social care, is probably not a wise course of action. Interestingly, following the cases involving retention of children's organs for many years for research purposes without explicit consent of the bereaved parents, guidance has been issued for hospitals, which must now obtain clear and detailed consent from families for post-mortem examinations of their relatives. Times have changed, and the assumption amongst the medical research profession that the parents would have given consent and did not need to be asked would now be seen as patronizing and plainly wrong. There have also been successful claims for psychiatric distress caused— for example, *AB and others v Leeds Teaching Hospital NHS Trust and another* (2004).

The nature of consent

Lawful consent has three qualities. First, the person must have the capacity or competence to consent; second, he or she must have sufficient information to enable them to give informed consent; and, third, consent must have been given voluntarily. (See **chapter 6** for a discussion of consent in respect of s. 20 accommodation.) Our main concern will be with the question of capacity.

What must be understood?

Clearly, if the law requires a total understanding of all of the implications of the decision, then few people are going to have legal capacity to consent. Before consenting to surgery, a patient will not need to be provided with the research papers in which risk is analysed and need not be capable of forming a useful judgement even if these were provided; but the patient is entitled to be informed of the nature and broad extent of risk of a particular type of complication, rather than being told merely not to worry. If the patient cannot understand at that general level, informed consent is not possible.

The Mental Capacity Act 2005 sets out to enable most people to make most decisions for themselves. Under s. 3(1) a person is able to make a decision for him- or herself if able to manage the following:

(a) to *understand* the information relevant to the decision;
(b) to *retain* that information;
(c) to *use* or weigh that information as part of the process of making a decision; and
(d) to *communicate* his or her decision.

The level of understanding can vary according to the situation: a woman about to lose her child through refusing a clearly medically indicated caesarean, where her own and the child's lives are otherwise at great risk, was considered not really able to understand the decision she was making, and therefore her refusal of consent was not an informed refusal and could be overruled by a court: *Bolton Hospitals NHS Trust v O* (2002). The difference in this case and that of *Re B* (see **Lawful authority**, p 61) may have been the fact that the life of the unborn baby was also at risk. It is hard to see any evidence that the woman did not clearly understand and accept that she was risking her life and that of her baby, and the decision that she did not understand appears to have been a fig leaf to get around the implications of letting both of them die when this tragedy could be so easily avoided.

Actual understanding or ability to understand?

This is another difficult question, to which the law provides no clear answer. It would be logical to require actual understanding, but then if the social worker or the doctor failed to provide sufficient information the person would be deprived of their capacity to consent. In *Gillick*—the leading case on the capacity of children to make informed decisions—the judges stated that what was important was that someone was capable of understanding the decision, and the gravity of the situation should be taken into account. In *Re L (Medical Treatment: Gillick Competency)* (1998) the court required actual understanding because of the consequences of a refusal of consent. Here the life of a 14-year-old girl was in danger as a result of serious and extensive burns. She was a practising Jehovah's Witness and refused to consent to the medical treatment as it might have required a blood transfusion. The court decided that what was required was actual understanding of the decision. The doctor had not explained to her the nature of the death she would endure if she did not undergo medical treatment. Because of that the court was able to decide that she did not have actual understanding of the decision and was therefore not competent to refuse the treatment. Her consent to receive the treatment, by contrast, would not have had such grave consequences and would probably have been sufficient, even against her parents' objections (though not had she been, say, aged eight, where a court order would have been necessary, if there was time to obtain it, to overcome her parents' refusal to consent on her behalf).

However, in the case of an adult, to override clear wishes is unusual. It can happen, for example, in the case of the woman in childbirth (**What must be understood?**, p 63), where the problem was temporary and urgent, and, in the opinion of the court, the woman could not at the time understand the consequences of what she was deciding. In *Malette v Shulman* (1991), a woman refused a blood transfusion and the court accepted this, and it inevitably led to her death. Interestingly, this same woman's refusal to consent before she turned 18 had been overruled and she had been treated under the court's consent, not her own.

Establishing competence to provide consent

We stated earlier that you need to start with the assumption that adults are competent. Legal authority for this comes, for example, from *Re T (Adult: Refusal of Treatment)* (1992). Section 8 of the Family Law Reform Act 1969 additionally provides that children aged between 16 and 18 are presumed competent. However, for both adults and 16–18-year-olds the presumption of competence is rebuttable. And the decision in the *Gillick* case means that the 1969 Act does not exclude under-16-year-olds from providing consent to their own treatment or, in principle, from refusing consent to treatment. An assessment of the child's competence is required in each case, and that assessment will vary according to the decision in question (as we discussed earlier when considering the gravity of a refusal of consent to a blood transfusion: **Actual understanding or ability to understand?**, p 63).

Competence to refuse treatment

There are a number of extremely clear statements that a competent person has freedom of choice, 'whether the reasons for making that choice are rational, irrational, unknown or even non-existent' per Lord Donaldson in *Re T*, cited above. The principle was revisited by Dame Elizabeth Butler-Sloss in the well-known case of *B* to which we referred in **Lawful authority**, p 61. Ms B, who had become completely paralysed following serious illness, sought declarations from the High Court that continued artificial ventilation against her wishes was unlawful. The judge was satisfied that Ms B was competent to make all relevant decisions and granted the declarations.

It should not be assumed that refusal of treatment is only possible where a person has no mental health problems. Each situation must be weighed up. In *Re C* (1993), a mental patient had gangrene but refused treatment. The court decided, on the evidence, that he knew enough about the issues to refuse amputation and take the risk. As it happens, his leg recovered. Similarly, in *Re W (Adult: Refusal of Medical Treatment)* (2002) a prisoner with severe psychosis wanted a transfer to a different hospital. To draw attention to his complaint, he cut his leg open repeatedly and forced foreign matter into the wound. He then refused treatment for the infection. The court refused an order to allow him to be treated. He clearly understood what he was doing and could not be treated against his will.

However, there are many situations with adults and children where competence to refuse treatment is found to be lacking. Competent children cannot, in general, withhold consent. In Re R (1991), the Court of Appeal held that although an anorexic 16-year-old girl could be said to be '*Gillick* competent', that fact did not prevent the court ordering that she be given drugs against her will. The court, in a much-criticized decision, drew the distinction between the ability of the girl to give consent and her right to refuse consent. It said that while she could give valid consent, if she refused this did not mean that others such as parents or the court could not still impose consent on her behalf.

The court said:

> The failure or refusal of the 'Gillick competent' child is a very important factor in the doctor's decision whether or not to treat, but it does not prevent the necessary consent being obtained from another competent source.

Similarly, in *Re W (A Minor) (Consent to Medical Treatment)* (1993), the Court of Appeal again overrode the refusal of an anorexic to accept treatment. The notion of a competent child involves limited competence. The courts consider that the welfare of the child is not something to be decided solely by the child. The welfare of the child can be decided by others, particularly the court.

Refusal of consent also raises problems for adults—for example, the refusal to undergo a caesarean, which the court overruled (see **What must be understood?**, p 63). *NHS Trust v T (Adult Patient: Refusal of Medical Treatment)* (2004) provides another example of particular interest because the patient had given a clear advance directive at a time when her mental competence was reasonably clear. She self-harmed to such an extent when in a state of temporary psychosis that she required frequent blood transfusions. Her advance directive stated that she knew the consequences of refusal, and she nevertheless did not consent to future transfusions. She believed her blood to be evil, though she acknowledged in her advance directive that this was a manifestation of her illness. She claimed in the directive that she had sufficient understanding of her situation and her illness at the time of making it to be able to refuse consent. Knowing the situation would arise again, the hospital which treated her applied in advance for court guidance. The judge used guidelines, set out in **Box 2.6**, from an earlier case (*Re MB (Medical Treatment)* (1997)), which are helpful to repeat:

BOX 2.6 Guidelines for capacity of consent—*Re MB (Medical Treatment)* (1997)

1   Every person is presumed to have the capacity to consent to or to refuse medical treatment unless and until that presumption is rebutted.

2   A competent woman who has the capacity to decide may, for religious reasons, other reasons, for rational or irrational reasons or for no reason at all, choose not to have medical intervention, even though the consequence may be the death or serious handicap of the child she bears, or her own death. In that event the courts do not have the jurisdiction to declare medical intervention lawful and the question of her own best interests, objectively considered, does not arise.

3   Irrationality is here used to connote a decision which is so outrageous in its defiance of logic or of accepted moral standards that no sensible person who had applied his mind to the question to be decided it could have arrived at it . . . it might be otherwise if a decision is based on a misperception of reality (e.g. the blood is poisoned because it is red). Such a misperception will be more readily accepted to be a disorder of the mind. Although it might be thought that irrationality sits uneasily with competence to decide, panic, indecisiveness and irrationality in themselves do not as such amount to incompetence, but they may be symptoms or evidence of incompetence. The graver the consequences of the decision, the commensurately greater the level of competence is required to take the decision . . .

4   A person lacks capacity if some impairment or disturbance of mental functioning renders the person unable to make a decision whether to consent to or to refuse treatment. That inability to make a decision will occur when:

(a) the patient is unable to comprehend and retain the information which is material to the decision, especially as to the likely consequences of having or not having the treatment in question;

(b) the patient is unable to use the information and weigh it in the balance as part of the process of arriving at the decision. If, as Thorpe J observed in *Re C* [see earlier in this section], a compulsive disorder or phobia from which the patient suffers stifles belief in the information presented to her, then the decision may not be a true one. As Lord Cockburn CJ put it in *Banks v Goodfellow* (1870): ' . . . one object may be so forced upon the attention of the invalid as to shut out all others that might require consideration'.

5   The 'temporary factors' mentioned by Lord Donaldson MR in Re T [**Establishing competence to provide consent,** p 64] (confusion, shock, fatigue, pain, or drugs) may completely erode capacity but those concerned must be satisfied that such factors are operating to such a degree that the ability to decide is absent.

6   Another such influence may be panic induced by fear. Again, careful scrutiny of the evidence is necessary because fear of an operation may be a rational reason for refusal to undergo it. Fear may also, however, paralyse the will and thus destroy the capacity to make a decision.

Balancing individual autonomy with welfare

When acting for children the position is clear. Section 1(1) of the Children Act provides that:

When a court determines any question with respect to—

(a)   the upbringing of a child; or

(b)   the administration of a child's property or the application of any income arising from it, the child's welfare shall be the court's paramount consideration.

'Upbringing' under the Act will include decisions about social or health care where for any reason parents cannot make this decision themselves. These are dealt with under s. 8 and are further discussed in **chapter 5**.

In cases involving children, respect for autonomy involves not only that of the child, but also that of the parent. The tension between autonomy and welfare can be seen, taking a case involving children, in *South Glamorgan County Council v W and B* (1993). Here Douglas Browne J was faced with the problem of a young person who clearly was beyond parental control. She was aged 15. She had refused to do anything she was told. She had, in fact, barricaded herself in the front room of her father's house for 11 months. The local authority wanted an interim care order to have the child assessed. The difficulty was the provisions in s. 38(6) of the Children Act 1989, which deal with the court's powers to make orders for assessments to be carried out when making interim care orders (see **chapter 8**). This particular subsection has provision for informed consent by the young person, stating, 'but if the child is of sufficient understanding to make an informed decision he may refuse to submit to the examination or other assessment'. The local authority and those acting for the girl put the view to the court that if she refused to submit to the assessment, then there was little that anyone could do. The judge would not accept this and gave directions under the inherent power of the court (s. 100) for the authority to remove the child. In effect, he bypassed the provisions of the Act relating to informed consent. He did this without making the girl a ward of court. He said:

> In my judgment the court can in an appropriate case—and they will be rare cases—but in an appropriate case, when other remedies within the Children Act have been used and exhausted and found not to bring about the desired result, can resort to other remedies, and the particular remedy here is the remedy of providing authority, if it is needed, for the local authority to take all necessary steps to bring the child to the doctors so that she can be assessed and treated.

Re B (Wardship: Abortion) (1991) illustrates the range of issues which can arise when balancing autonomy with welfare. A 12-year-old girl was pregnant. She herself consented to abortion and was supported by her grandparents. Her mother refused. The local authority and several medical witnesses thought aborting the foetus would be in the girl's best interests, physically and emotionally. The mother's experts thought the opposite. The court had to decide and decided in favour of a termination. The welfare, rather than consent issues, were uppermost, though what the child herself wanted influenced the assessment of what would also be in her best interests. There is a further discussion of consent in respect of s. 20 accommodation in **chapter 6**, see **The power to provide accommodation**, p 228.

Legal representation of children

There have been a number of cases concerning the ability of children or young people to appoint guardians or solicitors to act on their behalf. In *Re S (A Minor)* (1993), the

Court of Appeal held that a child of 11 could not remove the Official Solicitor as guardian. The court said:

> The 1989 [Children] Act enabled and required a judicious balance to be struck between two considerations. First was the principle, to be honoured and respected, that children were human beings in their own right with individual minds and wills, views and emotions, which should command attention. Second was the fact that a child was, after all, a child.

In *Re H (A Minor) (Care Proceedings: Child's Wishes)* (1993), the court said that a 15-year-old did not have the right to address the court on his own behalf. Guidelines for judges meeting children who were subject to family proceedings were given by the Family Justice Council in April 2010. The purpose of those guidelines was to encourage judges to enable children to feel more involved in proceedings in which important decisions were made in their lives, and to give them an opportunity to satisfy themselves that the judge had understood their wishes and feelings. It was noteworthy that the purpose of the guidelines was not to satisfy the judge that, if he saw the children, he would be better able to understand what their wishes were. Thus, such meetings were not for the purpose of gathering evidence. The decision in Re H was implicitly supported by a decision of the Court of Appeal in *Re W (Children)* (2008). The children clearly wanted to go with their mother to Sweden, but the judge hearing the application had refused to allow them to be taken out of the jurisdiction. Their mother's appeal was on the basis that the judge had refused to interview the children directly. The Court of Appeal thought this would not be a good course of action, though they did agree that the judge's decision itself was wrong. These were three *Gillick*-competent children who very clearly expressed to the court what they wanted, and it was wrong not to give their views considerably more weight.

These cases point to a view that, despite the apparent philosophy of legislation and statements supporting the right of children of understanding to participate in the decisions which concern them, and increasingly to make those decisions, the court retains the right to make the difficult decisions for itself, and, if it feels it must, to substitute its view for that of the child or young person. They appear to be particularly reluctant to allow a child to decide to participate in adversarial litigation. The Gillick-competent child is therefore only a competent person in a very limited sense.

Representation of adults

Family members may claim to speak for the adult, but there may be a conflict of interest. In straightforward litigation where there is no conflict—for example, a personal injuries claim following an accident—appointment of a litigation friend on behalf of an adult lacking capacity to conduct the proceedings is relatively straightforward. But where complex decisions have to be made about what is in the adult's own interests and whether he or she has capacity, a court will generally appoint the Official Solicitor to represent the adult's interests in the case.

Proxies

If people are not competent, then decisions have to be made for them and others must act as proxies for them.

For children, those people are generally parents. Each parent or other person with parental responsibility is able to exercise the right to consent individually. However, there may be a duty to consult the other parent in relation to major decisions. In the absence of agreement between parents, the courts may impose a limitation on the power of one parent to take the decision: for example, a decision to change a child's surname will require the approval of the court if the parents cannot agree. *In Re J (Child's Religious Upbringing and Circumcision)* (1999), it was held that ritual circumcision did not fall within the power of one parent to consent to, where there was disagreement between the parents.

As you will see (in **chapter 8**) local authorities may acquire parental responsibility under Part IV of the Children Act 1989. This enables them to consent to treatment, etc. on behalf of the children. Parents retain parental responsibility, but if a care order is made the local authority is allowed to restrict the exercise of that authority—see **chapter 8**.

The Children Act 1989 also provides for a further possible proxy. Section 3(5) provides:

A person who—

    (a) does not have parental responsibility for a particular child; but

    (b) has the care of the child,
    may (subject to the provisions of this Act) do what is reasonable in all the circumstances of the case for the purpose of safeguarding or promoting the child's welfare.

Teachers or grandparents are able to make necessary decisions with the authority of this provision.

The court is also a decision maker on behalf of children. The High Court has power as part of its inherent jurisdiction, and family proceedings courts in respect of s. 8 orders. We consider the power of the courts to make 'specific issues' orders and 'prohibited steps' orders in **chapter 5**.

All proxies must make decisions consistent with the welfare, or best interests, of the child.

The Mental Capacity Act 2005

The Mental Capacity Act 2005 provides a comprehensive framework for assessing whether a person of 16 and over has capacity to make decisions and making lawful an action to benefit the person who does not have capacity. **Box 2.7** give the principles, which are very clearly stated in s. 1:

BOX 2.7 Principles to assess mental capacity—s. 1 of the Mental Capacity Act 2005

(2) A person must be assumed to have capacity unless it is established that he lacks capacity.

(3) A person is not to be treated as unable to make a decision unless all practicable steps to help him to do so have been taken without success.

(4) A person is not to be treated as unable to make a decision merely because he makes an unwise decision.

(5) An act done, or decision made, under this Act for or on behalf of a person who lacks capacity must be done, or made, in his best interests.

(6) Before the act is done, or the decision is made, regard must be had to whether the purpose for which it is needed can be as effectively achieved in a way that is less restrictive of the person's rights and freedom of action.

A 'person *lacks capacity* in relation to a matter if at the material time he is unable to make a decision for himself in relation to the matter because of an impairment of, or a disturbance in the functioning of, the mind or brain'. The problem can be temporary—the decision has to be made according to the issue that has arisen at a particular time.

The Act talks in terms of hypothetical figures D (the person intervening) and P (the person whose capacity is being considered). For our discussion, we limit it to social worker and service user, though please do not conclude that the Act is limited to this context. Anyone—benign relative, passer-by, doctor, etc.—is protected if they act on behalf of another person without consent under the terms of this Act.

The social worker who decides a service user lacks *capacity to make a decision* is protected if, at the time, and on the balance of probabilities (which means that something is more likely than not) the service user is 'unable to understand the information relevant to the decision, [or] to retain that information, [or] to use or weigh that information as part of the process of making the decision, or to communicate his decision (whether by talking, using sign language or any other means)'.

Actions taken must always be in the best interests of the service user. This is based on all the circumstances, but in particular 'whether it is likely that the person will at some time have capacity in relation to the matter in question, and if it appears likely that he will, when that is likely to be'. This means that there is no point acting now if there is a good chance the service user will have capacity for him- or herself to take the necessary action later. Even though lacking capacity, the service user must, as far as possible, 'participate, or to improve his ability to participate, as fully as possible in any act done for him and any decision affecting him [in the light of] the person's past and present wishes and feelings [and] the beliefs and values that would be likely to influence his decision if he had capacity', and must consult if appropriate 'anyone named by the person as someone to be consulted on the matter . . . anyone engaged in caring for the person or interested in his welfare . . . anyone of a lasting power of attorney granted by the person' (we discuss these in **chapter 14**).

The result of going through this checklist is that if the social worker 'reasonably believes that what he does or decides is in the best interests of the person concerned' he or she is acting lawfully, so long as the actions which follow are neither negligent nor criminal and are compliant with the terms of any advance directive (see **chapter 14**). The powers to act include physical restraint and payment out of the service user's available funds for goods and services. We strongly suggest taking legal advice in advance of taking such steps, unless physical restraint is needed in an emergency.

Working with lawyers

Lawyers, like social workers, have a professional identity. They belong to a professional body—the Law Society or the Bar Council, dependent upon whether they are solicitors or barristers—and are bound by a code of conduct. The code of conduct for solicitors, however, focuses on less complex dilemmas, such as not acting for people where you have a conflict of interest, and having to hold money that belongs to clients in a separate account from your own money. This is because lawyers have a more straightforward relationship with their clients than you have with the service user. If the lawyer and the client disagree on what is the best course of action, then the client can sack the lawyer. The child or vulnerable adult who is your service user does not have that freedom.

Lawyers are originally not creations of statute; they are creatures of the market, though you will perhaps be reassured to know that the law now regulates them closely. There has always been a demand for lawyers to interpret the law and to argue for an interpretation which best suits the client who is paying them. This is not to say that the individual lawyer does not have ideals; indeed, the prime motivation for working in social welfare law is an idealistic one, since other areas of law pay far more. However, being a lawyer does not in itself require an idealistic vocation, perhaps in contrast with the social worker. If there is an overarching ideal it is perhaps best expressed as a commitment to the rule of law, which includes the right of all to have the best professional help to argue their case on an equal footing.

Lawyers also have different skills from social workers. Their skills lie in the interpretation of complex statutes and cases and in defending the interests of their clients through negotiation and advocacy.

However, it is probably at the quite different level of their view of the world that the essential difference between the social worker and the lawyer is seen most clearly. Social workers want what is best for the service user, which is not always the same as what the service user actually wants; lawyers are interested in achieving for the client what he or she wants, and the question of whether it should be what they want is wholly irrelevant. This is best illustrated by an incident involving one of our colleagues, a lawyer. When she was working at a law centre, she was approached by a 16-year-old woman clutching the hand of a 35-year-old man. The young woman explained that she was in care and she wanted to marry her boyfriend. Our colleague explained the legal process of getting permission from the magistrates. Our colleague was then telephoned by the young woman's social worker, who was outraged at the advice. Marrying the boyfriend was not in the best interests of the young woman, in the opinion of the social worker, and therefore it was inappropriate to advise her how to go about it. Our colleague was perplexed; she considered she was only doing her job. The social worker was perplexed; the lawyer did not understand the best interests of the young woman. Our opinion is that both of these roles are important. When there are two conflicting sets of wants, the lawyer's role is to represent one, not both, sides. The lawyer does so within a framework which prevents any invention of evidence, any collusion in crime, or any attempt to mislead an opponent or a court. The lawyer should also help a client to reach an informed decision before acting on the client's instructions. So, there is still a lot of professional responsibility and scope for some personal concern. But it does not go so far as telling the client she cannot do what she is legally entitled to do. The social worker in that situation should not have criticized the lawyers. She or he could and should have got advice from their own lawyer on what legal measures—if any—were available to protect this child's welfare.

 SUMMARY

- Social workers employed by public authorities are required to carry out tasks set down in law. Failure to do so is likely to lead to potentially significant censure.

- Social workers should conduct themselves according to agreed sets of professional ethics or standards. Similarly, their decisions should be ethically defensible.

- Social Work England has been established as the new regulator for the profession. The title of social worker is a protected in law and to practise social work requires that one should be appropriately registered with the relevant regulator.

- Social workers' responsibilities are complex, especially when it comes to acting in the best interests of service users. Service users' wishes and feelings should be taken into account but the nature of social workers' tasks means that wishes and feelings should not always be followed. Social workers' tasks are largely defined by the Local Authority Social Services Act 1970. This act lists a large number of social work tasks, but not in any coherent or organized fashion.

- Local authorities have been sued in the courts for breaches of statutory responsibilities to children.

- Social workers are accountable to their employers and may be liable if they make mistakes. However, if social workers have taken reasonable care and acted within an acceptable level of professional competence, they will have a reasonable defence in respect of their liability if something goes wrong. Equally, employers have responsibilities to social workers to ensure they are kept safe from harm, including emotional harm.

- Social workers should ensure they always maintain service users' confidentiality and act on the consent of service users, unless there is a public interest in dispensing with that consent. The Mental Capacity Act 2005 sets out the criteria for deciding when a person lacks capacity to consent and acting on their behalf for their benefit.

EXERCISES

1 Do you think your role is about justice, care, or social order?

2 A neighbour reports the Lee family to social services because of fears for the welfare of the children. You are admitted to the home by Jasmine Lee and discover the following.

   (a) Her daughter Susan Lee, aged 13, appears anorexic and seriously underweight. She also has an unrelated skin disorder. Her mother does not want her to receive treatment for either condition. Susan would like treatment for the skin disorder but does not accept that she suffers from anorexia.

   (b) Mrs Lee's mother-in-law, Selina Lee, is aged 75 and speaks no English. Jasmine Lee indicates that her mother-in-law is suffering from serious mental health problems and asks you to take her to a specialist unit for assessment. Mr Lee says he does not want you to take his mother anywhere and he is quite capable of deciding what is best for her.

   What are the principles involved in relation to issues of consent to treatment or assessment?

3 Ms C, the parent of two children who were sexually abused by a neighbour's child, wants to sue the local authority. She claims that she is suffering from psychiatric illness which is the result of the local authority's failure to act upon her concerns about the safety of her children. When she reported her concerns about the possibilities of sexual abuse, the local authority did not believe her and asked the social worker allocated to the abuser's family to investigate her complaints. Will the courts allow her to pursue her claim?

ONLINE RESOURCES

For guidance on how to answer these exercises, visit the online resources at www.oup.com/uk/carr-goosey15e.

WHERE DO WE GO FROM HERE?

This chapter builds upon **chapter 1**, which introduced you to the legal system. Here we have considered the relationship between the social worker and the law by identifying the multiple roles of the social worker and by demonstrating how the law, alongside ethics, determines each of those roles. We hope that this has provided an interesting introduction to your studies.

We may have given an impression that law and ideals are opposites. It is true that we have suggested that you should—indeed must—be guided by the powers and duties as laid down by law. If this might blunt your enthusiasm, we hope that **chapter 3** will show that law can be a vehicle for social change and the realization of ideals. We will be examining the Human Rights Act 1998 and follow this with an introduction to the legislation protecting people from inappropriate discrimination. These laws have changed, and are changing, the nature of our society. They require you, as a person working in a public authority, to respect individual rights, including the right not to be discriminated against unlawfully.

ANNOTATED FURTHER READING

Code of Ethics of the British Association of Social Workers, https://www.basw.co.uk/system/ files/resources/code-of-ethics.pdf—a comprehensive analysis of the standards of professional social work practice, including respect for human rights of service users, obligations to society, and issues concerning use of compulsory powers.

S. Nathanson, *What Lawyers Do—A Problem Solving Approach to Legal Practice* (Sweet & Maxwell, 1997)—if you want to look at the world through a lawyer's spectacles, this is readable and informative. Don't worry that it may be out of date; the core issues covered don't change.

J. Dickens, 'Risks and responsibilities—the role of the local authority lawyer in child care cases' (2004) *CFLQ* 16(1): 17. This article discusses key sticking points in the relationship between local authority lawyers and social workers. It suggests that awareness of each other's multiple and competing responsibilities will improve inter-professional relationships.

R. Bailey Harris and M. Harris, 'Local authorities and child protection—the mosaic of accountability' (2002) *CFLQ* 14(2): 117. This article, although now some years old, is particularly helpful in unravelling a difficult area of law. For a more recent analysis, see Seamus Burns, 'Rights versus duty' (2007) *New Law Journal* 157: 1002–3 and D. Nolan, 'Negligence and human rights law: the case for separate development' (March 2013) *Modern Law Review* 76(2): 286 for a discussion about the convergence of the law of negligence and human rights law.

J. Morrell and R. Foster, *Local Authority Liability* (6th edn, Jordan, 2015) has useful chapters covering liability for social service functions.

K. Greasley, 'A negligent blow to children at risk: *MAK and RK v United Kingdom* (European Court of Human Rights)' (2010) *Modern Law Review* 73(6): 1026.

We recommend getting into the habit of looking at—and acquiring—the texts of the major pieces of legislation relevant to your area. These can be easily found by searching electronically using the title of the Act. Cases can also usually be found through the same process.

Human rights law

3

OVERVIEW AND OBJECTIVES

The Human Rights Act 1998 (HRA) and the Equality Act 2010 have created a framework which to some extent pervades all other law. Human rights law, particularly that derived from the European Convention on Human Rights (ECHR), applies to the government and its employees and to other 'emanations of the state' and their employees—including social services departments, and hence social workers. This chapter comes early in the book because the principles we set out here underpin your practice as social workers. You may need to return to it as you become more familiar with the legal complexities of your work.

The Conservative Government has been looking for some years at the possibility of repealing the Human Rights Act, which requires UK courts to take account of the ECHR and human rights judgments from the European Court of Human Rights in Strasbourg. This possibility is discussed below.

Meanwhile look at this list of some of the main human rights enshrined in the ECHR. Consider how they might impact on your work, your relations with clients, and decision making as a social worker (some answers will be given later in the chapter):

- Article 2, right to life;
- Article 3, prohibition of torture and inhuman treatment;
- Article 5, right to liberty and security;
- Article 6, right to a fair trial or 'fair and public hearing within a reasonable time';
- Article 7, no punishment without law;
- Article 8, right to respect for private and family life;
- Article 9, freedom of thought, conscience, and religion;
- Article 10, freedom of expression;
- Article 13, right to an effective remedy 'notwithstanding that the violation has been committed by persons acting in an official capacity';
- Article 14, prohibition of discrimination in the application of human rights;
- Protocol 1 Article 1, protection of property and 'peaceful enjoyment of possessions'.

Some of these rights are qualified rights; they come with a second part indicating that a breach may not be unlawful if it is prescribed by law and 'necessary in a democratic society in the interests of public safety, for the protection of public order, health or morals, or for the protection of the rights and freedoms of others'. So, it might be necessary, for example, to restrain a person, contrary to the Article 5 right to freedom, for their own good or the safety of others. But such detention must be sanctioned by law and should occur only after the legal procedures have been undertaken.

Article 13 has an important warning for social workers, as for any state employee given authority over another person: you are not above the law simply because you have that authority. You must exercise it within the law even when you consider your decision to be for the good of the client or for the general good.

This means that you must know what powers you have in particular circumstances and should consider their use in the light of the human rights implications. It would be wise to record exactly how you arrived at a decision that might prove controversial, how you balanced necessity against rights. Courts will respect thought-out decisions and proper procedures and give due weight to fair decision making even in cases where breaches have occurred.

The first part of this chapter outlines how the HRA works, and indicates its impact on the work of a social worker (including if it is repealed). The second part of the chapter examines the protections provided by the Equality Act 2010. It is a little artificial to separate out human rights in general from equality law in particular, but that reflects the way the legislation is framed in England and Wales.

CASE STUDY

R (on the application of Johns) v Derby City Council (2011)

Why are we asking you to read this case?

This case is a controversial case and provokes strong reactions. It shows us that the application of human rights is not straightforward—human rights do not automatically trump other objectives. Courts are required to balance individual rights—here the right to freedom of religion—against other obligations—here the need to ensure that foster carers value and support the needs of all the children they may be asked to care for. It provides an answer to the question of whether people with fundamental religious beliefs are ever able to become foster carers because of the requirements of a liberal and diverse society. It also provides some indication of how local authorities should approach such conflicts of values.

What is at stake for the parties and beyond?

The potential foster parents wanted to demonstrate that their fundamental religious beliefs were not an obstacle which should prevent them from fostering children. The local authority was seeking to ensure that its commitment to diversity was not in conflict with the foster parents' legal rights and needed to know whether the procedure it had used to determine whose rights should prevail was a reasonable and fair procedure.

More broadly, this case shows the complexities involved in respecting religious beliefs in a liberal and diverse society. Perhaps it could be argued that the case suggests that no one with fundamental religious beliefs will ever be allowed to foster children, so what is at stake is the role of religion in contemporary society.

Background information

Mr and Mrs Johns were members of the Pentecostalist Church and believed that sexual relations other than those within marriage between one man and one woman were morally wrong. They applied to the local authority to be short-term foster carers. The local authority considered that Mr and Mrs Johns' views on same-sex relationships did not equate with the government's National Minimum Standards for Fostering Services, which required carers to value individuals equally and to promote diversity. The couple's application was considered by the local authority's fostering panel, which deferred a decision. The argument of the couple, who had fostered before, was that they should not be considered unsuitable to be foster carers solely because of their views. The local authority's response was that it could lawfully decide not to approve prospective foster carers who were unable to respect, value, and demonstrate positive attitudes towards homosexuality and same-sex relationships. Mr and Mrs Johns applied for a judicial review—a court's ruling on whether a public authority is acting lawfully. They argued that:

(1) the local authority's consideration of their Christian beliefs was an irrelevant consideration in the context of their application to become foster carers;
(2) the local authority's position constituted religious discrimination contrary to Article 9 of the ECHR;
(3) it was unreasonable for the majority of the population to be excluded from possible fostering because of their Christian beliefs.

The decision of the Court

The High Court refused to grant permission for judicial review.

(1) It held that the attitudes of potential foster carers to sexuality were relevant when considering an application for local authority approval. The *Statutory Guidance on Promoting the Health and Well-Being of Looked-after Children* issued under s. 10 of the Children Act 2004 (now superseded) provided that support in relation to the sexual health of looked-after children should be provided regardless of the children's sexual orientation and 'should not be affected by individual practitioners' personal views'. If children, whether they were known to be homosexual or not, were placed with carers who objected to or disapproved of homosexuality and same-sex relationships, there might be a conflict with the local authority's duty to safeguard and promote the welfare of looked-after children. There might also be a conflict with the National Minimum Standards and the 2009 Statutory Guidance. Religion, belief, and sexual orientation were protected characteristics under ss. 4, 10, and 12 of the Equality Act 2010. While there was no hierarchy of rights between religion and sexual orientation, there might be a tension between equality provisions concerning religious discrimination and those concerning sexual orientation. Where that was so, Standard 7 of the National Minimum Standards and the Statutory Guidance suggested that the equality provisions concerning sexual orientation should take precedence. Standard 7.1 said: 'The fostering service ensures that children and young people, and their families, are provided with foster care services which value diversity and promote equality.' (This wording has been removed from the latest 2011 version of the Standards: www.gov.uk/government/publications/fostering-services-national-minimum-standards.) The local authority was entitled to have regard to the extent to which prospective foster carers' beliefs might affect their behaviour and their treatment of a child being fostered by them, otherwise it might have found itself in breach of its own guidance and of the National Minimum Standards and the Statutory Guidance.

(2) The local authority's rejection of Mr and Mrs Johns would not be less favourable treatment than would be afforded to other people who, for reasons other than their religious views, expressed objection to, or disapproval of, homosexuality and same-sex relationships (in other words, they were being legitimately rejected for the effect their views might have, not because of their religion). Compliance with anti-discrimination legislation and with the local authority's

equal opportunities policies would justify any indirect discrimination (i.e. apparently discriminating against a religion because of legitimate concerns about the views its adherents might hold). Article 9 of the Convention only provided a *qualified* (not absolute) right to manifest religious belief, and interferences with that right were found to be justified in employment and analogous areas, even where the members of a particular religious group would find it difficult in practice to comply. That would be particularly so where someone in whose care a child was placed wished to manifest a belief that was against the interests of the children. By applying for approval as foster parents, Mr and Mrs Johns had agreed to subject themselves to the National Minimum Standards.

(3) It could not be argued that an examination of the attitudes to homosexuality of a person who had applied to be a foster carer was '*Wednesbury* unreasonable' (meaning unreasonable according to the legal definition in the case of *Associated Provincial Picture Houses Ltd v Wednesbury Corporation* (1948): 'So outrageous in its defiance of logic or accepted moral standards that no sensible person who had applied his mind to the question to be decided could have arrived at it').

WHAT DOES THIS CASE TELL YOU ABOUT SOCIAL WORK PRACTICE?

A reading of this case study demonstrates that human rights are not necessarily absolute and may be contradictory. If one person's right (e.g. to express religious views) might override another's right (e.g. to be brought up in a household sympathetic to his or her gender or sexuality choices), the law will probably require a balancing of respective claims. What you learn here is how the law might carry out the necessary balancing exercise. The claimants' religious views require respect and consideration, but they did not prevail because, on balance, they did not outweigh other considerations—including adherence to the National Minimum Standards and the Statutory Guidance. These require other values to be respected (those of diversity) and also the health (sexual and psychological) of any children who might be fostered with a couple.

This judgment was not uncontroversial (see the *Daily Mail*, 'Christian beliefs DO lose out to gay rights', 28 February 2011), and another message from this case is that the decisions of social workers about individual clients can be intensely political. Socially conservative voices objected to the undermining of Christianity implied by the judgment. Significantly perhaps, the Standard 7.1 wording of the Department for Education's National Minimum Standards on diversity no longer appears in the 2011 version. Instead, under the heading 'Valuing diversity through individualised care' Standard 2.1 simply says: 'Children are provided with personalised care that meets their needs and promotes all aspects of their individual identity.' The word diversity is not mentioned anywhere else in the document. Additionally, all mention of the words equality, gender, religion, ethnic origin, language, culture, disability, and sexuality have been removed. (Note: the Welsh government, with devolved powers over social services, retained the old version of the Minimum Standards, including the Standard 7 wording quoted in the court case.)

All this makes decision making for social workers in cases like *Johns* very difficult. Should you act according to the letter of the 2011 judgment and reject fosterers with strong religious views against homosexuality? Or can you assume that the new, less-specific wording would change a court's view, that a new context has been set by the government in order not to discourage religious people from fostering? The decision is all the harder given that a social worker cannot predict whether the issue would come up—whether any child will be gay or transgender and hence might at a future date have a grievance over his or her foster parents. The important point, as noted in the introduction to this chapter, is that you must be able to prove that you considered the issues and came to a reasonable, proportionate, and balanced decision—following legal advice where necessary. Keeping records and following procedures is crucial.

▊ Human rights law

By the end of this part of the chapter you will have some familiarity with:

- the origins of the ECHR;
- the extent of Convention rights;
- the legal mechanisms for enforcing human rights in England and Wales;
- the relevance of human rights for your practice as a social worker.

The background to the European Convention on Human Rights 1950

The ECHR was framed in 1950 after the Second World War to prevent a repeat of the oppression of individual rights in the name of the state seen in Germany and other Fascist and Nazi countries in the 1930s. As Lord Justice Sedley put it in his lecture for the Legal Action Group in 2003:

> The Convention is a child of its time—the post-war years when the states of western Europe tried to set their faces both against the devastation of the recent past and against any new form of totalitarianism. So the Convention says many important things about due process, personal integrity and free speech and ideas; but nothing directly about the most elementary of all human needs, a right to enough food and shelter to keep body and soul together.

> (Lord Justice Sedley, Legal Action, December 2003, p 19)

British lawyers were actively involved in the drafting of the Convention, which was designed to give legal force within Europe to the principles set out in the United Nations Declaration of Human Rights of 1948. Britain signed the ECHR in 1951 and the Convention became binding upon its signatories in 1953. However, the UK for many years refused to incorporate the Convention into its domestic law. Enforcement of its provisions was via the European Court of Human Rights (ECtHR) in Strasbourg—an expensive, drawn-out process with minimal redress (including relatively small compensation)—and not through the domestic courts.

The Human Rights Act 1998 was implemented on 2 October 2000. Its primary purpose is to enable individual Convention rights to be enforced through the UK courts, and to provide a legal check based on human rights principles on the activities of the government and public bodies. Parliament was to pass only 'Convention-compliant' legislation, meaning not at odds with the rights enshrined in the ECHR in the light of Strasbourg jurisprudence (i.e. as interpreted by cases that have been before judges at the ECtHR).

The HRA, crucially, allows courts to judge administrative actions not merely on the basis of English common law '*Wednesbury* unreasonableness' but also on the more European legal principle of proportionality: what is the harm or 'mischief' that the government or public authority (including local social services) is seeking to deal with and is the method used proportionate to that harm? '*Wednesbury* reasonable' means a decision 'no sensible person who had applied his mind to the question to be decided could have arrived at'—which allows the public authority or employee a fair range of decisions that some or even many people might think unreasonable. Indeed, a decision one way might be *Wednesbury* reasonable—but so might an opposite decision about exactly the same issue. The proportionality test is in many cases a stricter test than *Wednesbury*—giving authorities *less* leeway in their decision making. In effect, they must balance competing issues and make the *best* decision—not merely a reasonable one. You must decide: is what you want to do right and lawful? If so, is the means you employ to achieve it proportionate—the least restrictive measure, resulting in least detriment, given the good outcome you wish to achieve. One judge has described proportionality thus:

(1) whether the objective of the measure is sufficiently important to justify the limitation of a protected right,

(2) whether the measure is rationally connected to the objective,

(3) whether a less intrusive measure could have been used without unacceptably compromising the achievement of the objective, and

(4) whether, balancing the severity of the measure's effects on the rights of the persons to whom it applies against the importance of the objective, to the extent that the measure will contribute to its achievement, the former outweighs the latter. . . . In essence, the question at step four is whether the impact of the rights infringement is disproportionate to the likely benefit of the impugned measure.

(Lord Reed, *Bank Mellat* (2013), para. 79)

The HRA:

- requires judges in UK courts when interpreting new or already existing law to 'take account' of the ECHR and Strasbourg jurisprudence—s. 2(1);

- requires legislation to be interpreted in a way that is compatible with the Convention rights 'so far as it is possible to do so'—that is, 'expansively' but without stretching the meaning of words too far—s. 3(1);

- if it cannot do so, it allows the court to make a 'declaration of incompatibility'—a legal statement that a piece of British primary legislation (that has passed through the full parliamentary procedure and been signed into law by the monarch) is at odds with Convention law—s. 4(2). The government should then change the law by passing new legislation through Parliament (possibly using a remedial order that requires only limited parliamentary oversight rather than a new Act)—but how it changes the law is up to Parliament, not the judges.

A court can quash secondary (delegated) legislation that it finds non-compliant. Secondary legislation includes statutory instruments (orders in council, regulations, rules, and orders) containing amendments to statutes or details or updates added to them and also regulations issued by the government with minimal parliamentary input but under the authority of a piece of primary legislation. They can also be struck down by the courts if they are held to be *ultra vires*—beyond the powers Parliament intended when giving a minister the powers to issue such orders under the primary legislation (enabling Act).

Statutory guidance (which includes various codes of practice: see **chapter 1**) is another form of delegated legislation that may be quashed by courts. As HH Judge Anthony Thornton has noted: 'Statutory guidance is issued with statutory authority and it must therefore be complied with unless local circumstances indicate exceptional reasons to justify a departure from it in a specific case'—*R (RB & CD) v London Borough of Haringey* (2013). However, it may be challenged on human rights grounds—which raises the possibility that a practitioner is at liberty *not* to follow it if there is a human rights reason not to do so.

One compendium of guidance available to social workers is *Working Together to Safeguard Children*, issued by the government. Remarkably, since the 2013 edition it has made no reference to the ECHR or the HRA—or, indeed, 'human rights' at all. The previous 2010 version made clear that the guidance was grounded in human rights, particularly Articles 6 (right to a fair hearing) and 8 (family and private life). It required those who chair child protection conferences to have 'knowledge of relevant legislation, including that relating to children's services and human rights'. The 2018 edition only notes human rights in the context of information sharing, which we discuss in **chapter 4**. The purpose of the reference is to remind social workers that the Human Rights Act does not in itself prohibit the sharing of information. Nonetheless, human rights should remain at the core of your thinking as a social worker.

Human rights controversies

Opinions differ about the appropriateness of a human rights culture at the beginning of the twenty-first century. In particular, Labour and Conservative-led governments have suggested that human rights cannot work in the context of the so-called war on terror. Indeed, the government has the right to derogate (which means withdraw) from certain human rights obligations such as the ban on imprisonment without trial to deal with serious threats to security. In addition, most rights are conditional and may be breached if there is sufficient reason to do so. The ban on torture and inhuman treatment, however, has no such qualification (though there is evidence that UK security services use material gathered through torture abroad).

Former House of Lords (Supreme Court) judge Lord Steyn has noted:

> A constitutional democracy must protect fundamental rights. It is morally right that the state and all who act on its behalf in a broad functional sense, should respect the fundamental rights of individuals. Without such a moral compass the state is bound to treat individuals arbitrarily and unjustly.

> (Lord Steyn, '2000–2005: Laying the foundations of human rights law in the United Kingdom' [2005] *European Human Rights Law Review* 4: 349)

Social workers may be confronted with just such dilemmas: necessity on the one hand (the urgent need to deal with a problem); and the danger of acting arbitrarily (without legal authority and without reasoned justification) on the other. Again, the emphasis must be on being able to set out your reasons for making your decision, including understanding what powers you have and the discretion within those powers, as well as the limitations they impose. This, after all, is best practice for the social work profession and following best practice will often be the best defence against human rights claims.

An example of the issues social workers might face was the case of a social services department that put a camera in the bedroom of a couple with learning difficulties to assess whether they were fit to look after their baby (reported by the British Institute of Human Rights, 'The Human Rights Act—Changing Lives', 2008). Social services may place such parents in residential family centres and even use closed circuit television (CCTV) to help make a judgement. But can this include monitoring a couple in bed together? The proportionality test must be applied: the aim of the monitoring (the benefit of the baby) must be balanced against the clear breach of Article 8 privacy and family rights—surveillance of a couple in the most intimate circumstances. The council was eventually persuaded to turn off the bedroom camera when a friend of the couple cited the ECHR.

Such cases show that, although the human rights of suspected terrorists and prisoners tend to attract public attention (and controversy), the most significant impact of the HRA has been its effects on the ordinary lives of ordinary people—among them the clients of social workers. Perhaps one example will illustrate this. In *R (Bernard) v Enfield LBC* (2002), the High Court considered the application of Mrs Bernard, a severely disabled woman who lived with her family in inappropriate local authority accommodation. Social services assessed her needs and recommended special adaptations to the accommodation so that, for instance, she could access the toilet easily (she was doubly incontinent and hence frequently soiled herself) and gain a measure of privacy (six children lived in the small house and her bedroom was in fact the first-floor living room which was accessed directly through the front door and gave access to the stairs). The local authority failed to respond to the family's needs as assessed. The High Court found that the local authority had positive human rights obligations to enable the family to live as normal a life as possible and to secure Mrs Bernard's physical integrity and human dignity—meaning they had an obligation to act to achieve her rights under Article 8 of the ECHR ('everyone has the right to respect for his private and family life'). The lack of action by the local authority was a breach of Mrs Bernard's right under the Convention, though a claim under Article 3 ('no one shall be subjected to . . . inhuman or degrading treatment') was rejected despite the deplorable consequences of the local authority's inaction. Article 3 was conceived in terms of authoritarian states torturing or imposing other inhuman treatment. The judge in this case, Mr Justice Sullivan, did not wish to extend it to non-malevolent acts of a local authority: 'The claimants' suffering was due to the defendant's corporate neglect and not to a positive decision by the defendant that they should be subjected to such conditions.' However, it is not clear that a Strasbourg judge would necessarily come to the same conclusion when there is a clear responsibility and clear neglect.

Article 8 was originally conceived as seeking to curtail state interference with private family life, but here and elsewhere it is interpreted more widely as a duty on the local authority 'to take positive measures to secure respect for private or family life' (Mr Justice Sullivan, the judge in the case). The local authority's actions 'condemned the claimants to living conditions which made it virtually impossible for them to have any meaningful private or family life for the purposes of [Article 8]'.

The extent of human rights

Here we consider some concepts that underpin the workings of the ECHR and discuss the Articles of the Convention. We start by considering who can take proceedings under the Act, and against whom.

Victims

Only victims of breaches of Convention rights (with their legal representatives) can bring proceedings under the HRA. So only the person who has been affected by an act or by the decision of (generally) a public authority, including the government, local authorities, the NHS, police, and any state body, can take action in relation to that act or decision. This means that pressure groups cannot initiate legal proceedings, though they can help victims to pursue their case. Under the emerging doctrine of 'horizontality' there are opportunities for people to take action against private organizations (i.e. 'horizontally'—legal action between two private people/organizations—rather than 'vertically'—between a private person/organization and the state or state body). This is because the courts (which constitute a public body covered by human rights requirements directly) must interpret laws to be in conformity with the ECHR, since 'it is unlawful for a public authority to act in a way that is incompatible with a Convention right' (HRA, s. 6). Courts have, for example, imposed privacy obligations on the press by interpreting the common law principles of confidentiality in the light of Article 8 of the Convention. See, for example, *Campbell v Mirror Group Newspapers* (2004), in which the supermodel Naomi Campbell won a breach-of-privacy claim thanks to Article 8, even though in English law, for private individuals, there was 'no over-arching, all-embracing cause of action for invasion of privacy' (Lord Nicholls). The case established that the law now imposes a duty of confidentiality whenever a person receives information she 'knows or ought to know is fairly and reasonably to be regarded as confidential'—even if she had no pre-existing relationship of confidentiality with the individual.

Public authorities

Generally, a victim brings a case under the Act if the act or decision in question is one of a public authority. A public authority is a body carrying out a governmental or public function. Local authorities and their social services departments are public bodies. Other examples include schools, departments of central government such as the Home Office, hospitals, and prisons. Private companies that exercise public functions, such as organizations that run private prisons are also public authorities under the Act. In the case of private residential homes, however, the government had to pass legislation to ensure they complied with the Convention after the House of Lords (Supreme Court) ruled in 2007 that they were not carrying out a public function (see *YL v Birmingham City Council* (2007) in **Box 3.1**).

BOX 3.1 *YL v Birmingham City Council* (2007)

An 84-year-old woman with Alzheimer's lived in a private care home run by the care company Southern Cross. She was facing eviction because of what was said to be the bad behaviour of her family when they visited her. Medical opinion was that she would be put at considerable risk if moved. Lawyers for the woman, known as YL to protect her privacy, issued proceedings arguing that eviction would be a breach of her human rights regarding respect for family life (Article 8—see **Summary of the Convention rights**, p 90). The House of Lords decided by a three–two majority that the provision of care services by a private body did not engage the provisions of the HRA, even, as here, where a public body was paying the fees of the service user after assessing that she was in need of care because of her condition. This seems to contradict s. 6(3) of the HRA, which says: 'In this section "public authority" includes—. . . (b) any person certain of whose functions are functions of a public nature'. However, the Act also says at s. 5: 'In relation to a particular act, a person is not a public authority by virtue only of subsection (3)(b) if the nature of the act is private.' Care homes look after people paid for privately as well as those subsidized by the state.

Lord Scott explained: 'Southern Cross is a company carrying on a socially useful business for profit. It is neither a charity nor a philanthropist. It enters into private law contracts with the residents in its care homes and with the local authorities with whom it does business.' The main contractual relationship was with the family of YL. The home was not 'publicly funded' any more than any organization charging the government or local authorities fees for services, and it had no special statutory powers. Since the ECHR applies to public bodies, not private, its provisions did not apply to the care home.

Some bodies have mixed public and private functions. Many housing associations, for instance, carry out functions that courts may decide are public functions, but other functions would clearly be private functions. It is difficult to provide clear guidelines on whether a housing association is or is not a public authority for the purposes of HRA claims. In *Donaghue v Poplar Housing and Regeneration* (2002), the court decided that because the housing association had a particularly close relationship with and was performing very similar functions to a local authority, it was a public authority for the purposes of human rights legislation. However, in *R (Heather) v Leonard Cheshire Foundation* (2002), the charity, which provided residential care, was held not to be a public authority. This case highlights the limits of the HRA. Where a service is provided by a private organization, even though the provision is publicly funded, individual victims of bad treatment could not claim the protections of the ECHR. They are limited to their private law remedies, breach of contract for example. In 2008, the law was amended. The Health and Social Care Act 2008 says at s. 145(1): 'A person ("P") who provides accommodation, together with nursing or personal care, in a care home for an individual under arrangements made with P under the relevant statutory provisions is to be taken for the purposes of subsection (3)(b) of section 6 of the Human Rights Act 1998 (c. 42) (acts of public authorities) to be exercising a function of a public nature in doing so.'

Section 73 of the Care Act 2014 extends the HRA to all care home users *funded* by the state 'directly or indirectly, and in whole or in part'—even if the resident was placed by their family rather than a local authority. Previously only users of state-provided care or residential services *arranged* by the state were covered. It also extends the HRA to care provided in a person's own home: 'personal care in a place where the adult receiving the personal care is living'. We discuss the implications of this in **Part 3**.

Margin of appreciation

This is a technical term that means that the European Court of Human Rights (ECtHR) will allow domestic courts some space to make decisions which reflect their national domestic concerns, rather than impose its interpretation on the way the ECHR should operate. This is particularly relevant when the courts have to weigh up competing priorities, for instance individual liberty and national security. Of course, the margin of appreciation can only go so far; the ECtHR does ensure some consistency in the interpretation of the Convention, though it rejects the notion that it is a final appeal court, saying:

> The role of the Court is not one of final court of appeal or 'fourth instance'. Therefore, the main responsibility of ensuring the rights provided in the Convention rests with the Member States, and the role of the Strasbourg organs is limited to ensure whether the relevant authorities have remained within their limits.

> ('The Margin of Appreciation', Council of Europe)

UK Supreme Court justice Lord Hope has described the situation thus: 'By conceding a margin of appreciation to each national system, the court [ECtHR] has recognised that the Convention, as a living system, does not need to be applied uniformly by all states but may vary in its application according to local needs and conditions'—*R v DPP, ex p Kebilene* (2000).

Rights can be absolute, limited, or qualified

Rights are formulated in different ways under the Convention. Some rights are so fundamental that they are absolute. These rights include the right to protection from torture, inhuman and degrading treatment, and the prohibition on slavery. Others, such as the right to liberty, are limited under explicit and finite circumstances that are set out in the Convention itself. Finally, certain rights are qualified, which means that interference with these rights is permissible only if the interference is:

- prescribed by law;
- done with a permissible aim set out in the Convention; and
- necessary in a democratic society, which means that it must fulfil a pressing social need, pursue a legitimate aim, and be proportionate to the aims being pursued.

Proportionality is a particularly important requirement. Interference with rights is not justified if the means used to achieve a legitimate outcome are disproportionate.

Examples of qualified rights are the right to respect for private and family life and the right to freedom of expression. We can illustrate what we mean by qualified right by looking at the wording of Article 8, which sets out the right to respect for private and family life.

Paragraph 1 describes the right:

> Everyone has the right to respect for his private and family life, his home and his correspondence.

Paragraph 2 sets out its limits:

> There shall be no interference by a public authority with the exercise of this right except such as is in accordance with the law and is necessary in a democratic society in the interests of national security, public safety or the economic well being of the country, for the prevention of disorder or crime, for the protection of health or morals or for the protection of the rights and freedoms of others.

This leaves considerable discretion to the judges. They must exercise the discretion in the light of previous decisions of the Strasbourg Court and the body of human rights case law built up in this country. The 'rights and freedoms of others' may include other ECHR rights such as freedom of expression (Article 10). Much court time has been used in cases attempting to balance the Article 10 rights of media outlets with individuals' Article 8 rights: see *Campbell v Mirror Group Newspapers* discussed earlier in this section, and recently *PJS v News Group* (2016), which established that 'each right [Articles 8 and 10] has equal potential force in principle, and the question is which way the balance falls in the light of the specific facts and considerations in a particular case'.

Damages

There is no automatic right to damages for breach of one or more of the rights protected under the Human Rights Act 1998. The Act provides, at s. 8(3):

> No award of damages is to be made unless, taking account of all the circumstances of the case, including—
>
> (a) any other relief or remedy granted, or order made, in relation to the act in question (by that or any other court), and
>
> (b) the consequences of any decision (of that or any other court) in respect of that act, the court is satisfied that the award is necessary to afford just satisfaction to the person in whose favour it is made.

The courts have discretion about whether to make an award and, if so, how much is required to achieve 'just satsifaction'. This means that it is difficult to predict how the courts will treat cases where damages are sought. Some indication of what would be an appropriate level of damages in child protections cases was given in *Northamptonshire CC v AS* (2015). Here the child's guardian and the child's mother claimed damages for multiple breaches by the local authority of the child's human rights, in particular Article 6, Article 8, and Article 13. The local authority conceded that it was liable because:

- it had failed to take any protective action despite having concerns that the child was at risk;

- it had left the child in foster care, for 11 months without independent representation or anyone exercising parental responsibility;
- it had delayed filing necessary evidence and had generally mismanaged the case.

The local authority admitted that the breaches had been seriously prejudicial to the child's welfare and his and his mother's ability to enjoy a family life with a member of his extended family until shortly before the final order, and that those breaches might have irredeemable consequences for his future welfare and development. It agreed to pay damages of £12,000 to the child, £4,000 to the mother, and £1,000 to the maternal grandparents to help them in their care of the child. This level of damages was approved by the court.

Summary of the Convention rights

The full text of the Convention rights, which are included within the HRA, can be accessed directly via www.legislation.gov.uk/ukpga/1998/42/contents. We provide you with relevant extracts where it is important within later chapters. The key rights are summarized in the following paragraphs, with recent examples to illustrate their working.

Article 2 establishes a right to life. This could be relevant to a social services department that failed, for example, to protect a child who is killed by an abusive parent, or if there is a failure to properly investigate any such death.

Re OT (2009)

A baby had developed serious complications shortly after birth. By the age of nine months the brain stem had atrophied and breathing was sustained only by a ventilator. Feeding was via a gastric tube. The hospital sought an emergency order that they could cease providing care, saying it was not in the baby's interests to receive it. The parents opposed the application, on the basis of the child's right to life, and the fact that their own right to a fair trial under Article 6 (i.e. 'a fair and public hearing within a reasonable time'; see later in this section) meant this should not proceed as an emergency application. The High Court noted that the right to life under Article 2 was not absolute and to prolong it in breach of the baby's best interests was wrong. Withdrawal of treatment was lawful with a court order, and the parents' involvement in these proceedings gave them a fair hearing.

Anna Savage v South Essex Partnership NHS Foundation Trust & MIND (2007)

The claimant's mother, a known suicide risk, absconded from detention in a hospital and killed herself. It was held that the patient's right to life meant that she was entitled to be looked after in a way that would not have allowed her to abscond. Her right was breached because 'a duty to take steps to prevent a particular patient from committing suicide arises if the authorities know or ought to know that there is a real and immediate risk of her doing so'. The state and its organs have a positive obligation to protect life.

R (on the application of Verna Wilson) v Coventry City Council (2008)

The closure of a care home may engage the right to life, particularly where the resident is old and in a state of advanced dementia. HH Judge Pelling QC said that 'it was accepted before me that Article 2 is capable of applying to a council considering the closing of a care home. Article 2 imposes a positive obligation to take appropriate steps to safeguard the lives of relevant persons.' But here medical evidence as to whether moving a resident may increase mortality was found to be inconclusive. The council was aware of the potential risk and took measures to examine it, considering a fair summary on the medical literature regarding the risks. The judge noted that 'as a matter of law, the local authority is obliged to undertake individual assessments before deciding to move individual residents' and the council did so. The claimant had to prove 'the authorities did not do all that could reasonably be expected of them to avoid a real and immediate risk to life of which they have or ought to have knowledge'. This was not established.

Article 3 is the right not to be subjected to torture or inhuman or degrading treatment, and could be relevant to social workers' duties to protect children and vulnerable adults from abuse or, in extreme cases, failure of the state to provide economic support. As noted, this is an absolute right and cannot be violated under any circumstances. The issue therefore becomes: is the conduct complained of sufficiently serious to constitute torture or inhuman or degrading treatment? Lawyers describe this as reaching the necessary threshold to engage the Article. We have seen already in *R (Bernard) v Enfield LBC* (2002) that the judge was unwilling to consider non-malevolent treatment as falling within the definition, even though the outcome was degrading for the complainant. Severity of the treatment is also an issue. In *A v UK* (1998), the ECtHR stated that: 'ill-treatment must attain a minimum level of severity if it is to fall within the scope of Article 3. The assessment of this minimum is relative: it depends on all the circumstances of the case, such as the nature and context of the treatment, its duration, its physical and mental effects and, in some instances, the sex, age and state of health of the victim.'

A and S (Children) v Lancashire County Council (2012)
The local authority admitted breaching Article 3 (as well as Articles 5 and 6) in the cases of two brothers taken into care as young children and freed for adoption but without a placement ever being made in the 14 years thereafter. The boys 'suffered real, lifelong damage'. When adoption ceased to be an option the council did not lift the freeing orders, imposed in 2001, and the children therefore lost the chance of maintaining a connection with their family. Early on they were placed with abusive foster carers. A second placement ended when A was assaulted with a belt by one of the carers. 'A and S were by now [2008] deeply distressed and disturbed and showed formidably challenging and sometimes violent behaviour.' Over 12 years the boys 'had major placements, emergency placements, temporary placements, respite placements and respite for respite placements'. Their legal guardian described their lives as 'havoc' and 'permanently looked after disruption'. Mr Justice Peter Jackson said that 'the legal status of children in care has welfare consequences'. The boys' treatment during the two fostering placements was a violation of their Article 3 rights. (Note: legislation on freeing orders was repealed by the Adoption and Children Act 2002.)

R (on the application of A & B) v East Sussex County Council (2003)
A and B were young sisters who suffered learning disabilities and impaired mobility requiring assistance by their carers for many simple movements, such as getting out of bed. Their mother and stepfather and the council differed about how far this assistance

should be given by manual handling or by use of equipment—preferred by East Sussex (ESCC). The court considered the 'legality of what is said to be ESCC's policy of not permitting care staff to lift A and B manually'. The claim was that the ban on manual handling 'improperly failed to take into account the needs of the disabled people involved' but also that it amounted to degrading treatment.

The council cited a requirement in s. 2(1) of the Health and Safety at Work Act 1974 'to ensure, so far as is reasonably practicable, the health, safety and welfare at work of all his employees'. Mr Justice Munby saw Article 3 engaged in safeguarding (with Article 8) the right to respect for physical and mental integrity, particularly for vulnerable persons. Munby considered that the case law pointed to an increasingly strict application of Article 3 (i.e. shifting against public bodies) as the protection of human rights improves. 'Changes in social standards demand better provision for the disabled if their human dignity is not to be impaired.' So, he suggested: 'Article 3 might well be engaged, for example, in circumstances where the consequences of failing to lift A or B manually might result in them remaining sitting in bodily waste or on the lavatory for hours, unable to be moved.'

A council must decide its policy on manual handling but guided by the law. 'A lifting policy is most unlikely to be lawful which either on its face [ie in its wording] or in its application imposes a blanket proscription of all manual lifting' or allows it only in exceptional circumstances such as where other means are impossible or a life is in danger. So, it would be wrong, for example, to restrict the number of times the sisters could go out shopping, swimming, or horse-riding because manual handling was required, perhaps because the hoist was not working.

This is a crucial point in human rights law: very often a blanket policy decision, however reasonable it may seem, is the wrong decision because a balancing exercise has not been done (the health and safety issue balanced against the dignity and rights of the disabled person) and a disproportionate answer has been arrived at (a blanket ban that goes too far to achieve its end, such as health and safety). Again, human rights principles are also good social work practice principles: a proportionate response to the problem after balancing the competing issues. Munby accepted, though, that 'in a case such as this, there is a margin of appreciation and the court must afford some degree of deference to ESCC's assessments'.

Munby's view about the probable increased intensity with which Article 3 is imposed on public bodies seems to be at odds with Sullivan J in *R (Bernard) v Enfield*. Munby said 'thoughtless, uncaring and uncharitable actions can be quite as damaging and distressing to the victim as the vicious, wilful or malicious'. He seeks to extend the concept of 'torture' or degrading treatment into the ordinary and day to day; Sullivan was unwilling to do so unless there is a malevolent act. Often judges differ in their approaches and UK case law has tended to follow Sullivan rather than Munby. Dignity, or 'physical and psychological integrity', is held to be protected by the qualified rights of Article 8 (family life) rather than the unqualified rights of Article 3 (torture, etc). While this allows more leeway for public authorities, it does not allow them to avoid making the balancing considerations and the duty to act proportionately. This must be reflected in their policies.

Arguably the courts are beginning to apply wider duties to authorities regarding Article 3. For example, two victims of the 'black cab rapist' won damages from police in 2014 for breach of their right not to suffer inhuman treatment. The rapist had caused the harm but police had failed in their duty to investigate properly and in a timely manner—*DSD and another v The Commissioner of Police for the Metropolis* (2014).

Article 5 provides a right to liberty and security. This means that a person can be detained only following a proper, lawful procedure, and must have a speedy right to challenge any detention. This Article has led to a change in the procedures for detaining people who lack mental capacity, which we will discuss further in **chapter 14**.

Dorset County Council v EH (2009)

EH was living in her own home, but at 84 and with diagnosed Alzheimer's, was also largely out of touch with the real world. She did not seem to have capacity to consent to going into a care home and did not wish to be moved. The Court of Protection declared, and the High Court confirmed, that the best interests test applied—but there was conflict about what her best interests were. The Official Solicitor (who acts on behalf of those lacking capacity) argued that moving her to a home would deny her autonomy; but to stay at home put her at risk of cold, malnutrition, and fire. The courts found on balance that it was lawful to move her to and detain her in a particular care home (in other words, deprive her of liberty as an exception to Article 5), but because the evidence suggested she could be managed without physical restraint, powers of physical restraint were not included.

P v Cheshire West and Chester Council and P&Q v Surrey County Council (2014)

A person without capacity to give consent placed in a residential home without her permission may be enduring 'deprivation of liberty', even if it is in her best interests and albeit that the living arrangements may be 'benevolent', as Lady Hale called them in this Supreme Court case. Such a case therefore falls within Article 5, but this does not make it unlawful—as long as it is justified and 'in accordance with a procedure prescribed by law'. It may seem odd to declare residential homes or fostering to be a form of prison, at least for those residents incapable of giving consent to be there, but the practical result is that the resident gains certain rights beyond a simple assessment of best interests. As Lady Hale said: 'the deprivation has to be authorised, either by a court or by the procedures known as the Deprivation of Liberty Safeguards [DoLS], set out in the Mental Capacity Act 2005'. DoLS are examined in **chapter 15**. Basically, they require a local authority to examine whether deprivation of liberty is in the best interests of the individual, whether it is proportionate, and whether there is a reasonable alternative. Legal safeguards must be put in place with oversight by the courts—in effect requiring local authorities to take such cases to court themselves rather than waiting for the individual or family members to take legal action.

London Borough of Hillingdon v Steven Neary and others (2011)

The Steven Neary case shows how far things can go wrong if social workers fail to get the balance right between an urgent necessity and an individual's human rights. This is examined in detail in **chapter 15** on DoLS. In brief, Steven had been held 'in his own interests' in a support unit against his own and his father's wishes for a year.

Hillingdon had issued Deprivation of Liberty authorizations to its Adult Social Services Department, designed under the Mental Capacity Act 2005 to bring deprivation of liberty within the law, in particular Article 5 of the ECHR. However, the Court of Protection found that the local authority had breached Article 5 and Article 8 (right to family life). **Box 3.2** shows the principles (looked at in more detail in **chapter 15**) that can be taken from the case:

BOX 3.2 Principles at stake in *London Borough of Hillingdon v Stephen Neary and others* (2011)

- Your assessment of best interests is not enough to deprive someone of their liberty.
- A case should be approached on the presumption that liberty is better than deprivation of liberty.
- This presumption may be rebutted by good evidence with independent, objective oversight of that evidence.
- The authorizing body must approach the matter objectively, itself preferring liberty over deprivation of liberty rather than rubber-stamping a decision of social workers.
- Effective review must be built in and this must take on board the individual's desires and those of the family or another interested party.
- An independent mental capacity advocate must be appointed at the appropriate time to represent the individual.
- If disagreement remains, the local authority cannot leave it to the individual or interested parties to take the matter to court; it must be proactive to ensure Article 5(4) rights of a speedy hearing.

Article 6, right to a fair hearing, refers to the requirement for civil rights to be fairly determined, and criminal trials to contain full safeguards. The basic right is to a fair and public hearing within a reasonable time by an independent and impartial tribunal established by law. So, in *Northamptonshire CC v AS* (2015), the failure by Northamptonshire County Council to ensure that care proceedings were issued promptly in the case of a 15-day-old baby—it took them three months to make the decision to issue care proceedings and then a further five months to actually issue them—led to a breach of Article 6. The court described the local authority's conduct as inexcusable and deeply worrying.

The way you conduct case conferences and make decisions about use of your statutory powers, particularly in relation to children, can also be challenged under this Article. In other words, it does not just apply to formal legal hearings in tribunals and courts, but also constitutes a right to a fair hearing whenever an issue arises that might have a legal effect.

Article 8 provides a right to respect for family life and private life; any interference with this right must be lawful, necessary, and proportionate. Much of social work with children involves the use of compulsory powers, or the possibility of their use if other support fails. If the interference is carried out within the legal framework the first test for interference—lawfulness—is satisfied. It is unlikely that you will fall foul of the second test—was the interference necessary?—because the Children Act 1989, which is where most of your powers reside, requires a court to be satisfied that the interference was in the interests of a child. But there are some actions taken within other legal frameworks which also interfere with privacy or family life—for example, placing a child on an 'at-risk' register. These actions are lawful, but because they are not sanctioned by a court, your department and those who participate in the decision making must be satisfied that, on balance, the action was necessary and the procedure for making the decision fair under Article 6. Article 8 is probably the most important Article you will encounter.

Bury MBC v D (2009)

The court hearing took place as the mother was in labour. The local authority wanted a declaration that it would not be a breach of the mother's human rights to take immediate steps to remove the child as soon as it was born. (No order could be obtained in advance of the birth, because the Children Act does not cover unborn children.) They had not told the mother about their plans to do so. Her first child had already been made the subject of a care order. The mother held the view that if she could not be with her children, they would be better off dead. The local authority thought that if they discussed their intentions with her before the birth it would lead her to self-harm or to harm the child as soon as it was born.

Such secretive planning to remove a child once born engaged the right to respect for family life, and would normally not be justified, but the judge was satisfied that in the circumstances the secrecy was proportionate and justified.

Louisa Watts v UK (2010) (Strasbourg)

Mrs Watts, aged 106, claimed her removal from a home that was to be closed breached Articles 2, 3, 6, 8, and 14 (on discrimination). On Article 8 her claim was 'the move represented an unjustified interference with her private and family life'. The court found Article 8 engaged, but there was no suggestion that the move was not sanctioned by law; it was in pursuit of a legitimate aim (councils might be criticized for *not* closing dilapidated homes); and the interference with family or private life was proportionate to that aim. It was noted that Wolverhampton City Council had consulted with Mrs Watts before moving her. It was willing to place her with friends at a nearby home. The council did not overstep the 'margin of appreciation' allowed to signatories to the Convention in terms of pursuing social and economic policies. Her claim under the other Articles was also rejected.

Article 14 prohibits discrimination in the enjoyment of Convention rights. The grounds for discrimination are very broad; the Article forbids discrimination on any ground such as sex, race, colour, language, religion, political or other opinion, national or social origin, association with a national minority, property, birth, or other status. There is one important limit; it can only be invoked when there has been a breach of another Article of the Convention. In effect, it piggybacks on the other Articles of the

Convention. It means, for instance, that it is illegal to discriminate against looked-after children in respect of any of their Convention rights.

The legal mechanisms for enforcing human rights

Human rights claims may be attached to any other proceedings a claimant is bringing against a public authority. The time limit for the claim is the same as for the substantive cause of action. For example, if someone brings a personal injuries claim with additional arguments on human rights grounds, the limit is two years.

Generally, though, when someone has been the victim of a breach of their Convention rights, the appropriate legal action will be judicial review of the public body's action by the High Court. Judicial reviews should be started as soon as possible after the action complained of, or after no more than three months. However, a specific human rights claim under s. 7(5) of the HRA may be taken within one year of the action complained of. Courts have discretion to extend these periods. When the court considers the human rights issue, it will review the law to see if the public authority had any choice about the action it took. It will try to interpret the legislative basis of the public authority's action to see if it can be interpreted in a way that is compatible with Convention rights. If the legislation can be interpreted compatibly and the public authority is found to have acted in breach, then the court can remedy that breach using its usual powers.

We summarize the impact of the HRA on the law in **Table 3.1**.

TABLE 3.1 Overview of the Human Rights Act 1998

How HRA impacts on:	Obligations created by the HRA	Comment
Interpretation of statutes by courts	Judgments must 'take account of' Strasbourg judgments and opinions where relevant—HRA, s. 2(1). Words in statutes should be given a meaning compatible with Convention rights 'so far as it is possible to do so'—s. 3(1).	If statute conflicts with ECHR, statute prevails—s. 3(2)(b). A court may declare statute incompatible—s. 4(2). The incompatible law remains valid and continues to operate until remedied by Parliament—s. 4(6).
Interpretation of case law and delegated legislation by courts	ECHR rights prevail over common law (non-statute case law) and delegated/secondary legislation (rules made by government departments or public authorities)	All existing common law principles and all secondary legislation open to challenge as not human rights compliant

How HRA impacts on:	Obligations created by the HRA	Comment
Obligations of public authorities	Public authorities (including social service departments) must act at all times in ways which comply with the Convention rights—s. 6(1)	A public authority can be taken to court by a victim who alleges its actions are not compatible with Convention rights—s. 7(1)
Decisions of the European Court of Human Rights	Human rights law in England and Wales requires ECtHR case law to be taken into account when applying Convention law—s. 2(1)	Principles derived from cases involving human rights complaints in other countries are also relevant to challenges against the UK

The relevance of human rights for your work as a social worker

Circular LAC (2000)17 was issued to guide local authorities when the Human Rights Act came into force in 2000:

> Social Service Departments should actively develop good practice in a manner suited to the new human rights culture, linking as appropriate the equality and race relations agenda.

Human rights compliant practice is not defensive, but requires a proactive approach. We highlight the relevance of human rights in the context of your legal practice as a social worker throughout the chapters which follow. The Ministry of Justice has useful information—see www.justice.gov.uk. One particularly useful publication is its handbook on human rights for public authorities *Human Rights: Human Lives*: https://www. equalityhumanrights.com/sites/default/files/human_rights_human_lives_a_guide_for_ public_authorities.pdf. We reproduce the flow chart on human right-compliant decision making in **Figure 3.1**.

Good professional practice

Human rights and professional practice share an ethical basis of concern with citizens' (including service users') autonomy, privacy, and dignity. Even before the vocabulary of human rights was developed, good practice in the delivery of personal care recognized needs for privacy and dignity, and also recognized the tensions between these requirements and the need sometimes to protect vulnerable service users or the public from harm. Therefore, much of what is required for human rights compliance is already a prerequisite for ethical practice.

We have set out in **Box 3.3** two straightforward hypothetical scenarios where good social work practice reinforces service users' human rights.

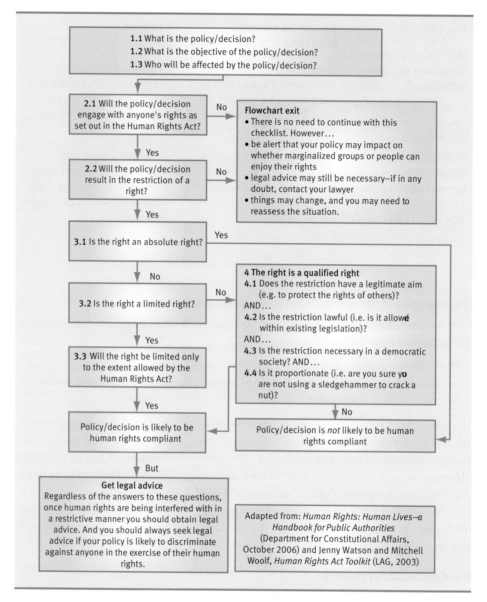

FIGURE 3.1   Human rights in policy and decision making—some key questions
Source: Department of Health.

    BOX 3.3 Examples of good practice

Samantha and Ben, who both live in a group home for people with learning disabilities, start a sexual relationship. Samantha's social worker talks to her independently about this decision and about the risks. Ben's community nurse has a similar conversation with him. The practitioners ensure as far as possible that both have consented to the relationship, and see their role as supportive rather than preventative.

Here the practitioners have worked with the service users to try to ensure that their best interests are considered but that also the service users have autonomy and a private life.

Carla, who lives in a supported housing project since leaving care, has put her health at risk by eating excessive cake and biscuits. The staff in the project decide that, as they owe her a duty of care, they should restrict her spending money so that she cannot binge on sweet things. Carla has capacity to make decisions, it is just that the staff think that what she is doing is not right for her. Carla's social worker explains to the project staff that they cannot restrict her money. Carla's Article 8 rights mean that she has a right to her money and to make decisions about how it should be spent. However, it is appropriate for the project staff to tell Carla of their concerns and to give her advice. It is also sensible to record this advice in writing.

Age Concern, along with a number of other organizations, has produced an excellent leaflet *Behind Closed Doors: Using the Toilet in Private*, which provides useful information on best practice for the preservation of human rights and dignity in the use of toilets. While the material applies to hospital settings, we think it can usefully be applied to other settings and you may find the suggested approaches helpful. See www.bgs.org.uk/resources/dignity-supporting-toilet-access-and-use-in-frail-older-people.

The British Institute of Human Rights has produced, with practitioners, a series of toolkits to support frontline staff to deliver compassionate, person-centred care. The primary toolkit is about how human rights apply in services supporting people with mental health and/or mental capacity issues. The seven specific toolkits focus on different practice areas:

- *Dementia and Human Rights: A Practitioner's Guide* (produced with Bristol Dementia Wellbeing Service)

- *Learning Disability and Human Rights: A Practitioner's Guide* (produced with Mersey Care NHS Foundation Trust)

- *Mental Health Care for Children and Young People and Human Rights: A Practitioner's Guide* (produced with The St Aubyn's Centre)

- *Mental Health Early Intervention: A Practitioner's Guide* (produced with Tees, Esk and Wear Valleys NHS Foundation Trust)

- *Mental Health Accommodation Support and Human Rights: A Practitioner's Guide* (produced with St Martin of Tours Housing Association)

- *Rehabilitation and Human Rights: A Practitioner's Guide* (produced with Avon and Wiltshire Mental Health Partnership NHS Trust)

- *Social Care Intervention and Human Rights: A Practitioner's Guide* (produced with Bristol City Council).

These are online at www.bihr.org.uk/connecting-human-rights-to-frontline-healthcare.

Equality law

By the end of this part of the chapter you will:

- have been introduced to the Equality Act 2010;
- understand the basic requirements of the law preventing direct and indirect discrimination on the grounds of race, sex, sexual orientation, age and disability discrimination, marriage or civil partnership, religious belief, and gender reassignment;
- understand the duty on public authorities to promote racial and disability equality.

The division between human rights law and equality law is not rigid. One example will illustrate this: *Young v UK* (2007). It involved a prisoner with cerebral palsy who had to use a wheelchair and had some impairment to cognitive function. She had little voluntary control of urine. She was in prison following breach of requirements of a probation order. She failed to supply a urine sample for a mandatory drug test, and at a disciplinary hearing 14 days were added to her sentence. She complained that in the hearing her disability was not taken into account. It was held that in the determination of her rights (alleged non-compliance with lawful order) she had not had a fair trial, under Article 6 of the Convention. The reason she had not had a fair trial was because her disability was not taken into account.

What do we mean by equality?

What good practice and law mean by equality is complex. All citizens are not equal in what they need. A child with a learning disability needs more care and educational support than other children. An old person may need services which a young person does not. A child has less autonomy than an adult and his or her decisions may have to be overridden. A pregnant woman may need to be protected from particular workplace demands. A blind person may need to be exempted from rules banning animals. People, at a particular time, may need particular forms of unequal treatment for a particular, identified, justifiable purpose. That unequal treatment should be restricted to achieving that purpose—so that they can live as equally respected members of society. These are relevant differences that can justify, indeed demand, discrimination to place them in the same position as other people when it comes to leading fulfilled lives.

By contrast, many differences between people have no relevance to how they should be treated. Sex, faith, skin colour, sexual orientation, or age, for example, should have no relevance in deciding who gets a job, what they are paid, where they live, what services they are entitled to, etc. The same applies for disability, once any appropriate adjustments are put in place to enable access, communication, etc. If such differences might become relevant, for example in dictating working hours, they should be respected so that, for instance, religious observances can take place.

The law has gradually developed to reflect these principles. It reflects what is sometimes called positive action (as opposed to 'positive discrimination'). Positive action occurs where a traditional but unjustifiable imbalance in the workforce can be addressed by favouring an under-represented group for additional training—or training managers to overcome traditional discrimination against particular groups with 'protected characteristics' (as set out in the Equality Act 2010; see later). This is different from 'positive discrimination'—appointing people to jobs for which other people are better qualified just to correct an imbalance. That is not permitted under equality laws in England and Wales.

The Equality and Human Rights Commission

Under the Equality Act 2006 the Equality and Human Rights Commission (EHRC) was created out of the merger of the Equal Opportunities Commission, the Commission for Racial Equality, and the Disability Rights Commission. It started work in October 2007. It promotes equality and tackles discrimination in relation to race, gender, gender reassignment, disability, sexual orientation, religion or belief, age, and human rights. It is able to help people to pursue court cases, including against the government. It does important work in researching and publicizing systemic breaches of human rights and equality law. One relevant example is its formal inquiry into the actions of public authorities to eliminate disability-related harassment and its causes. The website of the EHRC is www.equalityhumanrights.com. Its establishment was the first stage in producing a single and coherent framework for the promotion of equality in the UK. An even more significant step was the introduction of the Equality Act 2010.

The Equality Act 2010

The Equality Act came into force on 1 October 2010. It provides a legal framework to protect individuals from discriminatory and unfair treatment. It brings together more than 116 separate pieces of legislation into one Act and at the same time simplifies, and strengthens, the law.

In brief, the Equality Act works by: (a) prohibiting certain types of conduct towards individuals who have certain characteristics protected by the legislation; (b) requiring public bodies to consider how their policies, programmes, and service delivery will affect people with the protected characteristics; and (c) in limited circumstances enabling positive action to support inclusion of individuals with protected characteristics.

Protected characteristics

The protected characteristics are set out in s. 4 of the Equality Act. They are:

- age (which may be youth as well as old age);
- disability;
- gender reassignment (being or becoming a transsexual person);
- marriage and civil partnership (but not being unmarried);
- pregnancy and maternity (ie up to 26 weeks after the birth or while on maternity leave);

- race (including colour, nationality, ethnic or national origin);
- religion or belief (including philosophical belief and lack of religion/belief);
- sex;
- sexual orientation.

In s. 6 disability is defined thus:

> (1) A person (P) has a disability if—
>   (a) P has a physical or mental impairment, and
>   (b) the impairment has a substantial and long-term adverse effect on P's ability to carry out normal day-to-day activities.

Prohibited conduct

The Equality Act prohibits direct discrimination (including because of a combination of two relevant protected characteristics), discrimination arising from disability, indirect discrimination, harassment and victimization, and failure to make reasonable adjustments for a disability. What is meant by these terms is set out in the following sections.

Direct discrimination

Direct discrimination occurs when someone is treated less favourably than someone else in similar circumstances on the grounds of their gender/marital status/race/disability/age. A couple of examples will illustrate this.

Example: racially offensive graffiti appears on a tenant's property. The tenant complains to the landlord, but nothing is done to remove it. If the landlord normally takes prompt action to deal with complaints about other types of anti-social behaviour, the tenant could successfully argue that the landlord has not provided housing management services on a fair and equal basis and has directly discriminated against her.

Example: a social services department refuses to employ a qualified social worker because she is deaf. Her skills, experience, and abilities were appropriate to the job but had not been considered because the employer had assumed that a deaf person could not do the job.

Discrimination arising from a disability

Such discrimination occurs when a person (A) discriminates against a disabled person by treating them less favourably because of something arising in consequence of B's disability, and A cannot show that the treatment is a proportionate means of achieving a legitimate aim. Discrimination arising from a disability is not unlawful if A shows that A did not know, and could not reasonably have been expected to know, that B had the disability.

Indirect discrimination

This occurs when a condition or requirement is applied equally to everyone but in practice the proportion of one race or gender or person of a particular religion, etc. who can comply is considerably smaller than other groups and an employee is unable to comply because of, for example, their race or gender and the employer cannot show that the condition or requirement is objectively justifiable.

Note that it is lawful to discriminate indirectly if the condition or requirement imposed is objectively justifiable.

Example: a firm restricts recruitment to recent graduates—fewer older people would be able to meet this requirement and if the employer could not justify the requirement, then it would be unlawful.

Failure to make reasonable adjustments for a disability

Employers and service providers are required to make reasonable adjustments to the physical environment so that disabled people are not substantially disadvantaged. A successful claim would require that the employer knows, or should have known, that the person concerned had a disability.

Example: a social work student is dyslexic. She has informed her university of her disability. She has a specialist report from the university learning support unit stating that she needs additional time in examinations. Her law tutor refuses to extend the length of the examination for her. She is thus placed at a substantial disadvantage to her colleagues, who do not have a disability.

Victimization

A person is victimized if she is treated detrimentally because she has made a complaint or allegation or has given evidence against someone else in relation to a complaint of discrimination.

Example: a local authority employee gives evidence at an internal grievance hearing concerning a colleague who believes that he has been refused promotion on grounds of his visual impairment. Within weeks of giving evidence, the witness is moved to another post, where she considers she will not get sufficiently demanding work to enable her to apply for promotion.

Harassment

Harassment occurs when someone is subjected to harassment by their employer or by someone for whom the employer is responsible on the basis of their sex/race/disability/age.

Example: a social worker complains to her manager that a particular family of service users subjects her to racial abuse. Her manager says that this is one of those things that are part of a social work career and does nothing about it.

Example: a woman has a partner who is significantly younger than her and this is the basis of repeated comments and jokes from colleagues. This could be unlawful if she finds it humiliating or offensive, and the employer does not address the problem.

Disability discrimination

As we said earlier, the Equality Act is largely a consolidation and re-enactment of previous laws on discrimination. However, there are some significant changes, particularly in the field of disability discrimination. The definition of disability has been extended under the Equality Act 2010. A person has a disability if he or she has a physical or mental impairment that has a substantial and long-term adverse effect on that person's ability to carry out normal day-to-day activities. For the purposes of the Equality Act 2010, 'substantial' means more than minor or trivial; 'long-term' means that the effect of the impairment has lasted or is likely to last for at least 12 months; and 'normal day-to-day activities' include everyday things like eating, washing, walking, and going shopping. **Box 3.4** provides a summary explanation of the difference between the provisions in the Disability Discrimination Act 1995 and the Equality Act 2010.

BOX 3.4 Key differences between the Disability Discrimination Act 1995 and the Equality Act 2010

The Disability Discrimination Act 1995 provided protection for disabled people from direct discrimination in employment and related areas only. The Equality Act 2010 protects disabled people against direct discrimination in a broader range of areas, including the supply of goods, facilities, and services.

The Equality Act 2010 introduced improved protection from discrimination that occurs because of something connected with a person's disability. This form of discrimination can be justified if it can be shown to be a proportionate means of achieving a legitimate aim.

The Equality Act 2010 introduced the principle of indirect discrimination for disability. Indirect discrimination occurs when something applies in the same way to everybody but has an effect which particularly disadvantages, for example, disabled people. Indirect discrimination may be justified if it can be shown to be a proportionate means of achieving a legitimate aim.

The Equality Act 2010 applies one trigger point at which there is a duty to make reasonable adjustments for disabled people. This trigger point is where a disabled person would be at a substantial disadvantage compared to non-disabled people if the adjustment was not made.

The Equality Act 2010 extends protection from harassment that is related to disability beyond work.

The Equality Act 2010 provides protection from direct disability discrimination and harassment where this is based on a person's association with a disabled person, or on a false perception that the person is disabled.

The Equality Act 2010 contains a provision which limits the type of inquiries that a recruiting employer can make about disability and health when recruiting new staff. This provision will help to prevent disabled candidates from being unfairly screened out at an early stage of the recruitment process.

The Equality Act 2010 provides protection against indirect discrimination on the grounds of disability. This is a change from the previous position and is a useful extension of the law. **Box 3.5** provides an example of indirect discrimination.

BOX 3.5 Examples of indirect discrimination (taken from the leaflet provided by the Government Equalities Office)

Because of your disability, you might need to take more leave from work than people you work with. Your employer must not treat you unfavourably because you are off work, as long as it knows that you have a disability. However, your employer may be able to justify anything it does, and if its action can be justified, then it will not be against the law.

Your employer brings in a new shift pattern which means that everyone has to work fewer days, but longer days. You have a disability that means you are exhausted after two long days of working, so the new shift pattern puts you and other people who have the same disability as you at a disadvantage. Your employer will have indirectly discriminated against you if it cannot justify the new shift pattern.

Positive action

Section 158 of the Equality Act allows positive action enabling or encouraging people with a protected characteristic to overcome or minimize that disadvantage, meeting those needs, or enabling or encouraging people with the protected characteristic to participate in that activity. Any action must be proportionate. The proportionality of action will depend, among other things, on the seriousness of the relevant disadvantage, the extremity of need or under-representation, and the availability of other means of countering them. Positive discrimination remains illegal. Section 158(3) allows regulations to be made to specify actions, or descriptions of actions, that are not permitted as positive actions in order to provide greater legal certainty about what action is proportionate in particular circumstances.

Positive action in recruitment and promotion can be used where an employer reasonably thinks that people with a protected characteristic are under-represented. The profiles of the workforce and/or making inquiries of other comparable employers in the area or sector as a whole may provide information which would enable an employer to take action. However, positive action under s. 158 does not allow 'anything that is prohibited by or under an enactment other than this Act'. Positive action therefore cannot include positive discrimination, such as taking on more women when there are men more qualified for a job or instituting quotas for the numbers of those with protected characteristics employed in defiance of the qualifications of those who come forward.

Section 159 provides for much more specific action in connection with promotion or recruitment. It permits (but does not require) an employer to take a protected characteristic into consideration when deciding whom to recruit or promote, where people having the protected characteristic are at a disadvantage or are under-represented—this can be done only where the candidates are as qualified as each other and is sometimes called the 'tie-break rule' (i.e. it advantages, for example, a black candidate when a black and a white candidate are equally qualified, assuming black people are under-represented). The question of whether one person is as qualified as another is not limited to formal qualifications, but includes the criteria the employer uses to establish who is best for the job, so could include matters such as suitability, competence, and professional performance.

The section does not allow employers to have a policy or practice of automatically treating people who share a protected characteristic more favourably than those who do not have it. Rather, each case must be considered on its merits. Any action taken must be a proportionate means of addressing such disadvantage or under-representation.

You can find recent examples of the Equality and Human Rights Commission's legal work at www.equalityhumanrights.com/en/legal-casework/legal-cases.

Duties on public authorities

One of the most significant legal advances in combating inequality in recent years has been the move towards imposing a positive duty upon public bodies to take action to eliminate discrimination and advance equality of opportunity. The pre-existing equality duties in connection with gender, race, and disability have now been consolidated and extended. The duty known as the public sector equality duty is set out in s. 149 of the Equality Act 2010 (**Box 3.6** sets out the most important provisions), which came into force on 5 April 2011. What the general equality duty requires is for relevant organizations to consider how they could positively contribute to the advancement of equality and good relations. It requires equality considerations to be built into the design of policies and the delivery of services, including internal policies, and for these issues to be kept under review.

 BOX 3.6 Public sector equality duty—s. 149 of the Equality Act 2010

(1) A public authority must, in the exercise of its functions, have due regard to the need to—
   (a) eliminate discrimination, harassment, victimisation and any other conduct that is prohibited by or under this Act;
   (b) advance equality of opportunity between persons who share a relevant protected characteristic and persons who do not share it;
   (c) foster good relations between persons who share a relevant protected characteristic and persons who do not share it.

(2) A person who is not a public authority but who exercises public functions must, in the exercise of those functions, have due regard to the matters mentioned in subsection (1).

(3) Having due regard to the need to advance equality of opportunity between persons who share a relevant protected characteristic and persons who do not share it involves having due regard, in particular, to the need to—
   (a) remove or minimise disadvantages suffered by persons who share a relevant protected characteristic that are connected to that characteristic;
   (b) take steps to meet the needs of persons who share a relevant protected characteristic that are different from the needs of persons who do not share it;
   (c) encourage persons who share a relevant protected characteristic to participate in public life or in any other activity in which participation by such persons is disproportionately low.

(4) The steps involved in meeting the needs of disabled persons that are different from the needs of persons who are not disabled include, in particular, steps to take account of disabled persons' disabilities.

The general duty in s. 149 of the Equality Act 2010 is supplemented by specific duties set out in regulations. The specific duties, which impose obligations to publish information and set equality objectives, differ in England, Scotland, and Wales. The EHRC has published guidance on complying with the equality duties, an extract from which is set out in **Box 3.7**. The full guidance is available from the EHRC website, where it can be downloaded from www.equalityhumanrights.com/en/publication-download/essential-guide-public-sector-equality-duty.

 BOX 3.7 *The Essential Guide to the Public Sector Equality Duty*, The Equality and Human Rights Commission

Part 3 What the law requires

The general equality duty is not prescriptive about the approach a public authority should take in order to comply with their legal obligations. The specific duties are limited to requirements about publishing equality information and objectives.

Case law on the previous equality duties is still relevant to the public sector equality duty. The following principles, drawn from case law, explain that in order to properly have due regard to the general equality duty aims, each public authority should ensure that:

- Those who exercise its functions must be aware of the general equality duty's requirements. Compliance with the general equality duty involves a conscious approach and state of mind. General regard to the issue of equality is not enough to comply.

- The general equality duty is complied with before and at the time a particular policy is under consideration, as well as at the time a decision is taken. A public authority subject to the general equality duty cannot satisfy the general equality duty by justifying a decision after it has been taken.

- It consciously thinks about the need to do the things set out in the general equality duty as an integral part of the decision-making process. Having due regard is not a matter of box ticking. The duty must be exercised in substance, with rigour and with an open mind in such a way that it influences the final decision.

- It has sufficient information. A body subject to the general equality duty will need to consider whether it has sufficient information about the effects of the policy, or the way a function is being carried out, on the aims set out in the general equality duty.

- It takes responsibility for complying with the general equality duty in relation to all its functions to which the general equality duty applies. Responsibility for the general equality duty cannot be delegated to external organisations that are carrying out functions on its behalf.

- It consciously thinks about the need to do the things set out in the general equality duty, not only when a policy is developed and decided upon, but when it is being implemented. The general equality duty is a continuing one, so public authorities may need to review policies or decisions in light of the general equality duty, for example if the make-up of service users changes.

- Although a body subject to the general equality duty is not legally required to keep records of its consideration of the aims of the general equality duty in making decisions, it is good practice to do so and it encourages transparency. If a body is challenged it will be difficult to demonstrate that it has had due regard to the aims of the general equality duty if records are not kept.

There have been some significant cases in relation to the public sector equality duty regarding the provision of adult social care services. These are considered in **chapter 13**. Below we set out some examples of equality cases and some examples of the public sector equality duty, so that you can get some insight into how they operate.

Some examples from equality cases

Note: these mostly predate the 2010 Act but the principles are the same in the older legislation.

Azmi v Kirklees MBC (2007)

Ms Azmi was employed as a bilingual support worker at a school in Kirklees. She was a devout Muslim and wore a veil which covered her head and face when in the presence of adult males. Her request to wear a veil when teaching with male teachers was refused by the council's education department on the ground that obscuring the face and mouth impeded effective communication with the pupils. She was instructed to be unveiled at all times in the classroom but could continue to wear her veil in communal areas. Ms Azmi refused to remove her veil and was suspended for disobeying an instruction. She made a claim to an employment tribunal that she had been discriminated against directly and indirectly on the ground of her religion. The tribunal dismissed the claims. The veil ban was held to be indirectly discriminatory because a denial of work to veiled women disproportionately affected Muslim women. However, it was lawful as a proportionate means of achieving a legitimate aim—that children receive maximum benefit from their education. An Employment Appeal Tribunal agreed.

Derbyshire and others v St Helens MBC (Equal Opportunities Commission and others intervening) (2007)

The applicants were some of the 510 female catering staff employed by the council in its school meals service who brought equal pay claims against the council. The majority of the claims were agreed, but 36 did not accept the settlement, pursued their claims, and won compensation. But two months before the hearing of the claims the council wrote letters to all the catering staff, including the applicants, pointing out that a successful claim was likely to lead to the cost of school meals rising to such an extent that the council would have to consider ceasing to provide them except to those entitled to receive them by law, with a consequent reduction in the school meals service and loss of jobs. The applicants complained to the employment tribunal of victimization, contrary to the Sex Discrimination Act 1975, alleging that the letters had caused them anxiety and distress and had amounted to an attempt to induce them to abandon their claims. The House of Lords (Supreme Court) considered the question: 'did the Council . . . discriminate against the appellants . . . because . . . the appellants had brought proceedings against the Council under the Equal Pay Act 1970?' The Lords decided that the employment tribunal had been entitled to take the view that the council had gone further than was reasonable in protecting its interests in the equal pay litigation. What the council had done was 'effectively a threat', as Lord Neuberger put it, as a result of the women taking a discrimination claim.

R (on the application of Lunt) v Liverpool City Council (2009)

The council favoured the 'London Taxi' for the city, and believed it to be suitable for all wheelchair users. The claimant needed a longer wheelchair than most, and could only ride in the London Taxi sideways, without restraints, and therefore illegally. The council had refused a licence application from an applicant who proposed a different taxi vehicle adapted to take such a longer wheelchair. The Divisional Court held the council to be in breach of its duty under the Disability Discrimination Act 1995 to take all reasonable steps to develop policies allowing access to services by disabled people.

Islington LBC v Ladele (2009)

Lillian Ladele was a registrar of births, marriages, and deaths. She held strong convictions based on her Christian faith that, she felt, prevented her from being personally involved in registering civil partnerships for single-sex couples. The council's published policies were to promote equality of opportunity regardless of sexual orientation, and it did not agree that she could avoid this part of her duties. She applied to the employment tribunal on the basis that the requirement to conduct partnership registration was a form of direct discrimination on grounds of faith. The council said this was not discrimination: all registrars were asked to carry out identical duties. The Employment Appeal Tribunal agreed, finding that the appellant had been disciplined for failure to carry out her job, not because of her faith. In 2010 the Supreme Court refused her permission to appeal.

R (on the application of UNISON) (Appellant) v Lord Chancellor [2017]

We referred to this case at the beginning of **chapter 1** when we were talking about the Rule of Law. It is a case about the lawfulness of the level of fees prescribed by the government for people taking cases to the Employment Tribunal. Lady Hale in her judgment explains why the higher level of fees charged for complex cases such as discrimination claims indirectly discriminates against women and other protected groups. Statistics had been produced to the Court that women made proportionately more complex claims, and therefore were required to pay the higher fees more often. Whilst indirect discrimination can be justified by the authorities, the justification put forward in this case, that it transferred the cost of tribunals from the taxpayer to the users, that it deterred unmeritorious claims and that it encouraged earlier settlements, did not convince Lady Hale. She points out, for instance that people with good cases are going to be deterred from bringing their cases just as much as people with weak cases, that employers under this fee regime may well be less likely to settle, and that there was no evidence that the costs had been transferred to users as opposed to taxpayers. Overall, she concluded that charging higher fees for complex claims was not a proportionate means of achieving the stated aims of the fees regime.

Some examples of the public sector equality duty:

Blake and others v London Borough of Waltham Forest (2014)

The council had terminated the licence for a mobile soup kitchen run by Christian Kitchen on one of its car parks. There were claims that the kitchen was a focus for anti-social behaviour. The council decision engages the public sector equality duty (PSED) in s. 149(1) of the Equality Act (set out earlier in **Duties on public authorities**, p 104).

This duty applied even though it was not a council-run or funded soup kitchen. The claimants said that the council should have considered the likely impact of its decision on vulnerable, disabled, and elderly users of the soup kitchen. An alternative site in a lay-by a bus-ride away was not considered suitable for those reasons. The judge considered that the risk to the elderly and disabled 'was not addressed in any of the impact assessments set out in the Equality Analysis, nor are mitigating steps addressed to this risk'. A balancing exercise could not have been done without assessing that risk.

Some principles relating to the PSED were set out, based on case law:

- the duty applies to the exercise of all public authority functions even where the relevant decision relates to a public authority's private law arrangements such as the termination of a private contract or licence;

- the question whether a decision-maker has had due regard is a question of substance, not form or box-ticking. The duty must be performed with rigour and an open mind;

- the duty must be fulfilled before and at the time a particular policy is being considered, and not afterwards;

- there must be an analysis of the material 'with the specific statutory consideration in mind';

- in a case where large numbers of vulnerable people very many of whom fall within one or more of the protected groups, the due regard necessary is very high;

- in considering the impact, the authority must assess the risk and extent of any adverse impact and the ways in which such risk may be eliminated;

- the PSED may involve a duty of inquiry. If the relevant material is not available, there will be a duty to acquire it and this will mean some consultation with appropriate groups is necessary;

- 'The concept of due regard requires the court to ensure that there has been a proper and conscientious focus on the statutory criteria, but if that is done, the court cannot interfere with the decision simply because it would have given greater weight to the equality implications of the decision than did the decision-maker'—*Hurley & Moore v Secretary of State for BIS* (2012), per Elias LJ. The principles of '*Wednesbury* reasonableness' would apply;

- a sense of proportionality and reality is required. If a fair reading of the equality analysis makes clear that the decision-maker considered and conscientiously applied his or her mind to the relevant equality impact or impacts of the proposed decision, the court will not micromanage such decisions.

So, the decision maker must do a proper investigation, not a box-ticking exercise, and show that the results of that investigation are given due weight when the decision is made. Mrs Justice Simler said that 'the decision maker should be clear precisely what the equality implications are when he puts them in the balance, and that these equality implications should be given due consideration side by side with all the other pressing circumstances relevant to the decision.' If that can be shown, a court will not simply replace its decision with that of the decision maker on the ground, nor require some greater weight to be given to equality implications as long as the decision maker took a (*Wednesbury*) reasonable view of this. Waltham Forest's analysis was contradictory and made assumptions with no evidence or attempt to establish the accuracy of its assertions; the Equality Analysis 'fails to accord with reality or common sense'. The decision was quashed as unlawful.

R. (on the application of Law Centres Federation Ltd (t/a Law Centres Network)) v Lord Chancellor (2018)

This is a complex but important case as it involves protecting the housing rights of vulnerable people. Many Law Centres are funded to run duty possession schemes in local courts. These schemes enable individuals who are defending proceedings for possession to obtain emergency, on-the-day face-to-face legal advice, assistance, and advocacy services at court. The legal representative usually tries to obtain a brief adjournment to enable the matter to be resolved in a way that prevents the client from losing their home. These schemes provide a vital service for vulnerable individuals who face immediate homelessness. The challenge arose because the Lord Chancellor attempted to change the way that duty possession schemes were funded. Instead of awarding contracts to cover 100 geographical areas, it was decided to extend the geographical range of the schemes so that there were only 47 areas and to introduce price-competitive tendering for the scheme contracts. The Law Centre's Network argued that the Lord Chancellor had failed to make sufficient enquiries, leading in each case to a decision that was both illogical and irrational. It also argued that the Defendant failed to comply with the public sector equality duty ("PSED") in s. 149 of the Equality Act 2010.

The High Court found that the Lord Chancellor's decision to enlarge the geographic areas for which housing possession court duty scheme contracts were awarded was irrational and in breach of the public sector equality duty because he had failed to conduct a proper inquiry into the financial impact of the proposed changes on service providers or to give due regard to their effect on vulnerable clients.

The judge made the following observations about the decision maker's approach to the public sector equality duty:

> In my judgment if, as is the case, there is a real risk that in consequence of the restructuring of scheme areas, clients using the (duty possession scheme) will no longer have the same access to the 'wrap around' services that are not covered by Legal Aid and which may make all the difference to whether they end up homeless and destitute, that is something that the Ministers

should have been made aware of, and should have given due regard. I accept, of course, that the concept of 'due regard' is not the same as a requirement to give PSED considerations any specific weight. Weight is a matter for the decision maker alone.

1However, in this case, I regret to say that the evidence falls a long way short of demonstrating that any Minister (in person) gave due regard to the equality impact of the proposed changes. This is because the information collated by the LAA and placed in summary form before the Minister failed to identify in sufficiently unambiguous terms all the adverse effects that the proposed changes could have on users of the service (whose constituents contain a disproportionate number of people with protected characteristics under the Act). It portrayed the potential for agency arrangements as the cure for all ills, which it patently is not, and it failed to spell out what could happen if an agent were not used, or what the position would be in respect of those matters it had identified for which the ability to use agency services would not provide an answer.

Enforcement in race and sex discrimination cases

The victim of discrimination has two direct avenues of complaint, apart from enlisting the help of the EHRC. If discrimination is alleged at work, including unfair dismissal, he or she can bring a case in an employment tribunal; there must be no delay, as the time limit for starting the case is normally three months from the date of the last discriminatory act or dismissal. A tribunal can declare the rights of the individual, can order compensation to be paid (which can include a sum for distress to feelings, even if there is no other financial loss), and can order the employer to take specified steps to prevent further discrimination against this employee, failure to do so leading to a possible further award of compensation.

If the discrimination takes place outside the employment field (e.g. refusal to serve someone in a restaurant or to consider them for a partnership), the case is brought in the County Court. Proceedings have to be started within six months of the last act complained of, or eight months where the alleged discrimination was to do with education. The court can order damages to be paid, including compensation for distress to feelings, and an injunction requiring the discriminator to do or stop doing certain acts (e.g. ordering a landlord to cease harassing a tenant).

 SUMMARY

In this chapter, we have considered two important legal measures designed to protect individual rights and vulnerable people. In our discussion of human rights, we looked at:

- the background to human rights;
- the Articles of the Convention and their relevance for social work practice;
- the legal mechanisms for enforcing human rights.

In our discussion of equality law, we looked at:

- the Equality and Human Rights Commission;
- the Equality Act 2010, who it protects, and how it works;
- duties on public authorities and in particular the Public Sector Equality Duty.

EXERCISES

What effect does the law have in each of the situations set out in the bullet points?

1 The Jones family comprises Mr Jones, who is Welsh; Mrs Jones who is English, but of African racial background. They have adopted Gemma, who was born in China. They have two children, Matthew, age 12, who has attention deficit hyperactivity disorder, and Christine, age 6, who is confined to a wheelchair. Mr Jones has HIV. Mrs Jones has a severe facial disfigurement following a road accident.

• Mrs Jones, who has a science doctorate and a high-profile research and publication record, is refused several posts for which she meets all of the essential criteria. The University of Anytown told her that they might have trouble with the Home Office getting her a work permit. Science Labs plc told her that with her family problems she was unlikely to be committed to the work. Newtown College said the students would find her disfigurement difficult to handle.

• Gemma needs special English-language tuition but the school says it is not allowed to spend more money on her than on other children.

• Mr Jones is continuously taunted at work with offensive comments about his multi-racial family. The employer treats this as a joke, and up to now Mr Jones has tried to pretend that he does not mind.

• Mr Jones wants a clerical job. He is 45, and he has been told by the local authority that he is too old. He spent much of his twenties and thirties at home bringing up his first family, from whom he is separated, and his new family. He is told by his employer that they do not want anyone around with HIV as it will put off the other staff.

• Mrs Jones takes Christine to a cinema situated in an old building recently modernized. They are refused admission because Christine's wheelchair 'will create a safety hazard for other customers'.

• A social housing organization, the family's landlord, has written to say that Matthew's loud behaviour is anti-social and the family will have to leave.

2 You are a social worker for Careborough MBC. Your statutory service user is Maggie, a 14-year-old who has been sleeping rough and, you believe, taking drugs. You have been accommodating Maggie with her mother Jane's agreement. Because of Maggie's frequent absconding, you are considering secure accommodation. Jane has formed a relationship with John and wants Maggie to come home and the family to make a fresh start. Maggie's father Will wants Maggie to remain in local authority accommodation. You are about to set up a case conference. Maggie's headteacher does not want to participate if Will or Jane are present. Will wants to see copies of a psychologist's report which recommends that it would be disastrous for Maggie to return home or have contact with Will. John's former wife has phoned you to say she thinks John has sexually abused her daughter. Jane is deaf and can only communicate if a signer is present.

• What are the human rights law considerations you should be aware of before the case conference takes place?

3 Paragraph 2.5 of the Department of Health publication *Human Rights in Healthcare—A Framework for Local Action* (last published 2008 and now withdrawn) contains a table which

considers some Articles of the ECHR and their implications for health-care decisions. We reproduce an extract from this table in **Figure 3.2**. Decide which Articles of the ECHR are most significant for your practice as a social worker, then decide which aspects of social work practice might
raise possible compliance issues. Finally, illustrate your considerations with a specific example,
as the Department of Health has done.

HUMAN RIGHT	SOME RELEVANT ISSUES IN HEALTH CARE	AN EXAMPLE...
The right not to be tortured or treated in an inhuman or degrading way – Inhuman treatment means treatment causing severe mental or physical harm – Degrading treatment means treatment that is grossly humiliating and undignified Inhuman or degrading treatment does not have to be deliberate.	• Physical or mental abuse • Unchanged sheets • Leaving trays of food without helping patients to eat, when they are too frail to feed themselves • Excessive force used to restrain patients • Washing or dressing without regard to dignity • Staff not being protected from violent or abusive patients	A man with learning disabilities was living in a residential care home. He was regularly tied to a bed or his wheelchair for 16 hours at a time, to prevent him from hitting his head and face. This kind of situation could breach the right not to be treated in an inhuman or degrading way.
The right to liberty The right to liberty is not a right to be free to do whatever you want. The right to liberty is a right not to be locked in a cell or a room, or have any other extreme restriction placed on movement. The right to liberty is a limited right. It can be limited in a number of specific circumstances, for example the lawful detention of someone who has mental health issues.	• Informal detention of patients who do not have the capacity to decide whether they would like to be admitted into hospital, e.g. learning disabled or older patients • Delays in reviewing whether mental health patients who are detained under the Mental Health Act should still be detained • Excessive restraint of patients, e.g. tying them to their beds or chairs for long periods	A large number of patients throughout the UK who do not have capacity to make their own decisions are informally admitted into hospital. This kind of admission has been ruled to breach the right to liberty, as there are no clear rules about who decides that someone should be detained, and for what reasons. The government is currently exploring ways of protecting people who are admitted informally in this way, to make sure that their right to liberty is not breached.

FIGURE 3.2   Articles of the ECHR and their implications for health-care decisions
Source: Department of Health.

HUMAN RIGHT	SOME RELEVANT ISSUES IN HEALTH CARE	AN EXAMPL
The right to a fair trial The right to a fair trial contains a number of principles that need to be considered at *some stage* during the decision–making process. The person whose rights will be affected has the right to: – an independent and impartial tribunal; – be present at some stage during the decision–making process; – a reasonable opportunity to present their case before the decision is made; – an adversarial hearing; – disclosure of all relevant documents; – have their hearing take place within a reasonable time; and – be given reasons to enable them to understand the decision that has been made.	• Staff disciplinary proceedings • Compensation claims • Independence of tribunals, e.g. the Mental Health Review Tribunal	Ensure that there is robust and fair proce removing a doctor or dentist from the Perfo List.

FIGURE 3.2   (Continued)

ONLINE RESOURCES

For guidance on how to answer these exercises, visit the online resources at www.oup.com/uk/carr-goosey15e.

WHERE DO WE GO FROM HERE?

The duty to respect the dignity and the rights of all the people you work with, including those service users or their families in whose lives you are required to intervene, will become a fundamental aspect of your work. It must underpin your understanding of your legal powers. In this chapter, we have provided an introductory framework only. We will make reference to human rights and equality law in greater detail throughout the book and we will draw your attention to some significant cases. We have explained how one of your roles is to balance competing rights. The next chapter considers another important area where you must balance competing interests where human rights come into play: it concerns data protection and the obligations to and restrictions on sharing information.

 ANNOTATED FURTHER READING

The body set up in place of the race, gender, and disability rights commissions is the Equality and Human Rights Commission, which is charged with advising on and enforcing good practice in all aspects of human rights and discrimination, including types of discrimination not covered by the previous bodies (see www.equalityhumanrights.com).

Human rights

Liberty is the leading organization monitoring the effectiveness of the HRA and bringing test cases. It has a range of useful information at www.liberty-human-rights.org.uk.

The Department of Health has ceased to maintain a website on 'Managing Your Organisation: Human Rights', which included useful case studies with reference to actual court decisions on the impact of the HRA on areas of work which will be relevant to social workers and health professionals. You may still find it on the government's online archive.

The United Nations has all of the international charters on human rights and discrimination issues at www.un.org/en/rights.

Useful guidance to the HRA includes the following:

British Institute of Human Rights: Your *Human Rights Guides* (2006) at www.bihr.org.uk).

Ministry of Justice: *Human Rights, Human Lives: A Handbook for Public Authorities* (October 2006) www.equalityhumanrights.com/sites/default/files/human_rights_human_lives_a_guide_for_public_authorities.pdf.

J. Watson and M. Woolf, *Human Rights Act Toolkit* (2nd edn, Legal Action Group, 2008).

N. Kang-Riou,*Confronting the Human Rights Act 1998: Contemporary Themes and Perspectives* (Routledge, 2012).

K. Starmer, *European Human Rights Law: The Human Rights Act 1998 and the European Convention on Human Rights* (2nd edn, Legal Action Group, 2010).

J. Wadham, H. Mountfield, E. Prochaska, and R. Desai, *Blackstone's Guide to the Human Rights Act 1998* (7th edn, Oxford University Press, 2015).

The value of the United Nations Convention on the Rights of the Child is considered by:

U. Kilkelly and L. Lundy, 'Children's rights in action: using the UN Convention on the Rights of the Child as an auditing tool' (2006) *CFLQ* 18(3): 331.

The Equality Act 2010

J. Wadham, D. Ruebain, A. Robinson, and S. Uppal, *Blackstone's Guide to the Equality Act 2010* (2nd edn, Oxford University Press, 2012).

B. Hepple, *Equality: The New Legal Framework* (Hart, 2011).

More general articles on legal action around rights relevant to social work practice include:

Mark Simpson, 'Social rights, child rights, discrimination and devolution: untangling the web' (2018) *Journal of Social Welfare and Family Law* 40(1): 3–20.

Information security and information sharing

4

OVERVIEW AND OBJECTIVES

This chapter is designed to help you to understand the importance of the law on data protection and its relevance to you as a social worker. It considers what you need to take into account in order to ensure that the decisions you make about whether or not to disclose information belonging to or concerning the service user are lawful. The first part of the chapter outlines the General Data Protection Regulation (GDPR) and Data Protection Act 2018 (DPA), which together provide the legal framework for the protection of information in England and Wales. It also highlights the exemptions for social work data. The second part of the chapter is concerned with information sharing. This part begins with the government guidance on information sharing and explains the relevant provisions of the Human Rights Act 1998 (HRA) and the common law of confidentiality. These, together with the DPA and the GDPR, provide you with your basic tools for lawful practice in this area.

 CASE STUDY

BBC v Rochdale MBC [2005] EWHC 2862 (Fam)

Why are we asking you to read this case?

This case is about privacy—most particularly the privacy of social workers who gave evidence in a very controversial case involving allegations of satanic abuse. It introduces you to the competing interests in privacy and openness and suggests how the courts go about resolving the conflicts between the two. It is a strong reminder of why people want to defend their privacy. The social workers involved did not anticipate receiving sympathetic treatment from the BBC in its scrutiny of the case.

What is at stake for the parties and beyond?

The local authority wanted to protect its social work employees from media scrutiny that would expose them and their families to the public gaze. This would not only be potentially harmful for them personally and professionally, but could also impact upon the willingness of people to become social workers in the future. The BBC wanted to make a documentary about social work practice and the courts. More broadly, the case is about the balance between privacy and the public interest in freedom of expression.

Background

Rochdale Council applied for an injunction (a ban issued by a court) to prevent the BBC from publishing the names of two social workers who had given evidence in wardship proceedings. The children concerned had been returned to the care of their families after allegations of satanic abuse were rejected. Injunctions were made following the hearing to prevent disclosure of the identities of the children. The social workers had also been granted anonymity to prevent identification of the children. Several years later, the BBC intended to broadcast a documentary examining the criticisms made by the judge. It reached an agreement with the former wards—by now adults—who agreed to the use of materials protected by the injunction. The outstanding issue was whether the social workers could be identified in the documentary.

Their argument, and that of the council, was that social workers work in a confidential environment which should be protected by anonymity unless there had been dishonesty or bad faith. Under Article 8 of the European Convention on Human Rights (ECHR) (respect for private and family life: see **chapter 3**) maintenance of their anonymity was proportionate and being identified by the BBC would have a seriously detrimental impact on their families and their professional standing. The BBC argued that the social workers had failed to establish a pressing need to restrict the public interest in freedom of expression under Article 10 of the ECHR.

The decision of the Court

The application to uphold the injunction was refused. As a matter of general principle, there was nothing to prevent the identification of a witness who gave evidence in a case, including a witness in proceedings concerning the welfare of children. The court should conduct a balancing exercise between the competing rights, considering the proportionality of any interference with each right independently. What mattered here was the interface between Articles 8 and 10. The local authority had not established a pressing need for the injunction, and restraint would be a disproportionate interference with the BBC's Article 10 rights. While publication of the social workers' identities would interfere with their Article 8 rights to respect of private life, that interference was in pursuit of a legitimate aim, namely informed and open discussion of public-interest issues relating to the earlier proceedings and to family proceedings generally. It would be proportionate. The Article 10 rights of the BBC and the former wards, and the public interest in enabling public scrutiny of court proceedings and family justice, should prevail over the Article 8 rights of the social workers.

WHAT DOES THIS CASE TELL YOU ABOUT SOCIAL WORK PRACTICE?

The problem faced by the courts in this case was balancing the right of social workers' privacy with the right of the press to scrutinize the workings of the civil justice system. The decision involves a complex balancing exercise, which in this particular situation the court resolved in favour of the media and the former wards of court. Notice how the court used human rights principles in reaching its decision; also, how proportionality is crucial to the resolution of the conflict in rights.

You may remember from **chapter 1** that injunctions are equitable remedies. They are awarded at the discretion of the court. Using discretion means that each case has to be decided on its own facts—there is no one answer to the difficult questions posed when it comes to information sharing.

A more recent case, *Bristol City Council v C and others* (2012), has also asserted the Article 10 rights of the media where there is a public interest in care proceedings. A child, A, was removed from her father's care and fostered after an interim care order issued at family court proceedings. The local authority received information that a member of the foster household had accessed indecent images of children and another may have grabbed A by the throat. Police and social workers visited the house, computers were removed, and A was taken to another foster home. The following day the male foster carer was found dead, having apparently killed himself. The father of A approached the Sun newspaper to do a story based on his concerns about social services' handling of the case.

A court order banned media reports that could identify the child, foster carers, the local authority, or the social workers involved. Most care proceedings are held in private, and while accredited members of the press may attend, what they can report is restricted by s. 12 of the Administration of Justice Act 1960, which, broadly, treats reports involving minors as contempt of court. However, this Act must now be seen in the light of Article 10 freedom of expression rights of the press balanced against Article 8 privacy rights—here for the girl and her family (albeit that the father wanted the Sun to publish material about the case) and the foster family. Mr Justice Baker concluded that the reporting restrictions barring the naming of the social workers and local authority should be lifted; the names of the two families should remain unpublished but the fact of the apparent suicide should be published on the basis that that information would not lead to identification of A or his daughter. Baker also allowed the word 'strangling' to be used in relation to the assault on the girl, given similar wording was used by social services in reports on the case. In effect, the judgment suggests that there was potentially a public interest in how a particular social services department and particular social workers dealt with a case and hence the suicide following the indecent images claim and the seriousness of the assault were important elements of the Sun's potential article. So 'there is a clear public interest in facilitating an open discussion of the issues relating to child protection and fostering that arise in this case. In all the circumstances, I find no evidence of any pressing social need for a restricting exercise of the right to freedom of expression on that issue.' The principle of non-identification (hence Article 8 privacy) was preserved and balanced against Article 10 freedom of expression—for the father to make his complaint about social services known publicly and for the *Sun* to publish it.

◼ Introduction

Accurate and up-to-date information—data—is crucial for good social work practice. Information is required for proper decision making and is used to justify interventions in individual's lives. Local authorities and social workers gather information about people all the time. That information is then stored by those organizations and individuals. In the past it was stored on paper in files. Now it is generally stored electronically. Holding personal information about other people involves responsibilities. The law requires that the information is protected. Information also needs to be shared in order to maximize the protection of vulnerable people and crucial to the integrated system of child protection put in place by the Children Act 2004, as well as systems for safeguarding adults. Yet there is a tension between the requirements of security and privacy in the holding of data and the need to share information. There is a danger that social workers and those advising them will interpret the law in a way that prevents them from sharing information effectively.

Information security

The legal framework for information security has been overhauled by government. The previous legislation dated from the late 1990s; since then there has been unprecedented technological innovation. In particular, businesses and other organizations now hold masses of personal data on all of us. This poses risks, primarily that the data is used for commercial or political purposes which were unforeseen by us when we handed over the information. There are also risks that our data is not held securely, so that increasingly sophisticated criminal hackers can get hold of information and use it to gain access to our bank accounts.

The new laws aim to give individuals more control over the information that others hold about them and to ensure that those who hold data about us do so responsibly. There are two elements to the new legal framework: one is a European Union initiative, the General Data Protection Regulation, and the other is a piece of UK legislation—the Data Protection Act 2018.

The General Data Protection Regulation (GDPR)

You may have noticed the GDPR because your email inbox has been flooded with requests from individuals and organizations for you to consent to them holding information—data—about you as a result of GDPR coming into force. Those who hold data on us are required to tell us how it will be used, and in particular whether it will be given to another organization for another purpose. GDPR is European Union law, specifically Regulation (EU) 2016/679. It came into force in May 2018 and regulates the processing by an individual, a company, or an organization of personal data relating to individuals in the EU. GDRP grants new individual rights, such as easier access to the information companies hold on a person; imposes new obligations on companies, for instance a clear responsibility on companies to get consent to the holding of personal data; and sets up a much stronger enforcement regime. Fines of up to €10 million or two per cent of a firm's global turnover (whichever is greater) can be imposed for minor offences, with more serious offences attracting fines of up to €20 million or four per cent of a firm's global turnover (whichever is greater). Data breaches—defined as the 'destruction, loss, alteration, unauthorised disclosure of, or access to' people's data—have to be reported to the Information Commissioner's Office (ICO) within 72 hours of an organization finding out about the breach, and the people the breach impacts upon also need to be informed.

Key definitions

You need to understand particular terms in order to understand the rights and responsibilities imposed by GDPR.

The GDPR defines **personal data** as:

> Any information relating to an identified or identifiable natural person ('data subject'). An identifiable natural person is one who can be identified, directly or indirectly, in particular by reference to an identifier such as a name, an identification number, location data, an online identifier or to one or more factors specific to the physical, physiological, genetic, mental, economic, cultural or social identity of that natural person.

As you are aware, some information is more sensitive than others. The GDPR recognizes this and provides special protection for **special category personal data**. Special category personal data includes data on for example, information about an individual's race, politics, or sex life. Special protections apply to this more sensitive information.

The GDPR defines **processing** as:

> Any operation or set of operations which is performed on personal data or on sets of personal data, whether or not by automated means, such as collection, recording, organisation, structuring, storage, adaptation or alteration, retrieval, consultation, use, disclosure by transmission, dissemination or otherwise making available, alignment or combination, restriction, erasure or destruction.

The GDPR defines **a filing system** as:

> Any structured set of personal data which are accessible according to specific criteria, whether centralised, decentralised or dispersed on a functional or geographical basis.

The GDPR defines **controller** as:

> the natural or legal person, public authority, agency or other body which, alone or jointly with others, determines the purposes and means of the processing of personal data.

It is clear from these definitions that the GDPR applies to information you hold on your clients.

Lawful processing of data

You can only process data if you have a valid lawful basis to do so and it is necessary for you to process the data. So, if you can reasonably achieve the same result without processing data you won't have a lawful basis for data processing. You must decide on your legal basis before you begin processing data, and you need to document that basis.

The valid legal bases for processing data are:

- consent—data can be processed with consent. Note that there is a high standard for consent—individuals must be offered real choice and control and be able to withdraw consent easily;
- contract—if you need to process the data in order to fulfil your contractual obligations to the data subject, then this is lawful;
- legal obligation—you can legally process data if you have a statutory or common law obligation to do so. You should be able to either identify the specific legal provision or an appropriate source of advice or guidance that clearly sets out your obligation;
- vital interests of the data subject or someone else—i.e. if you need to process the data to save someone's life. This lawful basis is very limited in its scope, and generally only applies to matters of life and death;
- public task—data can be legally processed if it is done 'in the exercise of official authority'. This covers public functions and powers that are set out in law—public

task also covers data processing necessary to perform a specific task in the public interest that is set out in law;

- legitimate interests—this is the broadest and most flexible legal basis. It involves three elements to be lawful. The data processer needs to:

    o identify a legitimate interest;

    o show that the processing is necessary to achieve it; and

    o balance it against the individual's interests, rights and freedoms.

The legitimate interests can include commercial interests, individual interests, or broader societal benefits.

If you are processing special category personal data you need to do so drawing on one of the legal bases, and, in addition, you need to comply with the requirements of Article 9(2) of the GDPR. In **Box 4.1** we set out the relevant parts of Article 9(2):

 BOX 4.1 Processing special category personal data—Article 9(2) GDPR (2018)

(a) the data subject has given explicit consent to the processing of those personal data for one or more specified purposes, except where Union or Member State law provide that the prohibition referred to in paragraph 1 may not be lifted by the data subject;

(b) processing is necessary for the purposes of carrying out the obligations and exercising specific rights of the controller or of the data subject in the field of employment and social security and social protection law in so far as it is authorised by Union or Member State law or a collective agreement pursuant to Member State law providing for appropriate safeguards for the fundamental rights and the interests of the data subject;

(c) processing is necessary to protect the vital interests of the data subject or of another natural person where the data subject is physically or legally incapable of giving consent;

(d) processing is carried out in the course of its legitimate activities with appropriate safeguards by a foundation, association or any other not-for-profit body with a political, philosophical, religious or trade union aim and on condition that the processing relates solely to the members or to former members of the body or to persons who have regular contact with it in connection with its purposes and that the personal data are not disclosed outside that body without the consent of the data subjects;

(e) processing relates to personal data which are manifestly made public by the data subject;

(f) processing is necessary for the establishment, exercise or defence of legal claims or whenever courts are acting in their judicial capacity;

(g) processing is necessary for reasons of substantial public interest, on the basis of Union or Member State law which shall be proportionate to the aim pursued, respect the essence of the right to data protection and provide for suitable and specific measures to safeguard the fundamental rights and the interests of the data subject;

(h) processing is necessary for the purposes of preventive or occupational medicine, for the assessment of the working capacity of the employee, medical diagnosis, the provision of health or social care or treatment or the management of health or social care systems and services on the basis of Union or Member State law or pursuant to contract with a health professional and subject to the conditions and safeguards referred to in paragraph 3;

(i) processing is necessary for reasons of public interest in the area of public health, such as protecting against serious cross-border threats to health or ensuring high standards of quality and safety of health care and of medicinal products or medical devices, on the basis of Union or Member State law which provides for suitable and specific measures to safeguard the rights and freedoms of the data subject, in particular professional secrecy;

(j) processing is necessary for archiving purposes in the public interest, scientific or historical research purposes or statistical purposes in accordance with Article 89(1) based on Union or Member State law which shall be proportionate to the aim pursued, respect the essence of the right to data protection and provide for suitable and specific measures to safeguard the fundamental rights and the interests of the data subject.

There are additional requirements for processing sensitive personal data imposed by the DPA. We discuss these below.

Even if you have a lawful basis for processing data, your processing can still breach the regulations, unless it complies with the principles of data protection.

Seven principles underpinning GDPR

The General Data Protection Regulation sets out seven principles of data protection (see **Box 4.2**). This means that in order to avoid a breach of the regulation, data processing must comply with these principles.

BOX 4.2 The seven principles of data protection—GDPR (2018)

1. Lawfulness—Personal data shall be processed lawfully, fairly and in a transparent manner in relation to the data subject.

2. Purpose—Personal data shall be collected for specified, explicit and legitimate purposes and not further processed in a manner that is incompatible with those purposes.

3. Data minimisation—Personal data shall be adequate, relevant and limited to what is necessary in relation to the purposes for which they are processed.

4. Accuracy—Personal data shall be accurate and, where necessary, kept up to date; every reasonable step must be taken to ensure that personal data that are inaccurate, having regard to the purposes for which they are processed, are erased or rectified without delay.

5. Storage—Personal data shall be kept in a form which permits identification of data subjects for no longer than is necessary for the purposes for which the personal data are processed; personal data may be stored for longer periods insofar as the personal data will be processed solely for archiving purposes in the public interest, scientific or historical research purposes or statistical purposes.

6. Security—Personal data shall be processed in a manner that ensures appropriate security of the personal data, including protection against unauthorised or unlawful processing and against accidental loss, destruction or damage, using appropriate technical or organisational measures.

7. Accountability—The controller shall be responsible for, and be able to demonstrate, compliance with the principles.

Individual rights within the GDPR

The GDPR provides the following rights for individuals:

- The right to be informed.

  This means that you must be told about the collection and use of your personal data. This includes telling you why your personal data is being processed, how long your personal data will be retained and who it will be shared with.

- The right of access.

  This means you have the right to access your personal data. You can request access verbally or in writing and the individual or organization has a month to respond, and in most circumstances cannot charge a fee for provision of the information.

- The right to rectification.

  This means you have the right to have any inaccurate personal data held on you rectified, or completed if it is incomplete. You can make a request for rectification verbally or in writing and no fee can be charged. The individual or organization has one month to respond. There are some circumstances where there is no right to rectification.

- The right to erasure.

  This right, which can also be described as the right to be forgotten, is the right for you to have your personal data erased. A request for erasure can be made verbally or in writing and the individual or organization has one month to respond. There are some circumstances where there is no right to erasure.

- The right to restrict processing.

  You have the right to request the restriction or suppression of your personal data. This right only applies in certain circumstances. If processing is restricted, an individual or organization can only store your personal data, not use it. A request for erasure can be made verbally or in writing and the individual or organization has one month to respond.

- The right to data portability.

  You have the right to data portability, which means you can obtain and reuse your personal data for your own purposes across different services. This means you can move, copy, or transfer personal data easily from one IT environment to another in a safe and secure way, without affecting its usability.

- The right to object.

  You have the right to object to the processing of your personal data in certain circumstances. You have an absolute right to stop your data being used for direct marketing. In other circumstances where the right to object applies an individual or organization may be able to continue processing your data if it can be shown that there is a compelling reason for doing so. You must be told about your right to object. You can make an objection verbally or in writing and the individual or organisation has one month to respond.

- Rights in relation to automated decision making and profiling.

  The GDPR provides protections for individuals in connection with automated individual decision making (making a decision solely by automated means without any human involvement); and profiling (automated processing of personal data to evaluate certain things about an individual). This type of decision making can only be done where the decision is necessary for the entry into or performance of a contract, or authorized by Union or Member State law, or based on the individual's explicit consent. Individuals must be given information about this form of data processing, there must be simple ways for them to request human intervention or challenge a decision, and processors need to carry out regular checks to make sure that their systems are working as intended.

These rights reflect the principles of data protection, so they focus, for instance, on transparency, accuracy, and minimization of data held so as to provide individuals with maximum control of their personal data.

Exemptions from GDPR

Member States can introduce exemptions (known as derogations) from the requirements of GDPR. However, exemptions are only allowed which respect the individual's fundamental rights and freedoms and are necessary and proportionate measures in a democratic society to safeguard:

- national security;
- defence;
- public security;
- the prevention, investigation, detection, or prosecution of criminal offences;
- other important public interests, in particular economic or financial interests, including budgetary and taxation matters, public health, and security;
- the protection of judicial independence and proceedings;
- breaches of ethics in regulated professions;
- monitoring, inspection, or regulatory functions connected to the exercise of official authority regarding security, defence, other important public interests or crime/ethics prevention;
- the protection of the individual, or the rights and freedoms of others; or
- the enforcement of civil law matters.

GDPR and Brexit

We have already noted that GDPR is EU law. While the UK remains a member of the EU, all the rights and obligations of EU membership remain in force, and therefore GDPR remains in force. When the UK leaves the EU, the GDPR will be incorporated into the UK's domestic law under the European Union (Withdrawal) Bill, which is currently before Parliament.

The Data Protection Act 2018

The second element of information protection in England and Wales is the Data Protection Act 2018. The DPA implements a commitment in the 2017 Conservative Party manifesto to repeal and replace the UK's existing data protection laws to keep them up to date for the digital age in which ever increasing amounts of personal data are being processed. The Explanatory Notes to the Act say that it 'sets new standards for protecting personal data, in accordance with recent EU data protection laws, giving people more control over use of their data. The Act also helps prepare the UK for a future outside the EU.'

The DPA has to be read alongside the GDPR, and many of its provisions enact the GDPR into domestic law. In essence the DPA provides a legal regime which ensures that existing data processing can continue, subject to the enhanced rights provided by the GDPR. But it also goes beyond the GDPR—it uses the powers of the GDPR to create exemptions and it sets out a new legal regime for data protection for those areas which fall outside of EU law, for instance national security and immigration. Finally, it provides for the enhanced supervision of data handling required by GDPR by enhancing the role of the Information Commissioner and her office.

The Act is long and complex. For your purposes, understanding the principles and rights contained in GDPR should be sufficient, alongside knowledge of the particular exemption relating to social work data. This exemption is set out in Part 3 of Schedule 3 to the DPA, which is headed *Exemptions etc from the GDPR: Health, Social Work, Education and Child Abuse Data*. What Part 3 does is to restrict individual rights given by the GDPR in relation to social work data, that is personal data processed by a range of authorities or bodies pursuant to specified social services functions and by the courts in children's and family proceedings.

Restrictions apply where:

- the application of the GDPR would be likely to cause serious harm to the physical or mental health of the data subject or any other person;
- the information has been provided to a court and the court may withhold from the data subject;
- a request is made on behalf of the data subject for information the data subject has expressly indicated should not be disclosed.

The Explanatory Notes explain that in the context of health, social work, and education, there is sometimes information that is recorded about a person that is given on the condition that it is not disclosed to the person. If such information was disclosable, the information would not be given. This could, for example, result in safeguarding concerns or limit a Court's ability to properly assess the best interests of the child in proceedings concerned with the care of children. Disclosure of personal data could also result in serious harm to the data subject or another individual.

The other significant point for you to note about the DPA is that it imposes addition requirements for the processing of special category, i.e. sensitive personal data. Schedule 1 Part 1 of the DPA contains specific conditions for the various employment, health, and research purposes under Articles 9(2)(b), (h), (i), and (j).

Schedule 1 Part 2 contains specific 'substantial public interest' conditions for Article 9(2)(g).

In some cases, you must also have an 'appropriate policy document' in place to rely on these conditions.

These then are your basic tools. Essentially the law works to protect individual data, which can only be processed on a lawful basis and in a way that respects individual rights. The law also recognizes that social work data needs to be treated differently and provides exemptions, most particularly in circumstances where compliance would cause serious harm. However, in order to ensure that the information you hold is used effectively it has to be shared. The second part of this chapter turns to the requirements for lawful information sharing.

▨ Information sharing

The potential legal barriers to information sharing received careful scrutiny within the Laming Report, published in January 2003, into the death of Victoria Climbié. Paragraph 17.115 states:

> The evidence put to the Inquiry was that unless a child is deemed to be in need of protection, information cannot be shared between agencies without staff running the risk that their actions are unlawful. This either deters information sharing, or artificially elevates concern about the need for protection—each of which is not compatible with serving well the needs of children and families.

On the other hand, social workers may be using information given in the expectation of confidentiality, and individuals are entitled to have their privacy respected. Moreover, the state in its various guises holds a great deal of information about us all. If there is no check on its use, there is potential for oppression. Government has an interest in ensuring that the information it holds is seen to be used only for legitimate and proportionate purposes. It would be all too easy for individuals to lose their trust in the state if it was believed to have abused its powers. The government has provided user-friendly practitioners' guides on information sharing which are designed to help you to solve these dilemmas. These are:

- *Information Sharing Advice for Safeguarding Practitioners;*
- *Information Sharing: Further Guidance on Legal Issues; and*

- *How to Identify Which Rules Apply When Sharing Information.*

These are very helpful and we discuss them in **Information sharing advice for safe-guarding practitioners** at p 128. You should download them from www.gov.uk/government/publications/information-sharing-for-practitioners-and-managers.

We start, however, by reminding you of your ethical and legal responsibilities and considering why confidentiality is so important.

The Code of Ethics

The British Association of Social Workers (BASW) Code of Ethics for Social Work (updated 2014) is a key tool in helping you with the difficult conflicts that can arise in the relationships between professionals and their service users. Paragraph 10 of the Code sets out the ethical position on confidentiality and disclosure. We have set this out for you in **Box 4.3**.

You will see as you go through this chapter that the ethical principles are reflected in both the common law and the statutory framework. Confidentiality is the starting point, both legally and ethically. This is because social work, like many of the caring professions, is based upon the concept of respecting individual autonomy. Social workers obtain private information about individuals as a result of their privileged position in society. Unwarranted disclosure of that information is a breach of an individual's personal integrity. A relationship of confidentiality between a service user and the social worker promotes trust in social workers and allows people to discuss their problems knowing that the information will not be disclosed. Without this assurance, people may be unwilling to seek help.

Of course, there are circumstances when a social worker owes a greater duty to the community than to the individual who has disclosed information. The social worker may be obliged, or may have the discretion, to breach any obligation of confidence they owe to an individual. The difficulty is recognizing when those circumstances arise. Behaving ethically and legally in problematic circumstances and ensuring that an individual service user is appropriately protected involves difficult dilemmas (see **Box 4.4**).

BOX 4.3 Confidentiality and disclosure—para. 10 of BASW Code of Ethics for Social Work (updated October 2014)

Maintaining confidentiality

Social workers should respect the principles of confidentiality that apply to their relationships and ensure that confidential information is only divulged with the consent of the person using social work services or the informant. Exceptions to this may only be justified on the basis of a greater ethical requirement such as evidence of serious risk or the preservation of life. Social workers need to explain the nature of that confidentiality to people with whom they work and any circumstances where confidentiality must be waived should be made explicit. Social workers should identify dilemmas about confidentiality and seek support to address these issues.

Advice on sharing information

Government provides excellent advice on information sharing for social work practitioners. There are two particularly useful sources of advice.

Information sharing advice for safeguarding practitioners

This practitioners' guidance was published in 2018 and supersedes guidance published by the government in 2012. The guidance is influenced by the Munro Review of Child Protection (see **chapter 5**), which concluded that a new approach was needed: 'instead of "doing things right" (i.e. following procedures) the system needed to be focused on doing the right thing (i.e. checking whether children and young people are being helped)'. The idea was to relieve social workers from bureaucracy and form filling and enhance (and trust) their individual professionalism. Furthermore, in the light of the criticisms of social workers in the Victoria Climbié Inquiry, the emphasis is on prioritizing the safety and welfare of children. Lord Laming, in his Climbié report, 'recommended that all staff in every service, from frontline practitioners to managers in statutory services and the voluntary sector should understand the circumstances in which they may lawfully share information'.

There was a sense that social workers were so concerned about confidentiality and data protection that they failed to make decisions to reveal material to the right people at the right time so that the correct interventions could be made in cases such as Climbié. Confidentiality remains important—but it is crucial to recognize when and to whom to release information in order to safeguard children and vulnerable adults. The HRA and confidentiality should not be used as reasons barring proper and pertinent information sharing.

At the heart of the guidance are seven golden rules used to inform legal and ethical information sharing. These are set out in **Box 4.4.**

BOX 4.4 The seven golden rules to sharing information—*Information sharing advice for safeguarding practitioners (2018)*

1. Remember that the General Data Protection Regulation (GDPR), Data Protection Act 2018 and human rights law are not barriers to justified information sharing, but provide a framework to ensure that personal information about living individuals is shared appropriately.

2. Be open and honest with the individual (and/or their family where appropriate) from the outset about why, what, how and with whom information will, or could be shared, and seek their agreement, unless it is unsafe or inappropriate to do so.

3. Seek advice from other practitioners, or your information governance lead, if you are in any doubt about sharing the information concerned, without disclosing the identity of the individual where possible.

4. Where possible, share information with consent, and where possible, respect the wishes of those who do not consent to having their information shared. Under the GDPR and Data Protection Act 2018 you may share information without consent if, in your judgement, there is a lawful basis to do so, such as where safety may be at risk. You will need to base your judgement on the facts of the case. When you are sharing or requesting personal information from

someone, be clear of the basis upon which you are doing so. Where you do not have consent, be mindful that an individual might not expect information to be shared.

5. Consider safety and well-being: base your information sharing decisions on considerations of the safety and well-being of the individual and others who may be affected by their actions.

6. Necessary, proportionate, relevant, adequate, accurate, timely and secure: ensure that the information you share is necessary for the purpose for which you are sharing it, is shared only with those individuals who need to have it, is accurate and up-to-date, is shared in a timely fashion, and is shared securely (see principles).

7. Keep a record of your decision and the reasons for it—whether it is to share information or not. If you decide to share, then record what you have shared, with whom and for what purpose.

Working Together to Safeguard Children

Advice is also provided in the 2018 edition of the guidance to legislation on child welfare, *Working Together to Safeguard Children*. The starting point is that social work practitioners must have due regard to the relevant data protection principles which allow them to share personal information, as provided for in the Data Protection Act 2018 and the General Data Protection Regulation (GDPR).

To share information effectively:

*   all practitioners should be confident of the processing conditions under the Data Protection Act 2018 and the GDPR which allow them to store and share information for safeguarding purposes, including information which is sensitive and personal, and should be treated as 'special category personal data';

*   where practitioners need to share special category personal data, they should be aware that the Data Protection Act 2018 contains 'safeguarding of children and individuals at risk' as a processing condition that allows practitioners to share information. This includes allowing practitioners to share information without consent: if it is not possible to gain consent, it cannot be reasonably expected that a practitioner gains consent, or if to gain consent would place a child at risk.

The guidance also contains what it describes as a myth-busting guide to information sharing. This is set out in **Box 4.5**.

BOX 4.5 Myth-busting guide to information sharing—*Working Together to Safeguard Children (2018)*

Data protection legislation is a barrier to sharing information

No—the Data Protection Act 2018 and GDPR do not prohibit the collection and sharing of personal information, but rather provide a framework to ensure that personal information is shared appropriately. In particular, the Data Protection Act 2018 balances the rights of the information subject (the individual whom the information is about) and the possible need to share information about them.

Consent is always needed to share personal information

No—you do not necessarily need consent to share personal information. Wherever possible, you should seek consent and be open and honest with the individual from the outset as to why, what, how and with whom, their information will be shared. You should seek consent where an individual may not expect their information to be passed on. When you gain consent to share information, it must be explicit, and freely given. There may be some circumstances where it is not appropriate to seek consent, because the individual cannot give consent, or it is not reasonable to obtain consent, or because to gain consent would put a child's or young person's safety at risk.

Personal information collected by one organisation/agency cannot be disclosed to another

No—this is not the case, unless the information is to be used for a purpose incompatible with the purpose for which it was originally collected. In the case of children in need, or children at risk of significant harm, it is difficult to foresee circumstances where information law would be a barrier to sharing personal information with other practitioners.

The common law duty of confidence and the Human Rights Act 1998 prevent the sharing of personal information

No—this is not the case. In addition to the Data Protection Act 2018 and GDPR, practitioners need to balance the common law duty of confidence and the Human Rights Act 1998 against the effect on individuals or others of not sharing the information.

IT systems are often a barrier to effective information sharing

No—IT systems, such as the Child Protection Information Sharing project (CPIS), can be useful for information sharing. IT systems are most valuable when practitioners use the shared data to make more informed decisions about how to support and safeguard a child.

In order to follow the advice and the principles of effective information sharing you need an understanding of the HRA, the common law of confidentiality, the GDPR, and the Data Protection Act 2018—and need to be clear about when they restrict and when they allow for information sharing. We have already discussed the GDPR and the DPA. Now we turn to the Human Rights Act and the common law of confidentiality.

The Human Rights Act 1998

We have already described (in **chapter 3**) the significance and the impact of the HRA for social work practice. Every decision you make must comply with the Act. We set out the ECHR Articles of particular relevance to decisions about confidentiality in **Box 4.6**. We have emphasized the words that are important for this chapter in bold. The case study also demonstrated the importance of human rights in this context.

BOX 4.6 Confidentiality—extracts from key Articles of the European Convention on Human Rights

Article 6—Right to a fair trial

(1) In the determination of his civil rights and obligations or of any criminal charge against him, everyone is entitled to a fair and public hearing within a reasonable time by an independent and impartial tribunal established by law. Judgment shall be pronounced publicly but the press and public may be excluded from all or part of the trial in the interests of morals, public order or national security in a democratic society, where the interests of juveniles or the protection of the private life of the parties so require, or to the extent strictly necessary in the opinion of the court in special circumstances where publicity would prejudice the interests of justice.

. . .

(3) Everyone charged with a criminal offence has the following minimum rights:

    (a) to be informed promptly, in a language which he understands and in detail, of the nature and cause of the accusation against him;

    . . .

    (b) to examine or have examined witnesses against him and to obtain the attendance and examination of witnesses on his behalf under the same conditions as witnesses against him;

. . .

Article 8—Right to respect for private and family life

Everyone has the right to respect for his private and family life, his home and his correspondence.

There shall be no interference by a public authority with the exercise of this right except such as is in accordance with the law and is necessary in a democratic society in the interests of national security, public safety or the economic well being of the country, for the prevention of disorder or crime, for the protection of health or morals, or for the protection of the rights and freedoms of others.

Article 10—Freedom of expression

Everyone has the right to freedom of expression. This right shall include freedom to hold opinions and to receive and impart information and ideas without interference by public authority and regardless of frontiers . . .

The exercise of these freedoms, since it carries with it duties and responsibilities, may be subject to such formalities, conditions, restrictions or penalties as are prescribed by law and are necessary in a democratic society, in the interests of national security, territorial integrity or public safety, for the prevention of disorder or crime, for the protection of health or morals, for the protection of the reputation or rights of others, for preventing the disclosure of information received in confidence, or for maintaining the authority and impartiality of the judiciary.

Human rights and privacy

It is important at this stage to consider the distinction between privacy and confidentiality. Traditionally, there has been no right to privacy recognized in English law, as distinct from the legal protections given to confidential information. However, the European Court of Human Rights (ECtHR) is increasingly stressing the legal significance of privacy, as the two cases set out in **Box 4.7** indicate.

BOX 4.7 The increasing importance of privacy

Peck v UK (2003)

On the evening of 20 August 1995, at a time when he was suffering from depression, Mr Peck walked alone down Brentwood High Street, with a kitchen knife in his hand, and attempted suicide by cutting his wrists. He was unaware that he had been filmed by a closed-circuit television (CCTV) camera installed by Brentwood Borough Council.

The CCTV footage did not show the applicant cutting his wrists; the operator was solely alerted to an individual in possession of a knife. The police were notified and arrived at the scene, where they took the knife and gave the applicant medical assistance.

The council sought to publicize the value of CCTV and used the incident to demonstrate how CCTV had ensured prompt action was taken to protect Mr Peck's life. Footage of the incident was used in the local paper and in a national television programme. Mr Peck was identifiable from this footage.

The court observed that, following the disclosure of the CCTV footage, the applicant's actions were seen to an extent which far exceeded any exposure to a passer-by or to security observation and to a degree surpassing that which the applicant could possibly have foreseen. The disclosure by the council of the relevant footage therefore constituted a serious interference with the applicant's right to respect for his private life.

Perry v UK (2003)

Mr Perry was arrested in connection with a series of armed robberies. When he refused to take part in an identity parade, he was covertly videotaped in a police station and as a result identified by two witnesses. Mr Perry was subsequently convicted.

The ECtHR ruled that Mr Perry's right to respect for private life under Article 8 of the ECHR was breached. The covert videotaping had gone beyond the normal use of their station camera and was not in accordance with the law on identification procedures laid out in the code of practice. The police had not informed Mr Perry or his solicitor that the tape was being made or obtained his consent, and had not informed him of his rights in that respect.

These developments are very much in line with your ethical responsibilities set out in the BASW Code of Ethics and you should be aware that there has been an increasing emphasis on privacy in the courts. However, rights are not absolute and the state has responsibilities to protect its citizens' lives. Often, keeping vulnerable people safe requires that private information be disclosed. The starting point for decisions to disclose is the common law duty of confidentiality.

The common law duty of confidentiality

The common law provides individuals with a cause of action (a right to sue) for damages if there is a breach of the legal duty of confidentiality. We discussed what we mean by common law in **chapter 1**. The branch of common law that we are concerned with here is tort. A person (or organization) can sue in tort if they claim a breach of some duty: for example, a duty to take appropriate care (e.g. as a driver), a duty to respect persons or property, or in this case a duty to keep information confidential. In a case involving confidentiality a court can interfere, either by making an award of damages or by making an order, known as an injunction, prohibiting the disclosure of the relevant information. Note that the duty of confidentiality extends to children and adults who lack capacity, and even to the dead.

Breach of confidence is a tort that can apply to the collection, use, or disclosure of personal information. But not all information is protected by the law of tort. There are three basic requirements:

- where the information is no longer confidential, because, for instance, the individual to whom the information relates has consented to disclosure;
- where disclosure is necessary to safeguard the individual, or others, or is in the public interest;
- where there is a legal duty to disclose, for example a court order.

Information must be confidential

If someone consents to information that they provide being shared, then it is no longer confidential. Previous government guidance explained it like this:

> Confidence is only breached where the sharing of confidential information is not authorised by the person who provided it or to whom it relates. If the information was provided on the understanding that it would be shared with a limited range of people or for limited purposes, then sharing in accordance with that understanding will not be a breach of confidence. Similarly, there will not be a breach of confidence where there is explicit consent to the sharing.
>
> *Information Sharing: Guidance for Practitioners and Managers* (2010), para. 3.14 at http://webarchive.nationalarchives.gov.uk/20100625171628/http://publications. everychildmatters.gov.uk/eOrderingDownload/00807-2008BKT-EN-March09.pdf

So, information about service users can be shared if you get consent. Depending on the circumstances you may need the consent of the person who provided the information in confidence, and the consent of the person to whom the information relates. We explained some of the complexities of consent in **chapter 2**. Remember the person giving consent must understand the consequences of giving consent. Also, although consent may be implied, it is far better to get explicit consent to any sharing of information. Get the consent in writing and keep it on file. The best time to explain how you will handle confidential information is at the beginning of your relationship with the service user. More stringent rules apply to sensitive personal information, when consent should be explicit. But the guidance adds: 'even without consent, or explicit consent, it is still possible to share personal information if it is necessary in order to carry out your role, or to protect the vital interests of the individual where, for example, consent cannot be given'. We explain this further below. There must have been an *unauthorized* use of the information. If a service user gives you permission to divulge particular information, then the tort cannot arise. However, the service user could give you permission to disclose information only in certain circumstances or to certain people. Communication of the information in breach of those requirements would give rise to the tort. Moreover, the service user must have capacity to consent to the disclosure.

In addition, the courts will generally not protect information that is in the public domain or readily available from another source. That information is no longer confidential. The 'Spycatcher' case (*Attorney General v Observer Newspaper and others* (1989)) involved a former spy whose book revealing secrets gained in the course of his employment had been published in the United States and Australia. The House of Lords refused an injunction as there was nothing left to protect: nevertheless, they were clear that there had been a breach of confidentiality between employer and employee.

However, courts may act to limit further disclosure, even if the information is already in the public domain. This was true of the so-called 'three-in-a-bed case'— *PJS v News Group* (2016)—in which the *Sun on Sunday* wished to publish information about a celebrity's alleged adultery and said the information had already been published in the United States, Scotland (with a legal jurisdiction separate from the rest of the UK), and generally on the internet. Supreme Court justices nevertheless gave PJS an injunction preventing publication. Confidentiality might not be an issue, since the allegations were known publicly, but 'different considerations apply to privacy claims, where the impact of any additional disclosure on the likely distress to PJS and his family, and the degree of intrusion or harassment, continues to be highly relevant' (Supreme Court resumé of the judgment). Potential harm to the couple's children was particularly relevant in this case—which also confirmed there was no 'enhanced' Article 10 (freedom of expression) right. Article 10 and Article 8 (privacy) are of equal weight; which one prevails depends on the circumstances, including the public interest.

The cases point to an increasing importance of privacy indicating that the public/private divide is not clear-cut. Mr Peck's suicide attempt was in a public place, but he did not anticipate that it would be televised to nine million viewers, and he had the right to be protected from that dissemination.

To be legally confidential the information should have a degree of sensitivity and value that gives it the quality of confidentiality. Furthermore, it must have been communicated (or received, as in the *Campbell v MGN* case below) in circumstances giving rise to an obligation of confidence. If you guaranteed that you would not disclose the information, that guarantee would give rise to the obligation. However, the obligation can also be implied from the relationship between the person who communicated the information and the recipient. In the case of Max Mosley (*Mosley v News Group Newspapers* (2008)), for example, the Formula 1 boss involved in sadomasochistic sex with prostitutes, it was deemed that he was entitled to expect confidentiality from his fellow participants, and bringing in a secret camera was a breach of that expectation. In the case of *Campbell v Mirror Group Newspapers* (2004), the fact that a photographer had secretly taken pictures of supermodel Naomi Campbell leaving a drug rehabilitation centre was considered to establish confidentiality automatically even though the photographer had no pre-existing relationship of confidence with her. The photographs had the quality of confidential material because Campbell could reasonably expect her privacy to be protected—though the *Mirror* was not barred from *writing* about her attendance at the centre.

For social workers, the issue of confidence is more likely to arise when there is a pre-existing relationship (though you may come across information that has that quality of confidentiality without such a relationship—something the individual would obviously want to remain private, as in *Campbell*). If there is a professional relationship such as exists between a lawyer and their client or a social worker and service user, then information divulged is likely to give rise to the obligation of confidence. The obligation will extend to information you learn indirectly, for instance from a relative of a service user, because the information was received in your professional capacity.

The public interest

Confidentiality is not an absolute right and in particular circumstances even if there is no consent you can share confidential information. Having 'just cause or excuse' or acting in the public interest are defences to an action for breach of confidence. You can breach a duty of confidentiality to prevent serious crime. Paragraph 3.39 of the archived guidance referred to above explains:

> A public interest can arise in a wide range of circumstances, for example, to protect children or other people from harm, to promote the welfare of children or to prevent crime and disorder. There are also public interests, which in some circumstances may weigh against sharing, including the public interest in maintaining public confidence in the confidentiality of certain services.

Government departments and local authorities owe duties of confidentiality in the same way that individuals do. As there may be uncertainty about when it will be in the public interest to disclose information, legislation is sometimes used to provide clarity. Sometimes the legislation prevents the disclosure of information by imposing specific obligations of confidence, for instance in the Abortion Act 1967. Sometimes there is an obligation to inform a statutory authority. For instance, in the case of specific diseases there is an obligation to inform the NHS. Courts too can order the provision of information. The archived guidance says:

> If the information is confidential, and the consent of the information subject is not gained, then the responder needs to satisfy themselves that there are grounds to override the duty of confidentiality in these circumstances. This can be because it is overwhelmingly in the information subject's interests for this information to be disclosed. It is also possible that an overriding public interest would justify disclosure of the information (or that sharing is required by a court order, other legal obligation or statutory exemption).

The guidance says that the public interest threshold should not be difficult to meet, particularly in emergency situations, though for health information the threshold is higher.

A legal duty to disclose information

In particular circumstances there is a legal duty to disclose information, for instance when it is required by statute or when a judge orders you to disclose information. Legislation provides for some very specific circumstances when information must be disclosed to the police if they ask for it, for instance under the Prevention of Terrorism Act 1989, the Misuse of Drugs Act 1971, and the Police and Criminal Evidence Act 1984. If the particular provisions under these statutes apply, then social workers have no choice but to disclose confidential information. We do not have space to detail these provisions, and advise you to take legal advice as soon as a request to provide information is received. However, the more challenging scenario is where legislation gives only a *power* (i.e. not a duty) to disclose information. Section 115(1) of the Crime and Disorder Act 1998 provides:

> Any person who, apart from this subsection, would not have power to disclose information—
>
> (a) to a relevant authority; or
>
> (b) to a person acting on behalf of such an authority,
>
> shall have power to do so in any case where the disclosure is necessary or expedient for the purposes of any provision of this Act.

This is a broad provision, which impacts upon social services as members of Crime and Disorder Reduction Partnerships alongside the police and other local authority departments. This provision is not unique. For instance, s. 17 of the Anti-terrorism, Crime and Security Act 2001 extends the existing disclosure powers of public authorities contained in 66 Acts where disclosure would assist (amongst other things) criminal investigations, criminal proceedings, the initiation or bringing to an end of any such investigation or proceedings, or facilitating a determination of whether any such investigation or proceedings should be initiated or brought to an end. In these circumstances you should consider very carefully whether any decision you make to disclose information is lawful.

The guidance provides a useful flowchart (see **Figure 4.1**) of when to share information. What you have learned so far from consideration of your ethical responsibilities, the HRA, and the common law duty of confidentiality is that whilst the starting point is that information is confidential, there may be a range of circumstances which justify disclosure. Your role is to balance the competing interests, bearing in mind the need for proportionality. The archived practitioners' guide says, at para. 3.10:

> The key factor in deciding whether or not to share confidential information is proportionality, i.e. whether the proposed sharing is a proportionate response to the need to protect the public interest in question. In making the decision you must weigh up what might happen if the information is shared against what might happen if it is not, and make a decision based on a reasonable judgment.

In **Tables 4.1** and **4.2** we set out in summary the balancing exercise you must undertake.

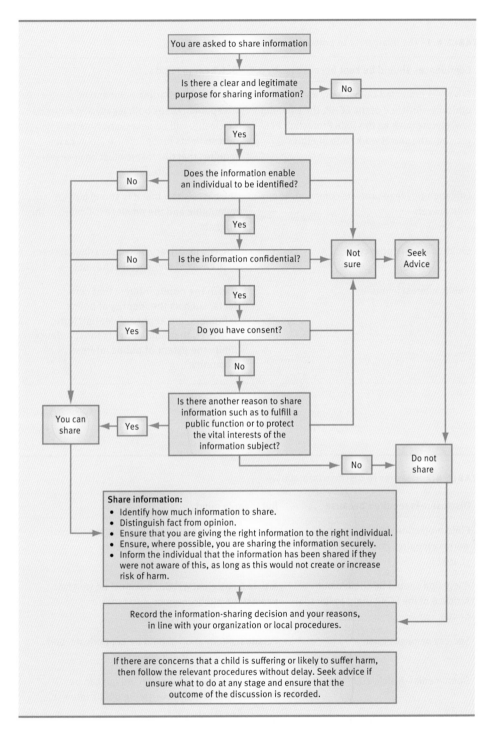

FIGURE 4.1   Flowchart on when and how to share information

Source: HM Government, https://www.gov.uk/government/uploads/system/uploads/attachment_data/
file/419628/Information_sharing_advice_safeguarding_practitioners.pdf.

TABLE 4.1 The basic duty to protect confidences

Confidences should be kept because . . .	But, bear in mind . . .
Privacy is protected both legally and ethically—Article 8 of the ECHR, the common law, statute such as the Data Protection Act, etc., and the social work code of ethics	This is only a starting point and in exceptional cases both legally and ethically disclosure will be necessary. Note that human rights jurisprudence (court cases) requires that disclosure must be necessary and proportionate.
Litigation privilege protects communications with lawyers	The cases show that it is strong but not immutable and the privilege is limited to the litigants
Children require privacy	There is no privacy in serious criminal cases, or in cases of anti-social behaviour
Public interest immunity	It is in the public interest that certain facts, such as the identity of police informers, are kept confidential. Note, however, that human rights jurisprudence limits the extent of public interest immunity

TABLE 4.2 Reasons to disclose information

Disclosure is required because . . .	But, bear in mind . . .
Child protection and partnership working requires information to be shared	There is no presumption of disclosure; each case must be considered on its own merits
Allegation should be spelled out—Article 6 of the ECHR (right to fair trial or hearing)	Article 6 has great weight, but must be weighed against the public interest
Secrecy damages trust	Personal information should be kept private, and disclosed only as far as necessary
Open media—Article 10 of the ECHR	Sources will have to be protected but can be disclosed if it is in the overriding public interest
Other reasons—particularly relating to the abuse of children by professionals and others	There must be disclosure only where there is evidence of a pressing need; disclosure must be limited to what is necessary

◼ Particular examples of disclosure dilemmas

Bear in mind that the decision to disclose information requires more rigorous analysis than the maintenance of confidentiality. Public interest, the general justification for disclosure, is a slippery concept. This is particularly so for social workers, whose role ranges from caring for the individual, through broader statutory responsibilities to protect the vulnerable, and beyond, to the investigation of harmful, often criminal, activities. Social workers are also required to work in partnership with a number of state agencies, including the police. The courts demonstrate an increasingly sophisticated understanding of the professional role of the social worker and provide some case-specific examples of appropriate and responsible information handling. Further, in this chapter we consider some common situations when confidentiality is a particular issue.

Disclosure of confidential material to the police

Many agencies hold their records under an express or implied undertaking to hold them in confidence. Police investigating crime can obtain warrants to search the records of agencies such as social services and, subject to judicial discretion, will be able to use the material in criminal prosecutions, notwithstanding the confidential nature of the contents. But while powers exist to force disclosure under a court order, those holding information must still start from an assumption of confidentiality, as para. 28 of circular Personal Social Services: *Confidentiality of Personal Information*, DoH Circular LAC (88)17 (now archived) indicated (emphasis added):

> The disclosure of personal information [to the police] may exceptionally be justified if it can help to prevent, detect or prosecute a serious crime . . . Before such a disclosure is made at least the following conditions must be satisfied:
>
> the crime must be sufficiently serious for the public interest to prevail. A record should be kept of when information is disclosed for this purpose;
>
> it must be established that, without the disclosure, the task of preventing or detecting the crime would be seriously prejudiced or delayed;
>
> satisfactory undertakings must be obtained that the personal information disclosed will not be used for any other purpose and will be destroyed if the person is not prosecuted, or is discharged or acquitted;
>
> request from a police officer of suitably senior rank, e.g. superintendent or above.

Paragraph 30 continues:

> In addition, evidence may come to the attention of staff that may justify disclosure on their own initiative to the police so as to protect another individual. The most common example of this is in cases of child abuse.

Decisions to disclose

When should social services choose to use these extensive powers to disclose information? Disclosure is allowed only if it conforms with the public interest exception to the common law duty and the proportionality and necessity requirements of the HRA. Disclosure may exceptionally be justified if it can help to prevent, detect, or prosecute a serious crime. However, the nature of the relationship between local authorities and the police has changed dramatically since 1988. Emerging partnerships mean that social services are likely to feel greater responsibilities to work with the police. Society has also become more risk-averse. What in the past may have been exceptional may become more routine to eliminate risks to children through criminal or anti-social activities.

Cases

In the matter of H (Children) (2009)

This case established that since rule changes in 2005 a more 'liberal approach' (i.e. favouring disclosure to police investigating crimes such as assaulting a child) was in place regarding disclosure of material garnered during and running up to care proceedings. The defendant lived with the mother of four children and was the father of the youngest. He confessed to causing serious head injuries to one of the other children, aged five months, in a witness statement to social services, at which point an interim care order was made regarding the children. The police then applied for disclosure of information about the assault, including medical reports and the confession. At the original hearing, the circuit judge refused disclosure and the police appealed.

Mr Justice Bodey noted that the new rules allowed disclosure without a court order to 'a professional acting in furtherance of the protection of children', which included a police officer investigating crime. Other such professionals 'were an officer of the local authority exercising child protection functions, any professional person attending a child protection case conference, or an officer of the NSPCC'. He added: 'It is undeniable that the rule change in 2005 introduced a far wider regime of disclosure without leave' (i.e. without permission of the courts).

Re X and Y (Children: Disclosure of Judgment to Police) (2014)

This case looked at the new Family Procedure Rules of 2010, which included the 2005 rule changes. It was about whether two care judgments that existed in anonymous form with redactions should be disclosed to the police given the father of Y admitted causing injuries to the child. In such family law proceedings, a witness cannot refuse to give evidence on the grounds that he might incriminate himself—but should be warned by a judge that this might be the case. In this case, no warning was given. Nevertheless, Mr Justice Baker ruled there should be disclosure because of the seriousness of the assaults on Y and the public interest in sharing the information by different agencies involved in child protection. 'The welfare of the children will not be significantly affected simply by the disclosure of the judgment, provided the police and the CPS are precluded from disclosing it, or any information contained in it, to any person without the court's permission.'

The 2010 Family Procedure Rules can be found at www.legislation.gov.uk/uksi/2010/2955/part/12/chapter/7/made. See also 'Practice Direction 12G—Communication of Information' at the Ministry of Justice.

The Regulation of Investigatory Powers Act 2000

Social workers do much more than provide support for families. They also investigate abuse. It may be that social services acquire information other than through direct information gathering. Local authorities, as public authorities, are able to engage in covert surveillance such as entry to or interference with property, following suspects, and use of informers. There are legal controls on these activities. Covert information gathering is governed by the Regulation of Investigatory Powers Act 2000. The Act aims to ensure that the use of powers to investigate individuals through surveillance or to intercept telecommunication complies with the HRA, in particular Article 8. (It also implemented Article 5 of EU Directive 97/66/EC, now Directive 2002/58/EC on privacy, which to some extent provides a European framework for handling such information and surveillance.) Public authorities have only the surveillance powers conferred by the Act, and if they exceed these powers they will be acting unlawfully. Surveillance operations to obtain evidence require prior authorization from a designated person. Local authorities can designate assistant chief officers and officers responsible for the management of investigations. A written record must be kept and include the reasons for granting the authorization and its terms. Necessity and proportionality are the bases for granting authorization. Proportionality is tested against the object to be achieved by carrying out the surveillance in question. The Act establishes a surveillance tribunal to oversee the Act and consider allegations that public authorities have infringed human rights by surveillance activities.

If a local authority fails to get activities authorized, then the evidence produced will be tainted if used in any court proceedings, as it will have been obtained in breach of s. 6 of the HRA ('It is unlawful for a public authority to act in a way which is incompatible with a Convention right'). Any prosecution using the evidence will be vulnerable to arguments that evidence acquired in breach of Convention rights should be excluded under s. 78(1) of the Police and Criminal Evidence Act 1984 (a court 'may refuse to allow evidence on which the prosecution proposes to rely to be given if it appears to the court that . . . the admission of the evidence would have such an adverse effect on the fairness of the proceedings that the court ought not to admit it'). Decisions to use these powers are likely to be taken at the highest level, but any social worker exceptionally involved in any covert activity should be fully briefed on what is and is not permissible.

Adoption and confidentiality

The difficulties and fragilities of adoption seem to pose particular challenges. Two ombudsman decisions indicate the dilemmas that can face social services. In Report 97/A/3857, Mrs W complained about the way a council placed two children with her and her husband with a view to adoption. One aspect of the complaint was the lack of information about the children's behavioural problems. The ombudsman accepted that social workers had to make difficult decisions about what they could disclose without improperly breaching confidentiality. Some of the information Mrs W asked for could not be disclosed, but the ombudsman said that the council did not tell her and her husband things which would not have entailed an improper breach of confidence and which they reasonably needed to know, such as information about the children's health and history of abuse. The ombudsman concluded that as it became clear to the prospective adopters that they had not been told enough about the children, they became increasingly anxious about what they did not know. That prolonged anxiety was an important element of the injustice caused by the way the council acted. This case emphasizes the need for appropriate and timely disclosure, which should not be held back by excessive fears of the legal regime of confidentiality, privacy, and data protection—the need to achieve the correct result, not just following the apparently correct procedure.

Inappropriate disclosure

The second case demonstrates that openness must be appropriate. Report 97/C/3985 concerned the induction process between the complainant and child she hoped to adopt, which was terminated without good reason, without proper notice, and without adequate explanation. One particular aspect of the complaint was that the council had allowed the child's foster parents full access to the complainant's adoption form. The ombudsman commented:

> Whilst it may be perfectly proper for a foster carer, who has an in depth knowledge and understanding of a child, to play some part in the selection process of a suitable adoptive parent, I can see no justification nor statutory basis for extending this to providing the foster carer with detailed personal and confidential information about the prospective adoptive parent. It appears to me to be totally inappropriate and unprofessional for such confidential information to be made available to anyone other than the most essential personnel.

The council's action exposed the complainant to unnecessary and unwarranted intrusion into her private affairs.

Perpetrators of abuse

Professionals who abuse

Professionals who abuse their own children are unlikely to be able to protect themselves from the disclosure of the information to their professional bodies. In *A County Council v W (Disclosure)* (1997), disclosure of the care proceedings to the General Medical Council where the father involved was a doctor was allowed on the basis that disciplinary proceedings would possibly protect other children.

In *Re L (Care Proceedings: Disclosure to Third Party)* (2000), the mother, a paediatric nurse suffering mental and emotional problems, had caused her child significant emotional harm, which resulted in an interim care order. The court gave leave to disclose the judgment and the medical reports to the UK Central Council for Nursing. The rights of the mother and child had to be balanced against the public interest in demanding protection from nurses who were or who were potentially unfit to practise.

In *London Borough of Brent v SK and HK (A Minor)* (2007), Brent applied to court for permission to disclose evidence from care proceedings, which arose from an assault by a mother upon her child, to the mother's employer, a residential home for the elderly. The judge gave permission for limited and confidential disclosure. The case is also useful because it reviews the existing case law in this area.

Other perpetrators

Even where perpetrators do not have professional responsibilities, disclosure may be ordered. In *R v Chief Constable of North Wales, ex p AB* (1997), a married couple released from prison after serving long sentences for serious sexual offences against a number of children rented a caravan on a caravan site as their home. The police informed the site owner of the convictions, and as a result the site owner required the couple to leave. They then sought a judicial review of the police decision to disclose the convictions. The Court of Appeal confirmed the Divisional Court's dismissal of the application. It was compatible with Article 8 because there was a pressing need for the police to disclose material already in the public domain to a caravan site owner, when the material related to paedophiles on the site who were a considerable risk to children and vulnerable adults who might come onto the site during the holidays.

What was critical here was the real evidence of a pressing need for disclosure. Without such evidence the authorities are much more vulnerable, as the following case demonstrates. In *R v Local Authority in the Midlands, ex p LM* (2000) the applicant, who owned a bus company, had his contract to transport school children terminated. This was because of social services and police concerns arising from an allegation against him of indecent assault on his daughter seven years previously, along with a further allegation against him of sexual abuse three years before that. He wished to take up a new contract for school bus services and therefore asked for assurances from the police and social services that such allegations would not be further disclosed. The authorities refused to give those assurances and he sought judicial review of the refusals. The court held that it was not compatible with Article 8 for the police to disclose stale and unproven allegations of sexual abuse to a county council which employed the applicant to provide school transport because there was no 'pressing need' for disclosure.

▉ Information governance

The law relating to confidential information illustrates the difficult and conflicting demands upon professionals striving to carry out their responsibilities. In the context of health services, the Caldicott review of personally identifiable information in 1997 recommended that 'guardians' of personal information be created to safeguard and govern the uses made of confidential information within NHS organizations. The review advocated a managerial approach, based upon a framework of quality standards for the management of confidentiality and access to personal information. The Caldicott approach has been extended by the government to councils with social services responsibilities which were required to appoint a Caldicott guardian. Full details are set out in LAC (2002)2 (now archived). Caldicott guardians must audit existing systems, procedures, and organizational capabilities relating to confidentiality and security. Principles set out by Caldicott for practitioners included:

- justifying every proposed use or transfer of client-identifiable information within or from an organization;
- no use of client-identifiable data items unless there is no alternative;
- providing access on a need-to-know basis;
- the fact that the duty to share information can be as important as the duty to protect patient confidentiality.

The Care Act 2014 and information sharing

Safeguarding Adults Boards (SABs) (see **chapter 14**) are local groups set up to facilitate joint working on protecting any vulnerable adult with needs for care and support or experiencing or at risk of abuse or neglect. The Act has put these on a statutory basis, with Schedule 2 requiring that they include representatives from the local authority and NHS clinical commissioning group and the chief officer of police. Others with care or support functions may be represented, such as providers of housing and organizations or individuals to be specified in later regulations. As is the case with local safeguarding children boards, there is now a duty on relevant organizations to supply SABs with information on request. The request must be made 'for the purpose of enabling or assisting the SAB to exercise its functions'; it must be made 'to a person whose functions or activities the SAB considers to be such that the person is likely to have information relevant to the exercise of a function by the SAB'; and the information must relate to: (a) the person to whom the request is made; (b) a function or activity of that person; or (c) a person in respect of whom that person exercises a function or engages in an activity.

The provision may be to deal with worries that bureaucratic interpretation of the DPA is standing in the way of perfectly sensible information sharing for legitimate purposes. As such, a rather wide and somewhat ill-defined power has been created to demand information from anyone who has 'functions or engage in activities such that the SAB considers it likely to have information relevant to a function of the SAB'. Explanatory notes list family members of the adult, carers, GPs, someone who has done voluntary work with the individual, or a church minister with knowledge of the family or the individual. The information may be used by the SAB or other person to whom it is supplied 'only for the purpose of enabling or assisting the SAB to exercise its functions'. The Act applies no sanctions against misuse of the information, which may be a worry, particularly given the wide range of non-professional people the government intends to be involved in SABs—who could include members of the family of a vulnerable adult. The rules on confidentiality certainly apply to all such information, as outlined earlier, as does the DPA once the SAB has gained the information. But presumably so too does the Article 10 right of freedom of expression. What if a SAB member received a controversial report as part of his or her SAB duties and felt it should be given wider publicity? Could family members on a SAB talk to their lawyers about what went on at its meetings? Or does the 'only to exercise its functions' provision act in effect to sterilize that information, putting it beyond use even as evidence in a court of law? At this stage we cannot really know.

◼ Data sharing—a summary

You are very likely to be involved in data sharing; perhaps you will receive a request for confidential data you hold, or perhaps you will be involved in a data-sharing partnership.

The government's information-sharing guidance provides a summary of the principles underpinning good practice.

- You should explain to children, young people, and families at the outset, openly and honestly, what and how information will, or could, be shared and why, and seek their agreement. The exception to this is where to do so would put that child, young person, or others at increased risk of significant harm or an adult at risk of serious harm, or if it would undermine the prevention, detection, or prosecution of a serious crime, including where seeking consent might lead to interference with any potential investigation.

- You must always consider the safety and welfare of a child or young person when making decisions on whether to share information about them. Where there is concern that the child may be suffering or is at risk of suffering significant harm, the child's safety and welfare must be the overriding consideration.

- You should, where possible, respect the wishes of children, young people, or families who do not consent to share confidential information. You may still share information, if in your judgement on the facts of the case, there is sufficient need to override that lack of consent.

- You should seek advice where you are in doubt, especially where your doubt relates to a concern about possible significant harm to a child or serious harm to others.

- You should ensure that the information you share is accurate and up to date, necessary for the purpose for which you are sharing it, shared only with those people who need to see it, and shared securely.

- You should always record the reasons for your decision—whether it is to share information or not.

The guidance also summarizes in a diagram the legal questions that need to be answered in deciding whether to disclose information. The diagram is provided in **Figure 4.1**.

SUMMARY

In this chapter we have considered the legal framework through which data is protected: the GDPR and the DPA 2018. We have made clear its relevance to your practice as a social worker. We have also considered information sharing. We looked at ethical considerations, human rights law, the law on confidentiality and privacy, and the advice government gives social work professionals on information sharing. We concluded by reminding you of some key principles: that information should be accurate, and only the minimum information necessary should be held; that decisions to share information should be recorded—in particular the legal justification; and that wherever possible you should get consent from those whose information you are sharing.

EXERCISES

1 One of us received the following email (no doubt you have received many similar emails).

> Dear Jazz Friends,
>
> You may have heard the news that the personal data laws are changing on 25 May 2018. As a result, we wanted to let you how we use your personal data, what your rights are with regards to your data, and to ensure that you are still happy for us to contact you in the future.
>
> We hold your information within a secure email system called MailChimp. At any point you can contact us via email and we will remove all your data from this system.
>
> Unless we hear from you, we will continue sending you occasional updates around the time of any Margate Jazz Festival activities. We won't ever pass on your data to anyone else, and you can choose to unsubscribe or manage your preferences at any time.
>
> If you'd like to continue receiving news and updates from us, you don't need to do anything. If you'd like to be removed from our mailing list, please click the 'unsubscribe' button below.
>
> As for the music . . . we hope to be making an announcement about this year's activities very soon.
>
> Thank you!

Explain why the email was sent and why it contains the information it does.

2 Why is confidentiality important? When do you think confidentiality should be breached? Does your thinking accord with the legal position? The ethical position? Are there ever circumstances when your ethical obligation is to breach a confidence?

3 In the following circumstances what issues are raised about human rights, your professional responsibilities, and confidentiality? How would you suggest they should be resolved? Do not forget to consider the Human Rights Act 1998 and the Data Protection Act 1998 in preparing your response.

(a) The Housing Department of a local authority asks the Social Services Department for any information it has about anti-social behaviour by a particular family.

(b) An anonymous caller rings social services because she has seen evidence of physical abuse of a child. The local authority asks the family's health visitor for information.

(c) You, a child care professional, tell the headteacher of a secondary school about your concerns for a particular child. The headteacher tells the child's form teacher.

(d) You suspect Mr X of sexual abuse of his grandchildren. Mr X has found himself accommodation with a housing association in a block of flats which also accommodates families. You want to tell the housing association of your concerns.

(e) When you were visiting a family, you overheard a telephone conversation which indicated that one of the adult children of the family was involved in criminal activities. You want to tell the police but your team leader says that the issue is not serious enough.

4 You have serious concerns about Fred, who you suspect of having physically and emotionally abused his two sons aged 12 and 14. You have recorded these concerns on both of the children's files. Fred has asked to see his file. He has obtained signed consents from his sons. What are his rights to do so? What information will he be allowed to see?

5 Why do you think there are specific provisions for information sharing within the Care Act 2014?

ONLINE RESOURCES

For guidance on how to answer these exercises, visit the online resources at www.oup.com/uk/carr-goosey15e.

WHERE DO WE GO FROM HERE?

Our overview of the common law duty of confidentiality and its interface with the HRA and information legislation illustrates the complexity of the area. Clearly, a balance needs to be reached between the necessity to protect children and other vulnerable people and the right to privacy. The law is moving towards greater sharing of information, provided the decision to share is one that is proportionate and necessary. On the other hand, we also see that public opinion is strongly in favour of privacy and resists state intrusion. It is this tension which causes legal uncertainty. We can understand and sympathize with the confusion and bewilderment the law creates for many social care professionals who are at the sharp end of this dilemma. The law does not necessarily make your decision making any easier—but it should help to clarify the issues you must consider.

This chapter concludes the first part of the book. You are now armed with the necessary tools to enable you to understand the more specific legal responsibilities we consider in Part 2 (relating to children) and Part 3 (relating to vulnerable adults).

ANNOTATED FURTHER READING

Confidentiality

R. S. Taylor, 'Re S (A Child) (Identification: Restrictions on Publication) and A Local Authority v W: children's privacy and press freedom in criminal cases' (2006) CFLQ 18(2): 269. This commentary considers the decisions in two difficult cases which raised the question of whether the courts can and should restrain publication of the identity of defendants in criminal trials in order to protect the welfare of their children. The cases reveal the ways in which the courts seek to reconcile press freedom and the privacy of the vulnerable.

T. Keyser and C. Dainty, The Information Governance Toolkit: Data Protection, Caldicott, Confidentiality (Radcliff Publishing, 2004). It is difficult to find anything specifically aimed at social work, but this is a good overview aimed at health-care professionals, and the issues are the same for social workers.

Information sharing

C. Cobley, '"Working Together?"—admissions of abuse in child protection proceedings and criminal prosecutions' (2004) CFLQ 16(2): 175. This article considers the way in which information is exchanged between the child protection and criminal justice systems. It suggests that tensions between the two systems increase as cases progress.

'Public Sector Data Sharing: Guidance on the Law' is available online: https://webarchive. nationalarchives.gov.uk/20150603223548/https://www.justice.gov.uk/downloads/information-access-rights/data-sharing/annex-h-data-sharing.pdf

Part 2

Responsibilities towards children

Part 2 Responsibilities towards children

The state has for many years taken on the role of looking after children when families cannot adequately meet their needs. On behalf of the state, this is a large part of what social workers do. Child protection and child welfare issues are far more prominent in social work than adult protection issues, and involve significantly greater use of the courts, so as a result this part of the book is considerably longer than **Part 3**.

This part of the book considers the range of statutory duties the social worker has towards children. The Children Act 1989 provides the legal framework for these responsibilities. The need to provide services for, or protect, children can often be triggered by family breakdown, so private family law needs to be considered as well.

Chapter 5 considers Part I of the Children Act 1989, which sets out the overarching principles of the law relating to children. We explain the critical importance of the welfare principle and the other principles which are set out in the legislation. The chapter also sets out how social services departments should work with other agencies which have a role in safeguarding children. Those agencies can be statutory, such as the police and health authorities, or voluntary. Working with these agencies ensures that the most effective outcomes for children are achieved. This chapter then explains the government's legislative response in the Children Act 2004, including *Working Together to Safeguard Children* (2018), before going on to consider inter-agency working.

Chapter 6 explains the responsibilities that local authorities have towards children in need, 'looked-after' children, and care leavers. The chapter also considers the extensive amendments made to the Children Act 1989 by the Children and Young Persons Act 2008.

Chapters 7–9 are concerned with the processes which are triggered when social workers take action to protect children. **Chapter 7** describes the local authority responsibilities to investigate cases where there are concerns about the welfare of children and to assess the needs of children. Investigations may be required by the court, or as a result of an agency or a member of the public expressing concerns about a child. It is vital for social workers to respond appropriately.

Chapter 8 sets out the law relating to applications for court orders. There is a variety of court orders available to the local authority, ranging from orders which provide for the long-term care of the child to short-term orders which enable the local authority to respond to emergency situations. Different considerations apply in each of these orders, reflecting the extent to which they interfere with the integrity of the family, the duration of the order, and the nature of the circumstances in which the application is made.

Chapter 9 moves on from the initial investigative role of local authorities to consider the role of local authorities in providing long-term security for children. Long-term plans need to be formulated as soon as possible, so as to avoid children 'drifting' in care, with local authorities failing to address their specific needs. This can involve consideration of adoption, and we explore the Adoption and Children Act 2002, which sought to modernize and increase the use of adoption. The Act also includes provision for special guardianship orders, which enable children to have long-term security in circumstances where there are good reasons for not permanently severing their links with their birth family.

Chapter 10 goes in a different direction. It explains how the criminal justice system deals with children when they are accused of crime. What is interesting is that the philosophy of the criminal justice system is quite different from that of the Children Act, despite the fact that in each arena we are concerned with the needs of children.

The principles of children's law

5

OVERVIEW AND OBJECTIVES

The aim of this chapter is to explore the overall structure and philosophy of the Children Act 1989 and some common definitions in relation to children and the law. It also describes the inter-agency context for safeguarding children. We consider in some detail the agencies which share your statutory responsibilities towards children and other vulnerable people and explain their roles. We also briefly consider the range of problems which vulnerable people may face and describe some voluntary-sector agencies which provide advice and assistance to those families. In subsequent chapters, we look at the more detailed provisions of the Children Act 1989. You will find it useful to have your own full copy of the statute via www.legislation.gov.uk/ukpga/1989/41/contents.

In this chapter we shall look at:

(a) the overall structure of the Children Act 1989;

(b) the philosophy behind the Children Act 1989;

(c) some relevant concepts;

(d) principles applicable to court proceedings under the Children Act 1989;

(e) the role of children's guardians and the Children and Family Support Advisory and Support Service (Cafcass);

(f) how your role complements the roles of other professionals concerned with vulnerable people, including an outline of the Children Act 2004, which provides the legislative framework for improving service provision for children.

You should note that Part 3 of the Children Act 1989 does not apply in Wales. The Social Services and Well-being (Wales) Act 2014, which came into force in April 2016, replaces some sections of the Children Act in Wales. For further details, see **chapter 6** and the online resources.

CASE STUDY

R (G) v Nottingham City Council **(2008) EWHC 400 (Admin)**

Why are we asking you to read this case?

There is an important principle that in carrying out duties in law to safeguard and protect children from harm, local authorities must ensure that parents' delegation of their parental responsibilities is voluntary. When a child is accommodated under s. 20 of the Children Act 1989, they effectively delegate their parental responsibility to the local authority. A parent's agreement to delegate should be voluntary and not forced. Without that voluntary consent, the local authority should not subvert the carefully crafted requirements under Parts IV and V of the Act. Local authorities cannot act unilateral to remove a child without a court order.

What is at stake for the parties and beyond?

The local authority pre-birth plan included actions to remove the child from the mother at birth. The plan lacked details about the legal authority necessary to do this. Judicial review proceedings were started by the mother following the baby's removal from her. The local authority was criticized by the court for its actions but immediately launched care proceedings in the County Court and the child was removed again from his mother under an interim care order. The local authority was seeking to protect the child from likely significant harm but it needed to do so by legal means rather than by asserting its authority.

Facts (taken from the judgment of Munby J)

G was born on 31 May 1989, so she is 18 years old. She has had a sad and troubled life. She has been in the care of Nottingham City Council. She has a history of alcohol and drug abuse. She has self-harmed. She is a very vulnerable young adult. In 2007, she became pregnant. The baby was due to be born on 3 February 2008. Unexpectedly . . . the mother went into labour. She gave birth in the small hours of Wednesday at about 2 a.m. Her son was born seemingly healthy and well. At about 4 a.m. her son was removed from her and placed in a different room in the hospital.

Application

An immediate application was made for mother and child to be reunited. The local authority produced two documents which explained the basis upon which the child had been removed. Munby explains:

The first was the minutes of an inter-agency child protection conference which had taken place on 18 December 2007. The minutes record the conference recommendation, inter alia, that the local authority 'apply for an Interim Care Order once the child is born [and] organise a care placement for when the child is born'. They recite that 'the birth plan for the baby is to remain in hospital until he is taken into foster care', further noting that 'the baby must not be removed from the ward by [G] . . . if necessary an Emergency Protection Order should be sought if the Interim Care Order is not in place'.

The minutes further record the recommendation that what was described as 'details of the agreed birth plan' be sent to all hospitals in the region.

The other document was the 'birth plan' prepared for the medical staff at the hospital by Nottingham City NHS Primary Care Trust. Referring to the child protection meeting that had been held on 18 December 2007, the Birth Plan said that 'Baby is to be placed in foster care.' In relation to delivery in hospital it said, 'please discuss with [G] at delivery if she wishes to see or hold baby'. It continued:

Baby will be removed at birth and there will be no contact without supervision. . . . The baby will not . . . be left in her sole care. . . . Further contact with baby on the ward will be supervised by Social Services.

There was no reference in that document to obtaining any emergency protection order or interim care order. So, the need for one or other of those steps to be taken if the child was to be removed from G was not brought to the attention of the midwives and other medical staff to whom the document was addressed.

Decision

The application was granted. There was no legal authority for separating mother and child. The judgment is worth reading for the clarity with which it explains the legal principles. The relevant paragraphs are set out below, with added emphasis.

15. The law is perfectly clear but perhaps requires re-emphasis. Whatever the impression a casual reader might gain from reading some newspaper reports, no local authority and no social worker has any power to remove a child from its parent or, without the agreement of the parent, to take a child into care, unless they have first obtained an order from a family court authorising that step: either an emergency protection order in accordance with section 44 of the Children Act 1989 or an interim care order in accordance with section 38 of the Act or perhaps, in an exceptional case (and subject to section 100 of the Act), a wardship order made by a judge of the Family Division of the High Court.

16. Section 46 of the Children Act 1989 permits a police constable to remove a child where he has reasonable cause to believe that the child would otherwise be likely to suffer significant harm, and that power can be exercised without prior judicial authority. But the powers conferred on the police by section 46 are not given to either local authorities or social workers.

17. Local authorities and social workers have no power to remove children from their parents unless they have first obtained judicial sanction for what they are proposing to do. Only a court can make a care order. Only if a court has authorised that step, whether by making an emergency

protection order or by making a care order or an interim care order or in some other way, can a local authority or a social worker remove a child from a parent. And the same goes, of course, for a hospital and its medical staff.

18. As I said during the course of the hearing, no baby, no child, can be removed simply 'as the result of a decision taken by officials in some room.'

19. This is all elementary. It is well known to all family lawyers. And it is, or ought to be, well known to all social workers. That is why, as the media accurately reported, I made the comment during the course of the hearing that 'The professionals involved in this case should have known better.' I went on to point out, however, that the midwives and doctors in a delivery room in the small hours could not have been expected to understand this. No doubt they acted as they did in accordance with the 'Birth Plan' that had been given to them by their superiors.

Munby J did make two points of clarification in his judgment. The first relates to the situation where a child is at risk of immediate harm.

21. In the first place, a social worker or a nurse is of course entitled to intervene if that is necessary to protect a baby from immediate violence at the hands of a parent. That is not, however, because they have any special power or privilege entitling them to intervene. It is merely an application of the wider principle that anyone who happens to be present is entitled, whether by restraining the assailant or by removing the defenceless victim from his assailant's reach, to intervene in order to prevent an actual or threatened criminal assault taking place before his very eyes.

The second point relates to s. 3(5) of the Children Act 1989, which provides that:

A person who—

(a) does not have parental responsibility for a particular child; but
(b) has care of the child,

may (subject to the provisions of this Act) do what is reasonable in all the circumstances of the case for the purpose of safeguarding or promoting the child's welfare.

What Munby says about the operation of that section is helpful.

24. Now section 3(5) could not avail the local authority, because it did not have the 'care' of G's son. But there might be circumstances in which a hospital could rely upon section 3(5) as justifying action taken in relation to a child in its medical care, despite the absence of parental consent and the absence of any court order.

25. For instance, medical intervention might be required in order to preserve the child's life or to protect a child from irreversible harm in circumstances of such urgency that there is not even time to make an urgent telephone application to a judge. In such a situation of emergency a doctor can act without parental or judicial consent and, if parents are acting unreasonably or contrary to the child's best interests, even despite a parental refusal of consent: see Grubb et al, Principles of Medical Law, ed 4.

26. Doctors, midwives and nurses do not have to stand idly by waiting for a court order if, for example, a premature baby desperately needs to be put in a special unit or placed on a ventilator. They are of course entitled to separate the child from the mother if medical necessity dictates, and even if she objects. Law, medical ethics and common-sense march hand in hand.

WHAT DOES THIS CASE TELL YOU ABOUT SOCIAL WORK PRACTICE?

Munby J's decision provides a valuable opportunity to re-emphasize one of the most important principles of the Children Act 1989.

- The state can only interfere in the lives of its citizens if it has legal authority to do so. That has to be your starting point. The fact that the local authority was about to make an urgent application to the family proceedings court for an interim care order or an emergency protection order was not relevant to the legality of separating the mother and child prior to any order being made by the court.
- In subsequent years several cases have come before the courts which have resulted in judicial criticism of local authority use of s. 20 agreements and the matter of obtaining appropriate parental consent to accommodate children. As Hedley J comments in *Re CA (A Baby)* (2012), 'However, the use of Section 20 is not unrestricted and must not be compulsion in disguise. In order for such an agreement to be lawful, the parent must have the requisite capacity to make that agreement' (para. 27). Hedley subsequently provided guidance on the use of s. 20 and the seeking of consent (see **chapter 6**).

The overall structure of the Children Act 1989

The Act has over 100 sections and 15 schedules. It is a very large piece of legislation. It is divided into Parts. The Parts group together different sections under headings. We reproduce, in **Table 5.1**, an outline of the Parts in the Children Act and the main chapters in this book in which we consider those Parts. We do not have the space to examine every Part in great depth here, so we concentrate on those Parts the 'field' social worker will have to be familiar with.

TABLE 5.1 The Parts of the Children Act 1989

Part number	Title	Chapter number and comment
Part I	Introductory	**Chapter 5**
		Outlines key principles underpinning the legislation
Part II	Orders with respect to Children in Family Proceedings	**Chapter 5** This deals with the private law proceedings Key section is s. 8

Part number	Title	Chapter number and comment
Part III	Local Authority Support for Children and Families (This Part of the Act does not apply in Wales)	**Chapter 5** Children in need Key section is s. 17 Concerned with public law proceedings
Part IV	Care and Supervision	**Chapter 8** Deals with care orders and supervision orders concerned with public law proceedings
Part V	Protection of Children	**Chapter 6** Sets out the key s. 47 local authority duty to investigate
		Chapter 8 Provides for emergency protection orders and other short-term measures to protect children concerned with public law proceedings
Part VI	Community Homes	Essentially regulatory
Part VII	Voluntary Homes and Voluntary Organizations	This Part and those below, whilst important, fall outside the scope of this textbook
Part VIII	Registered Children's Homes	
Part IX	Private Arrangements for Fostering Children	
Part X	Child Minding and Day Care for Young Children	
Part XA	Child Minding and Day Care for Children in England and Wales (inserted by the Care Standards Act 2000)	
Part XI	Secretary of State's Supervisory Functions and Responsibilities	
Part XII	Miscellaneous and General	

▨ The philosophy of the Act

Guidance and regulation

You are advised to read this chapter in conjunction with the Children Act 1989 statutory guidance. Five volumes can be found at www.gov.uk/government/publications/children-act-1989-court-orders--2.

A word of clarification and warning: these volumes contain guidance which has to be considered by all local authorities, as they are issued under s. 7 of the Local Authority (Social Services) Act 1970 (LASSA) (see **chapter 1**). They are not the final statement of the law. They reflect the government's view of what it hopes the words of the Act say. Therefore, while you should read them, do not take them to be the final, definitive statement of the law.

It is the courts that finally decide what the law means and, whilst helped by guidance, the social worker has to consult with his or her lawyers for the best interpretation.

The underlying philosophy

It may be easier to understand the philosophy of the Children Act 1989 if you have some knowledge of the complex and perhaps contradictory forces which led to its implementation. One major impetus was the need to address a number of child abuse scandals. These ranged from reports of social service failure—for instance in *A Child in Trust—The Report of the Panel of Enquiry into the Circumstances Surrounding the Death of Jasmine Beckford* (Louis Blom-Cooper, London Borough of Brent, 1985), *Whose Child?*—Report on the death of Tyra Henry (London Borough of Lambeth, 1987), and *A Child in Mind—Report on the Death of Kimberley Carlile* (London Borough of Greenwich, 1987)—to reports of overzealous social work, for instance in the *Report of the Inquiry into Child Abuse in Cleveland 1987*. Another impetus was the need to provide a legal statement of the increasing importance of children's rights. These had been articulated in the courts as a result of the *Gillick* judgment (see **chapter 2**) and in international commitments, such as the United Nations Convention on the Rights of the Child 1989.

Finally, the Act provided a reaffirmation of the long-held belief that the best place to bring up children is usually within their family. This is clearly stated in the published guidance.

> A key principle of the 1989 Act is that children are best looked after within their families, with their parents playing a full part in their lives, unless compulsory intervention in family life is necessary.
>
> (*The Children Act 1989 Guidance and Regulations, Volume 2: Care Planning, Placement and Case Review*, para. 1.5)

Thus, the philosophy is that the child should be brought up with the child's family, and the local authority should be providing support to that end. This needs to be both understood and, more importantly, accepted by all those who carry out statutory work under the Children Act 1989.

Additional to this concept is the belief that the state, in the shape of the local authority, should not take control of a child's life unless some strict statutory criteria are met. These criteria—described as the threshold criteria—are the grounds for care and supervision orders contained in s. 31 of the Act—see **chapter 6**.

Some relevant concepts

The welfare of the child is paramount

There are three different welfare duties in the Act. These are set out in **Box 5.1**.

The Children Act 1989 requires the welfare of the child to be the paramount consideration only when the court is making a decision under its powers under the Act. Even then, if the Act lays down other statutory considerations, the welfare of the child is not paramount.

It is only when a court is dealing with a case that affects a child directly that that child's welfare is paramount. So, when the House of Lords was considering what should happen to a young baby born to a 16-year-old mother in care, it had to put the welfare of the baby as being paramount above that of the baby's mother (even though the mother was under 18 and, as such, a child). This was because the court was dealing with an application concerning the baby—not the mother (*Birmingham City Council v H (No 3)* (1994)).

BOX 5.1 The welfare duties in the Act

- A court making a decision as to the upbringing of a child must have the welfare of the child as the paramount consideration (s. 1(1)). This is unless there are statutory requirements that apply different criteria. (For example, the court can never make a care order if the significant harm test is not satisfied. This is true even if the welfare of the child would be best served by the care order.)

- A local authority must safeguard and promote the welfare of a child, in its area, who is in need (s. 17).

- A person who has the care of a child, but not parental responsibility can do what is reasonable in all the circumstances for the purpose of safeguarding or promoting the child's welfare (s. 3(5)).

Human rights and the welfare of the child

Article 8 of the European Convention on Human Rights (ECHR) specifically relates to respect for family life, which could potentially conflict with the welfare of the child unless the court is satisfied that interference by a public authority is warranted. Local authority and social work decision making will need to justify any interference in family life (see **chapter 8**). Decisions will need to be proportionate (see *Re B (A Child)* (2013), paras 33 and 34 and in general **chapter 3**). Overall, however, the requirement that the welfare of the child be the court's paramount consideration is consistent with Convention case law and within the margin of appreciation (allowance for local circumstances) permitted to national authorities under Article 8, and is therefore compatible with that Article.

Respect for the child

This is a concept that is difficult to define but which pervades all the questions of how the law considers the child. There are two particular aspects. First, the child, and not the parents, for instance, is the focus of your decision making and, second, you should take account of the wishes and feelings of the child in your decision making. It would be wrong, however, to consider the child's welfare as something which does not involve the parents. A famous British psychiatrist, D. W. Winnicott, argued, as long ago as 1953, that 'there is no such thing as a baby' (*Collected Papers: Through Paediatrics to Psycho-Analysis* (Tavistock Publishing)), meaning that without a parent it is difficult to consider a child in isolation. Empirical evidence from modern-day neuroscience would tend to agree. No matter how poor, neglectful, or abusive parenting is, the child should always be seen in relationship to the parent. Respect for a child includes respect for the child's relationships.

The child is your primary responsibility

In dealing with children you need to recognize that the law regards the child as your primary responsibility. You cannot escape the comment made on behalf of the British Association of Social Workers to the Jasmine Beckford inquiry, which fully endorsed:

> [the] clear and unequivocal view that in any child abuse case the primary client for the social worker is the child. The many conflicts are easier to resolve if social workers always bear in mind who is the primary client.

Social workers and other professionals working with adults who are parents should also remember that if a child in the family is at risk of significant harm, the child becomes their primary service user too.

The wishes of the child

Conflict is inevitable between parent and child at some stage of the child's development. Part of the growing process is the assertion of the child's independence. When the state becomes involved in the essentially private area of family life, the real difficulty is for the state to ascertain when that independence should be allowed to become a reality. Clearly, a six-month-old baby cannot be independent, and if the parents fail the child, then the state must step in and either assume parental responsibility or ensure that someone else takes it up. But what is to be said for a 12-year-old child or a 16-year-old young person? If their parents fail, what consideration must be given to the wishes of the child or young person?

For a statutory recognition of this concept we need to look at s. 22 of the Children Act 1989, which we set out in **Box 5.2**.

 BOX 5.2 The wishes of the child—s. 22 of the Children Act 1989

(4) Before making any decisions with respect to the child whom they are looking after, or proposing to look after, a local authority shall, so far as is reasonably practicable, ascertain the wishes and feelings of—

(a) the child;

(b) his parents;

(c) any person who is not a parent of his but who has parental responsibility for him; and

(d) any other person whose feelings the authority consider to be relevant, regarding the matter to be decided.

(5) In making any such decision a local authority shall give due consideration—

   (a) having regard to his age and understanding, to such wishes and feelings of the child as they have been able to ascertain;

   (b) to such wishes and feelings of any person mentioned in subsection (4)(b) to (d) as they have been able to ascertain; and

   (c) to the child's religious persuasion, racial origin and cultural and linguistic background.

The child is mentioned before the parents or any other person in this section. This suggests that the child's wishes are to be the first consideration. This applies whether or not the child is subject to a court order. It should also be borne in mind that if any matter concerning the child is taken to court, then the court will apply the welfare principle, placing the child's welfare as paramount; that is, coming before and overriding anyone else's welfare or convenience.

Respect for the child's autonomy

The statutory responsibilities are expanded by the decisions of the courts, notably the *Gillick* case discussed in **Informed consent**, p 165 and more fully in **chapter 2**. In dealing with any children, you have to ensure that an appropriate level of respect is given to the child as an individual who is entitled to separate consideration in his or her own right. As the Cleveland Report put it, 'the child is a person not an object of concern'. As a result of the respect principle, you will find that courts and local authorities are required, throughout the Act, to take into account the wishes and feelings of the child. (This does not necessarily mean carrying out those wishes.) Respect for the child does not mean that the child has absolute right above all other.

Partnership with parents under the Children Act 1989

Whilst partnership with parents is not a legal requirement under the Children Act, the guidance makes it clear that a local authority is required to work, as far as possible, in partnership with children and their families. For instance:

> parents should be encouraged to exercise their responsibility for their child's welfare in a constructive way and that where compulsory intervention in the family is necessary it should, where possible, support rather than undermine the parental role. The 1989 Act places a strong emphasis on the local authority working in partnership with parents when undertaking their statutory functions.
>
> (*The Children Act 1989 Guidance and Regulations, Volume 2: Care Planning, Placement and Case Review*, para. 1.7)

The principle is reflected in the statute in a number of ways, set out in **Box 5.3**.

There are several ways in which the state can and does promote the involvement of parents to participate in Children Act 1989 proceedings. Parents with parental responsibility are automatically parties to the proceedings and parents without parental responsibility have the right to be notified of public law proceedings. Parents are entitled to public funding in most public law proceedings without any means test, and in dealing with social services, parents of looked-after children have a right to be consulted, a right to have their views taken into account, and a right to participate in case conferences. The courts have also insisted on fair procedures, particularly since the advent of the Human Rights Act 1998 (see *Re L (Care Assessment Fair Trial)* (2002) and *Re J (Care; Assessment; Fair Trial)* (2006)). In addition, the 2014 Public Law Outline, Practice Direction 12A—Care, Supervision and Other Part 4 Proceedings: Guide to Case Management, establishes a pre-proceedings check-list which should include a range of assessments conducted on the family and in specific instances a Letter before Proceedings and a pre-proceedings meeting. As noted in **chapter 8**, a Letter before Proceedings indicates to parents the concerns held by the authority about their care of the child and what they and the authority will do to protect that child. This letter and the assessments conducted on the family rather suggest that local authorities should exhaust voluntary means to help parents and their children by seeking to work collaboratively with them before instigating proceedings.

BOX 5.3 Partnership with parents under the Children Act 1989

(a) Accommodation of children looked after should be provided as a consumer-led service (s. 22).

(b) That accommodation should be near the children's parents.

(c) Contact with parents is presumed if a child is in care (s. 34), and during emergency protection (s. 44) or police protection (s. 46).

(d) Care orders do not remove parental responsibilities (s. 2(6)).

(e) Abolition of care by stealth: that is, the placing of a child or young person into local authority accommodation cannot lead, of itself, to that child or young person becoming subject to any form of statutory control.

(f) The local authority has a duty to consult parents when they accommodate a child (s. 20) or provide services (s. 17).

Limits on partnership

It is important to note that the concept of partnership with parents and families does not remove the overriding duty of the local authority to safeguard and promote the welfare of the child. Allowing partnership to become paramount is both misapplying the law and bad practice. The death of Peter Connelly in 2007 has highlighted the difficulties inherent in a partnership-first approach.

Social workers must have the professional skills to recognize when partnership with parents is failing to protect a child. At that point, it must necessarily cease to be the underpinning strategy of child protection work. This is put clearly in *Court orders and Pre-proceedings: For Local Authorities*:

> Where concerns do arise and are identified by a local authority, the local authority is under a duty to act.
>
> (Department for Education, 2014, p 11)

Parental responsibility

The concept of continuing parental responsibility is critical to the Act. Married parents, unmarried mothers, and, since 1 December 2003, when the relevant section of the Adoption and Children Act 2002 was implemented, unmarried fathers who are registered on the birth certificate gain parental responsibility automatically; unmarried fathers who are not registered on the birth certificate or whose child was born before December 2003 have to apply to court to acquire parental responsibility. Parental responsibility is defined—as far as it can be defined—in s. 3 of the Act, set out in **Box 5.4**.

 BOX 5.4 The meaning of parental responsibility—s. 3(1) of the Children Act 1989

(3) In this Act 'parental responsibility' means all the rights, duties, powers, responsibilities and authority which by law a parent of a child has in relation to the child and his property.

Parents derive their authority from their commitment to bringing up their children, and not from anything else.

Once acquired, parental responsibility continues. The only way in which parental responsibility can be terminated is via an adoption order: see **chapter 9**. However, the extent of parental responsibility can vary. It is at its most extensive when exercised by parents and guardians. It is less extensive when it is given to non-parents in child arrangements orders (see **chapter 6**) and when given to local authorities as a result of a care order. It is most limited in scope when the child is the subject of an emergency protection order and parental responsibility is given to the applicant for the order (see **chapter 8**).

Informed consent

The principle of 'informed consent' permeates the Act. As a general rule, anyone (including a local authority) with parental responsibility can give a valid consent to the treatment of a child. (There are important limitations on the local authority's power when it has parental responsibility by virtue of an emergency protection order—see **chapter 8**.) However, there are limits on the powers of those with parental responsibility. First, irreversible medical treatment for non-therapeutic purposes (such as sterilization) should take place only with the leave of the court. Second, the age and understanding of the child are significant. The older and more mature a child becomes, the less the parent is entitled, as a matter of right, to know about and manage the child's affairs. The child does not have to wait for the age of majority (18) to be able to decide matters in his or her own right; that informed choice can be made at an earlier age. This statement of the law is based upon the decision of the House of Lords in *Gillick v West Norfolk and Wisbech Area Health Authority* (1986). The case concerned the question of whether or not a parent was entitled to be informed that a child under the age of 16 was going to be given contraception. The notion of the *Gillick*-competent child is built into the statute. There are several examples of statutory provisions along the lines of 'but if the child is of sufficient understanding to make an informed decision he may refuse to submit to the examination'. We discussed consent and capacity in **chapter 2**.

Limits on autonomy

Our discussion on the legal competence of children in **chapter 2** indicated that there are several difficulties in treating the *Gillick*-competent child as capable of having informed consent. Court decisions do not completely support the notion of autonomy for children, yet the statutory statements within the Act are clear. The social worker must follow the requirements of the Act. However, in some extreme circumstances there may be the need to seek court approval to override the wishes of children if you consider that their decision is not in their own best interests.

Refusal to consent

One difficulty that is raised by the idea of informed consent is 'What happens if the child refuses to consent?' Much will depend on the matter for which consent is refused and whether the child is deemed to be *Gillick* competent. It would be prudent to engage with a *Gillick*-competent young person's reasons for refusing treatment, since it would be an exception to give treatment in such circumstances against their will. However, the courts have overruled young people's refusal of treatment (*see Re R (A Minor) (Wardship: Consent to Medical Treatment)* (1992), *Re W (A Minor) (Medical Treatment: Court's Jurisdiction)* (1993), *Re M (Medical Treatment: Consent)* (1999), and *Re P (Medical Treatment: Best Interests)* (2003) EWHC 2327 (Fam)).

The position of parents

The court also has powers to override the decisions of parents to refuse medical treatment for their children. In *Re A (Children) (Conjoined Twins: Surgical Separation)* (2000), the Court of Appeal sanctioned the separation of conjoined twins against the wishes of the parents, even though the result would be the death of the weaker twin. The court in these circumstances makes its decision based on the best interests of the child and not on the reasonableness of the parents' refusal of consent.

Diminishment of court proceedings

This applies only in the public law area of the Act. Its provisions are to be found tucked away in Schedule 2, Part I, para. 7, which we set out in **Box 5.5**.

This provision imposes a duty on local authorities, and in carrying out your responsibilities you should be looking for ways in which to give effect to it. But that does not mean avoiding court proceedings when they would otherwise be necessary.

BOX 5.5 The diminishment of court proceedings—Schedule 2, Part I, para. 7 of the Children Act 1989

Every local authority shall take reasonable steps designed—

(a) to reduce the need to bring—

    (i) proceedings for care or supervision orders with respect to the children within their area;

    (ii) criminal proceedings against such children;

    (iii) any family or other proceedings with respect to such children which might lead to them being placed in the authority's care; or

    (iv) proceedings under the inherent jurisdiction of the High Court with respect to children;

(b) to encourage children within their area not to commit criminal offences;

(c) to avoid the need for children within their area to be placed in secure accommodation.

Principles applicable to court proceedings under the Children Act

There are three main principles that guide courts under this Act, all of which are found in s. 1 of the Act. They are:

(a) the welfare principle (s. 1(1));

(b) the non-delay principle (s. 1(2)); and

(c) the 'no order' principle (s. 1(5)).

The welfare principle

When a court (but only a court) considers any matter concerning the welfare of the child, the court shall treat the child's welfare as its paramount consideration. This means that although the Act tries to balance the rights of the child and the rights of the parents, finally the court must do what the court sees as being best for the child. That is the function of the court, to arrive at a hard decision with which not all the parties may agree.

Not all court decisions

The welfare principle in s. 1 does not apply to all decisions by the court. Within the Act there are sections that have specific statutory requirements for the court to consider. If the Act gives such requirements, the court must follow these. It cannot apply only the s. 1 paramount welfare principle. For example, s. 10(9) deals with applying for leave to make an application for an order by a private individual. There are specific grounds for the court to consider (*Re A and W* (1992)). Where an application is made to place a child in secure accommodation under s. 25, again, specific statutory criteria apply (*Re M (A Minor) (Secure Accommodation Order)* (1995)). The court (per Butler Sloss LJ) said in that case:

> This duty cast upon the local authority to safeguard and promote the welfare of the child is not the same duty cast upon the court by section 1 to place welfare as the paramount consideration. Other considerations can and frequently do affect the local authority's approach.

So, even if a court is dealing with a specific case involving children under the Children Act, the welfare principle may not be paramount. It cannot override statutory time limits, such as the length of time an emergency protection order may last. It will not allow the court to go behind established principles of law. In *Re M (A Minor) (Appeal) (No 2)* (1994), the guardian *ad litem* sought to introduce evidence before the Court of Appeal of the effect on the child of being told that the child would have to return home to the mother. The child became hysterical and distressed. The court would not allow the evidence to be introduced. Yet another example is the case of *Nottinghamshire County Council v P* (1993).

The non-delay principle

The court 'shall have regard to the general principle that any delay in determining the question is likely to prejudice the welfare of the child' (s. 1(2)). The 'question' here means the question on upbringing the court is deciding. In addition to the emphasis in the Children Act 1989, decisions of the European Court of Human Rights (ECtHR) in connection with Article 6 emphasize the need for appropriate speed in decision making. The Children and Families Act 2014 introduces a statutory time limit of 26 weeks to complete care or supervision proceedings.

Avoiding delay

In any proceedings involving children, both in private law and public law, there are sections which provide that the court shall:

(a) draw up a timetable with a view to determining the question without delay; and

(b) give such directions as it considers appropriate for the purpose of ensuring, as far as is reasonably practicable, that that timetable is adhered to.

These provisions are to be found for private law in s. 11 and for public law in s. 32. The rules, under the Children Act, require the holding of a directions hearing for the court to make arrangements for preparing the case and hearing it. The first item to be addressed is the timetable for the proceedings. The non-delay principle will be applied.

The Children and Families Act 2014 amends s. 32 so that when a court draws up a timetable for proceedings, it must in particular have regard to:

(a) the impact which the timetable would have on the welfare of the child to whom the application relates; and

(b) the impact which the timetable would have on the conduct of the proceedings.

In addition, when appointing experts, a court must consider, amongst other things, the impact which giving permission to admit expert evidence would be likely to have on the timetable for, and duration and conduct of, the proceedings. The Public Law Outline 2014—an agreed procedure for the handling of public law Children Act cases—replaces previous protocols. We discuss the Public Law Outline in **chapter 8**.

The 'no order' principle

The court should not make an order unless it considers 'that doing so would be better for the child than making no order at all' (s. 1(5)). It is important to realize that the 'no order' principle is a principle for the court, not for social workers.

The first *Annual Report on the Children Act* (Cm 2144) showed a considerable drop in the number of court proceedings taken under the Children Act compared with similar provisions under the former law.

Since that first report was published, there have been interesting fluctuations in the number of applications for orders to the court. In recent years there has been an upturn in applications, in response perhaps to the deaths of children known to social services, including Peter Connelly, Daniel Pelka, and Hamzah Khan, although the picture does fluctuate, particularly since the Supreme Court's judgment in *Re B* (2013) and the judgment in the Court of Appeal in *Re B-S* (2013) (see **chapter 9**).

- Between April 2017 and March 2018 Cafcass received a total of 14,223 care applications in England.

- This figure is slightly lower than the previous year, but demonstrates a progressive increase over the last eight or nine years since 2009/10, when the rate per 10,000 child population was eight per cent compared to the rate of 2016/17 of 12.5 per cent.

- In Wales, care applications increased by 24.4 per cent to 1039 in 2016/17 and by 1.1 per cent to 1050 in 2017/18. In 2008/09 the figure was 422.

However, the general point about the misunderstanding of the 'no order' principle remains true. The duty of the social worker is to promote and safeguard the welfare of children who are in need. Therefore, the 'no order' principle should not in any way inhibit the social worker from taking statutory steps, including going to court, to carry out this duty. It is not the function of the social worker to second-guess the court and to say, 'Well, the court may apply the no order principle and therefore I will not take any action.' Only when it is clear that it is a hopeless case should you consider not going to court because of the 'no order' principle.

In *T (A Child) (Care Order)* (2009), the Court of Appeal clearly restated the principle that it is the responsibility of the court and not the parties to the case to decide upon the appropriate order under the Children Act. The duty to treat the welfare of the child as the paramount consideration required the court to undertake the appropriate judicial investigation. In this case, all parties supported the care plan prepared by the local authority in which the child who had suffered non-accidental injuries would be returned to his parents' care under a supervision order which included provisions for monitoring the child. The judge, however, considered that the child remained at risk and imposed a care order. Whilst the Court of Appeal considered that the judge was acting perfectly properly in substituting the court's judgment for that of the local authority, it overturned the imposition of the care order. It considered that there were no strong and cogent reasons to force upon the authority a more draconian order than that which had been requested. In those circumstances, the care order would be varied to a 12-month supervision order.

In addition to these three main principles we find others, as set out in the following sections.

No compulsory intervention by the state without an application

This is a reflection of the philosophy of the Act and is applicable to both private and public law elements of the statute. The first point to be made here is that you cannot remove a child from its family without going to court. *R (G) v Nottingham City Council*, which we discussed at the beginning of this chapter, makes this absolutely clear. Second, the court cannot intervene to protect a child it perceives to be at risk without there being an application by the local authority or authorized person.

A salutary case to read is *Nottinghamshire County Council v P* (1993). In this case, the local authority applied for an order under s. 8 of the Children Act that a self-confessed child abuser stepfather vacate the household and that the children should have no contact except under supervision. The court held that, since the effect of the order was in fact to make a residence and contact order, it could not make that order.

Local authorities are specifically excluded from applying for such orders (s. 9(2)), now referred to as child arrangements orders. As the authority wished to ensure that the children were not put at risk by seeing their father unsupervised, they would have been better to apply for a care order. This is the view that the High Court judge and the Court of Appeal took. As the report of the judgment states:

> the route chosen by the council was wholly inappropriate. In cases where children were found to be at risk of suffering significant harm within s. 47 a clear duty arose on the part of the local authorities to protect them. . . . The council persistently and obstinately refused to undertake what was the appropriate course of action and thereby deprived the judge of the ability to make a constructive order. . . . The position was one which it was hoped would not recur.

Here the Court of Appeal found itself totally frustrated by being unable to make the order asked for. The local authority was seeking to obtain the effect of a care order by the back door. This is clearly contrary to the concept that the only basis on which statutory control can be obtained is by an application which satisfies the significant harm test. In more recent cases, local authorities have been criticized by the courts for exercising too much power. In *Coventry City Council v C, B, CA and CH* [2012] EWHC 2190 (Fam), the mother initially refused permission for her new-born child to be accommodated, but she subsequently agreed. However, the local authority accepted in court that they should not have sought her consent so soon after giving birth, when she was still under the influence of powerful painkillers. The local authority had breached the mother's Article 8 rights and had also acted disproportionately given the risks present at the time.

(See **chapter 6** for a further discussion of obtaining informed consent in respect of local authority accommodation.)

The welfare checklist

This is found in s. 1(3) of the Children Act 1989. It is applicable to all court proceedings in both private and public law, except court proceedings under Part V (the emergency protection of children). It consists of a uniform checklist to which the courts need to have regard when they are faced with a dispute concerning any child. It is applicable whether the dispute is between individuals, or whether a local authority is applying for an order. Section 1(3) is set out in **Box 5.6**.

BOX 5.6 The welfare checklist—s. 1(3) of the Children Act 1989

A court shall have regard in particular to—

(a) the ascertainable wishes and feelings of the child concerned (considered in the light of his age and understanding);

(b) his physical, emotional and educational needs;

(c) the likely effect on him of any change in his circumstances;

(d) his age, sex, background and any characteristics of his which the court considers relevant;

(e) any harm which he has suffered or is at risk of suffering;

(f) how capable each of his parents, and any other person in relation to whom the court considers the question to be relevant, is of meeting his needs;

(g) the range of powers available to the court under the Children Act in the proceedings in question.

Each point in the checklist is considered separately. There is no priority in the order in which the points appear. If you are seeking an order from the court, you must give careful attention to the checklist in your presentation of evidence and within your report. Also, expect in any disputed case to be cross-examined under each heading.

'Mix and match'

This is a useful expression derived from the Department of Health publication, *An Introduction to the Children Act*, where it states:

> [a] full menu of orders is also available to a court hearing a local authority application for a care or other order in respect of a child. Thus a court might, for example, order that a child live with a suitable relative or friend rather than make a care order in favour of the local authority. Or it may mix and match by, for example, ordering that a child live with a non-abusing parent and making a supervision order at the same time.

The best order in the circumstances

What this means is that the court should always seek to choose the best order for the child, and that choice is not limited to the orders that the parties have applied for. But the court cannot make a care or supervision order unless it has been applied for. How this works in practice can be seen in the case of *C v Solihull MBC* (1993). A 12-month-old child had suffered a non-accidental injury. The magistrates' court refused to grant a local authority application for a care order but returned the child subject to a supervision order with no conditions attached. On appeal, the High Court made a residence order which no one had applied for, with conditions attached, and an interim supervision order.

Family proceedings

Most proceedings in any area of family law are defined as 'family proceedings'. Inclusion in this category means that, if they have any family proceedings before them, the courts are free—in fact obliged—to apply the 'mix-and-match' principle, and make the best order for the child, not necessarily the one applied for, and quite possibly where no one has applied for an order under the Act.

The list of family proceedings is given in s. 8(3) and (4) of the Children Act 1989 as amended. We have reproduced this in **Box 5.7**. In **Box 5.8** we remind you of the orders that can be made in the context of family proceedings.

BOX 5.7 Family proceedings for the purposes of the Children Act 1989—s. 8(3) and (4)

(a) High Court proceedings relating to children under the residual powers of wardship;

(b) Parts I, II, and IV of the Children Act 1989;

(c) Matrimonial Causes Act 1973;

(d) Schedules 5 and 6 to the Civil Partnership Act 2004;

(e) Domestic Violence and Matrimonial Proceedings Act 1976;

(f) Adoption and Children Act 2002;

(g) Domestic Proceedings and Magistrates' Courts Act 1978;

(h) ss 1 and 9 of the Matrimonial Homes Act 1983;

(i) Part 3 of the Matrimonial and Family Proceedings Act 1984;

(j) Family Law Act 1996;

(k) ss 11 and 12 of the Crime and Disorder Act 1998.

BOX 5.8 Children Act orders in private disputes about the child

Section 8 covers disputes about the upbringing or treatment of a child. Orders can be made in favour of any person, not just the applicant and not just a parent: a grandparent, step-parent, unmarried father, friend, or even a sibling, for example. Courts must make the appropriate s. 8 order, regardless of which one was applied for. Anyone can apply, including a public authority; for example (a) instead of seeking care, social services can apply for an order that a child lives with a relative; or for example (b) a hospital can apply for an order that a child receives a blood transfusion against parental wishes.

A child arrangements order is an order regulating arrangements relating to with whom a child should live, spend time, or have other types of contact, or when they should do so. The 'other types of contact' a child arrangements order may provide for could include indirect contact such as a telephone call by the parent.

Specific issue order s. 8: where a person with parental responsibility normally makes (shares) decisions about a child (e.g. schooling, medical treatment) and there is dispute, any person (not just a parent—e.g. a local authority or another relative) can ask the court to make the decision about that specific issue. Specific issue orders have been used to determine religious issues (e.g. circumcision of boys), name changes, and consent to abortion.

Prohibited steps order s. 8: mirrors the specific issue order. The court order prevents parental responsibility being exercised in relation to a specified action, for example taking a child abroad or carrying out a non-therapeutic medical procedure.

What else can the court order when considering s. 8 applications? If a s. 8 application comes before a court, the court can make any other order under s. 8. As a s. 8 application is a family proceeding, a court could also make a family assistance order or order a s. 37 report from the local authority, which could then lead to care proceedings. In an extreme case an interim care order could be made.

Section 8 orders in public law proceedings: if it is in the best interests of the child, a court can (indeed must) make a s. 8 order instead of the care or supervision order which the local authority has applied for.

Section 5 order: where the child has no parent or guardian, the court can appoint a guardian, who will have parental responsibilities.

Not family proceedings

It is important to remember that proceedings under Part V of the Children Act (protection of children) are not family proceedings. So, there can be no 'mix and match', only an emergency protection order, or a child assessment order, or no order at all.

Family assistance orders

In any family proceedings the court can, under s. 16 of the Children Act 1989, make a family assistance order where the court is satisfied that there are exceptional circumstances and the people named in the order agree. Only the court can make the order; it cannot be applied for by a party. When a family assistance order is made, the officer named in the order is to advise, assist, and (where appropriate) befriend the person named in the order.

This order is intended to be a short-term order; it can last for only a maximum of six months. It is to help the family over the difficulties that have led to the court appearance.

In *Re C (Family Assistance Order)* (1996), when the local authority said that it did not have the resources to implement the order, the court held that it had no power to force the authority to do so. Nor would the court compel a local authority under a family assistance order to accompany a child to visit that child's father in prison (*S v P (Contact Application: Family Assistance Order)* (1997)). Practice Direction 12M which came into force in October 2007 states that:

> Before making a family assistance order the court must have obtained the opinion of the appropriate officer (LA [local authority] or Cafcass) about whether it would be in the best interests of the child in question for a family assistance order to be made and, if so, how the family assistance order could operate and for what period.

It further states that:

> Before making a family assistance order the court must give any person whom it proposes be named in the order an opportunity to comment upon any opinion given by the appropriate officer.

◼ The role of children's guardians

The role of the guardian is one, historically, that has been long known to the court. Out of the context of child care, the guardian—also known as the child's 'next friend'—acted on behalf of children in court actions such as a claim for damages arising from an accident.

Maria Colwell

Guardians were introduced into the statutory framework of child care law following the report of the Maria Colwell Inquiry published in 1974. In that case, Maria was killed by her stepfather, having been returned from the care of the local authority following the revocation of the care order with the consent of the local authority. It was felt that the tragedy could have been avoided if Maria had been separately represented in the proceedings. A person acting solely on behalf of Maria could have argued that it was not in Maria's best interest for the care order to be revoked.

The Children Act 1989 contains the duty for courts to appoint guardians *ad litem* 'unless it is satisfied that it is not necessary' to safeguard the child's interests (s. 41(1)). Following the creation of Cafcass (see **Children and Family Court Advisory and Support Service**, p 176) the term 'children's guardian' is used instead of 'guardian *ad litem*' (Family Proceedings (Amendment) Rules 2001). The guardian then has to appoint a solicitor for the child (Family Proceedings Rules 1991). The rules permit the older child who is *Gillick* competent and who is in conflict with the recommendations of the children's guardian, to instruct their solicitor directly.

The functions of the guardian

Rules of court set out the functions of the guardian. The way in which the guardian works is by a process of investigation involving interviewing the local authority personnel, the child, the parents, relatives, and any other persons the guardian considers relevant. The guardian then prepares a report stating what the guardian considers to be in the best interest of the child's welfare. This report must be made available to all parties to the proceedings in advance of the final hearing.

Resources

In tandem with the lawyer acting for the child, the system ensures that the child's interests are protected and his or her rights respected and upheld by the court. Since the commencement of the Children Act 1989, you can expect guardians to be involved in proceedings concerning children, even at the stage of the application for an emergency protection order. The practical difficulty in the past was one of resources, there not being sufficient suitably qualified people to act as guardians. In some parts of the country, this shortage delayed proceedings.

Inspection of records

The guardians have the advantage of s. 42 of the Children Act 1989, which provides that a guardian has the power to inspect any local authority or National Society for the Prevention of Cruelty to Children (NSPCC) records relating to the child who is the subject of the court proceedings. In addition, in *Re R (Care Proceedings: Disclosure)* (2000), the court held that the guardian had a right to see a report compiled by the Area Child Protection Committee on the child's half-sibling, who had been killed by the child's father. Having inspected those records, the guardian may take copies, and those copies shall be admissible as evidence both in the guardian's report and, if the guardian gives oral evidence, during the proceedings.

Your approach to the handling of any case must be carried out in the full knowledge that an officer of the court, the children's guardian, is possibly going to have the chance both to look at and produce in court all the records that you have made. More importantly, that person may be able to draw the court's attention to the fact that although you claim to have done a particular thing, there exists no record of this fact in your case notes. Accurately and comprehensively record all your actions and decisions as soon as possible after the events. Cafcass appoints the individual guardian, who might be a Cafcass employee or a self-employed contractor. Note that the Cafcass appointee should be invited to all formal meetings relating to the child. This includes statutory reviews of children who are accommodated or looked after, child protection conferences, and relevant Adoption Panel meetings.

Children and Family Court Advisory and Support Service

The Children and Family Court Advisory and Support Service (Cafcass) was created by ss 11–17 of Schedule 2 to the Criminal Justice and Court Services Act 2000. It is designed to carry out the functions set out in s. 12 of that Act, that is, to:

(a) safeguard and promote the welfare of children;

(b) give advice to any court about any application made to it in any family proceedings;

(c) make provision for the children to be represented in such proceedings; and

(d) provide information, advice, and other support for children and their families.

Cafcass—a non-departmental public body—came into operation on 2 April 2001. It united the Family Court Welfare Service (FCWO) (which advised the courts in private law cases), the Children's Guardian Service and Reporting Officers Service, and the Children's Division of the Official Solicitor's Department.

Private family law

We use the word 'private' to indicate that any recourse to law is initiated by individuals, not by the state. But family problems may well trigger an intervention by the state to provide services to children or to protect them. What we provide here is a brief glimpse of the various forms in which adults can come together in a relationship, and the legal provisions which can apply to them and to any children if that relationship falls apart.

Marriage, civil partnership, and other-couple relationships

Since March 2014, following the Royal Assent of the Marriage (Same Sex Couples) Act 2013, marriage is for two people of the same or different gender. Civil partnership was initially established as a formal commitment for people of the same gender (Civil Partnership Act 2004). However, the Supreme Court recently declared ss 1 and 3 of the Civil Partnership Act incompatible with Article 14 of the ECHR taken in conjunction with Article 8 (*R (on the application of Steinfeld and Keidan) (Appellants) v Secretary of State for International Development (in substitution for the Home Secretary and the Education Secretary)* [2018] UKSC 32). The government must now decide whether to change the law in respect of civil partnerships. In the case of either marriage or civil partnerships, the gender need not be the birth gender assigned (Gender Recognition Act 2004). In most respects, marriage and civil partnerships have the same legal consequences for the parties. In the following discussion, therefore, we use the word 'marriage' to cover both types of state-recognized partnership.

You should be aware that in different cultures different norms and different legal structures will exist. What is set out here is what is recognized in England and Wales.

A valid marriage cannot be polygamous, though a potentially polygamous marriage, if there is in fact only one spouse, does not present problems.

The law defines who has or lacks capacity to marry—for example, there is a minimum age of 16, there are prohibited relationships (such as marriage between siblings) and certain positive requirements (such as where it can be celebrated), and the need for genuine consent. A marriage is not valid if one of the parties is already married. This is the case even if that party obtained a divorce abroad which was recognized abroad, if that divorce was not also recognized in the UK. Foreign divorces are in general recognized in the UK, but some are not: for example, where the divorce involves a couple, one of whom is settled in the UK, and the divorce procedure is a 'bare talaq' (pronouncement of divorce by the man, with no involvement of the civil authorities).

Foreign marriages are also generally recognized in the UK, so couples who married abroad before settling in the UK can use courts here to obtain a divorce, and any orders open to the courts to deal with property and money. There are, however, exceptions to this principle. For example, in *Westminster City Council v C* (2008) an autistic child had a severe impairment of mental function, as well as a diagnosis of autistic spectrum disorder. He had no capacity to marry. However, he took part in a marriage ceremony in Bangladesh (his participation was by telephone from the UK, but that in itself is not an obstacle to recognition); under Bangladeshi law the marriage was valid, and such a marriage would normally call for recognition in the UK. The court, however, refused to recognize it for UK purposes as a valid marriage; the young man was a UK resident and needed protection, at least within the UK, from a marriage to which he could not consent.

Marriage is in principle an equal relationship. (This was not always the case. Until 1892 married women could not own their own property; and as late as the 1990s marital rape was not a crime.) So, a spouse or civil partner has no control over the other spouse's freedom of movement, over their ownership of property, or over their right to do what they please as an individual. Marriage does, however, create preferential status in relation to inheritance (which is tax-free between spouses), next-of-kin status (e.g. being consulted where a person lacks capacity to consent to medical treatment—see **chapter 8**), acting as the nearest relative to a mental patient (see **chapter 16**), and on death the right to receive part of the occupational payment paid to the late spouse/partner. Marriage confers a right of occupation of the marital home, whichever party is the owner or tenant; this right can be registered in the Land Registry if the property is owned by the other spouse, as a way to prevent it being sold off. The right to occupation on the basis of marriage ends on divorce, though it continues if there is another basis to remain there (ownership, tenancy, or court order).

Marital status confers the right to go to court to seek financial maintenance from the other spouse/partner, which is not available for cohabitees or for people in other close relationships, such as friends or siblings living together.

A marriage ends on death, of course, but can also be terminated by choice. A party petitions the court and has to show a recognized ground (living apart for at least two years, adultery, or unreasonable behaviour are the most common grounds in cases of married parties). Divorce or dissolution proceedings are almost never defended—what is the point?—so despite them being dealt with in court, it is in reality a bureaucratic procedure.

Where the courts do get involved is in dealing with disputes over children, property, and money—but courts can do that whether or not the parties are married. The difference is that without marriage, the courts are limited to dealing with disputes over children and disputes as to who owns what; they cannot make adjustments to ownership and they cannot award maintenance, except for the support of children.

It is widely, but wrongly, believed that there is also a legal status called common law marriage. It is true that people living together without being married, or in a civil partnership, are sometimes treated as a couple in law; this is when the state assesses their entitlement to social security as a couple. The result of being assessed as a couple is almost invariably a reduction of entitlement compared with what the claimant might get if not living with a partner.

Neither marriage, civil partnership, cohabitation, nor any other arrangement can compel people to live together. Housing and money problems, however, may lead to the same result, which is why those helping families need to know who to turn to for advice on escaping domestic violence, applying for housing, or seeking social security benefits. We will look at these topics in **Roles and responsibilities**, p 195.

Forced marriage

Government guidance on forced marriage (*The Right to Choose: Multi-agency Statutory Guidance for Dealing with Forced Marriage*) defines it as:

> . . . in forced marriage, one or both spouses do not consent to the marriage but are coerced into it. Duress can include physical, psychological, financial, sexual and emotional pressure. In the cases of some vulnerable adults who lack the capacity to consent, coercion is not required for a marriage to be forced.

> The provision of consent is essential within all marriages—only the spouses themselves will know if their consent is provided freely.

(p 7)

Figures from the Forced Marriage Unit, a UK joint Home Office and Foreign and Commonwealth Office organization, demonstrate that in the year to December 2018 it gave advice or support in 1,196 cases, of which 355 involved young people under 18. The Anti-social Behaviour, Crime and Policing Act 2014 made it an offence to force someone to marry, punishable by up to seven years' imprisonment. The provisions of the Act are set out in **Box 5.9**. You should note that the offence does not have to be committed in England or Wales. It is also an offence to breach a Forced Marriage Protection Order.

BOX 5.9 Forced marriage—The Anti-social Behaviour, Crime and Policing Act 2014

Section 121 of the 2014 Act provides that:

(1) A person commits an offence in England and Wales if he or she—

    (a) uses violence, threats or any other form of coercion for the purpose of causing another person to enter into the marriage, and

    (b) believes, or ought to reasonably believe, that the conduct may cause the other person to enter into the marriage without free and full consent.

(2) In relation to a victim who lacks capacity to consent to marriage, the offence under subsection (1) is capable of being committed by any conduct carried out for the purpose of causing the victim to enter into a marriage (whether or not the conduct amounts to violence, threats or any other form of coercion).

(3) A person commits an offence under the law of England and Wales if he or she—

    (a) practises any form of deception with the intention of causing another person to leave the United Kingdom, and

    (b) intends the other person to be subjected to conduct outside the UK that is an offence under subsection (1) or would be an offence under that subsection if the victim were in England and Wales.

Forced Marriage Protection Orders

Forced Marriage Protection Orders can also be made under s. 4A of the Family Law Act 1996. These orders can offer protection to children or adults whether they are being forced into marriage or have already been forced into marriage. The person who is seeking protection can apply for an order, but so too can the local authority. The order will last for a specified time, for example six months, and can include restrictions and requirements on a spouse, family member, or any other person involved to protect the victim. Remedies for the protection of children who are married against their consent can also involve emergency protection orders, care and supervision orders, or the inherent jurisdiction of the High Court (wardship) (see **chapter 8**).

Parental responsibility

Where more than one person has parental responsibility, they must agree on decisions about the child's care and upbringing, and, if unable to agree, the court may decide that issue. Under s. 8 of the Children Act 1989 (see **Private disputes involving children—s. 8 orders**, p 180), a court can limit the way either a mother or a father exercises their parental responsibility, and can (s. 31—see **chapter 8**) make a care order, which then gives the local authority the upper hand, allowing it to determine the extent to which the parents may exercise their parental responsibilities.

Step-parents do not have parental responsibilities unless a court orders it. Where there is no person with parental responsibility, a court can appoint a guardian—Children Act, s. 5.

Any person who does not have parental responsibility (e.g. a teacher or a babysitter) can take necessary action to safeguard the interests of a child who is in their actual care—Children Act, s. 3.

Private disputes involving children—s. 8 orders

Although we have drawn a distinction between public and private disputes concerning children, you should know from the outset that a local authority can be asked at any time in the course of private proceedings to provide a report to the court to help it to decide what is in the interests of the child, and a court can order an investigation by the local authority on whether child protection proceedings should be commenced (Children Act, s. 37).

You should also be aware that a court can make private-law-type orders while hearing a public law case: for example, in the course of care proceedings they might make a child arrangements order detailing that the child should live with a grandparent or directing to whom a child should have contact. The boundaries between public and private law are blurred—they will be crossed whenever the interests of the child require it.

We will briefly look at the three types of s. 8 order a court can make. The following can apply for a s. 8 order:

- a parent;
- a guardian;
- a step-parent who has treated the child as a member of the family;
- a person who lived with the child for at least three years (if they apply within three months);
- the child, if he or she has sufficient understanding to do so;
- anyone else, with the court's leave.

In deciding whether to make an order, s. 1 says that 'the child's welfare shall be the court's paramount consideration'. So, even though s. 8 orders are matters of private law, the private needs and desires of family members come second to the public interest in making an order for the benefit of the child. The court must take into account the child's wishes, needs, the likely effect of any change in circumstances, age, sex, and background; whether the child has suffered harm or is at risk; and who is best able to meet his or her needs. The courts should also presume, unless the contrary is shown, that involvement of a parent in the life of the child concerned will further the child's welfare (Children and Families Act 2014, s. 11(2A)). The court does not have to make any order if no order at all is thought to be in the best interests of the child (s. 1(5)). Or the court can make a different order from the one requested. Before making its decision, the court can also call for a report from Cafcass or the social services department (see **chapter 9**). It may call for the child to be separately represented by Cafcass. It may, as we noted earlier in this section, decide that the local authority should investigate with a view to care proceedings.

Section 8 allows the court to settle almost any dispute about the future arrangements for a child, but it does not touch on financial questions. A s. 8 order can be made in favour of any person the court thinks appropriate, after hearing all the evidence, not just the applicant and not just a parent; for example, a grandparent, step-parent, an unmarried father, or even a sibling. Let us look at the range of orders available.

Section 8 child arrangements order

A child arrangements order is an order regulating arrangements relating to with whom a child should live, spend time, or have other types of contact, or when they should do so. The right to contact is that of the child and the interests of the child are the court's paramount consideration. An order can provide that a person who the child is not living with shall have contact with the child. The court can lay down the exact nature and extent of the contact; for example, overnight stays, supervised visits, use of a contact centre, telephone contact, or in a difficult case, perhaps where a parent has been violent, just an annual birthday card.

Each case must be decided on its own facts, but some presumptions apply. For example, there is a presumption that children should have an ongoing relationship with both parents after family separation, where that is safe and in the child's best interests. In making decisions on contested s. 8 orders, a court should presume that a child's welfare will be furthered by the involvement of each of the child's parents in his or her life, unless it can be shown that such involvement would not in fact further the child's welfare. Involvement means any kind of direct or indirect involvement but not any particular division of the child's time. However, the best interests of the child should prevail in all decisions. In *Re (A Child) (Child Arrangements Order: Best Interests)* (2015) the Court of Appeal upheld an appeal by a family friend of a child whose mother had died of cancer. The mother and child lived with the friend before the mother died. The friend made an application for a special guardianship order, but the original judge had made a child arrangements order in favour of the father, who also had parental responsibility, indicating that there was a 'broad natural parent presumption'. The Court of Appeal dismissed this presumption. The position of the birth father should be given appropriate weight, but there is no presumption that it should prevail. The facts of each case must be examined.

If a child of sufficient understanding, or *Gillick* competence (see **chapter 2**), does not want contact, there is no point in imposing it: *Re S (Contact: Children's Views)* (2002).

Supported contact may be facilitated by the National Association of Child Contact Centres (www.naccc.org.uk).

A child arrangements order will also settle the arrangements as to with whom the child is to live. The arrangements stipulated in the order concerning where a child shall live will specify who will have parental responsibility for the child while it is in effect.

A child arrangements order can be made in favour of more than one person, even specifying exactly how the child's time will be split, if this serves the child's interests. The case study at the start of the chapter provides an example.

Section 8 specific issue order

This order ensures that, where there is disagreement, major decisions are brought before the court. It can be used in cases such as *Re B* (1991), where the court authorized a 12-year-old girl to have an abortion, overriding her mother's wishes. It has been used to authorize vaccination, where the mother feared the triple vaccine for MMR but the father wanted the child vaccinated: *B (Child)* (2003). The court accepted expert evidence that the treatment was in the child's best interests.

A common example of a specific issue order is to obtain a change to a child's surname where one parent objects. The courts, applying s. 1 of the Children Act, generally consider that the interests of the child are harmed by such a change, but not always: in *Re S (A Child) (Change of Name: Cultural Factors)* (2001), the father was Sikh and the child had a Sikh name. She lived with her mother, a Bangladeshi. The court ordered that she be known by a Bangladeshi name so as not to stand out in her community, but that she should keep her Sikh name in her own best long-term interests. The Court of Appeal, in *Re G* (2012), set out how a judge should decide in cases where there is a disagreement. In this case, an ultra-orthodox father disagreed with the children's mother that the children should be educated in a new co-educational school, where there were greater educational opportunities than in a traditional Talmudic school. The Appeal Court said:

> In the conditions of current society there are, as it seems to me, three answers to this question. First, we must recognise that equality of opportunity is a fundamental value of our society: equality as between different communities, social groupings and creeds, and equality as between men and women, boys and girls. Second, we foster, encourage and facilitate aspiration: both aspiration as a virtue in itself and, to the extent that it is practical and reasonable, the child's own aspirations. Far too many lives in our community are blighted, even today, by lack of aspiration. Third, our objective must be to bring the child to adulthood in such a way that the child is best equipped both to decide what kind of life they want to lead—what kind of person they want to be—and to give effect so far as practicable to their aspirations. Put shortly, our objective must be to maximise the child's opportunities in every sphere of life as they enter adulthood. And the corollary of this, where the decision has been devolved to a 'judicial parent', is that the judge must be cautious about approving a regime which may have the effect of foreclosing or unduly limiting the child's ability to make such decisions in future.

Section 8 prohibited steps order

This order prevents parental responsibility being exercised in relation to a specified matter. This could, for example, prevent a child being taken abroad or living with a certain individual. In *Re J (A Minor) (Prohibited Steps Order: Circumcision)* (1999), the court granted an order prohibiting a boy's circumcision. It was not in this child's interests to proceed unless both parents wanted it.

Arrangements for private law disputes

The Children and Families Act 2014 sets out procedures for the way the law deals with private disputes between parents. The Act requires a potential applicant to attend a family mediation, information, and assessment meeting (MIAM) to find out about and consider mediation before being able to apply for certain types of court order. The National Family Mediation organization provides information about MIAMs (see www. nfm.org.uk/index.php/family-mediation/mediation-information-meeting-miam). However, the success hoped for with mediation has not materialized. Private law cases have seen an increase in litigants in person since the abolition of legal aid (Legal Aid, Punishment of Offenders Act 2014). Mediation has not proved to be a suitable alternative, despite this.

Changing the safeguarding and inter-agency system

The Children Act 2004 was defined by the then Labour Government as 'the first step in a long-term programme of change'. It created the legislative spine for developing more effective and accessible services focused around the needs of children, young people, and their families. It described the principal purposes of the legislation as putting the improvement of children's well-being at the heart of government policies by creating:

- clear, shared outcomes embedded in legislation;
- an independent champion for the views and interests of children;
- robust partnership arrangements;
- improved local arrangements for child protection;
- clearer accountability for children's services;
- a new integrated inspection framework;
- a legislative basis for better sharing of information.

Fourteen years on, those objectives have been subject to considerable challenge, not least because child deaths have continued to occur and different political objectives have been established which involve less bureaucracy, smaller government, and potentially further involvement of the private sector in the running of services. The 'Every Child Matters' (ECM) policy and the five outcomes for children—stay safe, be healthy, enjoy and achieve, make a positive contribution, and achieve economic well-being—have been largely ignored. The ECM outcomes would not need a 'massive bureaucratic superstructure to police it' (Michael Gove's evidence to the Education Select Committee, 27 July 2010). Gove went on to say that he had no problem with ECM as a list but that it should be policed in a hands-off way, and signalled that the way to realize the outcomes was for children to achieve well in schools. The ECM website was removed and critically the five outcomes no longer form part of Ofsted's framework for the inspection of local authority arrangements for the protection of children. No announcements have been made to date about potential changes to the Children Act 2004, although some sections have not been implemented (see **The key provisions of the Children Act 2004**, p 188). Additionally, the multi-disciplinary statutory guidance, *Working Together to Safeguard Children*, has been updated. The most recent *Working Together to Safeguard Children* was published in July 2018. At 112 pages, it is still substantially shorter than previous versions (390 pages), in line with proposals made in the Munro Review of Child Protection (2012). It replaces *Working Together to Safeguard Children* (2010), the *Framework for the Assessment of Children in Need and their Families* (2000), and *Statutory Guidance on Making Arrangements to Safeguard and Promote* *the Welfare of Children under Section 11 of the Children Act 2004* (2007). The non-statutory sections have been cut out and the statutory sections shortened. However, several supplementary guides are referred to, and they can be downloaded from the UK government website:

> *Statutory Guidance on Children Who Run Away or Go Missing from Home or Care*
> www.gov.uk/government/publications/children-who-run-away-or-go-missing-from-home-or-care
> *Safeguarding Children Who May Have Been Trafficked: Practice Guidance*
> www.gov.uk/government/publications/safeguarding-children-who-may-have-been-trafficked-practice-guidance
> *Multi-agency Statutory Guidance on Female Genital Mutilation*
> www.gov.uk/government/publications/multi-agency-statutory-guidance-on-female-genital-mutilation
> *Child Sexual Exploitation: Definition and Guide for Practitioners*
> www.gov.uk/government/publications/child-sexual-exploitation-definition-and-guide-for-practitioners
> *Revised* Prevent *Duty Guidance for England and Wales*
> www.gov.uk/government/publications/prevent-duty-guidance

The Munro Review of Child Protection

Professor Eileen Munro was invited by Michael Gove, the Secretary of State for Education, to review the child protection system in England on 10 June 2010. She published three reports, with the final one, in May 2011, making a series of 15 recommendations. These are set out in **Box 5.10**, followed by a commentary on their implementation so far.

BOX 5.10 Recommendations—Munro Review of Child Protection (2010–11)

Recommendation 1: The government should revise both the statutory guidance, *Working Together to Safeguard Children* and *The Framework for the Assessment of Children in Need and their Families* and their associated policies to:

- distinguish the rules that are essential for effective working together, from guidance that informs professional judgment;
- set out the key principles underpinning the guidance;
- remove the distinction between initial and core assessments and the associated timescales in respect of these assessments, replacing them with the decisions that are required to be made by qualified social workers when developing an understanding of children's needs and making and implementing a plan to safeguard and promote their welfare;
- require local attention is given to:
  - timeliness in the identification of children's needs and provision of help;

- the quality of the assessment to inform next steps to safeguard and promote children's welfare; and
- the effectiveness of the help provided;

• give local areas the responsibility to draw on research and theoretical models to inform local practice; and

• remove constraints to local innovation and professional judgment that are created by prescribing or endorsing particular approaches, for example, nationally designed assessment forms, national performance indicators associated with assessment or nationally prescribed approaches to IT systems.

Recommendation 2: The inspection framework should examine the effectiveness of the contributions of all local services, including health, education, police, probation and the justice system to the protection of children.

Recommendation 3: The new inspection framework should examine the child's journey from needing to receiving help, explore how the rights, wishes, feelings and experiences of children and young people inform and shape the provision of services, and look at the effectiveness of the help provided to children, young people and their families.

Recommendation 4: Local authorities and their partners should use a combination of nationally collected and locally published performance information to help benchmark performance, facilitate improvement and promote accountability. It is crucial that performance information is not treated as an unambiguous measure of good or bad performance as performance indicators tend to be.

Recommendation 5: The existing statutory requirements for each Local Safeguarding Children Board (LSCB) to produce and publish an annual report for the Children's Trust Board should be amended, to require its submission instead to the Chief Executive and Leader of the Council, and, subject to the passage of legislation, to the local Police and Crime Commissioner and the Chair of the health and wellbeing board.

Recommendation 6: The statutory guidance, *Working Together to Safeguard Children*, should be amended to state that when monitoring and evaluating local arrangements, LSCBs should, taking account of local need, include an assessment of the effectiveness of the help being provided to children and families (including the effectiveness and value for money of early help services, including early years provision), and the effectiveness of multi-agency training to safeguard and promote the welfare of children and young people.

Recommendation 7: Local authorities should give due consideration to protecting the discrete roles and responsibilities of a Director of Children's Services and Lead Member for Children's Services before allocating any additional functions to individuals occupying such roles. The importance, as envisaged in the Children Act 2004, of appointing individuals to positions where they have specific responsibilities for children's services should not be undermined. The Government should amend the statutory guidance issued in relation to such roles and establish the principle that, given the importance of individuals in senior positions being responsible for children's services, it should not be considered appropriate to give additional functions (that do not relate to children's services) to Directors of Children's Services and Lead Members for Children's Services unless exceptional circumstances arise.

Recommendation 8: The Government should work collaboratively with the Royal College of Paediatrics and Child Health, the Royal College of General Practitioners, local authorities and others to research the impact of health reorganisation on effective partnership arrangements and the ability to provide effective help for children who are suffering, or likely to suffer, significant harm.

Recommendation 9: The Government should require LSCBs to use systems methodology when undertaking Serious Case Reviews (SCRs) and, over the coming year, work with the sector to develop national resources to:

- provide accredited, skilled and independent reviewers to jointly work with LSCBs on each SCR;
- promote the development of a variety of systems-based methodologies to learn from practice;
- initiate the development of a typology of the problems that contribute to adverse outcomes to facilitate national learning; and
- disseminate learning nationally to improve practice and inform the work of the Chief Social Worker.

In the meantime, Ofsted's evaluation [*sic*] of SCRs should end.

Recommendation 10: The Government should place a duty on local authorities and statutory partners to secure the sufficient provision of local early help services for children, young people and families. The arrangements setting out how they will do this should:

- specify the range of professional help available to local children, young people and families, through statutory, voluntary and community services, against the local profile of need set out in the local Joint Strategic Needs Analysis (JSNA);
- specify how they will identify children who are suffering or who are likely to suffer significant harm, including the availability of social work expertise to all professionals working with children, young people and families who are not being supported by children's social care services and specify the training available locally to support professionals working at the frontline of universal services;
- set out the local resourcing of the early help services for children, young people and families; and, most importantly
- lead to the identification of the early help that is needed by a particular child and their family, and to the provision of an 'early help offer' where their needs do not meet the criteria for receiving children's social care services.

Recommendation 11: The Social Work Reform Board's Professional Capabilities Framework should incorporate capabilities necessary for child and family social work. This framework should explicitly inform social work qualification training, postgraduate professional development and performance appraisal.

Recommendation 12: Employers and higher education institutions (HEIs) should work together so that social work students are prepared for the challenges of child protection work. In particular, the review considers that HEIs and employing agencies should work together so that:

- practice placements are of the highest quality and—in time—only in designated Approved Practice Settings;
- employers are able to apply for special 'teaching organisation' status, awarded by the College of Social Work;
- the merits of 'student units', which are headed up by a senior social worker are considered; and
- placements are of sufficiently high quality, and both employers and HEIs consider if their relationship is working well.

Recommendation 13: Local authorities and their partners should start an ongoing process to review and redesign the ways in which child and family social work is delivered, drawing on evidence of effectiveness of helping methods where appropriate and supporting practice that can implement evidence based ways of working with children and families.

Recommendation 14: Local authorities should designate a Principal Child and Family Social Worker, who is a senior manager with lead responsibility for practice in the local authority and who is still actively involved in frontline practice and who can report the views and experiences of the front line to all levels of management.

Recommendation 15: A Chief Social Worker should be created in Government, whose duties should include advising the Government on social work practice and informing the Secretary of State's annual report to Parliament on the working of the Children Act 1989.

Munro's recommendations did not lead to immediate changes in the structure of child protection agencies as was the case following Lord Laming's report into the death of Victoria Climbié. That report ultimately paved the way for the Children Act 2004 and the splitting of social services departments into children's and adults' services, which has led to criticism from some commentators. Munro's recommendations, which were accepted by the government, provided a more subtle approach to influencing how services are organized to protect children. In the introduction to her first report, Munro says:

> The problem is that previous reforms have not led to the expected improvements in frontline practice. Moreover, there is a substantial body of evidence indicating that past reforms are creating new, unforeseen complications. It is therefore important to think carefully before producing more recommendations for change.
>
> (E. Munro, *The Munro Review of Child Protection: Part One: A Systems Analysis* (Department for Education, 2010))

A year later, Munro further comments in *The Munro Review of Child Protection: Progress Report: Moving Towards a Child-centred System* (Department for Education, 2012) that 'progress is moving in the right direction but that it needs to move faster'. Perhaps this was inevitable since her recommendations, shown in **Box 5.10**, were not designed to change the law, certainly not substantially, nor were they designed to change the structure of the agencies involved in child protection. She was, however, interested in changing expectations about what could be achieved in the protection of children and in the provision of early help for them. She was also concerned to change the way social work is practised through influencing everyday decisions and behaviour. High-profile inquiries into the deaths of children have continued, with similar responses from the media. Local authorities all now have an early help strategy funded by grants from government. But the real test is whether social work practice has improved. Little widespread evidence of this is currently available, although some is contained in evaluations of social work innovations published in November 2017 (see *Children's Social Care Innovation Programme: Final evaluation report*, which can be downloaded from www.gov.uk/government/publications/childrens-social-care-innovation-programme-final-evaluation-report). One of Munro's recommendations which does have a tangible outcome was the appointment of the first Chief Social Worker for Children and Families, Isobel Trowler. In 2015, Trowler set out plans for the formal accreditation of social workers working with children, their supervisors, and leaders. The National Assessment and Accreditation System (NAAS) will involve social workers submitting evidence contained in portfolios, as well as examination success. This, taken together with provisions in the Children and Social Work Act 2017, to establish a new social work regulator, Social Work England, and new multi-agency arrangements for safeguarding, form the thrust of current government thinking about this area of social policy for children.

The key provisions of the Children Act 2004

The duty to cooperate to improve well-being

The Act is designed to create a holistic approach to children's services. Service providers must cooperate in order to improve children's well-being. Section 10 of the Act, which is set out in **Box 5.11**, creates the statutory framework for this to happen. It requires cooperation between local authorities, key partner agencies ('relevant partners'), and other relevant bodies ('other bodies or persons'), including the voluntary and community sectors, in order to improve the well-being of children in the area. 'Well-being' is defined in terms of five outcomes for children. The legislation describes these as:

(a) physical and mental health and emotional well-being;

(b) protection from harm and neglect;

(c) education, training and recreation;

(d) the contribution made by them to society;

(e) social and economic well-being.

The duty to make the arrangements to improve well-being is placed on the local authority and a duty to cooperate with the local authority is placed on the relevant partners, although, as already indicated, the five outcomes are now less influential than they once were. As well as underpinning wide cooperation arrangements, these duties and powers are also designed to provide the statutory context within which agencies will be encouraged to integrate commissioning and delivery of children's services, underpinned by pooled budgeting arrangements. As you read the section, notice the recognition of the range of bodies which are responsible for children's well-being, the extensive delegation of responsibilities, and the role of the local authority as the 'enabler' of effective provision. Notice also the specific mention of the importance of parents within the section.

The Children and Young Persons Act 2008 places a complementary duty upon the Secretary of State to promote the well-being of children and young people—this is discussed in **chapter 6**.

BOX 5.11 Cooperation to improve well-being—s. 10 of the Children Act 2004

(1) Each local authority in England must make arrangements to promote co-operation between—

(a) the authority;

(b) each of the authority's relevant partners; and

(c) such other persons or bodies as the authority consider appropriate, being persons or bodies of any nature who exercise functions or are engaged in activities in relation to children in the authority's area.

(2) The arrangements are to be made with a view to improving the well-being of children in the authority's area so far as relating to—

(a) physical and mental health and emotional well-being;

(b) protection from harm and neglect;

(c) education, training and recreation;

(d) the contribution made by them to society;

(e) social and economic well-being.

(3) In making arrangements under this section a [local authority] in England must have regard to the importance of parents and other persons caring for children in improving the well-being of children.

(4) For the purposes of this section each of the following is a relevant partner of a local authority in England—

(a) where the authority is a county council for an area for which there is also a district council, the district council;

(b) the local policing body and the chief officer of police for a police area any part of which falls within the area of the local authority;

(c) a local probation board for an area any part of which falls within the area of the authority;

(ca) the Secretary of State in relation to his functions under sections 2 and 3 of the Offender Management Act 2007, so far as they are exercisable in relation to England;

(cb) any provider of probation services that is required by arrangements under section 3(2) of the Offender Management Act 2007 to act as a relevant partner of the authority;

(d) a youth offending team for an area any part of which falls within the area of the authority;

(da) the National Health Service Commissioning Board;

(db) any clinical commissioning group for an area any part of which falls within the area of the authority; . . .

(f) a person providing services in pursuance of section 68 of the Education and Skills Act 2008 in any part of the area of the authority;

(fa) the governing body of a maintained school that is maintained by the authority;

(fb) the proprietor of a school approved by the Secretary of State under section 342 of the Education Act 1996 and situated in the authority's area;

(fc) the proprietor of a city technology college, city college for the technology of the arts or Academy situated in the authority's area;

> (fd) the governing body of an institution within the further education sector the main site of which is situated in the authority's area;
>
> (fe) the Secretary of State, in relation to the Secretary of State's functions under section 2 of the Employment and Training Act 1973.
>
> (5) The relevant partners of a local authority in England must co-operate with the authority in the making of arrangements under this section.

Children and Young People's Plans (CYPP)

Children's services authorities are no longer required by s. 17 of the Act to prepare and publish a strategic plan which will explain how they intend to carry out their responsibilities towards children and young people. The regulations requiring such plans were revoked in October 2010. Local partnership can produce plans if they see fit but there is no requirement to do so, or to do so in a particular format.

Safeguarding children

Section 11 of the 2004 Act imposes a duty on specified agencies (set out in **Box 5.12**) to make arrangements to ensure that their functions are discharged having regard to the need to safeguard and promote the welfare of children.

The aim of the duty (set out in **Box 5.13**) is to complement the general cooperation duty in the specific area of children's safeguards by:

- ensuring that agencies give appropriate priority to their responsibilities towards the children in their care or with whom they come into contact;
- encouraging agencies to share early concerns about safety and welfare of children and to ensure preventative action before a crisis develops.

Safeguarding and promoting the welfare of children is not statutorily defined in primary legislation but *Working Together* defines it as:

- protecting children from maltreatment;
- preventing impairment of children's health or development;
- ensuring that children grow up in circumstances consistent with the provision of safe and effective care; and
- taking action to enable all children to have the best outcomes.

It is somewhat distinct from the notion of child protection, which is key to the Children Act 1989 that we discuss in the following chapters. Child protection is linked to legally based state intervention and referred to by the first two bullet points above; safeguarding is a means of ensuring that children receive the support they need for their well-being.

The statutory duty requires agencies actively to consider the need to safeguard children and promote their welfare in the course of carrying out their normal functions. The duty requires agencies that come into contact with children to recognize that their needs are different from adults.

BOX 5.12 Specified agencies—s. 11 of the Children Act 2004

(a) a local authority in England;

(b) a district council which is not such an authority;

(ba) the National Health Service Commissioning Board;

(bb) a clinical commissioning group;

(c) ...

(d) a Special Health Authority, so far as exercising functions in relation to England, designated by order made by the Secretary of State for the purposes of this section;

(e) ...

(f) an NHS trust all or most of whose hospitals, establishments and facilities are situated in England;

(g) an NHS foundation trust;

(h) the local policing body and chief officer of police for a police area in England;

(i) the British Transport Police Authority, so far as exercising functions in relation to England;

(ia) the National Crime Agency;

(j) a local probation board for an area in England;

(ja) the Secretary of State in relation to his functions under sections 2 and 3 of the Offender Management Act 2007, so far as they are exercisable in relation to England;

(k) a youth offending team for an area in England;

(l) the governor of a prison or secure training centre in England (or, in the case of a contracted out prison or secure training centre, its director);

(la) the principal of a secure college in England;

(m) any person to the extent that he is providing services in pursuance of section 74 of the Education and Skills Act 2008.

BOX 5.13 The duty to make arrangements to safeguard and promote welfare—s. 11(2) of the Children Act 2004

Each person and body to whom this section applies must make arrangements for ensuring that—

(a) their functions are discharged having regard to the need to safeguard and promote the welfare of children; and

(b) any services provided by another person pursuant to arrangements made by the person or body in the discharge of their functions are provided having regard to that need.

Abolition of Local Safeguarding Children Boards

The Children Act 2004 provided that children's services authorities in England must establish Local Safeguarding Children Boards (LSCB) to ensure that the necessary local arrangements are in place for coordinating the work of the key agencies in safeguarding children. The Children and Social Work Act 2017 abolishes LSCBs and requires local authorities, chief officers of police, and clinical commissioning groups (health services) instead to make arrangements for them and relevant partners to 'work together in exercising their functions, so far as the functions are exercised for the purpose of safeguarding and promoting the welfare of children in the area'. Thus, the three major agencies should now take joint responsibility for safeguarding arrangements in each local area. It is noteworthy that education agencies are not specifically included, although *Working Together to Safeguard Children* strongly advises that educational institutions are included as relevant partners.

The Child Safeguarding Practice Review and Relevant Agency (England) Regulations (2018) sets out which agencies can be considered by the Safeguarding Partners as relevant agencies (see **Box 5.14**).

BOX 5.14 Summary of potential relevant agencies—Child Safeguarding Practice Review and Relevant Agency (England) Regulations (2018)

The following bodies/persons must be represented on the Board:

- Education and childcare
- The proprietor of an Academy school or governing body of a maintained school, nursey, pupil referral unit, independent school, FE college or Children's Centre
- Health and Social Care
- NHS trusts, adoption agencies, residential family centres or residential holiday schemes for disabled children
- Local Government
- District Councils, Cafcass, Prisons, Probation Services, Secure Training Centres, Young Offender Institutions, Youth Offending Teams
- Police and Immigration
- The British Transport Police, Border Authorities and Port Police services
- Miscellaneous
- Charities, Religious Organisations and any person or body involved in the provision, supervision or oversight of sport or leisure.

Section 16E of the Children Act 2004 sets out the crucial duties of safeguarding partners—see **Box 5.15**.

BOX 5.15 Duties of safeguarding partners—s. 16E of the Children Act 2004

1) The safeguarding partners for a local authority area in England must make arrangements for—

 (a) the safeguarding partners, and

(b) any relevant agencies that they consider appropriate, to work together in exercising their functions, so far as the functions are exercised for the purpose of safeguarding and promoting the welfare of children in the area.

(2) The arrangements must include arrangements for the safeguarding partners to work together to identify and respond to the needs of children in the area.

Section 16F sets out the duties of safeguarding partners to identify serious safeguarding cases and establish reviews of those cases. These reviews will be overseen by a national Child Safeguarding Practice Review Panel. The purpose of the reviews is to identify improvements to be made to the safeguarding arrangements locally. A summary of the functions of the safeguarding partners is found in s16G—see **Box 5.16.**

 BOX 5.16 Functions of the safeguarding partners—s. 16G of the Children Act 2004

1. This section applies in relation to arrangements made under section 16E or 16F by the safeguarding partners for a local authority area in England.

(1) The safeguarding partners must publish the arrangements.

(2) The arrangements must include arrangements for scrutiny by an independent person of the effectiveness of the arrangements.

(3) The safeguarding partners and relevant agencies for the local authority area must act in accordance with the arrangements.

(4) Subsection (6) applies where a person is specified in regulations under section 16E(3) for the purposes of the definition of 'relevant agency'.

(5) The regulations may make provision for the enforcement against the person of the duty imposed by subsection (4), if the Secretary of State considers that there would otherwise be no appropriate means of enforcing that duty against the person (but the regulations may not create criminal offences).

(6) At least once in every 12 month period, the safeguarding partners must prepare and publish a report on—

(a) what the safeguarding partners and relevant agencies for the local authority area have done as a result of the arrangements, and

(b) how effective the arrangements have been in practice.

The safeguarding partners are now the key statutory mechanism for ensuring that the relevant organizations in each local area effectively safeguard and promote the welfare of children. Details of the role and operation of safeguarding partners are set out in chapter 3 of the new *Working Together to Safeguard Children* (2018).

Safeguarding Boards in Wales

In Wales, the Social Services and Well-being (Wales) Act 2014 repealed those sections in the Children Act 2004 requiring LSCBs. The 2014 Act establishes a National Independent Safeguarding Board with the remit for both children and adults. The Act also establishes regulations which set out those areas where there are to be Safeguarding Children Boards (SCBs) (s. 134(1)). The objectives of these new SCBs are:

(a) to protect children within their area who are experiencing, or are at risk of, abuse, neglect, or other kinds of harm, and

(b) to prevent children within their area from becoming at risk of abuse, neglect, or other kinds of harm.

Local authority administration

Local authorities that are children's services authorities—that is, county-level or unitary authorities—have a number of specific duties to organize and plan services and to safeguard and promote the welfare of children. The Children Act 2004 required all children's services authorities in England to appoint a director of children's services and to designate a lead member for children's services prior to 1 January 2008.

The functions of the director of children's services include (s. 18(2)):

- local authority education functions (other than those relating to adults);
- social services functions for children;
- functions in relation to young people leaving care;
- functions under ss 10–12 and 17 of the Children Act 2004;
- any function delegated to the authority by an NHS body relating to children;
- any other function prescribed by regulations.

In addition, directors of children's services will take responsibility for local cooperation arrangements in relation to children's services. Two or more local authorities may appoint a director of children's services jointly.

The lead member for children's services is designed to ensure political leadership and accountability for the performance of children's services. Updated statutory guidance was published in April 2013, detailing the responsibilities of these roles. The guidance is available as a download from www.gov.uk/government/publications/directors-of-childrens-services-roles-and-responsibilities.

In Wales, the Social Services and Well-being (Wales) Act 2014 requires local authorities to appoint a Director of Social Services.

▓ Responsibilities on agencies

In this section of the chapter we discuss the ways in which agencies must take joint responsibility for outcomes for children. *Working Together to Safeguard Children*, the details of which we set out in **Changing the safeguarding and inter-agency system**, p 183, explains that safeguarding children is a shared responsibility.

Crime and child protection

Working Together to Safeguard Children also includes within the definition of safeguarding the responsibilities of agencies, particularly the police and probation services in respect of potentially dangerous persons who present a risk of harm to the public, including children. The Criminal Justice Act 2003 established the need for arrangements to assess risk to the public, including vulnerable children, posed by serious offenders. Multi-Agency Public Protection Arrangements (MAPPA) provide the mechanism for appropriate risk assessments to be carried out. MAPPA meetings are normally coordinated by the police service, but include representatives from probation services and children's services, amongst others. Designated agencies involved in MAPPA have a duty to cooperate, including by sharing information.

Roles and responsibilities

The following discussion of roles and responsibilities draws heavily on *Working Together to Safeguard Children* (2018). The guidance makes clear that all organizations which work with children have certain responsibilities. These are set out in Chapter 2, *para. 3* and are shown in **Box 5.17**:

BOX 5.17 Responsibilities of working with children—chapter 2, para. 3 of *Working Together to Safeguard Children* (2018)

- a clear line of accountability for the commissioning and/or provision of services designed to safeguard and promote the welfare of children

- a senior board level lead with the required knowledge, skills and expertise or sufficiently qualified and experienced to take leadership responsibility for the organisation's/agency's safeguarding arrangements

- a culture of listening to children and taking account of their wishes and feelings, both in individual decisions and the development of services

- clear whistleblowing procedures, which reflect the principles in Sir Robert Francis' Freedom to Speak Up Review and are suitably referenced in staff training and codes of conduct, and a culture that enables issues about safeguarding and promoting the welfare of children to be addressed

- clear escalation policies for staff to follow when their child safeguarding concerns are not being addressed within their organisation or by other agencies

- arrangements which set out clearly the processes for sharing information, with other practitioners and with safeguarding partners

- a designated practitioner (or, for health commissioning and health provider organisations/agencies, designated and named practitioners) for child safeguarding. Their role is to support other practitioners in their organisations and agencies to recognise the needs of children, including protection from possible abuse or neglect. Designated practitioner roles should always be explicitly defined in job descriptions. Practitioners should be given sufficient time, funding, supervision and support to fulfil their child welfare and safeguarding responsibilities effectively

- safe recruitment practices and ongoing safe working practices for individuals whom the organisation or agency permit to work regularly with children, including policies on when to obtain a criminal record check
- appropriate supervision and support for staff, including undertaking safeguarding training
- creating a culture of safety, equality and protection within the services they provide

In addition:

- employers are responsible for ensuring that their staff are competent to carry out their responsibilities for safeguarding and promoting the welfare of children and creating an environment where staff feel able to raise concerns and feel supported in their safeguarding role
- staff should be given a mandatory induction, which includes familiarisation with child protection responsibilities and the procedures to be followed if anyone has any concerns about a child's safety or welfare
- all practitioners should have regular reviews of their own practice to ensure they have knowledge, skills and expertise that improve over time

Local authority designated officer (LADO)

Working Together to Safeguard Children (para 4) sets out the arrangements which should be made to deal with allegations made against people who work with children. Allegations may be made against a person who has:

- behaved in a way that has harmed a child, or may have harmed a child
- possibly committed a criminal offence against or related to a child
- behaved towards a child or children in a way that indicates they may pose a risk of harm to children.

The role of the local authority designated officer (LADO) is to ensure that allegations made against persons who work with children are not dealt with in isolation. The LADO should provide advice and guidance to employers on how to deal with allegations effectively and efficiently. If an agency decides to remove an individual from work with children, they must inform the Disclosure and Barring Service. Failure to do so without good reason is an offence.

Duties to cooperate

The Children Act 1989 places two specific duties on agencies to cooperate in the interests of vulnerable children. The first of these is s. 27 of the Children Act 1989, set out in **Box 5.18**.

BOX 5.18 Agencies' responsibilities under s. 27 of the Children Act 1989

Section 27 provides that a local authority may request help from:

- any local authority;
- any local housing authority;
- the National Health Service Commissioning Board;
- any clinical commissioning group, Local Health Board, Special Health Authority, NHS Trust, or NHS Foundation Trust; and
- any person authorized by the Secretary of State in exercising the local authority's functions under Part 3 of the Act.

Part III of the Children Act 1989, which we discuss in **chapter 6**, places a duty on local authorities to provide support and services for children in need, including children looked after by the local authority and those in secure accommodation. The authority whose help is requested in these circumstances has a duty to comply with the request, provided it is compatible with its other duties and functions. Remember that in Wales Part III of the Children Act 1989 has been repealed and replaced with the Social Services and Well-being (Wales) Act 2014.

The second duty is in s. 47 of the Children Act 1989 set out in **Box 5.19**. We discuss s. 47 of the Children Act 1989 fully in **chapter 7**.

BOX 5.19 Agencies' duties under s. 47(11) of the Children Act 1989

Section 47 places a duty on:

- any local authority;
- any housing authority;
- the National Health Service Commissioning Board;
- any clinical commissioning group, Local Health Board, Special Health Authority, NHS Trust, or NHS Foundation Trust; and
- any person authorized by the Secretary of State to help a local authority with its inquiries in cases where there is reasonable cause to suspect that a child is suffering or is likely to suffer, significant harm.

The responsibilities of other agencies

Working Together outlines the main roles and responsibilities of statutory agencies, professionals, the voluntary sector, and the wider community in relation to child protection.

Education services

Schools and colleges, whether state or independent, have a critical role in the protection of children. Schools are often the place where abuse is first noticed. Schools do not have a direct investigative responsibility in child protection work, but schools and colleges should assist social services departments by referring concerns and providing information for s. 47 child protection inquiries. Further new guidance for schools and colleges was published in September 2018 and can be downloaded from www.gov.uk/government/publications/keeping-children-safe-in-education.

All educational settings should contribute to safeguarding and promoting children's welfare. **Box 5.20** sets out the safeguarding requirements listed in *Keeping Children Safe in Education*:

BOX 5.20 Safeguarding requirements in educational settings—*Keeping Children Safe in Education* (2018)

- All staff have a responsibility to provide a safe environment in which children can learn and all staff should be prepared to identify children who may benefit from early help.
- Early help means providing support as soon as a problem emerges at any point in a child's life, from the foundation years through to the teenage years.
- Any staff member who has a concern about a child's welfare should follow the referral processes . . .
- Staff should expect to support social workers and other agencies following any referral.
- Every school and college should have a designated safeguarding lead who will provide support to staff to carry out their safeguarding duties and who will liaise closely with other services such as children's social care.
- The designated safeguarding lead (and any deputies) are most likely to have a complete safeguarding picture and be the most appropriate person to advise on the response to safeguarding concerns.
- The Teachers' Standards 2012 state that teachers (which includes headteachers) should safeguard children's wellbeing and maintain public trust in the teaching profession as part of their professional duties.

Health services

Individual health professionals such as GPs, midwives, health visitors, and school nurses are extremely well placed to contribute to child protection. Hospital staff, particularly those working in accident and emergency departments, should be fully aware of child protection procedures. Mental health practitioners, particularly those working with child and adolescent mental health services, can provide evidence of child abuse or neglect. All staff working in health-care settings—including those who predominantly treat adults—should receive training to ensure they attain the competences appropriate to their role and follow the relevant professional guidance.

Strategic leadership should be provided by health authorities and clinical commissioning groups. *Working Together* highlights statutory responsibilities placed on health services.

NHS England is responsible for ensuring that the health commissioning system as a whole is working effectively to safeguard and promote the welfare of children. It is also accountable for the services it directly commissions, including primary care, and healthcare services in the under-18 secure estate (for police custody settings see **The Police Service**, p 200). NHS England also leads and defines improvement in safeguarding practice and outcomes and should also ensure that there are effective mechanisms for safeguarding partners and health and well-being boards to raise concerns about the engagement and leadership of the local NHS. Each NHS England region should have a safeguarding lead to ensure regional collaboration and assurance through convening safeguarding forums. Clinical commissioning groups (CCGs) will be the major commissioners of local health services. The CCG should employ or have in place a contractual agreement to secure the expertise of designated professionals, i.e. designated doctors and nurses for safeguarding children and for looked-after children (and designated paediatricians for unexpected deaths in childhood). Designated doctors and nurses, as senior professionals, clinical experts, and strategic leaders are a vital source of safeguarding advice and expertise for all relevant organizations and agencies, but particularly the clinical commissioning group, NHS England, and the local authority, and for advice and support to other health practitioners across the health economy. All providers of NHS-funded health services, including NHS Trusts and NHS Foundation Trusts, should identify a dedicated named doctor and a named nurse (and a named midwife if the organization or agency provides maternity services) for safeguarding children. In the case of ambulance trusts and independent providers, this should be a named practitioner. Named practitioners have a key role in promoting good professional practice within their organization and agency, providing advice and expertise for fellow practitioners, and ensuring that safeguarding training is in place. They should work closely with their organization's/agency's safeguarding lead on the executive board, designated health professionals for the health economy, and other statutory safeguarding partners. Health professionals and organizations have a key role to play in actively promoting the health and well-being of children. Section 11 of the Children Act 2004 places a duty on trusts to make arrangements to ensure that, in discharging their functions, they have regard to the need to safeguard and promote the welfare of children.

Day care services

Day care services including family centres, early years centres, nurseries, childminders, playgroups, and holiday and out-of-school schemes play an important role in the lives of large numbers of children. *Working Together* says:

Early Years providers must ensure that:

- they are alert to any issues of concern in the child's life
- they have and implement a policy and procedures to safeguard children. This must include an explanation of the action to be taken when there are safeguarding concerns

about a child and in the event of an allegation being made against a member of staff. The policy must also cover the use of mobile phones and cameras in the setting, that staff complete safeguarding training that enables them to understand their safeguarding policy and procedures, have up-to-date knowledge of safeguarding issues, and recognise signs of potential abuse and neglect

- they have a practitioner who is designated to take lead responsibility for safeguarding children within each early years setting and who must liaise with local statutory children's services as appropriate. This lead must also complete child protection training

The Police Service

The Police Service has a commitment under the Children Act 2004 to protect children from abuse. **Box 5.21** sets out the guidance of *Working Together* regarding the Police Service:

BOX 5.21 Commitments of the Police Service—*Working Together to Safeguard Children* (2018)

The police are subject to the section 11 duties. Under section 1(8)(h) of the Police Reform and Social Responsibility Act 2011 the police and crime commissioner must hold the Chief Constable to account for the exercise of the latter's duties in relation to safeguarding children under sections 10 and 11 of the Children Act 2004.

All police officers, and other police employees such as Police Community Support Officers, are well placed to identify early when a child's welfare is at risk and when a child may need protection from harm. Children have the right to the full protection offered by the criminal law. In addition to identifying when a child may be a victim of a crime, police officers should be aware of the effect of other incidents which might pose safeguarding risks to children and where officers should pay particular attention. For example, an officer attending a domestic abuse incident should be aware of the effect of such behaviour on any children in the household. Children who are encountered as offenders, or alleged offenders, are entitled to the same safeguards and protection as any other child and due regard should be given to their welfare at all times.

The police can hold important information about children who may be suffering, or likely to suffer, significant harm, as well as those who cause such harm. They should always share this information with other organisations where this is necessary to protect children. Similarly, they can expect other organisations to share information to enable the police to carry out their duties. Offences committed against children can be particularly sensitive and usually require the police to work with other organisations such as local authority children's social care. All police forces should have officers trained in child abuse investigation.

The police have emergency powers under section 46 of the Children Act 1989 to enter premises and remove a child to ensure their immediate protection. This power can be used if the police have reasonable cause to believe a child is suffering or is likely to suffer significant harm. Police emergency powers can help in emergency situations but should be used only when necessary. Wherever possible, the decision to remove a child from a parent or carer should be made by a court.

Adult Social Care Services

Local authorities provide services to adults who are responsible for children who may be in need. These services are subject to the section 11 duties . . .

When staff are providing services to adults they should ask whether there are children in the family and consider whether the children need help or protection from harm. Children may be at greater risk of harm or be in need of additional help in families where the adults have mental health problems, misuse substances or alcohol, are in a violent relationship or have complex needs or have learning difficulties.

Adults with parental responsibilities for disabled children have a right to a separate parent carer's needs assessment under section 17ZD of the Children Act 1989. Adults that do not have parental responsibility, but are caring for a disabled child, are entitled to an assessment on their ability to provide, or to continue to provide, care for that disabled child under the Carers (Recognition and Services) Act 1995. That assessment must also consider whether the carer works or wishes to work, or whether they wish to engage in any education, training or recreation activities.

Housing authorities

Housing and homelessness services in local authorities and others at the front line such as environmental health organisations are subject to the section 11 duties.

Professionals working in these services may become aware of conditions that could have an adverse impact on children. Under Part 1 of the Housing Act 2004, authorities must take account of the impact of health and safety hazards in housing on vulnerable occupants, including children, when deciding on the action to be taken by landlords to improve conditions. Housing authorities also have an important role to play in safeguarding vulnerable young people, including young people who are pregnant or leaving care.

National Offender Management Service

Probation services

Probation services are provided by the National Probation Service (NPS) and 21 community rehabilitation companies (CRCs). The NPS and CRCs are subject to the section 11 duties. They are primarily responsible for working with adult offenders both in the community and in the transition from custody to community to reduce reoffending and improve rehabilitation.

They are, therefore, well placed to identify offenders who pose a risk of harm to children, as well as children who may be at heightened risk of involvement in (or exposure to) criminal or anti-social behaviour and of other poor outcomes due to the offending behaviour of their parent/carer(s).

Where an adult offender is assessed as presenting a risk of serious harm to children, the offender manager should develop a risk management plan and supervision plan that contains a specific objective to manage and reduce the risk of harm to children. The risk management plan should be shared with other organizations and agencies involved in the risk management.

The Prison Service

The Prison Service has a responsibility to identify prisoners who pose a risk of harm to children. Where an individual has been identified as presenting a risk of harm to children, the relevant prison establishment:

- should inform the local authority children's social care services of the offender's reception to prison, subsequent transfers, release on temporary licence and release date, and of the release address of the offender;
- should notify the relevant probation service provider of 'presenting a risk of harm to children' status. The police should also be notified of the release date and address;
- may prevent or restrict a prisoner's contact with children. Decisions on the level of contact, if any, should be based on a multi-agency risk assessment. The assessment should draw on relevant risk information held by police, the probation service provider, and the prison service. The relevant local authority children's social care should contribute to the multi-agency risk assessment by providing a report on the child's best interests. The best interests of the child will be paramount in the decision-making process.

Youth Justice Service

Youth offending teams (YOTs) are multi-agency teams responsible for the supervision of children and young people subject to pre-court interventions and statutory court disposals. They are therefore well placed to identify children known to relevant organizations as being most at risk of offending and to undertake work to prevent them offending. YOTs should have a lead officer responsible for ensuring safeguarding is at the forefront of their business.

Under s. 38 of the Crime and Disorder Act 1998, local authorities must, within the delivery of youth justice services, ensure the 'provision of persons to act as appropriate adults to safeguard the interests of children and young persons detained or questioned by police officers'.

The work of YOTs is discussed further in **chapter 10**.

UK Visa and Immigration

Section 55 of the Borders, Citizenship and Immigration Act 2009 places responsibility upon the Secretary of State to ensure that immigration, asylum, nationality, and customs functions are discharged having regard to the need to safeguard and promote the welfare of children in the UK.

Cafcass

The Children and Family Court Advisory and Support Service (Cafcass) was established in April 2001 as a non-departmental government body. Note that the National Assembly for Wales carries out the functions of Cafcass for children who are ordinarily resident in Wales.

The principal functions of Cafcass are set out in the Criminal Justice and Court Services Act 2000. These are in respect of family proceedings in which the welfare of children is or may be in question to:

- safeguard and promote the welfare of children;
- give advice to any court about an application made to it in such proceedings;
- make provision for children to be represented in such proceedings;
- provide information, advice, and other support for children and families.

Advice and assistance to the service user

The service user is likely to be facing a number of problems. You have a range of statutory duties towards the service user, but he or she may need independent advice on a range of matters which fall outside your expertise, or the advice may even be needed to challenge your department's actions. **Table 5.2** sets out a number of agencies which may be able to provide advice and assistance to vulnerable people. Whenever you recommend an advice centre you should ensure that it offers a satisfactory standard of advice.

High-street lawyers

There are a huge number of solicitors' firms available. You are unlikely to find a solicitor with the expertise the service user requires in every firm. The Law Society runs a panel of specialist child care solicitors. These are solicitors who have undertaken specialist training and have expertise in public child care cases. Their names can be found from the Law Society website, www.lawsociety.org.uk.

TABLE 5.2 Advice agencies

Name of organization	Brief description of services	Contact
Citizens Advice Bureaux (CAB)	Free impartial advice by both volunteers and professional advisers in local bureaux throughout the country. Details of local citizens advice bureaux are available from the umbrella organization, Citizens Advice. The website also provides a useful advice guide.	www.citizensadvice.org.uk

Name of organization	Brief description of services	Contact
Law Centres	Law Centres provide free and independent professional legal services to people who live and work within their catchment areas. Law Centres tend to specialize in immigration, employment law, social security, mental health, housing, and community care issues. Information on Law Centres is available from their umbrella organization, the Law Centres Federation.	www.lawcentres.org.uk
Shelter	Shelter is a national organization which campaigns for homeless and inadequately housed people. It runs a number of Housing Advice Centres, a telephone advice line, and a website. You can access these services via the website.	www.shelter.org.uk
DIAL	DIAL is a national organization for a network of 140 local disability information and advice services run by and for disabled people. The website contains useful resources for disabled people and carers, including how to find a local DIAL, fact sheets, and links to other organizations	www.dialuk.info
Independent Advice Centres	There is a very large number of independent advice centres. Information about these advice centres is available from the Federation of Independent Advice Centres.	www.adviceuk.org.uk

SUMMARY

• The Children Act 1989 reaffirms the principle that children are best looked after within their families unless it is not safe for this to happen. A local authority should only intervene when strict statutory criteria are met. When courts make decisions about the future care of children, the child's welfare is paramount. Local authorities are under a duty to safeguard and promote the welfare of children in their areas.

- It is important that social workers are constantly curious about the wishes and feelings of children on their caseloads. Increasingly, as children grow older, their informed consent to decisions being made about them should be sought.

- Local authorities should work collaboratively with parents even when compulsory intervention is necessary. Ultimately, local authorities should protect children from significant harm.

- When carrying out social work tasks with families, it is important to recognize who has parental responsibility for the child.

- Courts should always have regard to the welfare principle, the need to avoid delay in proceedings, and to making an order in respect of a child only when it is necessary to do so.

- Section 8 orders can be used by the courts to regulate arrangements and decisions about children when there are disputes particularly arising between parents.

- The arrangements for safeguarding children remain subject to change by government. The Munro Review prompted some changes, but subsequent change continues, particularly the replacement of the Health and Care Professions Council with Social Work England.

- The Children Act 2004 establishes arrangements for a range of public authorities to cooperate to safeguard children. Amendments to this Act require local authorities in England to replace Local Safeguarding Children Boards with safeguarding partners (local authorities, health services, and the police).

EXERCISES

1 Read the whole of this chapter carefully and construct a checklist for yourself of the issues you will need to consider before recommending that your department makes a court application in respect of an individual child.

2 Locate and read one of the articles listed in **Annotated further reading**. Summarize the article in 100–150 words.

3 Try to construct a time line of events following the Children Act 1989.

4 What is the relationship between the Children Act 1989 and the Children Act 2004? Do you understand the difference between 'safeguarding children' as a concept and child protection?

5 Do you think that working in partnership with parents undermines the professional skills of social workers? Is there a need for greater intervention in family life in order to protect children?

6 You are investigating an anonymous phone call which expresses concern about a particular family. The caller tells you that there is a young baby and three other children under 10 in the family. Which agencies are likely to have information about the family? What is their role in protecting children? Can you ask for assistance from them?

7 A child has been assaulted by her father. What agencies are likely to become involved as a result of the assault? What duties do they have to help with investigations into the incident?

ONLINE RESOURCES

For guidance on how to answer these exercises, visit the online resources at
www.oup.com/uk/carr-goosey15e.

WHERE DO WE GO FROM HERE?

In this chapter, we have considered a number of aspects of Part I of the Children Act 1989, in particular its philosophy, structure, overarching principles, and the principles which guide decision making by the courts. This serves as an introduction to the remaining chapters about your responsibilities to children. However, it is more than an introduction. If you understand the purposes and the principles upon which the Act is based, you are going to be in a far better position to understand your role within the Act. In addition, this chapter is to help you to understand where social services fit into the organizational framework which exists to support and protect children. It has also suggested that you should be aware of other specialist advice organizations which may help your service user. You should not see your work with service users as separate from the poverty, poor housing, and vulnerability to crime and anti-social behaviour that affect their everyday lives. If you can do something to help, even if it is only pointing them in the right direction, you will have achieved something positive for them.

Chapter 6 considers Part III of the Act, local authority responsibilities to children in need.

ANNOTATED FURTHER READING

The welfare principle

J. Herring, 'The welfare principle and the children act: presumably it's about welfare?' (2014) *Journal of Social Welfare and Family Law* 36(1): 14. This interesting article explores the presumptions applied to the welfare principle by the courts.

R. Taylor, 'Putting children first? Children's interests as a primary consideration in public law' (2016) *CFLQ* 28(1): 45. Taylor explores the breadth of the duty to put children first in judicial decision making.

S. Jivraj and D. Herman, '"It is difficult for a white judge to understand": orientalism, racialisation, and Christianity in English child welfare cases' (2009) *CFLQ* 21(3): 283. This article analyses particular cases to discover how judges understand non-Christianity when applying the welfare principles.

M. Woolf, 'Coming of age?—The principle of "the best interests of the child"' (2003) *EHRLR* 2: 205. This article contrasts the approaches of the ECtHR and the English courts in decisions about the best interests of the child.

L. Ferguson, 'Not merely rights for children but children's rights: The theory gap and the assumption of the importance of children's rights' (2013) *The International Journal of Children's Rights* 21(2): 177–208. This is a fascinating account of whether children possess *children's* rights.

Informed consent

E. Cave, 'Goodbye Gillick? Identifying and resolving problems with the concept of child competence' (2014) *Legal Studies* 34(01): 103–22. This discusses the involvement of both parents.

F. Kaganas, 'A presumption that involving both parents is best: deciphering law's messages' (2013) *CFLQ* 25(3): 270. This article suggests that the provision in the Children and Families Act which requires courts to consider the involvement of both parents is part of a 'moral crusade' to uphold the importance of particular notions of the father and his role in the family.

Safeguarding or child protection

B. Featherstone, S. White, and K. Morris, *Reimagining Child Protection: Towards Humane Social Work with Families* (Bristol: Policy Press, 2014). This influential book establishes arguments for a reform of the safeguarding system for children.

Children's rights

There is a host of information available on children's rights.

You can access a variety of websites giving you access to the text of the UN Convention on the Rights of the Child, for instance www.unicef.org/crc or the vibrant and punchy website of the Children's Rights Alliance for England www.crae.org.uk.

The Howard League for Penal Reform

You may be interested in the other work on behalf of children in custody undertaken by the Howard League for Penal Reform, which took the case against the government that formed the case study featured in this chapter. They have produced reports on girls in prison, the use of anti-social behaviour orders against children, and deaths of children in custody. Their website, www.howardleague.org, provides a range of useful information.

Safeguarding system

The Munro Review of Child Protection includes three primary reports plus a progress report. These and other helpful material can be found at www.education.gov.uk/munroreview.

The Wood Report on Local Safeguarding Children Boards is available at www.gov.uk/government/publications/wood-review-of-local-safeguarding-children-boards

6

Local authority support for children and families

OVERVIEW AND OBJECTIVES

As you read this chapter, consider the extent of the services that social services departments can offer to children in need and the way in which those services underpin the philosophy of the Children Act 1989. Also consider the limited resources available to authorities, particularly deprived urban authorities. What impact does this have on the successful operation of the Children Act 1989? What risks does it pose to the new emphasis on 'safeguarding' children? By the end of the chapter you should know the range of powers and duties available to social services departments to assist children 'in need'.

CASE STUDY

R (on the application of G) v Barnet LBC; R (on the application of W) v Lambeth LBC; R (on the application of A) v Lambeth LBC (2003)

Why are we asking you to read these cases?

In the Children Act 1989, there are duties local authorities should carry for children in need and for looked-after children. The House of Lords in the cases above set out the limits of local authority duties in respect of housing. Reading these cases will help you to understand both the local authorities' responsibilities and duties and the limits of those duties.

What is at stake for the parties and beyond?

Each of these cases involve families that were homeless trying to elicit assistance from the local authority to provide suitable housing. The local authorities were concerned to balance their need to provide accommodation in specific circumstances within the context of limited resources. Ultimately, it is for the Housing Authority to provide housing.

Facts

These three cases were heard together by the House of Lords. They concern the lack of residential accommodation suitable for the children if they were to remain within the family unit without the risk of significant harm to their welfare. The children were children in need of adequate housing.

G was a person from abroad who was a Dutch national of Somali origin. Her son was born in 1999. G left the Netherlands because of social ostracism due to her child's illegitimacy and she came to the UK to look for the child's father. She was refused income support and housing because she did not satisfy the habitual residence test. She then sought assistance from Barnet Council, as the local social services authority. The council assessed the child's needs as best served by the return of both mother and child to the Netherlands, where they would be immediately entitled to accommodation and other benefits. G applied for judicial review of the decision. It was common ground that she was suitable to look after her son and that it was not in his best interests to be removed from her care. It was also common ground that if the mother refused to return to the Netherlands, the council intended to place the child with foster parents and to provide no accommodation for the mother. The judge granted her application, the local authority appealed, and the Court of Appeal allowed its appeal.

W, the mother of two children born in 1987 and 1998, was evicted from her home in February 2001. She was found by the local housing authority (Lambeth) to be intentionally homeless because there were substantial arrears of rent. She applied immediately to the local social services authority (also Lambeth) for assistance in securing private-sector housing for herself and her two children as a family unit, but that authority declined to help her. She was able to find temporary accommodation with a niece between August 2001 and January 2002. She said that no other member of her family was able to help her to house her family.

Assessments and judicial review

At her solicitors' request, Lambeth social services carried out assessments of the needs of her children in January 2002. The assessing officer found nothing exceptional and said that the council's social services department did not provide accommodation for the families of children in need. They would place the children with extended family members as a short-term measure whilst W sought alternative accommodation, but if the need arose, the authority would make provision for the children alone. Her application for judicial review of the refusal of the local social services authority to provide assistance with accommodation was dismissed. The Court of Appeal dismissed her appeal.

In A's appeal, two of her three children were in need because they were disabled. Assessments of the needs of A's children under the Children Act 1989 indicated that the family needed to be rehoused. A sought an order compelling the local social services authority to find and provide suitable accommodation which provided for the children's assessed needs. The High Court and the Court of Appeal held that the court had no power to intervene to make such an order.

In all three cases the parents argued that the effect of s. 17 of the Children Act 1989 was that, once there had been an assessment of the needs of an individual child in need, there was a specific duty on the local social services authority to provide services to meet the child's assessed needs, and that it followed that, if the identified need was the provision of residential accommodation, the child had an absolute right to that accommodation. In G's and W's appeal, the parents contend that the effect of s. 23 of the 1989 Act, which requires a local social services authority looking after a child to make arrangements to enable him or her to live with a parent or with relatives or friends, was to put the authority under a duty to make arrangements to enable the child to live with his or her parent.

Held: general duties provided by s. 17

The House of Lords decided (by a majority) that:

- s. 17 of the Children Act 1989 set out duties of a general nature only which were not intended to be enforceable as such by individuals. The 'general duty' was owed to all the children who were in need within the area of the local social services authority and not to each child in need individually. It provided the broad aims which the local social services authority was to bear in mind when it was performing the 'other duties' set out in Part III of the 1989 Act and the 'specific duties' set out in Part I of Schedule 2 to the 1989 Act, as to which it had a discretion as to how it should meet the needs of each individual child in need.
- Although the services which the local social services authority provided could include the provision of accommodation, the provision of residential accommodation to rehouse a child in need so that he could live with his family was not the principal or primary purpose of the legislation. Housing was the function of the local housing authority.
- Section 23 of the Act did not impose an obligation on a local social services authority to provide accommodation for the parent or other persons. Section 23 was concerned with the way a local social services authority was to discharge its obligation to provide accommodation for a child whom it was looking after. It required the local social services authority to make arrangements to allow the child to live with a parent or other specified person unless that would not be reasonably practicable or consistent with his welfare. The provision assumed the parent of the child already had accommodation which the child could live in with his parent. It was concerned with placement, not housing. Accordingly, the appeals were dismissed.

WHAT DO THESE CASES TELL YOU ABOUT SOCIAL WORK PRACTICE?

The House of Lords decided that the duty under s. 17 of the Children Act to an individual child is very limited. The duty is:
  - a general duty and not a targeted, specific duty owed to an individual child;
  - intended to be for the benefit of all the children in need in the local social services authority's area in general;

- discharged by providing a range and level of services appropriate to meet the various needs of children in its area.

Even assessment of a particular child's individual needs does not transform the general duty to a specific duty owed to the child as an individual.

So, although social services departments are able to provide accommodation under s. 17, this is not the principal purpose of the legislation. In other words, while a homeless child is very likely to be a child in need and should be accommodated by social services, this does not impose a duty upon the local authority to provide accommodation for the child's family as well. The decision demonstrates the desperate plight of some families who, for one reason or another, are excluded from welfare provision. It is clear that social services departments are inevitably constrained in the support they can give to children in need because of limited resources.

Introduction

Part III of the Children Act contains a range of duties which are imposed upon local authorities. These duties are summarized in **Table 6.1**. (In Wales the Social Services and Well-being Act (Wales) 2014 replaces Part III of the Children Act 1989.)

These duties have been amplified by four important pieces of legislation: the Children (Leaving Care) Act 2000, the Care Standards Act 2000, the Children and Young Persons Act 2008, and the Children and Social Work Act 2017. The 2008 Act in particular substantially amends the provisions of Part III of the Children Act.

TABLE 6.1 The duties contained in Part III of the Children Act 1989

Section	Description
17	The general preventive duty to 'children in need'
17A and 17B	Direct payments or vouchers for services to those with parental responsibility for disabled children, to disabled people with parental responsibility, or to disabled children aged 16 and 17
18(1), (3)	Day care for some under-fives who are 'children in need'
20	Provision of accommodation for some 'children in need'
22, 22C, 22F, 23, and 24(1)	Duties to children and young persons looked after by the local authority
23ZA and 23ZB	Duties to ensure visits to and contact with looked-after children and young people
23A, 23B, 23C, 23D, 23E, and 24	Duties to some people who have been in care; persons qualifying for advice and assistance

25	Secure accommodation
25A, 25B, and 26	Independent review and complaints
Schedule 2, Part 1	Provision of services in the community
Schedule 2, Part 2	Children looked after by local authorities
Schedule 2, Part 3	Contributions towards the maintenance of children looked after by local authorities

This chapter considers:

- the general duty in s. 17 of the Children Act to safeguard and promote the welfare of children within their area who are in need;
- the range of services which may be provided for children in need;
- local authority responsibilities to 'looked-after' and accommodated children;
- duties to people who have been in care;
- complaints/representation and planning/review procedures.

It will also note the provision of secure accommodation by local authorities, the particular problems facing 'looked-after' children, and the role of the voluntary sector in supporting vulnerable families.

The renewed emphasis on improving outcomes for children in need and looked-after children should be understood in the context of the Safeguarding Children programme that we discussed in **chapter 5**. The Children and Young Persons Act 2008 imposed a general duty upon the Secretary of State to promote the well-being of children. The meaning of 'well-being' in that Act is set out in s. 10 of the Children Act 2004. In the Children and Young Persons Act 2008, there is a particular emphasis on the role of the Secretary of State improving the well-being of care leavers. The statutory duty is designed to complement the role of the local authorities set out in Part III of the Children Act. In addition, the Children and Social Work Act 2017 establishes seven corporate parenting principles which local authorities must have regard to when exercising their functions in relation to looked-after children (see **Corporate Parenting Principles**, p 218).

The scope of Part III of the Children Act

Part III is extensive and affects every area of service provision under the Children Act 1989. It ranges from providing for very basic 'one-off' support to ensuring that young people who have left care still have support available to them.

▮ The provision of local authority support

Local authority support, designed to safeguard and promote the welfare of the child in need, and enabling the child to be brought up with his or her family, is a cornerstone of the

Children Act 1989. The local authority works in partnership with the child and the child's parents. The aim is to provide positive support to avoid the need, as far as possible, for the local authority to have to seek statutory control. This is probably the most important provision in the Children Act. All families need support and whilst some, maybe even the majority, find sufficient resources in family, friends, and communities, there remain those whose access to sufficient support is limited. Recent empirical evidence in UK shows that:

> Overall a child's chances of a formal child welfare intervention is much greater at higher levels of deprivation, but for any given level of deprivation a child in a less deprived local authority is more likely to be the subject of a formal intervention. (The rates also display a social gradient, not a simple analysis of deprivation resulting in increased levels of intervention but an incremental reduction in intervention rates as the deprivation rate reduces.)

> B. Featherstone, Children and Youth Services Review (2017),
> http://dx.doi.org/10.1016/j.childyouth.2017.06.009

The Children Act 1989 recognized that support available from local authorities could provide an important resource for families. However, lack of funding and the emphasis on child protection at the expense of support has ensured that families rarely get sufficient help.

The promotion of welfare

The welfare principle imposed upon the courts requires them to treat the child's welfare as the paramount consideration. For local authorities the requirement is distinct: they must safeguard and promote the welfare of children within their area who are in need. To discharge this duty the local authority has to carry out a balancing act. There will always be a conflict between what it may want to do for an individual child and what it can do, given its resources and the demands of other children whose welfare it has to safeguard and promote. This was the problem that social services departments faced in the case study at the beginning of the chapter.

Section 17

Section 17(1) of the Children Act sets out the general preventive duty which local authorities owe to 'children in need' in their area. We reproduce s. 17(1) in **Box 6.1**.

 BOX 6.1 The general duty on local authorities—s. 17(1) of the Children Act 1989

(3) It shall be the general duty of every local authority (in addition to the other duties imposed on them by this Part)—

(a) to safeguard and promote the welfare of children within their area who are in need; and

(b) so far as is consistent with that duty, to promote the upbringing of such children by their families by providing a range and level of services appropriate to those children's needs.

'Children in need'

The local authority's duty to safeguard and promote the welfare of a child extends only to those children who are 'in need'. Being in need is therefore a necessity if a child is going to benefit from the general duty.

Who are 'children in need'?

The latest Children in Need census indicates that there were 389,430 children in need at 31 March 2017 in England, which was a rate of 330.4 per 10,000 children. This overall rate hides a huge range across different local authorities. The rate throughout the year 2016/17 in Wokingham was 175.4 children in need per 10,000 children, in contrast to 831.2 children in need per 10,000 children in the Isles of Scilly.

Abuse and neglect are the biggest single reason for services and account for 49.4 per cent of all children served.

For a definition of a child in need we have to look at s. 17(10), which we set out in **Box 6.2**.

 BOX 6.2 Children in need—s. 17(10) and (11) of the Children Act 1989

(10)   For the purposes of this Part a child shall be taken to be in need if—

    (a)   he is unlikely to achieve or maintain, or to have the opportunity of achieving or maintaining, a reasonable standard of health or development without the provision for him of services by a local authority under this Part;

    (b)   his health or development is likely to be significantly impaired, or further impaired, without the provision for him of such services; or

    (c)   he is disabled, and 'family', in relation to such a child, includes any person who has parental responsibility for the child and any other person with whom he has been living.

(11)   For the purposes of this Part, a child is disabled if he is blind, deaf or dumb or suffers from mental disorder of any kind or is substantially and permanently handicapped by illness, injury or congenital deformity or such other disability as may be prescribed; and in this Part— 'development' means physical, intellectual, emotional, social or behavioural development; and 'health' means physical or mental health.

The majority of children and young people with whom the local authority is going to come into contact will fall within the definition of 'children in need'. The definition is broad to emphasize the preventive element of the local authority's role. There are three different elements of the definition:

(a) reasonable standard of health or development;

(b) significant impairment of health or development;

(c) disability.

The local authority must consider the provision of services for those who fall within any of the headings. It is the local authority that makes the decision as to whether or not a particular child is in need *(Re J (Specific Issue Order: Leave to Apply)* (1995)). In a more recent Supreme Court judgment, Lady Hale commented:

> where the issue is not, what order should the court make, but what service should the local authority provide, it is entirely reasonable to assume that Parliament intended such evaluative questions to be determined by the public authority, subject to the control of the courts on the ordinary principles of judicial review. Within the limits of fair process and 'Wednesbury reasonableness' there are no clear-cut right or wrong answers.
>
> (A v *London Borough of Croydon; M v London Borough of Lambeth* (2009), para. 26)

▨ Families with no recourse to public funds

Families can be excluded from children's services support if they are in one of the following five categories:

- European Economic Area (EEA) nationals who are not British citizens;
- people unlawfully present in the UK (including: visa overstayers, illegal entrants, and refused asylum seekers who claimed asylum in-country, rather than at port of entry);
- people with refugee status that has been granted by another EEA country;
- refused asylum seekers who have failed to comply with removal directions;
- refused asylum-seeking families that the Home Office has issued with certification confirming that they have failed to take steps to leave the UK voluntarily.

Any child who falls within one of these categories or is a dependent of someone who does may not receive support from the local authority unless they have a human rights application pending or are otherwise prevented from travelling back to their country of origin.

An infamous case for local authorities involved a family who had no recourse to public funds but did have an outstanding application for leave to remain. The Court of Appeal found in the family's favour. Dyson, LJ indicated the way forward when he said:

> The first question that Birmingham should have considered was whether the claimant and her family were destitute. If they were satisfied that they were destitute, it follows . . . that, upon learning that the claimant had made an application for indefinite leave to remain on grounds which expressly or implicitly raised article 8 of the Convention, they should then have considered whether the application was abusive or hopeless. If they considered that the application was not abusive or hopeless, they should not have refused assistance pending the determination of the application.
>
> (*Clue v Birmingham City Council* (2010))

More recently in *KA v Essex County Council* (2013), a Nigerian mother and her children were resident unlawfully in the UK and had had three applications for leave to remain turned down. They were living with a relative but had to leave. The local authority eventually supported the family with accommodation but following two assessments—a needs assessment of the children and a human rights assessment—the authority decided that the children would not be in need if they returned to Nigeria. In this instance, the mother refused to leave voluntarily, but the authority withdrew its support. This left the family with no right of appeal since removal directions had not been forthcoming. The Deputy High Court Judge, Robin Purchas QC concluded:

> Where on the facts of the case it is demonstrated that a person has a substantive convention claim, for example to a family or private life in this country, that would found an appeal against removal directions if made, a decision that effectively deprived the person of that protection would in my judgment be in breach of his convention procedural right.
>
> In my judgment, the proper approach on the facts of this case, should have been to provide support as far as necessary to preserve the procedural right to protection of the Claimant's and her family's article 8 rights unless the Defendant concluded that it was in effect obviously hopeless or abusive.

The No Recourse to Public Funds network of local authorities and partner organisations provides a useful website at www.nrpfnetwork.org.uk.

'Looked after'

This term is not actually defined specifically in the Children Act 1989. To become 'looked after', the child first has to be in need. In addition, to be looked after the child has either to be the subject of a care order or be supplied with accommodation by the local authority (including when remanded by a court to local authority accommodation or youth detention accommodation). This is explained in s. 22, set out in **Box 6.3**. The 'looked-after' child has access to the range of services the local authority provides for children in need. It is important to note that once a child is looked after, the child becomes subject to the Care Planning, Placement and Case Review (England) Regulations 2010. You are advised to also consider the *Children Act 1989 Guidance and Regulations, Volume 2: Care Planning, Placement and Case Review*. We discuss this and the responsibilities of local authorities to accommodate children more fully later in the chapter (**Local authority accommodation**, p 226). Looked-after children may be in more serious need than children in need living with their families.

 BOX 6.3 The general duty of the local authority in relation to children looked after by it—s. 22 of the Children Act 1989

(1) In this Act, any reference to a child who is looked after by a local authority is a reference to a child who is—

   (a) in their care; or

   (b) provided with accommodation by the authority in the exercise of any functions (in particular those under this Act) which are social services functions within the meaning of the Local Authority Social Services Act 1970 apart from functions under sections 17, 23B and 24B.

(2) In subsection (1) 'accommodation' means accommodation which is provided for a continuous period of more than 24 hours.

(3) It shall be the duty of a local authority looking after any child—

    (a) to safeguard and promote his welfare; and

    (b) to make such use of services available for children cared for by their own parents as appears to the authority reasonable in his case.

(3A) The duty of a local authority under subsection (3)(a) to safeguard and promote the welfare of a child looked after by them includes in particular a duty to promote the child's educational achievement.

Section 34 of the Children Act 1989 also places a duty on the local authority to allow contact (see **Box 6.4**).

BOX 6.4 The duty of the local authority to allow contact—s. 34 of the Children Act 1989

(1) Where a child is in the care of a local authority, the authority shall (subject to the provisions of this section and their duty under section 22(3)(a)) allow the child reasonable contact with—

    (a) his parents;

    (b) any guardian or special guardian of his;

    (ba) any person who by virtue of section 4A has parental responsibility for him;

    (c) where there was a residence order in force with respect to the child immediately before the care order was made, the person in whose favour the order was made; and

    (d) where, immediately before the care order was made, a person had care of the child by virtue of an order made in the exercise of the High Court's inherent jurisdiction with respect to children, that person.

Note: 'care' in subsection (1) means that the local authority has a court order for that particular child.

Corporate parenting principles

The Children and Social Work Act 2017 establishes seven key needs that local authorities must have regard to when they exercise their functions in respect of looked after children or care leavers, set out in **Box 6.5**:

BOX 6.5 Seven key needs in respect of looked-after children or care leavers—Children and Social Work Act (2017)

(a) to act in the best interests, and promote the physical and mental health and well-being, of those children and young people;

(b) to encourage those children and young people to express their views, wishes and feelings;

(c) to take into account the views, wishes and feelings of those children and young people;

(d) to help those children and young people gain access to, and make the best use of, services provided by the local authority and its relevant partners;

(e) to promote high aspirations, and seek to secure the best outcomes, for those children and young people;

(f) for those children and young people to be safe, and for stability in their home lives, relationships and education or work;

(g) to prepare those children and young people for adulthood and independent living.

It is too early to tell whether these principles will make a difference to the lives of children looked after by local authorities or those having left care. Most of these duties are set out elsewhere in legislation. Enforcing these duties will not be easy unless a child or young person has easy access to the court system. However, independent reviewing officers may find these principles useful when advocating for the young people for whom they have responsibility.

Services for a child in need

Once it is established that a child is in need, the local authority has the power to provide the appropriate services. Section 17(4A) (inserted by the Children Act 2004) requires the local authority to ascertain and take appropriate account of the child's wishes regarding the provision of services.

Services may be supplied direct to the child or to other members of the child's family (s. 17(3)). 'Family' is defined broadly (in s. 17(10)) so that it encompasses any family grouping you are likely to encounter. It is acceptable to target the services on someone other than the child, provided that this is done with the aim of promoting and safeguarding the welfare of the particular child in need. So, if a mother was finding it difficult to cope with a child because she also had the responsibility of looking after an elderly parent, it would be possible to use the budget for the provision of services to children under s. 17 to provide the elderly parent with day-care facilities, so as to enable the child's mother better to look after the child. However, a direct link needs to be made with the care of the children.

Cash help

The services can, if necessary, be provided by means of cash assistance, as s. 17(6)–(9) of the Children Act 1989, set out in **Box 6.6**, shows.

 BOX 6.6 Assistance in kind or in cash—s. 17(6)–(9) of the Children Act 1989

(6) The services provided by a local authority in the exercise of functions conferred on them by this section may include providing accommodation and giving assistance in kind or in cash.

(7) Assistance may be unconditional or subject to conditions as to the repayment of the assistance or of its value (in whole or in part).

(8) Before giving any assistance or imposing any conditions, a local authority shall have regard to the means of the child concerned and of each of his parents.

(9) No person shall be liable to make any repayment of assistance or of its value at any time when he is in receipt of income support under Part VII of the Social Security Contributions and Benefits Act 1992 of any element of child tax credit other than the family element, of working tax credit of an income-based jobseeker's allowance or of an income-related employment and support allowance.

These important powers mean that if the need can be met by cash, then there is nothing to stop the local authority giving cash. The local authority is entitled to take into account the resources of the child and the family before providing assistance. The majority of people who receive cash are likely to be in receipt of family credit or income support and therefore will not have to repay the money received.

Accommodation

Section 17 powers include the provision of accommodation—this power was made explicit by the insertion of a new phrase into subsection (6) of s. 17, which came into effect in November 2002. It is important to stress that s. 17(6) provides the local authority with the *power to provide* accommodation and not a duty to do so. However, local authorities should be wary of sidestepping their responsibilities. In *G v London Borough of Southwark* (2009), henceforth known as the Southwark judgment, the local authority suggested that G's needs could be met under the Housing Act 1996. The authority tried to suggest that he required *help with accommodation* rather than the *provision of accommodation*. Baroness Hale's lead opinion in this judgment was more than clear:

Under the Homelessness (Priority Need for Accommodation) (England) Order 2002 (SI 2002/2051), article 3, however, children aged 16 and 17 were expressly included in the list. So there was now a real possibility that they might be owed duties under the homelessness legislation. But two groups of children are excluded from those in priority need under article 3: those to whom a children's authority owe a duty under section 20 and 'relevant' children who have previously been looked after by a local authority (see para 6). As was said in the Hammersmith and Fulham case (R (M) v Hammersmith and Fulham London Borough Council [2008] UKHL 14), at para 31:

Such a young person has needs over and above the simple need for a roof over her head and these can better be met by social services. Unless the problem is relatively short-term, she will then become an eligible child, and social services accommodation will also bring with it the additional responsibilities to help and support her in the transition to independent adult living. It was not intended that social services should be able to avoid those responsibilities by looking to the housing authority to accommodate the child.

Direct payments

Sections 17A and 17B of the Act allow local authorities to make direct payments to persons with parental responsibility for a disabled child or provide vouchers instead of services which would otherwise have been provided for them by the local authorities. This increases the flexibility, for instance, in making arrangements for a carer's short-term break.

Specific duties

In addition to the general duty in s. 17 of the Children Act 1989, Part I of Schedule 2 to the Act contains a number of specific duties to provide services for the families of children in need. Part I of Schedule 2 is set out in **Box 6.7.**

BOX 6.7 Specific duties towards families of children in need—Schedule 2, Part I of the Children Act 1989

1. *Identification of children in need and provision of information*

    (1) Every local authority shall take reasonable steps to identify the extent to which there are children in need within their area.

    (2) Every local authority shall—

       (a) publish information—

         (i) about services provided by them under sections 17, 18, 20, 23B to D, 24A and B and

         (ii) where they consider it appropriate, about the provision by others (including, in particular, voluntary organisations) of services which the authority has power to provide under those sections; and

       (b) take such steps as are reasonably practicable to ensure that those who might benefit from the services receive the information relevant to them.

2. *Maintenance of a register of disabled children*

    (1) Every local authority shall open and maintain a register of disabled children within their area.

    (2) The register may be kept by means of a computer.

3. Assessment of children's needs

    Where it appears to a local authority that a child within their area is in need, the authority may assess his needs for the purposes of this Act at the same time as any assessment of his needs is made under—

    (a) the Chronically Sick and Disabled Persons Act 1970;

    (b) Part IV of the Education Act 1996;

       (ba) Part 3 of the Children and Families Act 2014

    (c) the Disabled Persons (Services, Consultation and Representation) Act 1986; or

    (d) any other enactment.

4. Prevention of neglect and abuse

(1) Every local authority shall take reasonable steps, through the provision of services under Part 3 of this Act, to prevent children within their area suffering ill treatment or neglect.

(2) Where a local authority believes that a child who is at any time within their area—

    (a) is likely to suffer harm; but

    (b) lives or proposes to live in the area of another local authority they shall inform that other local authority.

(3) When informing that other local authority they shall specify—

    (a) the harm that they believe he is likely to suffer; and

    (b) (if they can) where the child lives or proposes to live.

5. *Provision of accommodation [to the suspected abuser] in order to protect child*

(1) Where—

    (a) it appears to a local authority that a child who is living on particular premises is suffering, or is likely to suffer, ill treatment at the hands of another person who is living on those premises; and

    (b) that other person proposes to move from the premises; the authority may assist that other person to obtain alternative accommodation.

(2) Assistance given under this paragraph may be in cash.

6. *Provision for 'disabled' children*

(1) Every local authority shall provide services designed—

    (a) to minimise the effect on disabled children within their area of their disabilities;

    (b) to give such children the opportunity to lead lives which are as normal as possible; and

    (c) to assist individuals who provide care for such children to do so, or to do so more effectively, by giving them breaks from caring.

(2) The duty imposed by sub-paragraph (1)(c) shall be performed in accordance with regulations made by the Secretary of State.

7. *Provision to reduce need for care proceedings etc.* [This paragraph was considered in the previous chapter as the diminishment of court proceedings principle.]

8. *Provision for children living with their families*

(1) Every local authority shall make provision for such services as they consider appropriate to be available with respect to accommodated children.

(2) 'Accommodated children' are those children in respect of whose accommodation the local authority have been notified under section 85 or 86 or under section 120 of the Social Services and Well-being (Wales) Act 2014 (assessment of children accommodated by health authorities and education authorities).

(3) The services shall be provided with a view to promoting contact between each accommodated child and that child's family.

(4) The services may, in particular, include—

    (a) advice, guidance and counselling;

    (b) services necessary to enable the child to visit, or to be visited by, members of the family;

> (c)   assistance to enable the child and members of the family to have a holiday together.
>
> (5) Nothing in this paragraph affects the duty imposed by paragraph 10.
>
> 9.   *Family centres*
>
>   (1) Every local authority shall provide such family centres as they consider appropriate in relation to children within their area.
>
>   (2) 'Family centre' means a centre at which any of the persons mentioned in subparagraph (3) may—
>
>   (a)   attend for occupational, social, cultural or recreational activities;
>
>   (b)   attend for advice, guidance or counselling; or
>
>   (c)   be provided with accommodation while he is receiving advice, guidance or counselling.
>
>   (3) The persons are:
>
>   (a)   a child;
>
>   (b)   his parents;
>
>   (c)   any person who is not a parent of his but who has parental responsibility for him;
>
>   (d)   any other person who is looking after him.
>
> 10. *Maintenance of the family home*
>
>   Every local authority shall take such steps as are reasonably practicable, where any child within their area who is in need and whom they are not looking after is living apart from his family—
>
>   (a)   to enable him to live with his family; or
>
>   (b)   to promote contact between him and his family,
>
>   (c)   if, in their opinion, it is necessary to do so in order to safeguard or promote his welfare.
>
> 11. *Duty to consider racial groups to which children in need belong*
>
>   Every local authority shall, in making any arrangements—
>
>   (a)   for the provision of day care within their area; or
>
>   (b)   designed to encourage persons to act as local authority foster parents, have regard to the different racial groups to which children within their area who are in need belong.

Publicity

Paragraph 1 of the schedule requires the local authority to give publicity to services that the Act requires it to provide and also to services provided by voluntary groups.

The information must be published, and steps taken to ensure that it reaches the people who need it.

Prevention of neglect and abuse

Paragraph 4 of Schedule 2 focuses on the prevention of abuse and neglect. The appearance of the words 'reasonable steps' diminishes somewhat the duty set out in para. 4. The steps that may be taken are to prevent 'ill treatment or neglect'. This is a lower standard than the 'significant harm' test in s. 31 of the Act and therefore enables help to be given at an earlier stage. Neglect is not defined in the Act and therefore has to be given its normal meaning. Ill-treatment includes sexual abuse and forms of ill-treatment which are not physical: Children Act 1989, s. 31(9).

Accommodation of abusers away from the family home

Paragraph 5 gives a power to the children's services department to help a suspected abuser to find accommodation and pay for it. The limit in the power is that there can be no compulsion applied to the man (statistically, it is usually the man). This power is in addition to the power of a court to exclude a suspected abuser when making either an emergency protection order or an interim care order.

Breaks from caring for disabled children

Section 25 of the Children and Young Persons Act 2008 amends para. 6 of Schedule 2 to the 1989 Act (provision for disabled children) to impose a duty on local authorities to provide, as part of the range of services they provide for families, breaks from caring to assist parents and others who provide care for disabled children to enable them to continue to do so, or to do so more effectively. The intention is that breaks should not only be provided to those struggling to care for disabled children, but also to those for whom a break from their caring responsibilities will improve the quality of the care they provide. Local authorities must provide such services in accordance with regulations made by the appropriate national authority (see Chapter 6 of the *Children Act 1989 Guidance and Regulations, Volume 2: Care Planning, Placement and Case Review*). **Box 6.8** sets out the current regulations.

BOX 6.8 The Breaks for Carers of Disabled Children Regulations 2011

3. **Duty to make provision**

    In performing their duty under paragraph 6(1)(c) of Schedule 2 to the 1989 Act, a local authority must—

    (a) have regard to the needs of those carers who would be unable to continue to provide care unless breaks from caring were given to them; and

    (b) have regard to the needs of those carers who would be able to provide care for their disabled child more effectively if breaks from caring were given to them to allow them to—

        (i)   undertake education, training or any regular leisure activity,

        (ii) meet the needs of other children in the family more effectively, or

        (iii) carry out day to day tasks which they must perform in order to run their household.

4. **Types of services which must be provided**

    (1) In performing their duty under paragraph 6(1)(c) of Schedule 2 to the 1989 Act, a local authority must provide, so far as is reasonably practicable, a range of services which is sufficient to assist carers to continue to provide care or to do so more effectively.

(2) In particular, the local authority must provide, as appropriate, a range of—

    (a) day-time care in the homes of disabled children or elsewhere,

    (b) overnight care in the homes of disabled children or elsewhere,

    (c) educational or leisure activities for disabled children outside their homes, and

    (d) services available to assist carers in the evenings, at weekends and during the school holidays.

5. **Short breaks services statement**

(1) A local authority must, by 1st October 2011, prepare a statement for carers in their area (a 'short breaks services statement') setting out details of—

    (a) the range of services provided in accordance with regulation 4,

    (b) any criteria by which eligibility for those services will be assessed, and

    (c) how the range of services is designed to meet the needs of carers in their area.

(2) The local authority must publish their short breaks services statement, including by placing a copy of the statement on their website.

(3) The local authority must keep their short breaks services statement under review and, where appropriate, revise the statement.

(4) In preparing and revising their statement, the local authority must have regard to the views of carers in their area.

Support for children living with their families

Paragraph 8 requires the local authority, in accordance with the philosophy of the Children Act 1989, to support the child who is living with his or her family. The schedule provides a wide range of provisions that the local authority should consider.

Family centres

Paragraph 9 clearly states that the assistance of a family centre can be given to someone other than a particular child. This, again, is on the basis that the overall aim must be to safeguard and promote the welfare of a particular child.

Again, we see the philosophy spelt out, requiring the local authority to take steps to enable children they are not looking after to live with or to have contact with their families.

Housing

The responsibility upon the local authority implies the need to ensure that the family is kept together, although clearly it cannot take on an open-ended commitment to pay the rent and arrears. Ultimately, it may be that the authority might have to seek care orders to house the children, although this is also highly unlikely. This is because the statutory duty is to the individual children rather than to the family as a whole.

Diversity

This is a requirement for the local authority to take account of race and ethnicity in the provision of day care and recruiting foster parents. Where a local authority is 'looking after' a child, there is a requirement before making any decisions in respect of that child to give due consideration to the child's religious persuasion, racial origin, and cultural and linguistic background (Children Act 1989, s. 22(5)(c)). **Box 6.8** sets out the relevant provisions of Schedule 2.

Other sources of support

Voluntary-sector organizations

The Act recognizes, in s. 17(5) set out in **Box 6.9**, that the voluntary sector has a critical role in providing services for children in need.

There are hundreds of voluntary-sector projects working to support children and their families in a multiplicity of settings.

 BOX 6.9 The role of the voluntary sector—s. 17(5) of the Children Act 1989

Every local authority—

(a) shall facilitate the provision by others (including in particular voluntary organisations) of services which it is a function of the authority to provide by virtue of this section, or section 18, 20, 22A to 22C, 23B to 23D, 24A or 24B; and

(b) may make such arrangements as they see fit for any person to act on their behalf in the provision of any such services.

Local authority accommodation

Accommodation

The local authority may consider that the only way to safeguard and promote the welfare of a child is through the provision of accommodation. Accommodation is defined in s. 22(2) of the 1989 Act as meaning accommodation which is provided for a continuous period of more than 24 hours.

The status of accommodated children

If a local authority is providing accommodation for a child, the local authority is 'looking after' the child. 'Looked-after' children are defined in s. 22(1) of the Children Act 1989, which is set out in **Box 6.10**. The section makes it clear that 'looking after' covers both children subject to court orders and those who are not. The provision of accommodation does not in itself mean that the child is in 'care', it does not affect the parental responsibilities of any person, or give the local authority parental responsibility. It is only if the local authority has a court order that it has any control over the child. A child subject to a care order will automatically be looked after by an authority and provided with accommodation.

BOX 6.10 Looked-after children—s. 22(1) of the Children Act 1989

In this Act, any reference to a child who is looked after by a local authority is a reference to a child who is—

(a) in their care; or

(b) provided with accommodation by the authority in the exercise of any functions (in particular those under this Act) which are social services functions with the meaning of the Local Authority Social Services Act 1970 apart from functions under sections 17, 23B and 24B.

The exclusion of accommodation provided under ss 17, 23B, and 24B from the definition of looked-after children removes such children from the obligations placed upon local authorities under the Children Act 1989 (**Box 6.11**) and the Children (Leaving Care) Act 2000 (see **Box 6.16**).

BOX 6.11 The duty of local authorities towards looked-after children—s. 22(3)–(5) of the Children Act 1989

(3) It shall be the duty of a local authority looking after any child—

    (a) to safeguard and promote his welfare; and

    (b) to make such use of services available for children cared for by their own parents as appears to the authority reasonable in his case.

(3A) The duty of a local authority under subsection (3)(a) to safeguard and promote the welfare of a child looked after by them includes in particular a duty to promote the child's educational achievement.

(3B) A local authority must appoint at least one person for the purpose of discharging the duty imposed by virtue of subsection (3A).

(3C) A person appointed by a local authority under subsection (3B) must be an officer employed by that authority or another local authority

(4) Before making any decision with respect to a child whom they are looking after, or proposing to look after, a local authority shall, so far as is reasonably practicable, ascertain the wishes and feelings of—

    (a) the child;

    (b) his parents;

    (c) any person who is not a parent of his but who has parental responsibility for him; and

    (d) any other person whose wishes and feelings the authority consider to be relevant, regarding the matter to be decided.

(5) In making any such decision a local authority shall give due consideration—

> (a) having regard to his age and understanding, to such wishes and feelings of the child as they have been able to ascertain;
>
> (b) to such wishes and feelings of any person mentioned in subsection (4)(b) to (d) as they have been able to ascertain; and
>
> (c) to the child's religious persuasion, racial origin and cultural and linguistic background.

The local authority duty towards looked-after children

This duty is provided for in s. 22(3)–(5) of the Children Act 1989, which we have set out for you in **Box 6.11**. Notice the responsibilities upon local authorities to take into account the wishes of the child, his or her parents, and other people who are important to the child. The authority is also obliged to take into account the child's religious and cultural needs.

The power to provide accommodation

The local authority also has power to provide accommodation for a child even though there is someone who is willing and able to provide accommodation, if the local authority considers that the provision of accommodation would promote the child's welfare (s. 20(4)). This power may well be used to protect a child by removing the child from an unsatisfactory home setting. However, the provision of accommodation for a child under the age of 16 under this section is subject to parental consent (s. 20(7)). Without that consent no accommodation can be provided. If a child has been provided with accommodation and parental cooperation is withdrawn then, if you are seeking to protect the child, you should consider applying for an emergency protection order or care order. Recent case law demonstrates just how far social work practice has strayed from this principle. In *Re CA (A Baby) (Coventry City Council v C) (2012), Medway v MT (By her Children's Guardian) (2014), Re A (A Child) (2015), Darlington Borough Council v M (2015),* and *Northamptonshire County Council v S* [2015] EWHC 199 (Fam), the courts have criticized local authorities for ignoring the rights of parents. The Medway case is illustrative of the case law in this context. The judge commented on the 'remarkable extent of T [the child]'s unlawful accommodation by Medway Council and its additional ancillary failings'. Parental consent for s. 20 accommodation should follow principles which were set out by Hedley J in the Coventry case and added to by the President of the Family Division in *Re N (Children) (Adoption: Jurisdiction)* (2015), set out in **Box 6.12**:

BOX 6.12 *Re N (Children) (Adoption: Jurisdiction)* **(2015)**

i) Every parent has the right, if capacitous, to exercise their parental responsibility to consent under Section 20 to have their child accommodated by the local authority and every local authority has power under Section 20(4) so to accommodate provided that it is consistent with the welfare of the child.

ii) Every social worker obtaining such a consent is under a personal duty (the outcome of which may not be dictated to them by others) to be satisfied that the person giving the consent does not lack the capacity to do so.

iii) In taking any such consent the social worker must actively address the issue of capacity and take into account all the circumstances prevailing at the time and consider the questions raised by Section 3 of the 2005 Mental Capacity Act, and in particular the mother's capacity at that time to use and weigh all the relevant information.

iv) If the social worker has doubts about capacity no further attempt should be made to obtain consent on that occasion and advice should be sought from the social work team leader or management.

v) If the social worker is satisfied that the person whose consent is sought does not lack capacity, the social worker must be satisfied that the consent is fully informed:

  a)   Does the parent fully understand the consequences of giving such a consent?

  b)   Does the parent fully appreciate the range of choice available and the consequences of refusal as well as giving consent?

  c)   Is the parent in possession of all the facts and issues material to the giving of consent?

vi) If not satisfied that the answers to a)—c) above are all 'yes', no further attempt should be made to obtain consent on that occasion and advice should be sought as above and the social work team should further consider taking legal advice if thought necessary.

vii) If the social worker is satisfied that the consent is fully informed then it is necessary to be further satisfied that the giving of such consent and the subsequent removal is both fair and proportionate.

viii) In considering that it may be necessary to ask:

  a)   What is the current physical and psychological state of the parent?

  b)   If they have a solicitor, have they been encouraged to seek legal advice and/or advice from family or friends?

  c)   Is it necessary for the safety of the child for her to be removed at this time?

  d)   Would it be fairer in this case for this matter to be the subject of a court order rather than an agreement?

ix) If having done all this and, if necessary, having taken further advice (as above and including where necessary legal advice), the social worker then considers that a fully informed consent has been received from a capacitous mother in circumstances where removal is necessary and proportionate, consent may be acted upon.

x)   In the light of the foregoing, local authorities may want to approach with great care the obtaining of Section 20 agreements from mothers in the aftermath of birth, especially where there is no immediate danger to the child and where probably no order would be made.

xi) Wherever possible the agreement of a parent to the accommodation of their child under section 20 should be properly recorded in writing and evidenced by the parent's signature.

xii) The written document should be clear and precise as to its terms, drafted in simple and straight-forward language that the particular parent can readily understand.

xiii) The written document should spell out, following the language of section 20(8), that the parent can 'remove the child' from the local authority accommodation 'at any time'.

xiv) The written document should not seek to impose any fetters on the exercise of the parent's right under section 20(8).

xv) Where the parent is not fluent in English, the written document should be translated into the parent's own language and the parent should sign the foreign language text, adding, in the parent's language, words to the effect that 'I have read this document and I agree to its terms.'

More recently the Supreme Court has dismissed an appeal by parents in respect of the use of s. 20 and in doing so has both clarified the law and possibly muddied it at the same time. In *Williams (and another) v London Borough of Hackney* [2018] UKSC 37, Baroness Hale's leading judgment included nine points of guidance, as set out in **Box 6.13**:

BOX 6.13 *Williams (and another) v London Borough of Hackney* [2018] UKSC 37

a. In respect of parental responsibility (PR); a person with PR may arrange for some or all of his or her PR to be met by others acting on his or her behalf, but helpless submission in the face of asserted power does not amount to a delegation of PR or its exercise.

b. It may be confusing to talk about consent to removal or accommodation—doing so is simply delegating the exercise of PR for the time-being to the local authority. Any such delegation must be 'real and voluntary'.

c. Removing a child from the care of a parent is very different from stepping into the breach where a parent is not looking after a child; in the latter circumstances the active consent or delegation of PR is not required, but powers exercised in such circumstances are subject to the parents' right to object or to remove the child. In such cases, as a matter of good practice, local authorities should give parents clear information about what they have done and what the parents' rights are and the whereabouts of the child.

d. Parents may ask a local authority to accommodate their child and the local authority may have a power or even a duty to do so depending on the circumstances—this is a further example of the delegation of PR and again, as a matter of good practice, parents should be given clear information about their rights and the local authority's responsibilities.

e. The authority cannot accommodate a child if a parent with parental responsibility who is willing and able either to accommodate the child herself or to arrange for someone else to do so objects to the local authority doing so. It says nothing about the suitability of the parent or of the accommodation which the parent wishes to arrange.

f. It is absolutely clear that a parent with parental responsibility may remove the child from accommodation provided or arranged by a local authority at any time. There is no need to give notice, in writing or otherwise. The only caveat, is the right of anyone to take necessary steps to protect a person, including a child, from being physically harmed by another.

g. The right to object or to request return are qualified where court orders have been made determining where a child should live (s.20(9) and (10)) but are otherwise unrestricted.

h. There are separate provisions for children who have reached the age of sixteen (see s. 20(3), (4), (5) and (11)).

i. There is no time limit to s. 20 accommodation; however local authorities have duties to children whom they are accommodating under the Children Act 1989 and various regulations as well as a duty to act reasonably in general public law terms and to respect the child's and parents' rights under the ECHR.

Baroness Hale's observation that inserting a consent requirement into s. 20 when those words do not appear in the Children Act was inappropriate. Instead, she preferred the term 'real and voluntary delegation of parental responsibility'. It should be noted that those words do not appear in the Act, either. Nonetheless, real and voluntary delegation is what is required. Delegating parental responsibility is possibly what some parents intend when a child is accommodated by a local authority, although it is also possible that, for other parents, they simply require, perhaps on a short-term basis, for their child to be provided with accommodation and that delegating parental responsibility is a step too far.

A service for families

Section 20 makes it quite clear that the provision of accommodation without a care order is only provided on a 'service' basis. This is spelled out in s. 20(7) and (8), set out in **Box 6.14.**

 BOX 6.14 Provision of accommodation without a care order—s. 20(7) and (8) of the Children Act 1989

(7) A local authority may not provide accommodation under this section for any child if any person who—

  (a) has parental responsibility for him;

  (b) is willing and able to—

    (i) provide accommodation for him; or

    (ii) arrange for accommodation to be provided for him,objects.

(8) Any person who has parental responsibility for a child may at any time remove the child from accommodation provided by or on behalf of the local authority under this section.

A young person in accommodation

A young person of 16 or over is in control of whether or not he or she receives or stays in accommodation. This is because of s. 20(11):

(11) Subsections (7) and (8) [power of parents to refuse accommodation and to remove the child] do not apply where a child who has reached the age of sixteen agrees to being provided with accommodation under this section.

Accordingly, the parents may disagree about the future of the young person, but the choice is always that of the young person.

Disputes between parents

If one parent has a child arrangements order regulating where a child should live, the other parent cannot remove the child from accommodation without first successfully applying to the court for an order in their favour. If neither parent has a child arrangements order and both parents have parental responsibility, then either parent could remove the child, as stated in s. 20(8). This could mean that one parent places the child into accommodation and the other parent removes the child from that accommodation. This would be a good example of where the parent who wants the child to stay in the accommodation should apply to the court for a prohibited steps order under s. 8. Remember that s. 8 orders, other than a child arrangements order, cannot be made where the child is subject to a care order.

No child arrangements orders

Where there is no child arrangements order settling where a child should live, then there can be management difficulties. If during the breakdown of a marriage the mother were to place a child under the age of 16 into local authority-provided accommodation, what is to stop the father removing the child? The simple answer is nothing. The Act is quite clear that if a parent objects to the provision of accommodation, or seeks, at any time, to remove the child, *then the local authority cannot prevent it.*

The only guidance in this situation is to look to s. 3(5) of the Children Act 1989, which states that a person without parental responsibility but who has care of the child may, subject to the Act, do what is reasonable in all the circumstances of the case for the purpose of safeguarding or promoting the welfare of the child. The local authority is covered by this section, not having parental responsibility, and it has to do all it can to safeguard and promote the welfare of the child. Unfortunately, this does not give clear guidance as to what to do when the drunken father turns up at 2 a.m. It cannot be promoting the welfare of the child to allow the child to go with the father. In the *Williams* case above, Baroness Hale reminds us of the provision in s. 3(5) authorizing those caring for the child to do what is reasonable in all the circumstances to protect the child. What will be required here are negotiating skills. If these fail, then an application for an emergency protection order would have to be made, or a request should be made to the police to take the child into police protection (see **chapter 8**).

The supply of accommodation

The Children and Young People Act 2008 has substantially revised the system for provision of accommodation for children and young people. Section 8 of the Children and Young People Act 2008 replaces s. 23 of the Children Act with new ss 22A–22F. We will consider the planning and review obligations in **chapter 9**.

Section 22A re-enacts the duty on local authorities to provide accommodation for children who are in their care, and s. 22B re-enacts the duty to maintain all looked-after children other than providing for their accommodation. The duties and powers of local authorities to provide accommodation for children under ss 20 and 21 of the 1989 Act (i.e. those who are 'voluntarily accommodated' or accommodated for their own protection or by virtue of an order made in criminal proceedings) are unaffected by the changes.

Section 22C outlines the ways in which the local authority must perform its accommodation functions.

Placements with parents and others with parental responsibility

The local authority must make arrangements for a child they are looking after to live with their parents; any other person who has parental responsibility for the child; or, in the case of a child who is the subject of a care order (i.e. who is 'in care'), a person with whom a child lived under a child arrangements order immediately before the care order was made. This duty applies only where it is consistent with the child's welfare to do so and reasonably practicable. If the local authority is unable to place a child with a person specified in subsection (3), the local authority must place the child in the most appropriate placement available—s. 22C(5).

Placements

'Placement' is defined in s. 22C(6). This may include, for example, supporting young people to live independently in rented accommodation, residential employment, or in supported lodgings/hostels. When a local authority is deciding upon the most appropriate placement for a child, it must have regard to the other provisions of Part III of the 1989 Act—s. 22C(7). This includes the duty to safeguard and promote the welfare of the child (subsection (3)(a)) and the duty in particular to promote the child's educational achievement (subsection (3A)); the duty to ascertain the wishes and feelings of the child, his parents, and other relevant persons before making a decision with respect to the child they are looking after (subsection (4)); and the duty to give those wishes and feelings and the child's religious persuasion, racial origin, and cultural and religious background due consideration (subsection (5)).

The local authority must give preference to a placement with a relative, friend, or other person connected with the child over the other placement options.

Impact of placement

The local authority must, so far as is reasonably practicable in all the circumstances of the child's case, ensure that the placement:

- allows the child to live near their home;
- does not disrupt the child's education or training;
- if the child has a sibling who is also being looked after by the local authority, enables the child and that sibling to live together; and
- if the child is disabled, is suitable to the child's particular needs.

In general, local authorities are required to ensure that placements are within their own area.

Foster parents

A child in care or being looked after on a voluntary basis can, under s. 22C, be provided with accommodation by being placed with foster parents. Foster parents are suitable people selected by the local authority to provide accommodation and maintenance for a child being looked after. The selection and registration of foster parents are subject to detailed guidance, *Assessment and Approval of Foster Carers: Amendments to the Children Act 1989 Guidance and Regulations, 2013*. Section 22C allows the local authority to pay any person with whom it has placed a child, but the local authority can recover all or part of the costs from the parents unless the parents are in receipt of particular benefits.

Foster parents who wish to challenge the process by which they are approved by local authorities are supported by an independent review mechanism. The details of the independent review mechanism can be downloaded from www.gov.uk/government/organisations/independent-review-mechanism.

Services to accommodated children

Section 19 of the Children and Young Persons Act 2008 inserts a new para. 8A into Schedule 2 to the Children Act. This is set out in **Box 6.15**. This ensures that accommodated children receive the same range of services as other children in need and promotes contact between accommodated children and their families.

BOX 6.15 Provision for accommodated children—Schedule 2, Part 1, para. 8A of the Children Act 1989

(1) Every local authority shall make provision for such services as they consider appropriate to be available with respect to accommodated children.

(2) Accommodated children' are those children in respect of whose accommodation the local authority have been notified under section 85 or 86.

(3) The services shall be provided with a view to promoting contact between each accommodated child and that child's family.

(4) The services may, in particular, include—

    (a) advice, guidance and counselling;

    (b) services necessary to enable the child to visit, or to be visited by, members of the family;

    (c) assistance to enable the child and members of the family to have a holiday together.

(5) Nothing in this paragraph affects the duty imposed by paragraph 10.

Concern with the poor educational outcomes of looked-after children has led to another innovation. Section 20 of the Children and Young Persons Act 2008 requires schools to designate a member of staff to take responsibility for the educational attainment of looked-after children attending the school.

Responsibilities to care leavers

The local authority is acting as parent to the children it accommodates. One role of parenting is to prepare children for independence. Another is to provide continuing support after the child has left home. Research into the life chances of young people living in and leaving local authority care indicated that local authorities in general fail in these two roles. The Children (Leaving Care) Act 2000 attempts to address these failings. The explanatory notes to the Act state that its main purpose is to:

> help young people who have been looked after by a local authority move from care into living independently in as stable a fashion as possible.

To understand the amendments and new duties it introduces into the Children Act, it is necessary to explain some key definitions. We have set these out in **Box 6.16**.

 BOX 6.16 Definitions used in the Children (Leaving Care) Act 2000

(a) Eligible children—those children in care aged 16 and 17 who have been looked after for 13 weeks or more.

(b) Relevant children—those young people aged 16 and 17 who meet the criteria for eligible children but who leave care. The Regulations exclude certain groups, such as children who return home permanently and children who receive respite care.

(c) Former relevant children—those who before reaching the age of 18 were either eligible or relevant children.

(d) The responsible local authority—the local authority who last looked after an eligible or relevant young person.

Duties to care leavers

The Children (Leaving Care) Act introduced new paras 19A, 19B, and 19C into Part 2 of Schedule 2 to the Children Act 1989. Part 2 of Schedule 2 imposes duties on local authorities in connection with those children it looks after. The new paragraphs ensure that some responsibilities continue after the child leaves care. Paragraph 19A imposes a duty on local authorities which is set out in **Box 6.17**.

 BOX 6.17 Responsibilities after the child leaves care—Schedule 2, Part 2, s. 19A of the Children Act 1989

(19A) It is the duty of the local authority looking after a child to advise, assist, and befriend him with a view to promoting his welfare when they have ceased to look after him.

Subparagraph (4) of para. 19B requires that a local authority carry out an assessment of the needs of each eligible child for the advice, assistance, and support that would be appropriate for the local authority to provide. They will then prepare a pathway plan, which is defined in s. 23E. The pathway plan should take over from the care plan. The plan is to be reviewed regularly (s. 19B(5)).

Relevant and former relevant children

The amended s. 22 of the Act and the new ss 23A–23C impose duties on the local authority towards children and young people formerly looked after by them. Section 22 is amended so that local authorities can provide accommodation to a child who has left care, without the fact of their doing so classifying him or her as still being 'looked after'. Section 23B, set out in **Box 6.18**, contains the duties of the responsible local authority towards relevant children. Section 23C provides for similar duties towards former relevant children. This has been amended to include a duty to pay a contribution towards the costs of higher education of former relevant children. Section 23C was further amended by the Children and Families Act 2014 to allow for staying put arrangements. These are also set out in **Box 6.18**.

BOX 6.18 The duties towards relevant children—Schedule 2, Part 2, ss 23B and 23C of the Children Act 1989

Section 23B

(1) It is the duty of each local authority to take reasonable steps to keep in touch with a relevant child for whom they are the responsible authority, whether he is within their area or not.

(2) It is the duty of each local authority to appoint a personal adviser for each relevant child (if they have not already done so under paragraph 19C of Schedule 2).

(3) It is the duty of each local authority, in relation to any relevant child who does not already have a pathway plan prepared for the purposes of paragraph 19B of Schedule 2—

    (a) to carry out an assessment of his needs with a view to determining what advice, assistance and support it would be appropriate for them to provide him under this Part; and

    (b) to prepare a pathway plan for him.

Section 23C

(1) Each local authority in England have the duties provided for in subsection (3) in relation to a staying put arrangement.

(2) A 'staying put arrangement' is an arrangement under which—

    (a) a person who is a former relevant child by virtue of section 23C(1)(b), and

    (b) a person (a 'former foster parent') who was the former relevant child's local authority foster parent immediately before the former relevant child ceased to be looked after by the local authority,

    continue to live together after the former relevant child has ceased to be looked after.

(3) It is the duty of the local authority (in discharging the duties in section 23C(3) and by other means)—

    (a) to monitor the staying put arrangement, and

(b) to provide advice, assistance and support to the former relevant child and the former foster parent with a view to maintaining the staying put arrangement.

(4) Support provided to the former foster parent under subsection (3)(b) must include financial support.

(5) Subsection (3)(b) does not apply if the local authority consider that the staying put arrangement is not consistent with the welfare of the former relevant child.

(6) The duties set out in subsection (3) subsist until the former relevant child reaches the age of 21.

Sections 23D and 23E set out the details of personal advisers and pathway plans. Section 24 defines those qualifying for advice and assistance. The definition includes care leavers as a whole, as well as children and young people leaving accommodation provided by certain other providers.

Section 24(4) establishes a duty on a local authority to keep in touch as it thinks appropriate with any child whom it has looked after. Section 24B(5) obliges authorities to provide, or enable the young person to pay for, suitable vacation accommodation should it be needed, if they are in full-time higher education or further education. These provisions are amplified by the Care Leavers (England) Regulations 2010, which came into force on 1 April 2011. You are advised to read the revised volume of *Guidance and Regulations to the Children Act 1989, Vol 3: Planning Transition to Adulthood for Care Leavers*, which can be downloaded from www.gov.uk/government/publications/children-act-1989-transition-to-adulthood-for-care-leavers.

Assistance to pursue education and training

The Children and Young Persons Act 2008 inserts a new s. 23CA into the Children Act. This extends the duties of local authorities to appoint a personal adviser to include a former relevant child who informs the local authority who previously looked after him or her that he or she is pursuing or intends to pursue a programme of education or training but to whom the local authority would otherwise owe no duty under s. 23C because the young person is over 21 years of age and has completed (or abandoned) the programme set out in his or her original pathway plan.

As long as the young person is under 25, the local authority must also carry out an assessment of needs, prepare a pathway plan, and provide such assistance as the person's educational and training needs require.

Promoting educational achievement

The Children and Social Work Act 2017 has further amended the Children Act 1989 by requiring local authorities in England to make advice and information available in accordance with this section for the purpose of promoting the educational achievement of each relevant child educated in their area. The advice should be made available to anyone with parental responsibility for the child, school staff, and anyone else the local authority considers appropriate.

Regulatory framework

The whole field of 'looking after' is dominated by regulations that have been issued under the Children Act 1989:

- *Children Act 1989 Guidance and Regulations, Volume 4: Fostering Services* (1991);
- *Children Act 1989 Guidance and Regulations, Volume 2: Care Planning, Placement and Case Review* (2015);
- *Family and Friends Care: Statutory Guidance for Local Authorities* (2011);
- *Temporary Approval of Prospective Adopters as Foster Carers: Statutory Guidance for Local Authorities, Directors of Children's Services (DCSs) and Social Workers* (May 2013);
- *Children Act 1989 Guidance and Regulations, Volume 3: Planning Transition to Adulthood for Care Leavers* (2015);
- *Children Act 1989 Guidance and Regulations, Volume 5: Children's Homes Statutory Guidance for Local Authorities* (October 2013);
- *Looked-after Children: Contact with Siblings. Update to 'The Children Act 1989 Guidance and Regulations, Vol 2: Care Planning, Placement and Case Review'* (February 2014);
- *IRO Handbook: Statutory Guidance for Independent Reviewing Officers and Local Authorities on their Functions in Relation to Case Management and Review for Looked-after Children.*

Children Act 1989 Guidance and Regulations, Volume 4: Fostering Services and Children Act 1989 Guidance and Regulations and Volume 2: Care Planning, Placement and Case Review are essential reading for all social workers working with children in the public care system. The regulations set down procedures, specify dates, forms, the types and nature of review, and time limits. They govern who should be consulted about steps to be taken by a local authority concerning a child, and so on. In this chapter, we have the space only to give outline coverage of this large area, and you must read the guidance stated above.

Quality of services and accountability for provision are important. Services are regularly inspected and reports made to Parliament. The Education and Inspections Act 2006 transferred responsibilities for the inspection of children's services from a variety of inspectorates to the Office for Standards in Education, Children's Services and Skills—known as Ofsted. More information on inspection and audit is provided in **chapter 1**.

Promoting family links

One finding of research into children who have been looked after by local authorities in the past was the concept of the child being 'lost in care'. This arose when a child may have been provided with accommodation (placed in voluntary care under the old law) at some time of crisis within the family. The child being out of the family may have defused that particular crisis, but the reception of the child took place without any forward planning and the child just went on to 'hold' in the accommodation. The parents, relieved of the pressures, were often not encouraged to keep up contact and time passed, so that links were lost. Further crises with other families meant that the original child was not given attention and eventually the child became 'lost' in care.

The Children Act 1989 addresses this problem in a number of ways. It treats all children, regardless of the route by which they came to be looked after by a local authority, in the same way. We start with s. 23(6) and (7), which seeks to promote this contact between child and parent. These subsections are set out in **Box 6.19**.

 BOX 6.19 The promotion of contact with the family—s. 23 of the Children Act 1989

(6) Subject to any regulations made by the Secretary of State for the purposes of this sub-section, any local authority looking after a child shall make arrangements to enable him to live with—

  (a) a person falling within subsection (4) [that is a parent]; or

  (b) a relative, friend or other person connected with him, unless that would not be reasonably practicable or consistent with his welfare.

(7) Where a local authority provide accommodation for a child whom they are looking after, they shall, subject to the provisions of this Part and so far as is reasonably practicable and consistent with his welfare, secure that—

  (a) the accommodation is near his home; and

  (b) where the authority are also providing accommodation for a sibling of his, they are accommodated together.

The regulations set out the requirement for a written plan before any placement is made. All the people involved in the plan, including the child (as far as is consistent with age and understanding), should be consulted about it. The plan must include the proposals for contact. Volume 2 of the *Guidance and Regulations* sets out, at para. 2.44, the suggested contents of such a plan.

Schedule 2

There are comprehensive powers contained in Schedule 2 (see **Box 6.7**) to assist the maintaining of links with the child's family. By way of an example: one allegation that may be made against a social worker is that, having provided a child with accommodation, he or she then places the child with a foster parent remote from the child's parents. To visit the child, the parents may have to get two buses and a train, and find this difficult. As a consequence, the visits to the child drop off, and this is then used as an argument for saying that the parents do not really care for the child. The parents would say: 'This, of course, was what the authority was trying to prove all along. Indeed, this was the very reason why the child was placed with these particular foster parents.' Often the truth is closer to the fact that the harassed placement officer had only those foster parents available on the day the child had to be supplied with accommodation. Using the powers in Schedule 2, para. 16 should remove this argument. It provides that if the authority believes that visits could not be made without undue financial hardship, then the authority is permitted to make payments to any parent, or indeed any relative, friend, or person connected with the child. These payments can cover not only the cost of travel, but also subsistence and other expenses that may be involved. The payments need not be subject to a requirement for repayment, and indeed cannot be subject to that condition if the parents are in receipt of benefits.

In addition, new provision set out in the Care Planning, Placement and Case Review (England) Regulations 2010 requires that a nominated officer in the local authority must first approve a child's placement out of the local authority area. In doing so, before approving a decision under para. (1), the nominated officer must be satisfied that:

- the child's wishes and feelings have been ascertained and given due consideration;
- the placement is the most appropriate placement available for the child and consistent with his or her care plan;
- the child's relatives have been consulted, where appropriate;
- the area authority has been notified; and
- the independent reviewing officer has been consulted.

A child subject to a court order

All that we have said previously about the treatment of a child being looked after will be applicable to a child under a care order (see **Box 6.10**). We discuss care orders in **chapter 9**. However, there are some aspects of care orders which are relevant to our current discussion.

Links with families when children are subject to care orders

It is important to note that the statutory duty to consider placing the child with the child's family applies even if the child is subject to a care order. See the comments of the Court of Appeal in *Re T (A Minor) (Care or Supervision Order)* (1994). Put another way, the making of a care order does not require the local authority to remove the child from the child's home. This is often misunderstood, as in *Re A (Supervision Order: Extension)* (1995). This was resisted by the mother, and at that time by the local authority, in the mistaken belief that they would not be able to leave the child with her mother if a care order was made.

If such a placement is made, it must be done in accordance with Part 4, paras 15–20 of the Care Planning, Placement and Case Review (England) Regulations 2010.

Placement of the child with parents whilst in care

If it is intended to place a child in care with a parent of the child, s. 23(5) will permit this only if it is done in accordance with the Care Planning, Placement and Case Review (England) Regulations 2010. The purpose of these regulations is to ensure that when the decision is made to place at home a child who is the subject of a court order without the order being discharged, control and supervision is exercised over that procedure.

Before deciding to return the child, the 'respect for the child' principle dictates that the child's wishes be ascertained. The local authority must also obtain the written comments of all those agencies involved in the welfare and protection of this child, including the relevant health authority, the education authority, and the police, and must notify the people it has consulted, in writing, of the decision taken.

The regulations also provide a framework for the practical social work that will be needed to prepare the child and parent for the child's return. There has to be a written agreement with the parent recording the objective and plan of the placement, the arrangements for supervision, details of health, and educational arrangements. The agreement must record the fact that the child can be removed if the authority considers that the child's welfare is no longer being promoted. Whilst the agreement need not be signed, signing it may nonetheless be good practice.

Register of child placed at home but subject to care orders

On the return home, the register, which has to be kept of such returned children, must record the fact of the return and further record the regular visits of the social worker to the child that have to be undertaken. The first has to take place within one week and the visits then have to take place at intervals of six weeks at the most.

Having placed a child in care with the parents, the authority must not allow the situation to drift. It must review the placement within the first three months and then at six-month intervals. The reviews are to see whether the purpose of the placement is being met. If the placement is successful, the authority should consider whether to seek to discharge the care order. These reviews must be recorded in writing, as must the regular visits.

Contact

Under s. 34, where a child is under a care order there is a presumption that the child will have reasonable contact with his or her parents. Before the making of any care order, the authority shall inform the court of the plans it intends to make for contact between individuals and the child (s. 34(11)). The court can then define the extent of the contact that should take place. The presumption also applies whenever the local authority accommodates the child under an emergency protection order or a child assessment order.

At the stage of making a care order, the court has power under s. 34 to make what is in effect an interim contact order, with specific provision for a further hearing with a view to making provision for contact at the subsequent hearing *(Re B (A Minor) (Care Order: Review) (1993))*.

Contact decisions

At the same time as a care order is made or following a later application by either the local authority or the child, or the child's parents or others who had a residence order, the court may decide the amount of contact (s. 34(2), (3)). The court may instead make an order authorizing the local authority to refuse contact between the child and his or her parents (s. 34(4)). Section 34—with the rest of the Children Act—was written to ensure compliance with the European Convention. This judicial scrutiny of contact is necessary to satisfy the Human Rights Act 1998 and means that decisions to terminate parental contact are very likely to comply with Articles 6 and 8 of the Convention.

Local authority restriction of contact

There is also a general power given to the local authority in respect of contact under s. 34(6). If the authority believes that it would not promote the welfare of the child to allow contact, then it may refuse contact, but only as a matter of urgency and then only for a period of up to seven days. During that period, it would have to make an application to the court for an order. The use of the word 'urgency' implies that the situation which has arisen must have occurred within the recent past, this power not being available to solve long-standing difficulties. The Children and Families Act 2014 amends the Children Act 1989 to make it clear that the local authority's duty to allow reasonable contact between a child in the care of the local authority and his or her parents and other relevant people (any guardian or special guardian, any person who by virtue of s. 4A has parental responsibility for him or her, where there was a child arrangements order in force with respect to the child immediately before the care order was made, the person in whose favour the order was made, and where, immediately before the care order was made, a person had care of the child by virtue of an order made in the exercise of the High Court's inherent jurisdiction with respect to children) is subject to the local authority's duty to safeguard and promote the welfare of looked-after children under s. 22(3)(a) of the Children Act 1989. If allowing contact with any of those persons would not safeguard and promote the welfare of the child, the local authority should not allow the contact. It follows equally that preventing contact between a child and his or her parents should only be considered where a parent is likely to harm the child.

Variation or discharge

The parent can apply to the court to vary or discharge the order under s. 34(9). The child concerned may also use both s. 34(4) to stop a parent seeing him or her, and s. 34(6) to vary such an order.

Regulations concerning contact with looked-after children

Section 8 of the Care Planning, Placement and Case Review (England) Regulations 2010 covers contact between a child in care and the child's parents and others. The regulations are applicable to all children looked after by the local authority.

Reviewing the local authority plans for a child subject to a care order by contact application

Unless there has been an order to refuse contact under s. 34(4), or an order preventing a person from applying without leave of the court for contact under s. 91(14), the parents may apply to the court to consider the contact arrangements (s. 34(3)). If an application has been made and the application has been refused, then the parents must wait six months before applying again for contact unless they obtain the leave of the court (s. 91(17)).

Challenges to the local authority plans for the child in care can be made during the regular reviews. Importantly, the decision in *Re B (Minors) (Care: Local Authority's Plans)* (1993) has indicated that the Court of Appeal views s. 34 as another possible way of challenge. In this case it was argued that the discretion of the local authority with a care order could not be challenged and the court could not look at the local authority's long-term plans. The court would not accept this and said:

> If, however, a court was not able to intervene, it would make a nonsense of the paramountcy of the welfare of the child, which is the bedrock of the Act, and would subordinate it to the administrative decision of the local authority in a situation where the court is seized of the contact issue. That cannot be right.

This means that whilst the local authority has a wide discretion in caring for the child, this discretion can be reviewed by the courts when looking at the contact issue.

Independent visitor

One step that can be taken when links with the child's family have failed is the appointment of an independent visitor (ss 23ZA and 23ZB). The role of the visitor is to visit, befriend, and advise the child. In doing this, the authority must apply the 'respect for the child principle' and the child has the right of informed consent to object to the initial appointment and to the continuation of the appointment. The revised provisions for independent visitors (inserted into the Children Act by the Children and Young Persons Act 2008) extends the group of looked-after children for whom an independent person must be appointed to visit, befriend, and advise the child to include all those for whom an appointment would be in their interests. The purpose of an independent visitor is to:

- promote the child's developmental, social, emotional, educational, religious, and cultural needs;
- encourage the child to exercise his or her rights and to participate in decisions which will affect him or her;
- support the care plan for the child and his or her carers; and
- aim, as far as possible, to complement the activities of carers.

Reviews of children being looked after

One extremely important responsibility that local authorities have to looked-after children is the requirement to review regularly the position of and plans for each looked-after child (Children Act 1989, s. 26). Each authority is required to appoint an independent review officer (s. 25A) who must participate in and chair the review, monitor the performance of the local authority, and where appropriate refer a case to Cafcass (s. 25B).

The nature and format of the reviews are set down in the *Children Act 1989 Guidance and Regulations, Volume 2: Care Planning, Placement and Case Review* (2010). The regulations stipulate that the independent reviewing officer (IRO) should be independent of the matter in hand and be a registered and experienced social worker. Reviews must keep any s. 31A plan (see **Section 31A plans**, p 245) for the child under review and if there is no plan for the future care of the child one must be prepared. Reviews are to be held within four weeks of the initial placement, again not more than three months after that first review, and subsequently every six months. A review must also be carried out before the specified times if the IRO so directs. There are stipulations as to who should be consulted before a review, who should attend, and the matters for consideration. If cases are referred to Cafcass by the IRO, it may be appropriate to start court proceedings against the local authority seeking an order, requiring it to put right its failings in relation to the care plan. The options for court action are judicial review proceedings, a compensation claim, or a freestanding Human Rights Act 1998 application. Few cases have been referred to Cafcass by an IRO since 2004, when the first regulations for care planning were established. The government responded to this by increasing the powers of the IRO in new regulations in 2010 ('**Looked after**', p 217). The statutory duties of the IRO (Children Act 1989, s. 35B(1)) are to:

- monitor the performance by the local authority of their functions in relation to the child's case;
- participate in any review of the child's case;
- ensure that any ascertained wishes and feelings of the child concerning the case are given due consideration by the appropriate authority; and
- perform any other function which is prescribed in regulations.

The primary task of the IRO is to ensure that the care plan for the child fully reflects the child's current needs and that the actions set out in the plan are consistent with the local authority's legal responsibilities towards the child. As corporate parents, each local authority should act for the children they look after as a responsible and conscientious parent would act.

The primary purpose is one given to the individual IRO, not the authority for which he or she works. This is one of the very few instances where social workers have a duty accorded to them personally rather than as an officer of the local authority. The IRO can and has been cited in judicial review proceedings. In *A and S v Lancashire County*

Council (2012), two brothers applied for declarations under Articles 8, 6, and 3 of the Human Rights Act 1998. The defendants to the claim were Lancashire County Council and the IRO. The boys had been freed for adoption in 2001 and had moved from foster placement to foster placement, 77 times and 96 times, respectively. It was plain that the boys were unlikely to be adopted and yet the freeing order had not been revoked, thus preventing the boys from contact with the birth families. The IRO was found to have made no substantial challenge to the local authority's practice in respect of the boys. In effect, he had failed to execute the primary purpose of the role. He had a caseload of three times the recommended limit and had no access to training or independent legal advice.

Paragraph 2.13 of the IRO Handbook suggests that as part of the monitoring function, the IRO also has a duty to monitor the performance of the local authority's function as a corporate parent and to identify any areas of poor practice. This should include identifying patterns of concern emerging not just around individual children but also more generally in relation to the collective experience of its looked-after children of the services they receive. Where IROs identify more general concerns around the quality of the authority's services to its looked-after children, the IRO should immediately alert senior managers about these. Equally importantly, the IRO should recognize and report on good practice.

Section 31A plans

Section 31A of the Children Act 1989 provides that 'No care order may be made with respect to a child until the court has considered a section 31A plan.' Therefore, every child who is subject to a care order subsequent to the implementation of the section will have the benefit of a care plan which has been scrutinized by the courts. However, the Children and Families Act 2014 now requires the courts only to consider the 'permanence provision' in the plan; that is, the court is to consider whether the local authority care plan is for the child to live with a parent or any member or friend of the child's family, or whether the child is to be adopted or placed in other long-term care. The s. 31A plans will continue to be scrutinized by IROs.

The requirements of s. 31A care plans are set out in **Box 6.20.**

BOX 6.20 Care orders: care plans—s. 31A of the Children Act 1989

(1) Where an application is made on which a care order might be made with respect to a child, the appropriate local authority must, within such time as the court may direct, prepare a plan (a 'care plan') for the future care of the child.

(2) While the application is pending, the authority must keep any care plan prepared by them under review and, if they are of the opinion some change is required, revise the plan, or make a new plan, accordingly.

(3) A care plan must give any prescribed information and do so in the prescribed manner.

(4) For the purposes of this section, the appropriate local authority, in relation to a child in respect of whom a care order might be made, is the local authority proposed to be designated in the order.

(5) In section 31(3A) and this section, references to a care order do not include an interim care order.

(6) A plan prepared, or treated as prepared, under this section is referred to in this Act as a 'section 31A plan'.

The restriction on the liberty of a child being looked after

It is important for social workers to understand that the only basis on which the liberty of a child or young person accommodated by the local authority may be restricted is in accordance with s. 25 of the Children Act 1989 (unless the child is remanded from a criminal court—see **chapter 10**).

The restriction of liberty

The restriction of liberty does not only mean locking a door. Anything that goes beyond the bounds of ordinary domestic security will probably be a restriction of liberty. The failure to understand or accept this was the cause of the 'pin down' affair in Staffordshire (Allan Levy QC and Barbara Kahan, *The Pindown Experience and the Protection of Children* (Staffordshire County Council, 1991)).

What is secure accommodation?

Secure accommodation is accommodation that restricts the liberty of a child (s. 25). Detailed regulations have been issued under this section (written in the light of 'pin down') in respect of the type of accommodation and who may be placed in it. See the *Children Act 1989 Guidance and Regulations, Volume 5: Children's Homes* and the Children (Secure Accommodation) Regulations 1991.

Section 25 of the Children Act 1989

Section 25 prescribes that the restriction of liberty and the use of secure accommodation are available in strictly limited circumstances. A child may not be placed in secure accommodation unless:

(a) it appears that the child has a history of absconding; and
(b) is likely to abscond from any other type of accommodation; and
(c) if the child absconds, he or she is likely to suffer significant harm; or
(d) if the child is kept in any other type of accommodation, the child is likely to injure him or herself or other people.

Under the section, a child or young person whom a local authority is looking after may be placed in secure accommodation by a local authority only for a limited period of time; up to 72 hours in any period of 21 days.

It is not necessary for the child to be the subject of a care order before he or she can be placed in secure accommodation. But if the parent objects and there is no care order, in that situation the child must not be placed in secure accommodation.

Court application

If the authority wishes to keep the child in secure accommodation for a longer period than that prescribed by the regulations, then it must make an application for an authority from a court. A court can grant such an authority only if it is satisfied that the criteria of a history of absconding, etc., set out in s. 25 of the Children Act 1989 are fulfilled. In doing this, the court does not apply the welfare principle (*Re M (A Minor) (Secure Accommodation Order)* (1995)).

Legal representation

What is important from the social worker's point of view is the fact that the court cannot grant an authority unless the child is legally represented. Section 99 states that where an application for a secure accommodation order is being made, the child/ young person must be granted the necessary funding. Notice of the proceedings must be served on all relevant parties. A children's guardian should be appointed. Secure accommodation orders involve a serious deprivation of liberty, and therefore procedural safeguards are extremely important.

Cases

In the light of this, the decisions in *A Metropolitan Borough Council v DB (1997) and Re C (A Minor) (Medical Treatment: Courts' Jurisdiction)* (1997) are worrying.

In the first case, the court said that a maternity ward was secure accommodation and ordered that the 17-year-old be detained there. The young woman was a crack cocaine addict, who lived in squalor, and had received no antenatal care until very shortly before the birth of her child. Two days prior to the birth, she was admitted to hospital suffering from pre-eclamptic fits brought on by high blood pressure. She then discharged herself from hospital. The local authority obtained an emergency protection order and sought permission to detain her in the maternity ward. The court granted permission, saying that it was the restriction of liberty that made a particular place into secure accommodation.

In the second case, the local authority was granted authority to detain an anorexic young woman without reference to s. 25 under the court's inherent powers contained in s. 100. More recently, increased use of the courts' inherent powers has been made to restrict the liberty of some very vulnerable children. This has arisen because of the scarcity of secure accommodation provision. Indeed, the Children and Social Work Act 2017 has allowed children in England to be sent to Scottish secure units as a means of increasing the provision available to English local authorities. The use of the court's inherent powers under s. 100 of the Children Act 1989 is being used where no secure accommodation beds are available. The court can authorize that an existing placement or provision can restrict the liberty of a child. In *A Child (no approved secure accommodation available; deprivation of liberty)* [2017] EWHC 2458 (Fam) (see **Box 6.21**), Holman J said:

 BOX 6.21 *A Child (no approved secure accommodation available; deprivation of liberty)* [2017] EWHC 2458 (Fam)

. . . the local authority would have wished by last June to place the child in an approved secure accommodation placement. Such placements are currently very scarce, and they were unable to find one. So, it was that they hoped to place him in a unit which is not approved secure accommodation at X. Their plan was, however, that within X he should, if necessary, be subject to considerable restraint, including physical restraint, in order to keep him safe and prevent him from absconding, as he had done on occasions in the past. According to the case summary for today at paragraph 10, 'The staff of X are appropriately trained in de-escalation and physical restraint'.

Section 25 of the Children Act 1989 makes express and detailed provision for the making of what are known as secure accommodation orders. Such orders may be made and, indeed, frequently are made by courts, including courts composed of lay magistrates. It is not necessary to apply to the High Court for a secure accommodation order. However, as no approved secure accommodation was available, the local authority required the authorisation of a court for the inevitable deprivation of liberty of the child which would be involved.

There was a greater respect for the procedural safeguards in another case which established an important principle. In *LM v Essex County Council* (1999), Holman J expressed the view that once the criteria justifying a secure accommodation order ceased to be made out, the local authority should no longer keep the child in such accommodation. He also held that the court had no power to discharge or set aside such an order. If a local authority declined to release a child once it appreciated that the basis for the order was no longer present, a writ of habeas corpus would be appropriate. If the local authority failed to conclude that the grounds for the order no longer existed, the appropriate procedure might be judicial review.

The European Convention

The question arises whether secure accommodation orders made under s. 25 comply with Article 5 of the ECHR. Article 5(1) lists a finite set of circumstances in which persons may be deprived of their liberty, one of which is educational supervision. Despite the fact that the Children Act criteria make no reference to such supervision, the Court of Appeal in *Re K (Secure Accommodation Order: Right to Liberty)* (2001), rejected the argument that s. 25 was incompatible with the Convention, as the local authority has a duty to provide education for all those aged under 16. The court did, however, leave open the question of whether the words 'for the purposes of educational supervision' covered the facts of a particular case.

Seeking to place a child into secure accommodation will always cause the social worker the greatest of difficulties, both personally and professionally. It is difficult in such situations to see how to square your duty to the child with your wider duty to society.

Representations from children and others

It is one of the core principles of the UN Convention on the Rights of the Child that children's views and wishes should be at the forefront of the decision-making process. The Children Act 1989 enacts this principle.

We discussed the regulations which require local authorities to consider representations (complaints) about the exercise of its functions under Part III of the Act, made by or on behalf of any children looked after or in need in **chapter 1**. At this point we simply remind you about the significance of enabling and responding to complaints from children.

SUMMARY

- Local authority support, designed to safeguard and promote the welfare of the child in need, and enabling the child to be brought up with his or her family, is a cornerstone of the Children Act 1989.
- Children are in need if:
  - o they are unlikely to achieve a reasonable standard of health or development; or
  - o they experience a significant impairment of health or development; or
  - o they are disabled.
- Some children will not be eligible for support from local authorities if they are deemed to have no recourse to public funds.
- Children in need and their families can be offered a range of services, including cash.
- Children are looked after when they are provided with accommodation by the local authority, on a care order or remanded by the courts to local authority or youth detention accommodation. The placements of all children who are looked after are subject to regulation.
- When a child is looked after under s. 20 of the Children Act 1989, those with parental responsibility delegate some or all of their parental responsibility to the local authority, but that delegation must be voluntary.
- Local authorities must have regard to seven key corporate parenting principles when they exercise their functions in respect of children looked after.
- Normally, local authorities should promote contact between looked-after children and their parents and siblings (if they have any).
- Looked-after children should have periodic reviews of their care arrangements which are chaired by an independent reviewing officer. It is vital that all children look after (except those remanded) have robust permanency plans.
- In specific circumstances, courts can impose restrictions on a child's liberty by requiring them to reside in a secure establishment.
- Local authorities have a range of duties to care leavers. Each young person leaving care should have a pathway plan, which should be reviewed regularly. Local authorities are now under a duty to promote the educational achievement of relevant children.

EXERCISES

1 Sheila contacts the children's services department because she has concerns about her 14-year-old daughter, Claire. Claire has been refusing to go to school because she believes that her mother needs her to help at home. Sheila, a single mother, has two-year-old twins and she cares for her elderly mother at home. What help can you offer the family?

2 Fred contacts the children's services department. He wants you to assess the needs of his three children, all aged under 10, because he is about to be evicted by his housing association for non-payment of rent and the local housing department has found him intentionally homeless. On a brief consideration of the facts, you believe that Fred's children are not vulnerable. Is there any help your department can offer Fred?

3 Jameel has been living with foster parents for two years, since he was 13. He was placed there following his mother's remarriage to a man who has in the past been violent towards Jameel. Jameel's mother has now left her husband and would like Jameel to return to her care. Jameel does not want to return. What advice can you offer?

4 If Jameel's wishes are ignored and he is returned home, can he make a complaint? If he can, explain the procedure to him and the help that is available to him.

 ONLINE RESOURCES

For guidance on how to answer these exercises, visit the online resources at
www.oup.com/uk/carr-goosey15e.

 WHERE DO WE GO FROM HERE?

Part III of the Children Act contains a wide range of powers and duties necessary to ensure the welfare of children in need. Many children can be supported in their own families, and the Act contains a range of provisions to ensure that, where appropriate, children can remain with their families. Inevitably, some families will fail to support their children. Part III of the Act sets out the responsibilities of local authorities to those children that they are required to look after, including preparing children and young people for the time when they leave care. However, outcomes for 'looked-after' children are very poor and the government has set itself demanding targets to improve those outcomes. Part III straddles the two concerns of the Act, supporting families and caring properly for those children who require protection either through accommodation or through court orders. **Chapter 7** considers how social workers investigate concerns about children, and plan for the appropriate provision of services and, where necessary, for court applications.

 ANNOTATED FURTHER READING

More extensive information on Part III of the Children Act can be found in specialist texts on the Children Act 1989 such as:

I. Wise et al., *Children in Need: Local Authority Support for Children and Families* (Legal Action Group, 2014).

An influential report on the rising number of children in care was published in June 2018. The Care Crisis Review can be found at www.frg.org.uk/images/Care_Crisis/CCR-FINAL.pdf.

Advice for young people in care is provided by:

Coram Voice—a national organization offering advice, help, and advocacy to young people and care leavers, www.coramvoice.org.uk.

The limitations of s. 17 are made clear in a case commentary in:

E. Mitchell, 'R (LH and MM) v LB Lambeth—the provision of services for disabled children' (2007) CFLQ 19(4): 496.

Children in need and housing

D. Cowan (2004) CFLQ 16(3): 331. In a case commentary on the House of Lords case R (G) v Barnet LBC, discussed at the beginning of the chapter, Cowan considers Lambeth's policy, which survived the House of Lords' ruling, of offering accommodation only to children in need, without their family. He argues that these decisions make the general duty in s. 17(1) irrelevant; in addition, paradoxically, housing legislation gives greater protection to households with children than the Children Act 1989.

The following guide is a comprehensive exploration of the services for migrant families under s. 17:

Public Law Project, 'Social Services Support for Destitute Migrant Families: A guide to support under s 17 Children Act 1989' (August 2013; updated August 2014).

Coram Children's Legal Centre has also published a useful fact sheet on local authority support for migrant children: www.childrenslegalcentre.com/wp-content/uploads/2018/01/Section-17-support-January2018-FINAL.pdf

7 Investigation and case planning

OVERVIEW AND OBJECTIVES

This chapter focuses on the process of investigation and case planning. Our purpose is to ensure that you understand how to use the guidance and procedures and when to use your professional judgement, all informed by the law. Equally important is your role on planning for children. As you read this chapter, think about the steps involved from the initial expression of concern about a child to effective protection of the child, and finally through to a satisfactory long-term outcome. Achieving the latter depends upon a number of stages: investigation, assessment, and planning, and using court orders where necessary. You should not think of these as separate stages, but as overlapping. In particular, planning for the future of the child concerned is a critical stage which should begin as soon as possible.

CASE STUDY

R (on the application of A) v Enfield LBC (2008) [2008] EWHC 1886 (Admin)

Why are we asking you to read this case?

Social workers are frequently required by employers to 'follow procedures'. In this context, the procedures were set out in *Working Together to Safeguard Children* (2018). The procedures were followed, but equally the decision-making process was rationale, substantiated by evidence. Despite the parents' objections, the court agreed that decision of the CP conference was appropriate. It is important for social workers to justify their decision-making, grounding their work in the evidence in each case.

What is at stake for the parties and beyond?

The court's view was that the application of judicial review proceedings in the field of child protection should be rare. The judge quoted guidance from the Court of Appeal in respect of judicial review:

> It would also seem that recourse to judicial review is likely to be, and undoubtedly ought to be, rare. Local authorities have laid on them by Parliament the specific duty of protection of children in their area. The case conference has a duty to make an assessment as to abuse and the abuser, if sufficient information is available . . . In balancing adequate protection for the child and fairness to an adult, the interest of an adult may have to be placed second to the needs of the child. All concerned in this difficult and delicate area should be allowed to perform their task without looking over their shoulder all the time for the possible intervention of the court. The important power for the court to intervene should be kept very much in reserve, perhaps confined to the exceptional case which involves a point of principle which needs to be resolved.

> *R v Harrow London Borough Council ex parte D* [1990] Fam 133

In this instance, the local authority complaints procedure would have been more appropriate. Its use would not have led to the quashing of the original case conference decision, but it might have led to the vindication of the parents.

The factsThe parents of T applied for judicial review of a decision by the London Borough of Enfield to place T, their son, on the child protection register by reason of neglect. The decision to place T on the child protection register was taken at a child protection conference in 2006. T, who had been born in 2003 weighing 3.1 kg, was seriously underweight compared with similar children of his age. The conference noted that the parents had failed to attend numerous appointments in connection with T's progress. It considered that it was incomprehensible that the parents could not appreciate how dangerously underweight T had become. The parents argued that (1) on the evidence, no rational authority could have concluded that the case was one of neglect; rather, the parents had sought medical help and the local authority had overreacted because of the severity of T's condition; (2) the proceedings had been unfair, as insufficient account had been taken of the parents' views at the conference; moreover, the conference had approached the matter in the wrong way by failing to consider whether the parents posed any prospective risk of neglect so that T was at continuing risk of significant harm.

The parents' application for judicial review was refused.

- In the first place, the judge pointed out that recourse to judicial review should be rare in the field of child protection.
- Second, although one of the reports before the conference recorded that the parents loved their children, and because of that no doubt felt a genuine grievance at the finding of neglect, the issue to be decided was not whether T was in fact neglected, but whether there was a rational basis for the local authority's decision to place him on the child protection register. The material before the conference was sufficient to justify its decision.

  o It went considerably beyond evidence of severe malnutrition and nutritional rickets and it could reasonably be taken to point at least in part to parental responsibility for T's condition.
  o There had been failures to keep appointments, and it was open to the conference to conclude that the deterioration in T's health was caused by the parents' failure to seek medical attention and that T was at continuing risk of significant harm.
  o That decision reflected the unanimous view of all the professionals present at the conference.

- In response to the parents' second argument, their views had been properly taken into consideration at the conference and there was a proper evidential basis for the decision reached. The conference had asked itself the correct question, namely whether T was at continuing risk of significant harm, and its approach could not be faulted.
- The final observation of the judge was *obiter*—that is, it did not form part of the reasoning for the decision. He stated that the complaints procedure should have been followed by the parents as it would have provided an alternative remedy to proceedings for judicial review. A decision in the parents' favour as a result of making a complaint might not have resulted in the quashing of the original registration, but it could have resulted in their vindication.

WHAT DOES THIS CASE TELL US ABOUT SOCIAL WORK PRACTICE?

This case provides a useful overview of the framework of decision making. By s. 47 of the Children Act 1989, a local authority has a duty to investigate when it has reasonable cause to suspect that a child in its area is suffering, or likely to suffer, significant harm.

- There is no dispute that this duty was engaged in the case of T.
- The local authority followed the guidance in *Working Together to Safeguard Children*.
- The guidelines define neglect, which was the cause of concern in this case.
- The social workers followed the procedures laid down in the guidance.
- A child protection conference was called at which the relevant question, 'Is the child at continuing risk of significant harm?', was considered.
- The child protection conference was chaired by an independent chair and the parents were involved.
- The case arose because the parents thought that the outcome was unfair; they loved their children and they felt that they were being blamed for T's condition.
- The fact that statutory guidance and proper procedures were followed and rational decisions substantiated by evidence protected the social workers from the legal challenge. Just one point of clarification—the case refers to the child protection register. That mechanism for protecting children was replaced in April 2008 with a requirement that the child is made the subject of a *child protection plan* (CP plan).

Introduction

This chapter will look at three critical stages of child protection which follow from an initial expression of concern. In appropriate cases, these stages will be crucial to successful court proceedings by a local authority. We shall consider:

- the investigation of child protection concerns;
- the structures and processes designed to protect children; and
- case planning, including preparation for possible court proceedings.

Initial referral and assessment

The first step in the whole process of child protection is the initial referral. The protection of children is dependent upon everyone who works with children or is in contact with them being able to recognize indicators that a child's welfare or safety may be at risk. Many cases will not need to go beyond the initial referral. **Box 7.1** shows the most recent (October 2015) statistical data available showing referrals and outcomes. It is interesting to note that in the year ending 31 March 2015, 25 per cent of referrals led to a s. 47 inquiry, and an even smaller number (11 per cent) of referrals led to a child protection conference. It is also interesting to note that during the same year 62,200 children became the subject of a CP plan but 60,400 plans were ended. This suggests that in any one year there is a great deal of activity occurring in local authorities with children starting and ending CP plans.

 BOX 7.1 Child protection referral data

- There were 646,120 referrals to children's social care services in the year ending 31 March 2017. This is about 10,500 more referrals than two years ago when the previous edition of this book was published.
- There were 606,920 assessments completed in the year ending 31 March 2017, with a median duration of 29 days.
- The number of section 47 enquiries has increased, from 172,290 in 2016 to 185,450 in 2017, an increase of 7.6 per cent.

Children who were the subject of a child protection plan
- At 31 March 2013, there were 43,100 children who were the subject of a CP plan.
- In the year ending 31 March 2017, 51,080 children became the subject of a CP plan.
- 65,420 CP plans came to an end in the year.

Assessment

Hitherto, the assessment of children referred to children's services departments was set out in the *Framework for the Assessment of Children in Need and their Families* (The Stationery Office, 2000). This document issued under s. 7 of the Local Authority (Social Services) Act 1970 (LASSA), together with its associated volume of practice guidance, scales and questionnaires, and forms, prescribed how assessments of children in need should be carried out. Assessments would be divided into initial and core assessments and timescales were applied of seven days for the former and a further 35 days for the latter. These timescales, together with an inspection scheme which placed significant weight on adherence to the timescales, were overwhelmingly instrumental in encouraging local authorities to structure social work services with referral and advice teams at the front end followed by child in need/protection teams and looked-after children teams. Children and families could therefore expect a change of social worker as they progressed through the service, contrary to the importance of maintaining continuity.

The Munro Review of Child Protection recommended that the government look again at the emphasis on slavish adherence to timescales in assessments. In the *Progress Report: Moving towards a Child Centred System*, Munro says:

> The fixed timescale for assessments . . . has for many become the overriding concern so that an assessment is concluded because the deadline has been reached not because the worker

thinks they have acquired a good enough understanding of the child's needs to make a sound decision about what to do.

(para. 2.7)

The Final Report of the Munro Review recommends that both the *Framework for the Assessment of Children in Need and their Families* and *Working Together to Safeguard Children* should be revised (see **chapter 5** for further details). A new *Working Together to Safeguard Children* was published in March 2013 bringing together the multi-agency guidance, a revised assessment framework, and procedures in the case of child deaths. It was subsequently amended in 2015 and again in July 2018. **Box 7.2** shows key passages from *Working Together* concerning the assessment of children in need.

 BOX 7.2 Assessing need—*Working Together to Safeguard Children* (2018)

The purpose of an assessment

38. Whatever legislation the child is assessed under, the purpose of the assessment is always:
   - to gather important information about a child and family;
   - to analyse their needs and/or the nature and level of any risk and harm being suffered by the child;
   - to decide whether the child is a child in need (section 17) and/or is suffering or likely to suffer significant harm (section 47); and
   - to provide support to address those needs to improve the child's outcomes and welfare and where necessary to make them safe.

44. Assessment should be a dynamic process, which analyses and responds to the changing nature and level of need and/or risk faced by the child from within and outside their family. It is important that the impact of what is happening to a child is clearly identified and that information is gathered, recorded and checked systematically, and discussed with the child and their parents/carers where appropriate.

The principles and parameters of a good assessment

51. High quality assessments:
   - are child-centred. Where there is a conflict of interest, decisions should be made in the child's best interests: be rooted in child development: be age-appropriate; and be informed by evidence;
   - are focused on action and outcomes for children;
   - are holistic in approach, addressing the child's needs within their family and any risks the child faces from within the wider community;
   - ensure equality of opportunity;

   involve children, ensuring that their voice is heard and provide appropriate support to enable this where the child has specific communication needs;
   - involve families;
   - identify risks to the safety and welfare of children;

- build on strengths as well as identifying difficulties;
- are integrated in approach;
- are multi-agency and multi-disciplinary;
- are a continuing process, not an event;
- lead to action, including the provision of services;
- review services provided on an ongoing basis;
- are transparent and open to challenge.

Timeliness

69. The timeliness of an assessment is a critical element of the quality of that assessment and the outcomes for the child. The speed with which an assessment is carried out after a child's case has been referred into local authority children's social care should be determined by the needs of the individual child and the nature and level of any risk of harm they face. This will require judgements to be made by the social worker on each individual case. Adult assessments, for example, parent carer or non-parent carer assessments, should also be carried out in a timely manner, consistent with the needs of the child.

70. Once the referral has been accepted by local authority children's social care, the lead practitioner role falls to a social worker. The social worker should clarify with the referrer, when known, the nature of the concerns and how and why they have arisen.

71. Within one working day of a referral being received, a local authority social worker should acknowledge receipt to the referrer and make a decision about next steps and the type of response required. This will include determining whether:
   - the child requires immediate protection and urgent action is required;
   - the child is in need and should be assessed under section 17 of the Children Act 1989;
   - there is reasonable cause to suspect that the child is suffering or likely to suffer significant harm, and whether enquires must be made and the child assessed under section 47 of the Children Act 1989;
   - any services are required by the child and family and what type of services;
   - further specialist assessments are required to help the local authority to decide what further action to take;
   - to see the child as soon as possible if the decision is taken that the referral requires further assessment.

73. The child and family must be informed of the action to be taken, unless a decision is taken on the basis that this may jeopardise a police investigation or place the child at risk of significant harm.

75. The maximum timeframe for the assessment to conclude, such that it is possible to reach a decision on next steps, should be no longer than 45 working days from the point of referral. If, in discussion with a child and their family and other practitioners, an assessment exceeds 45 working days, the social worker should record the reasons for exceeding the time limit.

The Guidance retains the use of the dimensions associated with child developmental needs, parenting capacity, and family and environmental factors.

The next steps

The result of the assessment may be that no further action needs to be taken. It may be that the child is a 'child in need' and the family will benefit from additional support and practical help in promoting the child's health and development. **Chapter 6** sets out the responsibilities of the local authority to children in need. It may be that there are concerns sufficient to prompt a s. 47 inquiry—we discuss this in **The objective of local authority inquiries under s. 47**, p 262. It may be that there is a need for a parallel police investigation. It may be that the child's life is at risk, or that there is a likelihood of serious immediate harm. In that case, the children's services department must act quickly to secure the immediate safety of the child. Legal advice should be obtained as soon as possible. Full details of the emergency protection order and the other available court orders are set out in **chapter 8**. Details of the power to exclude perpetrators of violence or other abuse from the family home are set out in **chapter 6**. The s. 47 inquiries should proceed in parallel with seeking protection via the courts if appropriate. Whatever decision is made, it should be endorsed at managerial level and recorded in writing with the reasons. The family, the person who originally expressed concern, and other professionals and services involved in the assessment should be told what action has been taken, consistent with respecting the confidentiality of the child and the family.

▬ Referral from the courts

The vast majority of referrals are from social care and health professionals and others who have contact with children. In the course of any family proceedings not involving a local authority, a court may have legitimate reasons to be concerned about the care of a child. If that is the case, the court has the power under s. 37 of the Children Act 1989 to give directions to a local authority to investigate and consider whether care proceedings should be brought.

The powers of the court under s. 37

Section 37 is set out in **Box 7.3**. This is a comprehensive section that has wide implications for the local authority. It gives the residual power to the court to require the state, via the local authority, to consider intervention in the affairs of a family. The court can exercise the power in any family proceedings and the use of these powers can lead to a supervision order, or indeed a care order.

 BOX 7.3 Section 37 investigations—the Children Act 1989

(1) Where, in any family proceedings (i.e. other than care proceedings) in which a question arises with respect to the welfare of any child, it appears to the court that it may be appropriate for a care or supervision order to be made with respect to him, the court may direct the appropriate authority to undertake an investigation of the child's circumstances.

(2) Where the court gives a direction under this section the local authority concerned shall, when undertaking the investigation, consider whether they should—

(a) apply for a care order or for a supervision order with respect to the child;

(b) provide services or assistance for the child or his family; or

(c) take any other action with respect to the child.

(3) Where a local authority undertake an investigation under this section, and decide not to apply for a care order or supervision order with respect to the child concerned, they shall inform the court of—

(a) their reasons for so deciding;

(b) any service or assistance which they have provided, or intend to provide, for the child and his family; and

(c) any other action which they have taken or propose to take, with respect to the child.

(4) The information shall be given to the court before the end of the period of eight weeks beginning with the date of the direction, unless the court otherwise directs.

(5) The local authority named in a direction under subsection (1) must be—

(a) the authority in whose area the child is ordinarily resident; or

(b) where the child is not ordinarily resident in the area of a local authority, the authority within whose area any circumstances arose in consequence of which the direction is being given.

(6) If, on the conclusion of any investigation or review under this section, the authority decides not to apply for a care order or supervision order with respect to the child—

(a) they shall consider whether it would be appropriate to review the case at a later date; and

(b) if they decide that it would be, they shall determine the date on which the review is to begin.

Explanations of inaction are required

Even if a care or supervision application is not made, the local authority is still required to explain its actions, the reasons for non-action, and its plans for the future. If the court makes a direction under s. 37, it can appoint a guardian to act on behalf of the child.

The local authority decides

Although it is possible to envisage circumstances in which the local authority and guardian may disagree over the course of action, it remains solely the choice of the local authority whether or not to apply for an order. Even if the court prefers the views of the guardian, it cannot compel the local authority to make an application for a care order.

Interim care or supervision orders pending s. 37 investigations

There are provisions in s. 38 of the Children Act 1989 for making interim orders during the s. 37 investigations. **Box 7.4** sets out the court's power.

This section is a partial exception to the principle that no care or supervision order may be made without an application being made to the court. Under s. 37 of the 1989 Act, no application need be before the court for it to have the power to make an interim care or supervision order. However, before a full care or supervision order can be made it is necessary for a local authority actually to make an application, so the principle is essentially intact.

If the court has ordered a s. 37 investigation and is thinking of making an interim care or supervision order, it must be certain, first, that the normal test for an interim order is satisfied. Section 38(2) is set out in **Box 7.5**.

The words 'reasonable grounds for believing' mean that the grounds do not have to be 'proved' before an interim order can be made, but merely that there have to be some grounds for believing that a full order may be made. The making of an interim order does not presuppose that a full order will be made. You will find more information about interim care orders in **chapter 8**.

BOX 7.4 The power to make interim orders—s. 38 of the Children Act 1989

(1) Where—

    (a) in any proceedings on an application for a care order or supervision order, the proceedings are adjourned; or

    (b) the court gives a direction under section 37(1), the court may make an interim care order or an interim supervision order with respect to the child concerned.

BOX 7.5 There must be reasonable grounds for an interim order—s. 38(2) of the Children Act 1989

A court shall not make an interim care order or interim supervision order under this section unless it is satisfied that there are reasonable grounds for believing that the circumstances with respect to the child are as mentioned in section 31(2) [i.e. the grounds for a care order— the likelihood of significant harm, the child beyond parental control].

Section 8 child arrangements orders during or after s. 37 investigation

An alternative course open to the court would be to make a s. 8 child arrangements order. It has the power in any family proceedings to make a s. 8 order, even though it has not disposed of the main proceedings (s. 11(3)).

Time limits

One of the practical difficulties is the requirement that the investigation under s. 37 of the Children Act 1989 be completed within a period of eight weeks, unless 'the court otherwise directs'. The resource implications for s. 37 are immense, and in the absence of greatly increased resources the court may need to 'otherwise direct' in many cases.

The local authority's duty to investigate (s. 47)

Prompting the duty to investigate

If the initial assessment or the result of inquiries following referral from the court indicate that there is *reasonable cause to suspect that a child is suffering or is likely to suffer significant harm, then the local authority is placed under a statutory duty to investigate.* The duty also arises if a child is the subject of an emergency protection order or is in police protection. The meanings of significant harm, police protection, and emergency protection order are discussed in **chapter 8**.

Section 47 makes it clear that the main responsibility for the protection under the Act falls on local authorities. Section 47(1) is set out in **Box 7.6**.

 BOX 7.6 The local authority's duty to investigate—s. 47 of the Children Act 1989

(1) Where a local authority—

    (a) are informed that a child who lives, or is found, in their area—

        (i)   is the subject of an emergency protection order; or

        (ii) is in police protection; or

    (b) have reasonable cause to suspect that a child who lives, or is found, in their area is suffering or is likely to suffer significant harm,

    the authority shall make, or cause to be made, such enquiries as they consider to be necessary to enable them to decide whether they should take any action to safeguard or protect the child's welfare.

Low-level threshold

Note that the local authority has an overall duty to make inquiries as soon as it has 'reasonable cause to suspect' the possibility of significant harm. This is a relatively low-level threshold for triggering action and is lower than the threshold for justifying interim care or supervision orders, or emergency protection orders. These, by contrast with the s. 47 inquiries, involve a compulsory intervention in the lives of both child and family (see **chapter 9**) and therefore require a different balance to be drawn between the concerns of the state to protect children and the rights of individuals.

The objective of local authority inquiries under s. 47

Working Together to Safeguard Children makes it clear that the objective of the local authority is to decide whether and what type of action is required to safeguard and promote the welfare of the child who is suspected of suffering or likely to be suffering significant harm.

'Any action'

The 'any action' referred to in s. 47(1)(b) may constitute applying for a court order or providing any form of support under Part III of the Children Act—see **chapter 5**. Providing access to a wide range of support services to help children in need is likely to be the outcome in most cases.

Despite this emphasis, s. 47(3) goes on to state that the inquiries should in particular be directed towards establishing whether the local authority should make any application to court.

Statutory requirements

In making its inquiries, the local authority is required actually to see the child unless it is satisfied that it has sufficient information (s. 47(4)).

If in making the inquiries the local authority finds matters concerned with the child's education, it is required to consult the relevant education authority (s. 47(5)).

Where the local authority does try to carry out this statutory duty and is refused access to the child or is denied information as to the child's whereabouts, the authority is required to apply for an emergency protection order, a child assessment order, a care order, or a supervision order unless satisfied that the child's welfare can be satisfactorily safeguarded without doing so (s. 47(6)). These court orders are explained in **chapter 8**. The requirement to make an application to court if access is refused, again, is a statutory duty, albeit that there is a narrow area of discretion.

Next steps

Once the local authority has concluded its inquiries under s. 47, it has to consider what is to be done. Even a decision not to make a court application prompts a positive duty—to consider whether it is appropriate to review the case at a later date. Subsection (8) sets out the overriding statutory duty on the local authority if it concludes that action is necessary. It must take action—'so far as it is both within their power and reasonably practicable for them to do so'. If the local authority concludes as a result of its inquiries that the child needs some form of support, it must supply that support. If it fails to do so, then its decision may be liable to judicial review. If the local authority believes that court proceedings are required, the local authority must take proceedings. **Box 7.7** sets out s. 47(7) and (8).

BOX 7.7 The duty to take action—s. 47(7)–(8) of the Children Act 1989

(7) If, on the conclusion of any enquiries or review made under this section, the authority decide not to apply for an emergency protection order, a child assessment order, a care order or a supervision order they shall—

(a) consider whether it would be appropriate to review the case at a later date; and

(b) if they decide that it would be, determine the date on which that review is to begin.

(8) Where, as a result of complying with this section, a local authority conclude that they should take action to safeguard or promote the child's welfare they shall take that action (so far as it is both within their power and reasonably practicable for them to do so).

Recording of decisions

Whatever the outcome of the s. 47 inquiries, decisions should be recorded, and parents (together with professionals and agencies who have been significantly involved) should receive a copy of the record.

Cooperation from other agencies

The local authority may require assistance from other bodies and authorities. This duty, in s. 47(9), (10), and (11) is set out in **Box 7.8**. We considered the relationship between other agencies and local authorities in **chapter 5**.

BOX 7.8 The duty on other agencies—s. 47 of the Children Act 1989

(9) Where a local authority are conducting enquiries under this section, it shall be the duty of any person mentioned in subsection (11) to assist them with those enquiries (in particular by providing relevant information and advice) if called upon by the authority to do so.

(10) Subsection (9) does not oblige any person to assist a local authority where doing so would be unreasonable in all the circumstances of the case.

The nature of the duty

The local authority must do all within its power to safeguard or promote the welfare of a child brought to its attention as being at possible risk, in partnership with other agencies if appropriate. The aim of the legislation has been to avoid the local authority being put in a situation of saying 'We would like to do this but we do not have the legal power.'

This is merely emphasizing the concept of 'diminishment of court proceedings' discussed in **chapter 6** which, in turn, is a reflection of the overall philosophy of the current law relating to children. This is that the local authority shall do all that is within its power to safeguard children and should apply for court orders only as a final and last resort, but always bearing in mind that it should apply for a court order if that is necessary.

The inquiry process

Section 47 inquiries need to be carried out effectively and skilfully. *Working Together to Safeguard Children* no longer prescribes how assessments should be carried out.

Instead, emphasis is placed on describing the principles of assessment, including an emphasis to focus on the needs and views of the child, clear decision-making analysis which is focused on outcomes, and timeliness. Some of the key responsibilities of professionals are described in **Box 7.9**. It should be noted that the lastest version of *Working Together* omits 'managers' from Professional Responsibilities during s. 47 inquiries.

 BOX 7.9 Professional responsibilities during s. 47 inquiries—Working Together to Safeguard Children (2018)

Social workers and managers should:

- lead the assessment in accordance with this guidance;
- carry out enquiries in a way that minimises distress for the child and family;
- see the child who is the subject of concern to ascertain their wishes and feelings; assess their understanding of their situation; assess their relationships and circumstances more broadly;
- interview parents/carers and determine the wider social and environmental factors that might impact on them and their child;
- systematically gather information about the child's and family's history;
- analyse the findings of the assessment and evidence about what interventions are likely to be most effective with other relevant practitioners;
- determine the child's needs and the level of risk of harm faced by the child to inform what help should be provided and act to provide that help;
- follow the guidance set out in 'Achieving Best Evidence in Criminal Proceedings: Guidance on interviewing victims and witnesses, and guidance on using special measures', where a decision has been made to undertake a joint interview of the child as part of any criminal investigation.

The police should:

- help other organisations and agencies understand the reasons for concerns about the child's safety and welfare;
- decide whether or not police investigations reveal grounds for instigating criminal proceedings;
- make available to other practitioners any evidence gathered to inform discussions about the child's welfare;
- follow the guidance set out in 'Achieving Best Evidence in Criminal Proceedings: Guidance' on interviewing victims and witnesses, and guidance on using special measures, where a decision has been made to undertake a joint interview of the child as part of the criminal investigations.

Health professionals should:

- provide any of a range of specialist assessments. For example, paediatric or forensic medical assessments, physiotherapists, occupational therapists, speech and language therapists and/or child psychologists may be involved in specific assessments relating to the child's developmental progress. The lead health practitioner (probably a consultant paediatrician, or possibly the child's GP) may need to request and co-ordinate these assessments;
- ensure appropriate treatment and follow up health concerns, such as administration of missing vaccines

All involved professionals should:

• contribute to the assessment as required, providing information about the child and family;

• consider whether a joint enquiry/investigation team may need to speak to a child victim without the knowledge of the parent/carers;

• seek advice and guidance as required and in line with local practice guidance.

The structures and processes designed to protect children

The mechanisms for child protection in summary

The structures and processes for protection of children following initial referral consists of:

• safeguarding partnerships and their locally agreement arrangements (see *Working Together*);

• strategy discussions and the child protection conference;

• the CP plan.

In this chapter we discuss the short-term arrangements for the protection of children. In **chapter 9** we look at long-term planning.

Safeguarding partnerships

The core objects of safeguarding partnerships are set out in s. 16E of the Children Act 2004, as amended by the Children and Social Work Act 2017. We have set these out in **Box 7.10**.

 BOX 7.10 Local arrangements for safeguarding and promoting the welfare of children—the Children and Social Work Act 2017

(1) The safeguarding partners for a local authority area in England must make arrangements for—

(a) the safeguarding partners, and

(b) any relevant agencies that they consider appropriate,

to work together in exercising their functions, so far as the functions are exercised for the purpose of safeguarding and promoting the welfare of children in the area.

(2) The arrangements must include arrangements for the safeguarding partners to work together to identify and respond to the needs of children in the area.

The Safeguarding Partners are

(a) the local authority;

(b) a clinical commissioning group for an area any part of which falls within the local authority area;

(c) the chief officer of police for a police area any part of which falls within the local authority area.

Box 5.15 provides a summary of potential relevant agencies.

Purpose of local arrangements

Working Together (set out in **Box 7.11**) describes the purpose of local arrangements.

 BOX 7.11 The purpose of local arrangements—*Working Together to Safeguard Children* (2018)

The purpose of these local arrangements is to support and enable local organisations and agencies to work together in a system where:

- children are safeguarded and their welfare promoted;
- partner organisations and agencies collaborate, share and co-own the vision for how to achieve improved outcomes for vulnerable children;
- organisations and agencies challenge appropriately and hold one another to account effectively;
- there is early identification and analysis of new safeguarding issues and emerging threats;
- learning is promoted and embedded in a way that local services for children and families can become more reflective and implement changes to practice;
- information is shared effectively to facilitate more accurate and timely decision making for children and families.

In order to work together effectively, the safeguarding partners with other local organisations and agencies should develop processes that:

- facilitate and drive action beyond usual institutional and agency constraints and boundaries;
- ensure the effective protection of children is founded on practitioners developing lasting and trusting relationships with children and their families.

To be effective, these arrangements should link to other strategic partnership work happening locally to support children and families. This will include other public boards including Health and wellbeing boards, Adult Safeguarding Boards, Channel Panels, Improvement Boards, Community Safety Partnerships, the Local Family Justice Board and MAPPAs.

Functions in connection with serious case reviews

The Children and Social Work Act 2017 establishes a new Child Safeguarding Practice Review Panel to oversee serious case reviews in England. The function of the panel is:

(a) to identify serious child safeguarding cases in England which raise issues that are complex or of national importance; and

(b) where they consider it appropriate, to arrange for those cases to be reviewed under their supervision.

The purpose of a review is to identify any improvements that should be made by safeguarding partners or others to safeguard and promote the welfare of children. Serious case reviews should normally be published.

Working Together sets out the revised processes to be carried out in relation to continuous learning and in particular serious case reviews (**Box 7.12**).

 BOX 7.12 Revised processes for serious case reviews—*Working Together to Safeguard Children* (2018)

The responsibility for how the system learns the lessons from serious child safeguarding incidents lies at a national level with the Child Safeguarding Practice Review Panel (the Panel) and at local level with the safeguarding partners.

The Panel is responsible for identifying and overseeing the review of serious child safeguarding cases which, in its view, raise issues that are complex or of national importance. The Panel should also maintain oversight of the system of national and local reviews and how effectively it is operating.

Locally, safeguarding partners must make arrangements to identify and review serious child safeguarding cases which, in their view, raise issues of importance in relation to their area. They must commission and oversee the review of those cases, where they consider it appropriate for a review to be undertaken.

Serious child safeguarding cases are those in which:

• abuse or neglect of a child is known or suspected; and

• the child has died or been seriously harmed.

Serious harm includes (but is not limited to) serious and/or long-term impairment of a child's mental health or intellectual, emotional, social or behavioural development. It should also cover impairment of physical health. This is not an exhaustive list. When making decisions, judgement should be exercised in cases where impairment is likely to be long-term, even if this is not immediately certain. Even if a child recovers, including from a one-off incident, serious harm may still have occurred.

Strategy discussions

Working Together states:

> Whenever there is reasonable cause to suspect that a child is suffering or is likely to suffer significant harm there should be a strategy discussion involving local authority children's social care (including the residential or fostering service, if the child is looked-after), the police, health and other bodies such as the referring agency. This might take the form of a multi-agency meeting or phone calls and more than one discussion may be necessary. A strategy discussion can take place following a referral or at any other time, including during the assessment process and when new information is received on an already open case.

The discussion should be used to:

• share available information;

• agree the conduct and timing of any criminal investigation;

• decide whether enquiries under section 47 of the Children Act 1989 must be undertaken.

Where there are grounds to initiate an enquiry under section 47 of the Children Act 1989, decisions should be made as to:

- what further information is needed if an assessment is already underway and how it will be obtained and recorded;
- what immediate and short-term action is required to support the child, and who will do what by when; and
- whether legal action is required.

The timescale for the assessment to reach a decision on next steps should be based upon the needs of the individual child, consistent with the local protocol and no longer than 45 working days from the point of referral into local authority children's social care.

Initial child protection conference

Purpose
The purpose of the initial child protection conference is set out in *Working Together*—see **Box 7.13**.

BOX 7.13 Purpose of child protection conference—*Working Together to Safeguard Children* (2018)

To bring together and analyse, in an inter-agency setting, all relevant information and plan how best to safeguard and promote the welfare of the child. It is the responsibility of the conference to make recommendations on how agencies work together to safeguard the child in future. Conference tasks include:

- appointing a lead statutory body (either local authority children's social care or NSPCC) and a lead social worker, who should be a qualified, experienced social worker and an employee of the lead statutory body;
- identifying membership of the core group of professionals and family members who will develop and implement the child protection plan;
- establishing timescales for meetings of the core group, production of a child protection plan and for child protection review meetings; and
- agreeing an outline child protection plan, with clear actions and timescales, including a clear sense of how much improvement is needed, by when, so that success can be judged clearly.

Attendance and timing

Working Together suggests that the social worker has specific functions at the initial conference. This is set out in **Box 7.14**.

BOX 7.14 Functions of social worker and their manager at the initial conference—*Working Together to Safeguard Children* (2018)

The social worker and their manager should:

- convene, attend and present information about the reason for the conference, their understanding of the child's needs, parental capacity and family and environmental context and evidence of how the child has been abused or neglected and its impact on their health and development;
- analyse the information to enable informed decisions about what action is necessary to safeguard and promote the welfare of the child who is the subject of the conference;
- share the conference information with the child and family beforehand (where appropriate);
- prepare a report for the conference on the child and family which sets out and analyses what is known about the child and family and the local authority's recommendation; and
- record conference decisions and recommendations and ensure action follows.

If a Child Protection Conferences decides that a child has or is likely to suffer significant harm, a child protection plan should be drawn up and a core group established to carry out the tasks identified in the plan.

The purpose of a child protection plan

Working Together sets out the purpose of a child protection plan (see **Box 7.15**).

BOX 7.15 Purpose of a child protection plan—*Working Together to Safeguard Children* (2018)

The aim of the child protection plan is to:

- ensure the child is safe from harm and prevent them from suffering further harm;
- promote the child's health and development;
- support the family and wider family members to safeguard and promote the welfare of their child, provided it is in the best interests of the child.

Responsibilities of local authority children's social care:

- designate a social worker to be the lead professional as they carry statutory responsibility for the child's welfare;
- consider the evidence and decide what legal action to take if any, where a child has suffered, or is likely to suffer, significant harm; and
- define the local protocol for timeliness of circulating plans after the child protection conference.

Responsibilities of the lead social worker:

- be the lead professional for inter-agency work with the child and family, co-ordinating the contribution of family members and professionals into putting the child protection plan into effect;

- develop the outline child protection plan into a more detailed inter-agency plan and circulate to relevant practitioners (and family where appropriate);

- ensure the child protection plan is aligned and integrated with any associated offender risk management plan;

- undertake direct work with the child and family in accordance with the child protection plan, taking into account the child's wishes and feelings and the views of the parents in so far as they are consistent with the child's welfare;

- complete the child's and family's in-depth assessment, securing contributions from core group members and others as necessary;

- explain the plan to the child in a manner which is in accordance with their age and understanding and agree the plan with the child;

- consider the need to inform the relevant Embassy if the child has links to a foreign country;

- coordinate reviews of progress against the planned outcomes set out in the plan, updating as required. The first review should be held within 3 months of the initial conference and further reviews at intervals of no more than 6 months for as long as the child remains subject of a child protection plan;

- record decisions and actions agreed at core group meetings as well as the written views of those who were not able to attend, and follow up those actions to ensure they take place. The child protection plan should be updated as necessary;

- and lead core group activity.

To support joint working, responsibilities of the core group:

- meet within 10 working days from the initial child protection conference if the child is the subject of a child protection plan;

- develop the outline child protection plan, based on assessment findings, and set out what needs to change, by how much, and by when in order for the child to be safe and have their needs met;

- decide what steps need to be taken, and by whom, to complete the in-depth assessment to inform decisions about the child's safety and welfare; and

- implement the child protection plan and take joint responsibility for carrying out the agreed tasks, monitoring progress and outcomes, and refining the plan as needed.

SUMMARY

- The purpose of assessments of children should be to gather important information about children and families and analyse need and risk of harm, and to decide what support to offer. Assessments should be child centred and focused on outcomes. *Working Together to Safeguard Children* sets out the assessment requirements.

- Courts can require local authorities to carry out investigations under s. 37 of the Children Act 1989.

- Local authorities are under a duty (s. 47) to investigate whether a child is being or is likely to be significantly harmed, and to do something about it. Strategy discussions should normally follow s. 47 investigations. These are designed to coordinate information arising from investigation, including criminal investigations, and to decide further action.

- Initial child protection conferences are held to analyse information from s. 47 investigations and strategy discussions. Conferences should establish child protection plans or children in need plans.

- Local authorities, health services, and the police are the primary safeguarding partners in each locality and they should establish arrangements to support and enable local organizations and agencies to work together to safeguard children.

- Requirements for undertaking serious case reviews now lie with a national body, the Child Safeguarding Practice Review Panel.

EXERCISE

Consider the following evolving scenario and then answer the questions arising.

Mary, the six-year-old child of Tom and Ann, was found at school with a series of dark bruises on her back. She was examined by a paediatrician who said that they were the result of being hit and that there were some additional fingertip bruises on her arm. Mary said her dad had hit her. When questioned, Tom denies hitting Mary. Ann, whilst not saying what happened, talks about Tom's drinking and problems in the marriage. There are financial difficulties and the family want to be rehoused. There is a new baby, Peter, who is three months old. Ann appears to be finding coping a strain. Your initial conclusion (which may only be an instinctive feeling) is that the current pressures faced by the family are responsible for the situation in which Tom takes out his frustrations by hitting Mary.

1 What further inquiries would you make?

2 What, if any, statutory duties arise?

You discuss the case with colleagues; there is a child protection case conference.

3 Who would you expect to be present at the case conference?

4 What questions need to be decided at the initial case conference?

The case conference decides to make Mary the subject of a CP plan. You are the lead professional.

5 How would you explain that decision to Tom and Ann?

6 Who would you expect to be in your core group?

7 What action needs to be taken to record your decisions?

ONLINE RESOURCES

For guidance on how to answer this exercise, visit the online resources at
www.oup.com/uk/carr-goosey15e.

WHERE DO WE GO FROM HERE?

You have read in this chapter an account of the structures which have been set up to respond to concerns about children. They rely on effective cooperation and clear understanding of roles. You also know something of the process of responding to concerns about particular children, and the need to move from investigation of possible abuse to starting the planning process which is necessary for the future welfare of a child. The investigation and planning process prepares the social worker for a potential court application. However, the social worker also needs to consider the long-term future of children. **Chapter 8** focuses on preparing for court.

We return to planning for the long-term security of the child in **chapter 9**.

ANNOTATED FURTHER READING

Assessment

L. Devine, (2017) *The Limits of State Power and Private Rights: Exploring Child Protection and Safeguarding Referrals and Assessment* (London: Routledge). This book explores the theoretical, practical, and legal boundaries of State power following safeguarding and child protection referrals in England.

A. Bilson, B. Featherstone, and K. Martin, 'How child protection's "investigative turn" impacts on poor and deprived communities' *Family Law* 47: 316–19. This article explores the increase in child protection investigations.

Plans

J. Harwin and M. Owen, 'The implementation of care plans and its relationship to children's welfare' (2003) *CFLQ* 15(1): 71. An interesting piece of research into what constitutes a good or bad care plan.

A critical commentary on conjoined cases involving the question of whether the courts should monitor the implementation of care orders by local authorities is provided by N. Mole, a leading human rights lawyer, in '*Re W & B, RE W (Care Plans) and Re S (Minors) (Care Order: Implementation of Care Plan) Re W (Minors) (Care Order: Adequacy of Care Plan)*. A note on the judgment from the perspective of the European Convention for Protection of Human Rights and Fundamental Freedoms' (2002) *CFLQ* 14(4): 447.

Investigation and child protection

A new challenging text on child protection as published in 2014 examining whether services reinforce deprivation in families subject to child protection inquiries or ameliorate them is B. Featherstone, S. White, and K. Morris, *Re-Imagining Child Protection: Towards Humane Social Work with Families* (Policy Press, 2014).

N. Biehal, 'Balancing prevention and protection: child protection in England' in L. Merkel-Holguin, J. Fluke, and R. Krugman (eds), *National Systems of Child Protection. Child Maltreatment (Contemporary Issues in Research and Policy)*, vol 8 (Springer, 2018). This article examines the tensions at the heart of state intervention and the need to balance the rights of children and parents.

8 Applying to court

OVERVIEW AND OBJECTIVES

This chapter is concerned with Parts IV and V of the Children Act 1989. Part IV deals with care and supervision. Part V is concerned with child protection. These Parts of the Act contain the compulsory orders which require in general an application to a court. The exception to this requirement is the power of the police to remove a child to a place of safety under s. 46 of the Act. It is the courts which ensure that local authority action is legitimate. Legitimacy requires that the statutory provisions are observed and that the protections provided by the Human Rights Act 1998 are maintained. A key concept that justifies compulsory intervention in family life and which underpins both Part IV and Part V of the Act is significant harm, which we will discuss at length in this chapter. We summarize the range of orders available under the Children Act 1989. We then describe the longer-term orders available under Part IV of the Act (care orders and supervision orders), before turning to the short-term orders contained in Part V. As we set out the requirements and effects of each order, compare and contrast these. Which orders are easier to obtain? What impact does the order have on the parent(s)' parental responsibility? What constraints are there on the powers of the local authority? Why is s. 46 an exception to the general requirement of supervision by the courts?

Court orders cannot, of course, be obtained without proper preparation by those applying for them. Thorough preparation is necessary in order to minimize delay and to maximize the effectiveness of the courts in dealing with inevitably complex cases.

We begin this chapter by considering what local authorities need to do before applying to court.

All statutory references in this chapter are to the Children Act 1989, unless otherwise stated.

 CASE STUDY

MA, SA and HA (Children, by their Children's Guardian) v MA, HA, The City and County of Swansea

Why are we asking you to read this case?

The threshold signifying the point at which the state can intervene in family life or not is defined in the Children Act 1989 by the term 'significant harm'. This was a landmark case in respect of how the courts interpret the words in that term. Social workers working with children must have a comprehensive understanding of significant harm. This case is also important because the Court of Appeal accepted that one of the children had been harmed, but did not accept that there was a real possibility that the others would be harmed in the future.

What was at stake for the parties and beyond?

Importantly, much was at stake for the children. Their guardian was the one who appealed on their behalf. The older child had been treated appallingly and it was thought the witnessing of this would have caused the young children to be harmed. The guardian considered an appeal absolutely necessary. The court, however, painstakingly explored what Parliament had meant by the relevant wording of s. 31 of the Children Act and by a majority concluded that the original trial judge had been right.

Facts

M, S, and H, aged four years, 20 months, and four months respectively, had been placed in the care of the local authority following an allegation that their parents (P) had physically and sexually abused another child (X) who was living in the family home. During a fact-finding hearing, the judge found that P's treatment of X had been shocking and that M and S had been exposed to it. Findings of physical abuse against M were also made.

Issues

The issue before the judge was whether the evidence established to the satisfaction of the court on the balance of probabilities that the threshold set by s. 31 of the Children Act 1989 had been crossed. However, the judge concluded that in relation to M, S, and H, the threshold under s. 31(2) of the Children Act 1989 had not been crossed. The judge reached that conclusion on the basis of findings that:

(a) neither M nor S had suffered significant emotional harm as a result of their exposure to P's treatment of X;
(b) the emotional harm suffered by M as a result of her physical abuse could not be described as significant;
(c) it was not likely that M and S would suffer more harm through exposure to P's ill-treatment of X because X had been removed from the family home;
(d) there was a real distinction in the way that P chose to treat their own children from the way they treated X and so there was no basis for finding a likelihood of significant harm in relation to them.

The children's guardian appealed on behalf of M, S, and H. What the Court of Appeal had to decide was whether the judge, having decided that M had suffered some harm, was plainly wrong in concluding that she had not suffered significant harm. The court also had to determine whether the judge had erred in concluding that there was no likelihood of significant harm in relation to each or all of the children.

Decision

The appeal by the children's guardian was dismissed for two reasons:

(1) Given the underlying philosophy of the 1989 Act, the harm must be significant enough to justify the intervention by the state. It must be significant enough to enable the court to make a care order or a supervision order if the welfare of the child demanded it. In the instant case, the judge was fully entitled to conclude that the harm suffered by M was not significant.
(2) The judge had asked himself whether, on the proven facts, there was a real possibility of the children suffering or being likely to suffer significant harm in the future. Although P's treatment of X was truly shocking, the judge had not erred in concluding that it did not necessarily follow that P's biological children would suffer in the same or similar way. There had been good evidence before the judge that P's biological children were treated differently. Although P's treatment of X was to be deplored, the judge had been best placed to decide on the primary facts and was plainly not wrong in declining to find that the threshold of significant harm had been crossed.

One judge dissented—Lord Justice Wilson. He considered that the conduct of the parents towards X was so grossly abnormal as to show a capacity for cruelty towards children which, surely, gives rise to a real possibility that it would also be directed towards their own children. Nonetheless, the majority dismissed the appeal.

> **WHAT DOES THIS CASE TELL US ABOUT SOCIAL WORK PRACTICE?**
>
> The case demonstrates how important it is to appreciate the meaning of the words of the statute. Unless the children were suffering or were likely to suffer 'significant' harm, the necessary threshold for the making of a care order was not crossed. On the other hand, the dissent shows that the assessment of when harm is significant enough to justify intervention is likely to vary from judge to judge. Variations in judging the threshold for significant harm also affects the hundreds and thousands of decisions that social workers, managers, and lawyers face every week in local authorities.
>
> We will return to the words used in s. 31 of the Children Act later in this chapter. At this point what we want you to do as you work through the chapter is to notice how the legislation and the case law attempt to strike a balance between the need to protect children and the rights of individuals to a family life. The legislation sets out checks and balances on the responsibilities of the state. The courts supervise state intervention, ensuring that it provides appropriate protection for children, but preventing intervention which oversteps the boundaries set by Parliament. Having a thorough knowledge of significant harm is an essential prerequisite for any social worker working in the field of child protection.

Preparing for court proceedings

Review of the family justice system

David Norgrove was asked by Gordon Brown's Labour government to form a committee to review the family justice system. The committee began its work in March 2010 and provided a final report in November 2011. The government recognized the strain the system was working under and in its response to the Family Justice Review, it commented:

> Case volumes have increased in recent years and are still increasing. The number of children involved in public law applications was 10% higher in the last 12 months than the preceding 12 months. Similarly, it was 10% higher in 2010 than in 2006. Care and supervision cases are taking longer—applications take an average of 55 weeks. There are around 20,000 children currently waiting for a decision in public law, compared to some 11,000 at the end of 2008. The Family Justice Review estimated that the total cost of public law cases in 2009–10 was over £1bn.

Similar strains were identified for children in private law proceedings. Following this review, the Family Justice Board was established in March 2012 to drive forward changes identified in the Family Justice Review. The remit of the Board was to:

> provide the leadership and direction necessary to implement . . . ambitious plans for change. . . . The Board's overall aim is to drive significant improvements in the performance of the family justice system where performance is defined in terms of how effective (and

efficient) the system is in supporting the delivery of the best possible outcomes for children who come into contact with it.

The Board's terms of reference were:

i)   reducing delay in public law cases and making progress against the proposed 26-week time limit for care cases;

ii) resolving private law cases out of court where appropriate;

iii) building greater cross-agency coherence; and

iv) tackling variations in local performance.

Since the introduction of the 26-week limit the average duration of cases has reduced from 53.9 weeks in January–March 2012 to 30 weeks in January–March 2018, the highest average since early 2014. Forty-nine per cent of cases were disposed of within 26 weeks—down seven percentage points over the same period for 2017.

The proposed 26-week time limit for care proceedings has focused the minds of those in the court process, although it is clearly a constant battle.

The government also accepted another recommendation of the Family Justice Review to make the distinction between the role of the courts and local authorities in children's care plans clear. Lord Phillips and Lady Hale, Supreme Court justices, commented in their submission to the Family Justice Review:

> If parental rights and responsibilities are to be changed or rearranged, article 6(1) of the ECHR [European Convention on Human Rights] requires that the decision be made by a court after a fair hearing. A fair process is also required by article 8 where the state interferes with the right to respect for family life. But the court's current close involvement with the formulation of the care plan in care proceedings goes beyond what was originally envisaged when the Children Act was passed and probably beyond what is required by the ECHR. Article 8 requires that the courts have some control over the contact between parents and children in care and also over the decision to sever contact with the birth family. But it does not require that the courts have control over how the child is looked after in care. Courts cannot look after children or conjure up the resources with which to do so.

The Family Justice Review concluded:

- Courts must continue to play a central role in public law in England and Wales.
- Courts should refocus on the core issues of whether the child is to live with parents, other family or friends, or be removed to the care of the local authority.
- When determining whether a care order is in a child's best interests the court will not normally need to scrutinise the full detail of a local authority care plan for a child. Instead the court should consider only the core or essential components of a child's plan. We propose that these are:
  - planned return of the child to their family;
  - a plan to place (or explore placing) a child with family or friends;
  - alternative care arrangements; and
  - contact with birth family to the extent of deciding whether that should be regular, limited or none.

The Children and Families Act 2014 amends s. 31 so that courts are required to consider the permanence provisions for the child concerned only insofar as this addresses whether the child should:

(a) live with any parent of the child's or with any other member of, or any friend of, the child's family;

(b) be adopted;

(c) or remain in permanent fostering.

The Children and Social Work Act 2017, further amend s. 31 by requiring the courts to consider:

(a) such of the plan's provisions setting out the long-term plan for the upbringing of the child concerned as provide for any of the following—
   (i) the child to live with any parent of the child's or with any other member of, or any friend of, the child's family;
   (ii) adoption;
   (iii) long-term care not within sub-paragraph (i) or (ii);

(b) such of the plan's provisions as set out any of the following—
   (i) the impact on the child concerned of any harm that he or she suffered or was likely to suffer;
   (ii) the current and future needs of the child (including needs arising out of that impact);
   (iii) the way in which the long-term plan for the upbringing of the child would meet those current and future needs.

The purpose of these amendments is to raise the bar in respect of the standard of parenting to be expected from family and friends to promote adoption as a preferred outcome following the judgment in Re B-S (2013). See **chapter 9**.

These changes to s. 31 require the continued promotion of the enhanced role of the local authority independent reviewing officer in scrutinizing care plans and ensuring that they address the needs of the child. Indeed, the Government Response to the Family Justice Review has suggested that ongoing work to provide greater confidence in the scrutiny role of the independent reviewing officers (IROs) in England will be particularly important. Sadly, a recent national review of the IRO service concluded that 'the IRO role in ensuring high quality care planning is yet to be fully realised' (H. Jelicic et al., *The role of Independent Reviewing Officers (IROs) in England* (NCB, 2014)).

Revised guidance—Volume 1: *Court Orders and Pre-Proceedings April 2014*

The introductory remarks in this revised guidance summarize its aims and objectives:

> The Children and Families Act 2014 implements the Government's reforms in response to the Family Justice Review. These legislative changes are accompanied by a simplification of the court system with the majority of family cases heard by a Single Family Court. In private law, reforms make clear that, where safe and appropriate, a child should have the opportunity to benefit from the involvement of both parents. In public law new legislation addresses unjustified and potentially damaging delays in court proceedings.

The provision of early help for children and families is the bedrock of the reforms first muted in the Munro Review of Child Protection (see **chapter 5**). Local authorities and other agencies are urged to recognize that:

> Providing early help is more effective in promoting the welfare of children than reacting later. Local authorities will need to work with other agencies, as appropriate, to put processes in place for the effective assessment of the needs of individual children who may benefit from early help services and to ensure that support is provided.

What matters is that children's needs are met and this is clearly better done earlier than later. However, sometimes problems in families are more deep-seated and require more intensive intervention. In these instances, local authorities are likely to be called upon to undertake more detailed assessments and this is certainly the case if professionals are worried that a child is or is likely to be significantly harmed. Engaging both parents and children is nearly always essential when undertaking assessments in these circumstances and this is likely to increase the validity and reliability of reports. In turn, when social work reports are well written and based on carefully collected evidence, and which include all of the relevant historical information, decision making is improved. When these reports are used in care proceedings, courts are less likely to require expert evidence. The hope is that the duration of proceedings will reduce. Family Group Conferences are a way to promote understanding amongst wider family members of the seriousness of cases where significant harm is likely or has occurred, prompting action to protect children or relatives to come forward to provide alternative care. Once again, early intervention from wider family members can help to reduce delay in care proceedings, but only if family members are engaged early enough. Some current delays in care proceedings are created when family members come forward late in the cycle of the proceedings when matters might otherwise be settled.

Legal planning meeting

When the local authority is concerned that the threshold described in s. 31(2) has been met, it is likely to consult with legal advisers at a legal planning meeting. The *Statutory Guidance on Court Orders and Pre-Proceedings* states that the legal planning meeting should:

> [decide] in principle about whether the threshold criteria have been met. The local authority should then decide, based on a robust analysis of the level of assessed risk, whether it is in the best interests of the child to provide a further period of support for the family with the aim of avoiding proceedings, or whether proceedings should be initiated immediately. The meeting should also identify any evidence gaps, clarify whether additional assessments will be required, and consider what would be a suitable draft care plan for the child.

When a decision has been made to apply to the court under s. 31, the local authority should issue one of two letters to the parents and anyone else with parental responsibility. The Letter before Proceedings states that proceedings are being contemplated and the Letter of Issue states that proceedings are being initiated. Templates for these letters can be found in the statutory guidance, but you are advised to explore the templates available locally.

The social work documents which should accompany an application are:

- social work chronology;
- social work statement and genogram;
- the current assessments relating to the child and/or the family and friends of the child to which the social work statement refers and on which the local authority relies;
- the care plan.

In preparedness for proceedings under s. 31 it is vital that these documents are complete. **Box 8.1** sets out the headings under which the social work statement should be organized.

 BOX 8.1 The social work statement should contain—Practice Direction 12A—Care, Supervision and Other Part 4 Proceedings: Guide to Case Management

Summary

(a) The order sought;

(b) Succinct summary of reasons with reference as appropriate to the Welfare Checklist;

Family

(c) Family members and relationships especially the primary carers and significant adults/ other children;

(d) Genogram;

Threshold

(e) Precipitating events;

(f) Background circumstances—

(i) summary of children's services involvement cross-referenced to the chronology;

(ii) previous court orders and emergency steps;

(iii) previous assessments;

(g) Summary of significant harm and or likelihood of significant harm which the LA will seek to establish by evidence or concession;

Parenting capability

(h) Assessment of child's needs;

(i) Assessment of parental capability to meet needs;

(j) Analysis of why there is a gap between parental capability and the child's needs;

(k) Assessment of other significant adults who may be carers;

Child impact

(l) Wishes and feelings of the child(ren);

(m) Timetable for the child;

(n) Delay and timetable for the proceedings;

Permanence and contact

(o) Parallel planning;

(p) Realistic placement options by reference to a welfare and proportionality analysis;

(q) Contact framework;

Case management

(r) Evidence and assessments necessary and outstanding;

(s) Any information about any person's litigation capacity, mental health issues, disabilities or vulnerabilities that is relevant to their capability to participate in the proceedings; and

(t) Case management proposals.

The full range of orders and powers available under Parts IV and V of the Act is set out in summary tabular form in **Table 8.1**.

TABLE 8.1 The range of orders and powers in Parts IV and V

Order/power	Section	Comment
Care order	ss 31 and 33	Long-term orders which commit the child to the care of the local authority. They provide extensive powers to local authorities but require evidence which demonstrates to the court that a child is suffering, or likely to suffer, significant harm and that the harm or likelihood of harm is attributable to a lack of adequate parental care or control.
Supervision order	s. 35	An order which places the child under the supervision of a social worker or probation officer. The grounds upon which an order can be made are identical to the care order.

Order/power	Section	Comment
Interim care/supervision order	s. 38	An order made pending a full hearing of the application for a care order. An initial interim order cannot last longer than eight weeks. Subsequent interim orders cannot last longer than four weeks.
Child assessment order	s. 43	A short-term order (maximum seven days) which provides for the compulsory assessment of the child's state of health and development.
Emergency protection order	s. 44	A short-term order which either removes the child on a short-term basis, or allows the child to be kept in a place of safety or requires an alleged abuser to leave the family home. The grounds for the emergency protection order are much easier to prove but successful applicants gain limited powers.
Removal and accommodation of children by police	s. 46	No court order is necessary for the police to implement this power, which enables the police to remove a child or to keep a child in a safe place.
Child recovery order	s. 49	Enables the return of the child to a 'responsible person'.

The flowchart of pre-proceedings work issued as part of the statutory guidance is detailed in **Figure 8.1**.

Care plans for court

Since the implementation of s. 31A of the Children Act 1989, when any application is made upon which a care order might be made, the local authority must, within such time as the court may direct, prepare and submit to the court a s. 31A care plan which will set out basic information for the court, including details about the management of the child's case and long-term planning for the child. This should have been carefully scrutinized by the authority and should conform with the guidance set out in the *Children Act 1989 Guidance and Regulations, Volume 2: Care Planning, Placement and Case Review*. **Box 8.2** states that the care plan should include:

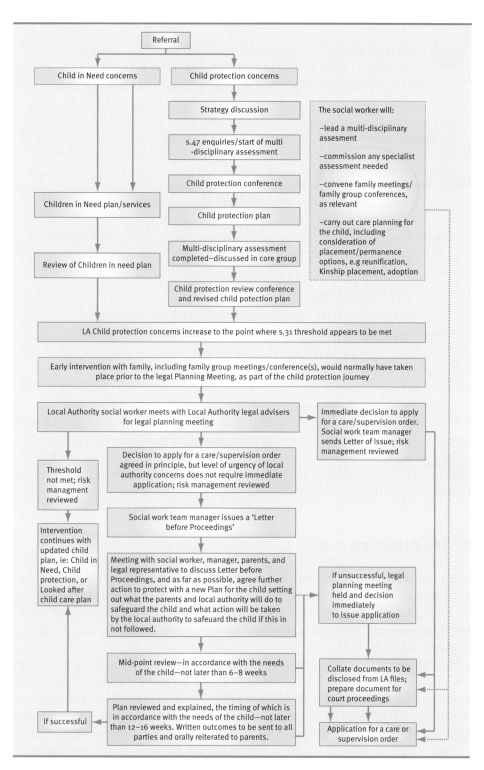

FIGURE 8.1 Guidelines prior to making an application for a care or supervision order

Source: Department for Education, April 2014.

BOX 8.2 Components of the care plan—*Children Act 1989 Guidance and Regulations, Volume 2: Care Planning, Placement and Case Review*

- the information about the long-term plan for the child, including timescales (the permanence plan);

- the arrangements to meet the child's needs in line with the child's developmental needs domain of the Assessment Framework, including arrangements for contact:

  - arrangements for contact with a brother or sister who is also looked after but not placed with the child;

  - details of any court orders made under s. 8 or s. 34; and

  - arrangements for promoting and maintaining contact with a parent and anyone else with parental responsibility;

- details of the placement plan and why the placement was chosen, unless the child is in care and not provided with accommodation by the responsible authority;

- the name of the child's IRO;

- details of the health plan and personal education plan (PEP);

- the wishes and feelings of relevant people about the arrangements for the child; and

- the wishes and feelings of these people about any proposed changes to the care plan;

- in drawing up a care plan, the responsible authority should have a contingency plan in the event that the care plan is not achievable.

It is the permanence plan that the court is most likely to scrutinize, although the paramountcy principle means that the court is not prevented from a more detailed analysis of the care plan if it considers it is in the child's best interests. Courts are less likely to carry out this detailed analysis when local authorities are able to demonstrate that they have carried out rigorous assessments.

The Public Law Outline

The purpose of the Public Law Outline Practice Direction 12A—Care, Supervision and Other Part 4 Proceedings Guide to Case Management is to ensure improved case preparation, active case management by judges, and the early identification of the key issues requiring determination by the courts in public law applications under the Children Act.

The Public Law Outline explains what judges must do in order actively to manage cases to ensure most effective outcomes for children. This is very much nuts-and-bolts procedural material and may seem a million miles away from your role as a social worker. Nevertheless, it is necessary for you to comply if you wish to make the most of your applications to the court and to gain the respect of the court for your professionalism.

There is a useful overview of what is required by the Public Law Outline in Appendix A to the guidance, which is copied in **Figure 8.2** and **Box 8.3**.

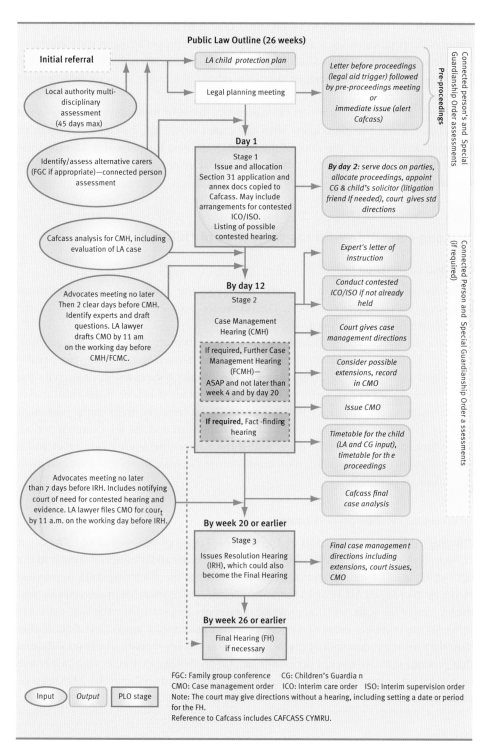

FIGURE 8.2 Court proceedings—Public Law Outline

Source: Department for Education, April 2014.

Although careful attention to procedure is crucial to ensure good and effective out-comes of court proceedings, it should never prevent the proper airing of the substantive issues in a case. Judges received a salutary reminder of this when, in *P and P (Children)* (2009) the Court of Appeal slapped down the refusal of a judge, in a case management conference, to allow the local authority to instruct a second expert paediatric patholo-gist on the ground that this would cause excessive delay. In its opinion, the judge acted prematurely. Until the judge knew what the expert would say, he could not make an informed decision about the value of the report. Moreover, the judge should respect the expertise of the local authority in determining what evidence it considers necessary to substantiate its application.

Long-term orders for the protection of children

Care and supervision orders

These orders provide for the long-term welfare of the child. They require identical grounds to be proved to the court. The difference between the two orders concerns control over the child involved.

A care order gives the local authority the power to protect a child through acqui-sition of parental responsibility. That may involve removing the child, but equally it can and does permit the child to be left at home. A supervision order puts the child under the supervision of a social worker or probation officer. If the court makes a supervision order, the child will not normally be removed from home, although there are powers to direct the child to live at a specified address for a limited period. Supervision orders are less intrusive, and if the balance between a care order and a supervision order is equal, the court should adopt the least interventionist and most proportionate approach.

Intervention must be proportionate

This was made clear by the Court of Appeal in *Re O (Supervision Order)* (2001). The Court of Appeal considered the relationship between a care order and a supervision order in the light of the need for intervention to be proportionate to the risk to the child, as required by the Human Rights Act 1998. In the particular case, the risk was felt by the court to be at the low end of the scale, and that provided the parents cooperated and the local authority delivered the necessary range of services to protect the child, a supervision order (rather than the care order requested by the local authority) was appropriate. The court indicated that previous case law was not necessarily helpful on this distinction, as each case has to be decided on its own facts and the requirements of the Human Rights Act 1998 must be considered.

BOX 8.3 Court proceedings—Public Law Outline

Stage 1—ISSUE AND ALLOCATION

Day 1 and Day 2 (see interpretation section)

On Day 1 (day of issue):

- The LA files the Application Form and Annex Documents and sends copies to Cafcass/CAFCASS CYMRU
- The LA notifies the court of the need for an urgent preliminary case management hearing or an urgent contested ICO hearing where this is known or expected
- Court officer issues application

Within a day of issue (Day 2):

- Court considers jurisdiction in a case with an international element
- Court considers initial allocation to specified level of judge, in accordance with the Allocation Rules and any President's Guidance on the distribution of business
- LA serves the Application Form, Annex Documents and evidential Checklist Documents on the parties together with the notice of date and time of CMH and any urgent hearing
- Court gives standard directions on Issue and Allocation including:
  - Checking compliance with Pre-Proceedings Checklist including service of any missing Annex Documents
  - Appointing Children's Guardian (to be allocated by Cafcass/CAFCASS CYMRU)
  - Appointing solicitor for the child only if necessary
  - Appointing (if the person to be appointed consents) a litigation friend for any protected party or any non subject child who is a party, including the OS where appropriate
  - Identifying whether a request has been made or should be made to a Central Authority or other competent authority in a foreign state or a consular authority in England and Wales in a case with an international element
  - Filing and service of a LA Case Summary
  - Filing and service of a Case Analysis by the Children's Guardian
  - Filing and Serving the Parents' Response
  - Sending a request for disclosure to, e.g., the police or health service body
  - Filing and serving an application for permission relating to experts under Part 25 on a date prior to the advocates meeting for the CMH
  - Directing the solicitor for the child to arrange an advocates' meeting no later than 2 business days before the CMH
  - Listing the CMH
- Court considers any request for an urgent preliminary case management hearing or an urgent contested ICO hearing and where necessary lists the hearing and gives additional directions
- Court officer sends copy Notice of Hearing of the CMH and any urgent hearing by email to Cafcass/CAFCASS CYMRU.

Stage 2—CASE MANAGEMENT HEARING

ADVOCATE'S MEETING (including any litigants in person)

CASE MANAGEMENT HEARING

No later than 2 business days before CMH (or FCMH if it is necessary)

CMH: Not before Day 12 and not later than Day 18

A FCMH is to be held only if necessary, it is to be listed as soon as possible, and in any event no later than Day 25

- Consider information on the Application Form and Annex documents, the LA Case Summary, and the Case Analysis
- Identify the parties' positions to be recited in the draft Case Management Order
- Identify the parties' positions about jurisdiction, in particular arising out of any international element
- If necessary, identify proposed experts and draft questions in accordance with Part 25 and the Experts Practice Directions
- Identify any disclosure that in the advocates' views is necessary
- Immediately notify the court of the need for a contested ICO hearing and any issue about allocation
- LA advocate to file a draft Case Management Order in prescribed form with court by 11a.m. on the business day before the CMH and/or FCMH

- Court gives detailed case management directions, including:
  - Considering jurisdiction in a case with an international element
  - Confirming allocation
  - Drawing up the timetable for the child and the timetable for the proceedings and considering if an extension is necessary
  - Identifying additional parties, intervenors and representation (including confirming that Cafcass/CAFCASS CYMRU have allocated a Children's Guardian and that a litigation friend is appointed for any protected party or non subject child)
  - Giving directions for the determination of any disputed issue about litigation capacity
  - Identifying the key issues
  - Identifying the evidence necessary to enable the court to resolve the key issues
  - Deciding whether there is a real issue about threshold to be resolved
  - Determining any application made under Part 25 and otherwise ensuring compliance with Part 25 where it is necessary for expert(s) to be instructed
  - Identifying any necessary disclosure and if appropriate giving directions
  - Giving directions for any concurrent or proposed placement order proceedings
  - Ensuring compliance with the court's directions
  - If a FCMH is necessary, directing an advocates' meeting and Case Analysis if required
  - Directing filing of any threshold agreement, final evidence and Care Plan and responses to those documents for the IRH
  - Directing a Case Analysis for the IRH
  - Directing an advocates' meeting for the IRH
  - Listing (any FCMH) IRH, Final Hearing (including early Final Hearing) as appropriate
  - Giving directions for special measures and/or interpreters and intermediaries
  - Issuing the Case Management Order

Stage 3—ISSUES RESOLUTION HEARING	
ADVOCATE'S MEETING (including any litigants in person)	**IRH**
No later than 7 business days before the IRH	As directed by the court, in accordance with the timetable for the proceedings
<ul><li>Review evidence and the positions of the parties</li><li>Identify the advocates' views of–<ul><li>the remaining key issues and how the issues may be resolved or narrowed at the IRH including by the making of final orders</li><li>the further evidence which is required to be heard to enable the key issues to be resolved or narrowed at the IRH</li><li>the evidence that is relevant and the witnesses that are required at the final hearing</li><li>the need for a contested hearing and/or time for oral evidence to be given at the IRH</li></ul></li><li>LA advocate to–<ul><li>notify the court immediately of the outcome of the discussion at the meeting</li><li>file a draft Case Management Order with the court by 11 a.m. on the business day before the IRH</li></ul></li></ul>	<ul><li>Court identifies the key issue(s) (if any) to be determined and the extent to which those issues can be resolved or narrowed at the IRH</li><li>Court considers whether the IRH can be used as a final hearing</li><li>Court resolves or narrows the issues by hearing evidence</li><li>Court identifies the evidence to be heard on the issues which remain to be resolved at the final hearing</li><li>Court gives final case management directions including:<ul><li>Any extension of the timetable for the proceedings which is necessary</li><li>Filing of the threshold agreement or a statement of facts/issues remaining to be determined</li><li>Filing of:<ul><li>Final evidence and Care Plan</li><li>Case Analysis for Final Hearing (if required)</li><li>Witness templates</li><li>Skeleton arguments</li></ul></li><li>Judicial reading list/reading time, including time estimate and an estimate for judgment writing time</li><li>Ensuring Compliance with PD27A (the Bundles Practice Direction)</li><li>Listing the Final Hearing</li></ul></li><li>Court issues Case Management Order</li></ul>

Source: Department of Education, April 2014.

Care orders

A care order should be applied for only when the principle of the diminishment of the need for court proceedings has been tried or considered and been found to be unsuccessful or inapplicable. Both the revised guidance and the Public Law Outline emphasize this.

Applications

Section 31(1) of the 1989 Act determines who may apply for a care order: **Box 8.4** sets this out. You will see that a distinction is made between the application, which can be made by any local authority or the National Society for the Prevention of Cruelty to Children (NSPCC), and the actual care order, which is made to a *designated* authority. The purpose of this is to ensure that the local authority close to the children concerned has the long-term responsibility for managing and implementing the care plan. The designated local authority is defined in s. 31(8) of the Children Act 1989 as the local authority where the child is ordinarily resident or, where the child does not reside in the area of a local authority, the authority within whose area any circumstances arose in consequence of which the order is made.

BOX 8.4 Who may apply for a care order—s. 31(1) of the Children Act

(1) On the application of any local authority or authorised person [only the NSPCC is authorized], the court may make an order—

    (a) placing the child with respect to whom the application is made in the care of a designated local authority; or

    (b) putting the child under the supervision of a designated local authority or a probation officer.

The grounds for a care order

The grounds, known as the 'threshold criteria', are contained in s. 31(2) set out in **Box 8.5**. They set out the minimum criteria necessary before the court can consider compulsory intervention in family life. The court will proceed to apply the welfare principles contained in s. 1 only if it is satisfied that the threshold criteria apply.

BOX 8.5 The grounds for a care order—s. 31(2) of the Children Act 1989

(2) A court may only make a care order or supervision order if it is satisfied—

    (a) that the child concerned is suffering, or is likely to suffer, significant harm; and

    (b) that the harm, or likelihood of harm, is attributable to—

        (i) the care given to the child, or likely to be given to him if the order were not made, not being what it would be reasonable to expect a parent to give to him; or

        (ii) the child's being beyond parental control.

Two questions require answering

You will notice that the section requires that the court answers two distinct questions.

When considering an application for a care or supervision order, a court must:

(a) be satisfied that the grounds in s. 31 (the threshold criteria) are met; and

(b) decide whether, by applying the grounds in s. 1, to make an order and what order to make.

Whilst there are two steps that the courts must take, these are not distinct, but inter-linked. This was made clear by Baroness Hale in *Re B (Children) (Care Proceedings: Standard of Proof)* (2008), which we will discuss further (see **Re B (Children) (Care Proceedings: Standard of Proof) (2008)**, p 298). The observation she made about the decision-making process is set out in **Box 8.6**.

BOX 8.6 Baroness Hale's observations in Re B *(Children) (Care Proceedings: Standard of Proof)*

74 Care proceedings are not a two-stage process. The court does have two questions to ask. Has the threshold been crossed? If so, what will be best for the child? But there are many cases in which a court has two or more questions to ask in the course of a single hearing. The same factual issues are often relevant to each question. Or some factual disputes may be relevant to the threshold while others are relevant to the welfare checklist: it may be clear, for example, that a child has suffered an injury while in the care of the mother, but whether the father or stepfather has a drink problem and has been beating the mother up is extremely relevant to the long term welfare of the child.

75 The purpose of splitting the hearing is not to split the two questions which the court must answer. It is to separate out those factual issues which are capable of swift resolution so that the welfare professionals have a firm foundation of fact upon which to base their assessments of family relationships and parenting ability.

The threshold criteria in detail

Understanding the threshold criteria is a prerequisite for effective social work with children. Later we examine exactly what is required by s. 31 of the Children Act.

Present or future harm

Notice that care orders are obtained either on the basis that the child is currently suffering significant harm or on the basis of the likelihood that the child will suffer significant harm in the future.

When does the child have to have suffered significant harm?

The temporal qualities of the suffering need careful attention. Whilst past harm cannot be the basis of a care order, the necessity for present suffering for the purposes of the section has caused some difficulty because the child is unlikely to be suffering at the time of the hearing. In *Northampton County Council v S* (1992), the court considered at what time the significance of the harm should be considered. In this case, the mother had two children, a girl born in 1986 and a boy born in 1989. The children had different fathers. Following a non-accidental injury, the children were taken into voluntary care under the old law. The Children Act then came into force. The local authority applied for a care order. The father of the boy sought a residence order that the boy only was to live with the boy's grandmother. The magistrates granted the care order. The father appealed to the High Court. The High Court had to consider the meaning of 'suffering significant harm'. What is the effect of the present tense? It held that the phrase referred to the period immediately before the action commenced. Ewbank J said:

> That means the court has to consider the position immediately before the emergency protection order, if there was one or an interim care order, if that was the initiation of protection, or, as in this case, when the child went into voluntary care. In my judgment, the family proceedings court was quite entitled to consider the position when the children were with the mother prior to going into care and was correct in doing so.

Harm

Harm is defined in s. 31. The relevant subsections (9) and (10) are set out in **Box 8.7**.

 BOX 8.7 The meaning of harm—s. 31(9) and (10) of the Children Act 1989

(9) In this section—

‘harm’ means ill treatment or the impairment of health or development;

‘development’ means physical, intellectual, emotional, social or behavioural development;

‘health’ means physical or mental health; and

‘ill treatment’ includes sexual abuse and forms of treatment that are not physical including for example impairment suffered from seeing or hearing the ill treatment of another.

(10) Where the question of whether harm suffered by a child is significant turns on the child's health or development, his health shall be compared with that which could reasonably be expected of a similar child.

The cause of the harm

The harm that a child suffers or is likely to suffer must emanate from a failure of parenting. However, there is no expectation that the care which has to be provided for a child is at the standard of a perfect parent. What is required is reasonable parenting.

The reasonable parent

The presence or likelihood of significant harm has to be attributable to the fact that the care given or likely to be given to the child (as appropriate) is not what a parent would reasonably be expected to give to the child. Therefore, you have to look at the child in his or her context (home, surroundings, locale, etc.) and ask what a reasonable parent in that situation would be expected to do. So, for instance, a reasonable parent in most, but not all, circumstances would ensure that a child attends school or takes prescribed medicine.

Being beyond parental control

'Being beyond parental control' in s. 31(1)(b)(ii) is largely a self-explanatory matter of fact for the court to decide. An example of the use of this concept can be found in *K (A Child) (Post Adoption Placement Breakdown)* 2012. No blame need be apportioned to the parents for the court to decide that a child is beyond parental control. The key question remains: is the child suffering or likely to suffer significant harm by reason of being beyond parental control?

Significant harm

Harm is not sufficient for the purposes of the threshold criteria. The key phrase within s. 31(2) is significant harm. Whether harm is significant is a matter for the court to decide as a question of fact. In *MA, SA and HA (Children, by their Children's Guardian) v MA, HA, The City and County of Swansea* (2009), the case we considered at the beginning of the chapter, the Court of Appeal made it clear that Article 8 of the European Convention on Human Rights informs the meaning of 'significant' in the phrase 'significant harm' and serves to emphasize that there has to be a relevant and sufficient reason for crossing the threshold. However, Lord Wilson, in *Re B* (2013), contends that the Court of Appeal added an inappropriate layer of complexity in suggesting that Article 8 informs the meaning of the word 'significant'. Lord Wilson says at para. 29:

> No interference (with the right to family life) occurs when a judge concludes that the threshold is crossed. The interference occurs only if, at the welfare stage, the judge proceeds to make a care or supervision order; and it is the order which must therefore not fall foul of article 8.

Lord Wilson went on to argue that the court should avoid explaining the meaning of the word 'significant'. To do so he said would merely be a gloss.

The statute provides little help in making decisions about when harm is significant. Section 31(10) (see **Box 8.8**) requires that the significance of the harm is measured via comparison with a similar child. This may be a difficult comparison to achieve when children come from a huge variety of cultural and social backgrounds. Social workers must be careful not to impose particular norms of development. In Re O (1992) the judge made these comments about the meaning of 'similar child' in the context of whether non-attendance at school caused significant harm:

> In my judgment, in the context of this type of case, 'similar child' means a child of equivalent intellectual and social development, who has gone to school, and not merely an average child who may or may not be at school. In fact, what one has to ask oneself is whether this child suffered significant harm by not going to school. The answer, in my judgment, as in the magistrates' judgment is obvious.

Dictionary definitions indicate that 'significant' encompasses something more than the question of the magnitude of the harm. A broken arm, for instance, may not be 'significant' if it was suffered following a fall from playground equipment, but may be if it was suffered during a period when the child was left alone in the house or following a push from a parent. The use of a dictionary definition was endorsed in

Humberside County Council v B (1993), hence 'considerable, noteworthy or important' would describe significant. These terms rather imply that 'significant' harm is harm which is excessive, prominent, or critical to the child. Critical in this context is perhaps associated with damage to the child's developmental progress. But where does this leave you, the social worker? You have to decide, along with your colleagues, whether the harm done to a child is significant or not, and this judgement can be very difficult and not without controversy (see the case at the beginning of this chapter).

The categories of abuse are shown in **Box 8.8**, but these definitions are not without their inherent problems. The definition of physical abuse is merely a list of what might be classed as physical abuse and the definition of emotional abuse simply mentions the word 'maltreatment' so as to cause adverse effects on the child, which could mean many things. The definition of neglect is largely about the physical neglect of a child. What is not mentioned is emotional neglect, which might be thought to involve inadequate parents who are simply not able to provide 'good enough' parenting, despite their best endeavours. They are not 'abusive' but nonetheless their inadequacies lead to lasting damage to a child's developmental progress. Such parents probably make up the bulk of parents whose children come before the courts in care proceedings and yet the 'official' definitions give them little mention.

 BOX 8.8 Categories of abuse and neglect

Physical abuse	A form of abuse which may involve hitting, shaking, throwing, poisoning, burning, or scalding, drowning, suffocating or otherwise causing physical harm to a child. Physical harm may also be caused when a parent or carer fabricates the symptoms of, or deliberately induces, illness in a child.
Emotional abuse	The persistent emotional maltreatment of a child such as to cause severe and persistent adverse effects on the child's emotional development. It may involve conveying to a child that they are worthless or unloved, inadequate, or valued only insofar as they meet the needs of another person. It may include not giving the child opportunities to express their views, deliberately silencing them or 'making fun' of what they say or how they communicate. It may feature age or developmentally inappropriate expectations being imposed on children. These may include interactions that are beyond a child's developmental capability, as well as overprotection and limitation of exploration and learning, or preventing the child participating in normal social interaction. It may involve seeing or hearing the ill-treatment of another. It may involve serious bullying (including cyber bullying), causing the child frequently to feel frightened or in danger, or the exploitation or corruption of the child. Some level of emotional abuse is involved in all types of maltreatment of a child, though it may occur alone.

Sexual abuse	Involves forcing or enticing a child or young person to take part in sexual activities, not necessarily involving a high level of violence, whether or not the child is aware of what is happening. The activities may involve physical contact, including assault by penetration (e.g. rape or oral sex) or non-penetrative acts such as masturbation, kissing, rubbing, and touching outside clothing. They may also include non-contact activities, such as involving children in looking at, or in the production of, sexual images, watching sexual activities, encouraging children to behave in sexually inappropriate ways, or grooming a child in preparation for abuse (including via the internet). Sexual abuse is not solely perpetrated by adult males. Women can also commit acts of sexual abuse, as can other children.
Neglect	The persistent failure to meet a child's basic physical and/or psychological needs, likely to result in the serious impairment of the child's health or development. Neglect may occur during pregnancy as a result of maternal substance abuse. Once a child is born, neglect may involve a parent or carer failing to: • provide adequate food, clothing, and shelter (including exclusion from home or abandonment); • protect a child from physical and emotional harm or danger; • ensure adequate supervision (including the use of inadequate care givers); or • ensure access to appropriate medical care or treatment. It may also include neglect of, or unresponsiveness to, a child's basic emotional needs.

Lady Hale in her judgment in the case mentioned earlier in this section *(Re B* (2013)) set out five criteria which she hoped courts would find useful in determining whether the threshold criteria had been met. They are set out in **Box 8.9** as, by extension, you may also find these criteria helpful when you are considering whether a child has suffered significant harm:

BOX 8.9 Criteria for determining threshold criteria for abuse and neglect—*Re B* (2013)

(1) The court's task is not to improve on nature or even to secure that every child has a happy and fulfilled life, but to be satisfied that the statutory threshold has been crossed.

(2) When deciding whether the threshold is crossed the court should identify, as precisely as possible, the nature of the harm which the child is suffering or is likely to suffer. This is particularly important where the child has not yet suffered any, or any significant, harm and where the harm which is feared is the impairment of intellectual, emotional, social or behavioural development.

298

(3) Significant harm is harm which is 'considerable, noteworthy or important.' The court should iden-tify why and in what respects the harm is significant. Again, this may be particularly important where the harm in question is the impairment of intellectual, emotional, social or behavioural development which has not yet happened.

(4) The harm has to be attributable to a lack, or likely lack, of reasonable parental care, not simply to the characters and personalities of both the child and her parents. So once again, the court should identify the respects in which parental care is falling, or is likely to fall, short of what it would be reasonable to expect.

(5) Finally, where harm has not yet been suffered, the court must consider the degree of likelihood that it will be suffered in the future. This will entail considering the degree of likelihood that the parents' future behaviour will amount to a lack of reasonable parental care. It will also entail considering the relationship between the significance of the harmed feared and the likelihood that it will occur. Simply to state that there is a 'risk' is not enough. The court has to be satisfied, by relevant and sufficient evidence, that the harm is likely.

The meaning of the word 'likely'

In 2008 the House of Lords, in *Re B (Children) (Care Proceedings: Standard of Proof)*, clarified the law in respect of the meaning of 'likely'. This is an important and helpful case.

Re B (Children) (Care Proceedings: Standard of Proof) (2008)

The facts were as follows: the husband and wife lived in the family home with their two children, N, a girl aged nine, and A, a boy aged six, and with the wife's two children from a previous marriage, R, a girl aged 16 and S, a boy of 17. The husband left the family home and applied for residence orders in respect of N and A. Instead, the district judge made interim care orders in respect of R as well as N and A, on the basis of a plan to remove them from the wife and place them with the husband at his parents' home. Whilst they were being removed from the wife's home, R alleged that the husband had sexually abused her and had also physically assaulted both her and S. The husband denied the allegations. R was initially placed with foster carers and then returned to the wife. N and A were initially placed with the husband's parents and were subsequently moved to foster carers. The care proceedings were transferred to the High Court and a fact-finding hearing took place to ascertain whether the threshold criteria under s. 31(2) of the Children Act were satisfied.

The legal problem

The judge had found working out what had happened in the family difficult. He could not decide that it was 'more likely than not' that R was telling the truth in making the allegations, nor could he find that it 'was more likely than not' that the husband was telling the truth when denying the allegations. The judge decided that the sexual abuse allegations could not form any part of the findings which would be required to dem-onstrate whether or not the threshold criteria were met. He ordered that the basis for the instruction of expert witnesses and the basis for the final welfare hearing would be that R had not been sexually abused by the husband. The judge also recused (released) himself from the case. The children's guardian appealed. The Court of Appeal dismissed the appeal on the ground that it was bound by the House of Lords' authority to do so. The children's guardian appealed to the House of Lords.

Judgment

What the House of Lords decided was:

(a) The purpose of the threshold conditions was to protect children and their parents from unjustified intervention by the state.

(b) The court first had to be satisfied that the alleged significant harm to a child or likelihood of such harm existed and, if so satisfied, then to decide what outcome would be best for the child.

(c) Care proceedings are of a civil nature, intended not to punish or deter but to protect a child from harm.

(d) As the consequences of a wrong decision are equally serious either way, the standard of proof applicable in finding the facts necessary to establish the threshold criteria was the simple balance of probabilities, irrespective of the seriousness of the allegations or of the consequences.

(e) Care proceedings are not a two-stage process and the same factual issues were often relevant to questions as to whether the criteria had been crossed and if so, what was best for the child. Therefore, the same judge should hear both elements of the case.

Baroness Hale's judgment

Baroness Hale provides some clear answers to the questions which arise when trying to grapple with the concept of significant harm.

How is a court to be satisfied that a child is likely to suffer significant harm?

> This is a prediction from existing facts, often from a multitude of such facts, about what has happened in the past, about the characters and personalities of the people involved, about the things which they have said and done, and so on.

Do those facts have to be proved in the usual way?

Hale drew on previous authorities but also clarified them to answer this question in the affirmative.

> I . . . announce loud and clear that the standard of proof in finding the facts necessary to establish the threshold under section 31(2) or the welfare considerations in section 1 of the 1989 Act is the simple balance of probabilities, neither more nor less.

Does the seriousness of the allegation make a difference to the standard of proof?

> Neither the seriousness of the allegation nor the seriousness of the consequences should make any difference to the standard of proof to be applied in determining the facts. The inherent probabilities are simply something to be taken into account, where relevant, in deciding where truth lies.

Does it make a difference if it is impossible to determine who is responsible for the harm that a child has suffered?

No—the balance of probabilities applies in exactly the same way. What Hale said was:

> The court cannot shut its eyes to the undoubted harm which has been suffered simply because it does not know who was responsible.

Any confusion about the conduct of a case when there is uncertainty about which carer has perpetrated abuse, was clarified in a subsequent case, *Re D (Children)* (2009). Here the Court of Appeal was concerned that judges might consider that the effect of Re B was that they were required to identify the perpetrator of the significant harm. It observed:

> Nothing in Re B, in our judgment, requires the court to identify an individual as the perpetrator of non-accidental injuries to a child, simply because the standard of proof for such an identification is the balance of probabilities. If such an identification is not possible, because, for example, a judge remains genuinely uncertain at the end of a fact finding hearing, and cannot find on the balance of probabilities that A rather than B caused the injuries to the child, but that neither A nor B can be excluded as a perpetrator—it is the duty of the judge to state that as his or her conclusion.

What is the distinction between the role of the local authorities and the role of the courts?

> To allow the courts to make decisions about the allocation of parental responsibility for children on the basis of unproven allegations and unsubstantiated suspicions would be to deny them their essential role in protecting both children and their families from the intervention of the state, however well intentioned that intervention may be. It is to confuse the role of the local authority, in assessing and managing risk, in planning for the child, and deciding what action to initiate, with the role of the court in deciding where the truth lies and what the legal consequences should be. I do not underestimate the difficulty of deciding where the truth lies but that is what the courts are for.

In summary, then, the standard of proof is the balance of probabilities and neither the character of the abuse nor the difficulty in identifying perpetrators makes any difference to this. Interestingly, Baroness Hale commented on this case again in an academic journal as follows:

> In Re B, the House of Lords discarded the mantra once and for all. Inherent probabilities are not to be equated with the seriousness of the allegation. It may be unlikely that the animal you see while out walking in Regent's Park is a lion rather than a dog. But if you are in the zoo next door to the lion's enclosure and there is a great big hole in the fence, it is not unlikely at all. It may be unlikely that anyone would swing a tiny child by the arm and slam him into the wall. But when there is incontrovertible evidence that this is what happened, it is not unlikely at all.

> (B. Hale, 'The Children Act 1989 in the highest courts' (2006) *Journal of Children's Services 5(2): 17*)

The effect of a care order

Section 33—set out in **Box 8.10**—describes the effect of a care order. It gives the local authority parental responsibility; it makes the local authority the child's parent—with all the implications that are contained in that phrase.

 BOX 8.10 The effect of a care order–s. 33 of the Children Act 1989

(1) Where a care order is made with respect to a child it shall be the duty of a local authority designated by the order to receive the child into their care and to keep him in their care while the order remains in force.

(2) Where—
   (a) A care order has been made with respect to a child on the application of an authorised person [i.e. the NSPCC]; but
   (b) the local authority designated by the order was not informed that the person proposed to make the application (there is a requirement for the local authority to be informed of applications),

   the child may be kept in the care of that person until received into the care of the local authority.

(3) While a care order is in force with respect to a child, the local authority designated by the order shall—
   (a) have parental responsibility for the child; and
   (b) have the power (subject to the following provisions of this section) to determine the extent to which a parent or guardian of the child may meet his parental responsibility for him.

(4) The authority may not exercise the power in subsection (3)(b) unless they are satisfied that it is necessary to do so in order to safeguard or promote the child's welfare.

(5) Nothing in subsection (3)(b) shall prevent a parent or guardian of the child who has care of him from doing what is reasonable in all the circumstances of the case for the purpose of safeguarding or promoting his welfare.

Parental responsibility under a care order

Sharing parental responsibility

The mere fact of making a care order and giving parental responsibility to the local authority does not remove parental responsibility from the parents (s. 2(5) and (6)). What happens is that the principal responsibility rests with the local authority. Section 33(3)(b) echoes the philosophy of the Act. It seeks to encourage the local authority to consider how it can share the care of the child with the child's parent, albeit that this is a power and not a duty on the local authority.

The welfare of the child

Section 33(4) provides that although the local authority may share the care of the child with the parent, it may not exercise this power unless it is necessary to do so in order to safeguard or promote the child's welfare.

Limits on the local authority's parental responsibility

Section 33(6), (7), (8), and (9) imposes limitations on the power of the local authority in possession of a care order in respect of the child. We set out a summary of those in **Box 8.11**.

 BOX 8.11 Limiting the local authority's parental responsibility

Whilst a care order is in force the local authority may not:

(a) cause the child to be brought up in a different religious persuasion (this can present problems in the choice of foster parents);

(b) cause the child to be adopted without a court order;

(c) appoint a guardian for the child (that is a testamentary guardian for when the parents die); or

(d) cause the child to be known by a different surname (again, this needs to be watched with foster parents); or

(e) allow the child to be removed from the UK without the leave of the court (except for periods of less than four weeks).

Planning

In making applications to court it has always been necessary for the local authority to present its plans for contact (s. 34(11)) and its proposals for the future care of the child if a care order is made (*Manchester City Council v F* (1993)). This responsibility is made explicit as a result of the insertion of a new subsection (3A) into s. 31. This provides that 'no care order may be made with respect to a child until the court has considered a section 31A plan' (see **Care plans for court**, p 284).

Once a care order is made, the local authority has the task of deciding how to look after the child.

In care—but at home

The local authority's duty once a care order is made is still that contained in s. 17; that is, to safeguard and promote the child's welfare and, as far as is consistent with that duty, to encourage the child to be with his or her family. A care order adds to this a power, if necessary, to remove the child. Regulations still apply when a child is placed at home: see the *Children Act 1989 Guidance and Regulations, Volume 2: Care Planning, Placement and Case Review* (**chapter 3**).

Discharge of care orders

The procedure for the discharge of care orders is identical to that for supervision orders. Section 39 provides the powers for the variation and discharge of both care and supervision orders. Applications can be made by the authority, the child, or the parent. In the case of a supervision order, the child may be living with a person who does not have parental responsibility, for example a relative. In that case that person may apply for the supervision order to be discharged.

The welfare principle

There are no particular requirements for a court to consider when deciding an application to have a care or supervision order discharged except to do what is best for the welfare of the child (the welfare principle). The court does have the power, when an application is made to discharge a care order, to substitute a supervision order. In those particular circumstances, under s. 39(5), the court does not have to apply the significant harm test in s. 31, which would otherwise apply when considering a supervision order.

Unsuccessful applications

If an application to discharge a care or supervision order, or to have contact with a child in care, has been unsuccessful, then a further application may not be made for a period of six months (s. 91(15)). But there are provisions for the court to grant leave to make an application within the six-month period.

Rehabilitation

In attempting to rehabilitate a child, the local authority does not have available any particular court order. The choice is either a care order or a supervision order, or no order at all. The court does not have the power to make an order requiring either the local authority or the parents to undertake a rehabilitation plan. This is a situation in which the absence of the availability of wardship for local authorities is a real loss. The problem is that the court cannot impose restrictions or conditions on a full care order (see *Kent County Council v C* (1992)).

Discharge of care order by a child arrangements order

There is an alternative way to have a care order discharged and that is by an application for a s. 8 child arrangements order. Under s. 91(1), the making of a child arrangements order *with respect to the living arrangements* discharges any care order. Applications for a child arrangements order are made under s. 10(4) and (5). For the purposes of seeking to discharge a care order by this means, the following people could apply:

(a) the mother or father;

(b) any person with whom the child has lived for a period totalling at least three years out of the last five, ending at the latest three months ago;

(c) any person who has the consent of the local authority. A foster parent will come within this category unless the child has lived with the foster parent for a period of three years or the foster parent is a relative of the child. Then they can apply without consent. (A relative is defined in s. 105 as a grandparent, brother, sister, uncle, aunt, or step-parent.)

Applications with leave

In addition to these people, the court has power under s. 10(9) to grant leave to any person, except a foster parent, to apply for a s. 8 order. In considering whether to grant leave the court has to have regard to a number of points:

(a) what form of order is sought;

(b) the connection with the child;

(c) the risk that the application would disrupt the child so as to harm the child; and

(d) where the child is looked after by the local authority, what plans the authority has for the child and the wishes and feelings of the child's (actual) parents.

Whilst a hearing for leave ought to be shorter than the full hearing, experience does not always bear this out. In an extreme case an authority may be faced with a number of persons seeking leave to apply for a child arrangements order with respect to the living arrangements, with the consequent pressures on staff dealing with a series of legal proceedings. Of course, the granting of leave does not mean that the child arrangements order itself will be granted. That is decided at a full hearing on the basis of what is in the child's best interest.

Supervision orders

Identical grounds

The grounds for making a supervision order are exactly the same as those for a care order. They are set out in s. 31(2) (i.e. the likelihood of significant harm or the child being beyond parental control). Indeed, all the provisions of s. 31 are applicable to the making of a supervision order. Therefore, the questions of the meaning of 'significant harm', etc. which we discussed when looking at care orders, are just as applicable.

Choosing supervision orders

A supervision order is an alternative to a care order. In the Act there is no guidance on when a supervision order, rather than a care order, should be made. The decision is going to be the decision of the court, although the court will listen to the representations of all the parties, which can include a children's guardian, before coming to that decision. The order is made to either a local authority or a probation officer.

The Act creates three distinct supervision orders—the one made in the course of civil proceedings which we are considering here, the education supervision order which we look at later (**Education supervision orders (s. 36)**, p 306), and one made in criminal proceedings which we consider in **chapter 10**.

The value of a supervision order

An interesting case which considered the need for a supervision order is *Re K (Supervision Orders)* (1999). Here the local authority and the mother agreed that the threshold criteria in s. 31 were satisfied. They also agreed that a supervision order would be the appropriate way to safeguard the interests of the children. However, the children's guardian thought that the obligations of the local authority to safeguard the interests of the children under s. 17, as children 'in need' were sufficient to deal with their welfare. The judge found that as a concession had been made by the mother which appropriately reflected the gravity of the case, there was no need for a full investigation by the courts. He made it clear that a guardian should not lightly propose a contentious hearing. While accepting that the least intrusive order possible should be made, the supervision order imposed duties on the mother as well as on the local authority, which would be useful if the mother did not continue to cooperate, and that in practice the result of the supervision order would be to secure the allocation of a social worker and therefore greater protection for the children.

The effect of a supervision order

Section 35 of the Children Act sets out the effect of a supervision order. Its provisions are set out in **Box 8.12**.

BOX 8.12   The effect of a supervision order—s. 35 of the Children Act 1989

(1)   While a supervision order is in force it shall be the duty of the supervisor—
    (a)   to advise, assist and befriend the supervised child;
    (b)   to take such steps as are reasonably necessary to give effect to the order; and
    (c)   where—
       (i)   the order is not wholly complied with; or
       (ii)   the supervisor considers that the order may no longer be necessary, to consider whether or not to apply to the court for its variation or discharge.

There are no definitions of the terms 'advise', 'assist', or 'befriend' to give any guidance. The order need not specify a particular person in respect of a local authority. Note that a probation officer can be a supervisor only with the agreement of the probation authority and where the probation officer is already dealing or has dealt with another member of the child's household (Sch. 3, para. 9). This means that the majority of supervision orders will be made in favour of the local authority. Schedule 3 to the Act gives more detailed guidance on what a supervision order means.

The responsible person

The first paragraph of Schedule 3 introduces the idea of the 'responsible person' who is either a parent or someone with whom the child is living who consents to the role. This 'responsible person' can have duties imposed upon them in addition to any requirements that are imposed on the supervised child.

Requirements

The court, under a supervision order, can require the supervised person to obey certain directions given by the supervisor. Amongst these are that the supervised child:

(a) be required to live at a specified address for a specified period;

(b) present themselves to a specified person at a specified time and place; and

(c) participate in specified activities.

In addition, the responsible person can be required to:

(a) take all reasonable steps to ensure that the supervised child complies with directions given by the supervisor or contained in the order;

(b) keep the supervisor informed of the supervised child's address; and

(c) attend at a specified place to take part in any specified activities.

The supervision order can require the supervised child to submit to a medical or psychiatric examination, or to submit to such examinations as are required by the supervisor. This requirement is subject to the informed consent of the child, if the child has sufficient understanding. It is also possible for the court to require specified medical or psychiatric treatment but, if psychiatric, the court must have first heard the evidence of a Mental Health Act-approved doctor. The order can also require the child to keep the supervisor informed of his or her address.

Time limits

There are time limits on the supervision order. Any particular supervision order may not last, initially, for more than a period of one year, but the supervisor can apply to the court to have it extended for up to three years from the date on which the order was first made. The significant harm test need not be satisfied.

Can you replace a supervision order with a care order?

The answer is 'no'. The 'no order without an application' principle means there has to be a fresh application by the local authority. In making any new application the threshold criteria must be satisfied afresh. So in *Re A (Supervision Order: Extension)* (1995), the local authority obtained a 12-month supervision order in respect of an 11-year-old child. Before the expiry of the 12-month period, the local authority applied for an extension of the order. The guardian *ad litem* recommended that a care order be made in place of a supervision order. The Court of Appeal held that on an application for an extension of a supervision order, the court could make only a further supervision order and could not make a care order.

Discharge of a supervision order

This is dealt with in s. 39. We discuss the procedure, which is identical to that of the discharge of a care order earlier in the chapter (**Discharge of care orders**, p 302).

Education supervision orders (s. 36)

If a local education authority (which in most areas is the same authority as the social services department) can satisfy the magistrates' court that a particular child is both of compulsory school age and not being properly educated (s. 36(3)), the court may make an education supervision order. Section 36(4) defines a child as being properly educated only if the child is receiving efficient full-time education suitable to age, ability, and aptitude and any special educational needs that the child may have. An application for an order cannot be made if the child is in the care of the local authority, and the education department must consult with the social services department before the application is made. The order is designed to ensure that children do not go into care merely for school non-attendance.

The effect of an education supervision order

Under Schedule 3, Part III, there are detailed provisions as to the effect of the education supervision order. In essence, the supervisor has to advise, assist, and befriend the child and give directions to the child to ensure that the child is properly educated.

The directions might include directions for the child and parents to attend meetings to discuss the child's education or for the child to see an educational psychologist. Under the provisions there is the need to consult with the parents and child before the directions are made. If parents persistently fail to comply with directions that are reasonably given, they may be fined, on conviction, in the magistrates' court. There is no penalty for the child.

Time limits

The education supervision order lasts for 12 months or until the child is no longer of compulsory school age (whichever is the shorter). It can be extended for up to three years.

Appeals

There is a particular provision for appeals in s. 40. The aim is to allow the court to decide what will happen to a child where an application for an order is dismissed and there is to be an appeal. This is a safety net provision. No application will be made without an investigation by the local authority or authorized person, and it therefore follows that there should have been reasonable grounds for concern. The safety net that is provided gives the court the power to make an order of the type originally sought, pending the hearing of the appeal.

The requirement that needs to be satisfied is that there must have been an interim order made at an earlier stage in the proceedings. This means that at an earlier stage a court believed that there were reasonable grounds for believing that a final order might be made.

The order made pending appeal is not an interim order, since the dismissal of the application is an end to the proceedings as far as the lower court is concerned. The length of time that the order will last is strictly limited to the 'appeal period', which means that the order will last only until the hearing of the appeal. There are provisions for the appeal court to extend the period until it is practicable for it to hear the appeal. In *Re O* (1992), the court held that the magistrates had no power to stay (suspend) such an order pending an appeal.

As we have indicated earlier, if you are involved in a case where your application is dismissed, you should immediately seek the advice of your agency lawyer.

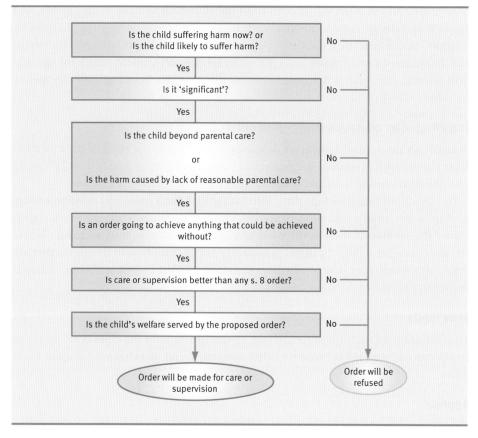

FIGURE 8.3   Getting a care order/supervision order

A flow chart setting out the key questions for determining the outcomes of an application for a care or supervision order is set out in **Figure 8.3**.

Interim care and supervision orders

Interim care or supervision orders are usually made when the full hearing cannot take place. Section 38(1) of the Children Act, set out in **Box 8.13**, provides the power for the court to make an interim care or supervision order. To make an interim order:

(a) the court must have reasonable grounds for believing there are grounds for the full care order;

(b) the making of the interim order does not mean that there will be a full order; and

(c) the court must act judicially in making an order.

BOX 8.13 Interim care or supervision orders—s. 38 of the Children Act 1989

(1) Where—

(a) in any proceedings on an application for a care order or supervision order, the proceedings are adjourned; or

(b) the court gives a direction under section 37(1),

the court may make an interim care order or an interim supervision order with respect to the child concerned.

Hearings are not always necessary

This does not mean that there will always have to be a hearing with evidence being given. Inevitably, after the first interim order is made, within the constraints of the timetable provisions listed in the following section, there are occasions on which everybody is agreed that for one reason or another a further interim order will need to be made—the medical report is not available, there is no available court time, etc. In this case, the court could make an interim order without hearing evidence but merely hearing representations from the applicant.

The timetable

Section 38(4) sets out a timetable for the granting of interim care or supervision orders. It is not reproduced verbatim here, since it is unnecessarily complex and unclear. What it appears to say is set out in **Box 8.14**.

 BOX 8.14 Timetabling interim care and supervision orders

(a) An initial interim order may not last more than eight weeks.

(b) If the initial interim order has been made for a period of less than eight weeks, then any subsequent orders may be made for a period or periods that will not exceed that eight-week period starting on the date on which the initial order was made.

(c) If any interim orders are made after that initial eight-week period, then those further interim orders may not exceed a four-week period, although they may be made for periods less than four weeks.

(d) Any number of interim orders could be made subject to the non-delay principle.

Directions

When making an interim order, the court has the power to give directions as follows (s. 38(6)):

Where the court makes an interim care order, or interim supervision order, it may give such directions (if any) as it considers appropriate with regard to the medical or psychiatric examination or other assessment of the child; but if the child is of sufficient understanding to make an informed decision he may refuse to submit to the examination or other assessment.

Section 38(7) specifies what directions may be given. This subsection is an exact reproduction of s. 44(8) and (9) relating to emergency protection orders, which is discussed later.

Medical examinations

If you are going to have any medical examination, investigation, or any other type of assessment carried out, you must obtain the leave of the court.

Assessments during interim care orders

In *Re C (A Minor) (Interim Care Order: Residential Assessment)* (1996), a four-month-old child was admitted to hospital suffering from non-accidental injuries. The child's parents, aged 16 and 17, were not able to give a satisfactory explanation of the injuries. An emergency protection order was made, and then an interim care order under s. 38 of the Children Act 1989. The social worker decided that an in-depth assessment of the child and the parents together needed to be undertaken as soon as possible at a residential unit. However, their managers refused to agree to, or pay for, the residential assessment and decided to apply for a care order so that the child could be placed in a permanent alternative placement with a view to adoption.

At first instance, the judge held that the social worker had jurisdiction under s. 38(6) to order a residential assessment. Having weighed the cost (estimated at £18,000–£24,000) against the recommendations from the professionals involved, she decided to exercise her discretion by ordering the local authority to carry out the residential assessment.

The House of Lords held that s. 38(6) and (7) conferred jurisdiction on the court to order or prohibit any assessment which involved the participation of the child and was to provide the court with the material to enable it to reach a proper decision at the final hearing. In exercising its discretion, the court would have to take into account the cost of the proposed assessment and the fact of local authorities' lack of resources. In this case, their Lordships ordered the assessment. The care plan here indicated that the local authority was going to place the child for adoption. To allow the local authority to decide what evidence was to go before the court at the final hearing would allow the local authority by administrative decision to pre-empt the court's judicial decision. However, not all parents can expect a residential assessment as a right. In *Re S* (2011), Black LJ rejected the submission that:

> parents should be given every reasonable opportunity of presenting a positive case . . . There is no right for a parent facing permanent removal of a child to have the assessment of their choice; rather, the relevant question is always whether the assessment in question would assist the judge in reaching the right conclusion at a final hearing.

Reducing delay

The final provision relating to interim orders is s. 38(10):

> Where a court makes an order under or by virtue of this section [an interim order] it shall, in determining the period for which the order is to be in force, consider whether any party who was, or might have been, opposed to the making of an order was in a position to argue his case against the order in full.

This is designed to cope with a situation where a parent has not had the opportunity to instruct lawyers to act on their behalf at the time of the interim hearing. The court should then consider making an interim order for just sufficient time to enable a lawyer to be properly instructed. This is another reflection of the Act's aim to try to reduce the delays that can be present in such cases. Section 14 of the Children and Families Act 2014 amends s. 32(1) of the Act to impose a strict timetable for care proceedings that they should be concluded in 26 weeks. In addition, s. 13 of the Children and Families Act lays out the conditions on which expert evidence can be submitted to the court. Subsection (7) says that in deciding whether permission should be granted for expert evidence the court shall consider:

(a) any impact which giving permission would be likely to have on the welfare of the children concerned, including in the case of permission as mentioned in subsection (3) any impact which any examination or other assessment would be likely to have on the welfare of the child who would be examined or otherwise assessed,

(b) the issues to which the expert evidence would relate,

(c) the questions which the court would require the expert to answer,

(d) what other expert evidence is available (whether obtained before or after the start of proceedings),

(e) whether evidence could be given by another person on the matters on which the expert would give evidence,

(f) the impact which giving permission would be likely to have on the timetable for, and duration and conduct of, the proceedings,

(g) the cost of the expert evidence, and

(h) any matters prescribed by Family Procedure Rules.

The Family Justice Review was concerned about the growth in the use of experts in care proceedings and the effect this was having on the duration of those proceedings. Reducing delay is important, but so too is the need for the consideration of cases to be carried out justly. These matters were explored in a recent case in which the President of the Family Division was giving the judgment. Sir James Munby said in *Re S (A Child)* (2014):

> Section 32(1)(a)(ii) does not describe some mere aspiration or target, nor does it prescribe an average. It defines . . . a mandatory limit which applies to all cases. It follows that there will be many cases that can, and therefore should, be concluded well within the 26 week limit. I repeat what I said in my first 'View from the President's Chambers: The process of reform', [2013] Fam Law 548: 'My message is clear and uncompromising: this deadline can be met, it must be met, it will be met. And remember, 26 weeks is a deadline, not a target; it is a maximum, not an average or a mean. So many cases will need to be finished in less than 26 weeks.'

This requirement places an onerous duty on case management judges, particularly in respect of the directions they give for expert evidence. The President, however, in *Re B-S* (2013) (which is also considered in **chapter 9**), indicated that:

> If, despite all, the court does not have the kind of evidence we have identified and is therefore not properly equipped to decide these issues, then an adjournment must be directed, even if this takes the case over 26 weeks. Where the proposal before the court is for non-consensual adoption, the issues are too grave, the stakes for all are too high, for the outcome to be determined by rigorous adherence to an inflexible timetable and justice thereby potentially denied.

Power to exclude alleged abuser while the interim order is in force

The Family Law Act 1996 amended the Children Act to include a new s. 38A—a power in interim care orders to require an alleged abuser to leave the house in which the child is living. The court would have to be satisfied of the following:

(a) that there is reasonable cause to believe that if a person is excluded from a dwelling house in which the child lives, the child will cease to suffer or cease to be likely to suffer significant harm; and

(b) another person living in the same house, whether or not a parent, is able and willing to give to the child the care which it would be reasonable to expect a parent to give; and

(c) that person consents to the inclusion of the exclusion requirement.

There are also powers of arrest available, subject to certain requirements. The difficulty with this power is that it does require the consent of the person who is to care for the child. This would normally be the mother. In the absence of her consent, it is not possible to compel the alleged abuser to leave. While this power is a welcome addition to the interim order, the requirement of consent may mean that it is not used as much as could be expected. There is an identical power in relation to the emergency protection order which we discuss later.

A fail-safe provision

Section 38(3) requires that the court makes an interim supervision order when making a residence order in certain circumstances. We set out s. 38(3) in **Box 8.15**.

BOX 8.15 Making an interim supervision order when making a residence order—s. 38(3) of the Children Act 1989

Where, in any proceedings on an application for a care order or supervision order, a court makes a residence order with respect to the child concerned, it shall also make an interim supervision order with respect to him unless satisfied that his welfare will be satisfactorily safeguarded without an interim order being made.

The court would need to be satisfied that the access was being unreasonably refused by the parent. The local authority would have to show that access was required as a matter of urgency. An application on these grounds may be simpler to obtain than one where you have to satisfy the court that the child is actually suffering significant harm.

This section covers the situation where the court, instead of making an interim care order, decides to make a a s. 8 child arrangements order, say to a grandparent. As a 'fail safe', the court is required to make an interim supervision order. An example of this in practice is *C v Solihull MBC (1993)*, which we discussed in **chapter 5**. It needs to be stressed again that the making of any particular interim order does not mean that type of order will be made as a final order.

Short-term orders to protect children

We will now discuss the orders and the police power set out in Part V of the Act. These provisions are all short term. The most important of these is the emergency protection order.

The emergency protection order—a summary

An emergency protection order is a short-term order that either:

(a) removes the child on a short-term basis; or

(b) allows the child to be kept in a place of safety (e.g. a hospital); or

(c) requires the alleged abuser to leave the family home (see **Power to exclude alleged abuser while the interim order is in force**, p 312).

An emergency protection order is not an end in itself. It is a critical step in the local authority's investigation under s. 47 which will lead to the local authority either being satisfied about the child's welfare or to care proceedings.

Emergency protection orders are provided for within s. 44 of the Children Act. Section 44(1) is set out in **Box 8.16**.

 BOX 8.16 The emergency protection of children—s. 44(1) of the Children Act 1989

(1) Where any person ('the applicant') applies to the court for an order to be made under this section with respect to a child, the court may make the order if, but only if it is satisfied that—

  (a) there is reasonable cause to believe that the child is likely to suffer significant harm if

    (i) he is not removed to accommodation provided by or on behalf of the applicant; or

    (ii) he does not remain in the place in which he is then being accommodated;

  (b) in the case of an application made by a local authority—

    (i) enquiries are being made with respect to the child under section 47(1)(b); and

    (ii) those enquires are being frustrated by access to the child being unreasonably refused to a person authorized to seek access and that the applicant has reasonable cause to believe that access to the child is required as a matter of urgency; or

(c) in the case of an application made by an authorized person—
   (i)   the applicant has reasonable cause to suspect that a child is suffering or is likely to suffer, significant harm;
   (ii) the applicant is making enquires with respect to the child's welfare; and
   (iii) those enquires are being frustrated by access to the child being unreasonably refused to a person authorized to seek access and the applicant has reasonable cause to believe that access to the child is required as a matter of urgency.

The key features of an emergency protection order

Duration
The emergency protection order may be granted for a period of up to an initial eight days, extendable, once only, for a period of up to a further seven days—s. 45. These are the maximum periods allowed. It may well be that the court will decide that the order should last for a shorter period.

The different forms of an emergency protection order
There are two forms the applications can take:

The 'any person basis' under s. 44(1)(a)
The 'any person' includes a social worker. The court, on the application of any person, may grant an order if a version of the significant harm test is satisfied. Where any person applies for it, the court may grant an emergency protection order only if the court is satisfied that there is reasonable cause to believe that the child is likely to suffer significant harm unless removed to accommodation provided by the applicant or unless allowed to remain in present accommodation.

'Likely to suffer significant harm'
This application is designed to cover situations where, for instance, a social worker is notified of a child with severe injuries and believes that the child should be removed from home for the protection of the child. The ground is that the child is likely to suffer significant harm. There will have to be evidence that there is a possibility that the harm which has already been inflicted will be repeated—so a 'one-off' incident cannot be a ground for granting an emergency protection order under this subsection.

Alternatively, the 'any person' emergency protection order envisages the situation where a child has been admitted to hospital and the parents are threatening to remove the child, and the court believes the removal would be likely to cause the child significant harm. It would also be possible to make an application where a child is being looked after by a local authority in accommodation and the parents are again threatening to remove the child.

The obstruction of investigation basis under s. 44(1)(b)
Here, if the investigations of a local authority or the NSPCC are obstructed, then the court may grant an emergency protection order without being satisfied on the significant harm test—but, like the child assessment order (see **Child assessment orders**, p 323), the applicant has to be satisfied that there is a risk of significant harm.

Part of continuing investigation

An application under s. 44(1)(b) is to be made by the local authority only as part of a continuing investigation under s. 47 of the Children Act. That is the investigation the authority or NSPCC has to carry out when it has reasonable cause to suspect that a child is suffering or is likely to suffer significant harm.

Parents

An order may be granted in the absence of the parents (i.e. without notice of the hearing), but as with the child assessment order there are provisions for the parents to seek to have the order discharged under s. 45(8). At that stage it would be possible for the parents to state that access will be granted and, if the statement is believed by the court, for the basis of the local authority application to be totally undermined.

Common elements between these different forms of emergency protection orders

Even though the court may be satisfied that the grounds for an emergency protection order exist, it still need not grant one, for it has to apply the 'welfare' principle and the 'non-intervention' principle, which are contained in s. 1 of the Children Act. This means that it has to be satisfied that the order is in the best interests of the child and necessary for its protection. It does not have to consider the welfare checklist in s. 1.

Safeguards

The various safeguards point to the need for the social worker to be adequately prepared before seeking an emergency protection order. Adequate preparation means that you will need to have answers ready for all the points that the court requires: the grounds (harm or obstruction of your investigation), the welfare of the child, and the need to intervene.

The operation of an emergency protection order

An emergency protection order does not give the applicant unfettered powers. **Box 8.17** sets out the relevant subsections of s. 44. Not to produce the child—showing the child to you—is a criminal offence (s. 44(15)). If you have such an order and ask for the child to be produced and he or she is not produced, you must draw the person's attention to the explanatory notes attached to the order and warn them that failure so to do will render them liable to criminal proceedings. If the child is produced, then you may take him or her to, and/or keep him or her in, accommodation.

 BOX 8.17 The operation of an emergency protection order—s. 44 of the Children Act 1989

(4) While an order under this section ('an emergency protection order') is in force it—

   (a) operates as a direction to any person who is in a position to do so to comply with any request to produce the child to the applicant;

   (b) authorises—

(i)   the removal of the child at any time to accommodation provided by or on behalf of the applicant and his being kept there; or

(ii) the prevention of the child's removal from any hospital or other place in which he was being accommodated immediately before the making of this order; and

(c) gives the applicant parental responsibility for the child.

(5) Where an emergency protection order is in force with respect to a child the applicants—

(a) shall only exercise the power given by virtue of subsection (4)(b) in order to safeguard the welfare of the child;

(b) shall take, and shall only take, such action in meeting his parental responsibility for the child as is reasonably required to safeguard or promote the welfare of the child (having regard in particular to the duration of the order); and

(c) shall comply with the requirements of any regulation made by the Secretary of State for the purpose of this subsection.

Power to exclude alleged abuser

The Family Law Act 1996 amended the Children Act to include s. 44A—which provides a power in an emergency protection order to require an alleged abuser to leave the house in which the child is living. There are also powers of arrest available, subject to certain requirements. **Box 8.18** sets out what needs to be demonstrated to the court.

BOX 8.18 Factors necessary for an exclusion requirement

(a) That there is reasonable cause to believe that if a person is excluded from a dwelling house in which the child lives, the child will cease to suffer or cease to be likely to suffer significant harm; and

(b) another person living in the same house, whether or not a parent, is able and willing to give to the child the care which it would be reasonable to expect a parent to give;

(c) that person consents to the inclusion of the exclusion requirement;

(d) the contact which is, or is not, to be allowed between the child and any named person;

(e) the medical or psychiatric examination or other assessment of the child.

The question of medical examinations is further dealt with in s. 44(7) and (8), which provide:

(a) that a child may give informed consent to any medical examination;

(b) that the court may order that there should be no medical or psychiatric examination, or that such an examination shall take place only if further permission is obtained from the court.

Consent

The difficulty with the exclusion power is that it requires the consent of the person who is to care for the child. This is normally the mother. In the absence of her consent it is not possible to compel the alleged abuser to leave. Note that an identical power to exclude an alleged abuser exists in relation to interim care orders (see **Power to exclude alleged abuser while the interim order is in force**, p 312).

Guidance on the exclusion requirement

In *Re W (Exclusion: Statement of Evidence)* (2000), the judge set out guidance on the relevant procedure. While it is not necessary for the local authority to make a specific application, there does need to be a separate statement of evidence supporting the case for an exclusion requirement. The consent can be given orally in court or in writing. If it is in writing, it should clearly state that the person giving consent understands the provision.

Limited power of removal under an emergency protection order

The power to remove the child is to be used only when necessary to safeguard the welfare of the child. This means that if you have obtained an order and then go to the house and find the child is safe, you are not permitted to remove the child.

It is easy to imagine an extreme case where this might be applied: you receive an anonymous telephone call stating that it sounds as if a child is being beaten in a certain house. You go to the house, knock on the door, get no answer, but hear the sounds of a child sobbing and screaming. You knock next door and are told that there is a child in the house and that 'they are an odd lot'. You go to court and are granted an emergency protection order under s. 44(1)(b) (on the ground that you are investigating, and your investigation is being obstructed). You go to the house with the emergency protection order, a surprised parent opens the door holding a cheerful, smiling toddler with no visible signs of injury. The parent readily agrees to you examining the child undressed and there are no signs of injury. When asked about the noise of crying, the parent says that they were listening to a play on the radio, about a child-beating case, which may explain the sounds, and they had the radio up very loud and therefore your knocks were not heard. Clearly, s. 44(5)(a) applies and you would have no grounds for the removal of the child, despite holding the emergency protection order.

Assistance of other professionals

Most cases are not like this and the particular subsection would prove challenging. To assist you in making the decision as to whether removal is necessary, you may want to have the assistance of some other professional person when you go to the house. In these circumstances, you may ask the court to make a direction under s. 45(12), which states that the court may direct that the applicant may be accompanied by a doctor, nurse, or health visitor, if the applicant so chooses.

Parental responsibility under an emergency protection order

The local authority, or whoever was the applicant, will also gain parental responsibility, but this does not mean that the parent of the child loses parental responsibility. The exercise of parental responsibility under an emergency protection order in accordance with s. 44(5) means that only steps that are reasonably required during the order (which will be eight, or at the very most 15, days) may be taken by the person with temporary parental responsibility. This does not mean that a child may, for instance, have their school permanently changed; only temporary educational provision can be made. It does not mean that a child may be allowed to undergo a cosmetic surgery operation, but it would allow for an emergency operation.

Contact

There is a general presumption that the parent will have reasonable contact with the child whilst an emergency protection order is in force, unless a direction under s. 44(6) is made.

Medical examinations

Medical examinations are allowed only for purposes that promote or safeguard the welfare of the child. This means that any examinations required for the purpose of preparing your case prior to applying for a care order would not be permitted unless you have the additional power contained in s. 44(6).

This subsection sets out the directions that the court can make at the time of granting the order. The court may decline to make any directions under this subsection.

The need for directions

If you are seeking an emergency protection order and you or your agency feel that there may be the need for some form of medical examination, then you should, at the time of the application, seek a direction from the court. If it is not sought at the time of the initial application and it is decided that such an examination ought to be carried out, then a direction should be sought under the provisions of s. 44(9).

Religious objections to treatment

The position of children of Jehovah's Witnesses and parents with similar religious objections to treatment needs particular mention. The use of emergency protection orders would not provide the degree of parental responsibility to override the parents' objections to treatment. In *Re R (A Minor) (Blood Transfusion)* (1993), Booth J stated that the use of an emergency protection order in such cases was not appropriate. Either the inherent jurisdiction of the High Court should be used, or the local authority should apply under s. 8 to a High Court judge.

Variation

Section 44(9) deals with applications to vary—change—the order whilst it is still in force. If directions have been made about contact with parents or other people, or medical examinations, then an application can be made to alter these.

Limits on the emergency protection order

Returning the child before the emergency protection order expires

The Act contains various provisions to mitigate the disruption caused to the child and family. Section 44(10) requires that although an emergency protection order may have been granted, the child should be kept away from 'home' only as long as necessary, and if it is safe the child should be returned 'home'. These provisions are set out in **Box 8.19**.

BOX 8.19 Mitigating disruption to the child and the family—s. 44(10) of the Children Act 1989

Where an emergency protection order is in force with respect to a child and—

(a) the applicant has exercised the power given by subsection (4)(b)(i) [removed a child] but it appears to him that it is safe for the child to be returned; or

(b) the applicant has exercised the power given by subsection (4)(b)(ii) [prevented the child from being removed from accommodation] but it appears to him safe for the child to be allowed to be removed from the place in question,

he shall return the child or (as the case may be) allow him to be removed.

In the case of a child needing an emergency operation, once the operation has taken place, then the child should be 'returned' (albeit that the child may stay in hospital). The duty to return in s. 44(11) is an important example of the necessary checks and balances built into the legislation. The state has a power to intervene in children's lives where it is necessary to protect them, but that power must not be excessive. You can return the child to a different person—not the parent or the person caring for the child at the time of the emergency protection order—only with the court's permission (s. 48(11)).

The emergency protection order continues

The return of a child under this subsection does not bring the emergency protection order to an end. Section 44(12) states that if, having returned the child at any time whilst the order is still in force, it appears to the applicant that the child should again be removed, then that can be done. This is without the need for a fresh application. So, suppose the parent of the child who had the emergency operation tried to remove the child against medical advice, the current emergency protection order would give the power to stop this.

Applications to discharge an emergency protection order

The next 'check' on the emergency protection order is the right of the parent to challenge the order—s. 45. There was a limit on this power set out in s. 9—it was not available for the first 72 hours of an emergency protection order. However, this restriction has been repealed by the Children and Young Persons Act 2008 following a decision of the Northern Ireland High Court in 2007 that such a restriction was contrary to Article 8 and Article 6 of the European Convention. Courts can now hear applications for discharge from the time that the emergency protection order is made.

The discharge provisions are not available for a parent who was present at the hearing of the application for the emergency protection order (i.e. was given the chance to put their side of the case to the court). Similarly, there is no right to have an order discharged after that order has been extended. This is because the relevant court rules require that an extension application take place only after notice has been given to all parties. So, again, the parents will have had their chance to put their side of the case. The application to discharge the order can be made by the child (through his or her guardian) or the child's parents.

No appeals

The Act allows for any particular emergency protection order only to be discharged, not to be appealed against.

Section 45(10) provides:

> No appeal may be made against the making of, or refusal to make, an emergency protection order or against any direction given by the court in connection with such an order.

This would not exclude an application for judicial review if the circumstances were appropriate. However, the case study at the beginning of this chapter indicates that the basis for an application for judicial review is very limited. There is a need to ensure that the expertise of the Family Proceedings Court is appropriately applied. If the emergency protection order was made by the High Court, there can be no judicial review of that decision.

Additional powers to protect children

Disclosure of information

Section 48 of the Children Act 1989 gives additional powers. For instance, you may not know the whereabouts of the child in need of emergency protection. The court may include a provision in the emergency protection order requiring a person who may have information about the child's whereabouts to disclose that information (s. 48(1)). The order may also authorize an applicant to enter premises and search for the child, although this section in any event requires that the parents, or whoever is in control of the premises, cooperate. If you are prevented from entering premises or gaining access to the child, or it appears to the court that you may be, the court can issue a warrant authorizing the police to assist the entry and search.

Other children

You may believe that there are other children on the premises who also ought to be the subject of an emergency protection order. If so, you may seek an order authorizing a search for them. If the child (or children) is found and you are satisfied that the grounds for an emergency protection order exist, the order authorizing the search has effect as if it were an emergency protection order. This is useful when you are not able to identify all the children in the family, or, for instance, where there is evidence of the existence of a paedophile ring, but the number and identities of the children involved are unknown.

Recovery orders

Finally, the Act gives you powers through the mechanism of recovery orders (s. 50) in respect of a child in care, or the subject of an emergency protection order, or in police protection, where the child has unlawfully been taken away, has run away, or is staying away from the 'responsible person'. A responsible person is anyone who has the care of the child by virtue of a care order or an emergency protection order. The order operates as a direction to produce the child, or to disclose his or her whereabouts, and authorizes the police to enter named premises and search for the child, using reasonable force if necessary.

Practical considerations for emergency protection orders

Record keeping

Meticulous records must be kept by the social worker involved so that there is evidence of the investigation, which is one branch of the grounds for an emergency protection order, together with the details of any obstruction by the parents.

Before taking action

Always stop to think clearly about why you want an emergency protection order and what you are going to do with it. Always try and consult with a colleague, even if your particular management guidelines allow you to take such steps without consultation.

Refusal of an emergency protection order

If an emergency protection order is refused then, in principle, there does not appear to be any bar to making another application. This is particularly true if further information becomes available concerning the likelihood of potential harm to the child.

Identification

Under s. 44(3) of the Children Act a person seeking access to a child for an investigation must produce some duly authenticated document stating that they are authorized to seek access. All local authority social workers are such authorized persons. Failure by you to produce such proof, if asked for, is just the sort of point that a lawyer acting for a parent would love to have as an opening question in cross-examination. The mere failure to have identification does not on its own prevent you obtaining the order, but it makes you look less professional to the court. In addition, the explanatory notes that are part of the statutory form of the emergency protection order have a box telling the parent to ask anyone who tries to carry out the order for evidence of their identity.

Out-of-hours applications

The magistrates' courts' rules allow a single justice (magistrate) to hear an application for an emergency protection order. If the hearing is to be made without notice, leave of the clerk to the justices has to be obtained.

Time limits

There is a long list of tasks for the social worker to complete in the short period of time that the emergency protection order lasts. Fifteen, let alone eight, days is a very short period of time, especially when lawyers and courts are involved. Given the chance for parties to seek a discharge of the order and to seek contact with the child, the entire time between the granting and expiration of the order could be occupied with court hearings instead of carrying out the intended assessment.

To set this in some context, we reproduce in **Box 8.20** a list of possible tasks following an emergency protection order.

 BOX 8.20 Tasks that may be necessary during the emergency protection order

(a) Arrange for accommodation for the child.

(b) Place the child with foster parents or in an institution and explain to the child what is happening and give sufficient information to those who will be caring for the child to do so appropriately.

(c) Explain to the parents why their child has been removed from them and discuss concerns and allegations with them.

(d) Spend further time with the child, to be satisfied that the child's welfare is being met, and also ask the child about any concerns or allegations.

(e) Take the child for medical examination and/or treatment, and obtain the doctor's diagnosis, having obtained leave of the court, if required.

(f) Make decisions about who the child should be allowed to have contact with (from those listed in s. 47(11)).

(g) Arrange for such contact to take place.

(h) Instruct the authority's solicitor in time for extension hearings. Consider making application for directions governing contact or medical examination. Instruct the local authority solicitor to commence appropriate proceedings and provide sufficient information for the solicitor to do so.

(i) Discuss the case with a children's guardian if one has been appointed.

(j) Convene a child protection conference, ensuring a sufficient number of those involved with the family attend.

(k) Keep under review whether it is safe to return the child home.

(l) Decide, with senior social work staff, whether action needs to be taken to promote or safeguard the child's welfare.

(m) Attend court in respect of an application for an interim care order.

(Taken from J. Bridge, S. Bridge, and S. Luke, *Blackstone's Guide to the Children Act 1989* (Blackstone Press, 1990), with slight adaptation.)

Summary of the key features of the emergency protection order

In **Table 8.2** we provide a summary of the key features of the emergency protection order.

TABLE 8.2 Key features of the emergency protection order

Feature	Provision	Section	Note
Grounds	Child likely to suffer significant harm or cannot be seen where child is at risk of suffering significant harm	s. 44(1)	See the full discussion of significant harm earlier in this chapter
	Must apply the welfare principle and the non-intervention principle, but not the welfare checklist		
Duration	Eight days—possible extension for additional seven days	s. 45(3), (5)	Could be for a shorter period
Application	Any person can apply		This includes the police
Discharge	Certain persons may be able to apply for discharge of the emergency protection order	s. 45(8), (9)	Cannot apply during extension of emergency protection order
Parental responsibility	Grants very limited parental responsibility to the local authority. The parent of the child does not lose parental responsibility.	s. 44(4)	This is a critical check on the scope of the emergency protection order
Directions	Court has the power to order contact, medical, and/or psychiatric reports, assessment, etc.	s. 44(6)	The child's informed consent is required

Child assessment orders

Section 43 of the Children Act allows the local authority to obtain a child assessment order. This provides for the compulsory assessment of the child's state of health and development, by removing the child from the home if necessary. **Box 8.21** sets out the relevant provisions of s. 43.

BOX 8.21 The child assessment order—s. 43 of the Children Act 1989

(1) On the application of a local authority . . . for an order under this section, the court may make the order if, but only if, it is satisfied that—

   (a) the applicant has reasonable cause to suspect that the child is suffering, or is likely to suffer, significant harm;

> (b) an assessment of the state of the child's health or development or of the way in which he has been treated, is required to enable the applicant to determine whether or not the child is suffering, or is likely to suffer, significant harm; and
>
> (c) it is unlikely that such an assessment will be made, or be satisfactory, in the absence of an order under this section.
>
> (2) ...
>
> (3) A court may treat an application under this section as an application for an emergency protection order.
>
> (4) No court shall make a child assessment order if it is satisfied—
>
> (a) that there are grounds for making an emergency protection order with respect to the child; and
>
> (b) that it ought to make such an order rather than a child assessment order.

The necessity of the order

To obtain an order you need to show to the court not that, objectively speaking, the child is at risk, but that you have reasonable cause to believe the child is at risk. Then you must show that an assessment of health and development is required actually to find out whether the child is suffering or is likely to suffer significant harm. Having satisfied the court of this, you then have to show that you could not make a satisfactory assessment without the order.

Is an emergency protection order more appropriate?

Whenever there is a child at risk, the question whether or not the child would be safe if left in his or her home will be uppermost in most people's minds. That is why this section states that the court shall not make a child assessment order if it thinks that the child should be removed from the home. This would be done by means of an emergency protection order. If there are no grounds for making an emergency protection order, then the court may grant the application for the child assessment order. This 'fail safe' measure may explain why the courts are reluctant to grant a child assessment order, preferring to grant an emergency protection order.

Planning for an assessment

Just as the child assessment order is not intended to be dealt with on a 'without notice' basis, neither does the assessment have to begin on the day the order is made. Section 43(5) specifies that the date on which the order may begin can be set by the court. This enables a plan for an assessment to be made, in advance, to begin at some future date.

Speed

The order may last for only seven days. It is difficult to make an adequate form of assessment within that timescale. Clearly, all that the assessment in a child assessment order is capable of achieving is showing whether other court orders should or should not be applied for.

If an order is granted, then its purpose will be to allow this limited type of assessment to be carried out. To this end, the order may include directions for the child to be produced for medical or psychiatric examination. Such examinations are subject to the informed consent of the child.

Removal for assessment only

The order does allow the child to be compulsorily removed from the home, but only for the purposes of the assessment, and, if that occurs, there are provisions for reasonable contact by the child with parents or other persons. These are contained in s. 43(9) and (10), which is set out in **Box 8.22**.

BOX 8.22 Limited removal from home under the child assessment order—s. 43(9) and (10) of the Children Act 1989

(9) The child may only be kept away from home—
   (a) in accordance with directions specified in the order;
   (b) if it is necessary for the purposes of assessment; and
   (c) for such period as may be specified in the order.

(10) Where the child is to be kept away from home, the order shall contain such directions as the court thinks fit with regard to the contact that he must be allowed to have with other persons while away from home.

Therefore, the child may be removed only if the court order says so. This would be where it was necessary for the child to attend for a short residential assessment. The order is not designed to protect the child by removal from the home—that is the function of the emergency protection order.

Parents must know of the application

An application for a child assessment order cannot be made on a 'without notice' basis. It must be made when the parents have been told of the hearing and have the chance to be represented there.

Variation and discharge of a child assessment order

It may be that the order having been made, the arrangements for the assessment cannot be carried out on the set date. The court can vary, or even discharge the order if required.

Removal by the police to accommodation

Police powers

The police are given powers under s. 46 of the Children Act to take children into police protection. The powers apply to children whom the police find and contain no provisions enabling the police to search for a child. They can be used for runaways or for abandoned children, or where the police come across children with drunk parents or living in unhygienic conditions.

A Home Office Circular, *The Duties and Powers of the Police under the Children Act 1989* (Home Office Circular 017/2008), provides guidance to the police about when and how they should use police protection powers under the Children Act 1989.

No court order necessary

The police are not equipped to deal with children at risk, and therefore the police are required to arrange to place the children in suitable accommodation. They also have the power to ensure that a child remains in suitable accommodation, such as a hospital (s. 46(1) (a) and (b)). Neither of these powers (to remove a child or to keep a child in a safe place) requires a court order. The police therefore have powers which a social worker does not.

Duties to notify

As soon as the police have taken a child into their protection they have to notify the relevant local authority, notify the child, if appropriate, of what steps are to be taken, take steps to discover the wishes of the child concerned, move the child to suitable accommodation, and inform the designated officer of the fact that a child has been taken into police protection (s. 46(3)).

The 'designated officer' within the police is the liaison point between the local authority and the police in these cases, and every social worker should be aware of who this person is—every police force is required to appoint one.

The police also have to inform the child's parent of the fact that the child has been taken into police custody. The police do not obtain parental responsibility for the child by taking the child into police custody but must do what is reasonable to safeguard or promote the child's welfare (s. 46(9)).

The relationship with emergency protection orders

If the police think that an emergency protection order should be sought, then they have to apply for it. They can do this whether or not the local authority is aware of the application or, more importantly, whether or not the local authority agrees with the making of such an application (s. 46(7) and (8)). If a child is in police protection that triggers the duty for a local authority to carry out an investigation under s. 47.

Time limits and contact

No child may be kept in police protection for more than 72 hours, and during that time the police must allow both the child's parent and anybody having a contact order under s. 8 to have reasonable contact with the child (s. 46(10)).

However, if the child in police protection has been placed in local authority accommodation, then it is for the local authority to arrange contact (s. 46(11)). Therefore, for the best of reasons, whenever the police take a child into their protection, they will wish to accommodate the child with the local authority as soon as possible. Either the police or, more probably, the local authority can apply for an emergency protection order if appropriate.

The relationship between the police and social services

The question whether the social worker should use their own powers under the Act or turn to the police will be a decision that will greatly depend on the circumstances of the particular case and the extent and nature of the cooperation and liaison between the local police and the social services department.

In an extreme case, if you believe that a child is in serious physical danger, you can ask a police officer to exercise their powers under s. 17 of the Police and Criminal Evidence Act 1984 to enter any premises and to search for and remove the child. No court order is required. The police may also arrest without warrant any person who has committed any offence where the arrest is necessary to protect a child from that person (Police and Criminal Evidence Act 1984, s. 25). The police also have powers under the Crime and Disorder Act 1998 to remove truants either to home, or to a place of safety.

SUMMARY

- When deciding care plans, courts must now consider the impact on the child of any harm suffered or likely to be suffered, the child's current and future needs, and how the plan could meet those needs. This requirement raises the bar in respect of the standards of parenting to be expected once a Care Order is granted.

- When the threshold in s. 31 is thought to be met, local authorities should convene legal planning meetings. These meetings consider the threshold evidence and make plans for compulsory intervention in family life.

- The Public Law Outline provides guidance on how the local authority should continue to work with parents for the protection of children, and it sets out a framework for the courts to follow when applications are made to the courts, including a timetable.

- Care plans are prepared by social workers for the courts to consider once threshold criteria have been agreed or determined.

- The long-term orders which a court can make are supervision orders, care orders, special guardianship orders, and placement orders, which normally precede adoption orders.

- The threshold criteria are concerned with significant harm, which is attributable to the parenting received or because the child is beyond parental control, or there is a likelihood of significant harm occurring in the future. Significant harm is harm that is considerable, noteworthy, or important. Likelihood is measured on the balance of probabilities; that is, is the harm more likely than not?

- Care orders give local authorities parental responsibility and they can determine the extent to which parents can exercise their parental responsibility towards their child. Care orders last until the child is 18 or until the order is discharged.

- The grounds for supervision orders are the same as for care orders. Supervision orders do not provide the local authority with parental responsibility, only that they will advise, assist, and befriend the child. They normally last for one year.

- Care proceedings should normally take no more than 26 weeks to conclude.

- Emergency protection orders are short-term (maximum eight-day) orders to secure the immediate protection of a child from significant harm. Child assessment orders allow the local authority to conduct an assessment of a child when the parents object. The police can exercise powers to protect children by removing them to a place of safety for up to 72 hours.

EXERCISES

1 What needs to be done by the local authority prior to making an application to court? What is the value of this pre-proceedings work?

2 Work through the various court orders in this chapter and produce a grid of their main features, such as duration, directions, discharge, etc.

3 In the following scenarios, consider what order you may be seeking and why:

(a) Jon has been found wandering in the street by the police. He is bruised and crying. He is about three years old.

(b) Tim is 11 years old. The headteacher of his school has contacted you with the following information. He is underweight and dressed in cast-off clothes. He is the youngest child of a family of seven. He has been absent from school on numerous occasions during the past year. When you consult your records, you find that two of the older children in the family have had short periods subject to a care order. There is a note on the file suggesting that Tim's mother finds it difficult to cope. You have talked to Tim, who seems depressed and tells you he is unhappy at home.

(c) Lizzie has serious drug addiction problems. She has tried to stop her drug abuse but frequently relapses. Her children, who are aged five and nine, are neglected. You suspect that in the long term the children would progress better with a foster placement.

4 Sarah is the subject of an emergency protection order. What are your responsibilities to Sarah and her parents during the period of the order?

5 Paula's child, Ian, is subject to a care order and has been placed with a foster family for the past six years. Ian has told Paula that he is unhappy in his placement. Paula would like to apply for the discharge of the care order. How does she go about this?

ONLINE RESOURCES

For guidance on how to answer these exercises, visit the online resources at www.oup.com/uk/carr-goosey15e.

WHERE DO WE GO FROM HERE?

This chapter has explained the range of court orders for which your department may apply to protect children. These orders must not be seen separately from the need to plan appropriately for children, which we discussed in **chapter 6**. One way of planning for children is to consider their needs for permanence. **Chapter 9,** on adoption and special guardianship, sets out the legal framework for finding children new families on a permanent basis.

 ANNOTATED FURTHER READING

Social work practice and the legal context

K. Holt and N. Kelly, 'Rhetoric and reality surrounding care proceedings: family justice under strain' (2012) *Journal of Social Welfare and Family Law* 34(3): 155. This article explores the issues surrounding the boundary of decision making between the courts and the local authority following the publication of the Family Justice Review.

K. Holt and N. Kelly, 'Limits to partnership working: developing relationship-based approaches with children and their families' (2018) *Journal of Social Welfare and Family Law*, 40:2, 147–63. This article explores relationship-based practice in social work with children in the context of recent legal reforms.

The work of the courts

J. Dickens and J. Masson, 'The courts and child protection social work in England: Tail wags dog?'(2014) *British Journal of Social Work* 46(2): 1.

Threshold criteria

There has been a wave of commentary on the *Re B* case which you will find helpful. For example, see A. Gupta and E. Lloyd Jones, 'Re B-S: a glass half full? An exploration of the implications of the Re B-S judgment on practice in the family courts' (2014) *Child and Family Social Work* 21(4): 539–47.

Similar commentary has emerged in the *MA, SA and HA (Children, by their Children's Guardian) v MA, HA, The City and County of Swansea* Court of Appeal case, which appears at the beginning of this chapter and makes for interesting reading.

H. Keating, '*Re MA*: the significance of harm' (2011) *CFLQ* 23(1): 115.

Protecting babies

M. Freel, 'Baby K's unlawful removal: practice issues in the emergency protection of children' (2010) *Child Abuse Review* 19(3): 158.

J. Masson and J. Dickens, 'Protecting unborn and newborn babies' (2014) *Child Abuse Review* 24(2): 107–19.

Historical overview

J. Masson, 'From Curtis to Waterhouse: state care and child protection in the UK 1945–2000' in S. Katz, J. Eekelaar, and M. Macken (eds), *Cross-Currents: Family Law and Policy in the United States and England* (Oxford University Press, 2000).

J. Eekelaar, 'Then and now—family law's direction of travel' (2013) *Journal of Social Welfare and Family Law* 35(4): 415. This article explores similarities and differences between cases from the 1960s and those of the present day to examine the direction of travel in family law.

9 Long-term planning for children

OVERVIEW AND OBJECTIVES

By the end of this chapter you should be familiar with the legal framework for domestic adoption discussed in this case and set out in the Adoption and Children Act 2002. You will also learn about the alternative to adoption—special guardianship. The chapter, however, starts by considering the responsibilities upon children's social care to start planning for the long-term future of children who become their responsibility from the time that any emergency problems are resolved. Long-term planning emerges from the investigative and immediate planning responsibilities that we considered in **chapter 8**.

CASE STUDY

F (A Child) (Placement Order) (2008), Court of Appeal; R (on the application of EL) v Essex CC

Why are we asking you to read these cases?

Social workers and local authorities have the difficult task of securing the long-term future of those children who are in their care, especially those subject to care orders. When the long-term plan is adoption, the local authority is required to secure that long-term future quickly, but they must also do so fairly. The severing of parental responsibility should only be done when nothing else will do. It is a decision of the gravest kind. Social workers are required to simultaneously hold in mind the welfare needs of the child and the human rights of parents.

What is at stake for the parties and beyond?

For parents seeking to challenge placement orders, their actions can be seen as last-ditch attempts to retain parental responsibility for their children and to stay in touch with them during their childhoods. For some parents, their challenges are their only possible attempts to demonstrate their love for their child. It may be of some comfort to them that they tried everything to retain their role as parent. For local authorities, there are significant pressures to make sure children who should be adopted are adopted as soon as possible. With increasing age, research evidence shows, the probability of placement breakdown increases.

F (A Child) (Placement Order) (2008), Court of Appeal The father (F) of a daughter (J) appealed against a decision that the court had no jurisdiction to grant him leave to make an application to revoke a placement order made in respect of his daughter. F had had a casual relationship with J's mother and had not initially been aware that he was J's father. DNA tests later established F's paternity after J had been placed in the care of the first respondent local authority. F subsequently learned that plans for J's adoption were well advanced. In fact, J had already been matched for placement. F sought information as to J's progress towards adoption and the authority informed him that she had not been placed but had been to a matching panel the previous day. F filed an application under s. 24 of the Adoption and Children Act 2002 for leave to revoke the placement order. Due to staff shortages, the County Court did not process F's application for nearly two weeks, when notices of a hearing were sent to the parties. In the meantime, however, and despite F's emerging challenge, the local authority's decision maker ratified the matching panel's decision. At the hearing, the local authority submitted that the terms of

s. 24(2)(b) of the Act removed the court's jurisdiction to grant F leave to make the application as J had already been placed for adoption. The judge upheld that submission. F contended that it was open to the court, in reliance on s. 3 of the Human Rights Act 1998 in giving effect to his rights both to a fair hearing and to family life under the European Convention on Human Rights, to interpret s. 24(5) of the Act so that the words 'an application for the revocation of a placement order has been made' could include the application for leave to make the application.

The Court of Appeal dismissed F's application. The words of s. 24 were clear, unambiguous, and capable of only one meaning. The words 'an application for the revocation of a placement order' in s. 24(5)(a) meant just that: they did not mean and could not be read as also meaning 'an application for leave to apply for the revocation of a placement order'. Further, s. 24 of the 2002 Act, properly applied and implemented, was compliant with the 1998 Act and the Convention. The fact that the 2002 Act had permitted the travesty of good practice which had occurred in the instant case was not a reason for declaring it incompatible with F's human rights or for construing s. 24(5), as F had contended. There was also a need for good practice to supplement the 2002 Act. The conduct of the local authority in the instant case had been disgraceful and was an example of the worst kind of sharp practice. Good practice demanded that what should have happened in the instant case was, first, that F should have invited the local authority to give an undertaking not to take any steps to place J with prospective adopters pending the hearing of his s. 24 application. Next, the local authority should have explained that its plans were at an advanced stage and about to be implemented. It could then itself have applied to the court, on short notice, for leave to place J for adoption under s. 24(5). Either way, there would have been a hearing on the merits. Local authorities and adoption agencies had to understand that it was the court which was in control and which had been given the responsibility for making those decisions by Parliament.

R. (on the application of EL) v Essex CC

As reported:

> The claimant mother sought judicial review of the defendant local authority's decision to place her daughter for adoption.

Care and placement orders had been made in May 2016. The mother was refused permission to appeal against those orders. In September 2016, the mother told the local authority that she would be seeking judicial review. By that stage, prospective adopters had been found. The local authority notified the mother of its intention to place the child. The placement plan was finalized. It provided for an initial meeting on 28 September, progressing to the child being taken to the adopters' home by 2 October. The mother was not informed of the timetable. She attended the Family Court on 29 September to apply to revoke the placement order. The court was unable to process her application due to errors. The court notified the local authority of the mother's actions. The legal services department advised the relevant social workers to carry on with the existing plans for the time being, since there was no application by the mother before the court. The Adoption and Children Act 2002 s.24(5) provided that, where an application for the revocation of a placement order had been made and had not yet been disposed of, the child could not be placed for adoption without the leave of the court. On 4 October, the local authority brought forward the date for the child to be placed with the adopters. The child was placed on 5 October. It was the mother's case that the decision was procedurally unfair, in the light of the guidance given in *F (A Child)*.

The mother's assertion that she would be seeking a judicial review had alerted the local authority to the fact that she still wanted to challenge the plan for adoption. The relevant social workers knew, ought to have known, or ought to have found out whether judicial review proceedings could be taken and what routes of challenge were open to the mother under the 2002 Act. In the circumstances of the case, before it embarked on the implementation of a placement plan, fairness, common sense, and straightforwardness required the local authority to inform the mother that unless she issued an application under s. 24 by a certain date, it would proceed with its placement plan by placing the child. The local authority's approach of not communicating with the mother about what it was doing and what she could do was not fair.

WHAT DO THESE CASES TELL US ABOUT SOCIAL WORK PRACTICE?

The judges in the Court of Appeal wanted their decision to be disseminated as widely as possible. What it emphasizes is the need for good practice as well as compliance with the letter of the law. It also reminds local authorities that birth parents deserve to be treated with dignity and respect. The more recent case also shows that despite the ruling in *F (A Child)*, local authorities' decisions can still fall outside what the law would describe as fair.

Perhaps we can have some sympathy for the local authorities. They were acting in the best interests of the children concerned and trying to provide them with long-term security as quickly as possible. Priority planning for the long-term future of children is of critical importance, but this must be done within the law. Adoption is one possible outcome for children who become the subject of child protection.

Introduction

Local authorities should plan for the long-term future of all the children they look after. *There is now a legal obligation to consider permanence at the four-month statutory review* of looked-after children, which we discuss later. When you consider permanent resolutions, you will inevitably find that there are some children who will never be in a position to return to their parents or any other family member. In those circumstances, the authority, to safeguard and promote the child's welfare, must look for an alternative permanent substitute family, unless there are compelling reasons not to do so.

If you have come to the conclusion that a permanent substitute family is the appropriate course of action, then you are likely to be considering adoption. However, there may be particular reasons why adoption is not appropriate for children; for instance, older children may be unhappy about severing legal links with their birth families. For this reason, the Adoption and Children Act 2002 introduced the legal status of special guardianship orders, which allow for a form of long-term placement with legal safeguards.

A note of caution: whilst we give you an overview of the law, for full details you may need a specialized text, and if you are involved in the adoption process you must consult specialist social workers and your agency lawyer.

Long-term planning

Good care plans should be prepared for all children looked after by the local authority.

 BOX 9.1 Key elements of care plans—para. 2.44, *Guidance and Regulations, Volume 2: Care Planning, Placement and Care Review* (2015)

- the information about the long-term plan for the child, including timescales (the -permanence plan) **[The Care Planning, Placement and Case Review (England) Regulations 2010 regulation 5(A)]**;

- the arrangements to meet the child's needs **[regulation 5(b)(i)–(vii)]** in line with the child's developmental needs domain of the Assessment Framework, including arrangements for contact:

- arrangements for contact with a brother or sister who is also looked after but not placed with the child;

- details of any court orders made under section 8 or section 34; and

- arrangements for promoting and maintaining contact with a parent and anyone else with parental responsibility **[regulation 5(b)(v) and para. 3, Schedule 1]**;

- details of the placement plan and why the placement was chosen, unless the child is in care and not provided with accommodation by the responsible authority;

- the name of the child's IRO;

- details of the health plan and personal education plan (PEP);

- the wishes and feelings of relevant people about the arrangements for the child; and

- the wishes and feelings of these people about any proposed changes to the care plan.

There is extensive advice available. Chapter 2 of the *Children Act 1989 Guidance and Regulations, Volume 2: Care Planning, Placement and Case Review June 2015* provides information about the planning process for children's placements. The guidance identifies four stages: assessment, planning, intervention, and review (see paras 2.18–2.34). This volume gives excellent suggestions and a checklist of whom to involve in the planning process and how to carry it out. Paragraph 2.44 sets out the key elements of a care plan, which we mentioned in **chapter 8** in respect of plans for care proceedings and which we have reproduced in **Box 9.1**. Long-term planning should start as early as possible. *Working Together to Safeguard Children (2018)* includes a flow chart which illustrates the process which follows the initial child protection conference (see p 52). We have copied this diagram for you at **Figure 9.1**. The process contains certain safeguards against 'drift', which we now discuss.

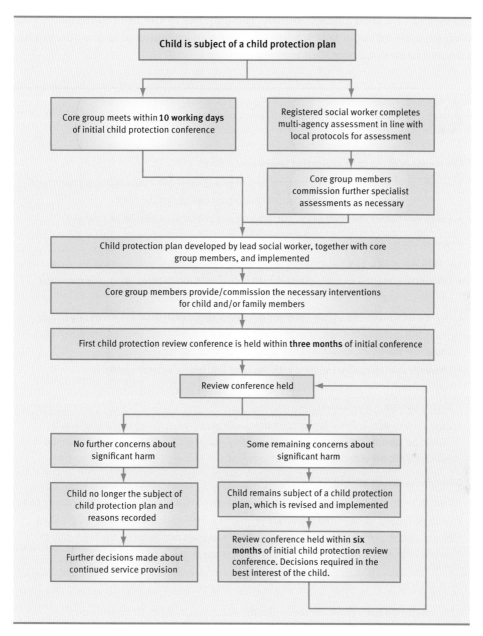

Figure 9.1 What happens after the child protection conference, including the review process?
Source: HM Government, July 2018.

The child protection review conference

Child protection review conferences should take place within three months of the initial child protection conference and then at six-monthly intervals whilst the child is the subject of a child protection plan. The purposes of the child protection review conference are set out in **Box 9.2**, including the responsibilities of local authority children's social care and how joint working is enabled.

 BOX 9.2 The child protection review conference—p 51 of *Working Together to Safeguard Children* (2018)

The purposes of the child protection review conference:

- Review whether the child is continuing to suffer, or is likely to suffer, significant harm, and review developmental progress against child protection plan outcomes.
- Consider whether the child protection plan should continue or should be changed.

Responsibilities of local authority children's social workers:

- Attend and lead organisation of the conference.
- Determine when the review conference should be held within three months of the initial conference and thereafter at maximum intervals of six months.
- Provide information to enable informed decisions about what action is necessary to safeguard and promote the welfare of the child who is the subject of the child protection plan, and about the effectiveness and impact of action taken so far.
- Share the conference information with the child and family beforehand (where appropriate).
- Record conference outcomes.
- Decide whether to initiate family court proceedings (all the children in the household should be considered, even if concerns are only expressed about one child) if the child is considered to be suffering significant harm.

Other professionals should:

- Attend, when invited, and provide details of their involvement with the child and family; and
- produce reports for the child protection review. This information will provide an overview of work undertaken by family members and professionals and evaluate the impact on the child's welfare against the planned outcomes set out in the child protection plan.

The core group has a collective responsibility, which is laid out in *Working Together*, to:

- meet within ten working days from the initial child protection conference if the child is the subject of a child protection plan;
- develop the outline child protection plan, based on assessment findings, and set out what needs to change, by how much, and by when in order for the child to be safe and have their needs met;
- decide what steps need to be taken, and by whom, to complete the in-depth assessment to inform decisions about the child's safety and welfare; and
- implement the child protection plan and take joint responsibility for carrying out the agreed tasks, monitoring progress and outcomes and refining the plan as needed.

As the social worker, you are likely to be the person who has the key responsibility for organizing the core group, ensuring its work is carried out, and for reporting back to the child protection review conference.

One important function of the child protection review conference is to consider explicitly whether the child continues to be at risk of significant harm. If not, then the child should no longer be the subject of a child protection plan. **Box 9.3** explains the decision-making process.

BOX 9.3 Discontinuing the child protection plan—*Working Together to Safeguard Children* (2018)

A child should no longer be the subject of a child protection plan if:

- it is judged that the child is no longer continuing to, or be likely to, suffer significant harm and therefore require safeguarding by means of a child protection plan;
- the child and family have moved permanently to another local authority area. In such cases, the receiving local authority should convene a child protection conference within 15 working days of being notified of the move, only after which event may discontinuing the child protection plan take place in respect of the original local authority's child protection plan; or
- the child has reached 18 years of age (to end the child protection plan, the local authority should have a review around the child's birthday and this should be planned in advance);
- the child has died, or has permanently left the UK.

Child protection conference and Public Law Outline

It is not unusual for a child protection conference to take place at the same time as the local authority is considering whether to apply for a care order in a legal planning meeting. Care should be taken to ensure that the decision making in each of these meetings is consistent. It has happened that a child has been discontinued on a child protection plan whilst, in another part of the authority, a legal planning meeting has decided that the threshold conditions under s.31 have been met and an application for a care order should be made. It would be challenging for most authorities to justify both conditions to be true at the same time.

Looked-after children

There are specific regulatory requirements upon local authorities to review looked-after children's care plans. These are set out in the *Children Act 1989 Guidance and Regulations, Volume 2: Care Planning, Placement and Case Review June 2015*. The regulations make provision for the minimum frequency of the review and the matters that must be discussed.

The role of the independent reviewing officer

The role of the independent reviewing officer (IRO) is set out in the *IRO Handbook: Statutory Guidance for Independent Reviewing Officers and Local Authorities on their Functions in Relation to Case Management and Review for Looked-after Children* (2010). The primary task of the IRO is to 'ensure that the care plan for the child fully reflects the child's current needs and that the actions set out in the plan are consistent with the local authority's legal responsibilities towards the child' (para. 2.10). The IRO will normally chair the review meeting. Their responsibilities, set out in s. 25B(1) of the Children and Young Persons Act 2008, are to:

(a) monitor the performance by the local authority of their functions in relation to the child's case;

(b) participate, in accordance with regulations made by the appropriate national authority, in any review of the child's case;

(c) ensure that any ascertained wishes and feelings of the child concerning the case are given due consideration by the local authority;

(d) perform any other function which is prescribed in regulations made by the appropriate national authority.

The first duty provides the IRO with considerable power to require the local authority to address the needs of the child at all times and not just at review meetings. The local authority must ultimately cooperate with the IRO.

In order to properly understand the role of the IRO, it is important to remind ourselves how it came about. In *Re S (FC)*, *In Re S and others*, *In Re W and others (First Appeal) (FC)*, and *In Re W and others (Second Appeal) (Conjoined Appeals)* [2002 UKHL 10], Lord Nicholls said:

> One of the questions needing urgent consideration is whether some degree of court supervision of local authorities' discharge of their parental responsibilities would bring about an overall improvement in the quality of child care provided by local authorities.

(para. 106)

This House of Lords judgment involved evidence of social services failure in the cases before the courts following Court of Appeal hearings which had resulted in 'starred care plans' where a court could exercise continued jurisdiction over local authority decision making in certain instances, post care order. The House of Lords rejected the provision of starred care plans, but in doing so it recognized a gap in the law regarding children's access to rights under Article 6 of the UN Declaration of Human Rights, namely:

> In the determination of his civil rights and obligations . . . everyone is entitled to a fair and public hearing within a reasonable time by an independent and impartial tribunal established by law.

Lord Mackay went on to add:

> . . . I do not see how a child who has no person to raise the matter on his behalf can be protected from violation of his or her Human Rights or the rights conferred on him or her by our domestic law, other than by reliance on an effective means by which others bring the violation to notice.

(para. 113)

It is this recognition, that some children subject to care orders may have no one who could bring to notice a violation of their human rights, that gave rise to the role of the IRO. Put simply, if drift, delay, or any other issue interferes with a child's human rights, the IRO has a duty in law to raise the matter with the appropriate authority and by implication to seek to resolve the matter to preserve the child's human rights. When this is not possible, the IRO ultimately has the responsibility to escalate resolution in the courts via referral to Cafcass. The IRO role is therefore a semi judicial one. It is primarily to ensure that children's human rights are observed. This task is given to the named IRO, not the local authority, thus the IRO personally carries the duty.

Coordinating the reviewing processes

As you have seen, there are two different types of review process applicable to looked-after children. The care planning regulations indicate that 'where a looked after child remains the subject of a child protection plan it is expected that there will be a single planning and reviewing process, led by the IRO, which meets the requirements of both the 2010 Regulations and guidance and *Working Together to Safeguard Children*'. If an IRO is used to chair the child protection review conference, the authority must ensure that their independence is not compromised. Their role is to ensure that the interests of the child are protected, which may be different from protecting the interests of the authority.

Considering the possibility that adoption may form part of planning for permanence, the rest of this chapter considers the law on adoption.

Adoption

The law on adoption is set out in the Adoption and Children Act 2002. The Act and the explanatory notes to the Act are available online at www.legislation.gov.uk/ ukpga/2002/38/contents. Note that amendments to the Act are not made to the internet version. The explanatory notes are extremely helpful in understanding the purpose of the statutory provisions.

The Adoption and Children Act 2002

In brief, the Adoption and Children Act 2002:

- aligns the principles of adoption law with the principles underpinning the Children Act where relevant to do so;
- improves and extends the regulation of adoption and adoption support services;
- sets out and modernizes the legal basis for the process of adoption;
- provides for both disclosure of and protection of information about adopted people and their birth relatives;
- regulates inter-country adoptions;
- regulates the advertising of children for adoption and payments in connection with adoption;
- provides the legal underpinning for an Adoption and Children Act Register;
- attempts to reduce delay in the adoption process.

▓ Human rights and adoption

The Adoption and Children Act 2002 addresses several human rights-based concerns about adoption. In particular, it clarifies the role of the unmarried father and sets up a system that allows adopted people access to information about their past. Independent reviews are available for crucial decisions about selection of prospective adopters and where access to information is denied by the state.

However, it is inevitable that the adoption process will raise Human Rights Act considerations for adoption agencies, as the case used at the beginning of the chapter demonstrated. First, any decision to remove a child from its birth parents must be proportionate and necessary. Second, the views of the birth parents must always be considered, and if the matter goes to court, they must be able to argue their case properly.

P, C and S v UK (2002) provides an excellent example of the way that precipitate action by the local authority can lead to a breach of the birth parents' and the child's human rights. The facts were as follows: P was convicted in the US in 1995 of deliberately administering laxatives to her young son and thus endangering his health. She was diagnosed as suffering from Munchausen's syndrome, which led her to induce illness in her child and exaggerate her own medical history. In 1996, P moved to the UK and married C. Before the birth of their child, S, the local authorities expressed concern about P's conviction in the US and sought to initiate care proceedings in relation to the unborn child. Upon birth, S was removed from P and C and freed for adoption—a procedure now abolished under the 2002 Act. Despite initial legal representation, P conducted her own legal case. The judge ordered S to be removed from P and C's care. His decision was based upon P's treatment of her previous child. Subsequent appeals were dismissed. P, C, and S applied to the European Court of Human Rights alleging that the adoption process had violated their rights under Article 6(1) (right to a fair trial), Article 8 (right to respect for family life), and Article 12 (right to marry and found a family) of the European Convention. The Court held that there had been a violation of Articles 6(1) and 8 both as regards the removal of S at birth and as regards the subsequent care and adoption procedures. It also held that there were no separate issues arising under Article 12. The Court pointed out that the key principle of Article 6 was fairness. In the light of the human rights principles of effective access to court and fairness, the complexity of the case, the importance of what was at stake, and the highly emotive nature of the subject matter, the Court concluded that P must receive the assistance of a lawyer. As regards Article 8, the Court made it clear that there must be extraordinarily compelling reasons before a baby can be physically removed from its mother, against her will, immediately after birth as a consequence of a procedure in which neither she nor her partner has been involved. In the particular circumstances of the case, the Court concluded that the draconian step of removing S from her mother shortly after birth was not supported by relevant and sufficient reasons and that it cannot be regarded as having been necessary in a democratic society for the purpose of safeguarding S.

Of course, concern for the birth family's rights will often be outweighed by the urgency of the need to protect the child. You may feel that this case is yet another instance where social workers are condemned for taking action but would also have been condemned for failing to act.

More recently, the Court of Appeal in *Re B-S* (2013) dismissed an appeal by a mother under s. 47(5) for leave to oppose the making of adoption orders in relation to her two children. The judgment has wider-ranging implications for practice in respect of adoption and human rights. The facts of the case are set out below.

> The mother has two children, the elder born in November 2007 and the younger in September 2008. In February 2011 they were removed from the mother's care. In October 2011 they were made the subject of care and placement orders, the court dispensing with the mother's consent in accordance with section 52(1)(b) of the 2002 Act. Contact between the mother and the children ceased in December 2011. The children were placed with prospective adopters in April 2012. An application for adoption followed in 2013. It was listed before Parker J on 7 May 2013. The mother applied under section 47(5) of the Act for leave to oppose the adoption. The basis of her application was that there had been what MacFarlane LJ described as 'an astonishing change of circumstances' since the making of the care and placement orders. Parker J gave a full judgment explaining why she refused the mother's application and then proceeded to make adoption orders. Parker J refused the mother permission to appeal.
>
> The mother filed an appellant's notice on 23 May 2013 setting out seven grounds of appeal and seeking a new trial. McFarlane LJ explained in some detail why he was giving permission to appeal on all except one of the grounds relied on. He was concerned that the full court should have the opportunity of considering the then very recent decision of the Supreme Court in In re B (A Child) (Care Proceedings: Threshold Criteria) [2013] UKSC 33 [see chapter 8].

The change of circumstances which the mother was relying on in her appeal was considered by the Court of Appeal and eventually dismissed, but not before the court provided detailed analysis of the law in respect of adoption. *Adoption is to be considered a last resort when nothing else will do, not merely being a good idea but where the child's circumstances require the making of an adoption order.* The judgment quotes a Strasbourg case, *YC v UK* (2012):

> Family ties may only be severed in very exceptional circumstances and . . . everything must be done to preserve personal relations and, where appropriate, to 'rebuild' the family. It is not enough to show that a child could be placed in a more beneficial environment for his upbringing

(para. 134)

The Court of Appeal judgment also stressed the need for local authorities and others to provide proper evidence so that all the options can be considered by the court. An analysis of the arguments for and against each option is necessary, echoing the views of the President of the Family Division when he said: 'I want to send out a clear message: local authority materials can be much shorter than hitherto, and they should be more focused on analysis than on history and narrative' ('The process of reform: the revised PLO and the local authority' [2013] Fam Law 680). In practice you might have heard social workers and lawyers talking about care plans being 'B-S compliant'.

This requires a balance-sheet where each realistic placement option is carefully considered for the pros and cons associated with it (see **Appendix, 'The Social Worker's Toolkit'**, p 598).

Adoption

'Nothing else will do'

The outcome of the judgment in *Re B-S* that adoption should be a last resort when nothing else will do, has led to a drastic decrease in the numbers of children being made subject to placement orders. There has been a 50 per cent reduction from the second quarter of 2013/14 (1,630) to the second quarter of 2015/16 (810). Similarly, the number of children being adopted has also fallen. These decreases alarmed the government and the prime minister. The Adoption Leadership Board published a paper clarifying the legal position following the reporting of *Re B-S* (see www.first4adoption. org.uk/wp-content/uploads/2014/11/ALB-Impact-of-Court-Judgments-on-Adoption-November-2014.pdf). The paper makes plain that the legal test for adoption was not altered by the judgment, nor should there be an increase in alternatives like special guardianship orders. However, that is exactly what did happen, which led to a review of special guardianship orders (see www.gov.uk/government/consultations/special-guardianship-review). Consequently, the regulations for special guardianship orders were amended (see **'Special guardianship orders'**, p 364). The government also published a strategy document on adoption to tackle the decrease in placement orders being made and to improve the overall performance of the sector. *Adoption: A Vision for Change* was published in March 2016 promising a change in the law on adoption. The Children and Social Work Act now amends s. 31 of the Children Act 1989 as set out in **Box 9.4**:

BOX 9.4 Amendments to the law on adoption—s. 31 of the Children Act 1989 as amended by the Children and Social Work Act 2017

(3B) For the purposes of subsection (3A), the permanence provisions of a section 31A plan are—

(a) such of the plan's provisions setting out the long-term plan for the upbringing of the child concerned as provide for any of the following—
  (i) the child to live with any parent of the child's or with any other member of, or any friend of, the child's family;
  (ii) adoption;
  (iii) long-term care not within sub-paragraph (i) or (ii);

(b) such of the plan's provisions as set out any of the following—
  (i) the impact on the child concerned of any harm that he or she suffered or was likely to suffer;
  (ii) the current and future needs of the child (including needs arising out of that impact);
  (iii) the way in which the long-term plan for the upbringing of the child would meet those current and future needs.

The purpose of these additional requirements places a greater hurdle on kinship carers to show how they can care for a child, thus increasing the chances of adoption. The proposed changes to s. 1 of the Adoption and Children Act 2002 are set out in bold in **Box 9.6**. The impact of these changes will emerge in case law in due course although currently there is a relatively settled view that, when considering care and placement orders, the court should not be considering the optimum adoptive home for a child. In *Coventry County Council v CC and A* [2007] EWCA Civ 1383, Wilson LJ said:

> The application for a placement order required the magistrates to consider the principle whether the best interests of A required that she be adopted but not to determine the identity of the optimum adoptive home for her.

(para. 24)

Similarly, in *Re T (A Child) (Early Permanence Placement)* [2015] EWCA Civ 983, Sir James Munby, the then President of the Family Division said:

> The care judge is concerned at most with consideration of adoption in principle, not with evaluating the merits of particular proposed adopters. There is no need for the prospective adopters to be joined, for it is the children's guardian . . . who has the task, indeed is under the duty, of subjecting the local authority's care plan to rigorous scrutiny and, where appropriate, criticism.

(para. 50)

However, as reported, in *B (A Child) (care proceedings)* [2018] EWCA Civ 20, the Court of Appeal considered an appeal from HH Judge George's order making care and placement orders that a baby girl, B (born in 2016), be adopted by the adoptive parents of her older brother (born in 2015). The other option considered, and dismissed, by Judge George was to place the child in the care of her father's cousin. One of the father's arguments on appeal was that Judge George had misapplied the principles in *Re T* by comparing the adopters with the kinship carers and deciding 'which would be the "better" placement'. The Court of Appeal found that the judge could not ignore the crucial fact that the child's sibling had been adopted and that his adoptive parents were willing to adopt B. The original judge's careful consideration of the factors to be considered was commended.

Timescales

We have already made it clear that social workers should treat as urgent the need to provide for the long-term security of a child. The statutory guidance on the Adoption and Children Act 2002 sets out the timescales for decisions about adoption. The relevant paragraphs are set out in **Box 9.5**.

BOX 9.5 Timescales—Adoption Statutory Guidance (July 2014)

1.1 Unnecessary delays in the adoption process may have an adverse effect on the child's development and welfare and may reduce their chances of being adopted. The child's need for a permanent home must be addressed and a permanence plan should be made as early as possible;

> well before and no later than the second statutory review (four months after the child becomes looked after) (see *Children Act 1989 Guidance and Regulations: Volume 2: Care Planning, Placement and Case Review*). The adoption scorecards expect that children for whom adoption is the plan will be placed with their prospective adoptive family, on average, within 14 months of entering care by 2016.

The child's welfare

Decisions about adoption must be shaped by the legal requirements set out in the Adoption and Children Act 2002. Section 1 is the linchpin of the Act. It sets out the overarching principles upon which decisions made either by courts or by adoption agencies relating to the adoption of children should be based. The principles dovetail with the principles of the Children Act 1989. The child's welfare is placed at the centre of decision making (s. 1):

> (2) The paramount consideration of the court or adoption agency must be the child's welfare, throughout his life.

Note, however, that in s. 1(1) of the Children Act, it is court decisions only, and not those of social services or other agencies, which must be guided by the paramount consideration of the welfare of the child. There remains, therefore, a contrast between the welfare principle in adoption and in other proceedings in respect of children.

The statute then sets out a checklist of matters which a court or an adoption agency must consider. This welfare checklist is very similar to the checklist within the Children Act. It does not provide an exhaustive statement of what needs to be considered, nor is it written in order of priority. However, you should notice that decision makers must bear in mind that the decision is one which affects the rest of the child's life—and the long-lasting impact of adoption decisions must be reflected in their decision-making process. We have set the checklist out in **Box 9.6**. Note that the requirement for local authorities and adoption agencies to give due consideration to the child's religious persuasion, racial origin, and cultural and linguistic background has been repealed by the Children and Families Act 2014. These factors are no longer prefaced as being more important than other factors, but are factors which will be taken into account by s. 1(2)–(4).

The importance of s. 1 of the Act cannot be overemphasized. All decisions relating to adoption are to be based upon it. (Changes mentioned in the Children and Social Work Act 2017 are set out in bold.)

 BOX 9.6 The Adoption and Children Act checklist—s. 1, Adoption and Children Act 2002

(2) The paramount consideration of the court or adoption agency must be the child's welfare, throughout his life.

(3) The court or adoption agency must at all times bear in mind that, in general, any delay in coming to the decision is likely to prejudice the child's welfare.

(4) The court or adoption agency must have regard to the following matters (among others)—

    (a) the child's ascertainable wishes and feelings regarding the decision (considered in the light of the child's age and understanding),

    (b) the child's particular needs,

    (c) the likely effect on the child (throughout his life) of having ceased to be a member of the original family and become an adopted person,

    (d) the child's age, sex, background and any of the child's characteristics which the court considers relevant,

    (e) any harm (within the meaning of the Children Act 1989) which the child has suffered or is at risk of suffering,

    (f) the relationship which the child has with relatives, **with any person who is a prospective adopter with whom the child is placed** and with any other person in relation to whom the court or agency considers the relationship to be relevant, including—

        (i) the likelihood of any such relationship continuing and the value to the child of its doing so,

        (ii) the ability and willingness of any of the child's relatives, **with any person who is a prospective adopter with whom the child is placed,** or of any such person, to provide the child with a secure environment in which the child can develop, and otherwise to meet the child's needs,

        (iii) the wishes and feelings of any of the child's relatives, **with any person who is a prospective adopter with whom the child is placed** or of any such person, regarding the child.

Placement for adoption

There are two stages to the adoption process. The first is placement for adoption. Placement allows adoption agencies to plan effectively for any subsequent adoption. In most circumstances this will not require court intervention. Placement can either be actual placement with the prospective adopters or it can act as an authority to place with prospective adopters once these have been identified.

Placement of children by adoption agencies for adoption is covered by ss 18–29 of the Act. An adoption agency may place a child for adoption only with the consent of the parent or guardian under s. 19, or under a court placement order under s. 21. The consent of both birth parents is necessary to avoid court proceedings. Babies under six weeks old cannot be placed for adoption. The purpose of the placement provisions is set out in the explanatory notes to the Act:

> The intention is to ensure key decisions are taken earlier in the adoption process than at present, with court involvement where necessary. This is intended to provide greater certainty and stability for children by dealing with consent to placement for adoption before they have been placed (at present this issue is often not addressed until the final adoption order hearing); to minimize the uncertainty for prospective adopters, who under the current system possibly face a contested court hearing at the adoption order stage; and to reduce the extent to which birth families are faced with a 'fait accompli' at the final adoption hearing (as they may be under the current system, where their child has not been freed for adoption but has been placed with an adoptive family for some time before the application or an adoption order is made).

Section 18(1) provides that an adoption agency (except in the case of a child who is less than six weeks old) may place a child for adoption with prospective adopters or, where it has already placed a child with any persons, leave the child with them as prospective adopters only if it does so with consent under s. 19 or under a placement order. Section 18(2) makes it clear that an adoption agency may place a child for adoption with prospective adopters only if the agency is satisfied that the child ought to be placed for adoption. So, there are two placement routes, one with parental consent and the other by court order.

Placement with consent

Section 19 provides the mechanism by which children may be placed for adoption with parental consent and without a court order. Parents or guardians may consent either to the child being placed for adoption with prospective adopters identified in the consent or being placed for adoption with any prospective adopters who may be chosen by the agency. Consent can be withdrawn at any point before an application for the final adoption order is made. As we explain later, if care proceedings have already been launched under the Children Act, s. 19 consent is not possible. Instead, the local authority which is proposing an adoption must apply under s. 22(2) for a placement order—see **Placement by court order**, p 346. Section 20 provides that parents or guardians may consent at the same time or subsequently to the making of a future adoption order.

Placement by court order

If parents do not consent, then a court order is necessary. Section 21 provides that placement orders, court orders authorizing local authorities to place children for adoption with prospective adopters, may be made only if (s. 21(2)):

(a) the child is subject to a care order;

(b) the court is satisfied that the conditions for a care order are met; or

(c) the child has no parent or guardian.

The placement order can be made only if either the parent or guardian has consented to the placement or the court is satisfied that the parent's or guardian's consent should be dispensed with.

In determining whether the conditions are met, a clear link is made with the Children Act 1989. The Adoption and Children Act explanatory notes explain:

> The same threshold for compulsory intervention in family life is to apply where a local authority seeks authority to place a child for adoption without parental consent as applies where an authority seeks to take a child into care under a care order. In placement order cases, where the court is satisfied that the 'significant harm' threshold is met, it will then consider whether a placement order should be made.

That decision will be made using the s. 1 welfare criteria.

Section 22 sets out the circumstances when the local authority must apply for a placement order. We have set these out in **Box 9.7**.

BOX 9.7 Circumstances requiring a placement order—s. 22(1) of the Adoption and Children Act 2002

(a) the child is placed for adoption by them or is being provided with accommodation by them,

(b) no adoption agency is authorised to place the child for adoption,

(c) the child has no parent or guardian or the authority consider that the conditions in section 31(2) of the 1989 Act are met, and

(d) the authority are satisfied that the child ought to be placed for adoption.

What happens if the child's future is already being considered by the courts? Subsection (2) provides that, if an application has been made the outcome of which may be a care order, or the child is subject to a care order, and the parents have not consented to the placement for adoption, the authority must, if satisfied that the child ought to be placed for adoption, apply for a placement order. However, if the child is subject to a care order and the parents are prepared to consent, the authority can choose whether to apply for a placement order or to place with parental consent under s. 19.

Fostering for adoption

The Children and Families Act 2014 amends s. 22C of the Children Act so that when a local authority is considering placing a child for adoption but does not yet have the court's permission to do so, it has a duty to consider placing the child in a fostering for adoption placement. The foster parents in these placements are also approved as prospective adopters. The local authority must first have considered placing the child with relatives, friends, or other connected persons and have ruled them out as not being the most appropriate potential carers for the child.

Parental consent to placement and adoption

Either the birth parents must consent to the placement or the court must decide that consent can be dispensed with. Consent, and when it can be dispensed with, are obviously critical to the placement and, indeed, the whole adoption process. The following discussion about consent in relation to placement orders is equally relevant to adoption orders (see **Adoption orders**, p 352).

Section 52 sets out the necessity for consent, the circumstances in which the court can dispense with consent, and the meaning of consent. We have set out the key subsections for you in full in **Box 9.8**.

BOX 9.8 Consent—s. 52 of the Adoption and Children Act 2002

(1) The court cannot dispense with the consent of any parent or guardian of a child to the child being placed for adoption or to the making of an adoption order in respect of the child unless the court is satisfied that—

> (a) the parent or guardian cannot be found or is incapable of giving consent, or
>
> (b) the welfare of the child requires the consent to be dispensed with.
>
> (2) ...
>
> (3) Any consent given by the mother to the making of an adoption order is ineffective if it is given less than six weeks after the child's birth.
>
> (4) The withdrawal of any consent to the placement of a child for adoption, or of any consent given under section 20, is ineffective if it is given after an application for an adoption order is made.
>
> (5) 'Consent' means consent given unconditionally and with full understanding of what is involved; but a person may consent to adoption without knowing the identity of the persons in whose favour the order will be made.

Dispensing with consent

In the light of s. 52, it is apparent that consent can be dispensed with only in limited circumstances. The decision of the court will be based upon the criteria in s. 1 of the Act. Each case will be based upon its own facts. Careful judgements will have to be made about the best possible future for the child.

Parental responsibility

The impact of placement for adoption on parental responsibility is set out in s. 25. If a child is placed for adoption under s. 19 or an adoption agency is authorized to place a child for adoption under s. 19 or a placement order is in force in respect of a child, then parental responsibility for the child is given to the agency. While the child is placed with prospective adopters, then parental responsibility is given to them. The agency may restrict the exercise of parental responsibility of any parent or guardian, or of prospective adopters, in the same way as they can under a care order (see **chapter 8**).

Contact while the child is placed

Section 26 empowers the court to make orders for contact with the child placed for adoption or authorized to be placed. Applications for such contact may be made by the child or the agency, a parent, guardian, or relative, and any person who previously had contact under the Children Act 1989. Applications may also be made by a person who was caring for a baby under six weeks old and had the benefit of a residence order or child arrangements order settling the living arrangements of the child immediately before the adoption agency was authorized to place the child for adoption or placed the child for adoption. Applications may, in the rare cases where this occurs, be made by someone who had the care of a child prior to wardship. Finally, any person may apply who has obtained the court's leave to make the application.

Courts may on their own initiative make contact orders under s. 26. It may, for instance, become apparent during the court proceedings that the child gains great benefit from contact with a particular person.

Contact orders under s. 26 may be varied or revoked by the court on application by the child, the agency, or a person named in the order. If there are urgent short-term problems with contact, for instance where a child has become extremely upset following a visit and the social worker thinks that a cooling-off period is required, then, despite the existence of the contact order, s. 27(2) enables the agency to stop contact for up to seven days in order to safeguard or promote the child's welfare. Clearly, where there are longer-term concerns, then agencies should make proper application to the court for variation or revocation.

Legal implications

Sections 28 and 29 set out the legal relationship between placement, adoption, and other orders. Once a child is placed for adoption or authorized to be placed, then the parent or guardian may not apply for child arrangements orders unless an application for an adoption order has been made and the parent or guardian has obtained the court's leave. Likewise, once an application is made for an adoption order, a guardian of the child may not apply for a special guardianship order without the court's leave. We discuss special guardianship later in the chapter (**Special guardianship orders**, p 364). These provisions operate to restrict the availability of court proceedings and prevent unnecessary disruption to the placement process.

Children placed for adoption, authorized to be placed, or subject to a placement order cannot be given new surnames or removed from the UK without the leave of the court or the consent of each parent or guardian. Removal for a holiday of less than one month by prospective adopters does not require permission of the court or the parents or guardians.

There are additional legal implications of placement orders. When a placement order is in force it supersedes any care order, any supervision order, and any s. 8 orders. Nor can prohibited steps orders, child arrangements orders, specific issues orders, supervision orders, or child assessment orders be made in respect of the child—s. 29(3). There is an exception in respect of child arrangements orders. These can be applied for where an application for an adoption order has been made in respect of the child and the applying parent or guardian has the court's leave under s. 47 of the Act, or other applicants given leave by the court under s. 29—see earlier in this section. Similarly, special guardianship orders may be made in respect of a child when an application has been made for an adoption order only when the person applying has the leave of the court. This allows for applications which compete with the adoption, but only with the leave of the court.

Modifying the 'looked-after' status under the Children Act 1989

The Adoption and Children Act extends the 'looked-after' status under s. 22 of the Children Act 1989 (see **chapter 6**) to children authorized to be placed for adoption, which ensures that the local authority retains clear legal responsibilities for the welfare of the child. However, it would be inappropriate if all the requirements of the 'looked-after' status applied to children authorized to be placed for adoption. For instance, it may not always be necessary to consult the child's parent before making decisions in respect of that child. Regulations modify the operation of s. 22 of the Children Act 1989 in these circumstances.

Removal and recovery

Removal means taking a child away from where he or she has been placed. Section 30 sets out extensive general restrictions on the removal of children involved in the placement process. No one can remove children who have been placed for adoption with prospective adopters except the adoption agency; no one, unless they have the leave of the court, may remove children accommodated by the local authority while a placement order is under consideration by the court; and no one can remove a child from accommodation provided by an adoption agency once the agency is authorized to place the child for adoption under s. 19 (this also applies where consent has been given and then withdrawn). In these circumstances, only the agency may remove the child. Any person who removes a child in contravention of the section commits an offence.

There are, however, some circumstances where the removal of a child is allowed. First, where the child is arrested and, second, in particular circumstances set out in ss 31 and 32. These sections cover the situation where the child is not subject to a care order. If the child either has been placed for adoption or is being provided with accommodation by an adoption agency prior to being placed, and any parent or guardian withdraws consent to placement and requests that the child is returned to him or her, then the agency must return the child within seven days if the child has not been placed, or within 14 days if the child has been placed. Prospective adopters who do not return the child to the agency commit an offence. If the agency wishes to prevent the removal, then it must apply for a placement order. If a placement order is refused and the parent or guardian wishes the child to be returned to him or her, then the court which refused the placement order will determine when the child is returned.

Where a placement order is in force or has been revoked but the child remains with the prospective adopters or remains accommodated by the local authority, then no one other than the local authority may remove the child except in accordance with any order made by the court. If prospective adopters wish to return a child placed for adoption, or the adoption agency decides that the child should not remain with the prospective adopters, then the child should be returned within seven days of the decision and the parents or guardian of the child should be informed by the agency.

Sections 36–40 apply to a child who is the subject of an application for an adoption order and:

- where notice of intention to adopt has been given; or
- there has been an application for leave to apply for an adoption order; and
- where the child has not been placed in its current home by an adoption agency.

There is a limit on who can remove children in these circumstances. Generally, only someone who has the leave of the court, someone with parental responsibility, or the local authority may remove the child.

Recovery orders

Section 41 provides for recovery orders. Where it appears to the court that a child has been or may be removed in contravention of the provisions of the Act, then s. 41(2) permits the court to:

(a) direct any person who is in a position to do so to produce the child on request to any person mentioned in subsection (4);

(b) authorize the removal of the child by any person mentioned in that subsection;

(c) require any person who has information as to the child's whereabouts to disclose that information on request to any constable or officer of the court;

(d) authorize a constable to enter any premises specified in the order and search for the child, using reasonable force if necessary.

Key features of placement

We summarize the key features of placement in **Table 9.1**.

TABLE 9.1 A summary of the key features of placement

Feature	Section	Comment
Parental consent required	ss 19 and 20	• Consent can be withdrawn at any time • Consent may at the same time or subsequently be given for adoption • Prospective adopters do not need to have been identified
Placement order necessary if no consent	s. 21	• Child must be subject to a care order, or the conditions for care order made out, or the child has no parent or guardian
Parental responsibility	s. 25	• With the adoption agency • With prospective adopters once placed • With birth parents • Agency may restrict birth parents', guardians', or prospective adopters' parental responsibility
Contact	s. 26	• Contact under Children Act 1989 ceases to have effect • Contact may be ordered by the court with anyone following application from a wide range of persons and anyone with the leave of the court

Lack of consent	s. 52	• Either parent cannot be found, or is incapable of giving consent, or the welfare of the child requires consent to be dispensed with
Quality of consent	s. 52	• Consent must be unconditional and given with full understanding
		• All decisions are underpinned by s. 1 criteria

Adoption orders

Preliminaries to adoption

Section 42 of the Act requires that the child must live with the adopter(s) before the application to adopt is made. The time periods depend upon the identity of the applicant or applicants and who has placed the child for adoption. We have set the time periods out in **Table 9.2**.

The section also requires that the court is satisfied that the adoption agency or the local authority has had sufficient opportunities to see the child with the applicant or applicants together in the home environment.

Reporting requirements

Section 43 sets out the reporting requirements imposed on an adoption agency:

> . . . the agency must—
>
> (a) submit to the court a report on the suitability of the applicants and on any other matters relevant to the operation of section 1, and
>
> (b) assist the court in any manner the court directs.

TABLE 9.2 Time periods prior to application

Placed by/applicant	Time period
Placed by adoption agency	Ten weeks preceding application
Applicant a parent	Ten weeks preceding application
Applicant or one of applicants is partner of parent	Six months
Applicant(s) local authority foster parents	One year
Any other applicant	Not less than three years out of the period of five years preceding application (the three-year period does not need to have been continuous)

Notice of intention to adopt

Where proposed adopters wish to adopt a child, who is not placed for adoption with them by an adoption agency, s. 44 requires them to give notice of intention to adopt to their local authority. They can give this notice as much as two years before applying, or as little as three months. The local authority must then investigate and report to the court on the suitability of the proposed adopters and other matters relevant to s. 1 of the Act.

Regulations provide the detail of the matters to be taken into account in the investigation and report. Section 45(2) provides:

> In particular, the regulations may make provision for the purpose of securing that, in determining the suitability of a couple to adopt a child, proper regard is had to the need for stability and permanence in their relationship.

This is designed to ensure that all couples who wish to adopt jointly, whether married or unmarried, demonstrate the strength of their relationship. Individual people can, of course, adopt. We will discuss the different requirements for individual people and couples who wish to adopt in **Adoption by a single person–s. 51**, p 355 and **Adoption by a couple–s. 50**, p 355.

Adoption orders

The adoption order is the court order which gives effect to the adoption. Section 46 of the Act gives parental responsibility for a child to the adopters or adopter. The order extinguishes any other person's parental responsibility and any order under the Children Act 1989, the Children (Northern Ireland) Order 1995, and the Children (Scotland) Act 1995. It also extinguishes any obligation to make payments for the maintenance of the child after the making of the adoption order, whether that obligation arises under an agreement or a court order. Section 46(6) provides that:

> Before making an adoption order, the court must consider whether there should be arrangements for allowing any person contact with the child; and for that purpose, the court must consider any existing or proposed arrangements and obtain any views of the parties to the proceedings.

Section 47 is a key section of the Act. It sets out the three conditions, one of which must be met, before the court may make an adoption order. The first condition is in s. 47(2) in **Box 9.9**. The first condition will be appropriate where, for instance, the child is being adopted by a parent and step-parent.

 BOX 9.9 The first condition—s. 47(2) of the Adoption and Children Act 2002

In the case of each parent or guardian of the child the court must be satisfied that—

(a) the parent or guardian now consents to the making of the adoption order,

(b) the parent or guardian consented at the time of the placement order under s. 20 (and has not withdrawn the consent) and does not oppose the making of the adoption order, or

(c) parent's or guardian's consent should be dispensed with.

The second condition is set out in **Box 9.10**. The second condition will be appropriate where the adoption follows a placement by an adoption agency.

 BOX 9.10 The second condition—s. 47(4) of the Adoption and Children Act 2002

(a) the child has been placed for adoption by an adoption agency with the prospective adopters in whose favour the order is proposed to be made,

(b) either—

   (i) the child was placed for adoption with the consent of each parent or guardian and the consent of the mother was given when the child was at least six weeks old, or

   (ii) the child was placed for adoption under a placement order, and

(c) no parent or guardian opposes the making of the adoption order.

Parents or guardians may not oppose the making of adoption orders under either the first or second condition unless they have the leave of the court. The court can only give leave if it is satisfied that there has been a change in circumstances since the consent of the parent or guardian was given or when the placement order was made—s. 47(7). In *A and B v Rotherham MBC* (2014), an adoption order was not granted, despite the child being placed with the adoptive parents for 13 months, because the evidence showed that the child's welfare throughout his life required him to live with his paternal aunt. The facts of this case are that the applicant couple applied for an adoption order in relation to a child who had been placed with them for adoption at the age of seven months. The child had been removed from his mother at birth and fostered. The social workers, guardian, and court all accepted the mother's assertion that her partner at that time was the genetic father. There was an unopposed care order and placement order. When he was seven months old, the child was placed for adoption with the applicants and the instant application was issued three months later. Another man then came forward and proved that he was the genetic father. Although he could not care full time for the child himself, the father stated that he wanted the child to live with his sister (the aunt) so that he would grow up within his birth family and have the opportunity to enjoy a normal relationship with his father, paternal half-sibling, and other members of his extended, genetic paternal family. The father and the aunt also emphasized that they and their family were black African; the child was clearly of mixed race; but that the applicants were white. The aunt had been assessed as a good parent to her own son, who was only a little older than the child, and as a suitable carer. At the date of the instant hearing the child had lived with the applicants for 13 months and was very well attached to them. Holman J refused to grant an adoption order because whilst the list of advantages to the adoption order was longer than that of the disadvantages, it was not the number of factors which counted but their respective importance. The court did not consider that making an adoption order would be better for the child than not doing so. Holman J concludes his judgment thus:

I have found this decision extremely painful, for I sincerely and deeply appreciate the intense grief it will cause to A and B and to their extended families and friends. But I have not, in the end, found it difficult; and, as I said at the outset of this judgment, it is not one which I reach narrowly or marginally. At the directions hearing in Leeds, when I had read few of the papers (and there were several key documents still to come) and before I had heard any of the oral evidence or argument, I described this as a finely balanced case. By the end, I do not think that it is. I am clear that the welfare of C throughout his life decisively requires that he is not adopted but moves to live with the aunt. It is my duty to make that welfare paramount.

The third condition is that the child is free for adoption under s. 18 of the Adoption (Scotland) Act 1978 or under article 17(1) or 18(1) of the Adoption (Northern Ireland) Order 1987.

Adoption orders may be made even if the child to be adopted is already an adopted child—s. 46(5). However, adoption orders may not be made in relation to someone who is or has been married (s. 47(8)) or who is 19 or older (s. 47(9)). An application for adoption can be made only if the person to be adopted is at the time of the application under 18—s. 49(4). Applications for adoption may be made by a couple or one person.

Adoption by a couple—s. 50

If the application is made by a couple, then at least one of them must be domiciled in a part of the British Islands and both must have been habitually resident for one year prior to the making of the application. Domiciled means that their settled home is in the British Islands. Both should be over 21 unless one is the birth parent of the child to be adopted and is over 18, in which case the other must be over 21. The definition of 'couple' is set out in s. 144(4) of the Act:

... a couple means—
  (a) a married couple, or
  (b) two people (whether of different sexes or the same sex) living as partners in an enduring family relationship ...

Therefore, unmarried heterosexuals and gay and lesbian couples can adopt as couples as long as they can demonstrate an enduring family relationship. Allowing couples who are not married to adopt widens the pool of potential adoptive parents and therefore supports the aim of increasing the number of children who are adopted. Of course, no couple, however stable their relationship, is automatically entitled to adopt. It will be up to the adoption agencies and ultimately the courts to decide upon each individual couple's suitability.

Adoption by a single person—s. 51

Single people who are 21 and over and not married and are domiciled in a part of the British Islands may adopt. One member of a couple who is 21 or over may adopt if the court is satisfied that the person is the partner of a parent of the person to be adopted.

Section 51(3) of the Adoption and Children Act 2002 states that someone who is married may adopt as a single person if the court is satisfied that:

(a) the person's spouse cannot be found;

(b) the spouses have separated and are living apart, and the separation is likely to be permanent; or

(c) the person's spouse is by reason of ill health, whether physical or mental, incapable of making an application for an adoption order.

Parental consent

Parental consent or a court decision that parental consent should be dispensed with is critical to the adoption process. The discussion on the meaning of consent and the circumstances when it can be dispensed with in the context of placement for adoption is equally relevant here.

Key features of the legal process of adoption

We set out the key features of the legal process of adoption in **Table 9.3**.

TABLE 9.3 The key features of the adoption process

Feature	Section	Comment and details
The child must live with adopters prior to application	s. 42	• Parent of child—ten weeks • Placed by agency—ten weeks • Placement order—ten weeks • Partner of parent—six months • Foster parent—one year • Anyone else, total of three out of last five years
Proposed adopters of child not placed by agency must give notice of intention to adopt to local authority	s. 44	• To be given not more than two years or less than three months before application is made

Local authority to prepare reports for court	ss 44 and 45	• Regulations to provide detailed requirements but include:
		  - suitability of applicant(s);
		  - stability and permanence of couple's relationship;
		  - s. 1 matters

Adoption orders	ss 46, 47, and 48	• Give parental responsibility to adopters • Extinguish previous parental responsibility • One of three conditions in s. 47 must be complied with, the most important being consent of parents, or the court is satisfied that consent should be dispensed with

Feature	Section	Comment and details
Potential applicants	ss 49, 50, and 51	• Couples • Single people • Domiciled in British Islands • Habitually resident for one year or more • Aged 21+ (unless one of a couple and the birth parent, in which case must be 18+)
Lack of consent	s. 52	• Either parent cannot be found, or is incapable of giving consent, or the welfare of the child requires consent to be dispensed with
Quality of consent	s. 52	• Consent must be unconditional and given with full understanding • Decisions underpinned by s. 1 criteria

The status of adopted children

Section 67 sets out the status of adopted children. We have reproduced this in **Box 9.11**.

The section has effect from the date of the adoption. You may recall that s. 51(2) is about adoptions by one of a couple where the partner is the birth parent of the child.

BOX 9.11 An adopted person is to be treated in law as if born as the child of the adopters or adopter—s. 67 of the Adoption and Children Act 2002

(1) An adopted person is the legitimate child of the adopters or adopter and, if adopted by—

   (a) a couple, or

   (b) one of a couple under section 51(2) is to be treated as the child of the relationship of the couple in question.

(2) An adopted person—

   (a) if adopted by one of a couple under section 51(2), is to be treated in law as not being the child of any person other than the adopted and other one of the couple, and

   (b) in any other case, is to be treated in law, subject to subsection (4), as not being the child of any person other than the adopters or adopter;

but this subsection does not affect any reference in this Act to a person's natural parent or to any other natural relationship.

Information about a person's adoption

The Act attempts to achieve a balance between information being properly recorded and maintained and available to an adopted person and ensuring that private information is properly controlled. It also sets up a 'gateway' for access to information about adopted persons. The provisions apply only to adoptions which take place after the Act has been implemented.

Adoption registers

The Act provides the statutory basis for three adoption registers. The first two registers provide the infrastructure for the maintenance of key information about adoption. The first is the Adopted Children Register originally set up under the Children Act 1989 which the Registrar General must continue to maintain—s. 77. Entries are made in the Adopted Children Register following adoption orders or following registrable foreign adoptions (Sch. 1 to the Act—not covered in this chapter). The Registrar General must make traceable the connection between any entry in the registers of live births or other records which has been marked 'Adopted' and any corresponding entry in the Adopted Children Register—s. 79.

The second register which must be kept is the Adoption Contact Register. The register contains information about adopted people who wish to make contact with their birth relatives and birth relatives who wish to make contact with adopted people—see s. 80.

A third adoption register, the Adoption and Children Act Register, is provided for in another Part of the Act. This must contain (s. 125(1)):

(a) prescribed information about children who are suitable for adoption and prospective adopters who are suitable to adopt a child;

(b) prescribed information about persons included in the register in pursuance of paragraph (a) in respect of things occurring after their inclusion.

This provision puts onto a statutory basis the Adoption and Children Act Register for England and Wales, launched in August 2001. Information about the operation of the register can be found on the adoption register website, www.adoptionmatch.org.uk. This site also lists a range of other useful websites. By far the most used service is Link Maker. This is a social enterprise founded and run by adoptive parents and is thus adopter led. They provide an on-line platform of children and prospective adopters with near-to-real time data (see www.linkmaker.co.uk).

Prescribed information

Protected information

Some prescribed information will be protected information. Protected information is information which allows the adopted person, or any other person connected with the adoption to be identified—see s. 57. Any information held by an adoption agency which the agency has obtained from the Registrar General and any other information which would enable the adopted person to obtain a certified copy of the record of his or her birth, or information about an entry relating to the adopted person in the Adoption Contact Register, is identifying information.

Section 57 restricts the circumstances in which an adoption agency may disclose prescribed information to anyone other than the adopted person except where there has been an agreement to which the adoption agency is a party. Section 58 provides for the disclosure of information which is not protected by an adoption agency where it is necessary for its functions. Such disclosures will be governed by regulations. The explanatory notes suggest, 'This could, for example, be background information about the child's progress to be disclosed to his birth family without disclosing his new identity or his whereabouts.'

Adopted adults' rights to information

Section 60 sets out the rights of an adopted adult (someone over 18) to any information from the adoption agency which enables him or her to obtain his or her birth certificate (unless the adoption agency successfully applies to the High Court for an order preventing this) and any information disclosed to the adopters by the agency. In this way, the adoptive adult is able to access some part of the story of the adoption.

Procedure for disclosure

Not all applications for disclosure of protected information will succeed—see ss 60 and 61. An agency is not required to proceed with an application unless it considers it appropriate to do so. In making a decision, the agency must consider the welfare of the adopted person, the views of the person to whom the information relates, and all the other circumstances of the case, including matters which will be prescribed by regulation. Where the information relates to a child, there are additional requirements to consider the views of any parent or guardian of the child and the views of the child, if appropriate to do so having regard to the child's age and understanding and to all the other circumstances of the case. If the child is an adopted child, the child's welfare must be the paramount consideration of the adoption agency in processing the request, and in the case of any other child, the agency must have particular regard to the child's welfare.

▉ Transnational adoptions

Lady Hale in the Supreme Court has noted:

> Free movement of workers and their families within the European Union has led to many children living, permanently or temporarily, in countries of which they are not nationals. Inevitably, some of them will come to the attention of the child protection authorities, because of ill-treatment or neglect or the risk of it.
>
> (*In the Matter of N (Children)* [2016] UKSC 15)

Which authorities should deal with such children if they are taken into care—those of the UK or of the parents' homeland? How should one decide whether the British authorities (including UK courts) or the authorities of the parents' homeland are 'best placed' to deal with the child? The issue is particularly controversial given the UK's greater willingness to have children adopted without parental consent than is generally the case on the Continent. What seems to some as excessive interventionism, particularly for 'non-consensual adoption' (without the parents' permission), has angered some EU countries, which are much more wary of compulsory adoption except as an emergency measure. The then President of the Family Division of the High Court, Sir James Munby, noting the rising number of cross-national care cases in the UK, has said:

It is one of frequently voiced complaints that the courts of England and Wales are exorbitant in their exercise of the care jurisdiction over children from other European countries.

(In the matter of N (Children) [2015] EWCA Civ)

He has even suggested there is an element of 'social engineering' involved on the part of social workers: 'It might be said that we are prepared to contemplate with equanimity in a case with a foreign element what many would say is a much greater degree of social engineering than we would be prepared to tolerate in a purely domestic case.'

International agreement: Brussels II (Revised)

The law on where such cases are to be dealt with, the legal jurisdiction for deciding them, is covered in an EU Regulation called Brussels II (Revised) ((EC) No. 2201/2003—BIIR or BIIa, or even B2a for short). This covers certain family matters of EU citizens living in countries other than their own, including social care, adoption, and divorce issues such as parental responsibility. It establishes which jurisdiction (i.e. the courts of which country) such matters should be heard in depending on the couples' circumstances, particularly where they are habitually resident.

The fundamental point is that the legal jurisdiction 'best placed' to hear a case is the one where it is in the best interests of the child for the case to be heard. So, according to Article 8 of BIIR the general rule is that 'jurisdiction lies with the courts of the Member State of the child's habitual residence' at the time proceedings begin. But Article 15 adds that a case may be transferred to another court 'if they [judges] consider that a court of another Member State, with which the child has a particular connection, would be better placed to hear the case, or a specific part thereof, and where this is in the best interests of the child'.

So, if a child is taken into care in the UK, the parents may be habitually resident in the UK, even if nationals of another EU country, so the case would be heard in the UK—unless it was in the best interests of the child to refer it to the home country of the parents. Similarly, if they are habitually resident in their home country, that is where the case would be heard—unless it was in the child's best interests to hear it in the UK.

It is important to note that best interests in this case should not include a notion that UK courts and social care systems are *better* than those of the country of parental origin. The systems have to be recognized as equal, so 'it is not permissible for the court to enter into a comparison of such matters as the competence, diligence, resources or efficacy of either the child protection services or the courts of the other State' (*J and E (Children: Brussels II Revised—Article 15)* [2014] EWFC 45). Best interests may, however, include a wish to see a child brought up in circumstances relevant to her culture or ethnicity or close to other members of her family.

The issues were raised in the case of N *(Children)*—with contrasting views expressed in the Court of Appeal by Sir James Munby and in the Supreme Court by Lady Hale.

■ Court of Appeal: *In the matter of N (Children) (Adoption: Jurisdiction)* [2015] EWCA Civ 1112

JN (later called Janetta by Hale) was born in 2012 in the UK and EN (Ella) was born in 2013. The mother of the two girls, known as AM, and her partner, ZN, both of Hungarian Roma background, had come to London in 2011. AM could speak no English and ZN very little. They initially lived in a caravan with no electricity, running water, or sanitation.

By 2013, they were living in a squalid multi-occupied house in a single room. According to Hounslow social services the shared kitchen was filthy. The family had almost no food—the fridge contained one packet of custard creams. There were no clothes for either child. There was no bed or cot for Janetta and no Moses basket for Ella. The mother had sought no antenatal care in the case of either child. Ella was born in the room. Police protection orders under s. 46 of the Children Act 1989 were issued and Janetta was taken in by Hounslow. A few days later the parents agreed both children should be accommodated by Social Services under s. 20 of the Children Act 1989. The two children were placed with a white family that the legally appointed guardian noted was not a cultural match, so the children were learning only English. In January 2014, Hounslow issued care proceedings. The parents opposed the order and sought to have the case transferred to Hungary under Brussels II Revised Article 15. The High Court ordered that the case be transferred there. In the Court of Appeal Munby recognized the issue as one of non-consensual adoption, since that was Hounslow's plan, and said: 'Thus the outcome of care proceedings in England and Wales may be that a child who is a national of another European country is adopted by an English family notwithstanding the vigorous protests of the child's non-English parents.' He raised his concerns about 'social engineering' noted above.

But Munby said social services were obliged to consider 'the likely effect on the child (throughout his life) of having ceased to be a member of the original family and become an adopted person'—Adoption and Children Act 2002 s. 1(4)(c). Additionally, 'the court must always be sensitive to the cultural, social and religious circumstances of the particular child and family' (*See Re K; A Local Authority v N and others* [2005] EWHC 2956 (Fam)). Munby expressed his worries about claims that the UK overuses non-consensual adoption. He also considered the argument that 'the status of the child's natural parent(s) and their parental rights cannot be extinguished by the English court dispensing with their consent and making an adoption order except in accordance with and as permitted by the law of the state of the parental domicile'. Hungary's constitutional law does not allow foreign adoptions of its nationals' children—and Hungary's authorities are particularly vociferous in objecting to the UK's use of non-consensual adoption.

Weighing up all these matters, Munby ruled that Hounslow should be denied its care order, pointing out the danger of creating 'limping infants' whose adopted status would be recognized in the UK but not elsewhere—particularly in the homeland of their parents. (The term 'limping infant' comes originally from Cheshire's *Private International Law* (7th edn, Butterworth, 1965), p 382.)

With regard to Article 15 of BIIR the issues were:

(1) Does the child have, within the meaning of Article 15(3), 'a particular connection with another Member State'?

(2) Would the court of that other Member State 'be better placed to hear the case, or a specific part thereof'?

(3) Will a transfer to the other court be 'in the best interests of the child'?

All three questions must be answered 'yes' before a court can transfer the case to a foreign court—and in this case they were so answered, Munby ruled. He upheld the decision of the High Court to transfer the case to Hungary. He criticized Hounslow for misuse of s. 20 accommodation, which should be short term only, and for taking eight months to bring the case to court.

Hounslow appealed against this judgment to the UK Supreme Court.

■ Supreme Court: *In the matter of N (Children)* [2016] UKSC 15

In her judgment in this case, Lady Hale said: 'The court is deciding whether to request a transfer of the case. The question is whether the *transfer* is in the child's best interests. This is a different question from what eventual *outcome* to the case will be in the child's best interests.' This implicit criticism of Munby's approach suggests he was putting the cart before the horse, in effect deciding in advance what the long-term best interests of the children were (to be brought up within their own culture, for example) then deciding which court would be most likely to deliver that (a Hungarian court).

Hale, in contrast, suggested there may be shorter-term 'best interests', among them the simple need to deal with the case as speedily as possible, which might suggest the English court is 'best placed' to ensure 'best interests'. 'The question is not what eventual outcome to the case will be in the best interests of the child but whether the *transfer* will be in her best interests.'

In this case the delay and disruption of transferring the case to Hungary, and by implication moving the children from settled foster parents in the UK to the uncertainties of the Hungarian care system, was not in their best interests. So:

> The factors relevant to deciding the question will vary according to the circumstances. It is impossible to be definitive. But there is no reason at all to exclude the impact upon the child's welfare, in the short or the longer term, of the transfer itself. What will be its immediate consequences? What impact will it have on the choices available to the court deciding upon the eventual outcome? This is not the same as deciding what outcome will be in the child's best interests. It is deciding whether it is in the child's best interests for the court currently seized of the case [i.e. the court with jurisdiction following service of the proceedings] to retain it or whether it is in the child's best interests for the case to be transferred to the requested court.

The judges in the lower courts had 'left out of account the vital factor that to transfer the case would preclude one possible outcome [for the children to remain in the UK and be adopted] which might be in the best interests of the children concerned, whereas retaining jurisdiction would allow all the possible outcomes to be considered'. In other words, Hungary's insistence that the children of Hungarian parents should be dealt with in Hungary would exclude a Hungarian court considering fostering and adoption in England at all—even though this might in reality be in their best interests:

> The short-term consequence was that these little girls would be removed from the home where Ella had lived for virtually all her life and Janetta had lived for most of hers, where they were happy and settled, and doing well (Janetta's behaviour having been seriously disturbed when they first arrived). They would be transferred to a foster placement [in Hungary] about which the court knew nothing other than that the foster carer spoke English. The country, the language and the surroundings would be completely unfamiliar to them . . . It would not be in the best interests of these children to transfer a dispute about their future to a court which would be unable to consider one of the possible outcomes, indeed the outcome which those professionals with the closest knowledge of the case and the children now consider would be best for them.

The case should therefore be remitted to the Family Division, where the future of the children could be decided.

What does this case tell us?

In a sense Lady Hale's judgment has left the law in some confusion. The principles set out by Munby are not incorrect regarding the process of deciding on which country has jurisdiction—recognizing the other country's systems as equivalent to that of the UK; establishing habitual residence of the parents; establishing whether, as an exception, another jurisdiction (which might be the UK or the homeland) is best placed to deal with the case; making this decision in light of the best interests of the child, which can involve considering her 'particular connection' with that jurisdiction.

Munby's judgment, however, was informed by a debate about 'social engineering', by which is meant UK authorities, particularly social workers, imposing British standards in judging migrant workers' lifestyles when deciding to draw children into the UK social care and adoption system.

How far Hale's judgment rejects those concerns is difficult to say without more cases responding to her judgment. She has, in effect, opened a gap in the principle of 'recognition'—the idea that other EU court systems are no worse than ours in 'competence, diligence, resources or efficacy'—by suggesting they may be deficient in not looking at a range of best-interest possibilities for children, including remaining in the UK. Or she may simply be suggesting that this concern is restricted to Hungary and one or two other countries that take the constitutional view about the children of their citizens having their futures decided by their own national authorities.

In *Child and Family Agency v D (C-428/15)*, the Court of Justice of the European Union considered the case of an Irish mother who having had one child removed in the UK, went to Ireland, where her second child was born. The Irish Supreme Court referred to the Court of Justice of the European Union for a preliminary ruling on amongst other things, how the concepts of the court which was 'better placed' and of 'the best interests of the child' referred to in Article 15(1) were to be interpreted. The European Court held that the court having jurisdiction had to be satisfied that the transfer of the case would provide 'genuine and specific added value' to the examination of the case and that the court having jurisdiction had to be satisfied that the transfer was not liable to be detrimental to the child's situation, to which end it had to assess any negative effects of such a transfer on the child's familial, social, and emotional attachments. It also declared that if a possible transfer of the case were liable to be detrimental to the child's right of freedom of movement, that would be a factor to consider when applying Article 15(1).

A note on withdrawing from the EU

At the time of writing (and probably at the point of reading) there still remains uncertainty about the nature of Britain's withdrawal from the EU following the 2016 referendum. It is likely there will remain a legal relationship, and the Brussels II Revised regulations suggest that there is far more to that relationship than whether Britain is in the EU Single Market. It seems most unlikely that BIIR will cease to apply, certainly in the near future or in the further future, since it serves a very important purpose.

Regional adoption agencies

The Education and Adoption Act 2016 amends the Adoption and Children Act 2002 by inserting s3ZA so that the Secretary of State may give directions requiring one or more local authorities in England to make arrangements for all or any of their functions within subsection (3) to be carried out on their behalf by:

   (a) one of those authorities, or

   (b) one or more other adoption agencies.

The government's aim is to 'see all local authorities being part of regional agencies. We want to accelerate the pace of change to ensure those children, for whom adoption is the right path, are given the best chance of finding a loving, forever family as quickly as possible.'

   Requiring local authorities to establish regional adoption agencies will see a structural shift in the provision of children's services where the traditional organization of the local authority will be separated from its adoption services. It is currently too early to tell whether regionalization will make much difference to reforming adoption services for the better, or whether it will in fact make matters worse.

Special guardianship orders

There are some children for whom adoption is not appropriate but who cannot return to their birth parents and could benefit from the permanence provided by a legally secure family placement. The explanatory notes to the Act explain:

> Special guardianship is not, however, a replacement for adoption. In AJ *(A Child) (Adoption Order or Special Guardianship Order)* (2007), the Court of Appeal made clear that each case

had to be decided on what was in the best interests of the particular child on the particular facts of the case. Adoption provides carers with assurance that a placement will not be disturbed. Special guardianship cannot do this.

Section 115 of the Act amends the Children Act 1989 to insert provisions, ss 14A–14G, which create special guardianship. Statutory references in this section of this chapter are therefore references to the Children Act 1989 as amended.

The special guardianship order, as the explanatory notes set out, is intended 'to provide the child with the stability he needs', and therefore 'the special guardian has clear responsibility for all the day-to-day decisions about caring for the child or young person and for taking decisions about his upbringing'.

Section 14A sets out the basic legal requirements which we reproduce in **Box 9.12**.

BOX 9.12 Special guardianship—s. 14A of the Children Act 1989

(1) A 'special guardianship order' is an order appointing one or more individuals to be a child's 'special guardian' (or 'special guardians').

(2) A special guardian—
    (a) must be aged eighteen or over; and
    (b) must not be a parent of the child in question.

Special guardianship orders may be made following an application from someone who is entitled to make an application or from someone who has the leave of the court to make the application. The people who are entitled to apply for a special guardianship order with respect to a child are set out in s. 14A(5): see **Box 9.13**.

BOX 9.13 Those entitled to apply—s. 14A(5) of the Children Act 1989

(a) any guardian of the child;

(b) any individual in whose favour a residence order is in force with respect to the child;

(c) any individual listed in subsection (5)(b) or (c) of section 10 (as read with subsection (10) of that section);

(d) a local authority foster parent with whom the child has lived for a period of at least one year immediately preceding the application.

Subsection (6) provides for circumstances where the court may make a special guardianship order. Its provisions are set out in **Box 9.14** with respect to a child in any family proceedings in which a question arises with respect to the welfare of the child if:

(a)   an application for the order has been made by an individual who falls within subsection (3)(a) or (b); or

(b)   the court considers that a special guardianship order should be made even though no such application has been made.

BOX 9.14 Other circumstances when a court may make a special guardianship order—s. 14A(6) of the Children Act 1989

The court may also make a special guardianship order with respect to a child in any family proceedings in which a question arises with respect to the welfare of the child if—

(a)   an application for the order has been made by an individual who falls within subsection (3)(a) or (b); or

(b)   the court considers that a special guardianship order should be made even though no such application has been made.

No individual may make an application unless they give written notice of their intention to do so, either to the local authority which is looking after the child in question or otherwise to the local authority in whose area the individual is ordinarily resident.

Subsection (8) provides that on receipt of such a notice, the local authority must investigate the matter and prepare a report for the court dealing with:

(a)   the suitability of the applicant to be a special guardian;

(b)   such matters (if any) as may be prescribed by the Secretary of State; and

(c)   any other matter which the local authority consider to be relevant.

The court may itself ask a local authority to conduct such an investigation and report on the results. The court may only make a special guardianship order if it has received a report from the local authority. The Special Guardianship (Amendment) Regulations 2016 place additional requirements on the local authority in preparing a report for the court. The local authority is now required to consider:

• any harm which the child has suffered;

• any risk of future harm to the child posed by the child's parents, relatives, or any other person the local authority consider relevant.

In addition, prospective special guardians will also be assessed on:

(i)   their understanding of, and ability to meet the child's current and likely future needs, particularly, any needs the child may have arising from harm that the child has suffered;

(ii)   their understanding of, and ability to protect the child from any current or future risk of harm posed by the child's parents, relatives or any other person the local authority consider relevant, particularly in relation to contact between any such person and the child;

(iii)   their ability and suitability to bring up the child until the child reaches the age of eighteen.

Section 14B sets out other matters to be considered when a special guardianship order is made. We have set this out in **Box 9.15**.

 BOX 9.15 Additional matters to be considered—s. 14B of the Children Act 1989

(1) Before making a special guardianship order, the court must consider whether, if the order were made—

    (a) a contact order should also be made with respect to the child, and

    (b) any section 8 order in force with respect to the child should be varied or discharged.

(2) On making a special guardianship order, the court may also—

    (a) give leave for the child to be known by a new surname;

    (b) grant the leave required by section 14C(3)(b) either generally or for specified purposes.

Section 14C(3)(b) prevents the removal of the child from the UK, without either the written consent of every person who has parental responsibility for the child or the leave of the court. However, the special guardian can remove the child for a period of up to three months.

The effect of a special guardianship order is set out in s. 14C—see **Box 9.16**.

 BOX 9.16 The effect of special guardianship—s. 14C of the Children Act 1989

Whilst the order is in force then—

(a) a special guardian appointed by the order has parental responsibility for the child in respect of whom it is made; and

(b) subject to any other order in force with respect to the child under this Act, a special guardian is entitled to exercise parental responsibility to the exclusion of any other person with parental responsibility for the child (apart from another special guardian).

Special guardianship orders may be varied or discharged following an application by someone listed in s. 14(D)(1), set out in **Box 9.17**.

 BOX 9.17 Who can apply for variation and discharge—s. 14D(1) of the Children Act 1989

(a) the special guardian (or any of them, if there are more than one);

(b) any parent or guardian of the child concerned;

(c) any individual in whose favour a residence order is in force with respect to the child;

(d) any individual not falling within any of paragraphs (a) to (c) who has, or immediately before the making of the special guardianship order had, parental responsibility for the child;

(e) the child himself; or

(f) a local authority designated in a care order with respect to the child.

The court may also of its own motion vary or discharge a special guardianship order if it considers that it should be varied or discharged during the course of any family proceedings. Anyone listed in paras (b)–(e) of s. 14D will require leave of the court before they can apply for variation or discharge. In all applications for leave other than that of the child, leave will be granted only if there has been a significant change in circumstances since the making of the special guardianship order.

Special guardianship is therefore distinct from adoption. The distinctions lie in the ability to vary or discharge the order and in the continuation of the legal link, although diluted, with the birth parents. As the explanatory notes to the Act put it 'unlike adoption, there is the possibility of discharge or variation of the order, and the child's legal relationship with his birth parents is not severed. They remain legally the child's parents, though their ability to exercise their parental responsibility is limited.'

Section 14F sets out the responsibilities of local authorities to make provision for special guardianship support services, which include counselling, advice and information, and financial support. Following a request for support services, the local authority may carry out an assessment of that person's needs for support and must do so if the regulations prescribe. If the assessment leads to a decision by the local authority that a person has needs for support services, then it may decide to provide them, and if it does it must prepare a plan of provision and keep the plan under review. Regulations will provide the detailed requirements of the assessment, planning, and review procedures. Finally, s. 14G provides that local authorities must establish a procedure for considering representations, including complaints about the discharge of responsibilities to provide support services.

Key features of special guardianship orders

We summarize the key features of special guardianship orders in **Table 9.4**.

TABLE 9.4 Special guardianship orders

Feature	Section of the Children Act	Comment and details
Special guardians	s. 14A(2)	Must be over 18 Must not be a parent of the child

Feature	Section of the Children Act	Comment and details
Applications	s. 14A(3) and (5)	Guardians Individuals with residence orders Local authority foster parents Others with leave Can be appointed on court's own motion
Notice of intention of application	s. 14A(7) and (8)	Must be made Notice initiates investigation and report
Parental responsibility	s. 14C	Special guardian gains parental responsibility Birth parents retain residual parental responsibility
Variation and discharge	s. 14D	Applications may be made as of right or with leave Child can apply with leave Court may make of own motion
Entitlement to support from local authority	s. 14F	Counselling, advice, and information, etc.

SUMMARY

- Permanent arrangements for all children looked after (except those remanded) are vitally important and should be considered at the child's four-month statutory review.

- Independent reviewing officers (IROs) should ensure that the care plan for the child fully reflects the child's current needs and that the plan is consistent with the local authority's legal obligations. IROs should also monitor the performance of the local authority in relation to each child.

- One type of permanent arrangement is adoption. Adoption orders should be granted only when nothing else will do. The Adoption and Children Act 2002 sets out the requirements for adoption orders, including a checklist. The paramount consideration of the court when considering adoption is the child's welfare throughout his life.

- Parents can consent to their child's adoption. However, normally adoption orders are granted when the court dispenses with the parents' consent. Specific criteria must be applied in these instances. Children can be placed with prospective adopters only when a placement order is granted. Prospective adopters normally apply for an adoption order several months following the child being placement with them, but not before 10 weeks has elapsed.

- Adoption orders sever existing parental responsibility. The adopters gain parental responsibility for the child. The child ceases to be looked after. Married couples and non-married couples can adopt, as can single people.

- International agreements exist concerning which jurisdiction has responsibility for the adoption of foreign-born national children.

- Special guardianship orders (SGOs) can be granted to settle the permanent living arrangements for children which falls short of adoption. Existing parental responsibility is not severed on granting an SGO, but the applicant can determine the extent to which parental responsibility can be exercised by parents. The child ceases to be looked after when an SGO is granted.

- Support for special guardians and adopters can be provided by local authorities.

 EXERCISES

Sonia has three children, Anita who is 12, Ben who is six, and Caitlin who is two. Sonia suffers from chronic alcoholism. Unfortunately, her sober intervals are becoming increasingly rare. She had a serious relapse about 18 months ago. The children were found on their own in Sonia's flat and it appeared that she had been gone for some days. Care orders were obtained on all three children. Anita is now settled with her grandmother. Ben and Caitlin are living with foster parents. You have been allocated this case and you would like to achieve some permanence for the children. Sonia has recently reluctantly begun to accept that she is unlikely to be able to care for her children again. The three children are very close to each other, and Anita is particularly close to Caitlin as she was her primary carer for large parts of her babyhood. Anita is very happy living with her grandmother. She has made it quite clear that she does not want to end her relationship with her mother. Ben and Caitlin are settled with the foster parents who have expressed a wish to adopt them. Caitlin in particular is very attached to them. The foster parents are white and in their mid-forties. Ben and Caitlin are mixed race.

What suggestions would you make to provide for the children? Why? What further information would you need? Assuming you decide that adoption may be appropriate, explain the procedure to Sonia. What contact provisions would you recommend?

 ONLINE RESOURCES

For guidance on how to answer these exercises, visit the online resources at
www.oup.com/uk/carr-goosey15e.

 WHERE DO WE GO FROM HERE?

This chapter has been concerned with local authority responsibilities to plan for the long-term future of the children who are in their care. The following chapters have a quite different focus—they are concerned with children who get caught up in the criminal justice system and the complex responsibilities that arise in these circumstances.

ANNOTATED FURTHER READING

M. Higgins, 'The judgment in Re W (A child): National and international implications for contemporary child and family social work' (2018) *British Journal of Social Work* 49(1): 44–58. This thoughtful article explores the implications for social work of the judgement in *Re W (A Child)*.

D. Kirton, '"Kinship by design" in England: reconfiguring adoption from Blair to the coalition' (2013) *Child and Family Social Work* 18(1): 97. This article analyses recent efforts to reform adoption in England, arguing that they represent an attempt to curtail the powers of adoption professionals and their established practices of assessing and responding to risk.

J. Doughty, '"Where nothing else will do": judicial approaches to adoption in England and Wales' (2015)

Adoption and Fostering 39(2): 105–18. This article argues that the unintended outcome of the *Re B-S* judgment was greater influence by the courts over the increased rate of adoptions.

K. Holt and N. Kelly, 'When adoption without parental consent breaches human rights: implications of *Re B-S (Children)* [2013] EWCA Civ 963 on decision making and permanency planning for children' (2015) *Journal of Social Welfare and Family Law* 37(2): 228. The authors are concerned that following the decision in *Re B-S* the courts appear to be more willing to grant leave to appeal an adoption order, especially where parents are not legally represented. Members of the judiciary may be concerned to uphold the Article 6 rights of parents, but this must be carefully balanced against the welfare of the child.

Brexit and adoption

R. Lamont, 'Not a European family: implications of "Brexit" for international family law' (2017) *Child and Family Law Quarterly* 29(3): 267–80. This article provides a thorough discussion of the implications of Brexit on family law in Europe and in the UK.

10 Youth justice

There seems to be a shift away from hard rhetoric about crime and young people. In 2012, Theresa May, the then Home Secretary, wrote in the forward to *Putting Victims First: More Effective Responses to Anti-Social Behaviour* (Cm 8367, 2012):

> We will introduce faster and more effective powers to stop the dangerous and yobbish behaviour of those who make victims' lives a misery. We will replace 19 complex existing powers with six simple new ones. The powers will include a new court order available on conviction that will stop the behaviour of the most destructive individuals and will address the underlying causes of that behaviour —addressing one of the main failings of the ASBO. There will be a new civil injunction that agencies can use immediately to protect victims and communities; simpler powers to close premises that are a magnet for trouble; and a more effective police power to stop anti-social behaviour in public places. We will also help speed up the eviction of anti-social tenants to stop 'nightmare neighbours' who ruin the lives of those around them.

This contrasts with different thinking in 2018. The *Serious Violence Strategy* says:

> We want to make clear that our approach is not solely focused on law enforcement, very important as that is, but depends on partnerships across a number of sectors such as education, health, social services, housing, youth services, and victim services. In particular it needs the support of communities thinking about what they can themselves do to help prevent violent crime happening in the first place and how they can support measures to get young people and young adults involved in positive activities. Our overarching message is that tackling serious violence is not a law enforcement issue alone. It requires a multiple strand approach involving a range of partners across different sectors.

It goes on to say:

> The strategy is framed on four key themes: tackling county lines and misuse of drugs, early intervention and prevention, supporting communities and partnerships, and an effective law enforcement and criminal justice response. This strategy represents a step change in the way we think and respond to serious violence, establishing a new balance between prevention and law enforcement.

And thus, the pendulum swings towards prevention and welfare-oriented policy. Any history of youth crime during the past 100 years show these shifts between policies emphasizing either justice or welfare. But punishment has never been part of the statutory role of a social worker. The welfare of the child and the reduction of crime are, as we see shortly, the main statutory principles. Working with children suspected or convicted of crime means working with them when they are highly vulnerable, in order to help get them through the process with minimum damage and in a way that reduces future criminality.

In this chapter, we look at your statutory responsibilities, then we work chronologically through the criminal process, focusing on those parts where a social worker is most likely to be involved: the police station interview; decisions to prosecute and alternative outcomes; youth courts and their sentencing powers; and consideration of how children can end up being sent for trial and sentence in adult courts. We will consider how social services can be involved in accommodating the child during the trial process, and we will look at helping the court make fair sentencing decisions.

Social workers can be involved when vulnerable adults are suspected of crime, particularly those with a mental disorder, in the police station, and we will flag up those responsibilities too.

CASE STUDY

V v UK (1999) Case 24888/94 (also *T v UK* (1999) Case 24724/94), European Court of Human Rights

Why are we asking you to read this case?

When children commit serious crimes, in this case a brutal murder, society struggles to understand how it can have happened. The brutality of this case shocked the nation. Members of the public insisted upon the maximum punishment for those convicted. Despite this, the children convicted were still entitled to the preservation of their human rights.

What is at stake for the parties and beyond?

One of the boys convicted of killing James Bulger appealed, claiming he has been subject to inhuman and degrading treatment by the state because he was too young to be convicted, 10 years. This was rejected but his claim under Article 6 of the European Convention on Human Rights (ECHR) was upheld.

The facts: Two boys, aged 10 and 11 at the time, were convicted in the Crown Court for abducting and murdering a two-year-old boy, James Bulger. It was a highly publicized case. They were vilified in the press before, during, and after the trial.

V did not appeal against conviction but brought proceedings which eventually came before the European Court of Human Rights (ECtHR). He complained:

- of a breach of Article 3 (the right not to suffer inhuman and degrading treatment);
- of a breach of Article 6 (right to a fair trial); and
- of a breach of Article 14 (he claimed that, as a 10-year-old, he had been discriminated against; if he had been nine years old, he would not have been tried, since he would have been below the age of criminal responsibility);
- that indefinite detention ('at Her Majesty's pleasure', the sentence instead of life imprisonment for those under 18) breached his right to liberty (Article 5);
- finally, that the Home Secretary's personal decision to increase the 'tariff' (the time he would actually spend in custody) was made by a politician and not an independent body (breach of the Article 6 requirement for a fair determination of his rights).

The ECtHR ruled that the welfare of the child, even one accused of a horrific crime, must be a guiding factor in all decisions within the criminal justice process. The right to understand and participate in his trial was the right of the child, not of his lawyers. He should have been personally able to follow and understand. The procedure of the case in an adult court was deemed 'incomprehensible and intimidating' to the boys, and they had been unable to discuss the case with their lawyers because they were suffering post-traumatic shock after having killed James.

Sentence should be determined impartially, by a court, not by a politician. However, the claim that V had been subjected to inhuman or degrading treatment was rejected. The Court ruled that the age of criminal responsibility in each state had to start at some arbitrary age, so he had not been discriminated against because of his age.

It noted:

> Special measures were taken in view of the applicant's young age and to promote his under-standing of the proceedings: for example, he had the trial procedure explained to him and was taken to see the courtroom in advance, and the hearing times were shortened so as not to tire the defendants excessively. Nonetheless, the formality and ritual of the Crown Court must at times have seemed incomprehensible and intimidating to a child of 11.

WHAT DOES THIS CASE TELL YOU ABOUT SOCIAL WORK PRACTICE?

What this case tells you is really straightforward. The investigation and trials of children accused of crime—however ghastly—affect real children whose welfare must be taken into account as a matter of law.

Children's age in the justice system

Almost every European country sets the age of criminal responsibility higher than 10 (in Scotland it is 12), but in the case study we saw that the ECtHR did not find that prosecuting a 10-year-old was in itself a breach of human rights. So, at the age of 10 a child can be charged with, tried, and convicted of a criminal offence, and in a range of courts, including the Crown Court.

But a child under 10 cannot, in English law, commit a crime, and therefore cannot be prosecuted (Children and Young Persons Act 1933, s. 50). Below that age, conduct which would otherwise be criminal must be dealt with informally by the police and/or social services (a telling-off and a word with the parents) or through statutory procedures. One might be an application for a child safety order (Crime and Disorder Act 1998, s. 11), which could put the child under the supervision of a youth offending team (YOT) set up by local authorities and made up of social workers liaising with other local authority workers, police, and probation officers (see **Youth offending teams—liaison with police and other agencies**, p 379 and **chapter 8**); or a local curfew order could be issued; or care, supervision, or emergency protection orders (**chapter 8**). The behaviour of the child could be evidence of significant harm under s. 31 of the Children Act 1989. **Box 10.1** sets out the law in respect of child safety orders:

BOX 10.1 Child safety orders—s. 11 Crime and Disorder Act 1998

Child safety orders.

(1) ... if the family court, on the application of a local authority, is satisfied that one or more of the conditions specified in subsection (3) below are fulfilled with respect to a child under the age of 10, it may make an order (a 'child safety order') which—

   (a) places the child, for a period (not exceeding the permitted maximum) specified in the order, under the supervision of the responsible officer; and

   (b) requires the child to comply with such requirements as are so specified.

(3) The conditions are—

   (a) that the child has committed an act which, if he had been aged 10 or over, would have constituted an offence;

   (b) that a child safety order is necessary for the purpose of preventing the commission by the child of such an act as is mentioned in paragraph (a) above;

   (d) that the child has acted in a manner that caused or was likely to cause harassment, alarm or distress to one or more persons not of the same household as himself.

(4) The maximum period permitted for the purposes of subsection (1)(a) above is twelve months.

   A responsible officer is

   (a) a social worker of a local authority; and

   (b) a member of a youth offending team.

Under 18-year-olds in most of the legislation are designated children (aged 10–13) or young persons (aged 14–17). Age is relevant to how children are treated in the justice system, but it is not as simple as applying safeguards to all children under 18.

- Defendants under 18 are called juveniles (but the old juvenile courts are now called youth courts, part of the magistrates' court system with specially trained magistrates).
- Children under 17 are considered vulnerable when being questioned by police.
- Children under 18 refused bail (i.e. not freed pending the case coming to court) should generally be accommodated by social services.
- Available sentences vary according to the age of the convicted child (and in some circumstances according to their sex).
- Secure children's homes run by local authorities take child offenders who are 10–14, those who have been in care, and those with mental health problems.
- Older children may be sent to secure training centres, which offer education and training and are run by private companies.
- Young offender institutions, run by the Prison Service or private firms, can take those from 15 to 21, though social workers will not be involved after age 18.

■ Youth justice philosophy—tough on crime or concern for a vulnerable child?

Section 44 of the Children and Young Persons Act 1933 (CYPA 1933) makes the *welfare of the juvenile* the number one priority in the criminal justice system, as does the 1989 United Nations Convention on the Rights of the Child (UNCRC, to which the UK is a signatory). From 1933 to 1998 that core principle was taken for granted as the starting point for social workers, magistrates, police, and everyone else. But more recently the 'tough on crime' political mood led to s. 37 of the Crime and Disorder Act 1998 (CDA):

> It shall be the principal aim of the youth justice system to *prevent offending* by children and young persons. [Emphasis added]

Tied to this, under s. 17(1) of the CDA the local authority must:

> exercise its various functions with due regard to the likely effect of the exercise of those functions on, and the need to do all that it reasonably can to prevent, crime and disorder in its area.

The wording covers not just social services functions—housing services, for example, must also be managed for crime reduction. Indeed, every local authority (at district, borough, or county level, not just those with social service functions) must have a youth justice plan (CDA, ss 6 and 40) setting out their strategy and targets for reducing crime and disorder.

Government policy on naming young offenders is an example of the conflict between protecting young offenders and the new punitive agenda. Court cases involving adults can be freely reported. Since the 1933 Act, the principle for young offenders was generally to separate them from the adult justice system, maintain their anonymity, and hope that they could enter adulthood without the stigma of youthful offending and without having been drawn into the adult criminal world (including in prison). The absolute anonymity provision in youth courts was originally contained in s. 49 of the 1933 Act. If they were tried in an adult court, as the Bulger killers were, the anonymity assumption would not apply but the judge could use his or her discretion to ban identification (s. 39).

The issue was considered in *McKerry v Teesdale and Wear Valley Justices* (2001) in which a 15-year-old, who was guilty of taking a car, appealed against a court's action in allowing a newspaper reporter to address the court on dispensing with reporting restrictions and the resultant lifting of the restrictions regarding his name (though not address). His argument was that 'naming and shaming' should not be used as punishment and the reporter had no right to address the court on the matter. The order lifting anonymity was upheld, however, the test being, according to an amendment to the 1933 Act (s. 49(4A) inserted by the Crime (Sentences) Act 1997, s. 45) whether the court is 'satisfied it is in the public interest to do so'. On the one hand, were the child's privacy rights (Article 8 of the ECHR and Article 40 of the UNCRC guaranteeing the right of a child defendant 'to have his or her privacy fully respected at all stages of the proceedings').

On the other were freedom of expression rights (Article 10 of the ECHR). However, Lord Bingham (then Lord Chief Justice) said:

> It is in my judgment plain that power to dispense with anonymity, as permitted in certain circumstances . . . must be exercised with very great care, caution and circumspection. It would be wholly wrong for any court to dispense with a juvenile's *prima facie right to anonymity as an additional punishment.*

It is not clear that government (of either hue) sees matters that way. For example, anti-social behaviour orders (ASBOs) are made in open civil court without anonymity (unless imposed by the court) and they may also be published by the authorities after assessing the need to do so and the vulnerability of the young person involved. The Serious Organised Crime and Police Act 2005 included a provision—s. 141(2)(a)—abolishing s. 49 anonymity for those sent to youth courts for breaching ASBOs (treated as a criminal offence) unless the court imposed an anonymity order. The Anti-social Behaviour, Crime and Policing Act 2014, s. 17 also removes reporting restrictions for children and young people in respect of any injunction resulting from anti-social behaviour.

The anomalous, even contradictory, position in which local authorities are put as a result of the move against anonymity is illustrated by the case of *Medway Council v BBC* (2001). The local authority obtained ASBOs on eight children from the magistrates' court. The authority's motivation, the court noted in the case, had been in part to make an example of these problem children. But these problem children were also troubled children; indeed, they soon came to be recognized as children in need under s. 17 of the Children Act and children at risk of significant harm under s. 47. The same council now had to view the children from its Children Act perspective. It applied for a care order for one of the children. Given its responsibilities to the child's welfare it now needed to restrict, not encourage, publicity. Any information revealed in the care proceedings themselves was protected (Children Act 1989, s. 97(2)), but the council additionally sought an injunction to prevent the broadcast of an interview with the child's mother about the ASBO. The Family Division refused an injunction: the publicity related to proceedings over which it had no control, and (to paraphrase) it was too late to lock the stable door.

In other criminal cases prosecutors are now encouraged to ask for the anonymity of young people to be lifted after conviction. In the past it was generally only local papers that felt they had an interest in making such applications. The Crown Prosecution Service (CPS) has issued guidelines (updated in 2018) about 'circumstances where it will be appropriate for the prosecutor to make representations that there is a strong public interest in favour of lifting restrictions' (*Guidance on Imposing and Lifting Reporting Restrictions in Cases Involving Youths Who are Convicted*). These include where there has been significant public disorder (the guidance was issued after the 2011 riots in England), 'where the public will rightly need to be satisfied that offenders have been brought to justice and there is a need to deter others'; serious offences 'which have undermined the public's confidence in the safety of their communities'; and hate crimes 'which can have a corrosive impact on the confidence of communities'. Previous guidance had said anonymity should be lifted when the offences were 'persistent, serious, affected a large number of people and where identifying the offender might prevent further offences'.

As a social worker, you additionally have duties under s. 17 of and Schedule 2 to the Children Act 1989 which require you to promote the welfare of children and keep them out of the criminal courts (see **chapter 6**).

The Court of Appeal has considered the purpose of the youth justice system in *R v Shoban Butt* (2009) and made clear that while adults could be sentenced on a punitive basis (i.e. to reflect society's abhorrence of an offence), this was not the purpose of sentencing a juvenile. The sentence should be no longer than was required to deter crime.

Youth offending teams—liaison with police and other agencies

The CDA created a Youth Justice Board (YJB) to set standards and coordinate all parts of youth justice work, and to advise the government on policy.

The YJB is concerned with the funding of local YOTs, your most likely point of contact with the youth justice process, also set up under the CDA in 1998. There are 155 YOTs in England and Wales. Social services departments are at the heart of the YOT. Under s. 38 of the CDA, the social services department must secure all necessary youth justice services. It does this, under s. 39, by setting up YOTs for its area, or jointly with another area. The cooperation of police, probation, health, and education authorities is required by statute. The functions of the YOT must be secured by the social services department but need not necessarily be provided directly by it. Curiously, none of these appears in the Local Authority Social Services Act 1970 as a statutory duty (see **chapter 2**).

You are likely to work with the police at four levels: to work with children in general or a particular child to steer them away from criminality (a long-term process involving self-esteem, protection, education, housing, etc.); to attend a police station when a child has been brought in as a suspect; to advise the police on welfare issues when they and the CPS are deciding whether to charge a child; and, if there is a conviction, to advise a court on sentence, consistent with the welfare of the child, most likely to cut future offending.

In an individual case police are likely to consult social services before making any but the most obvious decisions. Even if they do not consult you, the police must notify social services if they decide to prosecute a child (CYPA 1969, ss 5 and 34).

The social worker in the police station

A suspect may have been arrested and taken to the police station or bailed by the arresting officer with a requirement to attend at a future date. Or the child may attend 'voluntarily'—that is, without compulsion but having been told to.

What goes on when a suspect is held in the police station is governed by the Police and Criminal Evidence Act 1984 (PACE), and the PACE Codes made by the Home Office. The important code is Code C on Detention, Treatment and Questioning, last updated in 2018. Code C can be consulted in every police station and downloaded from www. gov.uk/government/publications/pace-code-c-2018 (Annex L details the regulations for searching transgender people).

The code recognizes two groups as being vulnerable in the police station. The first is 'juveniles'. Until recently a juvenile was a child under 17. (Following a High Court judgment (*HC (A Child)* (2013)) indicating the incompatibility of 17-year-olds being treated as adults with the UNCRC, the law was changed via s. 42 of the Criminal Justice and Courts Act 2015, which amends the Police and Criminal Evidence Act 1984 so that all under 18-year-olds are now consider juveniles.) The other is suspects who are mentally vulnerable (Code C, Part 11). Under Code C, para. 1.5, if the police have any suspicion, or are told in good faith, that a person is a juvenile, they must act accordingly unless they have reliable evidence to the contrary. An 'appropriate adult' (usually parent or guardian) should be called to assist the suspect; no questioning should normally take place until an appropriate adult has arrived.

Where a parent cannot or will not come, or is deemed not to be suitable, a social worker will frequently be asked to be the appropriate adult.

Identifying the appropriate adult

Code C contains several references to the appropriate adult: see **Box 10.2**.

BOX 10.2 Who is an appropriate adult, with emphasis added to show where social workers can be involved—para. 1.7, Code C on Detention, Treatment and Questioning (updated 2018)

(a)　in the case of a juvenile:

    (i)　the parent, guardian or, if the juvenile is in local authority or voluntary organisation care, or is otherwise being looked after under the Children Act 1989, *a person* **representing** *that authority* or organisation;

    (ii)　*a social worker of a local authority*;

    (iii)　failing these, some other responsible adult aged 18 or over who is not a police officer or employed by the police.

(b)　in the case of a person who is vulnerable:

    (i)　a relative, *guardian*, or other person responsible for their care or custody;

    (ii)　someone experienced in dealing with vulnerable persons but who is not a police officer or employed by the police;

    (iii)　failing these, some other responsible adult aged 18 or over who is not a police officer or employed by the police and not themselves vulnerable.

Note: someone experienced or trained in the person's care is to be preferred unless the individual wants a relative rather than a qualified stranger.

Where the police detain a juvenile or vulnerable person, para. 3.15 of Code C requires them to identify who they think is the appropriate adult and to inform the appropriate adult as soon as practicable of the grounds for detention, and where the suspect is being detained. They will then request the appropriate adult to come to the police station. This is not least because if they interview the suspect without an appropriate adult, any evidence obtained is likely to be seen as unreliable or unfair under ss 76 and 78 of PACE, and therefore not available if there is a trial (see **Exclusion at trial of evidence obtained in police questioning**, p 387).

However, in exceptional cases, Code C, para. 11.18 allows the police to interview a juvenile or a person who appears unable to appreciate the significance of questions and their answers; or understand what is happening because of the effects of drink, drugs, or any illness, ailment, or condition without an appropriate adult. This must be authorized by a superintendent or more senior officer, who must certify that delay will (not might) lead to:

(a) interference with, or harm to, evidence connected with an offence;
   • interference with, or physical harm to, other people; or
   • serious loss of, or damage to, property;

(b) alerting other people suspected of committing an offence but not yet arrested for it; or

(c) hindering the recovery of property obtained in consequence of the commission of an offence. The Code warns that the evidence obtained may be unreliable (and, consequently, as we see later, may be unusable):

11C Although juveniles or people who are mentally disordered or otherwise mentally vulnerable are often capable of providing reliable evidence, they may, without knowing or wishing to do so, be particularly prone in certain circumstances to provide information that may be unreliable, misleading or self-incriminating.

Special care should always be taken when questioning such a person, and the appropriate adult should be involved if there is any doubt about a person's age, mental state or capacity. Because of the risk of unreliable evidence, it is also important to obtain corroboration of any facts admitted whenever possible.

As well as enlisting an appropriate adult before interviewing, the police must attempt to inform the person responsible for the child's welfare (usually a parent or guardian) of the arrest and detention of any juvenile (CYPA 1933, s. 34(2)); if the juvenile is under supervision, they must inform the supervisor, and, if in local authority care or accommodation, the local authority.

A social services department must have appropriate adults available, but there is no statutory duty for one to be sent or for the police to approach a social worker rather than a parent. Clearly, where a juvenile is in your care, a social worker from that authority is the appropriate adult. But in other situations, it may be better for a parent or other relative to attend. It will depend on your knowledge of the circumstances. Worryingly, in 2011 a joint inspection of the appropriate adult provision for children detained in police custody (*Who's Looking Out for the Children?*) found that:

(The) Appropriate Adult provision has evolved into being another part of the custody process, with a focus on complying with PACE 1984 rather than safeguarding and promoting the welfare of children and young people.

An individual social worker to whom the juvenile has previously admitted the offence is not the appropriate adult—another social worker will be required (Code C Notes for Guidance 1C). In that case, of course, your reason for not attending in person should not be given to the police (see **chapter 4** for guidance on confidentiality).

An appropriate adult has only one task, that of assisting the detainee, and must never double as an interpreter.

Attending as an appropriate adult

It is important to get to the police station as soon as possible, to minimize the period of detention. Once you arrive, you should obtain basic details from the custody officer or suspect's solicitor—suspected offence, time of arrest, and what the police are intending to do, in particular.

Your role is described in the following sections. Your objective is not that of helping the police. Resist the police advice along the lines 'Between you and me, if you could persuade him to tell us what happened, he'll be out of here much quicker . . . '. Section 1.7A of Code C describes the role, which is to:

- support, advise and assist them when, in accordance with this Code or any other Code of Practice, they are given or asked to provide information or participate in any procedure;
- observe whether the police are acting properly and fairly to respect their rights and entitlements, and inform an officer of the rank of inspector or above if they consider that they are not;
- assist them to communicate with the police whilst respecting their right to say nothing unless they want to as set out in the terms of the caution;
- help them to understand their rights and ensure that those rights are protected and respected.

The detainee is entitled to consult you privately at any time (Code C, para. 3.18). Make sure that your discussion is entirely in private: conversations overheard can be used in evidence at trial (*R v Ali* (1991)). If a solicitor has been called, he or she may wish to hold the first interview without you being present. This is because the solicitor's duty of confidentiality is virtually absolute, whereas something said in front of a social worker could, exceptionally, be ordered to be revealed in court. (We say '*virtually* absolute' in the light of the case of *Re McE* (2009), where the House of Lords accepted that police can in law eavesdrop even on solicitor–client interviews in circumstances set out in the Regulation of Investigatory Powers Act 2000.) The National Appropriate Adult Network has published National Standards for appropriate adults. These standards have been approved by the Secretary of State for Justice and published in October 2018 (see www. appropriateadult.org.uk/index.php/downloads/national-standards).

Police powers of detention

The only lawful purpose of detention is for the police to obtain evidence to decide whether to charge or not—not to obtain evidence to use at trial. They should charge or release as soon as possible, which means as soon as they have enough evidence to decide (s. 37 and Code C, para. 16.1).

Home Office Circular 60/2003 states that a child should not be detained for more than 24 hours unless the offence is a serious, arrestable offence and bail is considered inappropriate. As well as the obvious serious crimes of rape, possessing firearms, or grievous bodily harm (GBH), any arrestable offence can be serious if the consequences are serious, such as causing death or serious injury, or substantial financial gain or loss. Code C para 15.2A says that detention of a juvenile or vulnerable person beyond 24 hours will involve consideration of:

(a) special vulnerability;
(b) the legal obligation to provide an opportunity for representations to be made prior to a decision about extending detention;
(c) the need to consult and consider the views of any appropriate adult; and
(d) any alternatives to police custody.

The police cannot in any event detain beyond 36 hours after arrival at the police station (PACE, s. 41). But a magistrates' court can renew the period for a further 36 hours, and again up to a final total of 96 hours (s. 43). (In a terrorism cases detention can be extended even longer: currently 28 days.)

Decisions concerning detention and charge are made by an officer called the custody officer (ss 37 and 38), who must be independent of the investigation. Any complaints or problems should be addressed to the custody officer. One of the first things the appropriate adult should ask the custody officer is whether the suspect has in fact been detained. If the suspect is not detained, they are a 'volunteer' and they are free to leave. Of course, once they say they wish to leave this may trigger an arrest; but at least at that point the time clock for maximum periods of detention has started to run.

Right to legal advice
Section 58 of PACE and Code C give detainees and volunteers a right to legal advice in person or on the telephone, in private, at any time, day or night, before they are questioned and during police interview. This legal advice is paid for by the Legal Aid Agency and is not means-tested. The detainee can nominate an adviser or ask for the duty solicitor (or representative).

A detainee who declines legal advice must sign the custody record to confirm this decision. However, it is possible to 'just sign the custody record here, and again, here, please' without realizing the importance of the right which has been declined. The s. 58 right to advice never stops, and the appropriate adult can call a legal adviser even if the suspect declined to do so. But it is the decision of the suspect whether to actually see the solicitor or not (Code C, para. 6.5A).

If a solicitor is called, the advice on law should be left to him or her. Nevertheless, it will help you to communicate between solicitor and detainee if you know what is going on.

Right to have someone informed of the detention
A detainee is entitled on request to have the police notify a person who is likely to have an interest in their welfare (s. 56 of the Act, para. 5.1 of the Code—the notification

condition). If the police cannot contact the person chosen, they must try at least two further people chosen by the suspect. The police should normally allow the detainee to speak to the person by telephone.

Informing the suspect of PACE rights

On arrival, the suspect must be told of these rights, and the right to consult the Code. When the appropriate adult arrives, the suspect should be told this again, in the adult's presence. Suspects are entitled to written notice of their rights under the Code, which must be available in a range of languages and in audio (Code, Notes for Guidance to s. 3).

Denial of PACE rights

Refusal or delay in the right to legal advice and to have someone notified requires the authority of a superintendent or higher-ranking officer and can only occur where the offence is a serious, arrestable offence (discussed in **Attending as an appropriate adult**, p 382). The officer must be satisfied that the exercise of the right *will* (not may) lead to harm to others, interference with evidence, or a tip-off of other suspects, or hinder the recovery of property (PACE, s. 58, and Annex B to Code C). But as refusal necessarily requires the police to believe that the adviser intends to commit a criminal offence, this is most unlikely. After 36 hours in the police station, no delay in the right to advice can be authorized.

Once an adviser has been requested, there must be no further questioning until he or she arrives, unless the superintendent believes that delay will lead to immediate risk of harm to persons or serious damage to property, or will unreasonably delay the investigation, or unless the suspect and the appropriate adult both consent (it is hard to think of circumstances where this is appropriate).

We stated earlier that the purpose of detention is to decide whether or not to charge. That decision is taken by the custody officer. This officer must formally review the detention after six hours, and then every nine hours, to confirm whether detention is required or consider whether the decision could be made now.

Once charged, the accused person should, normally, be released on bail, which we discuss shortly. If a decision is made not to charge, the suspect must be released. If the police realize that they need more time and more information before they can decide whether to charge, the suspect may be bailed to report to the police station on a later date.

Drug testing children in the police station

Section 63B of PACE enables urine or non-intimate samples to be taken, in approved police stations, to test detainees for Class A drugs. For those aged at least 14 but below 18 it can be done only if they have been charged with a 'trigger offence' (e.g. theft, burglary, robbery, and others set out in Sch. 6 to the Criminal Justice and Court Services Act 2000) or charged with an offence that an officer of at least the rank of inspector believes was linked to drug taking. The notification condition must also have been met, as outlined in **Right to have someone informed of the detention**, p 383. The suspect must be informed that refusal to give a sample without good cause may result in prosecution. Detainees should be told or reminded that they have a right to get legal advice before the sample is taken (Code C), and the sample must be taken in the presence of the appropriate adult where the suspect is below the age of 18.

Conditions of detention

As soon as someone is detained (but not helping as a 'volunteer') at the police station, a custody record must be opened, to record all events, decisions, and reviews, as well as listing the property of the detainee. Code C gives the detainee and the appropriate adult a right to inspect the record. You will particularly be looking to see reasons for any refusal of the right to legal advice, either by the detainee or by the police. If any complaints are made, they must be noted in the record—this includes complaints by the appropriate adult.

Code C sets out how detainees must be treated. Requirements include adequate heating and lighting, temperature, toilet facilities, and sufficient meals, taking account of special dietary requirements. A juvenile should not be kept in a cell unless no other suitable accommodation or supervision is available; the reason must be entered in the custody record. If you suspect treatment may be improper, check s. 8 of Code C (you must be allowed to see a copy) and if appropriate make your complaint, which has to be recorded.

Under s. 9 of Code C, a police surgeon must be called if there is any indication of physical illness or mental disorder, injury, or other apparent need, or upon request by the detainee. If the police surgeon is unavailable, another GP must be called, or the detainee taken to hospital. It is therefore vital that you check whether the detainee has a medical problem or needs medication and inform the custody officer.

Under s. 5, the police should allow the detainee to receive visits (but may refuse if short-staffed). A social worker can assist in this by contacting family or friends of a detainee. (Be careful, of course, not to inadvertently pass on messages that may help to dispose of evidence or enable another suspect to avoid arrest.)

Any interview should not proceed while the suspect is unfit through drink or drugs—if you think this applies, you need to insist on a delay. If necessary, insist on a delay and ask for a doctor.

When the interview starts, the first thing that happens is that a tape recorder, with two tapes, is switched on and the parties present identify themselves. One tape is used as a working copy and the other is sealed in front of the parties as a secure copy. The suspect will later be provided, via the solicitor, with a transcript, and can ask for the tape as well. A suspect must be cautioned or re-cautioned before any questioning starts.

If, before the interview, the suspect has made any statement that may be important if the case goes to court, or alternatively failed to answer any significant question which a court could take into account, the police must put it to him or her at the start of the formal interview (Code C, para. 11.4).

There should be a break at least every two hours and at usual mealtimes. There must normally be a break of eight continuous hours every 24 hours, usually at night time. Inducements to confess should not be offered, although if a suspect asks what course the police will take if he or she divulges certain information ('If I tell you, will I be out of here quicker?') the police are allowed to answer.

Code D, the Code of Practice for the Identification of Persons by Police Officers, like the other codes, is available at the police station for consultation, and covers fingerprinting and identification procedures. The detainee, or you on his or her behalf, should exercise the right to legal advice before consenting. If the police insist on proceeding before the solicitor arrives, ensure that the reasons are given and recorded, and stay with the detainee to observe what happens and also to reduce the risk of an informal interview taking place.

Fingerprints and DNA samples may be taken after arrest or charge for a recordable offence (all but the most minor offences such as breach of the peace). The appropriate adult cannot give consent to fingerprints or DNA samples on behalf of a juvenile. Consent in the case of a child—aged 10–14—is the consent of parents alone; in the case of a young adult—aged 14–17—of the parents and the juvenile.

Police can only authorize taking samples if they believe they will confirm or disprove the suspect's involvement in the offence. Intimate samples can only be taken by a medical practitioner with written consent. A refusal without good reason may be used as evidence of guilt in a court case. Non-intimate samples (hair that is not pubic hair, a swab from the skin or mouth but not any other orifice, and a sample from a nail or under a nail) can be taken by use of reasonable force if consent is not forthcoming and an officer of the rank of inspector or above authorizes it. Photographs may be taken without consent if consent is not forthcoming.

The detainee has the right to refuse an identification parade but should be aware that alternative methods of identification—direct confrontation or identification by photographs—are more likely to lead to a positive identification.

The role of the appropriate adult at the police station

If an appropriate adult is present at an interview, they shall be informed:

- that they are not expected to act simply as an observer; and
- that the purpose of their presence is to:
  - advise the person being interviewed;
  - observe whether the interview is being conducted properly and fairly; and
  - facilitate communication with the person being interviewed.

(Code C, para. 11.17)

As an observer, your presence should ensure that correct procedures are followed, and you should formally complain if they are not, insisting your concerns are noted in the custody record: evidence of breach of procedures could lead to evidence from questioning being excluded, which the police do not want. See **Exclusion at trial of evidence obtained in police questioning**, p 387, for more detail on how courts decide whether to exclude this evidence.

As an adviser you are not being requested to advise on the law: that is for the legal adviser. The Code is not clear on what advice it is for you to give, but if it is not legal, it will be everything else: how to cope with the ordeal, in particular.

Your third task is to help the suspect communicate with the lawyer and with the police. This means you need to understand what advice is being, or should be, given. So, we need to look at some of the legal issues which can arise in the police station or as a result of what happens there.

There is also an important role as an advocate of the detainee's rights and interests. If, for example, a senior officer wishes to delay the right to see a solicitor, to continue to detain for questioning, or to refuse bail after charge, the police ought to listen to your views before deciding. It means interrupting if the questioning is oppressive (e.g. repetition of questions already dealt with) or incomprehensible (e.g. asking an over-complex question). If the interview is extremely oppressive, you will need to consider whether to state your concerns and then leave. Advocacy includes insisting on breaks for refreshment.

Legal issues during police questioning

The right to remain silent under interrogation is an ancient feature of the common law as well as a human right under Article 6, which states:

> Everyone charged with a criminal offence shall be presumed innocent until proved guilty in accordance with the law.

However, the Criminal Justice and Public Order Act 1994 (ss 31–38) permits a court, and in particular a jury, to draw adverse conclusions from silence. So, there is a risk in failing to answer questions, and this must be explained to the suspect. The wording of the obligatory police caution (Code C, para. 10) is quite complex:

> You do not have to say anything. But it may harm your defence if you do not mention when questioned something which you later rely on in court. Anything you do say may be given in evidence.

The legal adviser will have to explain the consequences of not answering questions before questioning starts. Adverse inferences can be drawn, even if he or she stayed silent on the advice of a solicitor (*R v Daniel* (1998)) and even where the detainee was of low intelligence (*R v Friend* (1997): a 14-year-old with an IQ of 63).

A lawyer might nevertheless advise a detainee not to answer questions, for example where the police have failed to outline the allegations which have to be answered. Failure to provide this information is in fact a breach of Article 6(1) (right to a fair trial); the case of *Edwards v UK* (1992) establishes that a right to disclosure of the prosecution case applies at all stages of the criminal process. The lawyer, of course, must be the person giving advice to the suspect on the issue of whether or not to answer questions.

If the police interview a suspect who has requested an adviser but before one is available, no inferences can be drawn from silence. So, a simpler caution is then used:

> You do not have to say anything, but anything you do say may be given in evidence.

Exclusion at trial of evidence obtained in police questioning

When a confession is part of the prosecution case, it is up to the prosecution to prove that there was no oppression and there were no other circumstances in play at the time which might cause it to be unreliable (PACE, s. 76).

To decide whether the circumstances at interview amounted to oppression, or led to unreliability, the court holds a 'trial within a trial'. Prosecution and defence present evidence of how the confession was obtained (in the Crown Court the jury is sent out). On rare occasions, an appropriate adult may be called as a witness in this mini-trial. Just in case, you should always go to the police station with paper, pens, and an accurate watch. You should record the time, to the minute, of every stage of the procedure—arrival, talking to the custody officer, waiting to see the detainee, length of interview, etc.—and the names, rank, and numbers of the people you deal with. If the police see you noting these details, they should respect your professional approach, and may resist the temptation to do anything in breach of the code. If you are called as a witness, you can refresh your memory from these notes.

Courts also look at confessions in the light of s. 78 of PACE, which requires a court to exclude evidence if to admit it would be unfair. An example would be tricking the suspect by lying about having found fingerprint evidence against the detainee.

Taking Code C, ss 58, 76, and 78 of PACE, and Article 6 into account, courts tend to exclude confessions obtained in a non-urgent case in the absence of an appropriate adult (*R v Delaney* (1989)).

The police may have talked to the suspect about the offence 'informally' before you or the lawyer are allowed to see him or her and obtained damaging evidence. You obviously cannot prevent this. But if at the same time you have a record that you were waiting in the foyer and available, it is possible that any evidence obtained will be ruled inadmissible (*R v Franklin* (1994)). If you are kept waiting unnecessarily, make a complaint to the custody officer, so that it is registered in the custody record. Code C (para. 11.1) forbids this type of informal questioning, except where there is a risk to property or people, or the likelihood of evidence being tampered with.

Charges, youth cautions, or no action

At some point during the detention of the juvenile, the police must make a decision. The options are to charge and prosecute, to give a youth caution (under the Legal Aid, Sentencing and Punishment of Offenders Act 2012 (LASPO) s. 135, which abolishes the old reprimand and warning system in the CDA 1998), or to take no further action. With a juvenile the decision may take time, in which case police bail should be granted until the decision is made.

A decision to charge must be approved by the CPS, which will wish to be sure that adequate evidence is there for a conviction, and that prosecution is in the public interest. But as well as consulting the CPS, if the suspect is a juvenile the police should consult with the YOT. They can only avoid this if it is obvious that there should be a charge because of the seriousness of the offence, or the case is so trivial that no charge is appropriate. In between these clear-cut cases, liaison with appropriate agencies is normal before a decision is made; but the decision is still that of the police and CPS. Guidance on whether to prosecute in the public interest is found in the Code for Crown Prosecutors (www.cps.gov.uk/publications/code_for_crown_prosecutors/codetest.html). The Code states in relation to young suspects:

> The criminal justice system treats children and young people differently from adults and significant weight must be attached to the age of the suspect if they are a child or young person under 18. The best interests and welfare of the child or young person must be considered including whether a prosecution is likely to have an adverse impact on his or her future prospects that is disproportionate to the seriousness of the offending. Prosecutors must

have regard to the principal aim of the youth justice system which is to prevent offending by children and young people. Prosecutors must also have regard to the obligations arising under the United Nations 1989 Convention on the Rights of the Child.

As a starting point, the younger the suspect, the less likely it is that a prosecution is required.

However, there may be circumstances which mean that notwithstanding the fact that the suspect is under 18, a prosecution is in the public interest. These include where the offence committed is serious, where the suspect's past record suggests that there are no suitable alternatives to prosecution, or where the absence of an admission means that out-of-court disposals which might have addressed the offending behaviour are not available.

In principle, the High Court, on judicial review, can quash a decision to prosecute if it is demonstrably not in the public interest to prosecute. But it is very unlikely an application will succeed. For example, in *R (on the application of S) v DPP* (2006) a boy of 15 was charged with rape of a 12-year-old girl. She could not give consent to intercourse in view of her age, though on the evidence the sex was consensual. The court refused to stop the prosecution as the defendant, while young, was still three years older than the victim.

Reprimands, warnings, and youth cautions

The system of reprimands and warnings was formerly governed by ss 65 and 66 of the CDA 1998. These sections have been removed by LASPO and replaced with sections on youth cautions (new ss 66ZA and 66ZB of CDA).

Reprimands used to be issued for a first offence if it was not too serious; a warning was the next step for a person who had previously been reprimanded, or for a first more serious offence. The new youth cautions can cover both these situations; they may be more flexibly issued, not necessarily for first offences.

New s. 66ZA(1) says:

A constable may give a child or young person ('Y') a caution under this section (a 'youth caution') if—

(a) the constable decides that there is sufficient evidence to charge Y with an offence,
(b) Y admits to the constable that Y committed the offence, and
(c) the constable does not consider that Y should be prosecuted or given a youth conditional caution in respect of the offence.

The Secretary of State has published guidance on the appropriate circumstances for youth cautions (see www.gov.uk/government/publications/youth-cautions-guidance-for-police-and-youth-offending-teams). For all children under 18 years of age cautions have to be given in the presence of the appropriate adult. That child's admission must be genuine and not obtained by inducement or pressure (*R v Commissioner of Police of the Metropolis, ex p Thompson* (1997)). It must be unambiguous (*R (on the application of M) v (1) Leicestershire Constabulary (2) Crown Prosecution Service* (2009), where a juvenile admitted unsolicited sexual activity with a girl but nothing amounting to attempted rape. He should not have been given a warning).

The guidance on the old warnings and reprimands made clear that they should not be administered where the evidence against the juvenile is weak. If the police do not consider, on the evidence they have, that a conviction is more likely than an acquittal, the case should simply be dropped. Police must reveal their evidence, so a suspect can, on advice, decide whether to accept the youth caution.

Under new s. 66ZB of CDA:

(1) If a constable gives a youth caution to a person, the constable must as soon as practicable refer the person to a youth offending team.

(2) . . . on a referral of a person under subsection (1), the youth offending team—
   (a) must assess the person, and
   (b) unless they consider it inappropriate to do so, must arrange for the person to participate in a rehabilitation programme.

While a youth caution is not a criminal conviction, for example for job applications, if a person is later found guilty of an offence, it may be taken into account for sentencing. Under the old system, if someone was convicted of an offence within two years of a warning, the court would not consider a discharge but moved to a more serious sentence. A warning in relation to a sexual offence resulted in the offender being placed on the register of sex offenders. The same is likely to apply to youth cautions.

Legal advice and representation in criminal cases

Help from a solicitor out of public funds is governed by the Access to Justice Act 1999, modified by the Legal Aid, Sentencing and Punishment of Offenders Act 2012. In the police station, as we have seen under s. 58 of PACE, any suspect can insist on seeing a solicitor. The scheme is known as the police station duty solicitor scheme. A move to means test this service through the 2012 Act was withdrawn by the government under intense political pressure.

A similar scheme operates at court for an accused person who is brought directly to court following police detention or police bail. The court duty solicitor can deal with bail applications, ask for an adjournment, and make a plea in mitigation if there is an immediate guilty plea and no adjournments for reports.

For representation and advice beyond this, a specialist criminal solicitor has to be sought. This will normally be a solicitor working in a private firm. Legal aid for representation in criminal proceedings of under 16s, or under 18s without independent income, is free.

▧ Waiting for the final hearing—bail or custody

Police bail after charge

If a juvenile is charged, he or she should normally be released on bail. Police are not required to liaise with social services on bail decisions, though it is likely they will do so.

Police, like courts, can make bail conditional—for example, requiring that the accused live at a certain address or does not approach a witness. Another person can be asked to stand surety, which means that person is liable to pay a penalty if the accused absconds. A court can also impose bail conditions which have nothing to do with preventing offending or with securing attendance at court, and under s. 3(6)(ca) of the Bail Act 1976 (as amended in 2003) can impose conditions 'for his own protection or, if he is a child or young person, for his own welfare or in his own interests'.

A breach of police bail is a criminal offence. It also makes it less likely that the court will grant bail when an application is made.

Refusal of police bail

The police can refuse bail only on grounds set out in s. 38 of PACE:

(a) the custody officer is not satisfied of the identity or address of the person charged;

(b) the custody officer believes that the person will not answer bail, will interfere with evidence or witnesses, cause injury to themselves or others, or damage to property;

(c) the custody officer believes that it is necessary for the person's own protection; or

(d) granting bail would not be in a juvenile's own interests.

Section 38 does not offer guidance on what the interests of the juvenile are in this situation; but on refusal of bail the juvenile must be transferred to local authority accommodation, and it will be this transfer pending trial that the police may see as being in the juvenile's interests.

If a suspect is charged and bail is refused, he or she must be brought before a court at the earliest practicable time. Until that point, s. 38(6) of PACE requires the custody officer to make arrangements for the juvenile to be taken into local authority accommodation. The subsection makes it lawful for the local authority to detain the juvenile in secure accommodation (but there is no obligation to do so). It will be up to the authority to transport the juvenile to court.

Under s. 38(6), following a refusal of bail, the custody officer can refuse to transfer the detained juvenile to local authority accommodation on one of two grounds.

(a) If the juvenile is 15 or older, the custody officer considers that the juvenile is a danger to the public and that the local authority lacks adequate secure accommodation.

(b) It is not practical to make the arrangements for a transfer. This should be exceptional, for example social services are on strike or the roads are blocked by snow.

The custody officer must give a certificate to this effect and may then detain the juvenile in the same way as an adult until the first court appearance; that is, in the police station (but not in a cell if this can be avoided).

Court bail

Courts which adjourn before they have completely disposed of a case can either release the accused unconditionally or on bail or in custody.

The grounds in s. 4 of the Bail Act 1976 for a court to refuse bail are almost identical to those for police bail under PACE (see **Refusal of police bail**, p 391). Breach of court bail or bail conditions is a criminal offence and will make further bail applications more difficult.

Court remand into custody

If bail is refused and the child is at least 12 and below 18 years of age, the remand will normally be to local authority accommodation (formerly under CYPA 1969, s. 23; now under LASPO, ss 91 and 92).

The court designates a local authority (LASPO, s. 92(3)), which is (a) in the case of a child who is being looked after by a local authority, that authority; or (b) the local authority in whose area it appears to the court that the child habitually resides or the offence or one of the offences was committed.

The court can impose conditions on the child and hence under s. 93(3) of LASPO on the local authority (a) to secure compliance with any conditions imposed on the child; or (b) requirements stipulating that the child must not be placed with a named person (e.g. the parent or someone involved in the alleged offence).

Among conditions may be electronic tagging of a child aged 12 or over who is alleged to have committed one of certain serious, imprisonable offences and where the YOT has told the court electronic monitoring would be suitable for the child (LASPO, s. 94; s. 95 for those where the offence gives rise to extradition proceedings).

In the case of serious offences, the child may be remanded to youth detention accommodation to protect the public or prevent any further imprisonable offence (LASPO, s. 98); or if, additionally, the child has a history of absconding or there is a history of the child committing imprisonable offences or there is a high likelihood of him or her receiving a custodial sentence (LASPO, s. 99). Sections 100 and 101 have similar conditions for cases involving the possibility of extradition.

Serious offences are defined as a violent or sexual offence, or an offence punishable in the case of an adult with imprisonment for a term of 14 years or more.

In the case of remand into youth detention, a local authority will be designated for various responsibilities (including potentially the cost of youth detention) and consulted about the detention. The child will have 'looked-after child status'; that is, 'is to be treated as a child who is looked after by the designated authority' (LASPO, s. 104(1)—in local authority care or accommodated by the authority under the Children Act 1989, s. 22(1)). The *Children Act 1989 Guidance and Regulations, Volume 2: Care Planning, Placement and Case Review* will regulate these placements (see Chapter 8 of the Guidance).

It is for the authority to decide how to accommodate the juvenile. The considerations are the same as for any child it is looking after (see **chapter 6**). However, when a young person becomes looked after solely as a result of being remanded, the local authority is not required to prepare a plan for permanence (Reg 5(a)). This to recognize that some young people in these circumstances are looked after for a short period of time. But the Guidance also states that 'consideration must be given to what longer term support or accommodation the child will need following the remand episode'.

Remand to youth detention accommodation (YDA)

When a young person is remanded to youth detention accommodation the duties of the local authority are set out in the *Care Planning* regulations.

> In these circumstances the local authority is not required to prepare a care plan and a placement plan, instead the authority must carry out an initial assessment of the child's needs and use this

information to prepare a Detention Placement Plan (DPP). This should describe how the YDA will meet the child's needs and record the roles and responsibilities of the other partner organisations (the local authority and the YOT specifically). The DPP should also take into account the circumstances that contributed to the child's alleged involvement in any offending and the support s/he should be offered when they return to the community to prevent (re)offending.

If a young person is subject to a care order or if they are a 'relevant child' and remanded to YDA, care/pathway planning will continue once the remand ceases, even if the young person is sentenced to custody.

Table 10.1 sets out the content of the detention placement plan.

TABLE 10.1 Matters to be dealt with in a detention placement plan

1	How the child will be cared for on a day-to-day basis and how their welfare will be safeguarded and promoted by the staff of the YDA	Does the child know about the arrangements in the YDA to keep them safe—e.g. to prevent bullying? Is there a risk of self-harm? What strategies will the YDA follow to minimize this? How well does the child understand their circumstances? What are their wishes and feelings?
2	Any arrangements made for contact between the child and their parent; and any person who is not their parent but who has parental responsibility and between the child and any other connected person including, if appropriate—(a) the reasons why contact with any such person would not be reasonably practicable or would not be consistent with the child's welfare; (b) if the child is not in the care of the responsible authority, details of any order made under s. 8 of the 1989 Act; (c) if the child is in the care of the responsible authority, details of any order concerning contact made under s. 34 of the 1989 Act; (d) the arrangements for notifying any changes in the arrangements for contact	Are the child's parents able to fulfil their parental responsibilities to the child whilst in custody? Is action needed by the local authority to facilitate family contact?
3	The arrangements made for the local authority's representative to visit the child, the frequency of visits, and the arrangements made for advice, support, and assistance to be available to the child between visits in accordance with regulation 31 of the Care Planning Regs 2010	Children must be visited at no less than the statutory intervals. As with other looked-after children, more frequent visiting and contact with the YDA may be required based on the assessment of the child's vulnerability and needs.

4	If an independent visitor (where the child is already looked after) is appointed, the arrangements made for them to visit the child whilst remanded in YDA	
5	The arrangements made by the staff of the YDA for meeting the child's health needs (including physical, emotional, and mental health) and dental care	Where children who are looked after solely as a result of being remanded, 'the 2013 Regulations' disapply local authority duties for arranging health assessments. Health provision for children looked after solely as a result of remand to YDA will be the same as those for any other detained child. The local authority must be satisfied that health professionals and establishment staff are fully aware of the child's health needs and that arrangements are in place to respond appropriately to these. It will be necessary for arrangements to be in place so that health staff in YDA share information about their assessment of each looked-after child's health needs with community health staff responsible for the oversight and monitoring of looked-after children's health.
6	The arrangements made by staff of the YDA for the child's education and training: (a) the name and address of any educational or training institution the child was attending, or any other person providing the child with education or training, immediately before his detention; (b) where the child has a statement of special educational needs, details of the local authority that maintains the statement	The local authority must establish that the YDA's education staff are aware of, and able to meet, the child's educational needs, including any special needs.
7	The child's personal history, religious persuasion, cultural and linguistic background, and racial origin	What arrangements does the YDA have in place for meeting the child's religious, cultural, or linguistic needs? (Are these appropriate for the child concerned?) This may involve establishing a child's immigration status and whether there is any adult with parental responsibility for the child resident in the UK.

8	The child's development of self-care skills	How will the routines of the YDA and the support provided to the child offer him/her any necessary opportunities to develop independent living skills? Does the child need money, clothes, books, or other practical support?
9	The name and contact details of: (a) the IRO; (b) the independent visitor (if one is appointed); (c) the local authority's social worker; (d) (if the child is an eligible child) the personal adviser; (e) the Virtual Head Teacher for the designated authority responsible for the child's care; (f) the YOT caseworker; and (g) the YDA caseworker	
10	Details of any support required by the child when the remand ceases and they may no longer be looked after. The DPP must include details about any arrangements for the child's support when s/he ceases to be looked after following the remand, perhaps as a result of their receiving a custodial sentence.	In particular the plan will need to cover: (a) whether the child will need to be accommodated by the designated authority or by another local authority on release; and (b) whether any other services should be provided by the designated authority or by another local authority under the 1989 Act. These could include the provision of support to the child's family or arranging for the child to be referred to other appropriate services.

Remand to hospital

A court can remand any person accused of a criminal offence who may be mentally disordered to a hospital for the purpose of obtaining a medical report, or for treatment: Mental Health Act, ss 35 and 36.

Allocation of the juvenile to youth court, magistrates' court, or Crown Court for trial and sentence

Most cases involving a juvenile are dealt with in the youth court. The exceptions arise where the alleged offence is serious, or where an adult is a co-accused. **Box 10.3** explains these exceptions. Where a child becomes an adult during the course of the proceedings he or she can be sent to the adult court for trial or sentence (Crime and Disorder Act 1998, s. 47). If the youth court decides not to do so, it must sentence him or her as if still under 18 (CYPA 1969, s. 29: *A v DPP* (2002), where an 18-year-old was sentenced to a detention and training order, a sentence not available for adult offenders).

BOX 10.3 Use of adult courts for juvenile cases

Case factually connected to an adult defendant (CYPA 1933, s. 16; CYPA 1969, s. 18; Magistrates' Courts Act 1980, s. 24):

- magistrates **must try** the juvenile with an adult if the adult is to be tried by magistrates and the juvenile and the adult are jointly charged with same offence;
- the juvenile may be sent to a youth court for separate trial if the adult is pleading guilty and the juvenile is pleading not guilty, or charges are factually connected but not joint;
- Crown Court committal for an adult: magistrates **must** separate juvenile from adult if in the interest of justice—for example wide difference in ages; evidential issues not closely connected.

Murder and grave crimes (Powers of Criminal Courts (Sentencing) Act 2000 (PCCSA), ss 90 and 91); grave crime means:

- it could attract a 14-year prison sentence if committed by an adult;
- indecent assault;
- death by dangerous driving, careless driving while under the influence of alcohol or drugs, or firearms offence and the accused is at least 14.

If more than two years custody is likely to be the sentence (Magistrates' Courts Act 1980, s. 24):

- a youth court must commit the case to Crown Court for trial if the powers of punishment of a youth court (maximum two years' custody) would be insufficient. The decision must be made before conviction.

Case involves a child witness (CDA 1998, s. 51B).

In *R v Ghafoor* (2002), the Court of Appeal reminded sentencing courts that it is a breach of human rights to impose a harsher penalty on an offender than could have been applied at the date the offence was committed. In this case an 18-year-old convicted of riot had been sentenced to four-and-a-half years in a young offender institution; but he was only 17 at the time of the offence and the maximum for a 17-year-old was 24 months' detention and training.

Supporting a child appearing before the criminal court

Where the trial takes place in the Crown Court the Lord Chief Justice has published guidelines for measures to reduce formality and stress, such as regular breaks, removal of wigs, access to social workers and guardians, etc: *Criminal Practice Direction* [2015] EWCA Crim 1567. These guidelines are the result of the criticism voiced by the ECtHR in relation to the trial arrangements in the James Bulger murder trial, where the young boys on trial had been intimidated by the formality (see the case study at the beginning of the chapter).

We do not have space to describe the trial process. Some of this was discussed in **chapter 1**. Your role will be supporting the child through this process rather than participating. The guidance in **Box 10.4** is an extract from *Youth Court Cases—Defence Good Practice*, which was prepared by the Law Society for lawyers using the youth court. It is no longer published on the Law Society website, but remains useful to social workers as well as defence lawyers when children are on trial.

BOX 10.4 Extract from Law Society Guidance for Lawyers, *Youth Court Cases—Defence Good Practice*

[E]xplain the layout of the court and the roles of all those present. This need not take long as few are allowed to be present and if this is a pre-trial hearing should usually consist of:

- the client, who in most courts, wherever possible, sits next to his or her legal representative—if not, the client sits in the 'front row' before the bench;
- the parent, guardian or appropriate adult who sits behind;
- the YOT court officer who sits usually behind a table at right angles to the bench, to the right of the prosecutor;
- the bench of three lay magistrates, or single district judge who sits at the 'top' of the room opposite all other seating places;
- the court clerk who sits next to or sometimes in front of the bench; and
- the prosecutor who sits to the left of the defence.

The Youth Court 2001—The Changing Culture of the Youth Court—Good Practice Guide (March 2001) suggests that parents should be seated next to their dependent children, and that justices should be moved from a raised bench to sit at or near the same level as defendants. However, the Guide recognizes that existing architecture in courts around the country may restrict what can be achieved, though all courts should aim for a more approachable court layout.

The layout of courts varies and you should not be embarrassed to ask the usher where the personnel all sit. Some courts have a picture of the layout of the court in the waiting area outside the court. If there is any other person in court and you don't know their identity, then ask the usher.

You should explain the procedure you expect at the hearing to the client but warn them that sometimes other issues come up and the procedure may change. Prepare the client for what their involvement might be. For example, where you are trying to persuade the bench to adopt a community disposal, some benches routinely ask the defendant's advocate if they can address the client directly, and in some cases, permission is not sought at all. Technically you can decline permission or intervene, but this approach may not always assist the client's best interests. Unless there is good reason such as mental health problems or communication problems, you should prepare the client for this possibility. All magistrates sitting in the Youth Court receive 'engagement' training and you may find that your clients are increasingly expected to engage with the court.

If questions are put to the client and parents, you should be invited to make representations on what has been said. Before considering sentence, if the defendant has pleaded guilty or been found guilty, the chairman is likely to try to talk to the defendant and parents/guardians, focusing on the offending behaviour and how to change it. Adverse inferences should not be drawn by the failure or the inability of the defendant to reply.

The informality of the Youth Court is generally observed, but within limits. You should also advise the client about the impact of their body language and physical attitude—it won't help your client if he or she is slouching, chewing, or apparently ignoring the proceedings, even if their attitude is clearly a result of fear or bravado. In the atmosphere of the court a youth may behave in a disruptive manner, including in the public area, to impress other youths in the vicinity. You should advise such a client that excessive disruptive behaviour may lead to exclusion from the court building and will not make a good impression with the court.

A guide to going to youth courts for children with learning disabilities also offers a wide range of information (see www.kent.ac.uk/tizard/sotsec/CJSbooklets/Youth court_safer IDD.pdf).

Drug testing after conviction

A court can order a sample to be taken from anyone if it is contemplating a community or suspended sentence. This must be done in the presence of the appropriate adult if the child is under 17. The results can be used to help to decide the appropriate sentence. This may include a drug rehabilitation requirement under s. 209 of the Criminal Justice Act 2003 (CJA) if 'the offender is dependent on, or has a propensity to misuse, drugs' and would be amenable to treatment. Similarly, under s. 212 an alcohol treatment requirement may be imposed.

Section 76 of LASPO also introduces an alcohol abstinence and monitoring requirement (inserting a new s. 212A into the CJA 2003) if alcohol was an element in the offence of which the individual was convicted. The new requirement (in force in certain areas only until April 2019) was to be introduced by order of the Secretary of State with an initial pilot scheme. The implication seems to be to move away from seeing alcohol abuse as an illness that can be treated but rather as bad behaviour that can be deterred. LASPO also lifts the six-month limit on the drug rehabilitation and alcohol treatment laid down in the CJA, leaving the court to set an appropriate time.

■ Sentencing of juveniles

You are likely to be involved in the sentencing process because you will be required to prepare a pre-sentence report for the court. You will need to know which court is dealing with sentencing and what its powers are.

The CJA states at s. 142A that the principal aim of the youth justice system is to prevent offending and reoffending as under s. 37(1) of the CDA. Courts must have regard for the welfare of offenders as under s. 44 of the CYPA 1933. The purpose of sentencing juveniles is:

- punishment;
- reform and rehabilitation;
- protection of the public; and
- reparation by offenders to persons affected by their offences.

The sentencing powers of courts are largely found in the Powers of Criminal Courts (Sentencing) Act 2000 (PCCSA) with amendments in the CJA and LASPO. In what follows, section numbers are references to the PCCSA. Central to the government's approach when amending this Act in 2003 was the creation of a Sentencing Guidelines Council. Courts must refer to the Council's guidelines and must justify any departure from these. Guidelines are available at www.sentencingcouncil.org.uk/about-sentencing/about-guidelines. In addition, in March 2017 the Sentencing Council published Definitive Guidelines of Sentencing Young People (see www.sentencingcouncil.org.uk/wp-content/uploads/Sentencing-Children-and-Young-People-definitive-guideline-Web.pdf).

The principles of sentencing juvenile offenders are set out in the Guidelines as:

> The principal aim of the youth justice system (to prevent offending by children and young people), and the welfare of the child or young person
> Sentencing should be focused on the individual child not the seriousness of the offence
> Custody should always be a last resort
> Criminalising children should be avoided, better to encourage them to take responsibility for their own actions
> Account should be taken of the child not fully appreciating the effect of their actions on other people
> Children should have the opportunity to change their conduct
> Offending is often a passing phase in childhood
> The impact of punishment is likely to be felt more by a child than an adult
> Any restrictions on liberty must be proportionate to the offence.

The Guidelines go on to state how the courts should regard the welfare of the child when sentencing (see **Box 10.5**).

When sentencing juveniles, the courts must take account of s. 44 of the CYPA 1933:

> Every court in dealing with a child or young person who is brought before it, either as an offender or otherwise, shall have regard to the welfare of the child or young person, and shall in a proper case take steps for removing him from undesirable surroundings, and for securing that proper provision is made for his education and training.

BOX 10.5 Regard to the welfare of the child or young person—Definitive Guidelines of Sentencing Young People (Sentencing Council)

In having regard to the welfare of the child or young person, a court should ensure that it is alert to:

- any mental health problems or learning difficulties/disabilities;
- any experiences of brain injury or traumatic life experience (including exposure to drug and alcohol abuse) and the developmental impact this may have had;

> - any speech and language difficulties and the effect this may have on the ability of the child or young person (or any accompanying adult) to communicate with the court, to understand the sanction imposed or to fulfil the obligations resulting from that sanction;
> - the vulnerability of children and young people to self-harm, particularly within a custodial environment; and
> - the effect on children and young people of experiences of loss and neglect and/or abuse.

Your pre-sentence report must take account of relevant guidelines.

This does not mean that the child's welfare is paramount, for the court has a statutory duty—as do social workers as part of the youth justice system—'to prevent offending by children and young persons' (CDA, s. 37). But welfare must be a factor in deciding on the appropriateness of a sentence and gives you some leverage if you wish to suggest outcomes which will benefit the child as well as punish. The Court of Appeal frequently notes that juveniles should receive shorter custodial sentences than adults, and that reform of the young offender is the best way of protecting society. When we look at community sentences, you will see that a community sentence must not only be appropriate to the seriousness of the offence, but also to reforming the offender.

When sentencing a juvenile offender, a court must not impose a greater penalty than it could have imposed on an adult.

Sentencing powers of the adult magistrates' court

These powers are strictly limited. This court can sentence a juvenile only where it has already dealt with the juvenile together with a connected adult. It only has power to fine or discharge the juvenile or require parents to enter a recognizance. If it wishes to impose a custodial or community sentence following a conviction, it must send the case to the youth court (s. 8).

Sentencing powers of the youth court

This court's maximum power is to impose a two-year detention and training order.

Sentencing powers of the Crown Court

The Crown Court may be dealing with a juvenile offender not because the offence is serious, but because it also tried a linked adult. In this case, it should not in principle sentence a juvenile but remit the case to the youth court. However, the judge can declare him- or herself satisfied that it would be undesirable to do so (s. 8) and in practice the judge will do this, rather than delay a sentencing decision by sending the case to a youth court. This also enables the sentences of the adult and the juvenile to be considered together by the court which has heard all the evidence.

If the youth court has sent the case to the Crown Court for trial, this would have been because its maximum sentencing power of a two-year detention and training order was considered insufficient, or because it was a charge of murder. Under ss 90–92, the Crown Court then has the power to order detention of the juvenile for a period up to the maximum period that could have been imposed on an adult. So, a juvenile can be detained 'during Her Majesty's pleasure' for crimes which carry a life sentence. (However, the court must set a target date for eligibility for release. Failure to do so leaves this decision in the hands of the Home Secretary rather than an independent body and was a breach of the human rights of the juveniles who murdered James Bulger: see *T v UK* (2000).) The Sentencing Council Guidance on Mandatory Life Sentences in Murder cases states that for an offender under 18 when they committed the offence the appropriate starting point for the length of detention at Her Majesty's pleasure is 12 years, although aggravating and mitigating factors can be taken into account (see www.cps. gov.uk/legal-guidance/sentencing-mandatory-life-sentences-murder-cases).

Sentencing procedure

A court cannot lawfully impose custody if there is no pre-sentence report (CJA, Part 12). The Magistrates' Courts (Children and Young Persons) Rules 1992 require the court to have evidence on the child's circumstances before sentencing, though lack of a report does not invalidate a non-custodial sentence.

The report writer will be a social worker for any convicted child under 14, but after that age the local authority can by agreement leave this to probation officers.

You can quite reasonably be asked for your report before conviction, if it is known that the child will admit the offence. In any event s. 9 of the CYPA 1969 requires you to start making investigations and preparing the information as soon as the young person is charged, and not to wait until conviction. There is no reason to expect the juvenile to cooperate with the preparation of a pre-sentence report if he or she intends to deny the charge. The preparation of the report may well make the child think their guilt has been pre-judged. So, if you have not been able to prepare the report by the time of conviction, the case will need to be adjourned; as with all adjournments, the child may be released on bail, remanded to the accommodation of the local authority, or remanded in custody.

Your report will be in writing. You do not have to be in court to give it, but a representative of your department must be there. The court, or the defence, may wish you to be present to explain and justify what has been put in the report. You are reporting to the court as an officer of the court. The child is not your client and it is not your job to push for a lenient, or indeed any particular, outcome. Your task is to advise on the individual needs and circumstances of the juvenile, something which cannot be done by the court without your help.

Seriousness and sentencing

Courts (unless sentencing for murder, when there is only one sentence of life imprisonment) exercise discretion in sentencing decisions. They cannot exceed the maximum penalty, and they must take into account Court of Appeal and Sentencing Council guidelines, including the Guidelines on Sentencing Children and Young People. They are likely also to take into account the Magistrates' Court Guidelines. All of these can be accessed from the Sentencing Council's website at www.sentencingcouncil.org.uk.

The starting point is how serious this offence is, and the guideline punishment appropriate to that seriousness. The Magistrates' Association guidelines can be used as an example, as it is quite specific on the range of offences and does not just talk about principles. The Association sets an 'entry point' for each offence, then looks at aspects of the offence that are 'aggravating' or 'mitigating'. For example, the defendant has been convicted of taking a vehicle without the owner's consent (TWOC) under s. 12 of the Theft Act 1968, where the statutory maximum punishment is six months' custody (more if it is 'aggravated vehicle-taking'—a different offence). The guidelines suggest that as a Category 3 rating for harm caused, a fine or community penalty is a starting point. Factors listed in the guidelines pushing the seriousness upwards could be, for example, driving while disqualified, offending while on bail, driving badly, or premeditation. Mitigating factors could be, for example, that no damage was caused, the owner left the keys in the car, or the driving was not itself bad. The sentencing court then looks at any case law guidance, which may be in relation to the offence itself or general. The CJA gives statutory guidance on some aspects of seriousness. Under s. 153, racial aggravation explicitly increases seriousness. Pleading guilty—the sooner the better—reduces seriousness under s. 152. The Act additionally requires seriousness to be calculated with reference to culpability, and any harm caused which was intended or foreseeable; it says that seriousness is aggravated by each previous offence on the offender's record, particularly recent offences. It is also aggravated if an offence was committed while the offender was already on bail and if it involves racial or religious aggravation, or hostility towards gay or disabled persons. Section 73 of the Serious Organised Crime and Police Act 2005 requires courts to take account of cooperation with the authorities as reducing seriousness.

Each penalty that a court is thinking of imposing—whether custody, a community penalty, or a particular level of fine—should be imposed only if the court considers the offence to be so serious that only that level of sentencing is appropriate. But under s. 166 of the CJA the court must take into account any mitigating factors, and not decide the sentence just on seriousness. Mitigating factors may include, for example, remorse or the effect that the punishment will have on the offender and/or other people.

There is, therefore, much for the probation officer or social worker to say in a pre-sentence report. A good record, or a bad record with redeeming features, can be used to mitigate the sentence—to reduce it below the sentence the court would think of imposing if seriousness alone were taken into account.

Box 10.6 shows a simplified, step-by-step approach to deciding on sentence which mirrors the court's decision-making process.

 BOX 10.6 Choosing the right sentence

(a) Does the court have a choice, or is the sentence fixed by law?

(b) How serious is the offence? (Consider issues such as violence; effect on the victim; amount of gain or loss; planning; breach of trust; racial aggravation.)

(c) Is it so serious that only custody is appropriate?

(d) If not, is it so serious that only a community sentence involving restrictions on liberty is appropriate? Is such a sentence appropriate for this offender?

(e) If not, is another community sentence appropriate, or a fine?

(f) If not, a discharge should be ordered, unless a warning or a reprimand was given within the last two years (youth caution if LASPO is in force).

Custody where court has no discretion

The penalty for murder is fixed, even for a juvenile (see **Seriousness and sentencing**, p 401).

The CJA creates the concept of the *dangerous offender*, who also must be sentenced to custody for life. This applies under s. 226 if the offender:

- is under 18;
- has committed a serious offence;
- will pose a significant danger to the public;

Section 124 of LASPO creates extended sentences for certain violent or sexual offences where there is considered to be serious risk to the public. (This amends the CJA with a new s. 226B.)

The minimum penalty for a number of other offences is fixed, unless there are exceptional circumstances, if the offender has a previous record of such offending. See ss 109–115 of the PCCSA where, for example, domestic burglary committed for a third time attracts at least three years' imprisonment. These minimum sentences do not apply to offenders aged under 18. However, juvenile offences will be taken into account if the person is later convicted before the adult court.

Custody where court has discretion

Children in custody are also children in need under s. 17 of the Children Act: *R (on behalf of the Howard League) v Secretary of State for the Home Department* (2002). The local authority must continue to assess and meet the needs of children whom the courts have locked up in the prison system, insofar as a prison sentence allows.

The minimum period for custody for a juvenile is four months and it cannot be suspended. There is no corresponding minimum for an adult of 21 or over. Is this unfair on the juvenile? The idea is that courts are deterred from the idea of a short, sharp shock; the thinking is that custody is wrong unless the offence is serious enough to merit longer periods.

Nevertheless, custody is required in certain circumstances. There are then two regimes for locking up children.

(a) *Custody for murder or grave crimes* (PCCSA, ss 90–92, see **Sentencing powers of the Crown Court**, p 400). The Crown Court sentences the juvenile to be detained for a defined term or 'during Her Majesty's pleasure', and the place of detention is left to the Home Secretary to determine. It can include detention in local authority accommodation (CYPA 1969, s. 30). While the offender is under 21, prison is not used; the offender is held in a young offenders' institution.

(b) *A detention and training order.* This comprises a custodial part, which is served in a young offenders' institution or at a secure training centre (STC), and a training part, which is served in the community.

Even if the court decides that custody is justified, it is still entitled to consider whether what is known about the offender mitigates the sentence in favour of something non-custodial. Under s. 166 of the CJA it must always take into account any mental disorder before considering a custodial sentence, even if the offence is otherwise sufficiently serious for custody.

It may help you, if you are called on to prepare a pre-sentence report where custody is likely, to recall that the statutory purpose of the criminal justice system (see **Sentencing of juveniles**, p 398) is the prevention of offending. A pre-sentence report can contain very important information about the likely effect on this offender's future risk of offending, of custody versus community, or other sentences. The actual imposed custodial sentence should be no longer than is necessary to reflect the seriousness of the offence or the need to protect the public from violence: CJA, s. 153. However, we referred earlier to sentencing 'dangerous offenders' to custody for life for 'grave' crimes where the juvenile has committed a sexual or violent offence and there is significant danger to the public (new s. 226B of the CJA, amended by LASPO, s. 124). If the conditions are otherwise met, but it is not a grave crime as defined, the court has the power not only to impose the appropriate custodial sentence, but to add a period on licence of up to five years (for a violent offender) and eight years (for a sexual offender). This means he or she can be recalled to custody for breach of licence conditions or continue to be detained if the Parole Board consider that he or she continues to present an unacceptable risk to the public. The licence still runs after the juvenile becomes an adult.

If a young offender is still serving a period of detention at the age of 21, he or she is transferred to a prison sentence for the remainder of the custodial term (s. 99).

Custody under a detention and training order

These custodial sentences are governed by ss 102–107 of the PCCSA. The seriousness and statutory custody criteria must be satisfied. For offenders below the age of 15, the courts also must find that the child is a 'persistent' offender. Courts will, it seems, define 'persistent' for themselves. See *R v C (A Juvenile) (Persistent Offender)* (2000), where C was convicted of burglary and aggravated vehicle-taking, committed while on bail for an earlier burglary. This was enough to make his offending persistent, even though he had no convictions.

The maximum term is two years. The actual term has to be one of the following: four months; six months; eight months; ten months; 12 months; 18 months; or 24 months. Half of the term is served in custody undergoing training, with some reduction for good behaviour. The detention is served in an STC, a young offenders' institution, or in local authority secure accommodation.

After release, the offender is supervised for the remaining period by a social worker, probation officer, or YOT member. The offender must comply with the requirements of the supervisor. Breach can be reported to the court, which has the power to fine or to order detention for up to three further months. Commission of an imprisonable offence during the period can put the offender back into custody for some or all of the remaining supervision period, with additional custody for the new offence. (New provisions have been added by s. 80 of LASPO.)

The referral order under ss 16–32 of the PCCSA

A court *must* make a referral to the youth offender panel following conviction for any offence if the following conditions apply:

- the offender is under 18, pleads guilty to all the offences, and has no previous convictions;
- the court decides that custody is not appropriate but something greater than an absolute discharge is required. (LASPO, s. 79(1) allows conditional discharge as a further option.)

A court *may* make a referral where such an offender has pleaded guilty to at least one of the offences of which he or she was eventually convicted.

The essence of the order is that the court passes the responsibility to a panel nominated by the local YOT. A new panel is constituted for each offender. Together with that panel the offender works out a contract of behaviour for between three and twelve months (the period is predetermined by the court). The consequence of not agreeing a contract is that the offender will be sent back to court for sentencing.

You need to understand and apply the concept of restorative justice to work with referral orders—this is beyond the scope of our book, but the government maintains a restorative justice website (www.justice.gov.uk/youth-justice/working-with-victims/restorative-justice).

A parenting order can be made at the same time as a referral order. These require a parent to attend counselling sessions.

Principles of community sentencing

An offender must consent to a community sentence. But refusal is not advisable, as this is a ground for triggering custody and enables the court to bypass the seriousness requirement.

A key feature of the community sentence is that it is a punishment. To count as punishment, the offence must be serious enough to warrant the particular type of community order chosen. Seriousness as a concept has already been discussed in terms of custodial sentences, but s. 148 of the CJA repeats similar seriousness criteria for deciding if a community sentence, including a youth rehabilitation order (YRO: see **Available community sentences for juvenile offenders**, p 406), is appropriate, as set out in **Box 10.7**:

BOX 10.7 Criteria for deciding of a community sentence is appropriate—s. 148 of the Criminal Justice Act 2005

(1) A court must not pass a community sentence on an offender unless it is of the opinion that the offence, or the combination of the offence and one or more offences associated with it, was serious enough to warrant such a sentence.

(2) Where a court passes a community sentence—

    (a) the particular requirement or requirements forming part of the community order or YRO must be such as, in the opinion of the court, is, or taken together are, the most suitable for the offender, and

    (b) the restrictions on liberty imposed by the order must be such as in the opinion of the court are commensurate with the seriousness of the offence, or the combination of the offence and one or more offences associated with it.

(3) Where a court passes a community sentence which consists of or includes one or more youth community orders—

    (a) the particular order or orders forming part of the sentence must be such as, in the opinion of the court, is, or taken together are, the most suitable for the offender, and

    (b) the restrictions on liberty imposed by the order or orders must be such as in the opinion of the court are commensurate with the seriousness of the offence, or the combination of the offence and one or more offences associated with it.

Under s. 151 of the CJA a juvenile offender of 16 or over with three previous convictions and fines can be given a community order or YRO, even if the seriousness criteria are otherwise not met.

Available community sentences for juvenile offenders

The Criminal Justice and Immigration Act 2008 introduced the YRO in an attempt to combine a number of juvenile community sentences into a single generic sentence with various requirements that may be attached to it. They are listed in **Box 10.8** and include curfews, residence in a particular local authority area or particular residence, exclusion from a particular area, mental health treatment, drug testing and treatment, electronic monitoring, intensive supervision or fostering, unpaid work, or education (see Criminal Justice and Immigration Act 2008, s. 1). The rules on seriousness in ss 147–148 of the CJA apply: any restriction of liberty must be proportionate to the offence. So, with intensive supervision and surveillance (ISS) or intensive fostering the offence must be an imprisonable one and custody would otherwise be warranted. Those under 15 must be persistent offenders. Custody may be an option for breach of a YRO only if it could have applied to the original offence or there is 'wilful and persistent' non-compliance and ISS or intensive fostering have been tried.

 BOX 10.8 Requirements that may be attached to a Youth Rehabilitation Order

The court can impose a community order lasting up to three years (unless a shorter period is specified) containing one or more of the following requirements, supervised by probation officers, not YOT members:

- Activity Requirement;

- Curfew Requirement (up to 16 hours a day for up to 12 months, as amended by LASPO);
- Exclusion Requirement;
- Local Authority Residence Requirement;
- Education Requirement;
- Mental Health Treatment Requirement;
- Unpaid Work Requirement (16/17 years);
- Drug Testing Requirement;
- Intoxicating Substance Misuse Requirement;
- Supervision Requirement;
- Electronic Monitoring Requirement;
- Prohibited Activity Requirement;
- Drug Treatment Requirement;
- Residence Requirement;
- Programme Requirement;
- Attendance Centre Requirement;
- Intensive Supervision and Surveillance (based on the current ISSP);
- Intensive Fostering.

The YRO, which courts are not obliged to impose if another penalty (e.g. custody) is thought more appropriate, replaced various community sentences such as supervision orders, community rehabilitation orders, and community punishment orders. The intention is to have available a range of options to suit the situation of the juvenile that may be used several times (possibly with increased levels of severity) when in the past custody would have been likely for a repeat offender. The requirements attached to the YRO should be only those necessary to address the risk of serious harm to others and reduce the likelihood of reoffending and should be proportionate to the offence. The individuals involved must indicate willingness to comply. Sections 81–84 of LASPO make some amendments to the YRO regime.

Pre-sentence reports from YOTs will be crucial in deciding whether an individual is suitable for a YRO, in particular whether he or she would benefit from some of the treatments and interventions involved (see s. 156(3) of the CJA).

The pre-sentence report will have to specify the supervision and other arrangements, and where cooperation from others (e.g. family or work with other agencies) is needed, confirmation that their cooperation is available.

When a YRO is imposed, an officer in charge of an individual's YRO will be appointed from a YOT or, for 16- and 17-year-olds, the probation service through a private firm may be the responsible officer if the only requirement is electronic monitoring for a curfew. If an attendance centre requirement is the only imposition, the responsible officer will be whoever is in charge of the centre.

Breach of a YRO

The officer in charge will deal with failure to comply with a YRO under Schedule 2 to the Criminal Justice and Immigration Act 2008. Two warnings may be given, and on the third failure within a 12-month warned period the matter should be referred back to court unless the responsible officer/YOT manager considers that there are exceptional circumstances. If not, they can seek a summons or warrant for the individual's arrest. A court may fine someone up to £2,500 (under LASPO assuming it is in force—formerly only £250 for a child under 14, £1,000 for someone older); impose another tougher YRO, including imposing an ISS even if the original offence would not have warranted it; and re-sentence on the basis of other sentences that would have been available originally, including imprisonment. The young person or responsible officer may seek a revocation of a YRO if good progress has been shown. They may apply for variation if circumstances require it (e.g. if the individual subject to a residence order moves home). If the young person reoffends during the period of a YRO, it may be revoked and the individual may be re-sentenced for the original offence as well as the new one.

Binding parents over

When a court convicts a juvenile of under 16, it must normally also bind over the parents (but it cannot bind over the local authority where the child is in care). If the juvenile is over 16, it can still choose to do this. This means the parent or guardian promises to exercise proper control over the child to prevent reoffending (PCCSA, s. 150). A sum is fixed by the court, which can be forfeited if a further offence is committed. The maximum sum is £1,000, and the period during which the parent is at risk lasts up to three years, or the offender's eighteenth birthday. The court should take into account whether the parents could have had or will have any influence over the juvenile's behaviour in deciding whether to use its power not to bind over.

A parent can refuse to be bound over, but if the court thinks a refusal is unreasonable, it can fine the parents up to £1,000 on top of any fine imposed for the juvenile's offence.

Deferred sentence

Under PCCSA, s. 1, a court can defer (i.e. postpone) the decision on sentence for up to six months. It should do so only if some change is imminent—for example, leaving school and taking up employment—which the court ought to take into account. The offender must consent, and the court can impose conditions with which the offender must comply pending the return to court. Compliance will usually be monitored by a probation officer, though the court can appoint another person. Breach of any conditions can lead to arrest and return to the court. All being well, however, a day is fixed for the return to court and the court will sentence in the light of the new circumstances—conduct after conviction, including any appropriate reparations that may have been made and compliance with requirements regarding conduct imposed by the court. It will not normally be appropriate to order custody after deferment if the offender's circumstances are now looking more stable. The court can only order what the court could have ordered at the time of deferment—so if the offender is now 18, the court cannot use adult powers of sentencing.

Discharge

This is an option where in all the circumstances (the offence and the offender's past history) no punishment is appropriate. It is governed by PCCSA, ss 12–15. If the offender had been prepared to admit the offence before charge, it might with hindsight have been more appropriate to reprimand or warn the offender. If the court orders an absolute discharge then, apart from showing on the offender's record, it does not count as a conviction. A discharge can be conditional for a period of up to three years. If the offender commits an offence within that period, the court can sentence for the original offence as well as the new offence. A conditional discharge is available only in exceptional circumstances if an offender has already had a warning in the past two years (CDA, s. 66) or, presumably, a youth caution under LASPO.

Compensation orders

Any person found guilty of an offence can be ordered to pay compensation to the victim. (This is one reason why a caution is sometimes inappropriate—there must be a conviction for a compensation order.) Indeed, a court must consider making such an order if appropriate, or give its reasons for not doing so (PCCSA, s. 130(3)). This order can stand alone, without the court making any other order against the offender, or it can accompany any other order made by the court. As with a fine, the juvenile's means are taken into account; and the parents can be ordered to pay the compensation (but not where they were not in control of the juvenile at the time of the offence—e.g. the child was in local authority accommodation). Where the offender has limited means, a compensation order should be made before a fine.

Parenting order

If the appropriate conditions apply, a sentencing court can order the parents of a convicted child to attend counselling sessions to receive support via a parenting order. They involve a parenting skills course or weekly counselling. There may be other conditions applied by the court over a period of up to 12 months, for example that the parent ensures the child is at home during set hours or ensures that the child attends school on time.

SUMMARY

- The age of criminal responsibility in England and Wales is 10 years. Children under 10 who have committed a crime and who may harass, alarm, or distress others can be subject to a child safety order, which puts them under the supervision of a responsible person, such as a youth offending team member or social worker.

- Those under 18 are considered to be juveniles by the courts. Juveniles under 17 are automatically considered to be vulnerable persons when questioned by police. The welfare of the juvenile is the key priority in the criminal justice system.

- Youth offending teams are multi-professional and established by local authorities.

- Social workers may be required to act as an appropriate adult when a juvenile or vulnerable adult is questioned by police. The duties of the appropriate adult are set out in Code C of the Police and Criminal Evidence Act 1984.

- Juveniles detained by police should only be detained to enable police to obtain evidence to decide whether or not to charge the child with an offence in law. Lawful detention periods are set out in Code C, as are a series of rights for the detained person.

- Decisions to charge juveniles should be made with the approval of the Crown Prosecution Service.

- Youth cautions can be made by the police when a juvenile admits an offence.

- When a juvenile has committed a serious offence, they can be remanded in custody awaiting trial or granted bail. When remanded into the care of the local authority or a youth detention centre the juvenile becomes a looked-after child.

- The principle aim of sentencing juveniles is to prevent offending. Courts must have regard for the welfare of the juvenile. Pre-sentence reports help the courts to decide the type of sentence. Juveniles can be detained under detention and training orders for a maximum period of two years. Half of the term is served in a secure training centre or similar institution and half supervised in the community.

- Referral orders require juveniles to be referred to a youth offender panel to establish a contract of behaviour for 3–12 months. The juvenile must have pleaded guilty to the offence and have no previous convictions.

- Youth rehabilitation orders can combine various requirements for the juvenile for a period up to three years. Juveniles must agree to YROs. A YOT officer is appointed to oversee the specific requirements to be met.

 EXERCISES

Consider the statutory responsibilities of a social worker and appropriate actions you might take in each of the following situations:

1 Jennifer, who is 14, is currently in local authority accommodation because her mother cannot cope. You feel you have established quite a good relationship with her and, having begun to gain her trust, you have been able to talk to her about her life, which has included recent shoplifting and drug use. The police inform you that they have arrested her for supplying cannabis and wish to question her.

2 You have arrived at Sunderfield police station following a request to be present as appropriate adult for the questioning of Abdul, who is 16 and is suspected of arson at a local school. The police sergeant tells you that Abdul has refused legal advice and therefore they are ready to interview him. He has been in the police station for 20 hours, and when you see him you can see he is tired. The police have not told you what evidence they have to connect Abdul with the offence, but Abdul tells you that he was with a group of friends and someone, perhaps himself, did accidentally drop a lighted match onto some paper. Abdul tells you the police have told him he will not be allowed to leave until he admits it.

3 Assume Abdul has been charged. You know he has no past history of offending and comes from what you believe to be a stable family. Consider his right to bail and what will happen if bail is refused.

4 If Abdul is found guilty, what opportunity would a social worker have to influence the court, and what approach might a court or courts take when deciding the appropriate sentence?

ONLINE RESOURCES

For guidance on how to answer these exercises, visit the online resources at www.oup.com/uk/carr-goosey15e.

WHERE DO WE GO FROM HERE?

We have completed our discussion of the statutory duties of social workers in relation to children. You will realize that when other measures are impossible, social workers and other agencies have to use the courts. In relation to children, this means child protection proceedings and criminal prosecution of abusers. You need to know how to use the courts. That means getting your evidence together. See the **Appendix, 'The Social Worker's Toolkit'**, p 598 for some hints on evidence.

ANNOTATED FURTHER READING

If you are really interested in the up-to-date and full details of a particular aspect of how the criminal process works, one of the standard reference works can provide the answer, if you use the contents or index carefully. The following are published annually: *Stone's Justices' Manual* (Butterworths) deals with the work of the youth courts; *Blackstone's Criminal Practice* (Oxford University Press) deals with all aspects of criminal law and practice, as does *Archbold's Criminal Pleading, Evidence and Practice* (Sweet & Maxwell). *Current Sentencing Practice* (Sweet & Maxwell), a loose-leaf encyclopaedia edited by L. Harris, is very useful for the detail on sentencing, including how the courts approach particular offences.

A. Edwards, *Advising a Suspect in the Police Station* (8th edn, Sweet & Maxwell, 2013). The author, Anthony Edwards, is a leading writer and practitioner, and this book is of value to anyone working as an appropriate adult, though it covers all suspects who are being questioned.

J. Muncie, *Youth and Crime* (4th edn, Sage 2015) is a good introduction to the study of criminology in respect of youth.

The Youth Justice Board is an agency with a statutory responsibility to prevent offending by children. Its website is usefully and accessibly organized, for example to take you through custodial and community sentences one at a time www.gov.uk/government/organisations/youth-justice-board-for-england-and-wales.

NACRO (National Association for the Care and Resettlement of Offenders) has an excellent list of publications, too long for inclusion here, but worth visiting: www.nacro.org.uk

Part 3

Responsibilities towards adults

Part 3 Responsibilities towards adults

This part of the book concentrates on the law which governs adult social care. Adult social care is in general organized by local authorities. Their role can be summarized in a relatively straight-forward way. Councils are required to assess the needs of vulnerable individuals for social care services, plan and then ensure the required services are delivered to meet those needs, and finally review and adjust provision to ensure the needs are met. Nonetheless, it is clearly more complicated than this; the Local Government Ombudsman and the Health Services Ombudsman receive complaints which demonstrate the difficulties that local authorities and health services have in meeting their legal responsibilities. The failure to assess service users' needs properly, the use of flawed criteria for assessments and for making decisions, the failure to follow government guidance, and the failure to provide services to meet assessed needs figure prominently in the complaints. These are serious issues for the individuals involved. If local authorities fail to make appropriate provision, there are consequences, not only for those individuals but for their families. There are a number of interlinked reasons for these failures. The limited resources available to local government to meet an increasing need for services is a major cause. The complexity of the legal framework and the lack of clarity in the policy drivers for social care also play significant roles. Since the last edition of this book, the Care Act 2014 has come into force. The hope is that with the modernization of the law, and the removal of some complexities, local authorities will make better, in the sense of more lawful, decisions about service provision.

Chapter 11 sets the scene by considering the legal and political context of adult social care and explains the principles behind the Care Act 2014. It also discusses the impact of some overarching legal requirements, such as human rights, and equalities legislation and policy approaches such as dignity and citizenship. **Chapter 12** provides a practical summary of the Care Act 2014. **Chapter 13** is concerned with the responsibilities placed upon local authorities to manage adult care services. Local authorities have to assess the needs of those wanting services, prioritize and plan for those needs, and then arrange delivery of the most pressing of those needs. What is critical in the chapter is the pressure on local authorities to ration resources, and we will examine some responses from the courts to cuts in provision. The final part of the chapter looks at the mechanisms that exist to improve the quality of care services. It considers the role of the Care Quality Commission in ensuring quality services, and the role of the Local Government Ombudsman, as well as complaints procedures. We provide more detailed references to the Care Act 2014.

The focus of **chapter 14** is the adult social care user. The chapter sets out the law on mental capacity. The Mental Capacity Act 2005 provides an excellent example of a careful balancing exercise between the right to autonomy and the need to be protected. It then turns to and explains current statutory and policy framework for safeguarding vulnerable adults—again, this area of law has been changed by the Care Act 2014. **Chapter 15** looks at the role of the Court of Protection and a particular area of legal difficulty facing social workers—the Deprivation of Liberty Safeguards. **Chapter 16**—the final chapter—provides an overview of a specialized area of law—mental health.

Adult social care

11

OVERVIEW AND OBJECTIVES

The chapter provides an introduction to the legal and policy framework for the provision of adult social care. It starts by setting out the need for, and the scope of, adult social services. It then introduces the Care Act 2014, explaining the legal and policy context of what is arguably the most important reform of the law relating to vulnerable adults since the implementation of the National Assistance Act 1948. Finally, it considers legal obligations that are overarching, such as human rights and anti-discrimination legislation, including the public-sector equality duty.

CASE STUDY

C v A Local Authority (2011), Court of Protection

Why are we asking you to read this case?

This case raises a typical dilemma faced by those give who social care to adults. It is concerned with how you balance the rights of individuals against the need to protect them and others from the consequences of the exercise of those rights. Note how guidance plays a key role in resolving the conflict. The case also introduces you to the Court of Protection, a specialist court, which has an important role in protecting the rights of people who lack capacity.

What is at stake for the parties and beyond?

For C, what is at stake are his individual human rights, in particular right not to be subjected to inhuman or degrading treatment, his right to liberty, and his right to respect for private life. For the local authority, which had responsibility for the residential special school, it was about its decision-making process, what is best practice when faced by challenging behaviour, and how it should interpret guidance provided on these issues. More broadly the case raises issues about how we treat people who lack capacity. Are there ways of maximizing an individual's dignity and freedom even when their behaviour is difficult?

Background

The court was required to make declarations about the treatment by a residential special school of an 18-year-old man (C), who suffered from severe autism and severe learning disabilities. C's challenging behaviour included severe anxiety, sensory impairment, aggressive and destructive traits, significant self-harm, and harm to his carers. One aspect of his sensory problems was a tendency towards nakedness. His behaviour management at the school included the use of a 'blue room', a small, specially constructed, padded room with a secure door and window. C was taken there whenever he was aggressive or naked. The amount of time C spent in the blue room had significantly increased because the school maintained that his behaviours were becoming increasingly uncontrolled. The Court of Protection was required to consider various issues, including: (a) the school's decision-making process under the Mental Capacity Act 2005; (b) best practice regarding the approach to C's nakedness; (c) best practice regarding the use of seclusion and restraint, particularly the use of the blue room, and its impact on C's right not to be subjected to inhuman or degrading treatment, his right to liberty, and his right to respect for private life.

The court decided that the school's policies and procedures needed to better acknowledge C's sensory needs and choices. It was in his best interests to be clothed in communal areas, but there should be minimal restrictions on his choice to be naked; nakedness was not to be punished with seclusion. Staff had to be trained in strategies to allow C to be naked in their presence and to encourage him to be naked in areas of his accommodation where it was acceptable to others. Further, in order to be lawful, seclusion had to comply with statutory guidance, and when used to control aggressive behaviour, it should be used only so long as necessary and proportionate, and it had to be the least restrictive option. It had to be exercised in accordance with an intervention and prevention plan designed to safeguard C's psychological and physical health. That plan, together with guidance for use of the blue room, had to be written up into a protocol forming C's care plan and all staff had to be trained in a manner that was specific to C. Seclusion was not to be used solely for nakedness, for punishment, as part of behaviour management, or as a way of dealing with self-harming. The blue room could be used when C chose to go there, but he had to be free to leave.

WHAT DOES THIS CASE TELL YOU ABOUT SOCIAL CARE LAW AND PRACTICE?

This case demonstrates the interface between managing challenging behaviour and the law, and the difficult issues that you as a social worker have to manage. There is a lot of guidance available to you, but it must be read and followed. Moreover, seclusion, which may be explained as a way of protecting a service user's dignity, can all too quickly become punitive and a deprivation of liberty. The questions that you have to ask of a scheme designed to manage an adult service user's behaviour derive from human rights (see **chapter 3**): is it a necessary action, is it proportionate, and is it the least restrictive option?

The scope of adult social care

The extensive statutory responsibilities that local social services authorities have for adults and their carers are summed up in the term 'adult social care'. The services that may be provided under the umbrella of adult social care range from community-based services such as home care, meals provision, the provision of equipment and adaptations, to residential care. The providers of services may be social service departments, health authorities, voluntary sector organizations, or commercial enterprises. Service user categories include older people, people with learning disabilities, physically disabled people, people with mental health problems, and carers. Age UK describes social care as follows:

Social care is any service *designed* to help people with support needs to live well. This could be someone coming in to your home to help with tasks like washing, dressing, getting in and out of bed and going to the toilet, right up to 24/7 support in a care home. Care services should protect people who are vulnerable, enable a decent quality of life, support independence and encourage people to remain active.

(Age UK, *Care in Crisis 2014*)

An indication of the extent of adult social care provision in England during 2017–18 is provided by **Box 11.1**, which replicates the key facts set out at the beginning of the Personal Social Services Adult Social Care Survey, England. These useful statistics can be found on the NHS Digital website at https://digital.nhs.uk/data-and-information/ publications/statistical/personal-social-services-adult-social-care-survey.

 BOX 11.1 The extent of adult social care provision in England—Personal Social Services Adult Social Care Survey, England, 2017–18

- There were 1,846,000 requests for support from new clients actioned in 2014–15. Of these, 72 per cent (1,327,000) were from clients aged 65 and over; the remaining 28 per cent of clients (519,000) were aged 18–64.

- The majority of these new requests for support (1,460,000 clients, or 79 per cent) came through the community. A further 18 per cent (333,000 clients) had been discharged from hospital.

- The most common sequel to requests for support was Universal Services/Signposted to Other Services (31 per cent, or 575,000 requests), followed by No Services Provided—any reason (28 per cent, or 520,000 requests). A further 16 per cent (304,000 requests) were offered ongoing low-level support, with Short Term Support to Maximise Independence and Long Term Support accounting for 12 per cent (218,000 requests) and 8 per cent (144,000 requests) respectively.

- Clients aged 65 and over account for two-thirds (68 per cent) of all clients accessing Long Term Support. Within this age group, nearly two-thirds (64 per cent) accessing Long Term Support during 2014–15 required Physical Support—Personal Care Support. Among those clients aged 18 to 64, the most common Primary Support Reason was Learning Disability support, accounting for 43 per cent of the age group.

- There were 334,000 instances of support being provided direct to carers, of which 6,000 (2 per cent) requests for carer support related to carers aged under 18. For 24 per cent of all requests for carer support, no direct support was provided.

The statistics reveal the extraordinary scale of service provision. Perhaps something that is not so clear is that the need for social care is, in part, determined by socio-economic circumstances. Statistics produced by the Office for National Statistics (ONS) suggest that in the most deprived areas of England healthy life expectancy was 19.0 years lower for men and 20.2 years lower for women than in the least deprived areas. This inequality is twice as wide as the difference seen in full life expectancy at 9.2 years for men; for women it is almost three times wider than the difference in life expectancy at 6.8 years (ONS statistical bulletin March 2016).

In August 2018, Age UK's Care in Crisis campaign pointed out that:

The current state of care
A number of issues need to be addressed:

- **Underfunding**—in the last 5 years there has been a £160 million cut in total public spending on older people's social care despite a rapidly increasing demand because of our ageing population
- **Postcode lottery**—despite the 2014 Care Act introducing a national system of eligibility, local variation is still leaving many older people without any support
- **Unmet need**—1.2 million people aged 65 plus don't receive the care support they need with essential living activities
- **Declining access**—cuts in local authority care services have placed increasing pressure on unpaid carers.

See www.ageuk.org.uk/our-impact/campaigning/care-in-crisis.

The role of local social services authorities

It is important to remember exactly what it is that local social services authorities are responsible for. Their role as provider of services is secondary and shared with other providers from the private and voluntary sectors. The primary role of local authorities with adult social care responsibilities is to ensure that:

- adult social care is delivered effectively;
- service users' wishes are taken into account; and
- services are delivered safely.

Therefore, social services authorities' responsibilities embrace planning for adult social care services, assessing individual needs for those services, promoting service user independence through direct payments, and maintaining appropriate safeguards for those using their services. This is made clear in s. 8 of the Care Act 2014 (see **Box 11.2**), which describes what local authorities may provide in response to adult social care needs and how they should provide it.

 BOX 11.2 Adult social care provision: how to meet needs—s. 8 of the Care Act 2014

(1) The following are examples of what may be provided to meet needs under sections 18 to 20—
  (a) accommodation in a care home or in premises of some other type;
  (b) care and support at home or in the community;
  (c) counselling and other types of social work;
  (d) goods and facilities;
  (e) information, advice and advocacy.

(2) The following are examples of the ways in which a local authority may meet needs under sections 18 to 20—
  (a) by arranging for a person other than it to provide a service;
  (b) by itself providing a service;
  (c) by making direct payments.

The health/social care divide

One important limit to the scope of adult social care services is that they are not health services. This is made clear in s. 22 of the Care Act 2014:

Exception for provision of health services

(1) A local authority may not meet needs under sections 18 to 20 by providing or arranging for the provision of a service or facility that is required to be provided under the National Health Service Act 2006 unless—

    (a) doing so would be merely incidental or ancillary to doing something else to meet needs under those sections, and

    (b) the service or facility in question would be of a nature that the local authority could be expected to provide.

This means it is unlawful for local authorities to provide services which can be provided by the National Health Service (NHS). One important distinction between health and social care services is that health services are free at the point of delivery, whereas charges can be made for social care services. Deciding whether services are health or social care services is therefore critical to the affordability of those services. Unfortunately, the divide is not clear, and causes confusion for local authorities, and considerable stress and anxiety for those who consider that the services they require are health services and yet are assessed as needing social care rather than health services.

The issue was litigated in *R v North and East Devon Health Authority, ex p Coughlan* (2002). This case is important, although technical. Miss Pamela Coughlan was tetraplegic. She was moved from hospital to a purpose-built facility that she was promised would be her home for life. She judicially reviewed the decision to close the purpose-built facility. She was successful; her nursing care had to be provided free by the NHS and could not be provided by the local authority on a means-tested basis where appropriate, and the Health Authority was in breach of its promise by closing the facility. The crucial paragraphs of the Court of Appeal decision are set out in **Box 11.3**. Note that the extract refers to s. 21 of the National Assistance Act 1948, which has been repealed and replaced by s. 22 of the Care Act 2014.

BOX 11.3 The health care divide—extract from the Court of Appeal decision in para. 30 of *R v North and East Devon Health Authority, ex p Coughlan* (2002)

(d) The fact that some nursing services can be properly regarded as part of social services care, to be provided by the local authority, does not mean that all nursing services provided to those in the care of the local authority can be treated in this way. The scale and type of nursing required in an individual case may mean that it would not be appropriate to regard all or part of the nursing as being part of 'the package of care' which can be provided by a local authority. There can be no precise legal line drawn between those nursing services which are and those which are not capable of being treated as included in such a package of care services.

(e) The distinction between those services which can and cannot be so provided is one of degree which in a borderline case will depend on a careful appraisal of the facts of the individual case.

However, as a very general indication as to where the line is to be drawn, it can be said that if the nursing services are (i) merely incidental or ancillary to the provision of the accommodation which a local authority is under a duty to provide to the category of persons to whom section 21 of the 1948 Act refers and (ii) of a nature which it can be expected that an authority whose primary responsibility is to provide social services can be expected to provide, then they can be provided under section 21. (This is known as the 'quantity and quality test' and is now enshrined in the Care Act 2014 s. 22(1).) It will be appreciated that the first part of the test is focusing on the overall quantity of the services and the second part on the quality of the services provided.

(f)   The fact that care services are provided on a means tested contribution basis does not prevent the Secretary of State declining to provide the nursing part of those services on the NHS. However, he can only decline if he has formed a judgment which is tenable and consistent with his long-term general duty to continue to promote a comprehensive free health service that it is not necessary to provide the services. He cannot decline simply because social services will fill the gap.

In summary, what the Court of Appeal decided was that it is wrong to say that if any nursing care is provided for a service user, then he or she is receiving health services which are the sole responsibility of the NHS and therefore free at the point of delivery. However, when the degree of nursing care that Miss Coughlan required was carefully examined, it was clear that her needs were far beyond what social services could provide. Therefore, she was not someone to whom a local authority could lawfully provide the nursing services she needed.

Gaps in provision

One of the consequences of the *Coughlan* case was that it left gaps in provision. The needs of the service user could be greater than social care support could provide for, yet fall below what the Department of Health specified as necessary to qualify for NHS continuing support. The legality of the gap was considered in *R (Grogan) v Bexley NHS Care Trust* (2006). The judge was critical of the Department of Health Guidance of the time, which led to serious problems in decisions about the provision of care. What he decided was that a gap could not be legal, and that as the definition of social care was statutory, that is, within s. 21 of the National Assistance Act 1948, and the definition of health care was provided in policy, the threshold for the provision of health care services had to fall to meet the upper limit of social care provision.

National Framework for NHS Continuing Healthcare and NHS-funded Nursing Care in England

The current divide between health and social care provision is determined by the *National Framework for NHS Continuing Healthcare and NHS-funded Nursing Care in England* 2018 edition. This says (in answer to the question 'Is there an authoritative definition of "beyond the responsibility of the Local authority?"'):

Local authorities have a duty to carry out an assessment of needs where it appears that an individual may have needs for care and support, and a duty to meet eligible needs (subject to means testing). However, local authorities cannot lawfully commission services that are clearly the responsibility of the NHS (such as registered nursing care and services that the NHS has to provide because the individual has a primary health need and is therefore eligible for NHS Continuing Healthcare).

We have provided an extract from the Framework in **Box 11.4**, which indicates how the social care/health care issue is to be decided in individual cases. What is important is whether an individual's primary need is a health need. If so, then they are eligible for NHS continuing health care.

BOX 11.4 Primary health need—*The National Framework for NHS Continuing Healthcare and NHS-funded Nursing Care*

54. To assist in determining which health services it is appropriate for the NHS to provide under the NHS Act, and to distinguish between those and the services that local authorities may provide under the Care Act 2014, the Secretary of State has developed the concept of a 'primary health need'. Where a person has been assessed to have a primary health need, they are eligible for NHS Continuing Healthcare and the NHS will be responsible for providing for all of that individual's assessed health and associated social care needs, including accommodation, if that is part of the overall need. Determining whether an individual has a primary health need involves looking at the totality of the relevant needs. In order to determine whether an individual has a primary health need, an assessment of eligibility process must be undertaken by a multidisciplinary team (MDT) which must use the national Decision Support Tool (DST).

55. An individual has a primary health need if, having taken account of all their needs (following completion of the Decision Support Tool), it can be said that the main aspects or majority part of the care they require is focused on addressing and/or preventing health needs. Having a primary health need is not about the reason why an individual requires care or support, nor is it based on their diagnosis; it is about the level and type of their overall actual day-to-day care needs taken in their totality.

56. Each individual case has to be considered on its own facts in accordance with the principles outlined in this National Framework.

It is clear that there is still potential for disagreement about decisions made about the health/social care divide. However, the framework provides the most recent statement of that divide and the one you will be required to work with.

This discussion has already highlighted the legal complexities involved. The divide continues to be a source of litigation. Recently, for instance, the Supreme Court, in *R (on the application of Forge Care Homes Ltd and others) (Appellants) v Cardiff and Vale University Health Board and others (Respondents)* [2017] UKSC 56, considered whether the National Health Service or local authorities (with means-tested contributions from clients) are responsible for paying for the work done by registered nurses in social rather than health care settings.

We are now going to consider the legal framework of social care itself. Resolving the health/social care divide was one of the aims of the Care Act 2014. However, as we shall see, there was a broader social and political context. A range of problems with the provision of adult social care stimulated legislative reform.

The context of the Care Act 2014—a crisis in adult social care?

The Coalition Government took office in 2010. It published a statement of its intentions for adult social care, *A Vision for Adult Social Care: Capable Communities and Active Citizens*, in November of that year. Its priorities—not remarkably different from those of the previous government—are set out in **Box 11.5**.

BOX 11.5 Statement of intentions for adult social care—*A Vision for Adult Social Care: Capable Communities and Active Citizens* (2010)

The Vision for a modern system of social care is built on seven principles:

* Prevention: communities are empowered to help people retain and regain independence.
* Personalisation: individuals not institutions take control of their care. Personal budgets, preferably as direct payments, are provided to all eligible people. Information about care and support is available for all local people, regardless of whether or not they fund their own care.
* Partnership: care and support delivered in a partnership between individuals, communities, the voluntary and private sectors, the NHS and councils—including wider support services, such as housing.
* Plurality: the variety of people's needs is matched by diverse service provision, with a broad market of high quality service providers.
* Protection: there are sensible safeguards against the risk of abuse or neglect. Risk is no longer an excuse to limit people's freedom.
* Productivity: greater local accountability will drive improvements and innovation to deliver higher productivity and high quality care and support services. A focus on publishing information about agreed quality outcomes will support transparency and accountability.
* People: we can draw on a workforce who can provide care and support with skill, compassion and imagination, and who are given the freedom and support to do so. We need the whole workforce, including care workers, nurses, occupational therapists, physiotherapists and social workers, alongside carers and the people who use services, to lead the changes set out here.

The priorities set out in the vision statement are not consistent with the legal framework that preceded the Care Act 2014. The law relating to the provision of adult social care was based on the immediate post-war welfare settlement. While this was a progressive vision at the time, as the years have gone by, its paternalism and the way in which it was expected that ordinary citizens would defer to the authority of experts, passively accepting what was offered to them, has become increasingly at odds with societal expectations of public services. As the Dilnot Commission (see later in this section) put it:

> Expectations have changed, people want more choice and control over their lives and care and support needs to change to meet this expectation.

The Care Act 2014 starts with a statement of principles which reflect much more clearly contemporary values. The provision is set out in full in **chapter 12**. What is important to note now is that the legislation is built upon the principle that the state has a responsibility to promote individual well-being.

The need for a reinvigoration of adult social care provision was underlined by a series of scandals that erupted in 2011. These included the collapse of Southern Cross, a private provider of residential care, leaving 31,000 vulnerable residents at risk of losing their homes. This raised the issue of how law and regulation can protect service users from the consequences of business failure by private providers—something that was not an issue when the state was the direct provider of services. Sections 53–57 of the Care Act 2014 gives the Care Quality Commission specific responsibility for overseeing financial probity of private providers. In addition, s. 48 provides that in the event of the business failure of a private provider of care services the local authority has a temporary duty to step in and make provision for the service users.

The physical safety of vulnerable adults has also become an issue. For example, in 2011 the BBC broadcast secret filming of the treatment of patients with learning difficulties and autism in a private hospital, Winterbourne View, which led to four arrests and an unreserved apology from the Care Quality Commission. Again, the difficulties that law and regulators face in protecting vulnerable adults from unacceptable behaviour became apparent. Nor were the failures of the system limited to institutional care. The Equality and Human Rights Commission published a report, *Close to Home*, detailing a lack of attention to human rights and dignity by many councils in their provision of domiciliary care. We discuss the provisions of the Care Act 2014 designed to improve adult safeguarding in summary in **chapter 12** and in detail when we consider adult safeguarding in **chapter 14**.

The current funding system for care and support in England and Wales is confusing, unfair, and unsustainable for a variety of reasons.

- The demographic time bomb—the population of older people is projected to grow by 50 per cent over the next 20 years as a result of longer life expectancy, while the proportion of the working-age adult population is falling. This means that there will be a considerable shortfall in money available to pay for increased demand for care and support.

- Means testing—the current system means that those with high care costs are required to support themselves in residential care until their assets are reduced to £23,250, leaving little to pass on to their families.

- The postcode lottery—local councils set local eligibility thresholds designed to reflect local priorities. This means that people with identical support needs can receive quite different levels of support depending upon where they live.

The Commission on Funding of Care and Support (the Dilnot Commission) was set up by the Coalition Government on 20 July 2010. The Commission published its report on 4 July 2011. Its recommendations included the following:

> Individuals' lifetime contributions towards their social care costs—which are currently potentially unlimited—should be capped. After the cap is reached, individuals would be eligible for full state support. This cap should be between £25,000 and £50,000. We consider that £35,000 is the most appropriate and fair figure.
>
> The means-tested threshold, above which people are liable for their full care costs, should be increased from £23,250 to £100,000.
>
> National eligibility criteria and portable assessments should be introduced to ensure greater consistency.
>
> All those who enter adulthood with a care and support need should be eligible for free state support immediately rather than being subjected to a means test.

The report estimated that its proposals for change would cost the government an initial £1.7bn a year—0.25 per cent of total public spending. The government's less-than-generous response to the Dilnot proposals is set out in the Care Act 2014. In essence the legislation 'caps' care costs, but not at the Dilnot levels. However, the relevant sections of the Care Act have not been implemented. The government explained that this was because of austerity. There was not enough money available both to fund current provision and to finance the cap. There was a promise from the government that the 'cap' would be implemented from 2020. Age UK responded to the delay as follows:

> For Age UK therefore, the major issue is not the delay in implementing the cap, but ensuring that the £6 billion that the government claims to have saved by this measure is used to prevent the collapse of the care system. If savings are used to ensure that older people who are in desperate need of care receive the help they need then the delay in implementing the spending cap is justifiable, but older people will understandably be asking for assurance that this is the intention.

(Age UK (July 2015), https://ageukblog.org.uk/2015/07/20/care-cap-delayed)

During the 2017 election campaign the Conservatives announced new plans for care reform that did not include a cap. This led to an intense public backlash. Their proposals were instantly labelled a 'dementia tax', there was a rapid U-turn, and a promise of a consultation paper to be published in the summer of 2018. We are still waiting for that consultation paper. In the meantime, the Government has ruled out introducing a cap on care costs by 2020. It's fair to say that a lot has happened since the last edition of this book in 2017, but nothing has changed!

There was another problem the Care Act 2014 was designed to overcome—the complex legal framework which comprised a multiplicity of statutes with overlapping provisions and significant gaps. You no longer need to know the details of the previous law, but in summary the legal limitations concerned:

- the lack of legislative provision for preventive measures;
- inadequacies in the legal framework in connection with carers' needs.

You may decide—once you have studied the rest of this book and spent some time in practice—that legislative reform deals better with modernizing legislation than with eliminating scandal and lack of resources from adult social care.

Overarching legal responsibilities

There are a number of statutes which are overarching in the sense that provisions of other statutes have to be interpreted consistently with their requirements. We considered some of these in **chapter 3**. They comprise equalities legislation, such as the Equality Act 2010, and information legislation, such as Data Protection Act 2018 and the Freedom of Information Act 2000. All social care legislation has to be read bearing in mind the obligations set out in these statutes.

The most important overarching obligations upon the state are those contained in the Human Rights Act 1998. Individuals have challenged the services that the state provides to them in a number of cases which have had important consequences for the delivery of services. Some examples are set out in **Table 11.1**.

TABLE 11.1 Human rights and adult social care

Case	Article	
Rabone and another v Pennine Care NHS Trust (2012)	Article 2—right to life	Failure to take reasonable steps to protect an informal patient under the Mental Health Act from the risk of suicide was a breach of Article 2
R (Limbuela) v Home Secretary (2006)	Article 3—right not to be subject to inhuman and degrading treatment	Failure to provide adequate means of support for asylum seekers was unlawful
R (A & B) v East Sussex (Manual Handling) (2003)	Article 8—right to respect for family and private life	A blanket ban on manual handling of disabled service users for health and safety reasons was a breach of Article 8. What is required are policies which strike a balance between the health and safety of carers and the rights of severely disabled people to be treated with dignity
R v Enfield London Borough Council, ex p Bernard (2002)	Article 8—right to respect for the home	The failure of the local authority to provide adaptations to the home of a severely disabled woman, despite it having assessed those adaptations as necessary, was unlawful
HL v UK (2004)	Article 5—right not to be deprived of liberty	The informal detention of a mentally incapacitated adult in a psychiatric hospital without any means of challenging that detention was unlawful

The non-discrimination provisions of Article 14 of the European Convention on Human Rights (ECHR) must also be considered to have potential for litigation, which may well prove productive for disabled people and other users of adult social care services.

United Nations Convention on Disability Rights

The UK government ratified the United Nations Convention on Disability Rights on 8 June 2009. The Convention is designed to promote, protect, and ensure the human rights, freedom, and dignity of disabled people. It explicitly sets out the rights that disabled people have and should be able to enjoy on the same basis as other people—for example, the right to dignity, freedom, equality, and justice. It also provides direction on how human rights should be interpreted from the perspective of disabled people all over the world. The UK has implemented the optional protocol to the Convention. This provides two additional procedures in respect of implementation and monitoring of the Convention, including an avenue that enables individuals who feel their rights have been breached to bring petitions to the UN Committee, set up to monitor implementation of the Convention.

In August 2017, the UK's progress against the Convention was reviewed by the United Nations Committee on the Rights of Persons with Disabilities. The Equality and Human Rights Commission has reported on the Committee's findings. The full report is available at www.equalityhumanrights.com/en/publication-download/how-well-uk-performing-disability-rights. In essence, the UN Committee was concerned that not enough was being done to apply the Convention consistently to all areas of life across the UK, to involve disabled people in decisions that affect their lives, and to put the human rights model of disability into practice.

Equalities legislation

We discussed the Equality Act 2010 in **chapter 3**. The discussion of disability discrimination in that chapter is of particular relevance for adult social care. Here we focus on the public sector equality duty, which has proved a productive legal tool to challenge cuts in provision of adult social care.

Duties on public authorities

As we indicated in **chapter 3**, the imposition of a positive duty upon public bodies to take action to eliminate discrimination and advance equality of opportunity has been one of the most significant legal advances of recent years. The duty known as the public sector equality duty is set out in s. 149 of the Equality Act 2010 and is fully discussed in **chapter 3**. Here we discuss some of the litigation in connection with the public sector equality duty that has become particularly pertinent because of financial cuts.

The public sector equality duty and financial cuts

There is no doubt that the financial crisis and cuts in public sector funding have reduced the resources available for adult social care. Local authorities are facing difficult choices about which services to cut, and where to increase contributions from users. The question arises: what role can the public sector equality duty play in ensuring that local authority decision making does not impact disproportionately upon the most vulnerable groups? In January 2013 the Equality and Human Rights Commission (EHRC) published useful non-statutory guidance on the public sector equality duty, which was updated in 2015. In **Box 11.6** we provide two extracts from the guidance.

BOX 11.6 Pre-2014 guidance from the Equality and Human Rights Commission—*Using the Equality Duties to make Fair Financial Decisions*

The public sector equality duty (the equality duty) does not prevent you from making difficult decisions such as reorganisations and relocations, redundancies, and service reductions, nor does it stop you from making decisions which may affect one group more than another group. The equality duty enables you to demonstrate that you are making financial decisions in a fair, transparent and accountable way, considering the needs and the rights of different members of your community. This is achieved through assessing the impact that changes to policies, procedures and practices could have on people with different protected characteristics.

Assessing the impact on equality of proposed changes to policies, procedures and practices is not just something that the law requires, it is a positive opportunity for you as a public authority leader to ensure you make better decisions based on robust evidence.

. . .

By law, your assessments of impact on equality must:

• Contain enough information to enable a public authority to demonstrate it has had 'due regard' to the aims of the equality duty in its decision-making

• Consider ways of mitigating or avoiding any adverse impacts.

Such assessments do not have to take the form of a document called an equality impact assessment. If you choose not to develop a document of this type, then some alternative approach which systematically assesses any adverse impacts of a change in policy, procedure or practice will be required.

Assessing impact on equality is not an end in itself and it should be tailored to, and be proportionate to, the decision that is being made.

Whether it is proportionate for an authority to conduct an assessment of the impact on equality of a financial decision or not depends on its relevance to the authority's particular function and its likely impact on people with protected characteristics.

We recommend that you document your assessment of the impact on equality when developing financial proposals. This will help you to:

• **Ensure you have a written record of the equality considerations** you have taken into account.

• **Ensure that your decision includes a consideration of the actions that would help to avoid or mitigate any impacts on particular protected characteristics.** Individual decisions should also be informed by the wider context of decisions in your own and other relevant public authorities, so that people with particular protected characteristics are not unduly affected by the cumulative effects of different decisions.

• **Make your decisions based on evidence**: a decision which is informed by relevant local and national information about equality is a better quality decision. Assessments of impact on equality provide a clear and systematic way to collect, assess and put forward relevant evidence.

- **Make the decision-making process more transparent:** a process which involves those likely to be affected by the policy, and which is based on evidence, is much more open and transparent. This should also help you secure better public understanding of the difficult decisions you will be making in the coming months.

- **Comply with the law:** a written record can be used to demonstrate that due regard has been had. Failure to meet the equality duty may result in authorities being exposed to costly, time-consuming and reputation-damaging legal challenges.

Litigation and the public sector equality duty

Three court decisions provide useful guidance on the legal expectations that arise from the public sector equality duty (PSED). The first is *R (Rahman) v Birmingham City Council* (2011). This was a judicial review of the decision of Birmingham City Council to close a number of legal advice centres in the city. It was accepted that the closure of the centres would disproportionally affect ethnic minority and disabled users. Whilst an equality impact needs assessment (EINA) was prepared in connection with the decision, it was not provided to the councillors who make that decision. Following the issue of the court proceedings, to avoid potential difficulties with the lawfulness of the decision-making process, the relevant councillors were asked to take the decision again, this time with the benefit of the EINA. They affirmed their previous decision. This, the judge, Mr Justice Blake, said, was not adequate. There were substantial defects in the EINA that had been prepared in November 2010. It was inadequate in its examination of the evidence and its compliance with the approach recommended by Birmingham City Council's own guidance code for such documents. As the judge put it, in para. 35 of his judgment:

> In a number of respects the content of that EINA seem to have been driven by the hopes of the advantages to be derived from a new policy rather than focusing upon the assessment of the degree of disadvantage to existing users of terminating funding arrangements until new arrangements can be put in place.

Moreover, the duty is not merely to have regard to the EINA but to have due regard to the PSED duty. Paragraph 46 of the judgment makes the requirements clear.

> Even where the context of decision making is financial resources in a tight budget, that does not excuse compliance with the PSEDs and indeed there is much to be said for the proposition that even in the straightened times the need for clear, well-informed decision making when assessing the impacts on less advantaged members of society is as great, if not greater.

The judge refers positively to the original non-statutory guidance produced by the EHRC set out in **Box 11.6**.

The second case that it is useful to note is *R (W) v Birmingham City Council* (2011). Here the judicial review challenged the defendant local authority's decision to reduce its budget for adult social care by restricting the provision of support for people with disabilities to those whose needs were assessed to be critical. The claimants were all severely disabled adults. They argued that the prospective change was unlawful, since the local authority had failed to have due regard to the disability equality duty set out in s. 49A of the Disability Discrimination Act 1995 (the duty which preceded s. 149 of the Equality Act 2010). The local authority argued that the courts should be careful not to intervene in questions involving the balancing of competing claims, which were matters for expertise, specialist knowledge, local policy, and democratic accountability. The judge, Mr Justice Walker, upheld the claim. At para. 176 he stated:

> It is difficult to see how, in the circumstances of the present case, 'due regard' could be paid to the matters identified in s. 49A without some attempt at assessment of the practical impact on those whose needs in a particular respect fell into the 'substantial' band but not into the 'critical' band.

He concluded:

> that there was a failure ... to address the questions which arose when considering whether the impact on the disabled of the move to 'critical only' was so serious that an alternative which was not so draconian should be identified and funded to the extent necessary by savings elsewhere.

He pointed out that:

> These cases indicate that the public sector equality duty may prove a very useful tool to protect the resources available for adult social care. What it requires is that local authorities take into account the potential. It is not that the cuts cannot go ahead, but they should only go ahead when the potential impact of decisions to cut services on those people with protected characteristics has been fully assessed and faced up to.

However, both these cases are High Court decisions. The third—and most recent case— is a Court of Appeal case—*Bracking v Secretary of State for Work and Pensions* (2013)—and therefore more authoritative. The legal challenge arose as a result of the decision to close the Independent Living Fund (ILF) from March 2015. The ILF, set up in 1988 as an interim measure pending the implementation of community care legislation and the reform of disability benefits, is funded by the Department for Work and Pensions (DWP) to provide services and direct payments to disabled people which help them to lead independent lives in the community. It has a complex bureaucratic history. Although wound up in 1993, its popularity meant that commitments were made to maintain funding to its existing recipients, and a new fund was established for applications made between 1993 and 2007. At the time of the Court of Appeal hearing it was estimated that more than 19,000 people were in receipt of assistance through the ILF, which cost the DWP over £350m. The government considered that the system was unsustainable and in July 2012 the DWP launched its consultation on a new model of provision. This made clear that closure was the preferred option, with funding being transferred to local government in England and the devolved administrations in Scotland and Wales. In December 2012, the government announced its decision to close the ILF from 2015. It published an Equality Impact Assessment (EIA), which concluded that any negative impact was 'justified by the policy aims of providing greater equity and fairness in the social care system and delivering this funding at a local level in a way which is account-able to local people through the electoral system' (quoted at para. 19).

The four claimants, each of whom had severe disabilities and were current recipients of ILF payments, made two substantive challenges to the lawfulness of the decision to close the fund. First, they argued that the consultation that preceded the decision was inadequate and, second, that the minister had failed to discharge the PSED. At the High Court Mr Justice Blake, remarking upon the legal limits of the duty to consult, determined that the consultation process was fit for purpose, and was nothing 'other than candid and open, having regard to what it was: a desire to know the consequences of a provisional decision to close the ILF'. He also determined that the PSED had been met. There was one caveat: the duty was a continuing one and in particular the government needed to continue to have regard to the express terms of the UN Convention on the Rights of Persons with Disabilities 2006, ratified by the UK in June 2009.

The claimants appealed to the Court of Appeal. Lord Justice McCombe upheld Mr Justice Blake's decision on the adequacy of the consultation. However, his review of the documentation presented to the minister in connection with the discharge of the PSED led him to conclude that there was insufficient evidence 'to demonstrate to the court that a focused regard was had to the potentially very grave impact upon individuals in this group of disabled persons, within the context of a consideration of the statutory requirements for disabled people as a whole' (para. 61). He therefore allowed the appeal and quashed the decision to close the fund. This decision seems to promise that the Court of Appeal will take the duty seriously.

Note: **chapter 3** considers the case of *Blake and others v London Borough of Waltham Forest* (2014) on the council's termination of a soup kitchen licence. The judge set out principles relating to the PSED and the process by which it must be fulfilled. A note on the PSED by Matrix Chambers, a leading set of barristers who specialize in equality and human rights law (available at www.matrixlaw.co.uk/wp-content/uploads/2016/03/27 _01_2016_12_40_30_Public-Sector-Equality-Duty-Update-and-OverviewvP.pdf) argues that there are two recurrent themes in cases where a breach of the duty is found: (i) the failure of public authorities to provide proper evidence of compliance with the PSED; and (ii) the failure of public authorities to provide evidence that all relevant protected characteristics have been considered. This shows the critical importance of carrying out reviews properly.

Just as equality has ethical and legal dimensions so does dignity, another mechanism for enhancing services to adult service users.

Human rights and dignity

Age UK includes the following case study in its 2015 publication *Older People and Human Rights*, www.ageuk.org.uk/documents/en-gb/for-professionals/equality-and-human-rights/older_people_human_rights__expert_series_pro.pdf.

> Help the Aged received a call from an older woman who was discharged from hospital without a proper assessment. When she got home, she found that she could not use the toilet as she needed rails to push herself up. She contacted the occupational therapist, who said she

would have to wait at least two months and could use incontinence pads in the meantime. She is not incontinent. She is upset by the indignity and feels suicidal.

This case study demonstrates the importance of dignity in dealing with adult social care users.

The Department of Health, as part of a drive to improve services for vulnerable adults, has actively promoted the concept of dignity. The Social Care Institute for Excellence (SCIE) has produced a practice guide on dignity which you may find useful. It can be downloaded from www.scie.org.uk/publications/guides/guide15. It contains the Dignity Challenge, accepted by the NHS, explaining what the concept of dignity can offer, and is set out in **Box 11.7.**

 BOX 11.7 The Dignity Challenge—The Social Care Institute for Excellence (SCIE)

High-quality care services that respect people's dignity should:

1) have a zero tolerance of all forms of abuse

2) support people with the same respect you would want for yourself or a member of your family

3) treat each person as an individual by offering a personalised service

4) enable people to maintain the maximum possible level of independence, choice and control

5) listen and support people to express their needs and wants

6) respect people's right to privacy

7) ensure people feel able to complain without fear of retribution

8) engage with family members and carers as care partners

9) assist people to maintain confidence and a positive self-esteem

10) act to alleviate people's loneliness and isolation.

Box 11.8 sets out a useful working definition of dignity taken from the SCIE practice guide.

 BOX 11.8 What is dignity?—SCIE practice guide Dignity in Care

Dignity consists of many overlapping aspects, involving respect, privacy, autonomy and self-worth. The provisional meaning of dignity used for this guide is based on a standard dictionary definition: a state, quality or manner worthy of esteem or respect; and (by extension) self-respect. Dignity in care, therefore, means the kind of care, in any setting, which supports and promotes, and does not undermine, a person's self respect regardless of any difference. While 'dignity' may be difficult to define, what is clear is that people know when they have not been treated with dignity and respect. Helping to put that right is the purpose of this guide.

SCIE also points out the factors that might indicate failure to treat people with appropriate dignity, which we have set out in **Box 11.9**.

 BOX 11.9 Factors that diminish dignity—extract from SCIE practice guide Dignity in Care

Factors that have been held responsible for the absence of dignity in care include bureaucracy, staff shortages, poor management and lack of leadership, absence of appropriate training and induction and difficulties with recruitment and retention leading to overuse of temporary staff.

There are also wider societal issues, including ageism, other forms of discrimination and abuse. A great deal of work is needed to tackle negative attitudes towards older people, to bring about a culture change and to ensure that such attitudes have no place in the health and social care sectors.

The idea of dignity is deeply embedded within human rights. Article 1 of the preamble to the Convention to the Universal Declaration of Human Rights, proclaims that:

> All human beings are born free and equal in dignity and rights. They are endowed with reason and conscience and should act towards one another in a spirit of brotherhood.

In the UK some judges refer to the importance of individual dignity when evaluating service provision. Perhaps the approach is best epitomized within the judgment of Mr Justice Munby in the case of *R (on the application of A & B) v East Sussex County Council* (2003). We looked more closely at this case on manual handling in **chapter 3** in connection with the Human Rights Act 1998. Here we want to use the case to demonstrate the legal importance of dignity. Mr Justice Munby, in his decision, made it clear that human dignity lies at the heart of the law—not just human rights law, but the common law as well. His judgment on this is well worth reading. We have set out paras 86 and 87 in **Box 11.10**.

 BOX 11.10 Dignity and the law—*R (on the application of A & B) v East Sussex County Council* (2003), paras 86 and 87

86 The recognition and protection of human dignity is one of the core values—in truth *the* core value—of our society and, indeed, of all the societies which are part of the European family of nations and which have embraced the principles of the Convention. It is a core value of the common law, long pre-dating the Convention and the Charter. The invocation of the dignity of the patient in the form of declaration habitually used when the court is exercising its inherent declaratory jurisdiction in relation to the gravely ill or dying is not some meaningless incantation designed to comfort the living or to assuage the consciences of those involved in making life and death decisions: it is a solemn affirmation of the law's and of society's recognition of our humanity and of human dignity as something fundamental. Not surprisingly, human dignity is extolled in article 1 of the Charter, just as it is in article 1 of the Universal Declaration. And the latter's call to us to 'act towards one another in a spirit of brotherhood' is nothing new. It reflects the fourth Earl of Chesterfield's injunc-

tion, 'Do as you would be done by' and, for the Christian, the biblical call (Matthew ch 7, v 12): 'all things whatsoever ye would that men should do to you, do ye even so to them: for this is the law and the prophets'.

87 Dignity interests are also, of course, at the core of the rights protected by article 3. Whether a particular set of circumstances constitutes 'inhuman or degrading treatment' is a matter of fact and degree. As the Court said in **A v United Kingdom** (1998) 27 EHRR 611 at 629 (para [20]):

> The Court recalls that ill-treatment must attain a minimum level of severity if it is to fall within the scope of Article 3. The assessment of this minimum is relative: it depends on all the circumstances of the case, such as the nature and context of the treatment, its duration, its physical and mental effects and, in some instances, the sex, age and state of health of the victim.

What Mr Justice Munby makes clear is that the law will not step in to protect a claimant from *any* claim that their dignity has been violated. Life is not that straightforward. Article 3, as we explained in **chapter 3**, has a relatively high threshold which must be crossed before the courts will intervene. Moreover, there are circumstances where one person's dignity has to be breached in order to protect another's dignity. In the circumstances of *A & B v East Sussex County Council*, the conflict was between the rights of the service users and the rights of those who were employed to care for them. Mr Justice Munby considers this conflict in his judgment. The relevant paragraphs are set out in **Box 11.11**. They contain a useful reminder of the value of compassion and the human touch as a prerequisite of humanity and dignity.

BOX 11.11 Dignified ends and undignified means—*A & B v East Sussex County Council* (2003), paras 120–122

120 I recognise of course that the compassion of the carer is itself a vital aspect of our humanity and dignity and that at a very deep level of our instinctive feelings we value and need the caring touch of the human hand. That no doubt is one of the reasons why the nobility of compassionate carers as different in their ways as Florence Nightingale, Leonard Cheshire and Mother Teresa resonates so strongly with us. . . . Even those who do not believe in any God know that a human being is more than a machine consisting of a few rather basic chemicals operated by electric currents controlled by some animalistic equivalent of a computer located in the skull—and that, no doubt, is why we have an instinctive and intuitive preference for the touch of the human hand rather than the assistance of a machine. As disabled persons or invalids our instinctive preference is to be fed by a nurse with a spoon rather than through a naso-gastric or gastrostomy tube.

121 But, and this is the first point, insistence on the use of dignified means cannot be allowed to obstruct more important ends. On occasions our very humanity and dignity may itself demand that we be subjected to a certain amount—sometimes a very great deal—of indignity. Dignified ends may sometimes demand the use of undignified means. The immediate dignity of a person trapped in a blazing building is probably the very last thing on his mind or in the mind of the fireman who bundles him undignified out of the window to save his life. And one thinks of the gross violence and indignity of the methods necessarily used by the crash team in its desperate efforts to save life in the Accident and Emergency Department. But this does not mean that means must be allowed to

triumph over ends. There is a balance to be held—and it is often a very difficult balance to strike. . . . Modern medical law and ethics illustrate the excruciating difficulty we often have in achieving the right balance between using undignified means in striving to achieve dignified ends.

122 The other point is this. One must guard against jumping too readily to the conclusion that manual handling is necessarily more dignified than the use of equipment. A disabled person or invalid may prefer manual handling by a relative or friend to the use of a hoist but at the same time prefer a hoist to manual handling by a stranger or a paid carer. The independently minded but physically disabled person might prefer to hoist himself up from his bath or chair rather than to be assisted even by his devoted wife. Dignity in the narrow context in which it has been used during much of the argument in this case is in truth part of a much wider concept of dignity, part of a complicated equation including such elusive concepts as, for example, (feelings of) independence and access to the world and to others. Hoisting is not inherently undignified, let alone inherently inhuman or degrading . . . It all depends on the context.

Munby J's words are moving and demonstrate the complexity of achieving dignity. There is never a clear answer which will protect dignity in all circumstances. You must be able to carry out the necessary balancing exercise, as described in **chapter 3**, and determine what the priorities are in particular circumstances. Neither should we get carried away with the idea that the law will intervene to protect the dignity of the service user regardless of resource implications. The decision of the Supreme Court in *R (McDonald) v Royal Borough of Kensington and Chelsea* (2011) made that absolutely clear. We will discuss this case further in **chapter 13**. For our purposes, what you need to know is that Ms McDonald argued that requiring her to use incontinence pads when she was not incontinent was a breach of her dignity. Whilst Lord Brown, giving the leading judgment, acknowledged the positive obligation under Article 8 to respect a person's private life, he considered that the consultation process and the attempts to reach agreement with Ms McDonald were sufficient to demonstrate the respect of the Royal Borough of Kensington and Chelsea (RBKC) for Ms McDonald's dignity and autonomy. Not only did he determine that there was no interference by RBKC with Ms McDonald's Article 8 rights, but he also added (at para. 19) that even if he were wrong any interference which was in accordance with the law would be justified:

on the grounds that it is necessary for the economic well-being of the respondents [i.e. the council and its taxpayers] and the interests of their other service-users and is a proportionate response to the appellant's needs because it affords her the maximum protection from injury, greater privacy and independence, and results in a substantial costs saving.

In May 2014 the European Court of Human Rights (ECtHR) heard Ms McDonald's challenge to the Supreme Court decision. Whilst the outcome was not very positive for Ms McDonald (see the discussion in **chapter 13**), the ECtHR did make it clear that dignity is to be given serious consideration in decisions about adult social care. It will be interesting to see how authorities and courts in England and Wales respond to the judgment.

The reluctance of the English and Welsh courts to take a strong stand of human rights is also seen in the litigation on the closure of care homes.

Care homes and the right to a home

The closure of care homes by local authorities has stimulated extensive litigation on behalf of residents of those homes, their carers, and those who use the homes as respite facilities. Their advocates have mounted human rights arguments in efforts to prevent closures. The relevant Articles of the European Convention which may be engaged by the closure of a residential home are Article 8—the right to respect for the home; Article 3—the right not to be subject to degrading treatment; and Article 2—the right to life. In *Dudley Whitbread and others v East Sussex County Council* (2003) the local authority had gone through a consultation exercise with all of those interested in the future of the home and had decided to close it. What the judgment in that case demonstrates is that where the proper processes have been completed, including a proper consideration of human rights arguments, the courts will be reluctant to interfere on the basis of breach of human rights. The issue was revisited in *R (on the application of Verna Wilson and others) v Coventry City Council* and *R (on the application of Victor Thomas and others) v London Borough of Havering* (2008). The main argument here concerned Article 2. The claimants' argument was that the published medical literature, buttressed by two expert reports produced to the court on behalf of the claimants, established that there was a statistically demonstrable increase in the rate of mortality of residents in care homes who are elderly and/or who suffer from dementia when they are moved from care homes where they have lived for a number of years, unless they are moved as a group from one home to another with the staff that have always looked after them. Therefore, if a decision was taken to close a care home without the decision maker being aware of these risks, the authorities had acted in breach of Article 2 of the ECHR in taking the decision. That argument was dependent upon demonstrating that the officers concerned had failed to take the relevant evidence into consideration. The judge rejected the argument following an interesting analysis of the medical evidence, which does not appear to have been quite as clear-cut as claimed, and decided that officials had thought very carefully and followed established protocols about the minimization of risk to residents prior to making the decision to close the home. The judge did concede that the claimants had a potentially arguable point about the necessity for careful timing of individual assessment of risk. The claimants had suggested that the decision was flawed because individual assessments of the residents had not been carried out prior to the decision to close the home. If those individual assessments were carried out subsequently and on a piecemeal basis, there was a risk that residents and staff would be split up, increasing the risk of a rise in mortality rates. However, there was no evidence in this case that this was going to happen, so such an argument would have to wait until a challenge based upon those particular facts.

What the cases demonstrate is that human rights arguments will not prevail in home closure cases as long as they are properly considered during the process of decision making. Officers must ensure that not only is consultation properly carried out, but also that risks are properly managed via competent assessment procedures, that agreed protocols are followed, and that there is clear justification for closure decisions. A good practice guide on care home closure has been published by the Care Quality Commission and

the National Health Service. It is available at www.nhs.uk/NHSEngland/keogh-review/
Documents/quick-guides/1577_QuickGuide-CareHomes_9.pdf.

See also *YL v Birmingham City Council* (2007) considered in **chapter 3**.

Asylum seekers

Judges may have been reluctant to extend the remit of the Human Rights Act in order
to protect the dignity of publicly funded elderly residents of private care homes; however, they have demonstrated much greater activism in response to the needs of asylum
seekers. This is an interesting area of law—30 years ago no one would have imagined
that you would have to show your passport in order to claim welfare benefits. The
combination of the state's increasing reluctance to provide generous benefits, global
migration, and the devastation that conflict and disease have caused to particular parts
of the world have meant that the individual needs of the asylum seeker in the UK have
become a political minefield. This account will only provide a brief outline of this area.

The term 'asylum seeker' is statutorily defined. The definition is set out in **Box 11.12**.

BOX 11.12 Statutory definition of asylum seeker—s. 94(1) of the Immigration
and Asylum Act 1999

a person who is not under 18 and has made a claim for asylum which has been recorded by the
Secretary of State but which has not been determined.

The meaning of a 'claim for asylum' is again statutorily defined. This is set out in **Box
11.13**.

BOX 11.13 A claim for asylum—s. 94(1) of the Immigration and Asylum Act 1999

claim that it would be contrary to the United Kingdom's obligations under the Refugee Convention,
or under Article 3 of the Human Rights Convention, for the claimant to be removed from, or require to
leave, the United Kingdom.

The basic position is that asylum seekers are entitled to accommodation and financial
support whilst they are in the UK. However, for a long time the UK has been concerned
that the generosity of its provisions to asylum seekers has made the UK disproportionately attractive to asylum seekers. Since 1996 there have been legislative efforts to
reduce the benefits that are available to them. A distinction was made between those
asylum seekers who made their claim for asylum at their port of entry on their arrival
in the UK and those who made their claim later, whilst in the country. Those who
made their claim later were excluded from benefits and from homelessness provisions.

The Immigration and Asylum Act 1999 set up the National Asylum Support Service (NASS) and from that time until March 2007 the needs of asylum seekers were to be provided for by this agency. In March 2007 NASS was replaced by the New Asylum Model (NAM)—designed to provide a more effective service. Despite the intentions of the government, however, neither NASS nor NAM actually provide for all of the needs of asylum seekers. Through particularly complex legal gymnastics, some asylum seekers with community care needs have those needs provided by local authorities. It is as a result of this that social workers become involved in asylum cases. We will try to summarize the legal journey below, before explaining the current position.

Clearly, those asylum seekers who claimed asylum too late to be entitled to benefits were in great difficulties. They used their destitution to make claims under the National Assistance Act 1948 (NAA 1948). Their entitlement to accommodation under the NAA 1948 was acknowledged by the Court of Appeal in *R v Hammersmith LBC, ex p M* (1997). Whilst this provided access to local authority support for those asylum seekers who met the criteria set out in the Act, it provided huge difficulties for local authorities, especially in London. The government therefore amended the NAA 1948 to exclude asylum seekers from its remit. The provision is substantially re-enacted within s. 21 of the Care Act 2014. This is set out in **Box 11.14**.

BOX 11.14 Exclusion of asylum seekers from local authority provision—s. 21 of the Care Act 2014

(1) A local authority may not meet the needs for care and support of an adult to whom section 115 of the Immigration and Asylum Act 1999 ('the 1999 Act') (exclusion from benefits) applies and whose needs for care and support have arisen solely—

(a) because the adult is destitute, or

(b) because of the physical effects, or anticipated physical effects, of being destitute.

Destitution itself is not a straightforward requirement. The government is seeking to ensure that as few people as possible are defined as destitute in order to limit its financial commitment. The meaning of destitution is set out in s. 95(3) of the Immigration and Asylum Act 1999 in **Box 11.15**.

BOX 11.15 Destitution—s. 95(3) of the Immigration and Asylum Act 1999

For the purposes of this section, a person is destitute if—

(a) he does not have adequate accommodation or any means of obtaining it (whether or not his other essential living needs are met); or

(b) he has adequate accommodation or the means of obtaining it, but cannot meet his other essential living needs.

The approach to destitution is amplified by the Asylum Support Regulations 2000, which require that when assessing whether or not an individual is destitute: (a) the whole family's circumstances must be taken into account; and (b) any other resources which the person might reasonably have access to must also be taken into account. So, for instance, community support for the individual, as long as it will provide essential needs for the next 14 days, must be taken into account.

Asylum seekers who are destitute, and their dependants, receive support, not through the NAA 1948, but through NAM managed by the Borders Agency.

The destitute and infirm asylum seeker

The 1999 amendment to the NAA 1948 used the word 'solely' in describing which asylum seekers are excluded from its remit. In *Westminster City Council v NASS* (2002), the House of Lords distinguished between destitute able-bodied asylum seekers and those who are destitute but infirm. It decided that those who have needs arising from infirmities over and beyond their destitution must have those needs provided for via the local authority. So, the government's efforts to ensure that local authorities have no responsibility to provide for asylum seekers failed. The local authority still has duties to asylum seekers to provide community care services when:

(a) the asylum seeker is destitute;

(b) in addition, the asylum seeker has a need for support services for infirmities caused other than by destitution;

(c) there is no other support available to the asylum seeker, including from NAM.

In these circumstances the local authority will have to assess the asylum seeker's needs.

In 2008, the House of Lords in *R(M) v Slough Borough Council*, considered whether an asylum seeker who was HIV positive, and required medication which needed refrigeration and a doctor's appointment every three months, was entitled to accommodation under s. 21 of the NAA 1948. Overruling the Court of Appeal, it decided that the applicant was not in need of the 'care and attention' that was an essential prerequisite to the provision of accommodation under the NAA 1948. In the opinion of Baroness Hale, the natural and ordinary meaning of 'care and attention' is 'looking after'. This means doing something for the person being cared for which he cannot or should not be expected to do for himself. It does not include the provision of medical care, and therefore the applicant's need for HIV medicine did not amount to a need for care and attention.

In *R (SL) v Westminster City Council* (2011), the Court of Appeal gave further consideration to the meaning of care and attention which was considered by the House of Lords in Slough. SL was a failed asylum seeker who had been granted indefinite leave to remain. He had been homeless and was later admitted to a psychiatric hospital, where he was diagnosed as suffering from mental health problems. Following his discharge, the local authority provided him with assistance in the form of regular weekly meetings with a care coordinator who provided advice and encouragement, monitored his condition and progress, and helped to arrange contact with counselling groups and a 'befriender'. SL also received medical attention. Westminster City Council refused to provide SL with residential accommodation on the basis that he was not in need of care and attention within the meaning of s. 21(1)(a). The Court of Appeal disagreed. It decided that SL was in need of care and attention, and that the judge at the High Court who had rejected SL's claim for judicial review had underestimated the support provided by his care coordinator. It would be absurd for it to provide assistance through a care coordinator without providing stable accommodation. However, Westminster City Council appealed the case to the Supreme Court, which overturned the decision of the Court of Appeal. The decision is reported at [2013] UKSC 27. In essence, the Supreme Court decided that the local authority was entitled to conclude that SL was not in need of 'care and attention' which was not 'otherwise available' to him, such as to require the provision of residential accommodation.

Lord Carnwath concluded:

> the present case is clearly distinguishable on the facts from the [*Westminster v*] *NASS* case. That case had been argued on the footing that the applicant's need for care and attention had arisen not solely because she was destitute 'but also (and largely) because she (was) ill' (Lord Hoffmann, para 49); and it was common ground that she had access to no other accommodation in which she could receive that care and attention (Lord Hoffmann, para 43). Furthermore, her needs affected both the nature and the location of the accommodation. In the present case, by contrast, care and attention can be, and is provided, independently of SL's need for accommodation or its location. Indeed, it was not in dispute that similar support services could be provided anywhere in the country.

Human rights and late asylum claims

There is a further complexity caused by the requirement for asylum seekers to claim asylum as soon as reasonably practicable after their arrival in the UK. If they fail to do so, then those applicants who do not have dependent children can be excluded from support under s. 55 of the Nationality, Immigration and Asylum Act 2002 (NIAA 2002). Moreover, those who if they had claimed in time would have been entitled to community care services under the NAA 1948 are excluded as a result of amendments made to s. 21 of the NAA 1948 by s. 54 of and Schedule 3 to the NIAA 2002. However, the government is required to 'secure to everyone within their jurisdiction' the rights contained within the ECHR. This includes failed asylum seekers. The government's responsibility is recognized within s. 55(5)(a), which provides that the Secretary of State is not prevented from making provision to the extent necessary to prevent a breach of an applicant's human rights.

In *R (Adam, Limbuela and Tesema) v SSHD* (2005), the House of Lords considered the severity of the consequences of denial of support that an asylum seeker must suffer in order for there to be a violation of his or her human rights. Lord Bingham, the senior Law Lord at the time of the judgment, indicated when such a situation would arise. The relevant paragraphs of his opinion are set out in **Box 11.16**.

BOX 11.16 Violation of human rights—Lord Bingham in R (Adam, Limbuela and Tesema) v SSHD (2005)

Treatment is inhuman or degrading if, to a seriously detrimental extent, it denies the most basic needs of any human being. As in all Art. 3 cases, the treatment, to be proscribed, must achieve a minimum standard of severity, and I would accept that in a context such as this, not involving the deliberate infliction of pain or suffering, the threshold is a high one. A general public duty to house the homeless or provide for the destitute cannot be spelled out of Art. 3. But I have no doubt that the threshold may be crossed if a late applicant with no means and no alternative sources of support, unable to support himself, is, by the deliberate action of the state, denied shelter, food or the most basic necessities of life. It is not necessary that treatment, to engage Art. 3, should merit the description used, in an immigration context, by Shakespeare and others in *Sir Thomas More* when they referred to 'your mountainish inhumanity'.

When does the Secretary of State's duty under s. 55(5)(a) arise? The answer must in my opinion be: when it appears on a fair and objective assessment of all relevant facts and circumstances that an individual applicant faces an imminent prospect of serious suffering caused or materially aggravated by denial of shelter, food or the most basic necessities of life. Many factors may affect that judgment, including age, gender, mental and physical health and condition, any facilities or sources of support available to the applicant, the weather and time of year and the period for which the applicant has already suffered or is likely to continue to suffer privation.

It is not in my opinion possible to formulate any simple test applicable in all cases. But if there were persuasive evidence that a late applicant was obliged to sleep in the street, save perhaps for a short and foreseeably finite period, or was seriously hungry, or unable to satisfy the most basic requirements of hygiene, the threshold would, in the ordinary way, be crossed.

It is unfortunate that the test cannot be stated simply. Nonetheless, the position of failed asylum seekers who are in need of accommodation under s. 21 of the NAA 1948 will receive those services if failure to provide them would mean that the government would be in breach of its obligations under the ECHR. Moreover, the judges appear to be determined to hold the government to account over its human rights responsibilities to asylum seekers.

Citizenship

So far in this chapter we have considered the concept of dignity as a driver to improve standards of service for the adult service user. There is another concept—citizenship—which is also used as a way of reminding service providers that decent services are an entitlement of service users, and not a privilege. Citizenship is an aspect of human rights, as Mr Justice Munby reminded us in his decision in *A & B v East Sussex County Council* (see **Box 11.17**).

BOX 11.17 Citizenship and social inclusion—extract from *A & B v East Sussex County Council* (2003)

The other important concept embraced in the 'physical and psychological integrity' protected by article 8 is the right of the disabled to participate in the life of the community and to have what has been described (see below) as 'access to essential economic and social activities and to an appropriate range of recreational and cultural activities'. This is matched by the positive obligation of the State to take appropriate measures designed to ensure to the greatest extent feasible that a disabled person is not 'so circumscribed and so isolated as to be deprived of the possibility of developing his personality'.

This aspect of article 8 appears from *Botta [v Italy:* ECtHR case 153/1996/772/973] itself, where the claim was brought by a physically disabled man who went on holiday to a seaside resort but was unable to gain access to a private beach and the sea because they were not equipped with disabled facilities. As the Court explained at 255 (para [27]):

> The applicant complained, firstly, of impairment of his private life and the development of his personality resulting from the Italian State's failure to take appropriate measures to remedy the omissions imputable to the private bathing establishments of Lido degli Estensi (Comacchio), namely the lack of lavatories and ramps providing access to the sea for the use of disabled people. He relied on Article 8 of the Convention . . . The applicant asserted that he was unable to enjoy a normal social life which would enable him to participate in the life of the community and to exercise essential rights, such as his non-pecuniary personal rights, not because of interference by the State but on account of its failure to discharge its positive obligations to adopt measures and to monitor compliance with domestic provisions relating to private beaches.

The Court dismissed the complaint, but the grounds on which it did so are revealing (at 257 paras [34]–[35]):

> [34] The Court has held that a State has obligations of this type where it has found a direct and immediate link between the measures sought by an applicant and the latter's private and/or family life . . .
>
> [35] In the instant case, however, the right asserted by Mr Botta, namely the right to gain access to the beach and the sea at a place distant from his normal place of residence during his holidays, concerns interpersonal relations of such broad and indeterminate scope that there can be no conceivable direct link between the measures the State was urged to take in order to make good the omissions of the private bathing establishments and the applicant's private life.

I have also been referred to the opinion of the Commission in *Botta* and, in particular, to the concurring opinion of, amongst others, Mr N Bratza (as he then was) at 250–252. His opinion, if I may say so, is important and merits quotation at some length: 'As the majority have recalled, although "the object of Article 8 is essentially that of protecting the individual against arbitrary interference by the public authorities", thereby imposing primarily negative obligations [i.e. not to interfere with a person's rights rather than actively to enhance them] on the Contracting States, this provision may nonetheless, in certain cases, impose on those States positive obligations inherent in an effective respect for private life. These positive obligations "may involve the adoption of measures designed to secure respect for private life even in the sphere of the relations of individuals between themselves".'

We believe this to be the case. Such positive obligations may exceptionally arise in the case of the handicapped in order to ensure that they are not deprived of the possibility of developing social relations with others and thereby developing their own personalities. In this regard, the Commission observes that there is no water-tight division separating the sphere of social and economic rights from the field covered by the Convention.

In the case of the physically handicapped, the above-mentioned positive obligations require appropriate measures to be taken, to the greatest extent feasible, to ensure that they have access to essential economic and social activities and to an appropriate range of recreational and cultural activities. The precise aim and nature of the measures undertaken may vary from place to place, and according to the priorities of facilitating access to sanitary facilities, footpaths, transport, entrances to buildings, historical sites, areas of natural beauty, and areas of recreational use. In the case of the mentally handicapped, the measures would necessarily be different. This is an area in which a wide discretion must inevitably be accorded to the national authorities. Nevertheless, the crucial factor is the extent to which a particular individual is so circumscribed and so isolated as to be deprived of the possibility of developing his personality.

As Mr Justice Munby indicates, citizenship is generally understood as the right to participate in the life of the community.

Ideas of citizenship are promoted by the government. This is evident in the statement, *A Vision for Adult Social Care: Capable Communities and Active Citizens*, published in November 2010, which we discussed earlier (**The context of the Care Act 2014—a crisis in adult social care?**, p 423). The vision claims to be a new direction but it continues the personalization agenda, the use of direct payments, and the empowerment of carers. There are also critical perspectives on these initiatives, which point out that the vision is a very consumer-orientated view of citizenship, attempting to transform the user of social care services into an effective participant in a market system. This may limit the effectiveness of citizenship as a driver for change.

The EHRC takes a different approach. Its understanding of citizenship is very much based upon the human rights of individuals. In a paper setting out its approach to the reform of adult social care, *From Safety Net to Springboard: A New Approach to Care and Support for all Based on Equality and Human Rights*, published in February 2009, it provides seven principles which it considers should underpin any reform. These are:

- Care and support based on clear outcomes and founded on human rights and equality.
- Access to publicly funded care and support based on clear, fair and consistent criteria.
- Individuals and families in control of their care and support.
- The right balance between safety and risk to promote choice and independence.
- Local strategic partnerships that play a central role in developing and maintaining local care and support.
- Funding that balances affordability and sustainability with fairness.
- Equality and human rights law and practice re-calibrated to respond to our ageing society.

These principles provide a very useful framework for you to evaluate the Care Act 2014 and other legal developments relating to adult social care.

SUMMARY

In this chapter we have considered:

- the meaning and scope of adult social care;
- the role of local authorities and the health/social care divide;
- the principles underpinning the Care Act 2014;
- overarching legal principles including human rights, dignity, and citizenship, as well as looking at the implications of the public sector equality duty.

EXERCISES

1 To what extent does the Care Act 2014 resolve the crisis of adult social care?

2 Find the latest statistics on adult social care provision. Does your local area have particular plans for cuts in adult social care provision? What do you think the impact of cuts will be?

3 Locate responses to the passing of the Care Act 2014. What do pressure groups think of the new legislation?

ONLINE RESOURCES

For guidance on how to answer these exercises, visit the online resources at www.oup.com/uk/carr-goosey15e.

WHERE DO WE GO FROM HERE?

This chapter has provided an introduction to adult social care, setting current provision in a legal and political context, in particularly introducing the Care Act 2014. **Chapter 12** focuses on the general legislative principles underpinning the Care Act 2014. It also introduces the equivalent piece of legislation for Wales, the Social Services and Well-being (Wales) Act 2014.

ANNOTATED FURTHER READING

The Equality and Human Rights Commission contains extensive information on age and disability issues. Age UK campaigns actively for improved outcomes for older people. Its policy pages provide information about dignity in care, equality and human rights, and adult safeguarding—www.ageuk.org.uk. You can obtain Age UK's 2014 edition of *Care in Crisis* from www.ageuk.org.uk/Documents/EN-GB/Campaigns/CIC/Care_in_Crisis_report_2014.pdf.

Other charities connected with adult social care run useful and informative websites. Mencap, for instance, is the leading campaign organization for learning disability—www.mencap.org.uk.

For something more academic, although with up-to-the-minute commentary on legal and policy developments on community care, we recommend the Small Places blog, authored by Lucy Series, a research assistant at Cardiff Law School, who has a background working in mental health: thesmallplaces.wordpress.com

For those of you who enjoy the legal approach, here are two pieces on the public sector equality duty written by a practising barrister and a judge, respectively:

T. Dyke, 'Judicial review in an age of austerity' (2011) *JR* 16 (3): 202

Mr Justice Sales, 'The public sector equality duty' (2011) *JR* 16 (1): 1.

A more academic and critical approach is taken in the following article:

S. Fredman, 'The public sector equality duty' (2011) *Industrial Law Journal* 40 (4): 405.

One particular article which focuses on the law and dignity is L. Clements, 'Disability, dignity and the *cri de coeur*' (2011) 6 EHRLR 675. This suggests that the judges treat the dignity of the prisoner with far greater respect than the dignity of the recipient of adult social care.

Finally, BBC Radio 4 has produced a number of programmes which cover the care crisis in the UK: www.bbc.co.uk/radio4/features/you-and-yours/care-in-the-uk-2010. They are well worth listening to.

12

The legislative framework for the provision of adult social care and support

 OVERVIEW AND OBJECTIVES

This chapter introduces two major and transformative pieces of legislation—the Care Act 2014 and the Social Services and Well-being (Wales) Act 2014. It summarizes each Act and then spends some time examining the principles underpinning the Care Act 2014 and what it might mean to social care practitioners in England. Although the chapter makes some references to the Welsh legislation, a more detailed analysis of the Welsh legislation is available in the online resources.

CASE STUDY

R (on the application of D) v Worcestershire County Council (2013)

Why are we asking you to read this case?

This case exemplifies the sort of legal challenges mounted by those whose care services are reduced as a result of financial constraints imposed upon local authorities. It challenges—by way of judicial review—the legality of the decision reached by the County Council alleging that its consultation process was flawed and that the council had failed to comply with the public sector equality duty (PSED) which we discussed in **chapters 3 and 11**.

What is at stake for the parties and beyond?

The claimant was resisting attempts to reduce the level of domiciliary care by using the benchmark of the costs of a residential care placement. The council was attempting to balance its budget and ration provision in a reasonable and fair way. More broadly, the case concerns the affordability of care provision. It also raises the issue as to whether the courts are the appropriate place to resolve such dilemmas.

Background

Following the financial crisis of 2008 and the election of the Coalition Government in 2010 the Government, as part of its austerity programme, set limits on local authority spending. In 2012 Worcestershire County Council, faced with a reduction in its income, and in common with many other local authorities, decided that cuts had to be made to its adult social care budget. It proposed a policy to reduce its expenditure on home care provision. In essence, unless there were exceptional circumstances, the proposal was that the maximum weekly expenditure on care in the community or domiciliary care for adults under 65 would be no more than the net weekly cost of a care home placement that could be commissioned to meet the individual's assessed eligible needs. If the support plan for care in the home exceeded the cost of residential care, then alternative care arrangements would be considered. The draft policy was accompanied by an equality impact assessment (EIA) which noted that the need to support people in a way reflecting their preferences had to be balanced against the local authority's responsibility to make best use of available resources. Following a number of consultation events, the policy was adopted in November 2012.

The proposals were challenged by D, a 17-year-old who received a high level of 24-hour care for his medical conditions in his home. He, and his mother, were concerned that the arrangements under the policy would not properly address his needs in the future. D was supported by a large number of campaigners who had grave concerns about the proposals. Note that the council had given assurances that it would not be applied retrospectively.

There were two grounds to the challenge. First, that the consultation process was flawed and, second, that the council had failed to comply with the PSED—Equality Act 2010, s. 149 (discussed in **chapter 11**).

The underlying concern of those campaigning against the proposals was that individuals with high levels of support needs would be forced to go into residential care. The council's response to that concern was as follows:

The cost of a residential home for the individual will only act as a benchmark for comparison with a community care package. Nobody will be forced to live in a residential home as a result of this policy, although some service users may feel it to be more appropriate to do so. It is important to be clear that there may be times when the Council cannot safely meet a person's needs in the community and it may be that residential care is most appropriate to meet their assessed eligible needs. This decision, however, is based on a best interest assessment for the person concerned where they lack mental capacity.

The decision of the court

The judge rejected both the claimant's arguments. He quoted from the Coughlan judgment (1999), discussed in **chapter 11**, to remind himself of the requirements of proper consultation.

> It is common ground that, whether or not consultation of interested parties and the public is a legal requirement, if it is embarked upon it must be carried out properly. To be proper, consultation must be undertaken at a time when proposals are still at a formative stage; it must include sufficient reasons for particular proposals to allow those consulted to give intelligent consideration and an intelligent response; adequate time must be given for this purpose; and the product of consultation must be conscientiously taken into account when the ultimate decision is taken . . .

On that basis he decided that the consultation, despite strenuous arguments from counsel for the claimant, was legally adequate. In particular he decided that:

> In all the circumstances, I am quite sure that, in failing to indicate that the policy would or might result in service users being put to choose between residential care with full support, or home care with less support than is required to meet his or her eligible needs, this consultation was not deficient at all, and certainly was not 'radically wrong'.

Turning to the PSED, and drawing on the particular factual circumstances, he stated that he had no doubt that the Cabinet had had due regard to its PSED, and in particular to the need to advance equality of opportunity.

WHAT DOES THIS CASE TELL YOU ABOUT SOCIAL CARE LAW AND PRACTICE?

Mr Justice Hickinbottom began his judgment with the observation that, 'these are times of considerable financial stringency, challenging for both those who rely upon public services and those who provide them. This is another claim that concerns the consequences of reduced public funding of services, this time adult community care in Worcestershire.' The problem is that it is very difficult to provide adequate care if resources are not available. Although the case predates the Care Act 2014, the challenges that face local authorities remain the same. The Act, as we shall see, places great emphasis on the well-being of individuals, and the need to tailor services to their needs. If individual well-being is continually compromised by lack of funding, the aspirations of the Care Act 2014 will not be achieved.

▩ A summary of the Care Act 2014

The Care Act 2014, which received Royal Assent on 14 May 2014, replaces a multitude of overlapping and complex statutes with a single statute to regulate the provision of adult social care. The purpose of the Act is to consolidate and modernize care and support law. It puts into legislative form an important policy shift: the move from adult social care as a provision-centred service to adult social care as a person-centred service. In other words, the law now supports the approach that requires local authorities to meet individual needs rather than provide standardized services.

The Act is in five Parts. It is the first Part that concerns you most closely. The other Parts relate to care standards and health provision, in part providing a legislative response to the Mid Staffordshire NHS Foundation Trust Public Inquiry.

The government policy that informs the legislation is set out in the White Paper *Caring for Our Future: Reforming Care and Support* (Cm 8378, 2012). Other important background information is contained in the Report of the Commission on the Funding of Care and Support, chaired by Andrew Dilnot, and the recommendations of the Law Commission in its report *Adult Social Care* (Law Com 326, 2011).

Part 1 (Care and Support) applies to local authorities in England only. This is because social care is a devolved matter for Wales. However, the provisions in relation to cross-border placements (s. 39(8) and Sch. 1), certain provisions on provider failure (ss 49–52), and the Human Rights Act 1998 provision (s. 73) also apply to Wales.

Part 1 of the Act sets out the legal framework for the provision of care and support. In summary, ss 1–7 set out the general responsibilities of local authorities. They describe local authorities' broader care and support role towards the local community, including services provided more generally, for instance those with the aim of reducing needs. Sections 8–41 map out the process of assessments, charging, establishing entitlements, care planning, and the provision of care and support. These sections are discussed more fully in **chapter 13**. Sections 42–47 outline the responsibilities of local authorities and other partners in relation to the safeguarding of adults, including a requirement to establish Safeguarding Adults Boards in every area. These sections are discussed more fully in **chapter 14**. Sections 48–57 set out local authorities' responsibilities for ensuring continuity of care where a provider sustains business failure and ceases to provide a service, and provide for the oversight of registered care and support providers by the Care Quality Commission (CQC). Sections 58–66 support the transition for young people between children's and adult care by giving local authorities powers to assess children, young carers, and parent carers. Sections 67–80 set out provisions in relation to independent advocacy (discussed in **chapter 14**), recovering charges owed to the local authority, reviews of funding provisions, appeals, and other miscellaneous matters, including making explicit when the provision of care and support is a function of a public nature being exercised for the purposes of the Human Rights Act 1998, and restating the law relating to delayed discharges.

■ A summary of the Social Services and Well-being (Wales) Act 2014

The National Assembly for Wales has passed its own legislation, the Social Services and Well-being (Wales) Act 2014. This is perhaps an even more ambitious piece of legislation than the Care Act 2014 as it aims to transform both adult and children's services. The Act was preceded by a White Paper, *Sustainable Social Services for Wales: A Framework for Action,* published in 2011. That White Paper highlighted a number of concerns about the provision of care and support services, including demographic changes, increased expectations from those who access care and support, and the problems of austerity.

The Act is in 11 Parts, all of which are of concern to social workers. Usefully, s. 1 of the Act provides a summary of its provisions, extracts from which are set out in Box 12.1.

BOX 12.1 An overview of the Act—extracts from s. 1 of the Social Services and Well-being (Wales) Act 2014

. . .

(3) Part 2 (general duties)—

   (a) requires persons exercising functions under this Act to seek to promote the well-being of people who need care and support and carers who need support (section 5);

   (b) imposes overarching duties on persons exercising functions under this Act in relation to persons who need or may need care and support, carers who need or may need support, or persons in respect of whom functions are exercisable under Part 6, so as to give effect to certain key principles (section 6);

   (c) requires the Welsh Ministers to issue a statement specifying the well-being outcomes that are to be achieved for people who need care and support and carers who need support and to issue a code to help achieve those outcomes (sections 8 to 13);

   (d) requires local authorities to assess the needs in their areas for care and support, support for carers and preventative services (section 14);

   (e) requires local authorities to provide or arrange for the provision of preventative services (section 15);

   (f) requires the promotion by local authorities of social enterprises, co-operatives, user led services and the third sector in the provision in their areas of care and support and support for carers (section 16);

   (g) requires the provision by local authorities of a service providing information and advice relating to care and support and support for carers and assistance in accessing it (section 17);

   (h) requires local authorities to establish and maintain registers of sight-impaired, hearing-impaired and other disabled people (section 18).

(4) Part 3 (assessing the needs of individuals) provides for—

   (a) the circumstances in which a local authority must assess a person's needs for care and support or a carer's needs for support;

   (b) how assessments are to be carried out.

(5) Part 4 (meeting needs) provides for—

    (a) the circumstances in which needs for care and support or support for carers may or must be met by local authorities;

    (b) how needs are to be met.

(6) Part 5 (charging and financial assessment) provides for—

    (a) the circumstances in which local authorities may charge for providing or arranging care and support or support for carers;

    (b) the circumstances in which local authorities may charge for preventative services and the provision of assistance;

    (c) how such charges are to be set, paid and enforced.

. . .

(8) Part 7 (safeguarding)—

    (a) requires local authorities to investigate where they suspect that an adult with care and support needs is at risk of abuse or neglect (section 126);

    (b) provides for adult protection and support orders to authorise entry to premises (if necessary by force) for the purpose of enabling an authorised officer of a local authority to assess whether an adult is at risk of abuse or neglect and, if so, what to do about it (section 127);

    (c) requires local authorities and their relevant partners to report to the appropriate authority where they suspect that people may be at risk of abuse or neglect (sections 128 and 130);

    (d) disapplies section 47 of the National Assistance Act 1948 (which enables local authorities to apply for a court order to remove people in need of care and attention from their homes to hospitals or other places) (section 129);

    (e) establishes a National Independent Safeguarding Board to provide support and advice in order to ensure the effectiveness of Safeguarding Boards (sections 132 and 133);

Even a quick scan of the Act's provisions demonstrates a considerable overlap with the Care Act 2014 in terms of priorities and approaches. Both pieces of legislation emphasize putting the individual and their needs at the centre of their care, prevention and early intervention, and well-being. One interesting feature of the Welsh legislation is that it specifically refers to the need to have due regard to the United Nations Principles for Older Persons adopted by the General Assembly of the United Nations on 16 December 1991.

In order to understand your responsibilities under either piece of legislation, you need not only the Act but the relevant regulations and statutory guidance. We will refer to the regulations relating to the Care Act 2014 where necessary in this chapter and those following. We also include extensive extracts from the statutory guidance to the Care Act 2014 within the text. Similar information with respect to the Social Services and Well-being (Wales) Act 2014 will be provided in the online resources. However, it is important that you read the statutory guidance in full and that you are familiar with its contents and its key messages. You can download the statutory guidance to the Care Act 2014, updated July 2018, from www.gov.uk/government/publications/care-act-statutory-guidance/care-and-support-statutory-guidance.

The Department of Health has produced some useful fact sheets (updated April 2016) to assist practitioners in understanding the law—see www.gov.uk/government/ publications/care-act-2014-part-1-factsheets/care-act-factsheets. The Social Care Institute for Excellence (SCIE) also provides useful and user-friendly guidance: www.scie.org.uk/care-act-2014.

In the rest of the chapter we explain the general principles underpinning the Care Act 2014, making reference to the corresponding sections of the Welsh legislation where appropriate.

The promotion of well-being

Section 1 of the Care Act 2014 is particularly important as a statement of the ethos that should inform the provision of adult social care in England. It sets out the principle that underpins the legislation—the responsibility of the state, and in particular local authorities, to promote individual well-being. From a policy perspective, this approach is not new but it has now been given legislative force.

Box 12.2 sets out the general duty to promote individual well-being—s. 1(1) and (2) of the Act. These indicate the breadth of the meaning of well-being for the purposes of the legislation.

BOX 12.2 General duty to promote well-being—s. 1(1) and (2) of the Care Act 2014

(1) The general duty of a local authority, in exercising a function under this Part in the case of an individual, is to promote that individual's well-being.

(2) 'Well-being', in relation to an individual, means that individual's well-being so far as relating to any of the following—
  (a) personal dignity (including treatment of the individual with respect);
  (b) physical and mental health and emotional well-being;
  (c) protection from abuse and neglect;
  (d) control by the individual over day-to-day life (including over care and support, or support, provided to the individual and the way in which it is provided);
  (e) participation in work, education, training or recreation;
  (f) social and economic well-being;
  (g) domestic, family and personal relationships;
  (h) suitability of living accommodation;
  (i) the individual's contribution to society.

Note that the duty is a general duty—this means that it is not directly enforceable as an individual right, but may well be taken into account when decisions are challenged via judicial review—see, for instance, *R (JF) v Merton LBC* (2017), where the High Court considered the impact of the duty on the local authority. You should also note *R (on the application of VI) v Lewisham LBC* (2018), where the High Court found that a holistic approach to the duty is sufficient.

Local authorities should review their provision to ensure that it complies with the duty. The statutory guidance points out (at para. 1.6) that *all* aspects of well-being set out in the section should be considered of equal importance when considering an individual's well-being 'in the round'.

The matters that a local authority must take into account when making decisions about individual service provision are set out in s. 1(3) and listed in **Box 12.3**.

 BOX 12.3 Individual service provision—s. 1(3) of the Care Act 2014

- the importance of beginning with the assumption that the individual is best placed to judge the individual's well-being;
- the individual's views, wishes, feelings, and beliefs;
- the need to ensure that decisions about the individual are made having regard to all the individual's circumstances (and are not based only on the individual's age or appearance or any condition of the individual's or aspect of the individual's behaviour which might lead others to make unjustified assumptions about the individual's well-being);
- the importance of the individual participating as fully as possible in decisions relating to the exercise of the function concerned and being provided with the information and support necessary to enable the individual to participate;
- the importance of achieving a balance between the individual's well-being and that of any friends or relatives who are involved in caring for the individual;
- the need to protect people from abuse and neglect;
- the need to ensure that any restriction on the individual's rights or freedom of action that is involved in the exercise of the function is kept to the minimum necessary for achieving the purpose for which the function is being exercised.

Note that what is required is active consideration of a service user's well-being at all stages of that user's involvement with the local authority, from the provision of information and advice to the reviewing of a care and support plan. The list is not set out in order of importance, nor is it exhaustive. There may be other factors that decision makers may need to take into consideration. The guidance indicates—at para. 1.8, set out in **Box 12.4**—the extent to which a local authority should respond to the particular circumstances and needs of the service user.

 BOX 12.4 Provision for particular circumstances and needs of the service user—para. 1.8 of Care and support statutory guidance (updated October 2018)

1.8 A local authority can promote a person's wellbeing in many ways. How this happens will depend on the circumstances, including the person's needs, goals and wishes, and how these impact on their wellbeing. There is no set approach—a local authority should consider each case on its own merits, consider what the person wants to achieve, and how the action which the local authority is taking may affect the wellbeing of the individual.

You may be surprised that independent living is not specifically mentioned within the section. The guidance indicates that this is because the government viewed 'independent living' as a relatively abstract term, and it wanted the legislation to focus on outcomes. However, paras 1.18–1.19 of the guidance, set out in **Box 12.5**, explains the centrality of independent living to the ethos of the Care Act 2014.

BOX 12.5 Independent living—paras 1.18 and 1.19 of Care and support statutory guidance (updated October 2018)

1.18 Although not mentioned specifically in the way that wellbeing is defined, the concept of 'independent living' is a core part of the wellbeing principle. Section 1 of the Care Act includes matters such as individual's control of their day-to-day life, suitability of living accommodation, contribution to society—and crucially, requires local authorities to consider each person's views, wishes, feelings and beliefs.

1.19 The wellbeing principle is intended to cover the key components of independent living, as expressed in the UN Convention on the Rights of People with Disabilities (in particular, Article 19 of the Convention). Supporting people to live as independently as possible, for as long as possible, is a guiding principle of the Care Act. The language used in the Act is intended to be clearer, and focus on the outcomes that truly matter to people, rather than using the relatively abstract term 'independent living'.

The Welsh legislation also starts by emphasizing well-being—see s. 2 of the Social Services and Well-being (Wales) Act 2014. There is a considerable overlap in the meaning given to well-being in both pieces of legislation. One interesting difference is that the Welsh legislation includes a specific reference to securing rights and entitlements. The Welsh legislation applies to child as well as adult well-being. There are additional meanings given to well-being in children for whom physical, intellectual, emotional, social, and behavioural development should be taken into account.

The question of whether there is substance to the legislative principle of well-being, particularly at a time when resources for care and support are being reduced, remains to be answered. In June 2016, the High Court gave permission for a disabled man to bring a legal challenge against a local authority's decision to reduce his care package—the first such challenge under the Care Act 2014. The challenge was made on the basis that it breached several statutory duties under the Care Act, including the duty to 'promote an individual's wellbeing' set out in s. 1 and the duty to meet an individual's unmet eligible needs set out in s. 18. It will be interesting to see whether the implementation of the Care Act makes a difference to how the judges determine challenges to reductions in provision.

Principal social workers

The guidance to the Care Act 2014 makes clear the importance of social work leadership in ensuring that the well-being ethos is properly embedded in adult social care and support. The guidance sets out the expectation that local authorities will appoint a principal social worker, who will:

• lead and oversee excellent social work practice;

- support and develop arrangements for excellent practice;

- lead the development of excellent social workers;

- support effective social work supervision and decision making;

- oversee quality assurance and improvement of social work practice;

- advise the director of adult social services (DASS) and/or wider council in complex or controversial cases and on developing case or other law relating to social work practice;

- function at the strategic level of the Professional Capabilities Framework.

The statutory guidance stresses that principal social workers can only be effective if they are given appropriate support by their local authority. The relevant paragraphs of the statutory guidance are set out in **Box 12.6**.

BOX 12.6 The local authority role in supporting principal social workers—para. 1.28 of Care and support statutory guidance (updated October 2018)

1.28 All local authorities should ensure principal social workers are given the credibility, authority and capacity to provide effective leadership and challenge, both at managerial and practitioner level and are given sufficient time to carry out their role. The principal social worker should also be visible across the organisation, from elected members and senior management, through to frontline social workers, people who use services and carers. Local authorities should therefore ensure that the role is located where it can have the most impact and profile.

Note that the principal social worker has an important role in keeping up to date with legislation and case law. The guidance specifically states that principal social workers should have extensive knowledge of the legal and social work response options to specific cases and in general (para. 1.31). Being on top of the law is essential to the provision of good services to vulnerable adults. This is particularly important in the context of adult safeguarding, which we discuss in **chapter 14**.

Preventative services

Section 2 of the Act—set out in **Box 12.7**—ensures that local authorities provide, or arrange to be provided, preventative services. This responds to particular concerns that previous legislation failed to provide for the need for services which prevented or delayed the need for care and support services. Norman Lamb, Minister for Health when the Care Bill was going through Parliament, explained its importance; 'For the first time (the law) creates a clear, legal duty on local authorities to ensure the provision of preventative services. It is across the board; it is not related to those individuals who have met the eligibility threshold; it is across the local community' (Hansard, 9 January 2014 col. 49).

BOX 12.7 Preventing needs for care and support—s. 2 of the Care Act 2014

(1) A local authority must provide or arrange for the provision of services, facilities or resources, or take other steps, which it considers will—

    (a) contribute towards preventing or delaying the development by adults in its area of needs for care and support;

    (b) contribute towards preventing or delaying the development by carers in its area of needs for support;

    (c) reduce the needs for care and support of adults in its area;

    (d) reduce the needs for support of carers in its area.

(2) In performing that duty, a local authority must have regard to—

    (a) the importance of identifying services, facilities and resources already available in the authority's area and the extent to which the authority could involve or make use of them in performing that duty;

    (b) the importance of identifying adults in the authority's area with needs for care and support which are not being met (by the authority or otherwise);

    (c) the importance of identifying carers in the authority's area with needs for support which are not being met (by the authority or otherwise).

The local authority's responsibilities for prevention apply to all adults, including:

- people who do not have any current needs for care and support;

- adults with needs for care and support, whether their needs are eligible and/or met by the local authority or not;

- carers, including those who may be about to take on a caring role or who do not currently have any needs for support, and those with needs for support which may not be being met by the local authority or other organization.

Note that the duty in s. 2(1) is not to *achieve* prevention/delay and/or reduction in needs but to do what the local authority considers will '*contribute towards*' prevention/ delay and/or reduction. This appears a weak duty for something which is a cornerstone of the legislation and designed to reduce future needs for care. The duty in s. 2(2) is also limited—the local authority '*must have regard to the importance of . . .*' . So as long as the local authority pays attention to the issue, there is nothing that prescribes what has to be done or achieved. It is arguable whether the preventive duty in s. 15 of the Social Services and Well-being (Wales) Act 2014 is more powerful. Section 15 provides that 'A local authority must provide or arrange for the provision of a range and level of services which it considers will achieve' the preventive purposes set out in the next sub-section of the statute. This provision will be discussed further in the online resources. Of course, both provisions are carefully worded so as to avoid too extensive a claim on the public purse. It is lack of money which is probably going to sound the death knell for preventive services. As Professor Luke Clements observes in his online and regularly updated overview of adult social services law (available at www.lukeclements.co.uk/category/whats-new).

> Given the very serious financial problems of most local authorities and the lack of any signifi-
> cant 'new' money to accompany this legislation—it is difficult to see how (in the short term)
> this duty can be made to be more than cosmetic. To invest in preventative services, without
> new money would require a local authority to disinvest in an existing area. In many local
> authorities this would require (in essence) disinvestment in crisis services and this is unrealistic.

The statutory guidance explains the broad scope of prevention. It stresses that prevention should be seen as an ongoing consideration rather than a single activity or intervention. It provides useful case studies of a variety of approaches to preventative action.

The Care Act 2014 pays much more attention than previous legislation to the role
of carers and to their needs for support. One example of this is the emphasis that the
statutory guidance places on preventive services for carers. **Box 12.8** sets out para. 2.16,
which explains interventions that can assist carers.

BOX 12.8 Carers and preventative interventions—para. 2.16 of Care and support
statutory guidance (updated October 2018)

2.16 Carers play a significant role in preventing the needs for care and support for the people they care
for, which is why it is important that local authorities consider preventing carers from developing needs
for care and support themselves. There may be specific interventions for carers that prevent, reduce or
delay the need for carers' support. These interventions may differ from those for people without caring
responsibilities. Examples of services, facilities or resources that could contribute to preventing, delay-
ing or reducing the needs of carers may include but is not limited to those which help carers to:

- care effectively and safely—both for themselves and the person they are supporting, e.g. timely
  interventions or advice on moving and handling safely or avoiding falls in the home, or training for
  carers to feel confident performing basic care tasks

- look after their own physical and mental health and wellbeing, including developing coping
  mechanisms

- make use of IT and other technology

- make choices about their own lives, for example managing their caring role and paid employment

- find support and services available in their area

- access the advice, information and support they need including information and advice on welfare benefits and other financial information and about entitlement to carers' assessments.

Preventative services, like other forms of care and support, are not necessarily provided free of charge. The Care and Support (Preventing Needs for Care and Support)
Regulations 2014 allow local authorities to make a charge for certain preventative services, facilities, or resources. The regulations also provide that some other specified
services must be provided free of charge. The statutory guidance, at paras 2.57–2.59 set
out in **Box 12.9** advises on how to approach charging for preventive services.

BOX 12.9 Charging for preventive services and activities—paras 2.57–2.59 of Care and support statutory guidance (updated October 2018)

2.57 Where a local authority chooses to charge for a particular service, it should consider how to balance the affordability and viability of the activity with the likely impact that charging may have on uptake. In some cases, charging may be necessary in order to make a preventative service viable or keep a service running.

2.58 When charging for any type of preventative support, local authorities should take reasonable steps to ensure that any charge is affordable for the person concerned. This does not need to follow the method of the financial assessment used for mainstream charging purposes; and the use of such a process is likely to be disproportionate.

2.59 However, local authorities should consider adopting a more proportionate or 'light-touch' approach which ensures that charges are only paid by those who can afford to do so. In any event, a local authority must not charge more than it costs to provide or arrange for the service, facility or resource.

2.60 The regulations require that intermediate care and reablement provided up to 6 weeks, and minor aids and adaptations up to the value of £1,000 must always be provided free of charge.

Information and advice

A person-centred service which prioritizes choice must ensure that service users and potential service users are fully appraised of the range of services that are available to them for both care and support. Section 4 of the Care Act 2014, set out in **Box 12.10**, imposes a duty.

A similar duty is provided for in s. 17 of the Social Services and Well-being (Wales) Act 2014.

BOX 12.10 A duty to provide information and advice relating to care and support—s. 4 of the Care Act 2014

(1) A local authority must establish and maintain a service for providing people in its area with information and advice relating to care and support for adults and support for carers.

(2) The service must provide information and advice on the following matters in particular—

    (a) the system provided for by this Part and how the system operates in the authority's area,

    (b) the choice of types of care and support, and the choice of providers, available to those who are in the authority's area,

    (c) how to access the care and support that is available,

    (d) how to access independent financial advice on matters relevant to the meeting of needs for care and support, and

    (e) how to raise concerns about the safety or well-being of an adult who has needs for care and support.

(3) In providing information and advice under this section, a local authority must in particular—

   (a) have regard to the importance of identifying adults in the authority's area who would be likely to benefit from financial advice on matters relevant to the meeting of needs for care and support, and

   (b) seek to ensure that what it provides is sufficient to enable adults—

      (i) to identify matters that are or might be relevant to their personal financial position that could be affected by the system provided for by this Part,

      (ii) to make plans for meeting needs for care and support that might arise, and

      (iii) to understand the different ways in which they may access independent financial advice on matters relevant to the meeting of needs for care and support.

(4) Information and advice provided under this section must be accessible to, and proportionate to the needs of, those for whom it is being provided.

The statutory guidance provides useful advice—set out in **Box 12.11**—on this important provision.

BOX 12.11 Information and guidance—paras 3.3–3.5 of Care and support statutory guidance (updated October 2018)

3.3 The local authority has an active and critical role in the provision of information and advice and must take an active role. To fulfil its duty under section 4 of the Act, a local authority is likely to need to go further than providing information and advice directly (though direct provision will be important) by working to ensure the coherence, sufficiency, availability and accessibility of information and advice relating to care and support across the local authority area. Importantly, this duty to establish and maintain an information and advice service relates to the whole population of the local authority area, not just those with care and support needs or in some other way already known to the system.

3.4 It is important to be clear that the duty to establish and maintain an information and advice service is distinct from the duty to meet eligible needs (see chapter 6): this is true for both people with care and support needs and their carers. While a person's eligible needs may be met by the provision of information and advice this will be an individual response following a needs or carers assessment. Local authorities cannot fulfil their universal information and advice duty simply by meeting eligible needs, and nor would information and advice always be an appropriate way of meeting eligible needs.

3.5 The local authority must ensure that information and advice services established cover more than just basic information about care and support and cover the wide range of care and support related areas set out in para. 3.22. The service should also address prevention of care and support needs, finances, health, housing, employment, what to do in cases of abuse or neglect of an adult and other areas where required. In fulfilling this duty, local authorities should consider the people they are communicating with on a case by case basis, and seek to actively encourage them towards the types of information and/or advice that may be particularly relevant to them.

Integration, cooperation, and partnership working

Three sections of the Care Act 2014—ss 3, 6, and 7—are relevant to a discussion of the statutory framework for the proper integration of care and support services for adults with other relevant services. Section 3—set out in **Box 12.12**—requires that local authorities ensure the integration of the health and support needs of service users. Paragraph 9 of the Social Services and Well-being (Wales) Act 2014 contains similar provisions.

BOX 12.12 Promoting integration of care and support with health services—s. 3 of the Care Act 2014

(1) A local authority must exercise its functions under this Part with a view to ensuring the integration of care and support provision with health provision and health-related provision where it considers that this would—

   (a) promote the well-being of adults in its area with needs for care and support and the well-being of carers in its area,

   (b) contribute to the prevention or delay of the development by adults in its area of needs for care and support or the development by carers in its area of needs for support, or

   (c) improve the quality of care and support for adults, and of support for carers, provided in its area (including the outcomes that are achieved from such provision).

Effective provision for vulnerable adults can only be achieved with the proper integration of care and support with health services. Note that health services include housing and leisure services. Chapter 15 of the statutory guidance provides a number of case studies as to how integration can be achieved.

Particular difficulties have arisen in connection with the relationship between the NHS and care and support services. Section 22 of the Care Act 2014 sets out the limits on what a local authority may provide by way of health care and therefore sets the boundary between the responsibilities of local authorities for the provision of care and support and those of the NHS for the provision of health care. Paragraph 15. 31 provides an explanation of the relationship between the local authority and the NHS (see **Box 12.13**).

BOX 12.13 The relationship between the local authority and the NHS—para. 15.31 of Care and support statutory guidance (updated October 2018)

15.31 Where the NHS has a clear legal responsibility to provide a particular service, then the local authority may not do so. This general rule is intended to provide clarity and avoid overlaps, and to maintain the existing legal boundary. However, there is an exception to this general rule, in that the local authority may provide some limited healthcare services as part of a package of care and support, but only where the services provided are 'incidental or ancillary' (that is, relatively minor, and part of a broader package), and where the services are the type of support that an authority whose primary responsibility if [*sic*] to provide social services could be expected to provide.

Difficulties in the integration of care and support services and health services are at their most acute and publicly charged in instances of 'bed-blocking'. 'Bed-blocking' refers to circumstances when a vulnerable adult who is well enough to be discharged from hospital, but because of needs for care and support services, cannot be discharged safely because those services are not available. Schedule 3 to the Care Act 2014 and the Care and Support (Discharge of Hospital Patients) Regulations 2014 ('the Regulations') sets out the current statutory regime designed to facilitate the discharge of these patients. In particular, the provisions enable the NHS to seek reimbursement from local authorities for the costs of delayed discharge. The statutory guidance provides additional explanation—set out in **Box 12.14**.

BOX 12.14 Reimbursement for delayed discharge of adults with care and support needs—paras 15.41 and 15.42 of Care and support statutory guidance (updated October 2018)

15.41 The NHS may seek reimbursement from local authorities for a delayed transfer of care in the circumstances set out in Schedule 3 to the Care Act and its Regulations. The potential for reimbursement liability is intended to act as an incentive to improve joint working between the NHS and local government, but should not be seen in isolation. It is a part of a wider picture in which joint and integrated working is embedded in the Act. The opportunity to seek collaborative solutions to address barriers locally in the first instance is reflected in the use of these reimbursements being made discretionary: see paragraphs 4(1) and (2) of Schedule 3 to the Act.

15.42 NHS and local authorities should develop and adopt collaborative approaches to working together in order to reduce the number of delayed days where a patient is ready to be transferred from NHS acute medical care to other settings regardless of whether the patient falls within the scope of the reimbursement regime. Both the NHS and local authorities owe a common law duty of care to the people within their care. The duties to cooperate in the Care Act 2014 also apply to all transfers of care.

Section 6 of the Act sets out the general duty to cooperate—see **Box 12.15**.

BOX 12.15 Cooperating generally—s. 6 of the Care Act 2014

(1) A local authority must co-operate with each of its relevant partners, and each relevant partner must co-operate with the authority, in the exercise of—
(a) their respective functions relating to adults with needs for care and support,
(b) their respective functions relating to carers, and

(c)   functions of theirs the exercise of which is relevant to functions referred to in paragraph (a) or (b).

(2)   A local authority must co-operate, in the exercise of its functions under this Part, with such other persons as it considers appropriate who exercise functions, or are engaged in activities, in the authority's area relating to adults with needs for care and support or relating to carers.

(3)   The following are examples of persons with whom a local authority may consider it appropriate to co-operate for the purposes of subsection (2)—

(a)   a person who provides services to meet adults' needs for care and support, services to meet carers' needs for support or services, facilities or resources of the kind referred to in section 2(1);

(b)   a person who provides primary medical services, primary dental services, primary ophthal-mic services, pharmaceutical services or local pharmaceutical services under the National Health Service Act 2006;

(c)   a person in whom a hospital in England is vested which is not a health service hospital as defined by that Act;

(d)   a private registered provider of social housing.

Note how wide the duty to cooperate is, and that the duty is not solely on the local author-ity to cooperate with partners in service delivery but is also on those partners to cooperate with it. The statutory guidance explains the importance of this—see **Box 12.16**.

BOX 12.16 Cooperation with and between partners—paras 15.15 and 15.16 of Care and support statutory guidance (updated October 2018)

15.15 All public organisations should work together and co-operate where needed, in order to ensure a focus on the care and support (including carers' support) and health and health-related needs of their local population. Whilst there are some local services where the local authority must actively promote integration, in other cases it must nonetheless co-operate with relevant local and national partners.

15.16 Co-operation between partners should be a general principle for all those concerned, and all should understand the reasons why co-operation is important for those people involved. The Act sets out 5 aims of co-operation between partners which are relevant to care and support, although it should be noted that the purposes of co-operation are not limited to these matters:

• promoting the wellbeing of adults needing care and support and of carers

• improving the quality of care and support for adults and support for carers (including the out-comes from such provision)

• smoothing the transition from children's to adults' services

• protecting adults with care and support needs who are currently experiencing or at risk of abuse or neglect

• identifying lessons to be learned from cases where adults with needs for care and support have experienced serious abuse or neglect.

In addition to the general duty to cooperate, s. 7 of the Act provides an express duty to cooperate where a local authority makes a specific request. The partner or authority to whom the request is made must comply unless it considers that doing so would: (a) be incompatible with its own duties; or (b) have an adverse effect on the exercise of its functions.

Diversity of provision

The Care Act 2014 places a great deal of emphasis on the need to produce a diverse market of care and support services in order to ensure that high-quality and personalized services can be provided—see paras 4.1–4.3 of the statutory guidance set out in **Box 12.17**.

BOX 12.17 The importance of market shaping and commissioning—paras 4.1–4.3 of Care and support statutory guidance (updated October 2018)

4.1 High-quality, personalised care and support can only be achieved where there is a vibrant, responsive market of service providers. The role of the local authority is critical to achieving this, both through the actions it takes to commission services directly to meet needs and the broader understanding of and interactions it undertakes with, the wider market, for the benefit of all local people and communities.

4.2 The Care Act places new duties on local authorities to promote the efficient and effective operation of the market for adult care and support as a whole. This can be considered a duty to facilitate the market, in the sense of using a wide range of approaches to encourage and shape it, so that it meets the needs of all people in their area who need care and support, whether arranged or funded by the state, by the individual themselves, or in other ways. The ambition is for local authorities to influence and drive the pace of change for their whole market, leading to a sustainable and diverse range of care and support providers, continuously improving quality and choice, and delivering better, innovative and cost-effective outcomes that promote the wellbeing of people who need care and support.

4.3 The market for care and support services is part of a wider system in which much of the need for care and support is met by people's own efforts, by their families, friends or other carers, and by community networks. Local authorities have a vital role in ensuring that universal services are available to the whole population and where necessary, tailored to meet the needs of those with additional support requirements (for example housing and leisure services). Market shaping and commissioning should aim to promote a market for care and support that should be seen as broadening, supplementing and supporting all these vital sources of care and support.

The relevant duty is set out in s. 5 of the Care Act 2014—see **Box 12.18**.

BOX 12.18 Promoting diversity and quality in provision of services—s. 5 of the Care Act 2014

(1) A local authority must promote the efficient and effective operation of a market in services for meeting care and support needs with a view to ensuring that any person in its area wishing to access services in the market—

  (a) has a variety of providers to choose from who (taken together) provide a variety of services;

  (b) has a variety of high quality services to choose from;

  (c) has sufficient information to make an informed decision about how to meet the needs in question.

(2) In performing that duty, a local authority must have regard to the following matters in particular—

  (a) the need to ensure that the authority has, and makes available, information about the providers of services for meeting care and support needs and the types of services they provide;

  (b) the need to ensure that it is aware of current and likely future demand for such services and to consider how providers might meet that demand;

  (c) the importance of enabling adults with needs for care and support, and carers with needs for support, who wish to do so to participate in work, education or training;

  (d) the importance of ensuring the sustainability of the market (in circumstances where it is operating effectively as well as in circumstances where it is not);

  (e) the importance of fostering continuous improvement in the quality of such services and the efficiency and effectiveness with which such services are provided and of encouraging innovation in their provision;

  (f) the importance of fostering a workforce whose members are able to ensure the delivery of high quality services (because, for example, they have relevant skills and appropriate working conditions).

In many ways s. 5 of the Care Act 2014 can be seen as the cornerstone of the Act. It is the means through which the outcomes, in particular individual well-being of both adult service users and carers, is to be achieved. Market shaping—defined in paras 4.6 and 4.7 of the statutory guidance, set out in **Box 12.19**—becomes the key function of local authorities.

BOX 12.19 Market shaping—para. 4.6 of Care and support statutory guidance (updated October 2018)

4.6 **Market** shaping means the local authority collaborating closely with other relevant partners, including people with care and support needs, carers and families, to encourage and facilitate the whole market in its area for care, support and related services. This includes services arranged and paid for by the state through the authority itself, those services paid by the state through direct payments, and those services arranged and paid for by individuals from whatever sources (sometimes called 'self-funders'), and services paid for by a combination of these sources. Market shaping activity should stimulate a diverse range of appropriate high quality services (both in terms of the types of services and the types of provider organisation), and ensure the market as a whole remains vibrant and sustainable.

In addition to a focus on outcomes, effective market shaping will seek to improve the quality of provision, in particular by emphasizing the need for a skilled workforce, and will ensure choice and support sustainability. This requires an understanding of the business environment which may not necessarily come naturally to local authorities. The statutory guidance provides extensive advice, an extract from which is set out in **Box 12.20**.

BOX 12.20 Supporting the sustainability of diverse provision—paras 4.33–4.35 of Care and support statutory guidance (updated October 2018)

4.33 Local authorities must work to develop markets for care and support that—whilst recognising that individual providers may exit the market from time to time—ensure the overall provision of services remains healthy in terms of the sufficiency of adequate provision of high quality care and support needed to meet expected needs. This will ensure that there are a range of appropriate and high quality providers and services for people to choose from.

4.34 Local authorities should understand the business environment of the providers offering services in their area and seek to work with providers facing challenges and understand their risks. Where needed, based on expected trends, local authorities should consider encouraging service providers to adjust the extent and types of service provision. This could include signalling to the market as a whole the likely need to extend or expand services, encourage new entrants to the market in their area, or if appropriate, signal likely decrease in needs—for example, drawing attention to a possible reduction in care home needs, and changes in demand resulting from increasing uptake of direct payments. The process of developing and articulating a Market Position Statement or equivalent should be central to this process.

4.35 Local authorities should consider the impact of their own activities on the market as a whole, in particular the potential impact of their commissioning and re-commissioning decisions, and how services are packaged or combined for tendering, and where they may also be a supplier of care and support. The local authority may be the most significant purchaser of care and support in an area, and therefore its approach to commissioning will have an impact beyond those services which it contracts. Local authorities must not undertake any actions which may threaten the sustainability of the market as a whole, that is, the pool of providers able to deliver services of an appropriate quality, for example, by setting fee levels below an amount which is not sustainable for providers in the long-term.

Closely related to the marketization of provision, and no doubt in part triggered by the problems posed by the collapse of Southern Cross, discussed in **chapter 11**, the Act contains a number of provisions to enable local authorities to deal with business failure. Section 48—set out in **Box 12.21**—provides that in the event of the business failure of a private provider of care services the local authority has a temporary duty to step in and make provision for the service users.

BOX 12.21 Temporary duty in the event of business failure—s. 48(2)–(4) of the Care Act 2014

(2) A local authority must for so long as it considers necessary (and in so far as it is not already required to do so) meet those of an adult's needs for care and support and those of a carer's

needs for support which were, immediately before the registered care provider became unable to carry on the regulated activity, being met by the carrying on of that activity in the authority's area by the provider.

(3) A local authority is accordingly required to meet needs under subsection (2) regardless of—

(a) whether the relevant adult is ordinarily resident in its area;

(b) whether the authority has carried out a needs assessment, a carer's assessment or a financial assessment;

(c) whether any of the needs meet the eligibility criteria.

(4) Where a local authority is meeting needs under subsection (2), it is not required to carry out a needs assessment, a carer's assessment or a financial assessment or to determine whether any of the needs meet the eligibility criteria.

Section 50 of the Care Act 2014 imposes a similar duty on local authorities in Wales.

Business failure is defined in the Care and Support (Business Failure) Regulations 2015. It includes situations where a business appoints a receiver, or an administrator, or is wound up, or, if the business is run by an individual, that person is made bankrupt. If a business providing care and/or support services does fail, it is very important that the local authority has contingency plans in place enabling it to react quickly to meet service users' needs, and to manage the anxieties and media interest which inevitably accompany such an event. There are additional provisions within the Act—at ss 53–57—which require the CQC to have market oversight of certain private providers. The Care and Support (Market Oversight Criteria) Regulations 2015 specify the particular circumstances when this additional oversight will apply. Relevant factors include the amount of social care provided by a registered care provider, the geographical concentration of a registered care provider's business, and the extent to which a registered care provider specializes in the provision of particular types of care. The role of the CQC is to monitor the financial sustainability of the providers. Some commentators have raised doubts about whether the CQC has the capacity to do this. The CQC is required to inform local authorities if provider failure is likely so that they can prepare for the local consequences of any business failure.

◼ Charging and financial assessment

The next set of sections we consider set out the new charging regime for adult social care. Local authorities will continue to charge for social care costs, following a means test. The principles underpinning charging regimes are set out in the statutory guidance as follows:

- people should not be charged more than it is reasonably practicable for them to pay;

- there should be a reduction in any variation in the way people are assessed and charged;

- rules should be clear and transparent, so people know what they will be charged;

- charging policies should promote well-being, social inclusion, and support the vision of personalization, independence, choice, and control;

- charging policies should support carers to look after their own health and well-being and to care effectively and safely;

- charging policies should be person-focused, reflecting the variety of care and caring journeys and the variety of options available to meet their needs;

- charging rules should apply equally so those with similar needs or services are treated the same and should minimize anomalies between different care settings;

- charging policies should encourage and enable those who wish to stay in or take up employment, education, or training or plan for the future costs of meeting their needs to do so;

- be sustainable for local authorities in the long-term.

Sections 14–17 set out the government's response to the recommendations of the Dilnot Committee. The sections cap costs, limiting what people will be required to pay for care during their lifetime, and enable the level of the cap to be reassessed annually. The original intention was to introduce a cap of £72,000 in April 2016. However, following expressions of concern from local authorities about the affordability of the cap its implementation was first deferred until 2020 and has now been abandoned (see discussion in **chapter 11**). We are now awaiting a government green paper on the future funding of adult social care.

Sections 34–36 of the Care Act 2014 provide for payments for care to be deferred, meaning that people in residential care will not have to sell their homes during their lifetime to pay for social care. Note that there is no requirement for a home to be sold if the service user's partner is living in the family home. The statutory guidance at paras 9.3–9.6 set out in **Box 12.22** provides some further explanation.

 BOX 12.22 Deferred payments—paras 9.3–9.6 of Care and support statutory guidance (updated October 2018)

9.3 The establishment of the universal deferred payment scheme means that people should not be forced to sell their home in their lifetime to pay for their care. By entering into a deferred payment agreement, a local authority agrees to:

- defer the payment of charges due to it from the adult, for the costs of meeting needs in a care home or supported living accommodation

or

- defer the repayment of a loan to the adult in instalments, to cover the costs of care and support in a care home or supported living accommodation.

> Deferring payment can help people to delay the need to sell their home, and provides peace of mind during a time that can be challenging (or even a crisis point) for them and their loved ones as they make the transition into care.
>
> 9.4 A deferred payment agreement can provide additional flexibility for when and how someone pays for their care and support. It should be stressed from the outset that the payment for care and support is deferred and not 'written off'—the costs of provision of care and support will have to be repaid by the individual (or a third party on their behalf) at a later date.
>
> 9.5 The scheme is universally available throughout England, and local authorities are required to offer deferred payment agreements to people who meet certain criteria governing eligibility for the scheme. Local authorities need to ensure that adequate security is in place for the amount being deferred, so that they can be confident that the amount deferred will be repaid in the future. Local authorities are also encouraged to offer the scheme more widely to anyone they feel would benefit who does not fully meet the criteria.
>
> 9.6 A deferral can last until death, however many people choose to use a deferred payment agreement as a 'bridging loan' to give them time and flexibility to sell their home when they choose to do so. This is entirely up to the individual to decide.

The details of the scheme are set out in the Care and Support (Deferred Payment Agreements) Regulations 2014.

▦ Final points

The next two provisions we draw your attention to in this summary are important ones, added at relatively late stages in the Bill's progress through Parliament. The first, at s. 72, provides for internal appeals against decisions made by local authorities in relation to Part 1 of the Act. It will be interesting to see what happens as a result of this provision. On the one hand, it will provide a facility for people to cheaply and simply challenge the local authority in relation to the provision of care and support. On the other hand, it will limit the extent to which local authority decision making in this area will be scrutinized by judicial review.

Section 73 of the Act extends the Human Rights Act to the private provision of care either in residential or domiciliary settings when that care is funded or arranged by local authorities. This important extension of the Human Rights Act particularly to care services provided in the home reminds us of the importance of human rights and other overarching legal requirements in connection with adult social care.

Finally, we should consider s. 8 of the Care Act 2014. This provides an indicative list of the sort of services that can be made available to service users. This is set out in **Box 12.23**. The section provides a useful end to this chapter and a springboard to considering in more detail individuals' journeys through the care and support system.

BOX 12.23 How to meet needs—s. 8 of the Care Act 2014

(1) The following are examples of what may be provided to meet needs under sections 18 to 20—

    (a) accommodation in a care home or in premises of some other type;

    (b) care and support at home or in the community;

    (c) counselling and other types of social work;

    (d) goods and facilities;

    (e) information, advice and advocacy.

(2) The following are examples of the ways in which a local authority may meet needs under sections 18 to 20—

    (a) by arranging for a person other than it to provide a service;

    (b) by itself providing a service;

    (c) by making direct payments.

SUMMARY

In this chapter we have considered in some detail the provisions of the Care Act 2014. In particular we have looked at:

- the promotion of well-being;

- principal social workers;

- preventative services;

- integration, cooperation, and partnership working;

- diversity of provision, including market provision;

- charging and financial assessment.

EXERCISES

1 Considering the cases referred to in the chapter, what difference, if any, do you think that the implementation of the Care Act 2014 has made to *R (on the application of D) v Worcestershire CC* (2013), the case considered at the start of the chapter?

2 Why was the costs cap within the Care Act not implemented? How do you think care should be funded?

3 Some years ago, your department provided John, who is disabled, with a radio following an assessment of his needs under s. 2 of the Chronically Sick and Disabled Persons Act 1970. John's ability to hear the radio has now declined. What provisions in the Care Act 2014 enable you to provide John with an audio-headphone?

ONLINE RESOURCES

For guidance on how to answer these exercises, visit the online resources at www.oup.com/uk/carr-goosey15e.

WHERE DO WE GO FROM HERE?

This chapter has explained the principles underpinning the Care Act 2014 and—in less detail—provided some information about the Social Services and Well-being (Wales) Act 2014. In **chapter 13** we consider how the adult service user and carers engage with support and care services in more detail, in particular assessment and planning work in the context of adult social care. Sections 8–41 of the Care Act 2014 provide the legislative underpinning for the chapter.

ANNOTATED FURTHER READING

The chapter has referred you to several sources of information about the Care Act 2014. Of particular value are the resources provided by SCIE at www.scie.org.uk/care-act-2014 and the leaflets provided by the Department of Health at www.gov.uk/government/publications/care-act-2014-part-1-factsheets. Many local authorities and charities such as Age UK produce their own briefings, which are very user friendly.

For a more lawyerly take on the Act, we recommend T. Spencer-Lane, *The Care Act Manual* (2nd edn, Sweet & Maxwell, 2015). Tim Spencer-Lane, a lawyer with the Law Commission, was very involved in the drafting of the Law Commission's proposals.

For a more critical approach to the Act read T. Collingbourne, 'The Care Act 2014: a missed opportunity?' in *Web JCLI* (2014) 20(3) at http://webjcli.org/article/view/365/464.

Professor Clements provides an online commentary on the Care Act 2014, which he regularly updates. It is available at www.lukeclements.co.uk/wp-content/uploads/2017/11/Care-Act-notes-updated-2017-08.pdf.

Managing adult social care

13

OVERVIEW AND OBJECTIVES

This chapter looks at what the Care Act 2014 describes as the individual's journey through the care and support system. It looks at the process of assessing someone's needs for care and support, establishing what a person is entitled to receive, care planning, and the provision of care and support. It also considers the relevance of resources to the decisions made about an individual's entitlements. It then looks at some of the mechanisms for ensuring that adult social care services are of sufficient quality. It considers complaints to both the care provider and the local authority, the role of the Care Quality Commission (CQC) (including its dealings with whistle-blowers), and the Local Government Ombudsman.

CASE STUDY

R. (on the application of VI) v Lewisham LBC 2018

Why are we asking you to read this case?

This case provides an early indication of the way the courts will interpret the various duties imposed on local authorities under the Care Act 2014. It also indicates what local authorities need to do in order to ensure that decisions to cut care services to vulnerable adults are lawful.

What was at stake for the parties and beyond?

For the claimant the importance of her case lies in the importance of maintaining a care package which in particular provides her with night-time carers. For her this is necessary for her health and well-being, and indeed her dignity. For the local authority it was about effective management of its increasingly scarce resources and how these are to be rationed amongst an increasing population of vulnerable adults.

Background

The claimant is a 55-year-old woman with muscular dystrophy, who is bed- and wheelchair-bound and requires carer support for all personal care. She is continent, but requires carer assistance and a hoist to use the toilet; she has to wear incontinence pads for periods during the day and night when no carers are in attendance. Lewisham has provided her with services since 2011. At that time, it assessed her needs and concluded that she required support 24 hours a day, with two carers in the morning and evening (a total of 185.5 hours a week). This level of support was in part because she was at risk of bedsores, which were exacerbated by her sitting in her own faeces and urine for hours at a time. In November 2014, a new care package was provided which reduced provision to 104 hours a week provided by direct payments. Her needs were assessed as requiring: (i) 'double-handed' care three times a day amounting to 48 hours (two carers x 24 hours) per week; and (ii) 56 hours' 'single-handed' night sitting (eight hours a night) 'to support with turning in bed at night and change incopad'. In December 2014 a hoist was installed in the Claimant's home, which eliminated the need for double-handed care. Despite the provision of a hoist, the Defendant failed to review the Claimant's care package until February 2016. In June that year, Lewisham wrote to the Claimant informing her that her care package would be reduced, in particular that night-time care (eight hours a night) would be removed as it was considered that this need could be managed through a pressure-relieving mattress and incontinence pads, which by this point the Claimant was already using during the night and day. In July 2016, the Defendant completed a care and support plan that reduced the Claimant's hours to 52 hours a week. In practice, no reduction was implemented, apparently due to administrative oversight on the part of the Defendant, and the Claimant continued to receive direct payments at the rate of 104 care hours a week. Both Citizens Advice and her GP wrote to Lewisham objecting to the reduction of her care package. In August 2016, Lewisham agreed to a reassessment of the Claimant's needs. This took time as it involved a multi-disciplinary team.

In August 2017, the new support plan was completed including a reduced care package of 40 hours a week, based on four one-hour, single-handed personal care visits a day (three visits on Sunday) (27 hours in total), seven hours a week meal preparation, three hours weekly domestic and shopping support, and three hours weekly community support. In relation to 'personal care' the plan stated:

> Care worker to support with full body wash a.m. and p.m. She is to be supported to shower once daily and body wash once daily at end of day. She needs contin[e]nce management support with pads x4 daily, un/dressing a.m. and p.m., grooming daily, medication as prescribed, transfer/mobility per visit as per need and food and drink support daily as per need and request. Food and drink can be provided within the pc [personal care] task 40 hours weekly DP [direct payments] to be used flexibly according to need.

The plan also indicated that '[the Claimant] needs support with social interaction and inclusion' in order to reduce living in isolation and to maintain social interaction, and that the direct payment hours were 'flexible for socialising and accessing the community'. There was to be no provision of night-time care. The plan was to be reviewed at six weeks by the social worker, with district nurse visits twice a week in the meantime to monitor and record. Following complaints from the Claimant, the care package was reassessed in 2018, at which point the Claimant was assisted by a Care Act advocate. In March 2018, the care package was finalized along the lines of the August 2017 care package. This led to a legal challenge by the Claimant.

She argued that the assessment was irrational, and/or unlawful in that it failed to comply with the Care Act 2014 and associated regulations, because:

- the Defendant's conclusion that the Claimant's needs for care and support could be met through a reduction of over 50 per cent in her carer hours was irrational. The Claimant's condition is degenerative and cogent reasons were therefore required for concluding that her care needs had reduced from the previously assessed level. The basis on which the Defendant asserts that the Claimant's needs had hitherto been 'over-provided' was seriously flawed;
- the assessment failed to give proper consideration to the factors in s. 9(4) of the Act, including the well-being factors in section 1(2);
- the Defendant failed to have regard to the need to prevent additional care needs arising through deterioration in the Claimant's mental health and physical well-being (s. 1(3));

- the assessment failed properly to assess the Claimant's care needs against the eligibility outcomes as set out in regulations made under the Act; and
- the Defendant failed to cooperate with NHS services, particularly with occupational therapy and physiotherapy, in assessing the Claimant's needs and the best way to prevent care needs arising in the future.

Decision

The Court found that there was nothing to substantiate the claim that Lewisham had behaved unlawfully. First whilst the judge agreed that the assessments were not detailed but rather conclusory in nature, he points out that 'the case law warns against over-zealous textual analysis and indicates that a social worker's assessment should be construed in a practical way with a view to finding the real substance of the decision. Viewing the assessment in the round, I consider that the decision-maker has not simply adopted the 2016 and 2017 decisions but has had regard to all the current circumstances in considering the Claimant's needs and well-being.' He also pointed to what the assessments did achieve.

> The assessment acknowledges that the Claimant's condition is degenerative (passage [i]). It notes that the trial removal of night care in August 2017 followed consultation with district nurses. It considers the evidence as it currently stands in relation to the Claimant's toileting needs, including the series of reports from the district nursing team referred to in passage [xiv] reporting an absence of pressure sores and intact skin. The Defendant has also recognised that this is a matter which needs to be kept under careful review, and has continued to do so with weekly district nurse visits and periodic social worker visits. The fact that the Claimant complained of wet leggings after outings on Sundays of approximately 5-5½ hours highlights the need for close monitoring of her needs at night during a longer period. However, viewing the assessment as a whole it is not possible in my judgment to conclude that the Defendant's approach has been irrational or that it has failed to have regard to the prescribed factors including the Claimant's individual well-being.
>
> (para. 79)

The assessments also referred to pain management and social isolation. In relation to the duties under the Care Act 2014, the judge concluded:

> I agree with the Defendant that the assessment gave holistic consideration to the well-being factors, including the impact of the revised care package upon the Claimant over the period of six months since it was first introduced in August 2017. The Defendant has monitored (and continues to monitor) whether the Claimant has any additional eligible care needs that may have arisen as a result. There is no or very limited evidence to support the Claimant's assertion that her mental health and physical well-being have significantly deteriorated to the extent that the care package needs to change. Neither the district nurses nor the evidence from the Claimant's GP has given reason to believe that the removal of night time care has led to deterioration in the Claimant's physical or mental well-being, whether in the form of pressure sores, increased pain or mental health problems.
>
> (para. 89)

In relation to the other claims, the judge considered that there was no failure to assess against eligibility outcomes and that there had been appropriate cooperation with other services.

WHAT DOES THIS CASE TELL YOU ABOUT SOCIAL CARE LAW?

The case demonstrates the importance of assessment of individual needs for services. But it also shows how assessment of needs informs part of the rationing of services, because local authorities cannot meet all needs—it would not be affordable. These problems are not new.

In 2012, the Supreme Court, in *R (on the Application of KM (By His Mother and Litigation Friend JM)) v Cambridgeshire County Council* (2012), considered the process of assessing needs, and the role of resources in determining which needs are met provides a useful statement of the law. What he said was that:

> when a local authority is required to consider whether it is 'necessary in order to meet the needs of that person for that authority to make arrangements for' the provision of any of the matters on the service list, it is required to ask itself three questions and should do so in three separate stages:
>
> (i)   What are the needs of the disabled person?
>
> (ii) In order to meet the needs identified at (i), is it necessary for the authority to make arrangements for the provision of any of the listed services?
>
> (iii) If the answer to question (ii) is affirmative, what are the nature and extent of the listed services for the provision of which it is necessary for the authority to make arrangements?

Resources become significant at the second stage. Lord Wilson explains:

> One important aspect of the question raised at the second stage is to ask whether the presenting needs of the disabled person can reasonably be met by family or friends (which I will describe as natural support) or by other organs of the state, such as the NHS, or by charities etc, or indeed out of the person's own resources. But it will by now be clear that the question at the second stage goes far further and, in particular, encompasses consideration of the relationship between the scale of the local authority's resources and the weight of other demands upon it, in other words the availability of its resources. The Care Act 2014 may have changed some of the processes of assessment; what it does not do is change the problems facing local authorities around managing its resources. Nonetheless the duties under the Act are important to ensure that assessments are lawful.

The duty to assess

The assessment process is central to the effective delivery of care and support. The duty to assess an adult's needs is provided by s. 9 of the Care Act 2014 and set out for you in **Box 13.1**. Notice how the needs assessment must place what a service user wishes to achieve in everyday life at the centre of the assessment process.

BOX 13.1 Assessment of an adult's needs for care and support—s. 9 of the Care Act 2014

(1) Where it appears to a local authority that an adult may have needs for care and support, the authority must assess—

   (a) whether the adult does have needs for care and support, and

   (b) if the adult does, what those needs are.

(2) An assessment under subsection (1) is referred to in this Part as a 'needs assessment'.

(3) The duty to carry out a needs assessment applies regardless of the authority's view of—

   (a) the level of the adult's needs for care and support, or

   (b) the level of the adult's financial resources.

(4) A needs assessment must include an assessment of—

   (a) the impact of the adult's needs for care and support on the matters specified in section 1(2),

   (b) the outcomes that the adult wishes to achieve in day-to-day life, and

   (c) whether, and if so to what extent, the provision of care and support could contribute to the achievement of those outcomes.

(5) A local authority, in carrying out a needs assessment, must involve—

   (a) the adult,

   (b) any carer that the adult has, and

   (c) any person whom the adult asks the authority to involve or, where the adult lacks capacity to ask the authority to do that, any person who appears to the authority to be interested in the adult's welfare.

(6) When carrying out a needs assessment, a local authority must also consider—

   (a) whether, and if so to what extent, matters other than the provision of care and support could contribute to the achievement of the outcomes that the adult wishes to achieve in day-to-day life, and

   (b) whether the adult would benefit from the provision of anything under section 2 or 4 or of anything which might be available in the community.

In R (Davey) v Oxfor*dshire CC and others* [2017], the High Court gave an indication as to how the duties within s. 9 would be understood by the courts.

First, the assessment duty is a duty upon the local authority and the assessment under section 9(1)(a) and (b) is an objective assessment made by the local authority (usually acting through its social workers or occupational therapist). Secondly, under section 9(4), there is no duty to achieve the outcomes which the adult wishes to achieve; rather it is a duty to assess whether the provision of care and support could contribute to those outcomes. On the other hand if, in the course of a needs assessment, the local authority does not assess the matters specified in section 9(4) (including the impact on well-being matters set out in section 1(2)) then there is a breach of the statutory duty. There is, thus, a duty on the part of the local authority to assess these factors.

Paragraph 6.3 of the statutory guidance to the Care Act 2014 (updated October 2018 and available at www.gov.uk/guidance/care-and-support-statutory-guidance) describes the different ways that assessment can be carried out (see **Box 13.2**). Note that any assessment must always be appropriate and proportionate.

 BOX 13.2 Carrying out assessments—para. 6.3 of Care and support statutory guidance (updated October 2018)

6.3 An 'assessment' must always be appropriate and proportionate. It may come in different formats and can be carried out in various ways, including but not limited to:

- a face-to-face assessment between the person and an assessor, whose professional role and qualifications may vary depending on the circumstances, but who must always be appropriately trained and have the right skills and knowledge

- a supported self-assessment, which should use similar assessment materials as used in other forms of needs or carers' assessments, but where the person completes the assessment themselves and the local authority assures itself that it is an accurate reflection of the person's needs (for example, by consulting with other relevant professionals and people who know the person with their consent)

- an online or phone assessment, which can be a proportionate way of carrying out assessments (for example where the person's needs are less complex or where the person is already known to the local authority and it is carrying out an assessment following a change in their needs or circumstances)

- a joint assessment, where relevant agencies work together to avoid the person undergoing multiple assessments (including assessments in a prison, where local authorities may need to put particular emphasis on cross-agency cooperation and sharing of expertise)

- a combined assessment, where an adult's assessment is combined with a carer's assessment and/or an assessment relating to a child so that interrelated needs are properly captured and the process is as efficient as possible

---

All that is required to trigger an assessment is that the authority has some awareness of someone's circumstances that indicates that they may have need of community care services. The threshold of knowledge required is very low—see *Bristol City Council, ex p Penfold* (1998) (**Box 13.3**). Local authorities must ensure that they have the necessary infrastructure to ensure that vulnerable individuals are referred for assessment as appropriate.

Notice also that all that is required is that the person *may* have needs—local authorities cannot refuse to carry out an assessment because they do not consider there is any likelihood that any assessed needs will be met. Again, *Bristol City Council, ex p Penfold* provides a useful illustration. The details are set out in **Box 13.3**.

BOX 13.3 *Bristol City Council, ex p Penfold* (1998)

Ms Penfold was a 52-year-old single mother of a dependent teenage daughter. She suffered from anxiety and depression, and received help and care from her family. Ms Penfold applied to Bristol City Council (BCC) for housing under the homelessness provisions of the Housing Act 1985. The council decided that it had an obligation to provide her with suitable accommodation and made two offers of housing, both of which were rejected by Ms Penfold as unsuitable. Ms Penfold then applied to be assessed for entitlement to community care services under s. 47 of the National Health Service and Community Care Act 1990, and for her daughter to be assessed under the Children Act 1989. The application was rejected on the basis that there was no prospect of her being granted any community care service because she did not 'appear' to be a person who required any of the services which the council's resources would enable it to give.

The judge held that under the 1990 Act, local authorities did not have the discretion to refuse to carry out an assessment simply on the basis that a lack of resources would mean that the authority would be unable to provide services to the applicant. On the facts, there had not been any assessment of the needs of either Ms Penfold or of her daughter. There was an obligation to carry out an assessment once she had crossed the threshold test that there may be some need for a service which BCC might be able to provide. BCC had no authority to refuse to carry out such an assessment based on a reasonable belief that no service could be provided in fact. Further, BCC's failure was unlawful on the basis that it did not comply with the policy guidance and because there had been no assessment of Ms Penfold's daughter under s. 21 of the Carers (Recognition and Services) Act 1995.

The purpose of assessment is to identify a person's needs for support and how best to achieve outcomes that maximize their well-being. Paragraphs 6.5 and 6.6 (set out in **Box 13.4**) of the statutory guidance provide further detail.

BOX 13.4 The purpose of assessment—paras 6.5 and 6.6 of Care and support statutory guidance (updated October 2018)

6.5 The aim of the assessment is to identify what needs the person may have and what outcomes they are looking to achieve to maintain or improve their wellbeing. The outcome of the assessment is to provide a full picture of the individual's needs so that a local authority can provide an appropriate response at the right time to meet the level of the person's needs. This might range from offering guidance and information to arranging for services to meet those needs. The assessment may be the only contact the local authority has with the individual at that point in time, so it is critical that the most is made of this opportunity.

6.6 The assessment and eligibility process provides a framework to identify any level of need for care and support so that local authorities can consider how to provide a proportionate response at the right time, based on the individual's needs. Prevention and early intervention are placed at the heart of the care and support system, and even if a person has needs that are not eligible at that time, the local authority must consider providing information and advice or other preventative services. Local authorities must also consider the person's own strengths or if any other support might be available in the community to meet those needs. The assessment and eligibility framework provides for ongoing engagement with the person so where they have eligible needs they are involved in the arrangements put in place to deliver the outcomes they want to achieve.

The important question of what the local authority should do if someone refuses an assessment is dealt with in s. 11 of the Care Act. This is set out in **Box 13.5**. The normal position is to accept the individual's right to refuse an assessment, but you will see in the section two important exceptions relating to incapacity and safeguarding. Of course, if someone changes their mind, or their circumstances change, then the local authority should offer to carry out an assessment.

BOX 13.5 Refusal of assessment—s. 11 of the Care Act 2014

(1) Where an adult refuses a needs assessment, the local authority concerned is not required to carry out the assessment (and section 9(1) does not apply in the adult's case).

(2) But the local authority may not rely on subsection (1) (and so must carry out a needs assessment) if—

    (a) the adult lacks capacity to refuse the assessment and the authority is satisfied that carrying out the assessment would be in the adult's best interests, or

    (b) the adult is experiencing, or is at risk of, abuse or neglect.

The assessment process

Section 12 of the Care Act 2014 provides that regulations will detail how assessment is to be carried out, including, among other things:

- the requirement to have regard to the needs of the family of the adult to whom the assessment relates;
- the need to ensure that the assessment is carried out in an appropriate and proportionate manner;
- the involvement where necessary of people with sufficient expertise in particular conditions;
- the requirement to refer a person to the NHS for assessment of their health needs;
- the circumstances in which joint or self-assessments can take place, and the ability of a local authority to require a third party to carry out the assessment.

There is an important duty within s. 12(3) of the Care Act, designed to protect service users. It is the duty to provide a written record of a needs assessment to the adult to whom the assessment relates, any carer that the adult has, if the adult asks the authority to do so, and any other person to whom the adult asks the authority to give a copy.

The relevant regulations are the Care and Support (Assessment) Regulations 2014. In addition to amplify the requirements above, the regulations also provide for supported self-assessment. An extract from reg. 2 of the Regulations is provided in **Box 13.6**.

BOX 13.6 Supported self-assessment—reg. 2 of the Care and Support (Assessment) Regulations 2014

(1) A supported self-assessment is an assessment carried out jointly by the local authority and the individual to whom it relates.

(2) A local authority proposing to carry out an assessment must ascertain whether the individual to whom the assessment is to relate wishes the assessment to be a supported self-assessment.

(3) A supported self-assessment must be carried out if the individual concerned is an adult and—

   (a) wishes the assessment to be a supported self-assessment; and

   (b) has the capacity to take part in a supported self-assessment.

Supported self-assessment plays an important role in placing the potential service user at the heart of the assessment process. However, this involves risks that the individual will not provide the authorities with an accurate picture of their needs. The statutory guidance provides information and advice to local authorities on how to manage the supported self-assessment process (see **Box 13.7**).

BOX 13.7 Managing supported self-assessment—paras 6.44–6.46 of Care and support statutory guidance (updated October 2018)

6.44 A supported self-assessment is an assessment carried out jointly by the adult with care and support needs or carer and the local authority. It places the individual in control of the assessment process to a point where they themselves complete their assessment form. Whilst it is the person filling in the assessment form, the duty to assess the person's needs, and in doing so ensure that they are accurate and complete, remains with the local authority. Local authorities can offer individuals a supported self-assessment, and must do so if the adult or carer is able, willing and has capacity to undertake it. If the person does not wish to self-assess, then the local authority must undertake an assessment following one of the other processes outlined above.

6.45 In order to support the person in carrying out a supported self-assessment, the local authority must give them any relevant information it has either about the person themselves or, for a carer's self-assessment, about the individual they care for. This is so that the person undertaking the assessment has a full picture of their care and support history and is equipped with the same information an assessor would have when undertaking an assessment. Before sharing any information, the local authority must ensure that the person consents to that information being shared. If the person lacks capacity, information must only be shared where the local authority is satisfied that doing so is in the person's best interests. In the case of a young carer, the local authority must also consider whether it is appropriate to share the information about the person the young carer cares for (see **chapter 16**).

6.46 Once the person has completed the assessment, the local authority must ensure that it is an accurate and complete reflection of the person's needs, outcomes, and the impact of needs on their wellbeing. The process of a supported self-assessment begins with first contact and is only complete when this assurance has been secured. Until the process of assurance is complete and the local authority has ensured that it is accurate, it will not have discharged its duties under section 9 of the Care Act. Where the person carrying out a supported self-assessment jointly with the local authority requires a specialist, for example people who are deafblind, then the professional leading this assurance process must be seen as the 'assessor' and so must have specific training and expertise relating to the individual's needs. When assuring itself that a self-assessment is comprehensive a local authority should not look to repeat the full assessment process again.

The assessment of carers' needs

The Care Act 2014 places carers at the centre of the system of support for vulnerable adults. Under s. 10 of the Act, a local authority must assess a carer's needs for support. The section provides the first clear articulation of the rights of carers to an assessment of their needs. The assessment must take into account the following:

- whether the carer is able, and is likely to continue to be able, to provide care for the adult needing care;
- whether the carer is willing, and is likely to continue to be willing, to do so;
- the impact of the carer's needs for support;
- the outcomes that the carer wishes to achieve in day-to-day life; and
- whether, and if so to what extent, the provision of support could contribute to the achievement of those outcomes.

The local authority must also take into account whether the carer works or wishes to do so, and whether the carer is participating in or wishes to participate in education, training, or recreation. The carer must be involved in the assessment, alongside any other person the carer wishes to involve. Paragraphs 6.18 and 6.19 of the statutory guidance, set out in **Box 13.8**, provide more details.

BOX 13.8 Assessing carers' needs for care and support—paras 6.18 and 6.19 of Care and support statutory guidance (updated October 2018)

6.18 Carers' assessments must seek to establish not only the carer's needs for support, but also the sustainability of the caring role itself, which includes both the practical and emotional support the carer provides to the adult. Therefore, where the local authority is carrying out a carer's assessment, it must include in its assessment a consideration of the carer's potential future needs for support. Factored into this must be a consideration of whether the carer is, and will continue to be, able and willing to care for the adult needing care. Some carers may need support in recognising issues around sustainability, and in recognising their own needs. This will allow local authorities to make a realistic evaluation of the carer's present and future needs for support and whether the caring relationship is sustainable. Where appropriate these views should be sought in a separate conversation independent from the adult's needs assessment.

6.19 The carer's assessment must also consider the outcomes that the carer wants to achieve in their daily life, their activities beyond their caring responsibilities, and the impact of caring upon those activities. This includes considering the impact of caring responsibilities on a carer's desire and ability to work and to partake in education, training or recreational activities, such as having time to themselves. This impact should be considered in both a short-term immediate sense but also the impact of caring responsibilities over a longer term, cumulative sense.

Eligibility criteria

Once a person—whether a service user or a carer—has had their needs for care and support assessed, a local authority has to determine which of those needs it will meet. The Care Act 2014, in a radical departure from previous provisions, puts the system for determining eligibility for care and support services into statutory form. Section 13 of the Care Act—in **Box 13.9**—sets out the basics of the national scheme. The fact that the scheme is nationwide is important. It is an attempt to get rid of local variations in care provision, which was a major criticism of the pre-Care Act 2014 system. On the other hand, Professor Clements is sceptical about whether a national statutory scheme will make a difference in practice. He argues that:

> Research suggests that for both carers and disabled/older people, the content of national criteria is less influential than local managerial culture, 'social work attitudes' and local interpretations of the national criteria. (see www.lukeclements.co.uk/wp-content/uploads/2017/11/Care-Act-notes-updated-2017-08.pdf at page 22).

BOX 13.9 The eligibility criteria—s. 13 of the Care Act 2014

(1) Where a local authority is satisfied on the basis of a needs or carer's assessment that an adult has needs for care and support or that a carer has needs for support, it must determine whether any of the needs meet the eligibility criteria (see subsection (7)).

(2) Having made a determination under subsection (1), the local authority must give the adult concerned a written record of the determination and the reasons for it.

(3) Where at least some of an adult's needs for care and support meet the eligibility criteria, the local authority must—

    (a) consider what could be done to meet those needs that do,

    (b) ascertain whether the adult wants to have those needs met by the local authority in accordance with this Part, and

    (c) establish whether the adult is ordinarily resident in the local authority's area.

(4) Where at least some of a carer's needs for support meet the eligibility criteria, the local authority must—

    (a) consider what could be done to meet those needs that do, and

    (b) establish whether the adult needing care is ordinarily resident in the local authority's area.

(5) Where none of the needs of the adult concerned meet the eligibility criteria, the local authority must give him or her written advice and information about—

    (a) what can be done to meet or reduce the needs;

    (b) what can be done to prevent or delay the development of needs for care and support, or the development of needs for support, in the future.

The details of the assessment process, including how a local authority must go about determining whether an adult's needs meet the eligibility criteria and which needs are 'eligible' needs, are provided for in the Care and Support (Eligibility Criteria) Regulations 2015.

Regulation 2 of the Regulations prescribes the minimum level of needs that local authorities must meet (see **Box 13.10**). Local authorities are able to decide to arrange services to meet needs at a lower level than the prescribed minimum. The decision about the minimum level will be crucial.

BOX 13.10 Needs which meet the eligibility criteria—reg. 2 of the Care and Support (Eligibility Criteria) Regulations 2015

2 (1) An adult's needs meet the eligibility criteria if—

    (a) the adult's needs arise from or are related to a physical or mental impairment or illness;

    (b) as a result of the adult's needs the adult is unable to achieve two or more of the outcomes specified in paragraph (2); and

    (c) as a consequence there is, or is likely to be, a significant impact on the adult's well-being.

(2) The specified outcomes are—

    (a) managing and maintaining nutrition;

    (b) maintaining personal hygiene;

(c) managing toilet needs;

(d) being appropriately clothed;

(e) being able to make use of the adult's home safely;

(f) maintaining a habitable home environment;

(g) developing and maintaining family or other personal relationships;

(h) accessing and engaging in work, training, education or volunteering;

(i) making use of necessary facilities or services in the local community including public transport, and recreational facilities or services; and

(j) carrying out any caring responsibilities the adult has for a child.

(3) For the purposes of this regulation an adult is to be regarded as being unable to achieve an outcome if the adult—

(a) is unable to achieve it without assistance;

(b) is able to achieve it without assistance but doing so causes the adult significant pain, distress or anxiety;

(c) is able to achieve it without assistance but doing so endangers or is likely to endanger the health or safety of the adult, or of others; or

(d) is able to achieve it without assistance but takes significantly longer than would normally be expected.

(4) Where the level of an adult's needs fluctuates, in determining whether the adult's needs meet the eligibility criteria, the local authority must take into account the adult's circumstances over such period as it considers necessary to establish accurately the adult's level of need.

The three conditions set out in reg. 2(1) are extremely important. Needs are only eligible needs if all three conditions are met. The guidance provides useful advice on each—see paras 6.101–6.110.

The first condition is that *the adult's needs for care and support arise from or are related to a physical or mental impairment or illness and are not caused by other circumstantial factors*. This requires local authorities to consider at this stage whether the adult has a condition as a result of either physical, mental, sensory, learning, or cognitive disabilities or illnesses, substance misuse, or brain injury. The authority should base its judgement on the assessment of the adult, and a formal diagnosis of the condition should not be required.

The second condition requires that *as a result of the adult's needs, the adult is unable to achieve two or more of the outcomes specified in the regulations*. The regulations also flesh out, in reg. 3, what 'unable to achieve' means. A person is unable to achieve an outcome if they are unable to achieve it without assistance, or even if they are able to achieve it without assistance, doing so causes the adult significant pain, distress, or anxiety, or endangers or is likely to endanger the health or safety of the adult, or of others, or it takes significantly longer to achieve the outcome than would normally be expected.

The third condition requires that *as a consequence of being unable to achieve these outcomes, there is, or there is likely to be, a significant impact on the adult's well-being.* Well-being is defined in s. 1 of the Care Act 2014, and is discussed in **chapter 12**. The sort of issues the local authority should be concerned with include the following:

- personal dignity (including treatment of the individual with respect);
- physical and mental health and emotional well-being;
- protection from abuse and neglect;
- control by the individual over day-to-day life (including over care and support provided and the way it is provided);
- participation in work, education, training, or recreation;
- social and economic well-being;
- domestic, family, and personal relationships;
- suitability of living accommodation;
- the individual's contribution to society.

The Care and Support (Eligibility Criteria) Regulations 2015 set out the national threshold for carers' eligibility for support. The threshold is based on the impact a carer's needs for support has on their well-being. A carer's needs are only eligible when all three of the following conditions are met:

- the needs arise as a consequence of providing necessary care for an adult;
- the effect of the carer's needs is that any of the circumstances specified in the Eligibility Regulations apply to the carer;
- as a consequence of that fact there is, or there is likely to be, a significant impact on the carer's well-being.

The statutory guidance, at paras 6.118–6.123, provides useful assistance in deciding whether or not carers have eligible needs. Some extracts are provided in **Box 13.11**.

BOX 13.11 The needs arise as a consequence of providing necessary care for an adult—paras 6.118–6.119, 6.122, and 6.123 of Care and support statutory guidance (updated October 2018)

6.118 Local authorities must consider whether the carer's need for support arises because they are providing care to an adult. Carers can be eligible for support whether or not the adult for whom they care has eligible needs. The eligibility determination must be made based on the carer's needs and how these impact on their wellbeing. The determination should be made without consideration of whether or not the adult the carer cares for, has eligible needs.

6.119 The carer must also be providing necessary care. If the carer is providing care and support for needs which the adult is capable of meeting themselves, the carer may not be providing necessary support. In such cases, local authorities should provide information and advice to the adult and carer about how the adult can use their own strengths or services available in the community to meet their needs.

The effect of the carer's needs is that any of the circumstances specified in the Eligibility Regulations apply to the carer.

6.120 The second condition that authorities must consider is whether the carer's physical or mental health is either deteriorating or is at risk of doing so, or whether the carer is unable to achieve any of a list of other outcomes which may apply.

6.121 Authorities must be aware that the regulations provide that 'being unable' to achieve outcomes, includes circumstances where the carer:

- is unable to achieve the outcome without assistance. This includes where the carer would be unable to achieve an outcome even if assistance were provided. A carer might, for example, be unable to fulfill their parental responsibilities unless they receive support in their caring role

- is able to achieve the outcome without assistance, but doing so causes or is likely to cause significant pain, distress or anxiety. A carer might for example be able to care for the adult and undertake fulltime employment, but if doing both, this causes the carer significant distress, the carer should not be considered able to engage in employment

- is able to achieve the outcome without assistance but doing so is likely to endanger the health or safety of the carer or any adults or children for whom the carer provides care. A carer might for example be able to provide care for their family and deliver necessary care for the adult, but, where this endangers the adult with care and support needs, for example, because the adult receiving care would have to be left alone while other responsibilities are met, the carer should not be considered able to meet the outcome of caring for their family.

6.124 The third condition that must be met is that local authorities must consider whether the carer's needs and their inability to achieve the outcomes above present a significant impact on the carer's wellbeing. 'Wellbeing' is defined by referring to examples of specific areas in Section 1 of the Care Act (see **chapter 1**). In doing so, local authorities should consider whether:

- the carer's needs and inability to achieve the outcomes impact on an area of the carer's wellbeing in a significant way

- the impact on a number of the areas of wellbeing is such that they have a significant impact on an adult's overall wellbeing.

6.125 The term 'significant' is not defined by the Regulations, and must therefore be understood to have its everyday meaning. Local authorities will have to consider whether the carer's needs and their inability to achieve the outcomes will have an important, consequential effect on their daily lives, their independence and their own wellbeing.

The local authority must, once a decision about eligibility has been made, provide a copy of that decision to the person who is the subject of the determination, whether an adult with care and support needs or a carer with support needs. If the person has no eligible needs, then the local authority must provide information and advice on meeting or reducing their needs, for instance information about available support in the community. If the person has eligible needs, then the local authority must:

- reach agreement with the person about which of the needs they wish the local authority to meet;
- consider how those needs might be met by the local authority; and
- establish whether the person meets the ordinary residence requirement.

Ordinary residence

The ordinary residence requirement establishes which local authority takes responsibility for the provision of care and support for someone with eligible needs. It is important because it has financial consequences for local authorities—ordinary residence establishes which local authority pays for provision. In most cases the ordinary residence test presents no difficulty as it is obvious where the service user resides and which local authority bears the costs. However, in some cases it is much more difficult to reach a conclusion about where someone is ordinarily resident. The key features of ordinary residence are that it is adopted voluntarily and represents a settled decision. The important paragraphs of the statutory guidance on the interpretation of ordinary residence are set out in **Box 13.12**.

BOX 13.12 Statutory guidance on ordinary residence—paras 19.14 and 19.15 of Care and support statutory guidance (updated October 2018)

19.14 The concept of ordinary residence involves questions of both fact and degree. Factors such as time, intention and continuity (each of which may be given different weight according to the context) have to be taken into account. The courts have considered the meaning of ordinary residence and the leading case is that of Shah v London Borough of Barnet (1983). In this case, Lord Scarman stated that:

unless . . . it can be shown that the statutory framework or the legal context in which the words are used requires a different meaning I unhesitatingly subscribe to the view that ordinarily resident refers to a man's abode in a particular place or country which he has adopted voluntarily and for settled purposes as part of the regular order of his life for the time being, whether of short or long duration.

19.15 Local authorities must always have regard to this case when determining the ordinary residence of adults who have capacity to make their own decisions about where they wish to live. Local authorities should in particular apply the principle that ordinary residence is the place the person has voluntarily adopted for a settled purpose, whether for a short or long duration. Ordinary residence can be acquired as soon as the person moves to an area, if their move is voluntary and for settled purposes, irrespective of whether they own, or have an interest in a property in another local authority area. There is no minimum period in which a person has to be living in a particular place for them to be considered ordinarily resident there, because it depends on the nature and quality of the connection with the new place.

The Supreme Court considered the ordinary residence test most recently in *R (on the application of Cornwall) v Secretary of State for Health* (2015). The case concerned a young incapacitated man who received accommodation and support at public expense. The question was whether the financial responsibility was that of South Gloucestershire Council, in whose area he had been 'ordinarily resident' when he reached adulthood; Wiltshire, where he had been born and lived for four years until Wiltshire placed him in foster care in South Gloucestershire; or Cornwall, where his parents, with whom he had strong links, had lived since he was four years old.

The Secretary of State (who has a role in determining disputes between local authorities) had determined that Cornwall was responsible as an incapacitated person is deemed to have the same ordinary residence as his parents until he reaches majority. The Court of Appeal disagreed. It found that the man no longer had any connection with Wiltshire, and that South Gloucestershire was responsible for him because that was where his social and family life had been concentrated in the years leading up to his eighteenth birthday. The Supreme Court disagreed. It found that whilst it was understandable that the Court of Appeal had chosen South Gloucestershire because of the language of the National Assistance Act 1948, it considered that there was no connection of any kind with South Gloucestershire, apart from a historic placement. The Supreme Court made the important point that it is undesirable to allow a local authority to export its social welfare responsibilities by placing a child for which it had fiscal and administrative responsibility in a different geographical area in the expectation that when he or she reached 18, the child would be regarded as ordinarily resident in that area for the purposes of the 1948 Act. The ordinary residence of a person entitled to accommodation and support should not be affected for the purposes of a local authority's responsibilities by the location of their placement. Before the young man moved to Somerset, he had been living in a place determined, not by his own settled intention, but by Wiltshire, the local authority statutorily responsible for him. The fact that Wiltshire had placed him outside its own area did not affect the form of his residence, which was to be found in the provisions of the 1989 Act. The placement in South Gloucestershire had, therefore, not changed his ordinary residence in Wiltshire for fiscal and administrative purposes.

Personal budgets and direct payments

Everyone eligible for statutory support should have a personal budget—that is, a sum of money based on the cost of meeting that person's care and/or support needs. Section 26 of the Care Act, set out in **Box 13.13**, puts the requirement for personal budgets into statute for the first time. It has, of course, been a policy priority for more than a decade.

BOX 13.13 Personal budgets—s. 26 of the Care Act 2014

(1) A personal budget for an adult is a statement which specifies—

(a) the cost to the local authority of meeting those of the adult's needs which it is required or decides to meet as mentioned in section 24(1),

(b) the amount which, on the basis of the financial assessment, the adult must pay towards that cost, and

(c) if on that basis the local authority must itself pay towards that cost, the amount which it must pay.

There are three ways personal budgets can be provided: first, via a managed account, where the local authority manages the personal budget in line with the care plan; second, where an account is managed by a third party, which is similar to a managed account other than that a third party, sometimes called a broker, manages the personal budget. The third way is via direct payments, when the service user him or herself is given the personal budget to spend on meeting their care and support needs in line with the care plan. The Care Act, at s. 31, gives a statutory right to a direct payment for adults with capacity.

The statutory guidance makes clear the importance of personal budgets to the delivery of person-centred care (see **Box 13.14**).

BOX 13.14 Personal budgets and person-centred care—para. 11.3 of Care and support statutory guidance (updated October 2018)

11.3 The personal budget is the mechanism that, in conjunction with the care and support plan, or support plan, enables the person, and their advocate if they have one, to exercise greater choice and take control over how their care and support needs are met. It means:

- knowing, before care and support planning begins, an estimate of how much money will be available to meet a person's assessed needs and, with the final personal budget, having clear information about the total amount of the budget, including proportion the local authority will pay, and what amount (if any) the person will pay

- being able to choose from a range of options for how the money is managed, including direct payments, the local authority managing the budget and a provider or third party managing the budget on the individual's behalf (an individual service fund), or a combination of these approaches

- having a choice over who is involved in developing the care and support plan for how the personal budget will be spent, including from family or friends

- having greater choice and control over the way the personal budget is used to purchase care and support, and from whom

Resource allocation systems

A significant challenge for local authorities is to calculate the sum of money required to fund the services that the service user needs. Many local authorities use a resource allocation system—RAS—to work out what should be paid. The statutory code of guidance discusses the role of RAS, set out in **Box 13.15**.

BOX 13.15 Resource allocation systems—paras 11.22–11.24 of Care and support statutory guidance (updated October 2018)

11.22 It is important to have a consistent method for calculating personal budgets that provides an early indication of the appropriate amount to meet the identified needs to be used at the beginning of the planning process. Local authorities should ensure that the method used for calculating the personal budget produces equitable outcomes to ensure fairness in care and support packages regardless of the environment in which care and support takes place, for example, in a care home or someone's own home. Local authorities should not have arbitrary ceilings to personal budgets that result in people being forced to accept to move into care homes against their will.

11.23 There are many variations of systems used to arrive at personal budget amounts, ranging from complex algorithmic-based resource allocation systems (RAS), to more 'ready-reckoner' approaches. Complex RAS models of allocation may not work for all client groups, especially where people have multiple complex needs, or where needs are comparatively costly to meet, such as in the case of deaf-blind people. It is important that these factors are taken into account, and that a 'one size fits all' approach to resource allocation is not taken. If a RAS model is being used, local authorities should consider alternative approaches where the process may be more suitable to particular client groups to ensure that the personal budget is an appropriate amount to meet needs.

11.24 Regardless of the process used, the most important principles in setting the personal budget are transparency, timeliness and sufficiency. This will ensure that the person, their carer, and their independent advocate if they have one, is fully aware of how their budget was calculated, that they know the amount at a stage which enables them to effectively engage in care and support planning, and that they can have confidence that the amount includes all relevant costs that will be sufficient to meet their identified needs in the way set out in the plan. The local authority should also explain that the initial indicative allowance can be increased or decreased depending on the decisions made during the development of the plan. This should prevent disputes from arising, but it must also be possible for the person, carer or independent advocate (on the person's behalf) to challenge the local authority on the sufficiency of the final amount. These principles apply to both the indicative upfront budget and the final signed-off personal budget that forms part of the care and support plan.

Legal challenges

The complexity of RAS, together with the increasing constraints imposed upon the budgets for adult social care, have made legal challenges inevitable. In **Box 13.16**, we consider three cases where issues of assessment, needs, and resource allocation have been considered by the courts. Although the cases precede the Care Act 2014, the principles set out by the courts will remain relevant to the post-Care Act position.

BOX 13.16 Assessment, needs, and resources

R (on the application of McDonald) v Royal Borough of Kensington and Chelsea (2011)

In this case the service user, Ms McDonald, challenged the process by which the local authority, the Royal Borough of Kensington and Chelsea (RBKC) had redesignated her needs from 'assistance to manage continence at night', a 'substantial need', with a high priority in terms of resource allocation to 'assistance at night to use the commode', a 'moderate need' with limited priority. In particular, RBKC considered that it would be preferable for Ms McDonald to use incontinence pads or special absorbent sheeting, which would avoid the need for a night-time carer and reduce the cost of Ms McDonald's care by more than £20,000 a year. Ms McDonald was unconvinced of the advantages of incontinence provisions over using a commode despite RBKC arguing that they provided greater safety, independence, and privacy. She strongly resisted RBKC's proposals; her argument was that she was not incontinent and did not wish to be treated as if she was. To suggest otherwise was an affront to her dignity. Nonetheless, RBKC implemented its change in provision.

The Supreme Court supported the local authority's decision to reduce the resources available to the adult service user and dismissed the argument that the failure to provide in the way that Ms McDonald wished was a breach of her human rights and her dignity.

Baroness Hale dissented. For her the decision of the local authority was 'irrational in the classic *Wednesbury* sense' because it characterized the appellant as 'having a different need from the one which she in fact has' (para. 78). She was concerned about the consequences of the local authority's decision. She argued that the logical conclusion of its decision could be the withdrawal of all assistance with mobility, during the day as well as at night, and, if Ms McDonald's physical condition deteriorated so that her bowels were affected, allowing her to lie in faeces until carers came in the morning. She echoed Lord Lloyd's dissent in *Barry*:

> In the United Kingdom we do not oblige people who can control their bodily functions to behave as if they cannot do so, unless they themselves find this the more convenient course. We are, I still believe, a civilized society. I would have allowed this appeal.

(para. 79)

Ms McDonald appealed to the European Court of Human Rights in Strasbourg. Its decision was handed down in May 2014. The Court held, unanimously, that the decision to reduce the amount allocated for Ms McDonald's care interfered with her right to respect for her family and private life, in respect of the period between 21 November 2008 and 4 November 2009 because the interference with her rights had not been in accordance with domestic law during this period. It held the complaint concerning the period after 4 November 2009 inadmissible as manifestly ill-founded because the state had considerable discretion when it came to decisions concerning the allocation of scarce resources and, as such, the interference with Ms McDonald's rights had been 'necessary in a democratic society'. She was awarded only €1,000 compensation and legal costs. However, the European Court decision may have more influence than the limited compensation suggests, as the judgment recognizes that a failure to consider a person's dignity can be a breach of human rights, which may lead to other challenges on this issue in future.

Savva v Kensington and Chelsea (2010)

The applicant, Mrs Savva, was 70 years old. She suffered from diabetes, heart and respiratory problems, and was arthritic with poor eyesight. She had had a stroke ten years previously and since then had been in receipt of adult social care services. In July 2009, Mrs Savva completed a Personal Budget Supported Self-Assessment Questionnaire (SAQ) with the support of her social worker. Using RAS Mrs Savva was allocated 16 points. This translated into a monetary value of £82.91 per week. The funding was adjusted to £132.56, and this was then increased to £170.45. The claimant completed another SAQ on 19 November 2009, after her discharge from hospital. This gave her 28 points which translated to a monetary value of £112.21. This sum, of course, was an increase from the £82.91 generated subsequent to the July SAQ. This sum was then adjusted to £142.02 per week. The local authority RAS then considered that the 'indicative budget' of £142.02 per week was too low and did not properly meet the claimant's needs, particularly in terms of meal preparation. Therefore, the panel increased the indicative figure and allocated a weekly budget of £170.45 to the claimant. Mrs Savva did not accept that this budget was reasonable to meet her assessed need. Her judicial review made three claims.

(a) The defendant's system for calculating budgets was inadequate to discharge the statutory duty to provide care services adequate to meet an individual's assessed needs.

(b) The defendant's reasons were inadequate to discharge the duty to provide adequate reasons for the decision to allocate the claimant a personal budget of £170.45 per week.

(c) The defendant assessed the claimant's needs to have increased substantially between July 2009 and December 2009, yet decided to keep the personal budget constant, at £170.45 per week. This, she argued, in the absence of a proper explanation, is irrational.

The judge at the High Court rejected the challenge based on the defendant's system of calculation but allowed the claim based on the failure to give adequate reasons. Mrs Savva appealed to the Court of Appeal on the lawfulness of Kensington and Chelsea's system of calculation and it cross-appealed on its duty to give reasons. The Court of Appeal decided that local authorities are entitled to use a RAS based on the assessed eligible needs of service users and those of others in the area, as long as the figures reached were used only as a starting point for calculating the level of payments required to meet the service users' needs. In this case the court found that the local authority had not lost sight of its absolute duty to meet the recipient's needs or to provide a budget with which to meet them. It rejected the cross-appeal, pointing out that while neither the Chronically Sick and Disabled Persons Act 1970 nor the Community Care, Services for Carers and Children's Services (Direct Payment) (England) Regulations 2009 imposed a duty on the defendant to provide reasons for the panel's decision, the common law required reasons to be given as a matter of fairness. Mrs Savva was entitled to be told how the sum assessed to meet her eligible needs had been calculated in order to satisfy herself either that it had been properly calculated or to challenge the decision, which could be achieved with reasonable brevity by the defendant listing the required services and assumed timings together with the assumed hourly cost. Anxious to avoid imposing too much of a burden on local authorities, the Court indicated that, as a matter of common sense, decision letters which include an offer of the provision of reasons on request would satisfy legal requirements.

KM (By His Mother and Litigation Friend JM) v Cambridgeshire County Council (2012)

KM suffered from physical and mental disabilities and required significant support in his everyday life. The local authority was responsible for the provision of KM's care. Under the Health and Social Care Act 2001 (HSCA 2001), support could be provided to an individual by way of direct payments: entitling the individual to decide how to spend his care funds. KM's needs were assessed by an independent social worker. The local authority then determined the level of funding required by using a RAS calculation. That figure was then checked against KM's care assessment to ensure that the funding level would reasonably meet his assessed needs. In particular, the RAS indicated that KM's need would exceed the upper limit of funding allowed by that system; the local authority utilized a second indicative tool called an Upper Banding Calculator (UBC). It reflected, in effect, three factors which, in Cambridgeshire's experience, often greatly elevate the requisite level of services, namely a requirement for a carer to remain awake at night, for two carers to operate simultaneously, and for a carer to have specialist expertise. The social worker later reassessed KM's needs and also produced an addendum report setting out services which he assessed as necessary to meet those needs and their cost in the sum of £157,060. The local authority accepted the later needs assessment but it stated that the services assessment suggested unnecessary services and awarded KM £84,678 a year. KM sought to claim judicial review of the sum awarded to him but the High Court refused him permission to seek judicial review on the basis that the local authority had properly arrived at the sum that it had awarded KM and that it had given adequate intelligible reasons for how the figure was arrived at. KM contended that the amount of the assessed direct payment did not fulfil the local authority's obligation to provide him with care, that it had not given adequate reasons, and that its decision was irrational. The High Court refused permission for judicial review and its decision was upheld by the Court of Appeal.

The applicant appealed to the Supreme Court. It was asked to decide whether RASs are a legitimate means for local authorities to apply to determine funding to be made available to persons in need by means of direct payment, and whether adequate reasons were given for the decision that it reached. Legal commentators were excited by the fact that the Supreme Court also accepted as a question to be considered on appeal whether *Barry* was correctly decided. In the event, the judges avoided considering *Barry*, pointing out that the question of whether the local authority was entitled to consider its resources to meet KM's needs was not relevant. Cambridgeshire had agreed to meet KM's needs, which were all decided to be critical.

The Supreme Court rejected KM's appeal. It was rational to use the RAS and the UBC provided that the result was cross-checked. The judges considered that the challenge to the adequacy of the *reasons* for the offer was more arguable. They suggested that Cambridgeshire should have made a more detailed presentation to KM of how in its opinion he might reasonably choose to deploy the offered sum than in the plans put forward in January and April 2010. In particular, Cambridgeshire should have made a presentation of its own assessment of the reasonable cost of the principal item of the appellant's future expenditure, namely the cost of paying for carers for him. Nevertheless, in the light of the amplification of Cambridgeshire's reasoning in the evidence filed in response to the application for judicial review, it would be a pointless exercise of discretion to order that it should be quashed so that the appellant's entitlement might be considered again, perhaps even to his disadvantage.

Care planning

Once the decision has been made that a person is eligible for particular community care services, then those services must be arranged. This is described as care planning. There is extensive statutory guidance on care planning. We have set out in **Box 13.17** a useful extract to demonstrate how to place the service user at the centre of the planning process.

BOX 13.17 Guidance on care planning—paras 10.31 and 10.32 of Care and support statutory guidance (updated October 2018)

10.31 The plan must detail the needs to be met and how the needs will be met, and will link back to the outcomes that the adult wishes to achieve in day-to-day life as identified in the assessment process and to the wellbeing principle in the Act. This should reflect the individual's wishes, their needs and aspirations, and what is important to and for them, where this is reasonable. This process is central to the provision of person-centred care and support that provides people with choice and control over how to meet their needs. The local authority should encourage creativity in planning how to meet needs, and refrain from judging unusual decisions as long as these are determined to meet needs in a reasonable way.

10.32 The guiding principle therefore is that the person be actively involved and is given every opportunity to influence the planning and subsequent content of the plan in conjunction with the local authority, with support if needed. Joint planning does not mean a 50:50 split; the person can take a bigger share of the planning where this is appropriate and the person wishes to do so. A further principle is that planning should be proportionate. The person should not be required to go through lengthy processes which limit their ability to be actively involved, unless there are very strong reasons to add in elements of process and decision-making. Wherever possible the person should be able to be fully involved in the development of their plan, and any revision if circumstances change, with minimum process.

The Care Act 2014 contains statutory provisions about care planning. Section 24—set out in **Box 13.18**—describes the next steps the local authority must take.

BOX 13.18 The steps for the local authority to take—s. 24 of the Care Act 2014

(1)   Where a local authority is required to meet needs under section 18 or 20(1), or decides to do so under section 19(1) or (2) or 20(6), it must—

(a)   prepare a care and support plan or a support plan for the adult concerned,

(b)   tell the adult which (if any) of the needs that it is going to meet may be met by direct payments, and

(c)   help the adult with deciding how to have the needs met.

(2) Where a local authority has carried out a needs or carer's assessment but is not required to meet needs under section 18 or 20(1), and does not decide to do so under section 19(1) or (2) or 20(6), it must give the adult concerned—

    (a) its written reasons for not meeting the needs, and

    (b) (unless it has already done so under section 13(5)) advice and information about—

        (i) what can be done to meet or reduce the needs;

        (ii) what can be done to prevent or delay the development by the adult concerned of needs for care and support or of needs for support in the future.

(3) Where a local authority is not going to meet an adult's needs for care and support, it must nonetheless prepare an independent personal budget for the adult (see section 28) if—

    (a) the needs meet the eligibility criteria,

    (b) at least some of the needs are not being met by a carer, and

    (c) the adult is ordinarily resident in the authority's area or is present in its area but of no settled residence.

Section 25 of the Care Act provides some detail as to what a care or support plan should contain—see **Box 13.19**.

 BOX 13.19 Care and support plans—s. 25 of the Care Act 2014

(1) A care and support plan or, in the case of a carer, a support plan is a document prepared by a local authority which—

    (a) specifies the needs identified by the needs assessment or carer's assessment,

    (b) specifies whether, and if so to what extent, the needs meet the eligibility criteria,

    (c) specifies the needs that the local authority is going to meet and how it is going to meet them,

    (d) specifies to which of the matters referred to in section 9(4) the provision of care and support could be relevant or to which of the matters referred to in section 10(5) and (6) the provision of support could be relevant,

    (e) includes the personal budget for the adult concerned (see section 26), and

    (f) includes advice and information about—

        (i) what can be done to meet or reduce the needs in question;

        (ii) what can be done to prevent or delay the development of needs for care and support or of needs for support in the future.

In preparing the plan the local authority must involve the vulnerable adult, the carer, and any other person that the carer or the vulnerable adult wish to involve. Section 27 of the Act requires that local authorities keep plans under review.

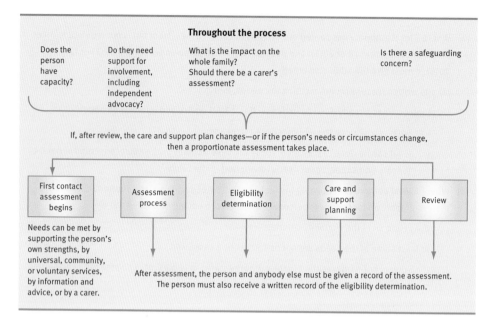

Figure 13.1 Summary of the assessment, eligibility, and care planning process

Source: https://assets.publishing.service.gov.uk/media/56d82def40f0b60376000008/5_Throughout-the-process.jpg.

A useful visual summary of assessment, eligibility, and care planning is provided by **Figure 13.1**, taken from the statutory guidance at para. 6.12.

▪ Managing quality

So far, in this chapter, we have considered how local authorities aided by the social care professionals that they employ, decide upon service provision. In this section of the chapter we consider how the quality of that provision is managed. Local authorities are clearly concerned that the services that they provide are delivered to a good and safe standard. In the immediate post-war welfare state, local authorities provided services themselves and they could be held accountable for any defects in those services via the ballot box. Now responsibility for the delivery of services has been dispersed and services are more likely to be provided by the private or voluntary sector than by local authorities themselves. However, local authorities retain responsibility for the quality of those services. Democratic accountability is not now (if it ever was) an appropriate mechanism. Instead local authorities use a range of techniques to ensure quality and manage risks. For instance, when they contract with a private or a voluntary sector provider they will put terms into the contract which require particular standards to be met. Another example is the use that local councils make of liaison groups, where adult social service users and their families meet council officers in an informal setting to discuss service provision.

We look at three more formal means of ensuring quality. The first is located in the local authority itself—the requirement for local authorities to have a statutory complaints procedure. The second is the Local Government Ombudsman. The third is the CQC, which is the national regulator of standards in health and social care. Each mechanism plays a part in ensuring that services do not fall below an acceptable level.

Statutory complaints procedure

The previous regime for local authority complaints about adult social care services was criticized for its bureaucracy and its inflexibility. Some complaints took a long time to resolve, and there was no system to ensure that complaints led to service improvement. Moreover, and in common with most complaint services, there was evidence that some people did not complain because they either did not know how to or they believed that doing so would be pointless.

From 1 April 2009, a single complaints system was introduced which covers all health and adult social care services in England. The aim of the new arrangements, known as 'making experiences count', is to encourage a flexible approach that aims to resolve complaints more effectively and ensure that opportunities for services to learn and improve are not lost.

The Local Authority Social Services and National Health Service Complaints (England) Regulations 2009 set out the procedures. What they require (in reg. 3(2)) is that:

(a) complaints are dealt with efficiently;

(b) complaints are properly investigated;

(c) complainants are treated with respect and courtesy;

(d) complainants receive, so far as is reasonably practical—

    (i) assistance to enable them to understand the procedure in relation to complaints; or

    (ii) advice on where they may obtain such assistance;

(e) complainants receive a timely and appropriate response;

(f) complainants are told the outcome of the investigation of their complaint; and

(g) action is taken if necessary in the light of the outcome of a complaint.

The process for investigating complaints is set out in reg. 14: see **Box 13.20**.

BOX 13.20 Investigating complaints—reg. 14 of the Local Authority Social Services and National Health Service Complaints (England) Regulations 2009

(1) A responsible body to which a complaint is made must—

    (a) investigate the complaint in a manner appropriate to resolve it speedily and efficiently; and

    (b) during the investigation, keep the complainant informed, as far as reasonably practicable, as to the progress of the investigation.

(2) As soon as reasonably practicable after completing the investigation, the responsible body must send the complainant in writing a response, signed by the responsible person, which includes—

    (a) a report which includes the following matters—

        (i) an explanation of how the complaint has been considered; and

        (ii) the conclusions reached in relation to the complaint, including any matters for which the complaint specifies, or the responsible body considers, that remedial action is needed; and

    (b) confirmation as to whether the responsible body is satisfied that any action needed in consequence of the complaint has been taken or is proposed to be taken;

    (c) where the complaint relates wholly or in part to the functions of a local authority, details of the complainant's right to take their complaint to a Local Commissioner under the Local Government Act 1974; and

    (d) except where the complaint relates only to the functions of a local authority, details of the complainant's right to take their complaint to the Health Service Commissioner under the 1993 Act.

Complainants have 12 months within which to make their complaint, although that time can be extended if it is reasonable to do so. Organizations must appoint someone, described as a complaints manager, to take responsibility for complaints; they must publicize their arrangements for handling complaints; and they must report annually on complaints received and their responses.

The Local Government Ombudsman

The Local Government Ombudsman considers complaints about councils and all types of care service for adults in England. This includes complaints about independent care providers as well as local authority provision. It does not matter whether the money for the service provided comes from the local authority or from private funds.

The Local Government Ombudsman produces a useful leaflet about how to complain, which can be downloaded from www.lgo.org.uk/adult-social-care. Following investigations of complaints, the Local Government Ombudsman produces reports which can provide you with a good insight into its expectations for a good service. It also provides, on an annual basis, summaries of its work, which provide an excellent overview of complaints received and a very useful statistical analysis. The reports are available at www.lgo.org.uk/information-centre/reports/annual-review-reports/adult-social-care-reviews.

The Care Quality Commission

The CQC is the national body which was set up by the Health and Social Care Act 2008 (HSCA 2008) to regulate the quality and safety of health and care service provision in

England, regardless of whether the services are provided by the public, the private, or the voluntary sector. The CQC exists, in its own words, to 'make sure health and social care services provide people with safe, effective, compassionate, high quality care and we encourage care services to improve' (see *A Fresh Start For Registration* (2015), available at www.cqc.org.uk/sites/default/files/documents/20131013_cqc_afreshstart_2013_final.pdf.

The CQC manages quality through a range of activities.

Registration

The primary activity of the CQC is to register providers of health and social care services. From April 2010 all health and adult social care providers are required by law to register with CQC if they provide 'regulated activities'. Failure to register is a criminal offence. Regulated activities are listed in Schedule 1 to the Health and Social Care Act 2008 (Regulated Activities) Regulations 2010. They include, for instance, the provision of personal care, provision of accommodation for people who require nursing or personal care, and accommodation for persons who require treatment for substance misuse. The CQC provides guidance on registration (as it is required to do by statute) at www.cqc.org.uk/content/guidance-providers.

The CQC explains the purpose of registration, in *A Fresh Start for Registration* (2015) as follows:

- Registration helps to protect people who use the regulated health and adult social care market. It provides a quality check at the point of market entry.
- Through our registration functions, we effectively control market entry. This is a very powerful regulatory tool and it is important that we use it well. Using this power disproportionately could prevent the public having access to services or raise costs by reducing supply.
- Registration is also linked to how we fund what we do. We charge registered providers fees to enter and remain in this regulated market.
- Through registration, we make sure that providers applying to us to run regulated health and care services are able to deliver services that are the right quality. We currently do this through a process which inspects and assesses applications against the regulations.

Monitoring and inspection

Once providers are registered, their activities are monitored through self-evaluation and inspection. There are three types of inspection:

- scheduled—these are inspections carried out on a rolling programme. Providers are not told the date of a scheduled inspection;
- responsive—these are carried out when concerns are raised over a provider's compliance with the standards;
- themed—these are carried out when the CQC reviews a particular type of service (e.g. learning disability services) or a specific set of standards (e.g, the use of medication in care homes). The results of thematic inspections will be published as a national report on the specific theme.

Enforcement

One purpose of the reforms set out in the HSCA 2008 was to provide a more rigorous enforcement regime than the previous one under the Care Standards Act 2000. The CQC can require providers to deliver a plan of action or it can use its enforcement powers. These powers include:

- issuing a warning notice requiring improvements within a short period of time;
- restricting the services that the provider can offer;
- stopping admissions into the care service;
- issuing fixed penalty notices;
- suspending or cancelling the service's registration;
- prosecution.

Box 13.21 summarizes the enforcement policy of the CQC.

BOX 13.21 The enforcement policy of the CQC

Our overarching concern and priority is to protect and promote the health, safety and welfare of people who use the services we regulate, and to improve the quality of care they receive.

We will be proportionate in how we work with registered persons and others to achieve—

- We will assess any risks to people using, working in and visiting services, and where necessary, take formal regulatory or enforcement action that is proportionate to those risks.
- Where a service fails to comply with legal requirements, we will take formal regulatory or enforcement action.
- Where legal requirements are not being met, we will choose the most proportionate way of achieving sustained compliance or we will remove the person's ability to provide or manage care if we consider that compliance could not be promptly achieved or sustained.
- Where legal requirements continue not to be met despite formal regulatory action being taken (compliance actions), we may escalate to enforcement action.

The Care Act 2014 imposes new responsibilities on the CQC. Part 2 of the Act, concerned with care standards, contains provisions which extend the remit of the CQC, introduce new criminal offences for bodies that provide false or misleading information about care services, and increase the independence of the CQC from government. In s. 55 of the Care Act, the CQC is given the responsibility of overseeing the financial sustainability of private providers. This follows the financial problems suffered by private care firms, particularly the failure of Southern Cross. Some commentators are sceptical about the ability of the CQC to take on this additional responsibility.

Criticism of the CQC

The performance of the CQC has been criticized by a number of bodies, particularly since the BBC's *Panorama* revealed abuse at Winterbourne View. Subsequent Panorama programmes have also revealed abuse not found by the CQC. Recent criticisms include a highly provocative working paper by John Burton, a social care commentator, called 'What's wrong with the CQC?' published by the Centre for Welfare Reform in January 2017, and available online at www.centreforwelfarereform.org/uploads/attachment/534/whats-wrong-with-cqc.pdf.

The introduction to the essay is set out in **Box 13.22.**

BOX 13.22 Introduction to John Burton, *What's Wrong with the CQC? (Centre for Welfare Reform, 2017)*

The Care Quality Commission is not effective or responsive; it doesn't understand how social care works; it rarely uncovers neglect and abuse, and it responds too slowly when they are brought to its attention; its judgements are flawed and its ratings inaccurate and unhelpful; its inspections reports are poorly written and constructed; it costs much more than it should and imposes vast unnecessary costs on social care providers; it dominates and distorts the whole social care sector, and the organisation is blinkered, risk averse, top heavy and hopelessly bureaucratic.

Burton's solution is to create a local system of inspection which would be more responsive and accountable to the communities it would serve.

SUMMARY

In this chapter we have considered:
- a service user's 'journey' through the assessment and planning process set out in the Care Act 2014;
- the assessment of carers' needs;
- quality control processes built into the adult social care system:
  - o the statutory complaints procedure;
  - o the role of the Care Quality Commission.

EXERCISES

1 Mrs Akuffo is about to be discharged from hospital, where she has been receiving treatment for bipolar disorder. She has chronic diabetes and severe arthritis and she has difficulty managing stairs and much of her personal care. She has no income or savings. She has no home to return to as her private landlord terminated her tenancy shortly before her hospital admission, as she was said to have been shouting abusive comments to neighbours. How would you assess her needs for social care services?

2 Mr O'Keefe is dissatisfied with the assessment of his care needs. How can he complain about this?

3 The funding available for domiciliary services has been cut in your local authority area. How does that impact upon your service users who have a care plan in place?

4 Why do you think that the government is constantly revisiting and reforming its mechanisms to ensure that adult social care services are of an adequate quality? Do you think that the current arrangements are effective?

ONLINE RESOURCES

For guidance on how to answer these exercises, visit the online resources at www.oup.com/uk/carr-goosey15e.

WHERE DO WE GO FROM HERE?

This chapter has concentrated on the strategic planning of adult social care services and the assessment and planning of individuals' community care packages. It has also considered mechanisms for ensuring the quality of service provision. **Chapter 14** addresses two key issues of autonomy and protection for adult social care users: mental capacity and adult safeguarding.

ANNOTATED FURTHER READING

Legal Action Group publishes two very useful and up-to-date practitioner orientated books on this area of law:

L. Clements, *Community Care and the Law* (Legal Action Group, 2017).

S. Knafler, *Adult Social Care Law* (Legal Action Group, 2016).

Resource allocation systems

L. Clements and L. Series, 'Putting the cart before the horse: resource allocation systems and community care' (2013) *Journal of Social Welfare and Family Law* 35(2): 207. The English Care Bill provides for all eligible community care service users to have a personal budget—and councils were required to ensure that 70 per cent of such users had one by April 2013. Almost all English authorities are experimenting with resource allocation systems (RASs) as a way of calculating these budgets. The article describes and critically analyses the nature of the RASs being used and the increasing body of case law they are attracting—in particular, the Supreme Court's 2012 judgment in *R (KM) v Cambridgeshire County Council*. The article draws on research involving 20 local authorities concerning their use of RASs and represents the first in-depth legal examination of the claims made by proponents of the use of RASs. It challenges many of the claims made concerning such systems—in particular that they are 'more transparent', 'more equitable', 'simpler', and less discretionary than the traditional social work-led community care assessment process.

The *KM* and *Barry* cases are also considered in *'R (KM) v Cambridgeshire—care and confusion: thinking legally'* at https://thinkinglegally.wordpress.com/2012/06/11/r-km-v-cambridgeshire-care-case-carers-rights.

Independent living

T. Collingbourne, 'Administrative justice? Realising the right to independent living in England: power, systems, identities' (2013) *Journal of Social Welfare and Family Law* 35(4): 475. Under Article 19 of the UN Convention on the Rights of Persons with Disabilities, disabled people have a right to live independently and to be included in the community. This article considers the potential for realization of that right through the English administrative justice system. It discusses models of administrative justice, and examines practical examples of the exercise of discretionary power in social care decision making, administration, and delivery. While some aspects of the current reconstruction in social care provision have succeeded in producing emancipatory outcomes, examples of continuing oppressive use of discretionary power still occur: in decision making, in the design of assessment questionnaires, and in the assessment experience. The article concludes that there is further to go before practice is aligned with meaningful, Convention-compliant change. Until then, realization in England of the right to independent living will remain partial, and the emancipatory purpose of the Convention compromised.

Complaints procedures

J. Gulland, 'Independence in complaints procedures: lessons from community care' (2009) *Journal of Social Welfare and Family Law* 31(1): 59. This article looks at internal complaints procedures and considers the role of independent elements in procedures that are designed to be simple, informal, and low cost. Taking the example of local authority community care services as a case study, it discusses research which looked at the views of complainants, potential complainants, and those who run the procedure. Most people do not make formal complaints at all and very few people seek an independent review of their complaint. When they do seek such a review, they expect it to be transparently independent of the body complained about. The article concludes that the current system of local authority complaints review panels or committees does not provide the independent element that complainants seek.

Ensuring quality

A. Stewart, 'Choosing care: dilemmas of a social market' (2005) *Journal of Social Welfare and Family Law* 27(3–4): 299. This article uses the lens of a personal experience of caring to reflect upon the provision of care services in England. It does so within the wider context of recent debates on the potential for a human rights culture within community care. The concept of independence, expressed as user choice in a social market of care, is central to government policy. The author, however, argues that this is a flawed approach and concludes that the starting point for policy and legal development should be the necessary interdependence of individuals.

14 Mental capacity and adult safeguarding

OVERVIEW AND OBJECTIVES

The first part of the chapter considers the Mental Capacity Act 2005. It is designed to ensure that the wishes of the service user are taken into account as far as is possible, and where that is not possible, to set in place mechanisms to ensure that the best interests of the service user are protected. The second part of the chapter considers the various safeguards to protect vulnerable service users from abuse.

CASE STUDY

A Local Authority v H (2012)

Why are we asking you to read this case?

This case demonstrates the role of the Court of Protection and the Mental Capacity Act 2005 in the lives of mentally incapacitated people. It demonstrates how the Court of Protection reaches its judgments on issues of mental capacity. Here the question was whether H had capacity to make decisions about sexual activity. If H is found to have capacity to make decisions about sex, then her freedom cannot be curtailed, even if she enters into some ill-judged relationships. If she lacks capacity, then she can be protected, as long as the local authority is acting in her best interests.

What is at stake for the parties and beyond?

For H, what is at stake is her bodily integrity. On the one hand, freedom to have sexual relations is a key human freedom and a crucial means of self-expression, even if its exercise can at times be mistaken or risky. On the other hand, if someone has no understanding of what they are doing when they agree to a sexual relationship, then they require protection.

The local authority is looking for confirmation from the Court of Protection that any decision it makes to restrict H's freedom to have sex is lawful.

More broadly, what is at stake is the correct balance between empowering people with learning difficulties and protecting them. The role of the Court of Protection is to reach that balance, using the tools given to it by the Mental Incapacity Act.

The background

A local authority sought a declaration from the Court of Protection on the capacity of H to consent to sexual relations. H, who was 29 years old, had mild learning difficulties, atypical autism, and an IQ of 64, and her history demonstrated a very early and a deep degree of sexualization. The local authority became aware of her sexual activities, vulnerability, and disinhibition. When interviewed, she gave an extensive and confused history of her willingness to have sex with strangers and indicated that she was engaging in sex with multiple partners at the same time, including a group of much older men. She saw herself as obligated to submit to what amounted to rape. H was compulsorily admitted to hospital under the Mental Health Act 1983 for nearly two years. After her discharge from hospital she lived in private accommodation provided by the local authority, but was supervised both in and out of the property at all times on a one-to-one basis. A Deprivation of Liberty Safeguard standard authorization (see **chapter 15**) under the Mental Capacity Act 2005, Schedule A1 was in force and a renewal was sought.

In other words, the local authority had permission from the Court to curtail H's freedom and it wanted to be able to continue to restrict her sexual activities.

The decision

The Court of Protection made the following judgment:

(1) For the purposes of s. 3(1) of the 2005 Act, a person was unable to make a decision for himself if he was unable:

(a) to understand the information relevant to the decision;
(b) to retain that information;
(c) to use or weigh that information as part of the process of making the decision; or
(d) to communicate his decision.

In this case the court had to apply s. 3(1) with the question of sexual relations specifically in mind. Clearly, a person had to have a basic understanding of the mechanics of the physical sexual act and that intercourse could lead to pregnancy. Moreover, it seemed that capacity required some grasp of sexual health issues. It would suffice if a person understood that sexual relations might lead to significant ill-health and that those risks could be reduced by precautions such as condoms. The question to ask was whether the person whose capacity was in question understood that they had a choice and that they could refuse sexual relations. That was an important aspect of capacity and was as far as it was possible to go over and above an understanding of the physical component. Learning difficulties impaired memory, and H was no exception. She had difficulty retaining information, but with patient explanation and repetition would be able to retain basic information. The court was reluctant to conclude that she lacked capacity on that basis. The question of using and weighing the relevant information was a difficult concept in the context of human sexual relations, since choices were made more by emotional drive and instinct than by rational choice. What was at issue was whether a person was able to deploy general knowledge into a specific decision-making act. H would struggle partly through an incomplete knowledge base and partly through an inability to deploy the knowledge she had when she was sexually aroused.

H lacked capacity to consent to sexual relations on two specific bases: first, she did not understand the health implications of sexual relations, a matter made more serious by her history of multiple partners indiscriminately accommodated; and second, she could not effectively deploy the information she had into the decision-making process (para. 31).

To protect H's best interests the court made a restrictive consequential order amounting to the deprivation of liberty.

WHAT DOES THIS CASE TELL YOU ABOUT SOCIAL CARE LAW AND PRACTICE?

This case illustrates the difficult task facing those concerned with both empowering vulnerable adults and protecting them. The Mental Capacity Act 2005 provides the tools with which this can be done, and the Court of Protection plays a very important role in making sure the necessary balancing act is carried out appropriately. The freedom to engage in sexual relationships is an important part of our identity as adults, and people with learning difficulties are as entitled to that freedom as others. However, if relationships appear to be abusive and an individual lacks capacity to consent to those relationships, then the authorities may be obliged to intervene. The Court of Protection has an important and controversial role in sanctioning the deprivation of liberty in particular cases.

Mental capacity

The capacity of service users to make decisions about their lives can often be an issue. For instance, is Mrs Smith able to refuse to go into a care home or refuse to be assessed for services? Can Mr Jones decide to give his savings to his grandson or gamble them away? The common law and best practice provided principles upon which the capacity of individuals to make decisions could be assessed. These principles have now been reformed and codified within statute.

There are three important tools that you require in order to understand how the law regulates mental capacity. The first is the Mental Capacity Act 2005; the second is the Code of Practice to the Mental Capacity Act (available from www.gov.uk/government/publications/mental-capacity-act-code-of-practice); the third is the statutory guidance to the Care Act 2014 (available from www.gov.uk/guidance/care-and-support-statutory-guidance), which provides extensive advice on the principles of the Care Act applied to the incapacitated service user.

The Mental Capacity Act 2005

The Mental Capacity Act (MCA) 2005 has its basis in the Law Commission Report No. 231 on Mental Incapacity, which was published in 1995 after extensive consultation. The Act basically deals with three areas.

- It sets out the legal rules that are used to determine whether an individual has sufficient mental capacity to make a particular decision.
- It sets out the principles upon which decisions are to be made when an individual is assessed as lacking capacity.
- It enables people to make decisions to refuse medical treatment if they lose capacity in the future.

The Code of Practice to the Mental Capacity Act

The Code of Practice to the Mental Capacity Act, which was published in 2007, provides guidance on how the MCA works on a day-to-day basis. It has useful case studies and explains the law in more detail.

Certain categories of people have a legal duty to have regard to the Code. These include:

- professionals and anyone who is paid for the work they do in relation to people who lack capacity. Clearly this includes social workers as well as doctors, nurses, care managers, solicitors, police officers, ambulance crew, and paid carers;
- attorneys appointed to act on someone's behalf under a Lasting Power of Attorney (LPA) or Enduring Power of Attorney (EPA); (we discuss these terms in **Lasting Powers of Attorney**, p 521);
- deputies appointed by the Court of Protection.

Family, friends, and unpaid carers do not have a duty to 'have regard' to the Code but they will still find the guidance helpful when they are caring for people who may lack capacity. The consequences of failure to comply with the Code are set out in the introduction to the Code, and provided for you in **Box 14.1**.

BOX 14.1 What happens if people don't comply with the Mental Capacity Act 2005 Code of Practice (2007)?

There are no specific sanctions for failure to comply with the Code. But a failure to comply with the Code can be used in evidence before a court or tribunal in any civil or criminal proceedings, if the court or tribunal considers it to be relevant to those proceedings. For example, if a court or tribunal believes that anyone making decisions for someone who lacks capacity has not acted in the best interests of the person they care for, the court can use the person's failure to comply with the Code as evidence. That's why it's important that anyone working with or caring for a person who lacks capacity to make specific decisions should become familiar with the Code.

How the MCA works

The MCA is underpinned by five principles set out in s. 1 of the Act. These are set out in **Box 14.2**. We examine these principles later.

BOX 14.2 The statutory principles—s. 1 of the Mental Capacity Act 2005

- A presumption of capacity—every adult has the right to make his or her own decisions and must be assumed to have capacity to do so unless it is proved otherwise.
- Individuals being supported to make their own decisions—a person must be given all practicable help before anyone treats them as not being able to make their own decisions.

- Unwise decisions—just because someone makes what might be seen as an unwise decision, they should not be treated as lacking capacity to make that decision.

- Best interests—an act done or decision made under the Act for or on behalf of a person who lacks capacity must be done in their best interests.

- Least restrictive principle—anything done for or on behalf of a person who lacks capacity should be the least restrictive possible to their basic rights and freedoms taking into account whether it is as effective as the proposed alternative.

Assessing capacity

A person lacks capacity if they meet the criteria of s. 2(1) of the MCA:

> For the purposes of this Act, a person lacks capacity in relation to a matter if at the material time he is unable to make a decision for himself in relation to the matter because of an impairment of, or a disturbance in the functioning of, the mind or brain.

The Act sets out a clear test for assessing whether a person lacks capacity to make a particular decision at a particular time. That test is in s. 3 of the MCA set out in **Box 14.3**.

 BOX 14.3 Inability to make decisions—s. 3 of the Mental Capacity Act 2005

(1) For the purposes of section 2, a person is unable to make a decision for himself if he is unable—

    (a) to understand the information relevant to the decision,

    (b) to retain that information,

    (c) to use or weigh that information as part of the process of making the decision, or

    (d) to communicate his decision (whether by talking, using sign language or any other means).

(2) A person is not to be regarded as unable to understand the information relevant to a decision if he is able to understand an explanation of it given to him in a way that is appropriate to his circumstances (using simple language, visual aids or any other means).

(3) The fact that a person is able to retain the information relevant to a decision for a short period only does not prevent him from being regarded as able to make the decision.

(4) The information relevant to a decision includes information about the reasonably foreseeable consequences of—

    (a) deciding one way or another, or

    (b) failing to make the decision.

As the statutory principles make clear, people must be helped to make their own decisions. Only if all appropriate help has been given should anyone conclude that someone cannot make their own decisions.

The presumption of capacity

The MCA states clearly that a person must be assumed to have capacity unless it is established that he lacks capacity—MCA, s. 1(2). What that means is that you cannot treat someone as if they lack capacity unless you have proof. The standard of proof is balance of probabilities—that it is more likely than not that the individual lacks capacity. The MCA makes it clear that lack of capacity cannot be established merely by reference to a person's age or appearance, or a condition of his, or an aspect of his behaviour, which might lead others to make unjustified assumptions about his capacity—MCA, s. 2(3).

Significantly, capacity is tested on the basis of the decision which has to be made. A person may have the capacity to decide what they want to wear, or whether they wish to buy new clothes, but not have the capacity to buy a house. This is set out in s. 2(1) of the MCA.

> For the purposes of this Act, a person lacks capacity in relation to a matter if at the material time he is unable to make a decision for himself in relation to the matter because of an impairment of, or a disturbance in the functioning of, the mind or brain.

Note that this test is a legal test and not a medical test. Doctors should only make decisions about capacity if they understand the law. What the section means in practice is illustrated by a scenario delineated in the Code of Practice which is set out in **Box 14.4**.

 BOX 14.4 Scenario: assessing a person's capacity to make decisions—Mental Capacity Act 2005 Code of Practice (2007)

When planning for her retirement, Mrs Arnold made and registered a Lasting Power of Attorney (LPA)—a legal process that would allow her son to manage her property and financial affairs if she ever lacked capacity to manage them herself. She has now been diagnosed with dementia, and her son is worried that she is becoming confused about money.

Her son must assume that his mother has capacity to manage her affairs. Then he must consider each of Mrs Arnold's financial decisions as she makes them, giving her any help and support she needs to make these decisions herself.

Mrs Arnold's son goes shopping with her, and he sees she is quite capable of finding goods and making sure she gets the correct change. But when she needs to make decisions about her investments, Mrs Arnold gets confused—even though she has made such decisions in the past. She still doesn't understand after her son explains the different options.

Her son concludes that she has capacity to deal with everyday financial matters but not more difficult affairs at this time. Therefore, he is able to use the LPA for the difficult financial decisions his mother can't make. But Mrs Arnold can continue to deal with her other affairs for as long as she has capacity to do so.

The statutory principles make it clear that people need to be supported in making decisions. An example of how this can be done is set out in the Code of Practice, provided for you in **Box 14.5**.

BOX 14.5 Scenario: taking steps to help people make decisions for themselves—Mental Capacity Act 2005 Code of Practice (2007)

Mr Jackson is brought into hospital following a traffic accident. He is conscious but in shock. He cannot speak and is clearly in distress, making noises and gestures.

From his behaviour, hospital staff conclude that Mr Jackson currently lacks the capacity to make decisions about treatment for his injuries, and they give him urgent treatment. They hope that after he has recovered from the shock they can use an advocate to help explain things to him.

However, one of the nurses thinks she recognises some of his gestures as sign language, and tries signing to him. Mr Jackson immediately becomes calmer, and the doctors realise that he can communicate in sign language. He can also answer some written questions about his injuries.

The hospital brings in a qualified sign-language interpreter and concludes that Mr Jackson has the capacity to make decisions about any further treatment.

Best interests

The law requires that decisions made in respect of individuals who lack capacity are made in the best interests of that person. 'Best interests' does not mean what you might think it means. Common sense would probably suggest that acting in someone's best interests means doing what is best for them objectively. However, the law is more complex; acting in someone's best interests has a subjective element—what would the person have decided to do for themselves if they had capacity. The relevant section of the MCA, s. 4, is set out in **Box 14.6**. What it does is provide a checklist to ensure that people act in someone's best interests.

BOX 14.6 Acting in a person's best interests—s. 4 of the Mental Capacity Act 2005

(1) The person making the determination must consider all the relevant circumstances and, in particular, take the following steps.

(2) He must consider—

  (a) whether it is likely that the person will at some time have capacity in relation to the matter in question, and

  (b) if it appears likely that he will, when that is likely to be.

(3) He must, so far as reasonably practicable, permit and encourage the person to participate, or to improve his ability to participate, as fully as possible in any act done for him and any decision affecting him.

(4) Where the determination relates to life-sustaining treatment he must not, in considering whether the treatment is in the best interests of the person concerned, be motivated by a desire to bring about his death.

(5) He must consider, so far as is reasonably ascertainable—

    (a) the person's past and present wishes and feelings (and, in particular, any relevant written statement made by him when he had capacity),

    (b) the beliefs and values that would be likely to influence his decision if he had capacity, and

    (c) the other factors that he would be likely to consider if he were able to do so.

(6) He must take into account, if it is practicable and appropriate to consult them, the views of—

    (a) anyone named by the person as someone to be consulted on the matter in question or on matters of that kind,

    (b) anyone engaged in caring for the person or interested in his welfare,

    (c) any donee (person who has been given) of a lasting power of attorney granted by the person, and

    (d) any deputy appointed for the person by the court, as to what would be in the person's best interests and, in particular, as to the matters mentioned in subsection (6).

'Best interests' is not defined. Explanatory notes to the Act said: 'Best interests is not a test of "substituted judgement" (what the person would have wanted), but rather it requires a determination to be made by applying an objective test as to what would be in the person's best interests.' What is required is that anyone acting on behalf of someone else goes through a rigorous process of decision making. This is inevitably going to be complex. Is it, for instance, in the best interests of someone who lacks capacity for the decision maker to make an unwise financial decision simply because that person habitually made unwise financial decisions when they had capacity? Perhaps not surprisingly, the Court of Protection in *Re P* (2009) decided that it was not. In **Box 14.7** we set out the judge's explanation of the process that a decision maker must follow. It demonstrates what a complex process acting in someone's best interests is. Even judges do not agree!

 BOX 14.7 Making decisions in someone's best interests—Re P (2009)

The goal of the enquiry is not what P [meaning 'a person' here, not specifically the P of the court case] 'might be expected' to have done; but what is in P's best interests. This is more akin to the 'balance sheet' approach than to the 'substituted judgment' approach.

The previous guidance [before the 2005 Act] was concerned with deciding what P would have wanted if he were not mentally disordered. But the 2005 Act requires the decision maker to consider P's *present* wishes and feelings, which . . . are wishes and feelings entertained by a person who lacks mental capacity in relation to the decision being made on his behalf.

The same structured decision making process applies to all decisions to be made on P's behalf, whether great or small . . . Moreover, it is a decision making process which must be followed, not only by the court, but by anyone who takes decisions on P's behalf.

In making his decision the decision maker must consider 'all relevant circumstances'. The Act expressly directs the decision maker to take a number of steps before reaching a decision. These include encouraging P to participate in the decision. The decision maker must also 'consider' P's past and present wishes, and his beliefs and values and must 'take into account' the views of third parties as to what would be in P's best interests.

Having gone through these steps, the decision maker must then form a value judgment of his own giving effect to the paramount statutory instruction that any decision must be made in P's best interests. In my judgment this process is quite different to that which applied under the former Mental Health Acts.

That is not to say that P's expressed wishes should be lightly overridden. On the contrary, the Act expressly requires them to be considered; and for particular consideration to be given to wishes expressed by P when he had capacity. In *Re S and S (Protected Persons)* (unreported 25 November 2008) Her Honour Judge Marshall QC . . . pointed out the stress that the Act lays on the ascertainment of P's wishes and feelings and on involving him in the decision making process. She concluded:

'55. In my judgment it is the inescapable conclusion from the stress laid on these matters in the Act that the views and wishes of P in regard to decisions made on his behalf are to carry great weight. What, after all, is the point of taking great trouble to ascertain or deduce P's views, and to encourage P to be involved in the decision making process, unless the objective is to try to achieve the outcome which P wants or prefers, even if he does not have the capacity to achieve it for himself?

'56. The Act does not of course say that P's wishes are to be paramount, nor does it lay down any express presumption in favour of implementing them if they can be ascertained. Indeed the paramount objective is that of P's best interests. However, by giving such prominence to the above matters, the Act does in my judgment recognise that having his views and wishes taken into account and respected is a very significant aspect of P's best interests. Due regard should therefore be paid when doing the weighing exercise of determining what is in P's best interests in all the circumstances of the case.

'57. As to how this will work in practice, in my judgment, where P can and does express a wish or view which is not irrational (in the sense of being a wish which a person of full capacity might reasonably have), is not impractical as far as its physical implementation is concerned, and is not irresponsible having regard to the extent of P's resources (i.e. whether a responsible person of full capacity who had such resources might reasonably consider it worth using the necessary resources to implement his wish) then that situation carries great weight, and effectively gives rise to a presumption in favour of implementing those wishes, unless there is some potential sufficiently detrimental effect for P of doing so which outweighs this.

'58. That might be some extraneous consequence, or some other unforeseen, unknown or unappreciated factor. Whether this further consideration actually should justify overriding P's wishes might then be tested by asking whether, had he known of this further consideration, it appears (from what is known of P) that he would have changed his wishes. It might further be tested by asking whether the seriousness of this countervailing factor in terms of detriment to P is such that it must outweigh the detriment to an adult of having one's wishes overruled, and the sense of impotence, and the frustration and anger, which living with that awareness (insofar as P appreciates it) will cause to P. Given the policy of the Act to empower people to make their own decisions wherever possible, justification for overruling P and "saving him from himself" must, in my judgment, be strong and cogent. Otherwise, taking a different course from that which P wishes would be likely to infringe the statutory direction in s [1(6)] of the Act, that one must achieve any desired objective by the route which least restricts P's own rights and freedom of actions.'

I agree with the broad thrust of this, although I think that HH Judge Marshall QC may have slightly overstated the importance to be given to P's wishes. First, section 1(6) is not a statutory direction that one 'must achieve' any desired objective by the least restrictive route. Section 1(6) only requires that before a decision is made 'regard must be had' to that question. It is an important question, to be sure, but it is not determinative. The only imperative is that the decision must be made in P's best interests. Second, although P's wishes must be given weight, if, as I think, Parliament has endorsed the 'balance sheet' approach, they are only one part of the balance. I agree that those wishes are to be given great weight, but I would prefer not to speak in terms of presumptions. Third, any attempt to test a decision by reference to what P would hypothetically have done or wanted runs the risk of amounting to a 'substituted judgment' rather than a decision of what would be in P's best interests. But despite this risk, the Act itself requires some hypothesising. The decision maker must consider the beliefs and values that would be likely to influence P's decision if he had capacity and also the other factors that P would be likely to consider if he were able to do so. This does not, I think, necessarily require those to be given effect.

The Code of Practice provides extensive assistance here. **Box 14.8** provides a scenario which illustrates how to follow the checklist.

 BOX 14.8 Scenario: following the checklist—Mental Capacity Act 2005 Code of Practice (2007)

Martina, an elderly woman with dementia, is beginning to neglect her appearance and personal hygiene and has several times been found wandering in the street unable to find her way home. Her care workers are concerned that Martina no longer has capacity to make appropriate decisions relating to her daily care. Her daughter is her personal welfare attorney and believes the time has come to act under the Lasting Power of Attorney (LPA). She assumes it would be best for Martina to move into a care home, since the staff would be able to help her wash and dress smartly and prevent her from wandering. However, it cannot be assumed *simply on the basis of her age, condition, appearance or behaviour* either that Martina lacks capacity to make such a decision or that such a move would be in her best interests. Instead, steps must be taken to assess her capacity.

If it is then agreed that Martina lacks the capacity to make this decision, all the relevant factors in the best interests checklist must be considered to try to work out what her best interests would be.

Her daughter must therefore consider:

- Martina's past and present wishes and feelings;
- the views of the people involved in her care;
- any alternative ways of meeting her care needs effectively which might be less restrictive of Martina's rights and freedoms, such as increased provision of home care or attendance at a day centre.

By following this process, Martina's daughter can then take decisions on behalf of her mother and in her best interests, when her mother lacks the capacity to make them herself, on any matters that fall under the authority of the LPA.

The Code of Practice also suggests that written records be kept of the decision-making process involved in working out what is in someone's best interests. This is important: demonstrably acting in someone's best interests protects a person from liability for what might otherwise be unlawful acts (e.g. touching or entering their home without permission) when they carry out care and treatment in connection with a person who lacks capacity. This is set out in s. 5 of the MCA, the effects of which are explained in the Code of Practice—see **Box 14.9**.

 BOX 14.9 What protection do people have when caring for those who lack capacity to consent?— extract from the Mental Capacity Act 2005 Code of Practice (2007)

6.1 Every day, millions of acts are done to and for people who lack capacity either to:

- take decisions about their own care or treatment, or
- consent to someone else caring for them.

Such acts range from everyday tasks of caring (for example, helping someone to wash) to life-changing events (for example, serious medical treatment or arranging for someone to go into a care home). In theory, many of these actions could be against the law. Legally, people have the right to stop others from interfering with their body or property unless they give permission. But what happens if someone lacks capacity to give permission? Carers who dress people who cannot dress themselves are potentially interfering with someone's body without their consent, so could theoretically be prosecuted for assault. A neighbour who enters and cleans the house of a person who lacks capacity could be trespassing on the person's property.

6.2 Section 5 of the Act provides 'protection from liability'. In other words, it protects people who carry out these actions. It stops them being prosecuted for acts that could otherwise be classed as civil wrongs or crimes. By protecting family and other carers from liability, the Act allows necessary caring acts or treatment to take place as if a person who lacks capacity to consent had consented to them. People providing care of this sort do not therefore need to get formal authority to act.

6.3 Importantly, section 5 does not give people caring for or treating someone the power to make any other decisions on behalf of those who lack capacity to make their own decisions. Instead, it offers protection from liability so that they can act in connection with the person's care or treatment.

> The power to make decisions on behalf of someone who lacks capacity can be granted through other parts of the Act (such as the powers granted to attorneys and deputies, which are explained in chapters 7 and 8 [of the Code of Practice]).

These protections are limited if the act done to or for the person who lacks capacity involves restraining that person. This is a complex area of law and practice, which we discuss fully in **chapter 15**.

The MCA and care planning

The Social Care Institute for Excellence (SCIE) estimates that around two million people lack capacity to make decisions about their care and support. There is a shared approach between the Care Act 2014 and the MCA. Both require the service user to:

- participate as fully as possible in decisions;
- have the information and support necessary to enable them to participate fully;
- have decisions made having regard to all the individual's circumstances (and not based only on the individual's age or appearance or other condition or behaviour); and
- keep any restriction on the individual's rights or freedom of action to the minimum necessary for achieving the purpose.

In 2014, SCIE published a report on the MCA and care planning. It is available at www. scie.org.uk/publications/reports/70-mental-capacity-act-and-care-planning/. The key messages from the report are set out in **Box 14.10**.

 BOX 14.10 Key messages—The Mental Capacity Act (MCA) and care planning report (reviewed September 2017)

- The Mental Capacity Act (MCA) 2005 is vital to ensuring person-centred care that respects people's rights.
- Local authorities and paid staff who provide care and support to people over 16 years of age are legally required to work within the framework of the MCA and have regard to the MCA Code of Practice (the Code).
- Care planning is a key mechanism for ensuring that the MCA is implemented in social care. Care planning should reflect the principles of the MCA.
- Care and support plans should promote people's liberty—the freedom to make decisions about their care and support as far as they are able.
- Care planning should show how people and their chosen representatives are supported to be involved in developing and reviewing their care and support.
- Care plans must provide evidence of consent, or, where people lack capacity to consent to their care and support plan, there must be a clearly recorded assessment of capacity with supporting evidence.

- Care planning documents must demonstrate how any decisions made on behalf of a person who lacks capacity are made in their best interests.

- Care and support plans must be regularly reviewed to make sure they continue to meet people's changing needs and choices.

- Care planning documents must demonstrate how people who are deprived of their liberty have their rights protected.

The statutory guidance to the Care Act 2014 provides useful specific advice in relation to persons who lack capacity and statutory functions. So, for instance, para. 10.49 (set out in **Box 14.11**) provides advice on how to involve a person who lacks capacity in the care planning process and paras 10.59–10.72 (an extract from which is set out in **Box 14.12**) are specifically targeted at planning for those who lack capacity.

BOX 14.11 Involving the person—para. 10.49 of Care and support statutory guidance (updated October 2018)

10.49 In addition to taking all reasonable steps to agree how needs are to be met, the local authority must also involve the person the plan is intended for, the carer (if there is one), and/or any other person the adult requests to be involved. Where the person lacks capacity to ask the authority to do that, the local authority must involve any person who appears to the authority to be interested in the welfare of the person and should involve any person who would be able to contribute useful information. An independent advocate must be provided if section 67 of the Act applies. The person, and their carers, will have the best understanding of how the needs identified fit into the person's life as a whole and connect to their overall wellbeing (see chapter 1). They are well placed to consider and identify which care and support options would best fit into their lifestyle and help them to achieve the day to day outcomes they identified during the assessment process. In practice, local authorities should give consideration to include a prompt to the person during the initial stages of the planning process to ask whether there is anyone else that the person wishes to be involved. Where the person lacks capacity, the local authority should make a best interests decision about who else should be involved.

BOX 14.12 Planning for people who lack capacity—paras 10.63–10.65 of Care and support statutory guidance (updated October 2018)

10.63 If a local authority thinks a person may lack capacity to make a decision or a plan, even after they have offered them all practicable support, a social worker or other suitably qualified professional should carry out a capacity assessment in relation to the specific decision to be made. For example, the local authority may assess whether the person has the capacity to decide whether family members should be involved in their care planning or whether the person has the capacity to decide on whether a particular support option will meet their needs.

10.64 Where an individual has been assessed as lacking capacity to make a particular decision, then the local authority must commence care planning in the person's best interests under the meaning of the MCA. Furthermore a person making a decision concerning a plan on behalf of a person who lacks capacity must consider whether it is possible to make a decision or a plan in a way that would be less restrictive of the person's rights and freedoms of action. Any restriction must be in the person's best interests and necessary to prevent harm to the person, and a proportionate response to the likelihood of the person suffering harm and the seriousness of that harm.

10.65 The duty to involve the person remains throughout the process. If lack of capacity is established, it is still important that the person is involved as far as possible in making decisions. Planning should always be done with the person and not for them; should always start by the identification of their wishes, feelings, values and aspirations, not just their needs, and should always consider their wellbeing in the wider context of their rights to security, to liberty, and to family life.

Independent advocacy

The statutory guidance to the Care Act 2014 makes reference to an independent advocate. Independent advocacy is an important service available to certain adult service care users. Section 67 of the Care Act 2014, set out in **Box 14.13**, places a duty on local authorities to provide access to independent advocacy to those who would have substantial difficulty in being involved in care and support 'processes' and have no appropriate individual(s)—carer, family, or friend—who can support their involvement. The duty applies to adults and also applies to children who are coming up to 'transition' to adult care. Independent advocacy means a service that is independent of the local authority.

BOX 14.13 Independent advocacy—s. 67(2)–(5) of the Care Act 2014

(2) The authority must, if the condition in subsection (4) is met, arrange for a person who is independent of the authority (an 'independent advocate') to be available to represent and support the individual for the purpose of facilitating the individual's involvement; but see subsection (5).

(3) The relevant provisions are—

   (a) **section 9(5)(a) and (b)** (carrying out needs assessment);

   (b) **section 10(7)(a)** (carrying out carer's assessment);

   (c) **section 25(3)(a) and (b)** (preparing care and support plan);

   (d) **section 25(4)(a) and (b)** (preparing support plan);

   (e) **section 27(2)(b)(i) and (ii)** (revising care and support plan);

   (f) **section 27(3)(b)(i) and (ii)** (revising support plan);

   (g) **section 59(2)(a) and (b)** (carrying out child's needs assessment);

(h) **section 61(3)(a)** (carrying out child's carer's assessment);

(i) **section 64(3)(a) and (b)** (carrying out young carer's assessment).

(4) The condition is that the local authority considers that, were an independent advocate not to be available, the individual would experience substantial difficulty in doing one or more of the following—

(a) understanding relevant information;

(b) retaining that information;

(c) using or weighing that information as part of the process of being involved;

(d) communicating the individual's views, wishes or feelings (whether by talking, using sign language or any other means).

(5) The duty under subsection (2) does not apply if the local authority is satisfied that there is a person—

(a) who would be an appropriate person to represent and support the individual for the purpose of facilitating the individual's involvement, and

(b) who is not engaged in providing care or treatment for the individual in a professional capacity or for remuneration.

The following points should be noted about the duty in s. 67.

- The duty applies in community and residential settings, including prisons.
- It is for the local authority to make a judgement about whether the individual would experience substantial difficulty in understanding relevant information, retaining that information, using or weighing that information as part of the process of being involved and/or communicating the individual's views, wishes, or feelings.
- The duty applies throughout the service user's journey through the social care system.

The statutory guidance to the Care Act 2014 explains the requirements for independent advocates—see **Box 14.14**.

BOX 14.14 Independent advocates—para. 7.43 of Care and support guidance (updated October 2018)

7.43 Advocates must have:

A suitable level of appropriate experience

This may, for example, be in non-instructed advocacy or in working with those groups of people who may have substantial difficulty in engaging with assessments and care and support planning

Appropriate training

This may, for example, initially be training in advocacy (non-instructed and instructed) or dementia, or working with people with learning disabilities. Once appointed, all independent advocates should be expected to work towards the National Qualification in Independent Advocacy (level 3) within a year of being appointed, and to achieve it in a reasonable amount of time.

Competency in the task

This will require the advocacy organisation assuring itself that the advocates who work for it are all competent and have regular training and assessment.

Integrity and good character

This might be assessed through: interview and selection processes; seeking and scrutinising references prior to employment and on-going DBS checks.

The ability to work independently of the local authority or body carrying out assessments, planning or reviews on the local authority's behalf

This would include the ability to make a judgement about what a person is communicating and what is in a person's best interests, as opposed to in a local authority's best interests, and to act accordingly to represent this.

There is a further duty to appoint independent advocates in the context of adult safeguarding. That duty is in s. 68 of the Care Act 2014 and is discussed later, in **Safeguarding Adults Boards**, p 527. Note that the appointment of independent advocates is for a wider constituency than those who are incapacitated. In the next section on **The Public Guardian**, we discuss protections that are more clearly focused on people who are lacking capacity.

The Public Guardian

The Public Guardian is a role created by the MCA to protect people who lack capacity by:

- setting up and managing a register of LPAs;
- setting up and managing a register of EPAs;
- setting up and managing a register of court orders that appoint deputies;
- supervising deputies, working with other relevant organizations (e.g. social services, if the person who lacks capacity is receiving social care);
- instructing Court of Protection visitors to visit people who may lack mental capacity to make particular decisions and those who have formal powers to act on their behalf, such as deputies;
- receiving reports from attorneys acting under LPAs and from deputies; and
- providing reports to the Court of Protection, when requested, and dealing with cases where there are concerns raised about the way in which attorneys or deputies are carrying out their duties.

Lasting Powers of Attorney

An LPA enables someone who has capacity to choose who they want to make decisions on their behalf when they lack mental capacity to make the decision themselves in advance of them losing mental capacity. It only comes into effect if and when the person making the LPA—the donor—loses capacity. Until that date they continue to make decisions themselves. If they lose capacity, the LPA is 'registered' with the Office of the Public Guardian. From this point on the other people—the attorney or attorneys—are able to make decisions on the donor's behalf.

There are two types of LPA:

- health and welfare (allowing decisions on treatment, care, medication, where you live, etc.);
- property and financial affairs (allowing an attorney to make decisions about paying bills, dealing with the bank, collecting benefits, selling your house, etc.).

Different attorneys can be appointed to make decisions under the different powers of attorney.

LPAs replaced Enduring Powers of Attorney (EPAs) as a result of the MCA. The important difference between LPAs and EPAs is the ability to appoint an attorney to make decisions concerning personal welfare matters. Although no new EPAs can now be created, you will come across EPAs made before the implementation of the MCA.

The Code of Practice provides advice on personal welfare LPAs, which is set out in **Box 14.15**.

 BOX 14.15 Personal welfare LPAs—para. 7.21 of the Mental Capacity Act 2005 Code of Practice (2007)

LPAs can be used to appoint attorneys to make decisions about personal welfare, which can include healthcare and medical treatment decisions. Personal welfare LPAs might include decisions about:

- where the donor should live and who they should live with
- the donor's day-to-day care, including diet and dress
- who the donor may have contact with
- consenting to or refusing medical examination and treatment on the donor's behalf
- arrangements needed for the donor to be given medical, dental or optical treatment
- assessments for and provision of community care services
- whether the donor should take part in social activities, leisure activities, education or training
- the donor's personal correspondence and papers
- rights of access to personal information about the donor, or
- complaints about the donor's care or treatment.

The types of action that may be carried out by an attorney with a property and affairs LPA are set out in **Box 14.16**.

BOX 14.16 Property and affairs LPA—para. 7.36 of the Mental Capacity Act 2005 Code of Practice (2007)

If a donor does not restrict decisions the attorney can make, the attorney will be able to decide on any or all of the person's property and financial affairs. This might include:

- buying or selling property
- opening, closing or operating any bank, building society or other account
- giving access to the donor's financial information
- claiming, receiving and using (on the donor's behalf) all benefits, pensions, allowances and rebates (unless the Department for Work and Pensions has already appointed someone and everyone is happy for this to continue)
- receiving any income, inheritance or other entitlement on behalf of the donor
- dealing with the donor's tax affairs
- paying the donor's mortgage, rent and household expenses
- insuring, maintaining and repairing the donor's property
- investing the donor's savings
- making limited gifts on the donor's behalf (but see paragraphs 7.40–7.42 below)
- paying for private medical care and residential care or nursing home fees
- applying for any entitlement to funding for NHS care, social care or adaptations
- using the donor's money to buy a vehicle or any equipment or other help they need
- repaying interest and capital on any loan taken out by the donor.

Advance decisions to refuse treatment

The MCA sets out statutory rules with built-in safeguards which allow people to make a decision in advance to refuse treatment if they should lose capacity in the future. If the advance decision is to refuse life-sustaining treatment, it must comply with the formalities set out in **Box 14.17**, which are taken from the Code of Practice.

BOX 14.17 The formalities required of advance decisions to refuse life-sustaining treatment—Mental Capacity Act 2005 Code of Practice (2007)

Advance decisions to refuse life-sustaining treatment must meet specific requirements:***

- They must be put in writing. If the person is unable to write, someone else should write it down for them. For example, a family member can write down the decision on their behalf, or a healthcare professional can record it in the person's healthcare notes.

- The person must sign the advance decision. If they are unable to sign, they can direct someone to sign on their behalf in their presence.

- The person making the decision must sign in the presence of a witness to the signature. The witness must then sign the document in the presence of the person making the advance decision. If the person making the advance decision is unable to sign, the witness can witness them directing someone else to sign on their behalf. The witness must then sign to indicate that they have witnessed the nominated person signing the document in front of the person making the advance decision.

- The advance decision must include a clear, specific written statement from the person making the advance decision that the advance decision is to apply to the specific treatment even if life is at risk.

- If this statement is made at a different time or in a separate document to the advance decision, the person making the advance decision (or someone they have directed to sign) must sign it in the presence of a witness, who must also sign it.

More information on advance directives, and indeed on all aspects of the law, can be found in the Code of Practice. We recommend you become very familiar with it. The law in connection with mental capacity reflects the complexity of balancing the right of an individual to autonomy and the need to protect those who need protection. The next section, **Safeguarding adults**, concentrates on recent developments to improve the law in connection with the safeguarding of adults.

■ Safeguarding adults

The televising of abuse in the private hospital Winterbourne, run by Castlebeck, by the BBC *Panorama* programme in summer 2011 highlighted the problem of abuse of vulnerable adults. Awareness of the issue has been growing for the past 15 years. A report from the House of Commons Health Select Committee published in 2004 about the extent of abuse and the lack of coherent responses to it provides useful background. Some paragraphs from the introduction to that report are set out in **Box 14.18**.

BOX 14.18 Extract from House of Commons Health Select Committee Report 2004

1 'The voice of older people is rarely heard by those who have a responsibility for commissioning, regulating and inspecting services.' This remark was made to us by Gary Fitzgerald, representing the charity Action for Elder Abuse. Mr Fitzgerald pointed out that many people would be familiar with the case of Victoria Climbié, a child tortured and murdered in the care of a relative, but few knew about Margaret Panting, a 78-year-old woman from Sheffield who died after suffering 'unbelievable cruelty' while living with relatives. After her death in 2001, a post-mortem found 49 injuries on her

body including cuts probably made by a razor blade and cigarette burns. She had moved from shel-tered accommodation to her son-in-law's home—five weeks later she was dead. But as the cause of Margaret Panting's death could not be established, no one was ever charged. An inquest in 2002 recorded an open verdict.

15 The prevalence of elder abuse is difficult to quantify for a number of reasons. Abuse is frequently hidden, may not be obvious even to the victim, and is likely to be under-reported. The Association of Directors of Social Services quoted research to suggest that 'reported alleged abuse is but a small proportion of the overall experience.' Moreover, a lack of staff awareness of what constitutes abuse (including poor practice), and inadequate knowledge and training in how to detect abuse can also lead to under-reporting of cases of abuse. Overall therefore, robust evidence is very hard to obtain.

34 A number of submissions drew particular attention to the potential for abuse to occur 'behind closed doors,' in situations where services were provided in a 'one-to-one situation', and where an older person was entirely dependent on the district nurse, or care worker, who came into their home. Gary Fitzgerald for AEA told us that it was almost impossible to quantify the level of 'unknown abuse' that occurred in such settings, but in terms of calls to his organisation's helpline it was clear that a great deal of reported abuse took place in people's own homes. Such concerns were also recently highlighted by the BBC Panorama programme broadcast in November 2003 which used an under cover reporter to investigate the vulnerability of older people cared for in their own homes.

Defining abuse has proved problematic. The relevant paragraphs of the statutory guid-ance to the Care Act provide a non-exhaustive list, extracts from which are set out in **Box 14.19**.

 BOX 14.19 What constitutes abuse and neglect—para. 14.17 of Care and support statutory guidance (updated October 2018)

Physical abuse including:

- assault
- hitting
- slapping
- pushing
- misuse of medication
- restraint
- inappropriate physical sanctions.

Domestic violence including:

- psychological
- physical
- sexual

- financial
- emotional abuse
- so called 'honour' based violence.

Sexual abuse including:

- rape
- indecent exposure
- sexual harassment
- inappropriate looking or touching
- sexual teasing or innuendo
- sexual photography
- subjection to pornography or witnessing sexual acts
- indecent exposure
- sexual assault
- sexual acts to which the adult has not consented or was pressured into consenting.

Psychological abuse including:

- emotional abuse
- threats of harm or abandonment
- deprivation of contact
- humiliation
- blaming
- controlling
- intimidation
- coercion
- harassment
- verbal abuse
- cyber bullying
- isolation
- unreasonable and unjustified withdrawal of services or supportive networks.

Financial or material abuse including:

- theft
- fraud
- internet scamming
- coercion in relation to an adult's financial affairs or arrangements, including in connection with wills, property, inheritance or financial transactions
- the misuse or misappropriation of property, possessions or benefits.

Modern slavery encompasses:

- slavery
- human trafficking
- forced labour and domestic servitude
- traffickers and slave masters using whatever means they have at their disposal to coerce, deceive and force individuals into a life of abuse, servitude and inhumane treatment.

Discriminatory abuse including forms of:

- harassment
- slurs or similar treatment
- because of race
- gender and gender identity
- age
- disability
- sexual orientation
- religion.

Organisational abuse:

Including neglect and poor care practice within an institution or specific care setting such as a hospital or care home, for example, or in relation to care provided in one's own home. This may range from one off incidents to on-going ill-treatment. It can be through neglect or poor professional practice as a result of the structure, policies, processes and practices within an organisation.

Neglect and acts of omission including:

- ignoring medical, emotional or physical care needs
- failure to provide access to appropriate health, care and support or educational services
- the withholding of the necessities of life, such as medication, adequate nutrition and heating.

The extent of abuse is also problematic. It is inevitably hidden. The Select Committee's report on elder abuse recommended that further research should be carried out. In response, King's College London (KCL) (Institute of Gerontology and Social Care Workforce Research Unit) and the National Centre for Social Research were commissioned by Comic Relief and the Department of Health to carry out the UK Study of Abuse and Neglect of Older People. This was the first dedicated study of its kind in the UK. More robust statistics are now being collated and are published by the Health and Social Care Information Centre. The statistical report contains information about instances where a concern has been raised to a council about an adult over the age of 18 who is at risk of abuse. The report also includes the results of investigations into these concerns. Types of abuse include physical, sexual, psychological, financial, neglect, discrimination, and institutional. The most recent statistics are set out in **Box 14.20**.

BOX 14.20 Extract from key facts from *Safeguarding Adults, England* 2016–17 (November 2017)

- For the 2016–17 reporting year there were 109,145 individuals that were the subject of a safeguarding enquiry under Section 42 of the Care Act that started within the year. This is an increase of 6 per cent on 2015–16.
- Of these individuals at risk, 60 per cent were female and 63 per cent were aged 65 or over.
- 364,605 concerns of abuse were raised during 2016–17, equating to an average of just under 1,000 per day. During the same period 151,160 formal safeguarding enquiries commenced.
- The most common type of risk in Section 42 enquiries that ended in the year was Neglect and Acts of Omission, which accounted for 35 per cent of risks.
- The location of risk in Section 42 enquiries that ended in the year was most frequently the home of the adult at risk (44 per cent of enquiries).

Safeguarding Adults Boards

Local Safeguarding Adults Boards are multi-agency partnerships made up of a wide range of statutory agencies and voluntary organizations. They are aimed at facilitating joint working in adult protection, and their responsibilities include ensuring that multi-agency policies and procedures are in place, conducting serious case reviews, and providing training and information. Sections 42–47 of the Care Act 2014 provide the statutory basis for the safeguarding of vulnerable adults, including the establishment of Safeguarding Adults Boards. Section 42, set out in **Box 14.21**, places a duty on local authorities to make enquiries in circumstances where an adult has needs for care and support (whether or not the local authority is meeting any of those needs, is experiencing, or at risk of, abuse or neglect and as a result of the care and support needs is unable to protect themselves from either the risk of, or the experience of, abuse or neglect).

BOX 14.21 Enquiries where an adult has needs for care and support—s. 42 of the Care Act 2014

(1) This section applies where a local authority has reasonable cause to suspect that an adult in its area (whether or not ordinarily resident there)—

    (a) has needs for care and support (whether or not the authority is meeting any of those needs),

    (b) is experiencing, or is at risk of, abuse or neglect, and

    (c) as a result of those needs is unable to protect himself or herself against the abuse or neglect or the risk of it.

(2) The local authority must make (or cause to be made) whatever enquiries it thinks necessary to enable it to decide whether any action should be taken in the adult's case (whether under this Part or otherwise) and, if so, what and by whom.

Enquiries must be carried out by experienced staff and in a sensitive manner. For instance, paras 14.68–14.69 of the statutory guidance, set out in **Box 14.22**, suggest the need for social work expertise, particularly when the abuse is within a complex situation.

BOX 14.22 Carrying out enquiries—paras 14.68–14.69 of Care and support statutory guidance (updated October 2018)

14.68 Professionals and other staff need to handle enquiries in a sensitive and skilled way to ensure distress to the adult is minimised. It is likely that many enquiries will require the input and supervision of a social worker, particularly the more complex situations and to support the adult to realise the outcomes they want and to reach a resolution or recovery. For example, where abuse or neglect is suspected within a family or informal relationship it is likely that a social worker will be the most appropriate lead. Personal and family relationships within community settings can prove both difficult and complex to assess and intervene in. The dynamics of personal relationships can be extremely difficult to judge and rebalance. For example, an adult may make a choice to be in a relationship that causes them emotional distress which outweighs, for them, the unhappiness of not maintaining the relationship.

Section 43 of the Care Act establishes Safeguarding Adults Boards. These are required to conduct Safeguarding Adults Reviews into certain cases in specific circumstances. The aim of a review is to ensure that lessons are learned from such cases, not to allocate blame but to improve future practice and partnership working, and to minimize the possibility of it happening again. The statutory guidance explains the strategic importance of Safeguarding Adults Boards—see the extract in **Box 14.23**.

BOX 14.23 The strategic role of Safeguarding Adults Boards—paras 14.105 and 14.106 of Care and support statutory guidance (updated October 2018)

14.105 The SAB has a strategic role that is greater than the sum of the operational duties of the core partners. It oversees and leads adult safeguarding across the locality and will be interested in a range of matters that contribute to the prevention of abuse and neglect. These will include the safety of patients in its local health services, quality of local care and support services, effectiveness of prisons and approved premises in safeguarding offenders and awareness and responsiveness of further education services. The SAB will need intelligence on safeguarding in all providers of health and social care in its locality (not just those with whom its members commission or contract). It is important that SAB partners feel able to challenge each other and other organisations where it believes that their actions or inactions are increasing the risk of abuse or neglect. This will include commissioners, as well as providers of services.

14.106 The SAB can be an important source of advice and assistance, for example in helping others improve their safeguarding mechanisms. It is important that the SAB has effective links with other key partnerships in the locality and share relevant information and work plans. They should consciously cooperate to reduce any duplication and maximise any efficiency, particularly as objectives and membership is likely to overlap.

The circumstances when a Safeguarding Adults Review is carried out are provided for in s. 44 of the Care Act 2014—see **Box 14.24**.

BOX 14.24 Safeguarding Adults Reviews—s. 44 of the Care Act 2014

(1) An SAB must arrange for there to be a review of a case involving an adult in its area with needs for care and support (whether or not the local authority has been meeting any of those needs) if—

    (a) there is reasonable cause for concern about how the SAB, members of it or other persons with relevant functions worked together to safeguard the adult, and

    (b) condition 1 or 2 is met.

(2) Condition 1 is met if—

    (a) the adult has died, and

    (b) the SAB knows or suspects that the death resulted from abuse or neglect (whether or not it knew about or suspected the abuse or neglect before the adult died).

(3) Condition 2 is met if—

    (a) the adult is still alive, and

    (b) the SAB knows or suspects that the adult has experienced serious abuse or neglect.

(4) An SAB may arrange for there to be a review of any other case involving an adult in its area with needs for care and support (whether or not the local authority has been meeting any of those needs).

(5) Each member of the SAB must co-operate in and contribute to the carrying out of a review under this section with a view to—

    (a) identifying the lessons to be learnt from the adult's case, and

    (b) applying those lessons to future cases.

Note that s. 68 of the Care Act 2014 requires the local authority to arrange, where necessary, for an independent advocate to support and represent an adult who is the subject of a safeguarding enquiry or a Safeguarding Adults Review.

Criminal offences and vulnerable adults

In theory, there should be no need to have additional legal protections for adult service users. The normal provisions of both civil and criminal law on assault and trespass to the person should adequately protect all citizens, regardless of their particular characteristics. However, increasing knowledge of the prevalence of abuse, and the particular problems of those who lack capacity, has required the law to respond.

Criminal provisions specifically relating to the victimization of adult service users who lack capacity have therefore increased in recent years. **Table 14.1** summarizes these.

TABLE 14.1 Criminal offences and vulnerable adults

Provision	Offence
Criminal Justice and Courts Act 2015, s.20	It is an offence for an individual who has the care of another individual by virtue of being a care worker to ill-treat or wilfully neglect that individual. The maximum penalty is five years' imprisonment.
Fraud Act 2006, s. 4	It is an offence for a person who occupies a position where he or she is required to safeguard, or not act against, the financial interests of another person, to dishonestly abuse that position, with the intent of self-benefit or to benefit others.
Mental Capacity Act 2005, s. 44	It is an offence for someone who has the care of a person who lacks capacity; a donee of a Lasting or Enduring Power of Attorney; or a deputy to ill-treat or wilfully neglect that person. The maximum penalty is five years' imprisonment.
Domestic Violence, Crime and Victims Act 2004, s. 5	It is an offence to cause or allow the death of a child or vulnerable adult. A vulnerable adult is defined as a person aged 16 or over whose ability to protect himself or herself from violence, abuse, or neglect is significantly impaired through physical or mental disability or illness, through old age, or otherwise. This applies if: (a) the person lived in the same household and had frequent contact with the victim; (b) there was significant risk of serious physical harm and the person either caused the victim's death, or was or ought to have been aware of the risk and failed to take steps to protect the victim; and (c) the act occurred in circumstances that the person foresaw or ought to have foreseen. The maximum penalty is 14 years' imprisonment.
Criminal Justice Act 2003, s. 146	Imposes a duty on the criminal courts to increase the sentence for any offence aggravated by hostility based on the victim's disability or perceived disability
Sexual Offences Act 2003	Establishes a number of criminal offences arising from sexual abuse. Specifically, these relate to: (a) the inability of a person with a mental disorder to refuse sexual activity where he or she lacks capacity or is unable to communicate refusal; (b) where a person with a mental disorder is induced, threatened, or deceived into sexual activity where the perpetrator knows or could reasonably be expected to know that the person is suffering from a mental disorder; and (c) situations involving care workers and sexual activity with mentally disordered people.

Mental Health Act 1983	Creates three offences of ill-treatment or neglect of mentally disordered persons by:
	(a) an employee or manager of a hospital or care home;
	(b) a guardian or some other person who has custody or care;
	(c) any person in respect of a person subject to supervised discharge.
	The maximum penalty was extended from two to five years' imprisonment as a result of the Mental Health Act 2007.

An offence of coercive and controlling behaviour in intimate and familial relationships was introduced into the Serious Crime Act 2015. The offence imposes a maximum five years' imprisonment, a fine, or both. The statutory guidance to the Care Act 2014 points out that, 'the offence closes a gap in the law around patterns of coercive and controlling behaviour during a relationship between intimate partners, former partners who still live together, or family members, sending a clear message that it is wrong to violate the trust of those closest to you, providing better protection to victims experiencing continuous abuse and allowing for earlier identification, intervention and prevention' (para. 14.22).

Conviction of the perpetrators of offences against vulnerable adults has been made easier by measures which enhance the ability of the victims of crime who have impaired mental capacity to give evidence in court proceedings. The special measures that may be available include:

- giving evidence through a TV link;
- video-recorded evidence: the witness's evidence is videotaped and played to the court;
- screens around the witness box;
- removal of wigs and gowns;
- evidence given in private, in the courtroom;
- use of communication aids, such as an alphabet board;
- examination through an intermediary, who can help a witness to understand questions that they are being asked, and can make his or her answers understood by the court.

It is useful for you to be aware of the Public Interest Disclosure Act 1998, which is designed to provide protection from dismissal or other disciplinary victimization for workers who raise concerns about abuse and malpractice in the workplace. These provisions may be particularly relevant for those who work in a care setting who suspect that abuse is occurring.

The Safeguarding Vulnerable Groups Act 2006 is a significant piece of legislation which directly impacts upon your practice as a social worker.

■ Safeguarding Vulnerable Groups Act 2006 (SVGA)

Whilst there have been statutory procedures since 2000 to prevent unsuitable people from working with vulnerable adults, they were criticized by the Bichard Inquiry arising from the Soham murders in 2002, when the schoolgirls Jessica Chapman and Holly Wells were murdered by Ian Huntley (a school caretaker). One recommendation of the Inquiry Report was that a single agency should be established to vet all individuals who want to work or volunteer with children or vulnerable adults and to bar unsuitable people from doing so. This was done in the SVGA. However, the Coalition Government considered the provisions of the SVGA to be too extensive. The Home Secretary announced a review, which reported in February 2011. Among other things, the report recommended that the requirement on those working with children and vulnerable adults to be monitored under the scheme should be dropped. The recommendations were put into legislative form in the Protection of Freedoms Act 2012.

The SVGA set up the Independent Safeguarding Authority (ISA). Some of its role survives the Protection of Freedoms Act. In particular, the requirement to make referrals are made to the ISA when an employer or an organization—for example a regulatory body—has concerns that a person has caused harm or poses a future risk of harm to children or vulnerable adults. In these circumstances, the employer or regulatory body must make a referral to the ISA. The range of organizations which are able to make referrals include:

- regulated activity providers;
- personnel suppliers;
- local authorities;
- education and library boards;
- health and social care (HSC) bodies;
- keepers of registers named in the legislation; and
- supervisory authorities named in the legislation.

Regulated activities cover a range of specified activities that involve close contact with children or vulnerable adults, other activities in key settings such as schools and care homes which provide an opportunity for contact, and key positions of responsibility such as the Children's Commissioner and the Director of Adult Social Services. It is a criminal offence if a barred individual engages in regulated activities.

If an organization dismisses or removes a member of staff/volunteer from working with children and/or vulnerable adults in a regulated activity because they have harmed a child or vulnerable adult, then that organization has a legal duty to inform the ISA. An organization that knowingly employs someone who is barred is breaking the law. A person barred from working with children or vulnerable adults is breaking the law if they work/volunteer or seek to work/volunteer with these groups.

SUMMARY

In this chapter we have considered two important ways the law intervenes to protect vulnerable service users:

- We have looked at the issue of mental incapacity and considered the Mental Capacity Act 2005, the Code of Practice to the Mental Capacity Act, and statutory guidance.
- We have also considered how the law safeguards vulnerable adults, both the provisions of the Care Act 2014 establishing Safeguarding Adult Boards, and the particular interventions made by the criminal law to protect the vulnerable victim of crime.

EXERCISES

1 Legislation relating to the abuse of adults has been categorized by Professor Clements in four different ways:

(a) that which bars certain individuals from working with vulnerable people;

(b) that which involves setting up protocols and procedures to prevent abuse;

(c) that which imposes duties to act in a person's best interests and restricts the actions they can take in relation to people who lack capacity;

(d) that which might act as a deterrent by criminalizing certain actions in relation to vulnerable adults.

Produce a table that sets out which legislation falls into which category. Which approach do you consider to be most effective?

2 Fiona Adair is 55 and has early onset Alzheimer's. She is living with her 19-year-old son Bill, having divorced her husband some years ago. She receives a teacher's pension, having retired early on health grounds, and the lowest rate of the care element of disability living allowance. She recently had a relationship with George but that ended with allegations that George had subjected her to violence. Her sister Lillian, who does not live locally, has contacted social services because she is concerned that Mrs Adair is at risk of exploitation. There is evidence that Bill is misusing her credit card to make internet purchases, that George has started visiting her again and may have access to her bank account, and that she is becoming increasingly at risk by leaving things on the stove and letting strangers into the house. Mrs Adair, George, and Bill all tell you and Lillian that Mrs Adair is coping fine and this is none of your business. What should you do?

3 John is 25 and lives in a residential home since a serious car accident left him brain damaged. He is unable to communicate other than through gestures. His parents would like him to have a further brain scan because they are convinced that brain surgery would alleviate his condition. John gets very agitated when he has to leave the care home, and when he is in confined spaces. Medical advice suggests that there is nothing to be gained from a further brain scan. The care home agrees to him having the further scan. Is their decision lawful?

4 Do you think there is a need to reform the Mental Capacity Act 2005? Give reasons for your answer.

ONLINE RESOURCES

For guidance on how to answer these exercises, visit the online resources at
www.oup.com/uk/carr-goosey15e.

WHERE DO WE GO FROM HERE?

This chapter and **chapters 12 and 13** have focused on the responsibilities of local authorities towards adult social care users who are in the community or residential care. **Chapter 15** examines in more detail an area relating to mental capacity which is particularly legally complex—the Deprivation of Liberty Safeguards. It also discusses the role of the Court of Protection, which is becoming increasingly important in the lives of vulnerable adults.

ANNOTATED FURTHER READING

Mental capacity

There are a number of useful books covering the law on mental capacity—though the Code of Practice is an excellent starting point. These include R. Jones, *Mental Capacity Act Manual* (3rd edn, Sweet & Maxwell, 2008) (targeted at lawyers) and R. Brown, P. Barber, and D. Martin, *The Mental Capacity Act 2005: A Guide for Practice (Post-Qualifying Social Work Practice)* (3rd edn, Learning Matters, 2015).

The Court of Protection has been the focus of media attention. One useful article by Amelia Hill in the *Guardian* was published on 6 November 2011: 'The court of protection: defender of the vulnerable or shadowy and unjust?' (www.theguardian.com/law/2011/nov/06/court-protection-defender-vulnerable-unjust). On the same date the *Guardian* published an interview with the president of the Court of Protection, Sir Nicholas Wall: 'Court of protection should be open to public scrutiny, says leading judge' (www.guardian.co.uk/law/2011/nov/06/court-of-protection-public-scrutiny).

The Small Places blog contains useful discussions of these issues: thesmallplaces.wordpress.com.

Adult safeguarding

A special issue of the *British Journal of Social Work on Elder Abuse: Research, Theory and Practice* (2018) 48(4) includes five excellent, up-to-date research-based articles on Elder abuse in England and Wales and beyond.

Professor Jill Manthorpe and Dr Stephen Martineau write about their research into Adult Safeguarding Reviews in 'Engaging with the new system of safeguarding adults reviews concerning care homes for older people' (2017) *British Journal of Social Work* 47(1): 2086–99.

Other law related articles around adult safeguarding include:

D. Galpin, 'Policy and the protection of older people from abuse' (2010) *Journal of Social Welfare and Family Law* 32(3): 247.

T. Spencer-Lane, 'Reforming the legal framework for adult safeguarding: The Law Commission's final recommendations on adult social care' (2011) *Journal of Adult Protection*

13(5): 275. These articles describe in useful detail the current state of the law and proposals for reform.

S. Hussein et al., 'Accusations of misconduct among staff working with vulnerable adults in England' (2009) *Journal of Social Welfare and Family Law* 31(1): 17. This article examines explanations and mitigation provided in response to accusations of misconduct amongst care staff.

J. Manthorpe, 'Local responses to elder abuse: building effective prevention strategies' in A. Wahidin and M. Cain (eds), *Ageing, Crime and Society* (Willan Publishing, 2006), 139–53. This chapter of an edited collection discusses local responses to the problems of elder abuse.

The *Journal of Adult Protection* provides regular articles and digests of information about practice and law in this area.

15 The Court of Protection and Deprivation of Liberty Safeguards

OVERVIEW AND OBJECTIVES

This chapter is designed to introduce you to the work of the Court of Protection and to help you consider how social work decisions may lead to deprivation of liberty and how to decide when that is lawful, taking account not merely of the best interests of the client but also the law, including the European Convention on Human Rights (ECHR), the Human Rights Act, and Deprivation of Liberty Safeguards (DoLS) introduced into the Mental Capacity Act 2005 (MCA) by the Mental Health Act 2007. It also looks at the controversy surrounding DoLS and proposed reforms to the system. The Mental Capacity (Amendment) Bill, which was introduced in the House of Lords in July 2018, seeks to address some of the problems of DoLS highlighted by the Law Commission and proposes a new regime covering deprivation of liberty called Liberty Protection Safeguards.

CASE STUDY

London Borough of Hillingdon v Steven Neary (2011)

Why are we asking you to read this case?

This case reminds us of the importance of liberty for everyone, including those who lack capacity. Not only should safeguards be in place to protect people from arbitrary decisions to remove their liberty, but those safeguards also have to be more than procedural; they need to ensure.

What is at stake for the parties and beyond

For Steven Neary and his father, what was at stake was Steven's right to be cared for by his family rather than in an institution. Further, it concerns the right of families to be involved in decision making about something as important as liberty and the right to a family life.

For the local authority, what was at stake was its ability to make lawful decisions, and the checks and balances which are inevitably involved in decisions about individual lives.

Background

Steven Neary was a 21-year-old with autism and a severe learning disability. He was cared for by his father. The local authority, Hillingdon, arranged care services to support Steven at home and provided respite care. In January 2010, Steven was placed in a support unit for a short period of respite care at the request of his father. Hillingdon started an assessment of Steven's needs and concluded that he could not get those needs met at home owing to his behaviour. There was concern, for instance, that food was used to control his behaviour and so Steven had gained a lot of weight. There was evidence that 'he can become moody and anxious . . . He can lash out, not in malice but rather in the manner of a small child.' The local authority refused to return Steven to the care of his father. Hillingdon said it was in his best interests to keep him beyond a period of respite care, that they had his father's permission at least until April 2010, and that he had not in fact been deprived of his liberty. From April to December, Deprivation of Liberty Safeguard authorizations (DoLS—see Deprivation of Liberty Safeguards, p 539) granted by Hillingdon to itself allowed the local authority to keep him in care.

Steven's father challenged Hillingdon but was informed that he could take the matter to the Court of Protection if he wanted to dispute the DoLS authorizations. In October 2010, the authority took the case to the Court of Protection itself.

The decision

The judge, Mr Justice Peter Jackson, found that Hillingdon had deprived Steven of his liberty throughout the year. 'It acted as if it had the right to make decisions about Steven, and by a combination of turning a deaf ear and force majeure [irresistible compulsion], it tried to wear down Mr Neary's resistance, stretching its relationship with him almost to breaking point. It relied upon him coming to see things its way, even though, as events have proved, he was right and it was wrong. In the meantime, it failed to activate the statutory safeguards that exist to prevent situations like this arising.' In particular Hillingdon should not have left it to Steven's father to bring the matter to the Court of Protection but should have done so itself at the earliest opportunity. The four months without court oversight was far too long. Jackson concluded that the local authority had breached Stephen Neary's right to respect for family life (Article 8 of the ECHR), and had unlawfully deprived him of his liberty in contravention of Article 5(1) of the ECHR. The court made clear that the local authority has a responsibility to bring deprivation of liberty cases to court in a timely fashion whenever there is any doubt regarding the DoLS, best interests, or proportionality.

WHAT DOES THIS CASE TELL YOU ABOUT SOCIAL WORK PRACTICE?

This case, which gained a good deal of media attention, provides salutary lessons for social workers seeking to admit people without capacity into care. Judge Jackson said the DoLS regime 'is not to be used by a local authority as a means of getting its own way on the question of whether it is in the person's best interests to be in [a particular place] at all'. It follows that the local authority, acting as the supervisory body over its own adult social care department, has an obligation to scrutinize an assessment like the department's regarding the Nearys, 'with independence and a degree of care that is appropriate to the seriousness of the decision and to the circumstances of the individual case that are or should be known to it'. Instead, it had offered authorization based on 'perfunctory scrutiny of superficial best interests assessments'.

The report of the best interests assessor authorizing the DoLS order should 'consider whether any care or treatment the person needs can be provided effectively in a way that is less restrictive of their rights and freedom of action'. The report flagged this up as an issue but it was not followed through. No doubt the local authority wanted a quick result. By now, looking at whether to return Steven home would have involved quite a complex inquiry. But in law that is no excuse for a 'perfunctory' assessment. Proper regard to keeping him at home was not given: 'Nowhere in their very full records of Steven's year in care is there any mention of the supposition that he should be at home, other things being equal, or the disadvantages to him of living away from his family, still less an attempt to weigh those disadvantages against the supposed advantages of care elsewhere.'

The following principles can be taken from the case:

- your assessment of best interests is not enough to deprive someone of their liberty;
- a case should be approached on the presumption that liberty is better than deprivation of liberty;
- this presumption may be rebutted by good evidence with independent, objective oversight of that evidence;
- the authorizing body must approach the matter objectively, itself preferring liberty over deprivation of liberty rather than rubber-stamping a decision of social workers;
- effective review must be built in and this must take on board the individual's desires and those of the family or another interested party;
- an independent mental capacity advocate (IMCA) must be appointed at the appropriate time to represent the individual.

If disagreement remains, the local authority cannot leave it to the individual or interested parties to take the matter to the Court of Protection; the local authority must be proactive to ensure Article 5(4) rights have a speedy hearing.

Deprivation of Liberty Safeguards

Until legislative changes passing through Parliament in 2018, deprivations of liberty in care homes and hospitals were covered by the Deprivation of Liberty Safeguards (DoLS) as set out in the Mental Capacity Act 2005. What was required under that Act was formal authorization by the supervisory body of the care home or hospital—that will be the local authority where the care home or hospital is located. Deprivations of liberty in community and domestic settings required the authorization of the Court of Protection—though under the 2019 proposed changes this may no longer be the case. Both these procedures to render a deprivation of liberty lawful are discussed in Deprivation of Liberty Safeguards.

You will note that the Court of Protection was very much involved in the case. The chapter begins by discussing the important role of the Court of Protection in the lives of people who lack capacity. You may find it useful to know that mentally incapacitated people who are parties to Court of Protection proceedings are generally known as P (for 'Person') unless the court has given permission for names to be used.

◼ The Court of Protection

The Court of Protection is the court that has jurisdiction relating to the Mental Capacity Act. It is the final arbiter on whether a person has capacity to make a particular decision for themselves. The work of the court is described on its web page, www.gov.uk/courts-tribunals/court-of-protection, and set out in summary for you in **Box 15.1**. The Court of Protection is a court of record and its decisions have precedent value—that is, they bind lower courts. The Code of Practice to the MCA provides information about how and when someone can make an application to the Court of Protection.

BOX 15.1 The work of the Court of Protection

We make decisions on financial or welfare matters for people who can't make decisions at the time they need to be made (they 'lack mental capacity').

We are responsible for:

- deciding whether someone has the mental capacity to make a particular decision for themselves
- appointing deputies to make ongoing decisions for people who lack mental capacity
- giving people permission to make one-off decisions on behalf of someone else who lacks mental capacity
- handling urgent or emergency applications where a decision must be made on behalf of someone else without delay
- making decisions about a lasting power of attorney or enduring power of attorney and considering any objections to their registration
- considering applications to make statutory wills or gifts
- making decisions about when someone can be deprived of their liberty under the Mental Capacity Act.

Note that under the proposed 2018 changes the Court of Protection is unlikely to retain such a wide role in *making* decisions about when someone can be deprived of their liberty under the MCA but will retain the role of reviewing such decisions where problems arise. Below we provide some additional detail on some of the court's areas of work.

Decisions on capacity

The Court of Protection does not usually get involved with disputes about whether a person lacks capacity. In most cases people can work it out between themselves, with some of the basic knowledge about the law on mental capacity that we discussed in **chapter 14**. However, there will be occasions when it is appropriate for an application to be made to the Court of Protection:

- when a person wants to challenge a decision that they lack capacity;
- when professionals disagree about a person's capacity to make a specific, usually serious, decision;
- when there is a dispute over whether the person has capacity (e.g. between family members).

If you read decisions made by the Court of Protection (and remember the requirement on principal social workers to keep up to date with the law on mental capacity), you get some understanding of the way the court approaches decisions about capacity. Decisions are available at www.bailii.org/ew/cases/EWCOP.

One recent decision that you might find informative is set out in **Box 15.2**. The case concerned a young woman who, obsessed with celebrity and social media, had taken risks with sexual relationships which may well have caused her harm in the past.

 BOX 15.2 A decision on capacity—*WBC v Z, X and Y* (2016)

Z was on the autistic spectrum with a diagnosis of Asperger syndrome, and had borderline learning disability. The local authority in whose area Z lived, had been involved in Z's life for a little over two years, and was very concerned that she was wanting to move out of the family home and live independently. Z had had a very harmful relationship with A, whom she had met online. In June 2014, the local authority issued proceedings in the Court of Protection seeking declarations as to Z's capacity to:

(a) choose her residence;

(b) make contacts with others;

(c) deal with her care;

(d) litigate in these proceedings.

The judge decided, after careful consideration and, on a fine balance, that the local authority had not rebutted the presumption of Z's capacity in relation to the matters under review in the case, at the present time.

At the heart of the dispute is the assessment of Z's ability to 'use or weigh' information (section 3(1) (c)) about risk to herself, and her ability to keep herself safe in independent living, and in her social contacts. Only if I were to find that Z is 'unable' (section 3 of the MCA) to process information relevant to risk (in the ways defined in section 3(1)MCA) could I find her incapacitous in relation to the matters in dispute. As the wording of the statute makes clear, the point in time at which I must find capacity is to be tested is now (i.e. 'at the material time').

. . .

In order to determine Z's capacity, it is not necessary for her to use or weigh every detail of the respective options available, merely the salient factors. In this case, it is apparent to me that Z does indeed understand the essential implications of living at home or living independently; as indicated above, Z acknowledged the benefit of having some 'guidance' on living independently. She recognised that she would reasonably expect to be allocated a flat, and was able to distinguish between the 'good' areas and 'bad' areas of town in which to live. I am . . . sufficiently persuaded that Z recognises at a material level the benefit of third party support in the event that she is to live on her own. She showed insight into the possible loneliness of living independently; she felt that one of the downsides of leaving home is that she will lose the benefit of having her mother's 'shoulder to cry on' when things are getting her down. She has an outline knowledge of her financial circumstances, and currently appears able to perform basic budgeting. She seems aware that her life is easy now, as all the bills are paid, and she is cared for; I felt that she recognised that she would be giving these comforts up if she were to move. Overall, I am satisfied that Z is able to 'use or weigh' the evidence relevant to the matters. . . .

. . .

In relation to social contacts, Z needs to be able to weigh up the risks of associating with strangers, particularly those whom she meets through the internet—something which she says that she has indeed learned to deal with through experience. Dr R (the medical expert) acknowledged that, other than with A, there was no evidence of Z making contacts through social media which were of any concern. The fact that she has rejected any ongoing support or care from Dimensions is not evidence in itself that she lacks the capacity to decide on its usefulness. She has articulated her reasons: she does not feel that she currently needs the package, and she feels that the workers are constantly talking about the past not the future, and they 'talk down' to her.

. . .

Dr. R expressed the view in November 2014 . . ., that with time and increased maturity, Z's ability accurately to assess risk may improve; it is my view that the evidence now available (December 2015) indicates that time and increased maturity, and the benefit of learning from experience, have indeed had that effect. There is no real issue but that 2015 has been a period of relative stability for Z; she has engaged (to a limited extent at least) with the support which is provided for her through Dimensions, and even within the limits of that work, she has impressed the workers with her display of increased maturity. In 2014, Dr. R advised that it would be sensible to re-assess Z's capacity in 'two to three years time', plainly contemplating a potential future change in capacity, but timescales of this kind are notoriously difficult to gauge, and in my view the evidence appears to have revealed change rather sooner.

. . .

While it may have been that Z showed an 'unusual' degree of interest in fame and celebrity in the past (to some extent in 2014, when first interviewed by Dr. R), and a limited appreciation of the quality of her talent-show performance, I do not find that she continues to hold or display these views. More recent discussions (including her evidence in court) reveal a good degree of awareness of the deficiencies of her performance, and a more realistic appraisal of her quest for fame. At the hearing before me, she impressed as someone who was more than just aware that 'people should treat you with respect', apparently mindful that people had not done so in the past. Dr. R expressed scepticism in her 2014 report about Z's ability to understand the evidence which was to be given in Court, process this information and use it to instruct her counsel appropriately; this scepticism was I believe misplaced. Z showed a good level of attention to the evidence, gave instructions to her solicitor and counsel, and—even on Dr. R's own view—answered questions in evidence better than she had during the three previous interviews.

. . .

Dr. R entirely fairly observed that young adults are generally able to learn from negative experiences, and use this to support their future decision making. She felt that Z had failed to do this; I do not agree. Z's behaviour in 2013 and 2014 was, I am prepared to accept for present purposes, intensely destructive; I accept Z's own assessment that she has at least to some extent 'learned how to make decisions'. I accept that she has changed, and I was impressed with her own assessment that '. . . everything has happened for a reason. It made me stronger and made me more mature'.

Dr. R indicated that she would be looking for Z to develop and display insight, that she is not putting herself in risky situations and is understanding of other people's motives; the trip to Brighton to stay with A was risky to some extent, but not more than usually risky for a young person who is in love, and who has met the object of her affections a number of times on home territory before heading off to see her at her home. Moreover, when the Brighton trip became intolerable, she left.

As indicated at the outset of this judgment, some risk-taking in adolescents and young adults can be perfectly healthy, such as in sporting activities, or artistic and creative pursuits . . . Some adolescent risk-taking can be unhealthy and dangerous—casual sexual relationships, unprotected sex, driving too fast on the roads, excessive consumption of alcohol, consumption of non-prescribed drugs, dealing with anger and confrontation. These forms of risk-taking are inherently unwise and unsafe. In dealing with risk issues in relation to a young person in the context of assessment under the MCA 2005, it is necessary to separate out as far as is possible the evidence which indicates that second category of risk taking (unhealthy, dangerous, unwise) from that which reveals or may reveal a lack of capacity.

. . .

In differing from Dr. R, I remind myself that her role and mine are distinct: the expert advises and the court decides. While the opinion of an independently instructed expert in a case such as this is 'likely to be of very considerable importance' . . ., the decision as to capacity is a judgment for the court . . ., weighing the expert evidence against my findings on the other evidence. I consider that Dr. R may well have been right in her assessment as to Z's capacity over a year ago (November 2014), but in my judgment, the passage of time and Z's greater maturity, coupled with some support from Dimensions and enhanced self-esteem through her music, Z appears to have matured, learned from her mistakes, and developed sufficiently in her capacity to make relevant decisions, and keep herself safe.

. . .

It is tempting for the court to take a paternalistic, perhaps overly risk-averse, approach to Z's future; but this would be unprincipled and wrong.

We have included extracts from the decision to illustrate how judges of the Court of Protection 'reason'—i.e. identify and weigh up the factors that need to be taken into account in reaching a decision which accords with the MCA. There are some useful summary points that can be identified.

- What matters is the individual's capacity at the time of the hearing. Individual capacity changes and this is particularly important in young people.
- Rejection of social work or community support is not necessarily indicative of a lack of capacity. There may be cogent reasons for that rejection.
- An expert's report is not determinative of the issue of capacity. The decision is a legal one, although an expert's report will be influential.
- There is a difference between unhealthy and unwise decision making and a lack of capacity.

One-off decisions on behalf of someone else who lacks mental capacity

The Code of Practice to the MCA describes when the Court of Protection may become involved in decision making for persons lacking capacity. The relevant paragraphs are set out in **Box 15.3.**

BOX 15.3 Making decisions and the Court of Protection—paras 8.3 and 8.4 of the Code of Practice to the Mental Capacity Act 2005

8.3 In most cases concerning personal welfare matters, the core principles of the Act and the processes set out in chapters 5 and 6 (of the Code of Guidance) will be enough to:

• help people take action or make decisions in the best interests of someone who lacks capacity to make decisions about their own care or treatment, or

• find ways of settling disagreements about such actions or decisions.

But an application to the Court of Protection may be necessary for:

• particularly difficult decisions

• disagreements that cannot be resolved in any other way (see chapter 15), or

• situations where ongoing decisions may need to be made about the personal welfare of a person who lacks capacity to make decisions for themselves.

8.4 An order of the court will usually be necessary for matters relating to the property and affairs (including financial matters) of people who lack capacity to make specific financial decisions for themselves, unless:

• their only income is state benefits (see paragraph 8.36 below), or

• they have previously made an Enduring Power of Attorney (EPA) or a Lasting Power of Attorney (LPA) to give somebody authority to manage their property and affairs (see chapter 7).

The sort of decisions that the Court of Protection might be asked to make include:

• which care home is in the best interests of the mentally incapacitated person when there is a disagreement between her children;

• whether someone should be allowed to visit the mentally incapacitated person when her carers disagree about whether it is in the person's best interests;

• decisions about property—for instance, should a house be sold, or a lease extension purchased.

Under the newly amended Court of Protection rules adopted on 1 December 2017 cases are allocated to one of three pathways:

• Personal welfare;

• Property and [financial] affairs;

• Mixed welfare and property.

Some areas are excluded from this procedure, such as uncontested applications, but particularly applications relating to serious medical treatment, applications for authorization of community deprivation of liberty, and appeals against standard authorizations under DoLS (s. 21A of the Mental Capacity Act 2005).

Decisions about medical treatment

Some decisions relating to the provision of medical treatment are so serious that, in those cases, an application should be made to the court for a declaration that the proposed action is lawful before the action is taken. Those decisions include:

- decisions about the proposed withholding or withdrawal of artificial nutrition and hydration (ANH) from patients in a permanent vegetative state (PVS);
- cases involving organ or bone marrow donation by a person who lacks capacity to consent;
- cases involving the proposed non-therapeutic sterilization of a person who lacks capacity to consent to this (e.g. for contraceptive purposes); and
- all other cases where there is a doubt or dispute about whether a particular treatment will be in a person's best interests.

Appointing deputies

In situations where there is a need for continuing or future decision making, the Court of Protection can appoint a deputy to act for and make decisions for that person. A deputy's authority should be as limited in scope and duration as possible. The Code of Practice to the MCA provides the following information on the appointment of deputies—**Box 15.4**.

BOX 15.4 The rules for appointing deputies—Mental Capacity Act Code of Practice (2007)

8.31 Sometimes it is not practical or appropriate for the court to make a single declaration or decision. In such cases, if the court thinks that somebody needs to make future or ongoing decisions for someone whose condition makes it likely they will lack capacity to make some further decisions in the future, it can appoint a deputy to act for and make decisions for that person. A deputy's authority should be as limited in scope and duration as possible (see paragraphs 8.35–8.39 below).

How does the court appoint deputies?

8.32 It is for the court to decide who to appoint as a deputy. Different skills may be required depending on whether the deputy's decisions will be about a person's welfare (including healthcare), their finances or both. The court will decide whether the proposed deputy is reliable and trustworthy and has an appropriate level of skill and competence to carry out the necessary tasks.

8.33 In the majority of cases, the deputy is likely to be a family member or someone who knows the person well. But in some cases the court may decide to appoint a deputy who is independent of the family (for example, where the person's affairs or care needs are particularly complicated). This could be, for example, the Director of Adult Services in the relevant local authority (but see paragraph 8.60 below) or a professional deputy. The OPG [Office of the Public Guardian] has a panel of professional deputies (mainly solicitors who specialise in this area of law) who may be appointed to deal with property and affairs if the court decides that would be in the person's best interests.

When might a deputy need to be appointed?

8.34 Whether a person who lacks capacity to make specific decisions needs a deputy will depend on:

• the individual circumstances of the person concerned

• whether future or ongoing decisions are likely to be necessary, and

• whether the appointment is for decisions about property and affairs or personal welfare.

There will usually be no need to appoint a deputy if the only income of a person who lacks capacity is social security benefits and they have no property or savings. Their benefits can be managed by an *appointee*, appointed by the Department for Work and Pensions.

A deputy must, of course, make decisions about whether the person concerned has capacity in relation to a particular decision, and if not, act in the best interests of the person lacking capacity. Deputies are accountable to the Court of Protection. Deputies can be appointed jointly, in which case they must make decisions together, or severally, in which case they can make decisions in relation to the matters about which they have been appointed independently. The court can cancel a deputy's appointment at any time if it decides the appointment is no longer in the best interests of the person who lacks capacity.

A major part of the work of the Court of Protection involves making decisions about when someone can be deprived of their liberty under the MCA. This is a complex and developing area of law. The next section, **Restraint and deprivation of liberty**, considers it in some detail.

■ Restraint and deprivation of liberty

We have seen in **chapter 14** that the law offers certain protections to people caring for those who lack capacity—s. 5 of the MCA. So, if someone ('D') does an act in connection with care and treatment of a person ('P') and 'takes reasonable steps to establish whether P lacks capacity in relation to the matter in question' and reasonably believes 'i) that P lacks capacity in relation to the matter, and ii) that it will be in P's best interests for the act to be done', then 'D' is protected from certain liabilities. These cover what otherwise would be unlawful acts that would require the person's consent—trespass, for example, including trespass to the person (touching someone) or entering someone's home. This does not, of course, protect you from 'civil liability for loss or damage, or . . . criminal liability, resulting from . . . negligence in doing the act'.

There are further limitations on the protections offered by s. 5 of the MCA set out in s. 6 of the Act. These concern acts of 'restraint', which are defined in s. 6(4).

(1)   For the purposes of this section D restrains P if he—

    (a)   uses, or threatens to use, force to secure the doing of an act which P resists, or

    (b)   restricts P's liberty of movement, whether or not P resists.

Simple, everyday acts such as using a seat belt, or stopping someone from crossing the road, or leaving the house are acts of restraint. Restraint can only be applied to someone if two conditions are met. These are set out in s. 6(2) and (3):

2)   The first condition is that D reasonably believes that it is necessary to do the act in order to prevent harm to P.

(3)   The second is that the act is a proportionate response to—

    (a)   the likelihood of P's suffering harm, and

    (b)   the seriousness of that harm.

Once more, the Code of Practice contains helpful advice. An extract from this is set out in **Box 15.5**.

BOX 15.5 Restraint—extract from the Mental Capacity Act 2005 Code of Practice (2007)

When might restraint be 'necessary'?

6.44 Anybody considering using restraint must have objective reasons to justify that restraint is necessary. They must be able to show that the person being cared for is likely to suffer harm unless proportionate restraint is used. A carer or professional must not use restraint just so that they can do something more easily. If restraint is necessary to prevent harm to the person who lacks capacity, it must be the minimum amount of force for the shortest time possible.

What is 'harm'?

6.45 The Act does not define 'harm', because it will vary depending on the situation. For example,

• a person with learning disabilities might run into a busy road without warning, if they do not understand the dangers of cars

• a person with dementia may wander away from home and get lost, if they cannot remember where they live

• a person with manic depression might engage in excessive spending during a manic phase, causing them to get into debt

• a person may also be at risk of harm if they behave in a way that encourages others to assault or exploit them (for example, by behaving in a dangerously provocative or sexual way).

6.46 Common sense measures can often help remove the risk of harm (for example, by locking away poisonous chemicals or removing obstacles). Also, care planning should include risk assessments and set out appropriate actions to try to prevent possible risks. But it is impossible to remove all risk, and a proportionate response is needed when the risk of harm does arise.

What is a 'proportionate response'?

6.47 A 'proportionate response' means using the least intrusive type and minimum amount of restraint to achieve a specific outcome in the best interests of the person who lacks capacity. On occasions when the use of force may be necessary, carers and healthcare and social care staff should use the minimum amount of force for the shortest possible time. For example, a carer may need to hold a person's arm while they cross the road, if the person does not understand the dangers of roads. But it would not be a proportionate response to stop the person going outdoors at all. It may be appropriate to have a secure lock on a door that faces a busy road, but it would not be a proportionate response to lock someone in a bedroom all the time to prevent them from attempting to cross the road.

6.48 Carers and healthcare and social care staff should consider less restrictive options before using restraint. Where possible, they should ask other people involved in the person's care what action they think is necessary to protect the person from harm. For example, it may be appropriate to get an advocate to work with the person to see if they can avoid or minimise the need for restraint to be used.

Deprivation of liberty

If the restraint involves the deprivation of someone's liberty, then different procedures apply. The Code of Practice for the Mental Capacity Act in 2007 provided guidance on the distinction between restraint and deprivation of liberty. What it said was:

> It is difficult to define the difference between actions that amount to a restriction of someone's liberty and those that result in a deprivation of liberty. In recent legal cases, the European Court of Human Rights said that the difference was 'one of degree or intensity, not one of nature or substance'. There must therefore be particular factors in the specific situation of the person concerned which provide the 'degree' or 'intensity' to result in a deprivation of liberty. In practice, this can relate to:
>
> • the type of care being provided
> • how long the situation lasts
> • its effects, or
> • the way in which a particular situation came about.

The case that the Code of Practice refers to is *HL v UK* (2004) (European Court of Human Rights). In this case the UK was found to have breached Article 5 of the ECHR—deprivation of liberty—because there were no procedural protections available for patients who were informally detained in care settings. The case had been taken to the European Court of Human Rights in Strasbourg after the House of Lords (now Supreme Court) had ruled in *R (L) v Bournewood NHS Trust* (1998) that an autistic man without capacity who was admitted into a psychiatric unit had not been unlawfully detained under English common law since the authorities acted reasonably in his best interests (see **chapter 3** for a definition of '*Wednesbury* reasonableness' and its limitations in terms of human rights). The Strasbourg judges, in contrast, said the UK had no 'procedure prescribed by law' to protect his Article 5 right to liberty, so admitting him to the unit without his consent was a breach of Article 5. This lack of procedure became known as the 'Bournewood gap'. There was also a contravention of Article 5(4) of the ECHR ('Everyone who is deprived of his liberty by arrest or detention shall be entitled to take proceedings by which the lawfulness of his detention shall be decided speedily by a court and his release ordered if the detention is not lawful'). HL had no means of applying quickly to a court to see if the deprivation of liberty was lawful.

In response to the judgment, the Deprivation of Liberty Safeguards system was introduced (DoLS) in 2009 in an amendment to the MCA. In 2018 quite sweeping amendments were proposed to this procedure in the Mental Capacity (Amendment) Bill (which will probably have passed into law by the time you read this—it is expected to come into force in late 2019). The following gives a resumé of the 2009 regime, though on the assumption that it will be replaced by the new procedures explained in **The proposed legislation: The Mental Capacity (Amendment) Bill**, p 555.

Under the 2009 system, a DoLS authorization was applied when someone did not have the mental capacity to make a decision about going into a care home or hospital for treatment (whether for mental or physical illness or injury) or their own well-being. The principle remains that a person should only be deprived of their liberty without consent if:

- they lack capacity to make decisions;
- it is in their best interests;
- it is 'proportionate' (not excessive given the danger it is intended to avoid, e.g. taking account of the likelihood of an individual suffering harm and the seriousness of that harm);
- there is no reasonable alternative.

An application was made to a supervisory body—a local authority (or primary care trust for keeping someone in a hospital). This body had to:

- ensure the person was over 18;
- ensure that he or she had no one who could make the decision for them;
- assess whether they could make the decision themselves;
- assess whether they had mental incapacity;
- check whether someone would meet the requirement to be detained instead under the Mental Health Act 1983;
- make sure the deprivation of liberty was necessary, proportionate, and in the best interests of the person.

If any of these conditions were not met, deprivation of liberty could not be authorized. The person would have to be cared for in a less restrictive way.

If the conditions were met, the supervisory body was to authorize the deprivation of liberty and inform the person and managing authority in writing. The deprivation of liberty order could last for 12 months, but should be for the shortest time possible to deal with the issue.

The supervisory body could make a 'standard authorization' within 21 days of the application unless there was an emergency (in which case an 'urgent authorization' could be sought for immediate deprivation of liberty, which could last for seven days— i.e. the provider of care self-authorized; the provider had to have a reasonable belief that a standard authorization would be granted). The assessments were made by at least two people. They could be challenged in the Court of Protection. *London Borough of Hillingdon v Steven Neary,* the case study set out at the beginning of the chapter, provides a useful illustration of the role of the DoLS and how it can protect the liberties of vulnerable adults.

The supervisory body could set conditions on the standard authorization to be followed by the managing authority. The managing authority must monitor the detention to ensure it is not continuing unnecessarily. Detention becomes unlawful once the period authorized is over and the authorization cannot simply be extended, though the managing authority could apply for a new authorization in advance.

In the Court of Protection, the lawfulness of the authorization could be challenged on one or more of the following grounds:

- whether the relevant person met one or more of the qualifying requirements for deprivation of liberty;
- the period for which the standard authorization was to be in force;
- the purpose for which the standard authorization was given;
- the conditions subject to which the standard authorization was given.

These grounds are likely to remain intact under the post-2018 system, but it is expected that far fewer cases will need to go to court.

An urgent authorization could also be challenged on:

- whether the urgent authorization should have been given;
- the period for which the urgent authorization was to be in force;
- the purpose for which the urgent authorization had been given.

The urgent authorization under the new system is being replaced by a more restrictive emergency authorization for life-sustaining treatment or taking action believed necessary to prevent a serious deterioration in the person's condition.

How do you know if there is potential deprivation of liberty?

Department of Health guidance in October 2015 noted that:

> A deprivation of liberty will only arise where an individual lacks capacity specifically to consent to the care/treatment arrangements that give rise to a deprivation of liberty. It is incorrect to assume that all individuals with a mental disorder will lack the capacity in this specific respect.

A state of unconsciousness is not regarded as a mental disorder (so the DoLS regime or its replacement would not apply) but the use of sedation for restraint would be regarded as a deprivation of liberty. The MCA Code of Practice noted that these factors were identified by the European Court of Human Rights as contributing to deprivation of liberty:

- restraint was used, including sedation, to admit a person who is resisting;
- professionals exercised complete and effective control over care and movement for a significant period;
- professionals exercised control over assessments, treatment, contacts, and residence;
- the person would be prevented from leaving if they made a meaningful attempt to do so;
- a request by carers for the person to be discharged to their care was refused;
- the person was unable to maintain social contacts because of restrictions placed on access to other people;
- the person lost autonomy because they were under continuous supervision and control.

To establish if there is a deprivation of liberty, the 'acid test' must be applied:

- Are they 'free to leave'? Just because they are physically unable to leave of their own accord does not mean they are not free to leave for the purpose of the test— they may, for example, be able to leave with family assistance.

- Are they under 'continuous control and supervision'? If the individual is in a private room and checked only every few hours then they may not necessarily be under continuous control and supervision.

Problems with DoLS

There has been extensive criticism of the DoLS regime, which is summarized in the House of Commons Library Briefing Paper 'The Deprivation of Liberty Safeguards' published in July 2018 and available at https://researchbriefings.parliament.uk/ResearchBriefing/Summary/CBP-8095#fullreport.

In 2015, the Government gave the Law Commission the task of examining the shortcomings of the DoLS and proposing a draft parliamentary Bill. A version of this, the Mental Capacity (Amendment) Bill was launched in the House of Lords in 2018 and included some of the main proposals of the Law Commission report (Law Com No. 372: www.lawcom.gov.uk/project/mental-capacity-and-deprivation-of-liberty).

Part of the reason for the changes was the sheer weight of bureaucracy required, according to the Law Commission's summary of its report. This said:

> The DoLS procedure requires a number of assessments to be carried out on behalf of the supervisory body in order to determine whether the deprivation of liberty is justified. This a paperwork-heavy process, involving six separate assessments of varying degrees of complexity. Much of the assessment process goes over the same ground as has already been gone over by health and social care professionals in deciding to make the placement in the first place. In many (though not all) cases there will be no realistic alternative to granting the authorisation because the person's condition makes a deprivation of liberty necessary. The 'best interests assessors' are, however, directed to consider whether the deprivation of liberty is in the person's best interests. It is not surprising that many best interests assessors told us that they feel they are engaged in a 'rubber-stamping' exercise, particularly where the deprivation of liberty is already in place.

But another pressing issue was that legal justification for deprivation of liberty became more complicated in 2014 when the Supreme Court decided the *Cheshire West* case. This case is very important for social workers and local authorities. It established that deprivation of liberty can occur 'in community and domestic settings where the State is responsible for imposing such arrangements', including supported living arrangements (Department of Health Guidance, October 2015). In other words, the person lacking mental capacity may suffer 'deprivation of liberty' even in residential homes or a person's own home if care provisions have been made for her. This placed new burdens on public authorities (mainly local authorities) to gain authorizations and provide safeguards for such extra deprivations of liberty. The new legislation seeks to tackle this problem, but does not give a definition of deprivation of liberty. The definition in *Cheshire West* therefore stands.

The key facts and learning points are set out in **Box 15.6**.

 BOX 15.6 *P v Cheshire West and Chester Council* and *P&Q v Surrey County Council* (2014)

The Supreme Court was hearing two separate appeals, by P, and P and Q, against decisions that living arrangements made for the appellants by their respective local authorities, Cheshire West and Surrey, did not amount to a deprivation of liberty under Article 5 of the ECHR.

P had cerebral palsy and Down's syndrome and required 24-hour care. He was in supervised local authority accommodation. Intervention was required to cope with his challenging behaviours, including use of restrictive clothing and the insertion of fingers into his mouth to prevent him from eating his continence pads. The Court of Protection had concluded that he was being deprived of his liberty, but that it was in his best interests. The Court of Appeal found that he was not being deprived of his liberty.

P and Q were sisters with significant learning difficulties. P was in foster care with intensive support in most aspects of daily living. She would be subject to restraint if she attempted to leave the house. Q was in residential care and under continuous supervision and control. The Court of Appeal had upheld a decision that P and Q's living arrangements were in their best interests and did not amount to deprivation of their liberty, referring to the 'relative normality' of their lives compared with the lives they might have had if still living with their family.

The Supreme Court decided that a person without capacity to give consent placed in a residential home without her permission may be enduring 'deprivation of liberty' even if it is in her best interests and albeit that the living arrangements may be 'benevolent', as Lady Hale called them in this case. Such a case therefore falls within Article 5 of the ECHR (right to liberty), but this does not make it unlawful—as long as it is justified and 'in accordance with a procedure prescribed by law'.

It may seem odd to declare residential homes or fostering to be a form of prison, at least for those residents incapable of giving consent to be there, but the practical result is that the resident gains certain rights beyond a simple assessment of best interests. As Lady Hale said: 'the deprivation has to be authorized, either by a court or by the procedures known as the deprivation of liberty safeguards [DoLS], set out in the Mental Capacity Act 2005'. DoLS require a local authority to examine whether deprivation of liberty is in the best interests of the individual, whether it is proportionate, and whether there is a reasonable alternative. Legal safeguards must be put in place with oversight by the courts—in effect requiring local authorities to take such cases to court themselves rather than waiting for the individual or family members to take legal action. In the *Surrey County Council* case, sisters with learning disabilities were removed from their home to protect them from sex abuse. (Their mother and stepfather were later convicted of sex attacks on their half-sister.) It was when they reached 16 and 17 that their case came before the Court of Protection (which has jurisdiction over people aged 16 or over, whereas a family court cannot make a care order once a child has reached 17: Children Act 1989, s. 31(3)). In 2010 Mr Justice Parker decided their living arrangements were in their best interests and did not amount to a deprivation of liberty.

Lady Hale, however, pointed to the Strasbourg judgment in *Austin v UK* (2012), where it was said that an underlying public interest motive 'has no bearing on the question whether that person has been deprived of his liberty . . . The same is true where the object is to protect, treat or care in some way for the person taken into confinement, unless that person has validly consented to what would otherwise be a deprivation of liberty.' *Austin* was about police 'kettling' demonstrators and others with police evidence that it was intended to curb violence and protect people within the 'kettle' (the police cordon they were not allowed to leave) and hence in their interests.

Strasbourg had not considered cases where the individual was placed without objecting 'in a small group or domestic setting which is as close as possible to "normal" home life', Lady Hale said in *Cheshire West* and *Surrey* cases. But she went on to say: 'We should not let the comparative benevolence of the living arrangements with which we are concerned blind us to their essential character if indeed that constitutes a deprivation of liberty.' Deprivation of liberty is one issue; justification is a separate one that then has to be considered. Benevolent and justified deprivation of liberty, without consent, remains deprivation of liberty. The person concerned 'was under continuous supervision and control and was not free to leave'. The issue then becomes: is it legal deprivation of liberty?

In the case of one of the sisters, 'the staff did exercise control over every aspect of her life. She would not be allowed out without supervision, or to see people whom they did not wish her to see, or to do things which they did not wish her to do.' For the other sister, 'her foster mother and others responsible for her care exercised complete control over every aspect of her life'. The deprivation is ultimately the responsibility of the state (even with a foster parent) so Article 5 is engaged. The proper safeguards (the DoLS regime) should be in place in order to render that deprivation of liberty lawful. Furthermore, periodic independent checks should be made to ensure the arrangements made for them remain in their best interests.

The Social Care Institute for Excellence summarizes the learning points from this decision as follows:

1. People with care and support needs have the same rights as everyone else under the Human Rights Act.

2. People cannot be deprived of their liberty without it being authorised by a legal process.

3. The Supreme Court judgment clarified what may constitute a deprivation of liberty but the Mental Capacity Act (MCA) and the Deprivation of Liberty Safeguards had not been changed by the judgment.

4. Even in a system under pressure, don't lose sight of the fundamental rights aspects of the MCA.

After the *Cheshire West* case, criticism of the legal requirements in connection with deprivation of liberty increased. In particular it has focused on the 'gilded cage' issue—a sense that the law is being heavy-handed if a person's home and residential homes are regarded as sites of potentially unlawful restraint; and the bureaucratic legalistic requirements imposed on caring bodies such as local authorities, which, as a result of the judgment, were in effect required to bring all cases to court even where there had been no complaint. The Department of Health in its October 2015 guidance note said: 'In 2013/14 (the year prior to the [*Cheshire West*] judgment) there were approximately 13,700 [DoLS] applications. In 2014/15 (the year following the judgment) there were 137,540.'

The *Cheshire West* judgment gave rise to what amounted to open defiance by one judge in the lower courts, HH Judge Mostyn, who declared:

> In the light of the decision of the Supreme Court, local authorities have to err on the side of caution and bring every case, however borderline, before the court. For if they do not, and a case is later found to be one of deprivation of liberty, there may be heavy damages claims (and lawyers' costs) to pay. I remain of the view that the matter needs to be urgently reconsidered by the Supreme Court.
>
> (*Bournemouth Borough Council v PS & DS* (2015), para. 40)

Earlier he had considered the case of Katherine, aged 52, in *Rochdale v KW* (2014). She was barely ambulatory and suffered the delusion that it was 1996 and she was at home with her young children—who were by then actually adults. Rochdale had made arrangements for her care in her home. Mostyn J noted:

> If it [the care] does amount to a deprivation of liberty then my order will have to provide for periodic reviews by this court. Such reviews plainly have significant resource implications for this hard-pressed local authority. Every pound spent on such reviews is a pound less for other vitally necessary projects.

Mostyn's view was that '[Katherine] is not in any realistic way being constrained from exercising the freedom to leave, in the required sense, for the essential reason that she does not have the physical or mental ability to exercise that freedom'. Mostyn's hope was that the case would be leapfrogged to the Supreme Court and the whole *Cheshire West* issue would be reopened and reconsidered. In the event, the case went no further than the Court of Appeal, which simply declared 'to the extent that the restrictions in place pursuant to the care plan are a deprivation of KW's liberty, such deprivation of KW's liberty is hereby authorized'. In other words, it refused to engage with Mostyn's point.

Law Commission report

An interim statement in 2016 from the Law Commission, then looking at the DoLS regime, said it was 'deeply flawed' and should be replaced. It was confusing to families, and clinicians reported that it was of no benefit to the individuals concerned. The result of *Cheshire West* was an increasing backlog of cases and huge expense to local authorities. The Commission recommended a new regime of Liberty Protection Safeguards. This should use the existing DoLS mechanisms and procedures but seek to remove the inefficiencies and elements detrimental to the individuals. For example, under DoLS, authorizations had to be gained when individuals were moved from one setting to another, even temporarily. The Commission proposed that:

> An authorisation under the Liberty Protection Safeguards could cover deprivation of liberty in any setting and in more than one setting so as to take account of, for example, planned admissions to hospitals and respite care, as well as arrangements for the person's travel between venues.

The proposed legislation: The Mental Capacity (Amendment) Bill

The 2018 Bill covering England and Wales (which will probably be an Act of Parliament by the time you read this) deletes Schedules A1 and 1A from the 2005 Act and replaces them with a new Schedule 1AA setting out the reformed procedure. It gives 'responsible bodies' the power to authorize arrangements giving rise to a deprivation of a person's liberty in any setting (when necessary and proportionate). Responsible bodies are a hospital manager if arrangements for the individual are taking place mainly in a hospital (whether NHS or private); or a clinical commissioning group or local health board under continuing health care arrangements; or, otherwise, the responsible local authority (the one where the cared-for person is mainly resident if more than one local authority is involved).

It also requires each responsible body to appoint an Independent Mental Capacity Advocate (IMCA) or an appropriate person to represent and support the person when an authorization is being proposed and while an authorization is in place. (Local authorities must ensure that there are enough IMCAs for the area.)

The conditions for an authorization are that:

(a) the cared-for person is 18 or over;

(b) the cared-for person lacks the capacity to consent to the arrangements;

(c) the cared-for person is of unsound mind; and

(d) the arrangements are necessary and proportionate.

There has to have been an assessment of the cared-for person to establish criteria (b) and (c), one that the responsible body or care home manager can reasonably rely on, bearing in mind the length of time since the assessment, its original purpose and 'whether there has been a change in the cared-for person's condition that is likely to affect the determination made on the assessment'.

The sort of arrangements envisaged are:

(a) for the cared-for person to reside in a particular place;

(b) for the cared-for person to receive care or treatment at a particular place;

(c) for the means and manner of transport for the cared-for person to, from or between particular places.

To establish whether the arrangements are 'necessary and proportionate', a determination must be made by someone with appropriate experience and knowledge to make such a determination. The Bill did not expand on this, but there may be a Code of Practice available to provide examples of when such an assessor should be a specialist or from a particular profession.

On the duty to consult, the new law says this (at para. 17 of the original Bill before Parliament, though numbering may change in the final Statute):

Consultation

(2) (a) anyone named by the cared-for person as someone to be consulted about arrangements of the kind in question,

(b) anyone engaged in caring for the cared-for person or interested in the cared-for person's welfare,

(c) any donee of a lasting power of attorney or an enduring power of attorney . . . granted by the cared-for person,

(d) any deputy appointed for the cared-for person by the court, and

(e) any appropriate person and any independent mental capacity advocate concerned.

(3) The main purpose of the consultation required by sub-paragraph (2) is to try to ascertain the cared-for person's wishes or feelings in relation to the arrangements.

(4) If it is not practicable or appropriate to consult a particular person falling within sub-paragraph (2) the duty to consult that person does not apply.

A pre-authorization review must be undertaken by someone not involved in the day-to-day care of the cared-for person or in their medical treatment. The review must be by an Approved Mental Capacity Professional if:

a) the arrangements provide for the cared-for person to reside in a particular place, and it is reasonable to believe that the cared-for person does not wish to reside in that place, or

(b) the arrangements provide for the cared-for person to receive care or treatment at a particular place, and it is reasonable to believe that the cared-for person does not wish to receive care or treatment at that place.

The Approved Mental Capacity Professional must meet the cared-for person if it seems appropriate and practicable to do so.

A record of the authorization must be kept specifying the arrangements made, the time from which they start to have effect (no later than 28 days after the authorization is given) and cease to have effect (up to 12 months unless reviewed) and the programme of reviewing authorization, plus other relevant information. Note that: 'An authorisation ceases to have effect if, at any time, the responsible body believes or ought reasonably to suspect that any of the authorisation conditions are not met'.

When the authorization ceases to have effect, 'reasonable steps must be taken to ensure any person likely to be carrying out the arrangements is notified'. In other words, those caring for the individual and their managers must be informed so that any potential deprivation of liberty ceases.

Care homes

Care home arrangements involving potential deprivation of liberty come under a different procedure that, according to the guidance notes to the original Bill, (https://publications.parliament.uk/pa/bills/lbill/2017-2019/0117/18117en06.htm or shortlink https://bit.ly/2xmAtbU) have the general effect that 'the care home manager must arrange the relevant assessments and take the other necessary steps before an authorization can be given by the responsible body'.

The responsible body may provide authorization if the care home manager sends a statement that certain criteria have been met (according to para. 14 of the original Bill):

- that the cared-for person is 18 or over;
- that they lack capacity;
- that an assessment has been made along the lines noted above;
- that an appropriate person has established the arrangements are necessary and proportionate;
- that necessary consultations have been undertaken (such as with anyone named by the cared-for person for the purpose or caring for her, any donee of a lasting power of attorney or an enduring power of attorney, any deputy appointed by the court, any 'appropriate person' or independent mental capacity advocate concerned).

The manager must have ensured that a review by an Approved Mental Capacity Professional has occurred if the arrangements involve residing in a particular place 'and it is reasonable to believe that the cared-for person does not wish to reside in that place' or that the cared-for person does not wish to receive treatment at that place.

Additionally, the care home manager must notify the responsible body if s/he considers an Independent Mental Capacity Advocate should be appointed for the cared-for person (under para. 36 of the Bill), i.e. if:

(a) that person has capacity to consent to being represented and supported by an IMCA, and

(b) makes a request to the relevant person for an IMCA to be appointed; *or*

(c) the cared-for person lacks capacity to consent to being represented and supported by an IMCA, and

(d) the relevant person is satisfied that being represented and supported by an IMCA would be in the cared-for person's best interests.

This requirement does not apply if there is already a suitable 'appropriate person' who has agreed to represent the cared-for person and who is not involved in the person's care. Again, the appropriate person must be someone the cared-for person has consented to have representing her or 'where the cared-for person lacks capacity to consent to being represented and supported by that person, the relevant person is satisfied that being represented and supported by that person would be in the cared-for person's best interests'. An IMCA may in this case also be appointed if the cared-for person has capacity and requests it or, not having capacity, the relevant person decides it would be in the cared-for person's best interests.

Protecting the cared-for person—and the professional

All this law seems very complex but it should be clear that the intention is to ensure that if someone is subject to deprivation of liberty as defined in the *Cheshire West* case, there is law and procedure to protect their interests (to some extent) and to ensure deprivation of liberty is lawful, with sufficient independent review, without needing to take vast numbers of cases to court (which, by implication, was what became necessary under *Cheshire West*).

Schedule AA1 makes provision for renewals of the authorizations (for 12 months or less on a first renewal or up to three years on a subsequent renewal) with similar safeguards as outlined above to protect, not merely the looked-after person's interests, but also their preferences insofar as they can be ascertained, and to establish that there is unlikely to be significant change in their condition during the renewal period. Variations can be made to the authorization as long as consultations are made again as already outlined (in para. 17 of the original Bill).

There is also protection for those carrying out the authorized arrangements (which would include the social workers and carers). An amendment adds this to the Mental Health Act as a new section 4C:

Carrying out of authorised arrangements giving rise to deprivation of liberty

(1) This section applies to an act that a person ('D') does in carrying out arrangements authorised under Schedule AA1.

(2) D does not incur any liability in relation to the act that would not have been incurred if the cared-for person—
(a) had had capacity to consent in relation to D doing the act, and
(b) had consented to D doing the act.

(3) Nothing in this section excludes a person's civil liability for loss or damage, or a person's criminal liability, resulting from that person's negligence in doing the act.

This allows those taking care of the individual under an authorized arrangement legal protection from civil damages claims and criminal liability in carrying out arrangements authorized under Schedule AA1 as long as they act without negligence. There is also protection if the authorization has terminated but someone caring for the individual could not reasonably have known.

Section 4B of the MCA is amended to provide express authority for a person to take steps to deprive another person of their liberty if four conditions are met:

Condition 1 is that the steps—

(a) are wholly or partly for the purpose of giving P life-sustaining treatment or doing any vital act, or

(b) consist wholly or partly of giving P life-sustaining treatment or doing any vital act.

A vital act is any act which the person doing it reasonably believes to be necessary to prevent a serious deterioration in P's condition.

Condition 2 is that the steps are necessary in order to give the life-sustaining treatment or do the vital act.

Condition 3 is that D reasonably believes that P lacks capacity to consent to D taking the steps.

Condition 4 is that—

(a) subsection (7) applies, or

(b) there is an emergency.

Subsection (7) in the Bill placed before Parliament (numbering may change in the final Statute) arises if a court case is pending regarding authorization of deprivation of liberty or 'a responsible body is carrying out functions under Schedule AA1 with a view to determining whether to authorise arrangements which would give rise to a deprivation of P's liberty'. This takes the place, in part, of the previous provision for urgent authorizations under DoLS. The person taking the decision must reasonably believe that the person to be deprived of liberty lacks the capacity to consent to the steps being taken.

Critique

The aim of these layers of protection for cared-for people facing potential deprivation of liberty is to protect the authorities from acting unlawfully in situations where individuals are receiving care arrangements—wherever they are living. Neither individual carers nor authorities should assume they know the best interests of a cared-for person who cannot express a view about where she would like to live to receive care or whose preference cannot be met. Let us remind ourselves of the crucial 'Right to liberty and security' in Article 5 of the European Convention on Human Rights:

1. Everyone has the right to liberty and security of person. No one shall be deprived of his liberty save in the following cases and in accordance with a procedure prescribed by law . . .

2. Everyone who has been the victim of arrest or detention in contravention of the provisions of this Article shall have an enforceable right to compensation.

The exceptions are largely to do with detaining criminals or stopping the spread of disease, or detaining 'persons of unsound mind, alcoholics or drug addicts or vagrants'. There is nothing specifically on detaining those who need care, which is why judges in *Bournewood* and *Cheshire West* have had to grapple with the issue. We must remember that before attention was given to the 'Bournewood gap', there was no legal authorization in England and Wales for detaining people in such circumstances.

But who is the new legislation protecting? There are certainly layers of consultation, with various experts and people representing cared-for people, and if the caring authorities go through the procedures, the intention of the Act is that it will keep them out of the courts. But is all this box-ticking designed only to have in place 'a procedure prescribed by law' and hence defeat the potential victim's 'enforceable right to compensation'? How far are the cared-for person's wishes and autonomy really protected?

Some critics of the new legislation certainly think it actually weakens protections for disabled people. There are particular concerns about the new powers for NHS and private health facilities to make their own authorizations, and the procedures giving care home managers a major role in making assessments. These are, in effect, new powers for care home managers to recommend deprivation of liberty for cared-for people. There are safeguards, of course, but also a certain amount of discretion for the manager to make judgements, for example, whether the cared-for person does or does not wish to reside in a particular place.

In short, the fear is that the new law is a legally watertight way of restricting liberty rather than an attempt to positively enhance the liberty and autonomy of cared-for people. Even the requirement that any arrangement be 'necessary and proportionate'—the sort of wording used in the ECHR for exceptions to basic rights—does not carry with it a duty to focus on the potential wishes of the cared-for person. (The Law Commission called for a 'particular' weight to be given to individuals' wishes in best-interest decision making under the MCA.) How far might 'necessity' depend on funding resources?

The Law Commission explained its own approach thus:

> The draft [i.e. Law Commission] Bill would amend the Mental Capacity Act to require that the decision-maker must, first of all, 'ascertain, so far as is reasonably practicable' the person's wishes and feelings. It further requires that, in making the best interests determination, the decision-maker 'must give particular weight to any wishes or feelings ascertained'. The draft Bill also places additional requirements on professionals to explain their decisions not to give effect to a person's wishes and feelings, in the context of restrictions of the defence to civil and criminal liability under section 5 the Mental Capacity Act.

The wording 'must give particular weight to any wishes or feelings ascertained' did not find its way into the parliamentary Bill.

One critique of the new legislation as presented to Parliament is available online from https://thesmallplaces.wordpress.com/2018/09/03/some-thoughts-from-the-lakes. There is also a shortlink: https://bit.ly/2OCiDbi

 SUMMARY

In this chapter we have considered:

- the work and role of the Court of Protection;
- the Deprivation of Liberty Safeguards;
- The Mental Capacity (Amendment) Bill.

Please be aware that the provisions of the Amendment Bill have been extensively debated and are very likely to change before becoming law. We will update you in the next edition.

EXERCISES

1 What is the difference between restraint and a deprivation of liberty?

2 Explain in your own words why it is necessary to protect incapacitated persons from unauthorized deprivations of liberty.

3 What do you think, if anything, was wrong with the DoLS regime?

4 Do you think legal safeguards against deprivation of liberty should apply in domestic and community settings?

5 Does the new legislation address the needs of people lacking mental capacity?

ONLINE RESOURCES

For guidance on how to answer these exercises, visit the online resources at
www.oup.com/uk/carr-goosey15e.

WHERE DO WE GO FROM HERE?

This chapter has focused on the work of the Court of Protection and in particular the problems posed by deprivations of liberty. **Chapter 16** retains the focus on adults, but turns to the more specialized area of mental health. It examines the legal rights of the mentally ill, and the responsibilities that social workers have to ensure that those rights are respected.

ANNOTATED FURTHER READING

There is a useful Social Care Institute for Excellence (SCIE) guide published in 2015, 'At a Glance 43: The Deprivation of Liberty Safeguards', available at www.scie.org.uk/mca/dols/at-a-glance.

In the light of *Cheshire West*, the Mental Capacity Law and Policy website has set up a special page of useful material, which it promises to update. It is worth watching for any new government Bill dealing with the issue: www.mentalcapacitylawandpolicy.org.uk/resources-2/cheshire-west-resources.

The Law Commission interim statement on DoLS reform (May 2016) can be accessed at their website: www.lawcom.gov.uk/wp-content/uploads/2016/06/mental_capacity_interim_statement.pdf

Those interested in Mostyn J's defiance of the Supreme Court may wish to read 'Deprivation of Liberty Safeguards descend into costly chaos', Thinking Legally blog: https://thinkinglegally.wordpress.com/2015/06/18/deprivation-of-liberty-safeguards-dols-descend-into-costly-chaos/ (or shortlink: http://bit.ly/29qIVvY).

The Court of Protection Handbook site (courtofprotectionhandbook.com) gives handy material such as legislation, court cases, and other updates: courtofprotectionhandbook.com/tag/deprivation-of-liberty.

16 Mental health and the law

OVERVIEW AND OBJECTIVES

The state, acting through social workers and doctors, has considerable powers over the lives of people with mental disorder. The law lays down the circumstances and procedures in which those powers can be exercised. If you step outside the law, your actions are unlawful. This chapter tells you about those circumstances and procedures.

Unless there is a need for compulsory powers over a patient, your involvement with mental disorder will be under community care legislation, as discussed in chapters 13–15. This chapter deals with the problems when community care is not enough and compulsory intervention may be needed.

These are the important issues:

- In what circumstances do doctors, social workers, and relatives have the power to override the wishes of people with a mental disorder?
- How does the Mental Health Act 1983 (MHA) (as amended by the Mental Health Act 2007) work to enable or require people to obtain assessment, treatment in hospital, treatment in the community, and after-care following discharge?
- To what extent are patients' rights safeguarded by tribunals and courts?

 CASE STUDY

Re S-C (Mental Patient: Habeas Corpus) (1996)

Why are we asking you to read this case?

This case demonstrates the importance of following the law, whatever you might think is the right outcome for the patient. If you fail to follow the law you are at risk of being publicly reprimanded.

What is at stake for the parties and beyond?

What was at stake for S-C was his freedom. For his father, his nearest relative, it was his right to be consulted over his son's detention. For the social worker and the local authority, it was about the importance of following legal procedures and the consequences of failing to do so. More broadly, what is at stake is the rule of law and the importance of a fundamental principle of liberal societies, that no one can be detained without proper legal procedures being followed.

Background

S-C had a history of mental disorder. He had been in hospital at least once before. As we will see, a specialist mental health social worker can apply to have a person detained (sectioned) under the MHA. The Act lays down a procedure for the application. Under s. 11(4)(a) and (b), the social worker cannot apply if the nearest relative objects and cannot apply without consulting the nearest relative (unless this is impossible).

The Act defines the nearest relative, and, where there are many family members, how to identify the right one, because in law only one person can be the nearest relative at any one time.

In this case the social worker misled the court. She said the mother of the patient was the nearest relative, that she had been consulted, and that she did not object. In fact, the father was the nearest relative. He had not been consulted, because the social worker knew he would object.

Having been sectioned, the patient applied for an order from the High Court for habeas corpus—a legal order requiring a person to be released immediately from unlawful detention. So, it was not an application to review the grounds for detention or whether the required nature or degree of mental disorder had been established. It was an application to require that the rights of the patient to liberty be restored because they had been taken away without due process of law.

The words of Sir Thomas Bingham MR should be noted:

> As we are all well aware, no adult citizen of the United Kingdom is liable to be confined in any institution against his will, save by the authority of law. That is a fundamental constitutional principle, traceable back to . . . Magna Carta . . . (1215). There are, of course, situations in which the law sanctions detention. The most obvious is in the case of those suspected or convicted of crime. Powers then exist to arrest and detain. But the conditions in which those powers may be exercised are very closely prescribed by statute and the common law . . . .
>
> [Mental patients] present a special problem since they may be liable, as a result of mental illness, to cause injury either to themselves or to others. But the very illness which is the source of the danger may deprive the sufferer of the insight necessary to ensure access to proper medical care, whether the proper medical care consists of assessment or treatment, and, if treatment, whether in-patient or out-patient treatment.
>
> Powers therefore exist to ensure that those who suffer from mental illness may, in appropriate circumstances, be involuntarily admitted to mental hospitals and detained. But—and it is a very important but—the circumstances in which the mentally ill may be detained are very carefully prescribed by statute. Action may only be taken if there is clear evidence that the medical condition of a patient justifies such action, and there are detailed rules prescribing the classes

of person who may apply to a hospital to admit and detain a mentally disordered person. The legislation recognises that action may be necessary at short notice and also recognises that it will be impracticable for a hospital to investigate the background facts to ensure that all the requirements of the Act are satisfied if they appear to be so. Thus, we find in the statute a panoply of powers combined with detailed safeguards for the protection of the patient. The underlying issue in the present appeal is whether those powers were properly exercised and whether the appellant was lawfully detained. One reminds oneself that the liberty of the subject is at stake in a case of this kind, and that liberty may be violated only to the extent permitted by law, and not otherwise.

WHAT DOES THIS CASE TELL YOU ABOUT SOCIAL WORK PRACTICE?

This case is a further reminder that you can only intervene in people's lives if you have their consent or if you act with legal authority. It is not enough justification to believe that you are acting in the best interests of the service user—no doubt that is what the social worker in this case thought. If the law requires that you consult with the nearest relative, then that is what you must do, however unpalatable that may be.

Is mental health law just for specialist social workers?

We will see that a social services department must appoint specialists to deal with hospital and guardianship admissions. But non-specialist social workers also need to be aware of mental health law.

For example, what are you going to do about a mentally disordered service user who threatens to jump off a window ledge, or to attack you? What about the service user who denies having a mental disorder and refuses appropriate care or medication? The question you face may be within the realm of consent, dealt with in chapter 2, but it may fall into the realm of compulsion. At the very least you need to be able to contact the right person, sometimes urgently; that involves knowing who does what, whether MHA powers to detain and treat in a hospital, to treat or care for released patients, or to make guardianship orders. It also helps to know what help you can get from the police.

Powers to detain and treat people who cannot consent can involve social workers who are not Approved Mental Health Professionals (AMHPs), even where the detention and treatment is for mental disorders.

Statutory framework of the Mental Health Act 1983

There are two distinct features of the MHA:

- decisions under the MHA are first and foremost medical decisions, though they may have social care consequences;

- the MHA gives the doctors, social workers, and relatives the possibility of using compulsory powers.

The Mental Health Act in its historical context

The 1983 Act is derived from the 1959 Mental Health Act, as amended in 1982. The 1959 Act was 'revolutionary' according to Brenda Hoggett (now the Supreme Court Justice Baroness Hale) in *Mental Health Law* (Sweet & Maxwell, 2017). Modern treatments, particularly medication, were to replace reliance on detention and restraint. Patients would obtain hospital treatment with as little fuss as any other medical treatment. Doctors would only use compulsory powers for exceptional circumstances. Patients who could not benefit from hospital treatment would be treated in the community. And criminals with mental disorder would receive the same medical care as anyone else.

This can be described as a medical model. It puts the state's powers of compelling individuals into the hands of doctors and, to a lesser extent, social workers. It is doctors, generally aided by social workers or other health professionals, and sometimes by relatives, who have powers to detain patients. It is usually doctors who decide to release patients.

Legal powers and constraints are grafted onto this medical model: criminal courts can send an offender to hospital for treatment, and in the case of dangerous offenders can restrict the power of doctors to release the patient; after detention has commenced a patient can apply to a Mental Health Tribunal for release, and the hospital must then prove that the detention remains justified in law.

A key concept of the 1959 and 1983 legislation was that compulsory treatment should be for the benefit of the patient. If the condition cannot be treated, the patient should not be detained. As we shall see, that concept has been watered down, so that a patient now can be detained if appropriate treatment is available, even if it cannot be shown that it will benefit the patient.

For almost 10 years the government planned to replace the whole of the legislation, but opposition from the medical profession and mental health organizations against the proposed powers of compulsory treatment in the community and preventive detention of those with psychopathic disorder eventually led to less ambitious plans. The Mental Health Act 2007 amended the 1983 legislation with effect from November 2008 and what we describe is not radically different from the previous regime. The core difference is that the definitions of mental disorder are not set out so narrowly, that new powers now exist to treat a patient in the community following release from detention, and that detention for treatment is not dependent on the treatment alleviating the condition.

Statutory duties

Section numbers below are from the 1983 Act. Any reference to regulations is to the Mental Health Regulations 2008 unless we indicate otherwise. Any reference to the Code is to the 2015 version of the Code of Practice to the Mental Health Act 1983, which you can locate at www.gov.uk/government/publications/code-of-practice-mental-health-act-1983. We also make reference to the Reference Guide to the Act, which was published at the same time as the Code of Practice and is designed to be read alongside it as statutory guidance.

The MHA confers statutory powers on social workers in three ways, all of which will be explored in more detail.

First, it creates specialist mental health professionals who make decisions alongside doctors. Previously called approved social workers (ASWs), the 2007 amendments changed their name and broadened the number of professions able to exercise these powers. Their new name is approved mental health professionals (AMHPs): members of other professions can be approved under the MHA, including nurses, occupational therapists, and psychologists. The panel of AMHPs is in the control of (but need not be employed by) social services authorities (s. 114), which must appoint enough AMHPs to provide 24-hour cover for admissions of mental patients and their treatment (DoH Circular LAC (93) 10 and Mental Health Act 1983 Code of Practice, para. 4.33). The AMHP exercises his or her powers personally, not under the direction of their employer.

The AMHP has powers, working with doctors, to detain for assessment or treatment or to admit to guardianship. The AMHP plays no statutory role in decisions to discharge, but social services are likely to be heavily involved in preparing for discharge and advising whether community facilities are ready and appropriate for the patient's discharge.

Second, a social services authority has statutory powers and duties relating to guardianship. It must either itself take on the role of guardian, or it must approve the appointment of an individual as guardian.

Third, the authority has duties under s. 117 to plan and provide after-care following discharge. We touched on that when looking at community care.

The scale of mental health problems

Statistics published by Mind (www.mind.org.uk) indicate that 30 per cent of the population experiences a mental health problem in any year. Most of these do not involve specialist help, though 10 per cent of the population is diagnosed with a specific condition each year. Government statistics, published in October 2017 and set out in **Box 16.1**, indicate the scale of use of formal powers under the legislation. The full statistics are available at https://digital.nhs.uk/data-and-information/publications/statistical/mental-health-act-statistics-annual-figures/mental-health-act-statistics-annual-figures-2016-17-experimental-statistics. Note that the way the statistics are sourced and produced has changed from previous years and coverage is also incomplete. As a result, 2016/17 figures are not directly comparable to previous years' figures, which we have discussed in previous editions. The intention is that when the system is fully working it will enable new insights into uses of the MHA. As those emerge, we will discuss them with you.

BOX 16.1 Key facts—Annual report on formal detentions under the Mental Health Act

There were 45,864 new detentions recorded in 2016/17 and 4,966 new Community Treatment Orders (CTOs).

This is estimated to represent a 2% increase on the previous year.

Known detention rates were higher for males (83.2 per 100,000 population) than females (76.1 per 100,000 population).

Known detention rates for the 18–34 age group (111.3 detentions per 100,000 population) were around a third higher than for those aged 50–64 (81.7 per 100,000 population).

Rates for 65+ age group have increased to 96.5 per 100,000 population.

Amongst the five broad ethnic groups, known rates of detention for the 'Black or Black British' group (272.1 detentions per 100,000 population) were over four times those of the White group (67.0 per 100,000 population).

Known rates of CTO use for males (11.4 per 100,000 population) were almost twice the rate for females (6.6 per 100,000 population).

Across age groups, those aged 35–49 had the highest rate of CTO use (15.6 known uses per 100,000 population compared to 9.0 uses per 100,000 population for all age groups).

Amongst broad ethnic groups, known rates of CTO use for the 'Black or Black British' group (60.1 uses per 100,000 population) were almost nine times the rate for the White group (6.8 uses per 100,000 population).

The need for compulsory powers over a patient is comparatively rare. By comparison with the numbers of people with some form of mental health problem, even voluntary admissions to hospital are rare. Out-patient hospital treatment, help from a GP or community mental health teams, social services support in the community, or simply coping without professional help, are how the bulk of mental health problems are dealt with.

Mental Health Act 1983 review

Below we discuss some of the details of the current legislative framework. However there have been longstanding concerns about the operation of the Mental Health Act 1983. In October 2017, the government commenced a review of the Mental Health Act. The particular concerns were:

- rising rates of detention under the act;
- the disproportionate number of people from black and minority ethnicities detained under the act;

- stakeholder concerns that some processes relating to the act are out of step with a modern mental health system, including but not limited to:

  o the balance of safeguards available to patients, such as tribunals, second opinions, and requirements for consent;

  o the ability of the detained person to determine which family or carers have a say in their care, and of families to find appropriate information about their loved one;

  o that detention may in some cases be used to detain rather than treat;

  o questions about the effectiveness of community treatment orders, and the difficulties in getting discharged;

  o the time required to take decisions and arrange transfers for patients subject to criminal proceedings.

An interim report was published in May 2018 which highlighted concerns about high rates of detention for people from black Caribbean, black African, and mixed black ethnicity. A number of explanations for these high rates were proffered, including discrimination, poverty, and social exclusion. It also considered possible changes to the law, for instance reform to the current rules of nearest relatives, which may be based upon outdated notions of family connections. The final report was published in December 2018 and is available at www.gov.uk/government/publications/modernising-the-mental-health-act-final-report-from-the-independent-review. It proposes an extensive overhaul of the law on the basis of the following principles:

Choice and autonomy—ensuring service users' views and choices are respected;

Least restriction—ensuring the Act's powers are used in the least restrictive way;

Therapeutic benefit—ensuring patients are supported to get better, so they can be discharged from the Act;

The person as an individual—ensuring patients are viewed and treated as rounded individuals.

Any reforms to the current legal framework are not likely to happen for some time.

Accountability to the Care Quality Commission

Those working in social care generally are accountable through complaints procedures (see **chapter 13**), through the courts and through the normal channels of democratic and media scrutiny. The Care Quality Commission (CQC), made up of laypeople, lawyers, doctors, nurses, social workers, psychologists, and other specialists (as we discussed in **chapter 13**), also has responsibilities under the MHA. It is required to:

- review MHA powers of detention;
- visit patients detained under the Act;
- investigate complaints;

- review decisions to withhold the mail of patients detained in high security hospitals;
- appoint medical practitioners and others to give second opinions;
- monitor the implementation of the Code of Practice.

Breaches of the Act and the Code of Practice are likely to trigger regulatory action from the CQC.

Accountability to the courts

It is a fundamental principle of health and social care law that service users and patients can choose whether they accept or refuse services or treatment. Only if they lack mental capacity does the law allow others to make decisions in their best interests (see **chapter 14**). However, compulsory detention under the MHA operates independently of capacity questions. The MHA allows health professionals to assess, detain, and treat patients, or impose guardianship or community treatment, even where they have adequate mental capacity to refuse.

This gives mental health professionals and—unless they have been barred from involvement (see **Barring discharge from hospital by the nearest relative**, p 589)— nearest relatives, a power to override the wishes of mentally disordered adults with mental capacity. Such powers have to be exercised with respect for human rights. The European Convention provides, in particular, the right to liberty. Article 5 states:

> No one shall be deprived of his liberty save in the following cases and in accordance with a procedure prescribed by law . . . [including] the lawful detention . . . of persons of unsound mind, alcoholics or drug addicts, or vagrants.

An example of the application of Article 5 in a mental health detention case was *Kay v UK* (1998). Mr Kay had been convicted of manslaughter and was subject to a hospital order with restriction. We will describe this in **Admission to hospital for treatment from a criminal court**, p 582.

Mr Kay was conditionally discharged from hospital in 1985 (the conditional release meant he was still subject to recall); he offended again, but this time was sentenced to prison, not sent to hospital. While in prison, he obtained evidence showing that he was no longer suffering from a mental disorder. Yet he was still liable to recall under the hospital order because of the restriction imposed on his previous conviction. A Mental Health Review Tribunal (MHRT) (now known as the First-tier Tribunal (Mental Health) or Mental Health Tribunal MHT) accepted that he had no mental disorder but refused to discharge the restriction order. The hospital then recalled him just before his release from prison, with the result that he was detained under the hospital order as soon as he left prison.

The European Court of Human Rights (ECtHR) said that if he was to be detained for treatment for mental disorder, the state must prove both that he had the mental disorder and that he needed the treatment. Deprivation of liberty was otherwise unlawful.

We will see later that MHTs are routinely involved where patients wish to challenge their continuing detention see **Discharge by the First-tier Tribunal (Mental Health)**, p 589.

Mental Health Act 1983 Code of Practice

The current Code of Practice was published in 2015 and it is quite different from previous versions. It clarifies much in relation to the interface between the Mental Capacity Act 2005, the Mental Health Act, and informal admissions. This code, the Mental Health Act 1983 Code of Practice (Department of Health, 2015) together with the Reference Guide to the Act, is essential reading. Extracts from the Code are set out in **Box 16.2**. The Code must (s. 118) conform to the following statutory principles:

(a) respect for patients' past and present wishes and feelings,

(b) minimising restrictions on liberty,

(c) involvement of patients in planning,

(d) developing and delivering care and treatment appropriate to them,

(e) avoidance of unlawful discrimination,

(f) effectiveness of treatment,

(g) views of carers and other interested parties,

(h) patient wellbeing and safety, and

(i) public safety.

 BOX 16.2 Principles set out in the Mental Health Act 1983 Code of Practice (2015)

1.1 It is essential that all those undertaking functions under the Act understand the five sets of overarching principles which should always be considered when making decisions in relation to care, support or treatment provided under the Act. This chapter provides an explanation of the overarching principles and stresses that should be considered when making decisions under the Act. Although all are of equal importance the weight given to each principle in reaching a particular decision will depend on context and the nature of the decision being made.

The five overarching principles are:

Least restrictive option and maximising independence

Where it is possible to treat a patient safely and lawfully without detaining them under the Act, the patient should not be detained. Wherever possible a patient's independence should be encouraged and supported with a focus on promoting recovery wherever possible.

Empowerment and involvement

Patients should be fully involved in decisions about care, support and treatment. The views of families, carers and others, if appropriate, should be fully considered when taking decisions. Where decisions are taken which are contradictory to views expressed, professionals should explain the reasons for this.

Respect and dignity

Patients, their families and carers should be treated with respect and dignity and listened to by professionals.

Purpose and effectiveness

Decisions about care and treatment should be appropriate to the patient, with clear therapeutic aims, promote recovery and should be performed to current national guidelines and/or current, available best practice guidelines.

Efficiency and equity

Providers, commissioners and other relevant organisations should work together to ensure that the quality of commissioning and provision of mental healthcare services are of high quality and are given equal priority to physical health and social care services. All relevant services should work together to facilitate timely, safe and supportive discharge from detention.

Independent mental health advocates

Mental patients are often unable to articulate their own views adequately. Independent mental health advocates (IMHAs) have a role independent of all other professionals to help the patient voice their wishes and concerns. Any detained patient (except detained in an emergency for six or 72 hours or in a place of safety) is entitled to this assistance, and to be told of its availability. The IMHA should have access to the patient and to records at all reasonable times. Clearly, as they aim to be the voice of the patient, what they say must be carefully listened to at all times. The Code provides more detail at Chapter 6 and the Reference Guide at Chapter 4.

Assessment of mental disorder with a view to admission

The MHA uses the word 'patient' for any person suffering from mental disorder. But it is not necessary to be an in-patient or even an out-patient for the MHA to apply.

A patient can be of any age for MHA powers to be available, except that for admission to guardianship the child must be at least 16. Of course, unless circumstances are exceptional, doctors and social workers are more likely to rely on Children Act powers where children have mental health problems.

The legal definition of mental disorder is simple: 'Any disorder or disability of the mind' (s. 1). Those with a learning disability are not considered to be suffering from a mental disorder unless 'that disability is associated with abnormally aggressive or seriously irresponsible conduct' (s. 1(2A)). Section 1(3) provides that 'dependence on alcohol or drugs is not to be considered a mental disorder'.

It is for mental health professionals to assess who has and who does not have a mental disorder. Courts and tribunals will not overrule such diagnoses, since they are matters of professional judgement. However, an MHT considering grounds for continuing detention must itself identify the nature and degree of the mental disorder where this triggers statutory powers to detain, so in theory the tribunal can disagree on clear evidence of a misdiagnosis.

Although mental disorder must not be diagnosed solely on grounds of alcohol or drug abuse (s. 1(3)), alcohol or drug abuse can be symptomatic of or can cause mental disorder and can lead to mental disorder. Anorexia nervosa has been found by a court to be a mental illness (*Re KB (Adult) (Mental Patient: Medical Treatment)* (1994)).

Assessment of the patient for MHA purposes should be carried out where possible by the doctors and the AMHP at the same time, but the conclusions are to be reached by each professional independently. While the AMHP acts on behalf of the local social services authority, they exercise their own judgement, deciding independently whether to apply for a patient to be detained on the basis of the medical evidence and whether there are alternatives (Reference Guide, para. 30.07). The AMHP must not defer to the doctor. It is for the AMHP to provide the social work perspective, and also to consult the nearest relative and others, such as a carer, before reaching a conclusion (Reference Guide, Chapter 8).

A diagnosis cannot be founded on unwise or irrational behaviour. *St George's NHS Trust v S* (1998) involved a woman who was refusing a caesarean section, even though she was, on the evidence, putting herself and her baby at grave risk. To get around the lack of consent, the hospital had her sectioned. This left her powerless, so she accepted the caesarean. Afterwards she applied to the court for a declaration that this use of MHA powers had been unlawful. No evidence was put forward that she had a mental disorder. The Court of Appeal ruling makes clear that the Act should be used to deal with mental health issues and not for social control.

The professional assessment can be reviewed by courts, for example where 'seriously irresponsible conduct' has to be identified. In *Re F (Mental Health Act: Guardianship)* (2000), the Court of Appeal disagreed with an assessment by doctors that a 17-year-old girl who chose to return to an unhappy, abusive home was behaving seriously irresponsibly, for the purpose of diagnosing mental impairment (now called learning disability).

MHA criteria for admission, as we shall shortly see, require that the patient 'is suffering'. However, a person can be liable to mental disorder, but presently symptom free, perhaps because the treatment is working. Does that person have the required mental disorder? In *R (on the application of P) v Mental Health Review Tribunal* (2002), the court agreed with the doctors that disorder (in this case psychopathic disorder) still exists while there is a risk of recurrence.

The Code contains extensive guidance on communicating with the patient and others. **Box 16.3** contains a flavour of this.

BOX 16.3 Assessment and communication—extracts from the Mental Health Act 1983 Code of Practice (2015)

Communicating with patients

4.3 Effective communication is essential in ensuring appropriate care and respect for patients' rights. It is important that the language used is clear and unambiguous and that people giving information check that the information that has been communicated has been understood.

4.4 Everything possible should be done to overcome barriers to effective communication, which may be caused by any of a number of reasons. For example, a patient's first language may not be English. Patients may have difficulty in understanding technical terms and jargon or in maintaining attention for extended periods. They may have a hearing or visual impairment, have difficulty in reading or writing, or have a learning disability. A patient's cultural background may also be different from that of the person speaking to them. Children and young people will need to have information explained in a way they can understand and in a format that is appropriate to their age.

4.5 Those with responsibility for the care of patients need to identify how communication difficulties affect each patient so that they can assess the needs of each patient and address them in the most appropriate way. Hospitals and other organisations should make people with specialist expertise (eg in sign language or Makaton) available as required. Often carers and advocates can help with or advise on best ways of communicating with a patient. Carers' centres and similar services can advise carers on their rights and can also answer general questions on the Mental Health Act Code procedures and other issues.

The nearest relative

Doctors and AMHPs have to work with the nearest relative. At any given moment a particular patient can have only one nearest relative. Section 26 of the Mental Health Act 1983 Code of Practice (2015) sets out how this person is identified, and this is summarized in **Box 16.4**.

 BOX 16.4 The nearest relative, in order of priority—extract from the Mental Health Act 1983 Code of Practice (2015)

The following order of priority is the starting point:

- spouse or civil partner (but not a spouse or partner who has deserted the patient or been separated by court order or formal agreement);
- cohabitee of six months' standing;
- son or daughter;
- parent;
- brother or sister;
- grandparent;
- grandchild;
- uncle or aunt;
- niece or nephew;
- any other person who has lived with the patient for at least five years (if there is no spouse).

A relative who actually lives with and cares for the patient takes precedence over some-one higher up the list. Anyone who lives abroad is ignored altogether. And, conversely, if the patient reasonably objects to the nearest relative (in *R (on the application of M) v Secretary of State for Health* (2003), where the patient had no relationship of trust with her adoptive father) that person cannot be a nearest relative. Where there is more than one person competing for the position on the same level in the list (e.g. a brother and a sister; two parents), then the oldest takes precedence. Relationships of the whole blood take precedence over those of half-blood (e.g. a sister comes before a half-sister).

If a child is in care under the Children Act 1989, the nearest relative is the authority named in the care order, even if the child is accommodated at home (s. 27).

The nearest relative can give written authorization to allow another person to dis-charge their role (reg. 14).

Discharge or replacement of nearest relative

Consulting with the family is important. But there may be no family, or no family will-ing to play the role. Alternatively, the nearest relative may, you think, be standing in the way of the patient's best interests, or of the interests of public safety. That was the problem, as the social worker saw it, in the case study at the beginning of the chapter.

Let us assume that it was entirely appropriate for S-C to be sectioned, and the father's objections were standing in the way of appropriate help being given. The correct approach would be to apply to the County Court to displace the nearest relative.

In either of these situations—unsuitability or unwillingness—any relative, any per-son with whom the patient normally resides, or an AMHP can apply to the County Court to be appointed or to have someone else appointed. The doctors, incidentally, cannot themselves make this application. They are reliant on the AMHP. The patient him- or herself (since 2008) can also apply to the court to displace the nearest relative.

A decision to make an application to displace the existing nearest relative itself raises human rights issues. It is a determination of the nearest relative's responsibilities and it triggers Article 6 of the Convention, so there must be a proper and fair process. In particular, the nearest relative who does not agree with being displaced has a right to see relevant documents: *R (on the application of S) v Plymouth City Council* (2002).

The court can make the s. 29 displacement order only if one of the following grounds is established:

(a) no nearest relative can be found; or

(b) the present nearest relative is incapable of acting because of mental disorder or other illness; or

(c) the nearest relative unreasonably refuses to consent to an application for admis-sion to hospital or guardianship under the MHA; or

(d) the nearest relative has unreasonably exercised his or her power to discharge the patient without taking into account the public interest or the welfare of the patient (s. 26(3)); or

(e) that the nearest relative is otherwise not a suitable person to act as such: *R (on the application of M) v Secretary of State for Health* (2003).

As soon as a s. 29 application is submitted—before any order is made—the current nearest relative loses the power to discharge the patient. This is the only means available to an AMHP to prevent a discharge. The doctors, as we will see, have other ways of preventing discharge by the nearest relative.

The nearest relative has the right, at any time, to appoint an independent doctor to visit the patient in hospital and look at relevant records. This is important, for the nearest relative (even if displaced) has rights to apply to the Mental Health Tribunal, and, if not displaced, to discharge a detained patient, and needs the best information before making that decision.

Informal admission to hospital

Some 70 per cent of mental health admissions are not compulsory. Section 131 of the Act and para. 13.2 of the Reference Guide explicitly encourage informal admissions. In fact, there is no power to detain a person in hospital under ss 2–5 if the patient genuinely consents to being admitted and to remain.

Any person of 16 or over can become an informal patient, regardless of the wishes of his or her parent or guardian. Below that age the informal admission requires consent of the parent or guardian (s. 131(2)). The local authority can admit a child informally, against the child's will, even if there are no grounds for a compulsory MHA admission: *R v Kirklees MBC, ex p C (A Minor)* (1993). Before admitting a child informally, the question of competence must be addressed. In *Kirklees*, the Court of Appeal accepted that if the child had been 'competent' she would have been entitled to refuse informal admission.

Nor can authorization be given to detain a patient informally if he or she has given an advance directive (see **chapter 14**) refusing consent, or where the patient has given a Lasting Power of Attorney covering health and welfare decisions (see **chapter 14**) and the donee has withheld consent.

Detention in these circumstances must be under the powers of the MHA or not at all. In fact, such a patient should have been admitted under the MHA and not the MCA.

Application for compulsory admission to hospital—'sectioning'

The compulsory route of most importance for social workers will be compulsory admission, or sectioning, for assessment or for treatment under ss 2 and 3 of the MHA.

Applicants should remind themselves of the least restriction principle set out in the Code. Liberty should only be restricted by compulsory admission in the absence of a suitable less restrictive approach. A full discussion of the problematic nature of Deprivation of Liberty Safeguards (DoLS) is included in **chapter 15**.

Who is the applicant? An AMHP is usually a better person to make the application than the nearest relative, given an AMHP's professional training and knowledge of the legislation and local resources, together with the potential adverse effect that an application by the nearest relative might have on their relationship with the patient. The AMHP must first consult with whoever appears to be the nearest relative (s. 11(4)). Consultation need not take place if it is 'not reasonably practicable or would involve unreasonable delay'. Knowingly consulting the wrong relative makes the ensuing admission and detention unlawful (*Re S-C (Mental Patient) (Habeas Corpus)* (1996), see the case study at the beginning of the chapter). Unilaterally deciding that it would be too difficult to consult the nearest relative before admitting the patient also amounted to unlawful detention, in circumstances where such consultation could have been arranged and had been deliberately avoided to secure the patient's admission: *GD v (1) Hospital Managers of the Edgware Community Hospital (2) Barnet LBC* (2008).

An application must be supported by two (or, in an emergency, one) doctors' statements.

The application is addressed to the managers of the proposed hospital (s. 11); this means the health authority or, if it is a private mental nursing home, the person registered with the CQC to run it, or, if the hospital is secure (e.g. Broadmoor), the Secretary of State for Health.

An AMHP *must* make an application where in his or her professional opinion that is the appropriate course (s. 13(1)). This is a matter for the AMHP; it is not a departmental decision. And he or she must reach the decision independently, even if it is a different decision from that of the doctors. This was spelled out in *St George's Healthcare NHS Trust v S* (1998), where the Court of Appeal stated that the approved social worker (predecessor to the AMHP) should have realized that a woman refusing a caesarean was not suffering from a mental disorder.

Before making the application, the AMHP must interview the patient 'in a suitable manner', and must be satisfied that compulsory admission is the most appropriate way of providing the care and medical treatment that the patient needs (s. 13(2)). A suitable manner means taking into account any language barriers, hearing difficulties, and other potential communication obstacles, such as cultural differences. Guidance is given in the Code, Chapter 4. As soon as the AMHP has made a decision—to apply or not to apply for compulsory admission—he or she must explain the decision to the patient, the doctors, the nearest relative (if possible), the patient's key worker and doctor (Reference Guide, paras 8.21 et seq.).

Patients do not always cooperate with an assessment. An assessment can be valid for admission purposes even if there is no conversation: *M v South West London and St George's Mental Health NHS Trust* (2008).

Certain pre-application requirements must be satisfied. The applicant for a compulsory admission must have seen the patient within the previous 14 days. The application must be supported by the signed medical recommendations of two doctors, one from a Department of Health-approved mental health specialist, the other, if possible, from a doctor who knows the patient. Both doctors must have examined the patient within five days of each other. They must sign the recommendations before the applicant signs the application, otherwise the application is invalid.

The five-day and 14-day time periods are shortened in the case of an emergency admission (which is discussed in **Compulsory admission for assessment**, p 578): the applicant must have seen the patient not more than 24 hours before making the application, and the admission must be carried out within 24 hours of the medical examination (s. 6(2)(b)).

Neither the managers nor the hospital doctors who receive the application actually consider its merits. They only consider whether they have space. Indeed, once the application for admission has been completed, even before it is delivered to the hospital, it gives rise to compulsory MHA powers: the applicant or his or her authorized agent is now empowered to take the patient to the named hospital. However, the detention ceases to be lawful if the hospital managers realize that the facts stated in the forms are untrue (*R v Central London County Court, ex p London* (1999)). Unless there is a clear abuse of process, in which case proceedings can be commenced, the detention can only be challenged through the Mental Health Tribunal, but a hearing will take time to arrange and until then the section continues to be lawful.

The power to convey the patient to hospital lapses 14 days after the last of the two medical examinations (s. 6(1)), so the medical information will be reasonably up to date at the time of the admission.

Once a patient is compulsorily detained, hospital managers must inform the patient of the grounds for detention, and their rights to a discharge and to apply to the Mental Health Tribunal. If the application was by an AMHP, the nearest relative must be similarly informed, unless the patient objects (s. 132).

Where the application was by a nearest relative, the managers must notify the patient's local social services department; a social worker (who does not have to be an AMHP) must then interview the patient and provide the hospital with a social circumstances report (s. 14). The report should set out not only the history of the patient and the disorder, but also state whether alternative methods of dealing with the patient are available and appropriate. Alternative methods mean looking after the patient in the community—can anything be organized under the powers described in the Code at Chapter 28?

◼ Compulsory admission for assessment

Application for an admission for assessment is under s. 2. It is possible even if the nearest relative objects, since there is no statutory requirement to consult the nearest relative. This is in contrast to an application for treatment under s. 3. (It remains good practice to consult, of course.) Note that there is a statutory requirement to inform the nearest relative that an application for detention under s. 2 is to be or has been made.

For compulsory admission for assessment under s. 2, the doctors must certify on the application that they are satisfied that (s. 2(2)):

   (a) he is suffering from mental disorder of a nature or degree that warrants the detention of the patient in a hospital for assessment (or for assessment followed by medical treatment) for at least a limited period;

(b) he ought to be so detained in the interests of his own health or safety or with a view to the protection of other persons.

A correctly completed application gives the applicant immediate powers to convey the patient to hospital. The hospital may detain the patient for up to 28 days (s. 2(4)). After that, the patient must be discharged unless he or she remains as an informal patient, or detention is authorized for treatment under s. 3 (see **Compulsory admission to hospital for treatment**, p 579).

In an emergency, s. 4 enables a brief detention on just one medical recommendation. The applicant must certify that the need for admission for assessment is urgent and that obtaining two recommendations would involve undesirable delay (s. 4(2)). The doctor should, if possible, be someone who knows the patient. The doctor must confirm that admission for assessment is a matter of urgency. Urgency requires for instance:

- immediate and significant risk of mental or physical harm to the patient or others
- danger of serious harm to property
- need for physical restraint of the patient.

Once the s. 4 application is completed the patient can be detained for up to 72 hours. During these 72 hours, if the second doctor's recommendation is received by the managers, the detention is converted into a s. 2, 28-day admission, starting from the day of the admission. Otherwise, at the end of the 72-hour period the patient is free to leave.

Compulsory admission to hospital for treatment

If the applicant is an AMHP, he or she must consult the person who appears to be the nearest relative before making the application for admission for treatment (s. 11(1)), unless it is 'not reasonably practicable or would involve unreasonable delay'. The nearest relative can then block the application (s. 11(4)), which means the AMHP may have to apply to the County Court to displace the nearest relative (see **Discharge or replacement of nearest relative**, p 575).

Medical grounds for admission for treatment are more rigorous than for assessment, which is not surprising given that the doctors are now, by definition, satisfied that treatment is appropriate. Mental disorder on its own is not enough. The doctors' recommendations must confirm that:

- the patient's 'mental disorder is of a nature or degree which makes it appropriate for him to receive medical treatment in a hospital';
- it is 'necessary for the health or safety of the patient or the protection of other persons' that he or she receives such treatment;
- the treatment cannot be provided without the detention; and
- appropriate medical treatment must be available.

Let us look at some of these requirements. Having a mental disorder is not sufficient if it can be treated entirely in the community; however, if the treatment has to be in or organized by the hospital, the patient may be allowed by the doctors to live in the community. The question is whether the patient would agree without compulsory powers to receive the treatment. A mental disorder can be cyclical, or the patient can be well when compliant with medication, but not otherwise. So, the nature of the condition must be such that detention for treatment is appropriate even if at this particular moment the patient is not necessarily unwell. A patient may therefore need treatment in a hospital under compulsory powers, even if not at present showing signs of severe disorder.

Popplewell J explained the distinction between nature and degree in *R v MHRT, ex p Smith* (1999). 'Nature' refers to the 'particular mental disorder from which the patient suffers, its chronicity, its prognosis, and the patient's previous response to receiving treatment for the disorder' and that it is not a static condition. 'Degree' refers to the 'current manifestation of the patient's disorder' and therefore allows the detention to be justified in relation to the current severity of the disorder. Degree and nature can be alternative grounds for assessing the patient as requiring admission—they do not both need to be satisfied for admission for treatment to be lawful.

Treatment must be available and appropriate. Treatment is a broad concept. Section 145 defines 'medical treatment' as including 'nursing, psychological intervention and specialist mental health habilitation, rehabilitation and care', and goes on to say that 'any reference in this Act to medical treatment, in relation to mental disorder, shall be construed as a reference to medical treatment the purpose of which is to alleviate, or prevent a worsening of, the disorder or one or more of its symptoms or manifestations'.

Force-feeding can be treatment where the patient is refusing to eat (*B v Croydon Health Authority (No 2)* (1996)). Group therapy is treatment, even if the patient is unwilling to participate: *B v Croydon Health Authority (No 2)* (1996). If the patient refuses available treatment, he or she is nevertheless treatable under the old legislation, and treatment would be available under the new legislation (*R v Canons Park MHRT, ex p A* (1994)).

The MHA was, as we mentioned earlier, designed on a medical model. Treatment for mental health was to be no different from treatment for other health problems. But what if there was no treatment to alleviate the condition? Formerly the power to detain for compulsory treatment under s. 3 did not apply if the patient was diagnosed as suffering from a 'minor' disorder—mental impairment or psychopathic disorder—unless the doctors certified that treatment was likely to alleviate the condition or stop it getting worse. The thinking was that, since the disorders were 'minor', no one should compulsorily be sent to hospital for treatment unless he or she would benefit from it. It was felt that even an untreatable psychopathic patient who was dangerous was not a problem that doctors should be required to solve.

In a controversial change opposed by psychiatrists and mental health organizations, the 'treatability test' for the patient has ceased to be a requirement. The government wanted to detain people in hospital even though there was no effective treatment for them so the requirement, under the new s. 3(2)(d), is the availability of 'appropriate medical treatment', meaning 'treatment which is appropriate in his case, taking into account the nature [the particular mental disorder] and degree [the current manifestation] of the mental disorder and all other circumstances of his case'. The definition in

s. 145(4) is 'medical treatment the purpose of which is to alleviate or prevent a worsening of the disorder or one or more of its symptoms or manifestations'. The treatment must actually be available to the patient. It need not be the best possible treatment, and it need only be available at this time, even if the long-term availability is unknown. Detention on its own cannot count as treatment.

On top of the required diagnosis of a disorder, the doctors must confirm that treatment is necessary 'for the health or safety of the patient or for the protection of other persons'—that is, the patient is a risk to him- or herself or others—and that 'it cannot be provided unless he is admitted under this section'. So, if the patient could be treated in the community, or be admitted voluntarily, the s. 3 grounds would not be established.

There is no emergency admission for treatment.

Detention for treatment then lasts up to six months unless it is renewed (see **Detaining the patient who is already in hospital,** p 586).

The Code of Practice provides useful advice as to when admissions should be made under s. 2 of the Act rather than s. 3. The relevant paragraphs are set out in **Box 16.5.**

 BOX 16.5 When to use which section of the Act—paras 14.26–14.29 of the Mental Health Act 1983 Code of Practice (2015)

14.26 An application for detention can be made under either section 2 or section 3 of the Act.

14.27 Section 2 should only be used if:

- the full extent of the nature and degree of a patient's condition is unclear

- there is a need to carry out an initial in-patient assessment in order to formulate a treatment plan, or to reach a judgement about whether the patient will accept treatment on a voluntary basis following admission, or

- there is a need to carry out a new in-patient assessment in order to re-formulate a treatment plan, or to reach a judgement about whether the patient will accept treatment on a voluntary basis.

14.28 Section 3 should be used if:

- the patient is already detained under section 2 (detention under section 2 cannot be renewed by a new section 2 application), or

- the nature and current degree of the patient's mental disorder, the essential elements of the treatment plan to be followed and the likelihood of the patient accepting treatment as an informal patient are already sufficiently established to make it unnecessary to undertake a new assessment under section 2.

14.29 The rationale for decisions to use section 2 or section 3 should be clearly recorded.

This clear statement in the Code of Practice corrects a widely held view that s. 2 was the preferable gateway to detention, even where the patient was well known to social workers. Key to this was a belief that s. 2 allowed for new situations and reasons for relapse to be explored, as well as speedy access to the tribunal for Article 5(4) purposes. This was wrong. Only if the patient's condition is unclear should s. 2 be used.

Getting the patient to hospital following admission

The completion of the admission procedures gives the applicant (usually, as we have seen, the AMHPs) power to convey the patient to hospital or to delegate that power.

Admission to hospital for treatment from a criminal court

Home Office Circular 66/90, *Mentally Disordered Offenders*, makes clear that police and Crown Prosecutors should avoid prosecution of a mentally disordered suspect unless this would be in the public interest. The circular also states that courts should, if possible, impose sentences that are therapeutic, not punitive.

The power to make a hospital order arises under s. 37 but only if the crime is one that would have led to a prison sentence. It requires that there has been a conviction, or if there is no conviction, the magistrates' court has to be satisfied that the accused did the act, otherwise there will have to be unqualified acquittal. Section 37 requires that the offender must be 'suffering from a mental disorder of a nature or degree which makes it appropriate for him to be detained in a hospital for medical treatment and appropriate medical treatment is available for him', and that:

> the court is of the opinion, having regard to all the circumstances including the nature of the offence and the character and antecedents of the offender, and to the other available methods of dealing with him, that the most suitable method of disposing of the case is by means of an order under this section.

The court can make this order where the offender is a child of 10 or more (since children under 10 cannot come before criminal courts).

A medical report is required by the court, and evidence that a hospital bed is available. The court must weigh up the likely effect of any custodial sentence on the offender's mental disorder (Criminal Justice Act 2003, s. 157(3)(b)).

There is no need for proof of a connection between the mental disorder and the criminal offence.

Once the offender is in the hospital, he or she is now a patient, and will be treated the same as any other patient. This means the detention expires after six months unless renewed (see **Detaining the patient who is already in hospital**, p 586). To avoid this risk of early release, the Crown Court can add to a hospital order a restriction order designed to protect the public from serious harm (MHA, s. 41). A youth court or magistrates' court does not have this particular power, but can commit an offender of 14 or over to the Crown Court in the expectation that the Crown Court will decide that such an order with restriction should be made.

The restriction period is indefinite. The result is that until it is discharged the detainee cannot be released, even for leave of absence, without an order of the Secretary of State for Justice or the Mental Health Tribunal. This is in contrast to other detained patients, who can and should be released by the hospital if the doctors think release is appropriate. The restriction will only apply until the earliest release date of the transferred prisoner, after which the restriction part of the order will lapse. If the patient remains in hospital, he or she will continue to be detained as if on a hospital order without restrictions from that date (called a 'notional s. 37'). We will consider restriction orders again when looking at discharge from hospital.

Transfer of mentally disordered offenders from prison to hospital is possible under s. 47 by a 'transfer direction' issued by the Home Secretary on the basis of reports from at least two medical practitioners. There is no role for the AMHP. The appropriate treatment must be available. Once admitted, the patient is treated like any other s. 2 patient, unless the Home Secretary places a restriction on the patient similar in effect to the restriction imposed by the Crown Court.

Admission from a police station

There is no special procedure for admission from a police station. We saw in **chapter 10** that a doctor should be called to assess a detainee in the police station when mental disorder is suspected. From there, informal or formal admission under ss 2–4 can take place. The decision whether to continue with any criminal proceedings will be taken by the police and Crown Prosecution Service. They should charge a mentally disordered suspect only if it is in the public interest.

Temporary detention by a police officer

At the beginning of the chapter, we talked about someone threatening suicide or violence. Your instinct may be to call the police. That is correct. The police can arrest someone, whether or not there is mental disorder, who is committing any kind of offence that is likely to be threatening, and in particular a person committing a breach of the peace. What then happens will be decided at the police station—see **Admission from a police station**, p 583.

Section 136 also enables a police officer to detain in a place of safety any person found in a public place, or a shared space, such as a communal garden or yard, who appears to be mentally disordered. This power of detention lasts only 24 hours. It may be extended by a further 12 hours if a medical examiner and superintendent police officer are in agreement per section 136B. Detention beyond this period requires an admission to hospital for assessment or treatment. A public place is defined in case law as somewhere to which the public have access (e.g. the landings in a block of flats—*Knox v Anderton* (1983)). The officer must consider that detention is necessary in the interests of the mentally disordered person or to protect another person. The place of safety can be a hospital, a person's own home, the home of a relative or friend, any other suitable place, or a police station only in exceptional circumstances. The Code provides guidance at Chapter 16 and makes clear that the patient should be assessed as soon as possible after removal to the place of safety.

Any person, not just a suspect, detained in a police station has the right to a lawyer under s. 58 of the Police and Criminal Evidence Act 1984 (PACE) and to the presence of an appropriate adult under PACE Code C (see **chapter 10**).

The power to detain in a place of safety is not given to a social worker, even an AMHP. You must call the police if you cannot yourself deal safely with the situation.

Searching out and protecting the mentally disordered

The power of removal to a place of safety does not extend to entering property. Section 135 enables a magistrates' court to issue a warrant for the police to enter premises, by force if necessary, and remove a mentally disordered person to a place of safety for up up to 24 hours, with a possibility of a further 12 hours if felt necessary by a medical examiner (see section 136B). The magistrate must believe, on the basis of information on oath from an AMHP, that there is evidence that either:

(a) a person suffering from a mental disorder has been or is being ill-treated, neglected, or kept otherwise than under proper control, or is living alone and unable to look after him or herself; or

(b) you are being denied access to a patient who has absconded from hospital or the place the patient is required to live by the guardian; or in respect of whom the proper admission procedures have been completed.

When the police officer executes the warrant, he or she should be accompanied by an AMHP and a doctor.

Admission to guardianship

We have seen that a person should not be compelled to go to hospital for treatment if they can be treated in the community. But this can leave a gap in terms of having some control of the mentally disordered person's life in the community. Applying the principles of the Code of Practice set out earlier (**Mental Health Act 1983 Code of Practice**, p 571), guardianship can be a less restrictive option than detention.

A guardian can be either an individual or a social services department. If the patient is under 16, however, MHA guardianship is not available: a person with parental responsibility is automatically the guardian.

The application procedure differs only slightly from that for admission for treatment. The application is submitted to a local authority social services department, either for the area where the proposed guardian lives or to the authority which is named as the proposed guardian (s. 11; Regulations, reg. 5). The application must be accepted before it is effective, unlike s. 3 applications for admission.

Procedures for an application for guardianship are otherwise the same as those for admission for treatment. The applicant is the AMHP or nearest relative, and must have seen the patient within the previous 14 days. If the AMHP is the applicant, the nearest relative must be consulted unless consultation is not practicable. An AMHP may not make an application if the nearest relative objects.

There must be two medical recommendations. The requirements (s. 7) are slightly different from those for admission to hospital. The patient must still be suffering from mental disorder, to a nature or degree that warrants reception into guardianship. The doctors must confirm that guardianship will either benefit the welfare of the patient or protect other persons. This is not such a stringent requirement as the need to show that detention is necessary for the health or safety of the patient under s. 3, which we saw is needed for admission for treatment. If the doctors think that guardianship would improve the quality of the patient's life, that is enough for guardianship.

As an alternative to the hospital order, s. 37 empowers any criminal court to make a guardianship order on the offender. The guardian will be nominated by social services and may well be the AMHP. The local authority will have to provide the court with details of how the guardian will exercise his or her powers. A guardianship order imposed by a court, once made, is identical in effect to any other guardianship order—see the following section.

Powers and duties of the guardian (s. 8 and Regulations, reg. 22)

If the local authority accepts the application, the guardian assumes certain powers over the patient: to specify where the patient shall live, to require the patient to go for medical treatment, to become involved in occupation, education, or training, and to require whoever the patient lives with to give access to a doctor, AMHP, or another named person. Any imposition of a requirement must be compatible with human rights, for example the right to family life. In *Re Connor's Application for Judicial Review* (2005) the patient had been subject to a condition that she must live in a particular institution, which meant that she could not live with her husband. The court held that such a requirement could be imposed if it was necessary and proportionate, but in this case the alternatives had not been considered.

There is no sanction against a patient who breaches these requirements, except the power discussed later to fetch back an absconding patient (see **Leave of absence and patients who abscond from detention or guardianship**, p 587). If the patient will not comply with the requirements, then guardianship is not appropriate and the order should be discharged (Code, para. 30.31).

Social services must see the patient every three months, and ensure that a doctor does so at least every 12 months (reg. 23).

Guardianship lasts initially for six months. The nominated doctor must review the guardianship during the last two months and report to the social services authority whether he or she is satisfied that the conditions for continuation of guardianship are fulfilled, including that appropriate medical treatment is available. If so, the guardianship is automatically renewed for six months on the first occasion, and each time after that for 12 months (s. 20).

Transfer from guardianship to hospital or vice versa

A patient under guardianship can be admitted to hospital as an informal patient, but if necessary, can be sectioned. The application procedure is similar to the s. 2 and s. 3 admission procedures, and in particular the same medical recommendations are required (s. 79). A transfer from a hospital section into guardianship, either to an individual or to a social services authority, is more straightforward. If the proposed

guardian and the relevant social services department agree, the hospital managers simply authorize the transfer (s. 19; reg. 7). Readmission to hospital after such a transfer
would either be informal or require an application under s. 2, 3, or 4.

Detaining the patient who is already in hospital

If hospital managers wish to detain an informal patient, the nearest relative or AMHP
should be asked to make an application under s. 3 for treatment, or consider applying
to the primary care trust or Welsh Assembly for authorization to detain a patient lacking mental capacity.

But if time is short—the patient is packing his or her bags, the taxi is waiting—
the informal patient can be temporarily detained using s. 5 powers. The psychiatrist
responsible for the patient, called in the legislation the 'responsible clinician' (RC),
or his or her delegate, can detain any existing hospital patient by delivering a report
to the hospital managers stating that such detention is necessary. This report creates
a 72-hour power of detention and a breathing space for the authorities to consider a
s. 3 application. If the doctor is unavailable and there is a crisis, a nurse (who must be
registered for mental disorder work under the Nurses, Midwives and Health Visitors Act
1979) can detain for up to six hours. In this case, the power of detention begins as soon
as the report is completed. Again, no second opinion is required.

Incidentally, these powers can apply to any hospital patient, not just a patient admitted informally for mental disorder. Although the nurse has to be a mental health specialist, and the patient has to be receiving treatment for a mental disorder, any type of
hospital doctor can exercise the 72-hour power of detention.

MHA detentions all have time limits. After the time limit expires, detention is unlawful unless compulsory powers are exercised to renew it. The possibilities for renewal or
upgrading are:

- a six-hour nurse's detention can become a 72-hour detention on receipt of the
report of the doctor treating the patient;

- a 72-hour doctor's detention can become an admission for treatment (or in theory
assessment) under s. 3 or s. 2 by obtaining the second medical recommendation;

- the 28-day detention for assessment can become a six-month detention for treatment by making an application under s. 3.

In all of these cases, any time already spent detained counts towards the new detention
period.

None of the powers of detention we have looked at so far last more than the six months
allowed for treatment under s. 3 (except a Crown Court hospital order with restriction).
However, s. 20 provides a procedure for review and, if appropriate, renewal of detention
for treatment. Review must take place in the last two months of a s. 3 detention, or the last
two months of an unrestricted s. 37 detention. The RC must do two things: first, examine
the patient and, second, consult at least one other person who has been professionally
concerned with the patient's medical treatment—such as a hospital social worker.

The doctor must then report to the managers stating whether he or she is satisfied that the requirements for continued detention apply. These requirements mirror the requirements for admission for treatment set out earlier: mental disorder of a nature or degree that makes it appropriate to be detained for treatment which is necessary for the health or safety of the patient or the protection of others. The renewal does not take effect until the expiry of the previous period of detention.

When the managers receive the signed report, they can detain the patient for treatment for a further six months on the first occasion, and on future occasions for 12 months at a time. The review must be repeated during the last two months of each new period of detention.

Leave of absence and patients who abscond from detention or guardianship

The RC (or the Secretary of State for Justice in the case of restricted patients) can give leave of absence under s. 17, and can recall a patient from such leave. The leave often is defined very closely: for example, it must be accompanied; it is limited to one hour a day; etc.

A patient who is absent without leave for less than six months, or a person subject to guardianship who disappears from the address specified by their guardian, can be detained and brought back by an AMHP, a member of the hospital staff, a police constable, or any person authorized by the hospital managers (s. 18).

Discharge of a detained patient

Except where there is a restriction order, it is good practice to discharge a patient if the criteria for detention in hospital no longer apply. Patients must be discharged if they are found not to be suffering from a mental disorder (*Kynaston v Secretary of State for Home Affairs* (1981)).

The power to discharge arises under s. 23 and can be exercised by hospital managers, the RC, or the nearest relative. However, the nearest relative has less power to discharge than the doctor or managers: this is because he or she has no power of discharge during the period of a hospital order made by a criminal court (s. 23 and Sch. 1); and because the nearest relative must give 72 hours' notice of intention. During that period the discharge can be barred by the RC (**Barring discharge from hospital by the nearest relative**, p 589).

The criteria for an 'order for discharge' are not stated in s. 23, but it implies that the RC should constantly be checking that the admission criteria are met; they should not wait until the automatic s. 20 review, which occurs towards the end of the detention period. The discharge does not have to be immediate (e.g. if after-care needs to be arranged), but must be within a reasonable time.

If the patient is subject to a restriction order imposed by the Crown Court, the release has to be approved by the Secretary of State unless discharge is ordered by the tribunal.

Discharge under community treatment order (CTO)

Discharge may be absolute or subject to supervised treatment in the community. The CTO replaces what used to be called supervised after-care and its framework is set out in ss 17A–17G. A CTO cannot be imposed unless the patient is currently detained under s. 3 or s. 37 without restrictions.

If a CTO is appropriate, it is—by definition—no longer necessary to detain the patient in hospital. The RC must consult with an AMHP and the AMHP must agree.

The criteria for discharge subject to the CTO are set out in s. 17A(5) and (6):

> (5) The relevant criteria are—
>> (a) the patient is suffering from mental disorder of a nature or degree which makes it appropriate for him to receive medical treatment;
>> (b) it is necessary for his health or safety or for the protection of other persons that he should receive such treatment;
>> (c) subject to his being liable to be recalled as mentioned in paragraph (d) below, such treatment can be provided without his continuing to be detained in a hospital;
>> (d) it is necessary that the responsible clinician should be able to exercise the power under section 17E(1) to recall the patient to hospital; and
>> (e) appropriate medical treatment is available for him.
> (6) In determining whether the power of recall is required, the RC shall, in particular, consider, having regard to the patient's history of mental disorder and any other relevant factors, what risk there would be of a deterioration of the patient's condition if he were not detained in a hospital (as a result, for example, of his refusing or neglecting to receive the medical treatment he requires for his mental disorder).

There can be requirements, enforced by the power of recall, imposed on patients in the community to ensure that they stay in contact with mental health services and practitioners can monitor them for signs of deteriorating health, and, if necessary, decide that they must be recalled to hospital. The patient can be recalled by the RC if the RC considers that he or she requires hospital treatment for mental disorder and there would be a risk of harm to the patient's health or safety or to others if not recalled. The recall will be for up to 72 hours, during which time the RC will have to decide if the CTO should be revoked or the patient sent out again on the CTO. If the RC decides to revoke, he or she must do so in writing with the agreement of an AMHP. The effect of revocation is that the original s. 3 or s. 37 is revived from the date of revocation (i.e. no need to do a fresh MHA assessment).

Conditions can be imposed under s. 17B(2) to ensure that the patient receives medical treatment, to prevent risk of harm to the patient's health or safety, or to protect others. The RC must agree these requirements with the AMHP. If treatment against a patient's will becomes clinically necessary, a patient can be recalled to hospital for treatment.

Renewal of the CTO occurs along the same time frame as renewal of detention under s. 3—that is, after six months from the time a patient leaves hospital, at one year and then at yearly intervals. Renewal is via a report to the hospital managers in the same way as renewal of detention.

Discharge by Parole Board

Section 74(5A) permits mental patients held under a restriction order to apply to the Parole Board for release, like any other prisoner. If the Parole Board orders release, the restriction order lapses.

Discharge from guardianship

Guardianship can be terminated before the end of the six- or 12-month period by the nearest relative, the social services authority, or the RC (s. 23)—but not by the guardian unless he or she is also the nearest relative.

Where guardianship was ordered by a criminal court, discharge under s. 23 can be made only by the social services department, not by the RC or the nearest relative (Sch. 1, Pt I, paras 2 and 8).

Barring discharge from hospital by the nearest relative

The doctors may not agree with the nearest relative that the patient should be discharged from hospital. The nearest relative must give 72 hours' notice of intention to discharge. The RC who wishes to bar this discharge must submit a report to the hospital managers stating that the patient would, if discharged, be a danger to him- or herself or to others. The barring order, once signed by the RC, bars the nearest relative discharge. The case must then be considered by the managers, who decide whether they should discharge the patient. Assuming the managers agree with the RC, the nearest relative is barred from discharging the patient for the next six months.

Neither the 72-hour notice period nor the barring order procedure apply to a discharge from guardianship by the nearest relative because the nearest relative has an absolute right to discharge the patient.

An AMHP can also block discharge by the nearest relative from hospital and from guardianship. But to do this the AMHP must apply to the County Court to displace the nearest relative (see **Discharge or replacement of nearest relative**, p 575). Under s. 29, once an application is filed with the court (which would have to be during the 72-hour notice period) discharge from hospital is blocked until the court makes its decision. It will probably be too late to use this power to block discharge from guardianship as there is no 72-hour notice requirement.

Discharge by the First-tier Tribunal (Mental Health)

The tribunal (known as a Mental Health Tribunal) can order a discharge from hospital, from guardianship, or from CTO (MHA, Pt V). Procedures are governed by the Tribunal Procedure (First-tier Tribunal) (Health, Education and Social Care Chamber) Rules 2008.

Although first-tier tribunals, as we saw in **chapter 1**, are in theory less orientated towards formal legal procedures than courts, in mental health cases it is recognized that applicants need free specialist legal representation. It is a good idea if the representative

TABLE 16.1 Time limits for applications to the tribunal—ss 66 and 68 of the Mental Health Act 1983

Application by the nearest relative	Time limit
Discharge of patient blocked by the RC	28 days from the date of being informed
Nearest relative displaced by county court order	12 months from order, then once every 12 months
Patient detained under a hospital order; patient under a restriction order	Not before six months; once during the second six-month period, then once in every 12-month period
Application by the patient	
Admission for assessment	14 days
Admission for treatment/reception into guardianship	Six months
Patient under CTO	No time limit

is a member of an approved panel of specialists, for there will be a need to marshal evidence of fact and medical opinion, and to cross-examine witnesses, including experts in mental health. However, there is no need for the patient's representative to be a panel member; the patient can appoint who they wish provided it is not another detained patient. Hospitals keep lists of local panel members. The AMHP does not have a statutory role, but a social circumstances report with detailed plans and recommendations for the patient if discharged must be provided, and social services are likely to be involved in providing this information.

Who can apply to the tribunal? The applicant will usually be the patient, but it may be the nearest relative if he or she has been barred from discharging the patient. Patients detained for treatment or in guardianship can apply once in each period of detention (i.e. first six months, second six months, and each subsequent period of 12 months).

If a patient detained under s. 3 is detained beyond six months and no one has made an application to the tribunal, the hospital managers must themselves refer the case to the tribunal within the first year. Subsequent references must be made if three years (or one year if the patient is under 18) have elapsed since the case was last considered by a tribunal. CTO patients must be referred to the tribunal if there has been no application in the six months since their original detention under s. 3 (see **Table 16.1**).

The tribunal hearing requires an up-to-date social circumstances report. The exact contents are specified in para. 14 of the First-tier Tribunal Health Education and Social Care Chamber Practice Direction on Statements and Reports in Mental Health Cases (2013) set out in **Box 16.6**.

BOX 16.6 Requirements for a social circumstances report submitted to the tribunal—para. 14 of the Practice Direction on Statements and Reports in Mental Health Cases (2013)

The report must be up-to-date, specifically prepared for the tribunal and have numbered paragraphs and pages. It should be signed and dated.

The sources of information for the events and incidents described must be made clear. This report should not be an addendum to (or reproduce extensive details from) previous reports, but must briefly describe the patient's recent relevant history and current presentation, and must include:

a) Whether there are any factors that might affect the patient's understanding or ability to cope with a hearing, and whether there are any adjustments that the tribunal may consider in order to deal with the case fairly and justly;

b) details of any index offence(s) and other relevant forensic history;

c) a chronology listing the patient's previous involvement with mental health services including any admissions to, discharge from and recall to hospital;

d) the patient's home and family circumstances;

e) the housing or accommodation available to the patient if discharged;

f) the patient's financial position (including benefit entitlements);

g) any available opportunities for employment;

h) the patient's previous response to community support or Section 117 aftercare;

i) so far as is known, details of the care pathway and Section 117 after-care to be made available to the patient, together with details of the proposed care plan;

j) the likely adequacy and effectiveness of the proposed care plan;

k) whether there are any issues as to funding the proposed care plan and, if so, the date by which those issues will be resolved;

l) the strengths or positive factors relating to the patient;

m) a summary of the patient's current progress, behaviour, compliance and insight;

n) details of any incidents where the patient has harmed themselves or others, or threatened harm, or damaged property, or threatened damage;

o) the patient's views, wishes, beliefs, opinions, hopes and concerns;

p) except in restricted cases, the views of the patient's Nearest Relative unless (having consulted the patient) it would be inappropriate or impractical to consult the Nearest Relative, in which case give reasons for this view and describe any attempts to rectify matters;

q) the views of any other person who takes a lead role in the care and support of the patient but who is not professionally involved;

r) whether the patient is known to any MAPPA meeting or agency and, if so, in which area, for what reason, and at what level—together with the name of the Chair of any MAPPA meeting concerned with the patient, and the name of the representative of the lead agency;

s) in the event that a MAPPA meeting or agency wishes to put forward evidence of its views in relation to the level and management of risk, a summary of those views (or an Executive Summary may be attached to the report); and where relevant, a copy of the Police National Computer record of previous convictions should be attached;

t)   in the case of an eligible compliant patient who lacks capacity to agree or object to their detention or treatment, whether or not deprivation of liberty under the Mental Capacity Act 2005 (as
amended) would be appropriate and less restrictive;

u)   whether (in Section 2 cases) detention in hospital, or (in all other cases) the provision of medical
treatment in hospital, is justified or necessary in the interests of the patient's health or safety, or
for the protection of others;

v)   whether the patient, if discharged from hospital, would be likely to act in a manner dangerous to
themselves or others;

w)   whether, and if so how, any risks could be managed effectively in the community, including the
use of any lawful conditions or recall powers;

x)   any recommendations to the tribunal, with reasons.

The tribunal must consider whether the criteria for continued detention, guardianship, or CTO are justified. The criteria are almost identical to the admission criteria so
we have not repeated them. The tribunal has a judge, and a specialist member (often
with mental health professional experience, such as a nurse), and also a medically
qualified member (invariably a psychiatrist). In the case of s. 2 appeals, this member
must examine the patient before the hearing and report findings to the hearing. The
automatic Pre-Hearing Examination for s. 3, CTO, and forensic applications was withdrawn by the Practice Direction and Guidance: Medical Examinations (2014) MHLO
43. The patient must now apply should they wish to see the medical member before
the hearing.

Unless it considers that the criteria for detention remain satisfied, a tribunal must
order the discharge of the patient—either now or at a future date (s. 72). As noted
already, these criteria are that the patient must be suffering from mental disorder of a
nature or degree which warrants the patient's detention in hospital for assessment or
treatment; if detained, for appropriate treatment, which must be available.

The facts leading to the decision on whether the section is to be lifted are determined
on the balance of probabilities. An attempt by a patient to argue that grounds for detention, as in criminal cases, should be proved beyond reasonable doubt did not succeed: *R
(on the application of N) v Mental Health Review Tribunal (Northern Region)* (2005). Failure
to order discharge where there is no continuing mental disorder was declared unlawful
by the ECtHR: *Johnson v UK* (1997). Such discharge need not necessarily be immediate.

Discharge can also be ordered—though it rarely happens—even if the original admission criteria continue to be satisfied. In unrestricted (but not restricted) cases, the tribunal also has an overriding discretion to discharge even if the criteria for detention are
still satisfied (i.e. even if it is not obliged to discharge).

If a patient has been transferred from prison to hospital under s. 47 (i.e. is still a serving prisoner), the MHT is allowed only to make a recommendation to the Secretary of
State for Justice and cannot direct release. However, the patient can apply for release to
the Parole Board (see **Discharge by Parole Board**, p 589).

Discharge by the tribunal does not prevent a compulsory readmission taking place under s. 3—but, unless the professionals are now aware of factors of which the tribunal was not aware and which would have affected its decision, this is an abuse of the patient's right to liberty: *R (on the application of Von Brandenburg) v East London and the City Mental Health NHS Trust* (2003). According to Sedley LJ at the Court of Appeal stage in, at para. 32:

> In such circumstances I do not see how an [AMHP] can properly be satisfied, as required by section 13, that 'an application ought to be made' unless aware of circumstances not known to the tribunal which invalidate the decision of the tribunal. In the absence of such circumstances an application by the AMHP should, on an application for judicial review, be held unlawful on the ground of irrationality.

Lord Bingham made the key point at para. 8 of his judgment: 'the rule of law requires that effect should be loyally given to the decisions of legally constituted tribunals in accordance with what is decided'.

If the hospital thinks the tribunal decision is wrong it should, instead, appeal to the Upper Tribunal. In this case, the court agreed that it was wrong to discharge the patient, since the patient was discharged in the absence of suitable after-care facilities.

If a discharge is ordered for a patient subject to Part 3, the tribunal can make it conditional on suitable after-care arrangements being made. It will not necessarily be a breach of the patient's human rights (Article 5, ECHR, right to liberty) if detention continues because the arrangements cannot in fact be made. In *R (on the application of W) v Doncaster MBC* (2004), the local authority did not have suitably trained staff to supervise the applicant in the hostel to which he would be discharged, so detention was prolonged for another seven months. The Court of Appeal held that this was a rational and lawful reason for refusing discharge. Additionally, the local authority was not responsible for detaining the patient, only for dealing with after-care, so the court could not make any order against it in relation to the detention itself.

The tribunal can defer an order for discharge in restricted cases under s. 73(7) until arrangements for after-care are in place; the tribunal can reconvene the hearing and reach a different decision if the arrangements it considers appropriate are not put into place within a reasonable time. In unrestricted cases, an order for discharge can be delayed to a specific date. Tribunals in unrestricted cases have powers of recommendation if they do not order discharge, for instance if the patient is transferred to another hospital or into guardianship or is given leave, or the RC considers making a CTO. There is no direct power of enforcement of recommendations, but the tribunal can reconvene if its recommendation is not complied with within a specified time. If discharge is ordered from civil detention, then it stands despite any problems with after-care. Even if the discharge is delayed by the tribunal, where after-care is not arranged in time, the patient is still discharged. The only alternative is to adjourn and reconvene on an arranged date with the hope that after-care has been arranged.

The tribunal hearing an application for discharge following the barring of a nearest relative's power to discharge must discharge if it is not satisfied that the patient would be likely on discharge to act in a manner dangerous to others or to him or herself. Evidence submitted to the tribunal must, among other things, address the dangerousness criterion as well as the need to detain the patient because of the nature or degree of the disorder. If the patient disputes the accuracy of allegations of events in the past, it will be essential to marshal reliable evidence to show them: vague file notes, sometimes based on vague information, are not a basis for detaining a person when what is at stake is not clinical judgement but proof of disputed facts.

Treatment in hospital for the mental disorder

The MHA and the Code of Practice provide detailed powers to treat a person for mental disorder where they are refusing consent to such treatment. As you are unlikely to be formally involved in the exercise of these powers, we have not described them here.

After-care following detention

Where a patient is discharged from detention in hospital or from guardianship, s. 117 imposes the duty jointly on the health authority and social services to provide after-care services for as long as they are needed. The authorities should cooperate with suitable voluntary agencies. Section 75 of the Care Act 2014 makes some clarifications and amendments to s. 117 of the MHA. The changes remove anomalies in determining the responsible local authority in relation to the provision of after-care services under the 1983 Act to people who have been detained in hospital for treatment of mental disorder and the provision of care and support services to which the Act applies. The section also inserts a new s. 117A into the 1983 Act. This is about enabling a person to express a preference for particular accommodation to be provided under s. 117. All discharged patients must have an individual care plan drawn up with an identified key worker, who will ensure that it is implemented. There is no statutory definition of what level of after-care is required. The decision on provision is made under community care law (see previous chapters), with the important difference that it must be paid for by the NHS.

Miscellaneous powers outside the MHA to control mentally disordered people

You would be forgiven for thinking that the powers of compulsory intervention in the lives of vulnerable people would be clearly set out in the legislation. Two interesting cases, taken together, cast doubt on this. They both concern the same mentally incapacitated young woman. She was 17 years old at the time of the first hearing—too old for a care order. The local authority tried guardianship as its preferred way of removing her from a sexually abusive home environment. There was no doubt that she suffered from a mental disorder under s. 1 of the MHA but her wish to return home, according to the Court of Appeal, did not amount to 'seriously irresponsible conduct', which also has to be shown in cases of learning disability. So, guardianship was not available (*Re F (Mental Health Act: Guardianship)* (2000)).

The local authority then tried another approach by resurrecting the common law doctrine of 'necessity'. The Court of Appeal in *Re F (Adult Patient)* (2000) held that it had the power to make a declaration as to the living arrangements to be made for a mentally incapacitated person, allowing the local authority control. It could do so if it was in F's best interests. The result is that the courts can declare it lawful for the state (the local authority in this case) to take control over a person's life, even where there are no statutory powers.

 SUMMARY

In this chapter we have introduced you to the law on mental health. In particular, we have considered:

- the statutory framework of mental health law;
- the scale of the use of powers under the Act;
- the protections available to those subject to the Act;
- the role of the Code of Practice;
- the procedures for admission and discharge;
- legal powers in community settings; and
- the role of the tribunal.

 EXERCISE

Steven, aged 20, has a developmental age of around four or five. As a child, he spent a significant amount of time in residential care, provided or paid for by the local authority, though he never required care under a care order. His parents struggled to cope, but managed. Recently his mother, to whom he was very attached, died. Now he is an adult and, though he receives day care, is living at home with his father, Cyril. Since his mother died, Steven has become quite aggressive towards Cyril, who finds it difficult to maintain a safe environment at home for Steven; also, Steven tends to wander off, talk with strangers, and stay out for long periods, sometimes having to be brought home by police or others. Recently, Cyril hit Steven. A social services assessment of Steven's needs and those of Cyril as his carer, which involved obtaining psychiatric evidence, now recommends that Steven should be accommodated elsewhere, as Cyril cannot cope. Cyril is strongly opposed to Steven being removed from his care and, insofar as it can be determined, Steven does not want to live away.

In the light of community care and mental health law, what options should the various agencies responsible for Steven's welfare consider?

ONLINE RESOURCES

For guidance on how to answer this exercise, visit the online resources at
www.oup.com/uk/carr-goosey15e.

 WHERE DO WE GO FROM HERE?

You have finished reading *Law for Social Workers*. After a short celebration, we suggest you keep
it handy as a reference source. If you have any comments, please contact Oxford University Press.
Your feedback may make the next edition even more useful. Thank you for reading our book, and
good luck.

 ANNOTATED FURTHER READING

Mental health

R. Jones, *Mental Health Act Manual* (21st edn, Sweet & Maxwell, 2018). This is used as a
handbook by lawyers and members of the MHRT.

P. Bartlett, L. Gostin, P. Fennell, J. McHale, and R. MacKay, *Principles of Mental Health Law*
(Oxford University Press, 2010). A collection of essays by leading academics in the field.

P. Bartlett and R. Sandland, *Mental Health Law: Policy and Practice* (4th edn, Oxford University
Press, 2013).

Two other good books are:

B. Hale, *Mental Health Law* (6th edn, Sweet and Maxwell, 2017).

P. Fennell, *Mental Health: Law and Practice* (2nd edn, Jordans, 2011).

Mind, www.mind.org.uk—access to a range of helpful materials to help those with mental
health problems.

Mental health law online—www.mentalhealthlaw.co.uk—is an amazing online resource which
provides the latest cases and updates in the law.

Department of Health and Social Care, www.gov.uk/government/organisations/department-
of-health-and-social-care—not an easy site to navigate, but you will need it to locate press
releases and official documents.

The Social Worker's Toolkit

Appendix: The Social Worker's Toolkit

In this toolkit we provide you with some quick reference points to guide you during your first years in practice. Undoubtedly the most testing experience in practice occurs when one has to attend court to give evidence but we begin with you as an employee. This chapter also provides quick reference tips on working with lawyers, report writing, whistle-blowing, and your responsibilities as an employed social worker. The sections on going to court and on care plans relate mostly to children and families social work. At the end of the toolkit there are some tips on how to approach issues of capacity.

You as an employee

Negligence and accountability

Many social workers are concerned that they may be personally liable if they make mistakes. There is no doubt that if things go wrong you will have to explain your decisions. If you have taken reasonable care, kept your written records properly, and acted within an acceptable level of professional competence then you will be able to do this. If you do make a professional misjudgement there may be several consequences:

- First, the case may become the subject of an inquiry and you may be personally blamed in the report. Many feel that such an emphasis on individual social workers is unfair. The Laming Report on the death of Victoria Climbié made this point:

  It is not to the handful of hapless, if sometimes inexperienced, front line staff that I direct most criticism for the events leading up to Victoria's death. Whilst the standard of work done by those with direct contact with her was generally of very poor quality, the greatest failure rests with the managers and senior members of the authorities whose task it was to ensure that services for children like Victoria were properly financed, staffed, and able to deliver good quality support to children and families. (para. 1.23)

- Second, you are subject to the risk that you will be disciplined, and even dismissed, as a result of your mistake. The incompetent social worker will always take this risk. As Laming points out, the risk to you is almost always greater than the risk to senior managers.

- Finally, the person who suffers may be able to sue for compensation for the effects of your mistake. He or she is far more likely to sue the local authority than you, and even if you are sued you will be indemnified by your employer.

Your rights as an employee

- You have obligations, as does any employee, to do the best you can for your employer. This may produce conflicts arising in individual cases. As an employee you are legally required to follow the instructions of your employer. However, your employer has hired you because you are a professional, and the exercise of professional judgement is part—a major part—of your duties to the employer. We hope conflict occurs rarely, but it remains a real possibility.

- In the event of irreconcilable conflict, you must do what the employer tells you to do, but this does not mean keeping quiet about your professional opinion. In fact, to express as your opinion a belief that you actually do not hold is itself a breach of your professional duty. If expressed in court it would be close to perjury (false testimony). It is, of course, rare that opinions differ in an irreconcilable way.

'Whistle-blowing' under the Public Interest Disclosure Act 1998

The Act is designed to encourage people to raise genuine concerns about malpractice in the workplace by providing legal protection against dismissal or victimization. If a social worker makes a disclosure in good faith to a manager or an employer, he or she will be protected as a whistle-blower if he or she has a reasonable suspicion that the malpractice has occurred, is occurring, or is likely to occur. The Act also protects disclosures made in good faith to prescribed regulatory bodies (such as the Health and Care Professions Council (HCPC), the Office for Standards in Education, Children's Services and Skills (Ofsted) or the Care Quality Commission (CQC), and presumably Social Work England when it is fully functional) where the whistle-blower reasonably believes that the information and any allegation in it are substantially true. The worker who makes a disclosure to a prescribed regulatory body has to have a reasonable belief that the disclosure was in the public interest and it must be related to an alleged criminal offence; breach of a legal obligation; a miscarriage of justice; danger to the health and safety of any individual; damage to the environment; or covering up any of these things. Wider disclosures (e.g. to the police, the media, MPs, and non-prescribed regulators) are protected if, in addition to the test for regulatory disclosure, they are reasonable in all the circumstances and:

- they are not made for personal gain;
- the whistle-blower must have reasonably believed that he or she would be victimized if he or she raised the matter internally or with a prescribed regulator; and
- he or she reasonably believed that a cover-up was likely and there was not a prescribed regulator, or had already raised the matter internally or with a prescribed regulator.

If the concern is exceptionally serious, a disclosure will be protected if it meets the test for regulatory disclosures and is not made for personal gain. The disclosure must also be reasonable, having particular regard to the identity of the person to whom it was made.

Where the whistle-blower is victimized in breach of the Act, he or she can bring a claim to an employment tribunal for compensation.

Information security

Social workers could not do their job if they did not have personal information about their users. They record that information and use it to make decisions. However, holding personal information about other people brings responsibilities. There are strong legal protections in respect of personal information held by third parties, including social workers and local authorities. The key legislative provisions of which you must be aware are:

- the General Data Protection Regulation (GDPR); and
- the Data Protection Act 2018.

The full details, and the exemptions available when information is held for health and or social reasons are discussed in **chapter 4**. You can check your knowledge using this BBC quiz: www.bbc.co.uk/news/technology-44224802.

The key points for you to note when you are in employment is that your employer will have information protocols in place, and you must comply with them. You must also be aware of your organization's privacy policy. These should be brought to your attention when you commence employment. If they are not, then you should find out what the expectations are about information security. Perhaps the most important principle of information security is that you must know why you are holding particular information about someone else and that reason must be a reason allowed for in the legislation.

Information sharing

 For a **VIDEO TUTORIAL** on this topic from author David Goosey please visit the **online resources,** www.oup.com/uk/carr-goosey15e.

Information sharing is a balancing act. The British Association of Social Workers (BASW's) Code of Ethics is worth remembering.

> Social workers should respect the principles of confidentiality that apply to their relationships and ensure that confidential information is only divulged with the consent of the person using social work services or the informant. Exceptions to this may only be justified on the basis of a greater ethical requirement such as evidence of serious risk or the preservation of life. Social workers need to explain the nature of that confidentiality to people with whom they work and any circumstances where confidentiality must be waived should be made explicit. Social workers should identify dilemmas about confidentiality and seek support to address these issues.

It is worth bearing in mind the following questions when considering whether to share information or not:

---

1 Is there a clear and legitimate purpose for you or your agency to share the information?

2 Does the information enable a living person to be identified?

3 Is the information confidential?

4 If the information is confidential, do you have consent to share?

5 If consent is refused, or there are good reasons not to seek consent to share confidential information, is there a sufficient public interest to share the information?

6 If the decision is to share, are you sharing information appropriately and securely?

7 Have you properly recorded your information-sharing decision?

For more detail on information sharing see **chapter 4**. You can also download further guidance on information sharing at www.gov.uk/government/uploads/system/uploads/attachment_data/file/419628/Information_sharing_advice_safeguarding_practitioners.pdf.

Risk analysis and assessment

  For a **VIDEO TUTORIAL** on this topic from author David Goosey please visit the **online resources,** www.oup.com/uk/carr-goosey15e.

Much has been written about risk analysis and assessment in social work and the profession has often been criticized for its errors in assessing the risk of harm to vulnerable adults and children. On the other hand, Munro, in *The Munro Review of Child Protection: Final Report. A Child Centred System* (Cm. 8062, 2011), was quick to point out that there is:

> a commonly held belief that the complexity and associated uncertainty of child protection work can be eradicated. (p 6)

This is true for social work with other services users, too. A natural consequence of this is that professionals talk about *risk management*, the means by which the likelihood of a negative outcome occurring is diminished.

Unfortunately, there are many examples in social work of risk management which borders on being unethical and sometimes illegal, as well as being ineffective. In **chapter 6** we explored the problems arising from authorities erroneously extending their powers to deny parents their rights to contact with their children on the grounds of managing risk.

The process of risk analysis is relatively simple. Munro's model is often helpful:

1. What is or has been happening?
2. What might happen?
3. How likely are these outcomes?
4. How undesirable are they?
5. The overall judgement of risk—a combination of the likelihood and the seriousness.

(E. Munro, Effective Child Protection (2nd edn, Sage, 2008))

The analysis of risk has to be based on what is or has happened. These matters normally lead someone to be 'concerned' about what might then happen. A risk analysis is an estimate of the likelihood that what might happen, will actually occur. You are advised to clarify the 'concerns' into statements of what might happen.

Being as specific as you can about what might happen will help your analysis. Sometimes it is difficult to be specific. Social workers and other professionals often talk about 'a gut feeling', in other words, an impression is formed. Some people describe this as intuition. There isn't enough space here to explore the science of intuition, but one view of intuition is:

> The situation has provided a cue: this cue has given the expert access to information in the memory and the information provides the answers. Intuition is nothing more and nothing less than recognition.

(H. Simon, 'What is an explanation of behaviour?' (1992) Psychological Science 3: 150)

Theory can be helpful in illuminating what gives rise to intuition and it also helps us to ask the right questions to tease out relevant evidence. A process to add to Munro's above, is called the TEER model:

- **Theory**
- **Evidence**
- **Evidence testing**
- **Reflection**

Relevant theory is normally very useful to help busy social workers to think about what they should be concerned about and what they should investigate. Their investigations will provide evidence. Given the gravity of decisions that social workers make about service users, the evidence collected should always be tested to ensure that it is reliable and valid. These three processes should be subject to systematic reflection so that the overall judgement or assessment, which Munro refers to in step 5 above, can be clearly determined.

(J. Keeling and D. Goosey, Safeguarding across the Life Span (Sage, forthcoming))

For example, it is possible to explain how a child's insecure avoidant attachment style has developed as a result of the care given by her clinically depressed mother (see D. Howe, *Child Abuse and Neglect: Attachment, Development and Intervention* (Palgrave Macmillan, 2005) for a discussion of how insecure attachments occur and C. Martins and E. Gaffan, 'Effects of early maternal depression on patterns of infant–mother attachment: a meta analytic investigation' (2000) *Journal of Child Psychology and Psychiatry* 41(6): 737, for research evidence on the impact of maternal depression on attachment styles). The consequences of living with an insecure attachment style can include an increased incidence of depression and anxiety in adolescence and adulthood (see A. Lee and B. Hankin, 'Insecure attachment, dysfunctional attitudes, and low self-esteem predicting prospective symptoms of depression and anxiety during adolescence' (2009) *Journal of Clinical Child and Adolescent Psychology* 38(2): 219). This type of theory and research evidence helps you to assess the likely outcome for a child in these circumstances. A risk management plan, which focuses on mitigating the effects of maternal depression on the child, should follow. Of course, all of this should occur within a legal framework. Social workers in local authorities cannot undertake assessments unless they either have permission from families to do so or there is an overriding duty to protect a vulnerable child or adult. When intervening to manage risk one should always be mindful of these legal hurdles. From time to time, permission to assess risk will need to be gathered for a second time, if circumstances change. Similarly, when exercising a duty to investigate at one point, as circumstances change, permission to continue might be not only a legal requirement but also an ethical duty.

Writing a report

 For a **VIDEO TUTORIAL** on this topic from author David Goosey please visit the **online resources,** www.oup.com/uk/carr-goosey15e.

Tips for report writing

- Use the appropriate template for your report to the court.
- Prepare the evidence carefully beforehand, including the completion of a comprehensive chronology.
- Leave plenty of time so that your report is not rushed and to allow you the opportunity to re-read the report before submission.
- Use straightforward sentences, the shorter the better.
- Ensure you have addressed the central question; for example, has the child suffered significant harm?
- Read the report out loud (you might want to do this in private). A badly written report is very difficult to read. If you stumble over reading it, it probably needs rewriting or editing.
- Supervision sessions are good places to reflect on and analyse evidence. Ensure you have discussed your report in supervision before completing it.

Child care plans

 For a **VIDEO TUTORIAL** on this topic from author David Goosey please visit the **online resources,** www.oup.com/uk/carr-goosey15e.

Since the judgment in *Re B (Children)* (see **chapter 8**) there has been renewed focus on the need for reports for courts to be analytical and evidence-based. In that particular case the local authority report and the report written by the children's guardian came in for some considerable criticism because they had not provided reasoned arguments for the various options open to the court in its decision making. Michael Jones's commentary on the implications of that case suggests that evidence should be organized as follows:

- The use of a pro-forma or 'balancing sheet' in respect of the available placement options is advisable.

- The contents of any such document must, however, be detailed in its analysis of the alternative options available and must carefully reason why each option is or is not suitable for the subject child.

- In the event that a care plan of adoption is sought, then the local authority should evidence that no other placement option available would be sustainable in the long term and that it is necessary to dispense with parental consent to adoption.

- The local authority should detail any support services which could be provided to the family and, if appropriate, why the provision of such services would not be sufficient to sustain any placement within the family.

- The local authority should be able clearly to evidence that it has had regard to concurrent care planning in each case.

- The evidence should acknowledge the gravity and the draconian nature of not only an adoptive care plan, but also of the making of a care order, and why this is necessary in the circumstances.

- This advice is obviously specific to cases involving the adoption of a child, but generalizations are also appropriate.

- Reports for court should clearly demonstrate the evidence on which decision making is proposed.

- Reasoned arguments for alternative options should be very clearly set out.

- Such arguments should try to explain what has happened, why it has happened, and what is likely to follow as a consequence.

Worked example of a balance sheet

What follows is a much-shortened case study of what should appear in a Social Work Evidence Template (SWET), which is written by the social worker (a copy of the form is provided at the end of this section). Below we provide a short case description, an analysis, and a balance sheet by way of illustration. When in practice you should famil-iarize yourself with real examples of completed SWETs. They will be much longer than what is provided here, perhaps reaching 30 or more pages.

Short case description

Jackie Smith, 19, gave birth to Erica Gondwe, 2 years and 5 months, when she was 17 years old. Erica's father, Victor Gondwe, 24 (as named on Erica's birth certificate) has an erratic relationship with Jackie, sometimes disappearing for weeks before returning for a few days. They frequently argue, even over minor issues, and these arguments turn to violence when Victor becomes frustrated. He has hit Jackie numerous times, often in front of Erica. On at least one occasion, Erica has been caught in the middle of this violence and was dropped. Despite this, Jackie is adamant that she wants Victor in her life. Victor has few relatives in the UK. He lives with a maternal uncle, but they don't get on well.

Jackie's early childhood was chaotic. Her mother, Joan, had numerous partners, many of whom were unkind to Jackie. In her early teenage years, Jackie took drugs regularly and was frequently drunk. She tried to kill herself on two occasions when she was 16 years old, once by hanging herself. Her relationship with her mother is volatile. They are frequently hostile to each other but regularly smoke cannabis together. Jackie lives with Joan most of the time, despite having her own accommodation. One consequence of this is that Joan does most of the caring for Erica. When she is distressed Erica tends to seek out her grandmother rather than her mother for comfort and support. Erica is still in nappies. She can say only a few words and no sentences. She is noticed to sleep frequently during the day and she has had a runny nose for months now.

Four months ago, an argument occurred at Joan's house resulting in Jackie leaving with Erica and returning to her own flat. Joan then consumed a lot of alcohol, becom-ing seriously intoxicated. Jackie found Victor had been staying at her flat and another argument was started. Shortly afterwards, Jackie ran out of the flat and tried to kill herself by taking 50 paracetamols in a local park. Sometime afterwards, Victor, also left the flat, leaving Erica alone. She was found by police after a neighbour, who could hear her crying, had alerted them.

Using their Powers of Protection under s. 46 of the Children Act 1989, the police take Erica to the local children's department, where staff arrange for her to be looked after. A day later, the local authority starts care proceedings. Erica is then subject to an interim care order. Through their solicitors, both Jackie and Victor accept that the threshold conditions in s. 31 have been met; that is, they accept that Erica was suf-fering significant harm at the time of the application. Jackie, Victor, and Joan all put themselves forward as long-term carers for Erica. No other wider family members do so. Reports on the viability of each of them are prepared. Despite his history of vio-lence to Jackie, Victor's report is largely positive in that he is able to show practical and emotional care towards Erica and demonstrates that he understands her needs, but he has no fixed abode since his uncle has moved back to Malawi. Jackie is diag-nosed with a dependent personality disorder and the reports on her rule her out. However, Joan's report is positive. She too demonstrates that she can care practically and emotionally for Erica and she has stopped smoking cannabis, but it is acknowledged that she may struggle to protect Erica from the influence of her mother's chaotic lifestyle in the future. The local authority and Erica's guardian recommend that Erica should be adopted.

Analysis

Erica's early life has been somewhat chaotic. She has moved frequently between her mother's flat and her grandmother's house. She has witnessed domestic violence and was on one occasion dropped, sustaining bruising. The hostile relationship between Jackie and Joan is also likely to have contributed to Erica's harm. Given the raised voices Erica has heard and the violence she has seen, she is likely to have been traumatized. Her speech was delayed, and her demeanour is indicative of a child who is desperately trying to shut out what is going on around her. Her general health also seems to be affected.

It is recognized that whilst Victor and Joan demonstrate that they can care for Erica at the moment, there remains scepticism about whether they can provide sufficient long-term stability for her and whether either of them has the capability of providing the quality of care needed for Erica to recover from being significantly harmed. Since being in care, Erica has blossomed. She is now talking much more, with an increased vocabulary, and she is constructing short sentences. She no longer uses nappies during the day and is more alert and attentive. Her nose has stopped running, too.

Whilst Erica is unable to verbalize her wishes and feelings, it is apparent from her behaviour that she responds well to a regular routine in the foster home. She is now turning to the foster mother when distressed and when cuddled she does now relax eventually, whereas she was unable to do either of these things a few months ago. It is likely that she now feels safe. She appears to be able to predict what is going to happen moment to moment given the daily routine. She does this by naming what is coming up, for example, 'yummy' before lunch and 'splash' before bath time. The consistent care provided to Erica and the attention the foster mother has given her when she is distressed, are reparative. Erica is likely to need that kind of attention for some time to come and probably throughout her childhood.

Whatever the outcome of the care proceedings, Erica will move from her current foster placement. If she returns to her grandmother or father, she is likely to exhibit distress, which is natural, but she may also remember times when she felt much less safe. The distress she may experience in these circumstances could be overwhelming. If she is placed with adoptive parents, she will also experience distress, but this is less likely to overwhelm her and is more likely to be short term.

Erica has experienced significant harm, and the impact of this harm on her development has already caused delay in her use of language. Emotionally she also appeared to be shutting down, given the amount of time she slept each day. Additionally, whilst she slept for long hours, she was also not able to engage with the world around her. To overcome this harm, Erica will need sustained, quality care from a parent or parents who are able to offer her real understanding (mindfulness) and a quality of response which is consistent and kind.

The viability assessments suggest that both Joan and Victor could provide Erica some of the care and attention that she needs. Of relevance would be Erica's continued contact with her Malawian heritage via either contact with her father if placed with her grandmother, or through being placed with him. Growing up with the influence of that heritage would be a significant advantage for Erica, since the culture would not only contribute to her identity, but she would also have the possibility of developing her father's first language, Chichewa. However, Victor has so far not spoken to Erica in his first language. During the first few years of her life, Victor has not been a consistent presence and therefore the influence he has already shown of his cultural heritage is small.

In weighing Erica's competing needs, recognition is given to the opportunity for her to grow up with some Malawian influence, but of even more importance is her need to receive quality care and attention so that she can recover from the harm she has experienced. The conclusion of this analysis is that neither her grandmother nor her father could provide the necessary quality of care that Erica needs. Furthermore, being placed with either of them would also be likely to rekindle feelings of being unsafe, which would further harm her. Therefore, only adoption will do. Erica should be placed with adoptive parents who are able to provide her with all the reparative care and attention that she clearly needs.

The balance sheet

Placement/order	Factors in favour	Factors against
Return to mother	• Erica will be cared for by her mother who has provided some of her care during her life. Erica and her mother's Article 8 rights will be preserved. • Erica is likely to still maintain a relationship with her father, thus preserving his Article 8 rights, and with her grandmother, who has been a significant carer to Erica. • With contact retained with her father, Erica will have access to her Malawian heritage and Chichewa language.	• Erica's mother has significant mental health problems which prevent her from adequately caring for Erica. It is likely she will not always prioritize Erica's needs over her own. • Jackie's relationships with both her mother and with Victor are characterized by hostility. Nothing in Jackie's life has changed sufficiently to result in anything other than more hostility in the future and further harm to Erica.

Placement/order	Factors in favour	Factors against
Return to father	• Erica will be cared for by her father, who has provided some of her care during her life. Erica and her father's Article 8 rights will be preserved. • It is likely that Jackie and Joan will have some contact with Erica if she is returned to her father, thus preserving her relationship with her maternal family. • Victor can provide practical and emotional care for Erica. He may need support from the local authority, which can be provided when requested. • Erica would have full access to her Malawian heritage and Chichewa language.	• Victor is no permanent accommodation currently and he has no employment. Without this he will struggle to provide Erica with the settled routine that she requires to continue to progress and to repair the harm she has experienced. • Victor will retain contact with Jackie and their hostility towards each other is more than likely to continue, adversely affecting Erica. • Victor has received no help or assistance to explore his violence to Jackie.
Placement with grandmother under a care order	• Erica would retain contact with her family of origin, thus preserving her Article 8 rights and theirs. The local authority would share parental responsibility and could monitor and assist the grandmother until such time as she is granted a child arrangements order. • A care order would ensure that the local authority's statutory duties to safeguard and protect Erica were continued. There would be oversight of contact arrangements with Erica's parents and involvement to reduce the negative effects of Jackie's mental health problems and the hostile relationships. • With contact retained with her father, Erica will have access to her Malawian heritage and Chichewa language.	• The day-to-day responsibility to protect Erica from her mother would rest with Joan, her grandmother. The local authority's supervision of the placement would not provide a guarantee that Erica would suffer further harm if Jackie continued to present at Joan's house. Joan would experience a conflict of interest between caring for her granddaughter and her daughter. • Joan has only been a parent or carer to Jackie. No other test of her ability to care for a child has occurred. The outcome of her parenting of Jackie could be repeated with Erica. • A care order would require the local authority's involvement in Erica's life until she was 18 or until it was discharged or replaced. This is significant state intervention.

Placement/order	Factors in favour	Factors against
Placement with Grandmother under a special guardianship order	• Erica would retain contact with her family of origin, thus preserving her Article 8 rights and theirs. • A special guardianship order would provide Erica with a permanent resolution. • The local authority could provide support to Joan throughout the duration of the order, via a support plan. • With contact retained with her father, Erica will have access to her Malawian heritage and Chichewa language.	• The day-to-day responsibility to protect Erica from her mother would rest with Joan, her grandmother. The local authority's support plan would not provide a guarantee that Erica would suffer further harm if Jackie continued to present at Joan's house. Joan would experience a conflict of interest between caring for her granddaughter and her daughter. • Joan has only been a parent or carer to Jackie. No other test of her ability to care for a child has occurred. The outcome of her parenting of Jackie could be repeated with Erica. • A special guardianship order would effectively make Joan the main parent of Erica. This would significantly reduce the exercise of Jackie and Victor's parental responsibility.
Adoption	• Erica would have a permanent placement lasting until her majority. • She would be provided with a consistent, regular routine with parents who are able to address the experience of harm that she has faced. • Erica will no longer experience significant harm. • Some contact could be maintained with Erica's birth family.	• Adoption would sever the ties between Erica and her parents and grandmother. This is the most significant intervention by the state and should only occur if nothing else will do. • Erica would lose access to her Malawian heritage through losing contact with her father. It is unlikely that adoptive parents can be found who have a Malawian heritage. • There is a chance that an adoptive placement is not found for Erica and this would prolong her experience of a lack of permanence. • There is a small chance the adoptive placement could breakdown thus exposing Erica to further damaging experiences.

Use of this document is recommended by the President of the Family Division, the Association of Directors of Children's Services, Cafcass, HM Courts and Tribunals Service, the Department for Education, the Ministry of Justice, and the Chair of the Family Justice Board, in compliance with the revised Public Law Outline (PLO) 2014.

The child(ren)—use one per template per family

Local authority social work evidence template (SWET)	In the family court sitting at	In the matter of the Children Act 1989

Names	Gender	Date of birth	Child's current placement status	Child's current legal status

Local authority and social worker details

Case number	
Filed by [local authority]	
Social work statement number in the proceedings, e.g. 1st, 2nd N.B. A final statement should be completed on the Final Statement Template (FST)	
Social work statement number for this witness e.g. 1st, 2nd, 3rd	
This author/witness's name, qualifications, experience, and office address	
This author/witness's HCPC registration number	
Set out which court order or order/s are being sought, and why.	

Contents page

1. Case details

1.1 Family composition

- This section should include family members and relationships, and should specify the relationship in respect of each child subject to the application. Please set out the family members' full names, their dates of birth, their nationality, ethnicity, and their current addresses.

- Where an address needs to be kept confidential, send the information to the court.

Name	Relationship	Parental responsibility	DoB	Nationality	Ethnicity	Address

1.2 Genogram (mandatory) (but format may be adapted)

  • Include family members and their relationship to each child.

1.3 Ecomap (risky and protective contacts) (optional)

2. The social work chronology

  • List significant events which can be evidenced.
  • Focus on the past two years unless prior events are significant.

Date	Incident or sequence of incidents relevant to the child's welfare	Significance

Date	Significant events happening in the near future which are relevant for the child (e.g. the transition from primary to secondary school)	Source of evidence/ document reference	Significance

3. Analysis of risk and protective factors

Key points before starting your analysis:

- The welfare checklist should be applied as appropriate throughout.
- Evidence can be primary (yours), or secondary (where you analyse what others say and think).

3.1 The social work analysis of the harm the child (or each child) has suffered and/or any risk of harm the child continues to face, including the analysis of the event/s that led to the application. Protective factors should also be identified.

3.2 List of previous assessments and interventions

Organization	Description of assessment/intervention	Date	Outcome and effectiveness

4. Child impact analysis (for each individual child)

4.1 Description of the child's daily life and experience during the period under consideration

4.2 Analysis of the child's needs, considering the welfare checklist (see Section 12)

- Set out the steps taken to meet these needs (e.g. any services provided and their outcomes, or their intended outcomes).

4.3 The child's wishes and feelings and how these have been identified

4.4 The child's own statement (where applicable)

4.5 The child's participation in the court case

- Set out the appropriate level of involvement in the author's judgement, with reasons.

5. Analysis of the evidence of parenting capability

- Analyse each parent's capability to meet each child's needs, including analysis of the evidence of any capability gap and whether/how this can be bridged in the child's timescale. Include unrelated members of the household/s where relevant.

Mother
Father
Other person with parental responsibility

6. Analysis of the evidence of wider family and friends' capability

- Analyse the evidence of wider family and friends' capability to meet each child's needs, including analysis of the evidence of any capability gap and whether/how this can be bridged in the child's timescale.

Key considerations for a viability assessment

1. The genogram and ecomap should routinely identify those relatives who are already protective contacts for the child. Both the genogram and the ecomap should be comprehensive and inclusive.

2. Risky contacts should be excluded from consideration through a robust filtering process.

3. This prima facie viability—for being a permanent carer—should be extended by three further tests before a full assessment is carried out, in compliance with the specific set of current Regulations that apply to the proposed permanent placement.

4. The three additional viability tests are:

   a) that the carer understands in broad terms the needs of the child subject to proceedings;

   b) that the carer understands the level and type of care the child will need throughout their childhood as a consequence of their experiences;

   c) that the carer expresses an authentic willingness to be part of the team around the child until matters are fully resolved.

7. The proposed S31A care plan—the 'realistic options' analysis

7.1 List of options discounted as they were assessed to be unrealistic

Discounted option	Reason why discounted

7.2 Table of realistic placement options

- Add additional tables for each child in a sibling group. Only list realistic options, whatever the number, i.e. 1, 2, 3, etc. Whilst the looked-after children care plan can be filed separately, the intention is for this template to be a single, integrated document.

Realistic options

1. To be defined as realistic, the proposed placement at the heart of the court care plan must be assessed as sufficiently resilient and sustainable to justify the label of 'permanent'. A robust filtering process is required to ensure each option assessed as realistic meets that standard.

2. In care proceedings, no arbitrary numerical limit can be placed on the number of realistic options available for the child, but one option must always be preferred. A clear reason or reasons must always be given for this preferred status in the body of this document.

3. Preferred status means that on the assessments and evidence available, the preferred placement should offer the child the prospect of recovering from any trauma she or he has experienced; personal growth and development within a family where the child is guaranteed unconditional love; strong educational prospects; good health outcomes; and—as far as can be predicted—one or more positive lifelong attachment/s which promote the child's unique identity.

4. Determining the rank order between realistic options is a matter of professional judgement about the relative importance to the child of various attributes of the carers and/or the relationship between the carers and the child, or the carers, child, and birth parent/s.

Child	First realistic option: [please describe option]	
	Factors in favour	**Factors against**
	Second realistic option: [please describe option]	
	Factors in favour	**Factors against**
	Third realistic option: [please describe option]	
	Factors in favour	**Factors against**

7.3 The preferred and proposed placement option for each child, with a proportionality evaluation that is a comparison of that option against other realistic options

- Analyse the likely impact on the child of the preferred option.

7.4 The contact plan

- The contact plan must be kept under review as circumstances change.

Child	Who contact is with and their relationship to the child	Brief rationale for the level of contact proposed	Level of support/ supervision required	Frequency and duration

8. The range of views of parties and significant others

- Set out and analyse individual views about what should happen for the child/children in the future.
- This section also has a vital opinion-sharing purpose.

8.1 Mother's views

8.2 Father's views

8.3 Views of wider family members

8.4 Views of other parties or significant others, e.g. Cafcass, the independent reviewing officer (IRO), court-appointed experts

9. Case management issues and proposals

- List any case management issues, e.g. delay factors, special factors relevant for the child, vulnerability of any key participant, any further proposed assessments and why they are necessary, etc.

10. Statement of procedural fairness

- Have the contents of this statement been communicated to mother, father, significant others, and the child in a way which can be clearly understood? If not, what has been tried?

11. Signature

Print full name	
Role/position held	
	The facts in this application are true to the best of my knowledge and belief and the opinions set out are my own.
Signed	
Date	

12. The welfare checklist in full for reference

The full Children Act checklist, to be used in care and supervision proceedings is found at section 1(3) (a)—(g) and requires the court to have regard to the following matters:

  (a) the ascertainable wishes and feelings of the child/children concerned (considered in the light of his/her/their age and understanding);

  (b) his/her/their physical, emotional and educational needs;

  (c) the likely effect on him/her/them of any change in his/her/their circumstances;

  (d) his/her/their age, sex, background and any characteristics of his/hers/theirs which the court considers relevant;

(e) any harm which he/she/they has/have suffered or is/are at risk of suffering;

(f) how capable each of his/her/their parents, and any other person in relation to whom the court considers the question to be relevant, is of meeting his/her/their needs;

(g) the range of powers available to the court under this Act (Children Act 1989) in the proceedings in question.

The full Adoption and Children Act welfare checklist, to be used in care proceedings where the plan is for adoption and in placement proceedings, is found in section 1 (4) (a)—(f) and requires the court and the adoption agency to have regard to the following matters (among others):

(a) the child's ascertainable wishes and feelings regarding the decision (considered in the light of the child's age and understanding);

(b) the child's particular needs;

(c) the likely effect on the child (throughout his life) of having ceased to be a member of the original family and become an adopted person;

(d) the child's age, sex, background and any of the child's characteristics which the court or agency considers relevant;

(e) any harm (within the meaning of the Children Act 1989 (c. 41)) which the child has suffered or is at risk of suffering;

(f) the relationship which the child has with relatives, and with any other person in relation to whom the court or agency considers the relationship to be relevant, including:

   i) the likelihood of any such relationship continuing and the value of the child of its doing so,

   ii) the ability and willingness of any of the child's relatives, or of any such person, to provide the child with a secure environment in which the child can develop, and otherwise to meet the child's needs,

   iii) the wishes and feelings of any of the child's relatives, or of any such person, regarding the child.

Adult social care—decisions about capacity and best interests

- Your starting point here is that you should not be making these decisions unless you have been trained. However, you can get guidance on assessments of capacity from the following questions, which are extracted from COP3, the Court of Protection form which social workers must complete before making an application under the Deprivation of Liberty Safeguards (DoLS).

Assessment of capacity

7.1 The person to whom the application relates has the following impairment of, or disturbance in the functioning of, the mind or brain. Where this impairment or disturbance arises out of a specific diagnosis, please set out the diagnosis or diagnoses here: (complete box).

This has lasted since: (complete box).

As a result, the person is unable to make a decision for themselves in relation to the following matter(s) in question: (complete box).

7.2 The person to whom the application relates is unable to make a decision in relation to the relevant matter because:

- he or she is unable to understand the following relevant information (please give details);

and/or

- he or she is unable to retain the following relevant information (please give details);

and/or

- he or she is unable to use or weigh the following relevant information as part of the process of making the decision(s) (please give details);

and/or

- is unable to communicate his or her decision(s) by any means at all (please give details).

7.3 My opinion is based on the following evidence of a lack of capacity: (complete box).

7.4 Please answer either (a) or (b).

(a) I have acted as a practitioner for the person to whom the application relates since [DDMMYY] and last assessed him or her on [DDMMYY].

(b) I assessed the person to whom the application relates on [DDMMYY] following a referral from [NAME].

7.5 Has the person to whom this application relates made you aware of any views they have in relation to the relevant matter? (yes or no)

If yes, please give details.

7.6 Do you consider there is a prospect that the person to whom the application relates might regain or acquire capacity in the future in respect of the decision to which the application relates?

Yes—please state why and give an indication of when this might happen. No—please state why.

7.7 Are you aware of anyone who holds a different view regarding the capacity of the person to whom the application relates?

If yes, please give details.

7.8 Do you, your family or friends have any interest (financial or otherwise) in any matter concerning the person to whom the application relates? (yes or no)

If yes, please give details.

7.9 Do you have any general comments or any other recommendations for future care?

These questions provide a useful starting point. Depending on the individual's responses to the questions asked, the practitioner would ask more questions if they felt the question hadn't been understood or if the response wasn't clear. For example, if you were assessing someone regarding capacity to manage finances, they might know what a bank account was used for and that bills were paid out of it but not necessarily how direct debits or PIN cards worked. It would depend on what the individual needs in order to make the specific decision at hand.

If you are required to make a decision about someone who lacks capacity you have to act in their best interests. The following questions, extracted from Deprivation of Liberty Safeguards Form 3 help you decide whether a course of action is in the best interests of the person and ensure you are fully informed in making that assessment.

BEST INTERESTS ASSESSMENT	
MATTERS THAT I HAVE CONSIDERED AND TAKEN INTO ACCOUNT	
I have considered and taken into account the views of the relevant person.	
I have considered what I believe to be all of the relevant circumstances and, in particular, the matters referred to in section 4 of the Mental Capacity Act 2005.	
I have taken into account the conclusions of the mental health assessor as to how the person's mental health is likely to be affected by being deprived of liberty.	
I have taken into account any assessments of the person's needs in connection with accommodating the person in the hospital or care home.	
I have taken into account any care plan that sets out how the person's needs are to be met while the person is accommodated in the hospital or care home.	
In carrying out this assessment, I have taken into account any information given to me, or submissions made, by any of the following: (a) any relevant person's representative appointed for the person (b) any donee of a Lasting Power of Attorney or Deputy (c) any IMCA instructed for the person in relation to their current or proposed deprivation of liberty.	
BACKGROUND INFORMATION *Background and historical information relating to the current or potential deprivation of liberty.* *For a review look at previous conditions and include comments on previous conditions set.*	
VIEWS OF THE RELEVANT PERSON *Provide details of their past and present wishes, values, beliefs and matters they would consider if able to do so:*	
VIEWS OF OTHERS	

Working with lawyers

For a **VIDEO TUTORIAL** on this topic from author David Goosey please visit the **online resources,** www.oup.com/uk/carr-goosey15e.

- Lawyers belong to a professional body—the Law Society or the Bar Council, dependent upon whether they are solicitors or barristers—and are bound by a code of conduct.

- The code of conduct for solicitors focuses on less complex dilemmas, such as not acting for people where you have a conflict of interest and having to hold money that belongs to clients in a separate account from your own money.

- Lawyers have a more straightforward relationship with their clients than you have with the service user. If the lawyer and the client disagree on what is the best course of action, then the client can sack the lawyer.

- Lawyers are committed to the rule of law, which includes the right of all to have the best professional help to argue their case on an equal footing.

- Lawyers' skills lie in the interpretation of complex statutes and cases and in defending the interests of their clients through negotiation and advocacy.

- Lawyers are interested in achieving for the client what he or she wants, and the question of whether it should be what they want is wholly irrelevant.

- The local authority lawyer's role is to advise the social worker as to the legal strengths and weakness of the case.

- The local authority lawyer, however, may not always do as the social worker suggests since their 'client' is in fact the local authority.

Going to court

For a **VIDEO TUTORIAL** on this topic from Wendy Pullen, a Court Team Manager in the London Borough of Bromley, please visit the **online resources,** www. oup.com/uk/carr-goosey15e.

In chapter 1 we gave you an outline of the English legal system and how it impacts upon you. Here we provide you with some useful pointers on evidence and cross-examination—two issues which can cause stress to social workers who are required to give evidence in court and are likely to be cross-examined on that evidence.

Giving evidence in court is a vital part of the role of a social worker. The role of the court is to determine the truth so far as this can be ascertained and to agree plans for the future. These are fundamental processes for the social work task.

See **Figure 1.1** for a reminder of the court system.

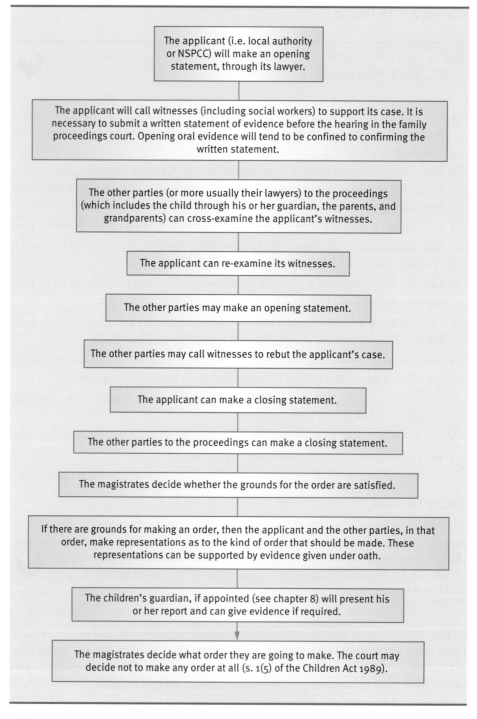

FIGURE A   The procedure in family proceedings

What will happen at court?

Figure A, a flow diagram of the procedure in family proceedings, is a useful way of understanding what happens in court.

The making or refusing of the order ends the proceedings, unless there is an appeal (see **chapter 1**, **Courts and tribunals**, 'Appeal hearings', p 29).

Preparing for court

The best advice for going to court is to be prepared. You should know the case inside out and back to front. It is important to have thought carefully about the evidence you have for the threshold criteria and reasons for your care plan. Something to avoid is finding yourself being cross-examined on aspects of the statement that were drafted in the lawyer's words, not your own. Courts will be angry if you express doubts about what is in your statement. Before you sign it, read your statement and ask yourself if you are ready to be cross-examined on it. It is worth anticipating very hard questions on any opinions you have stated in your evidence; if you cannot justify them, perhaps they are unjustifiable, or perhaps you are the wrong person to call as the witness on this point.

Tips for presenting

- You are likely to be nervous and most nervous people speak faster than usual. Try to slow down deliberately.
- Face the magistrate or judge when speaking, even though the question put to you will have come from one of the lawyers, who will be in a physically different part of the court.
- If you do not understand the question, ask for clarification.
- Wear smart but comfortable clothes.

Be prepared for the apparently friendly question which softens you up for the sharp follow-up question. You may wonder what the questioner is getting at. If you are unsure, then the best advice is to answer the question in as matter-of-fact a way as you can, and let the questioner reveal the strategy. Long, complex answers, given under pressure, may well contain things that you are not confident about, or even that contradict your earlier evidence. But giving evidence is an art and giving short answers may itself allow a false picture to be constructed. Consider the following exchange:

Q: You were concerned about June?
A: Yes.
Q: Very concerned?
A: Yes.
Q: Did you discuss this with your management?
A: Oh yes, we had many meetings and case conferences.

Q: There was considerable concern throughout the department?
A: Yes.
Q: June was a constant preoccupation?
A: Yes.
Q: Then why did you visit only twice before you applied for a protection order?

How should the witness have answered these questions? Perhaps he or she was too eager. There is no correct answer except what you consider to be the truth. A skilled cross-examiner will know how to trip you up. You will say something which you think on reflection is wrong. The immediate temptation is to cover your tracks. But you risk digging a deeper hole, and a good cross-examining lawyer will allow you to dig deep before pointing out the inconsistencies in what you have just said. We suggest: 'I think I have just said something which gives the wrong impression', or even 'I made a mistake when I said that; what I meant to say was . . . '.

Evidence

Social workers' evidence is largely about what they have seen and heard in the families in question or in relation to the context of family life, or what other professionals have said or done. This evidence is normally put together as a statement for the court. You might be drawing on more formal documents, such as assessments completed.

We would argue that in compiling a statement, and indeed in giving evidence in court, a useful question to bear in mind is 'How can I assist the court to make a decision?' For example, in care proceedings, the primary questions for the court are the following.

(a) Has this child been significantly harmed and is the harm attributable to the parent's care?

(b) What are the best interests of the child?

Your statement should answer these questions. You will inevitably draw on evidence from other people, including other professionals, and you may have commissioned assessment reports to help you to analyse what is happening in the family.

What is evidence?

Evidence is information which supports a conclusion. When you are in court you are arguing for a particular outcome. In order to justify that outcome, you require evidence. Evidence can come in a variety of forms. A court will place a different weight on different types of evidence. Another way of putting this is that successful court proceedings are all about facts—the social worker in a case should get the facts straight, based on a thorough analysis of the evidence, and then draw conclusions from those facts as to the appropriate next steps.

Types of evidence

- Factual evidence—you are likely to have to give evidence in relation to the facts of the case: for instance, the names and dates of birth of children involved in the case, the dates of significant events, and of interventions by your department. If your statement and the chronology has been carefully prepared and checked for accuracy this should present you with no difficulties. However, you should be prepared to be cross-examined closely on the facts—see 'Cross-examination' below. You will be allowed to refer to your witness statement and chronology in court.

- Real and documentary evidence—real evidence refers to tangible things, such as items used perhaps to injure someone or stolen items. Documentary evidence refers to documents containing information, such as social work reports, minutes of meetings, etc. You are most likely to be relying on documentary evidence when you are explaining your position on a court application.

- Hearsay evidence is evidence presented to the court by someone who is not present to be cross-examined. So, if you give evidence that X told you he did something to Y, then that is hearsay evidence. Whilst in general such evidence is admissible in civil proceedings (but not in criminal proceedings), because the evidence cannot be challenged it is not given the same weight as direct evidence. In addition, the court requires that notice is given that the evidence is going to be relied upon, and that an explanation as to why direct evidence cannot be given is provided. Nonetheless it is always better that first-hand evidence is given, as Lord Munby President of the Family Court has pointed out:

  Of course the court can act on the basis of evidence that is hearsay. But direct evidence from those who can speak to what they have themselves seen and heard is more compelling and less open to cross-examination.

  (View from the President's Chambers [2013] Fam Law 680)

- Opinion evidence—your opinion is not what is required by the court. After all, your opinion is likely to be biased, as you are employed by the local authority. The court will think, 'You would say that wouldn't you?' So, you must give factual evidence to demonstrate that the threshold criteria are met in child care cases, and not simply assert your opinion. However, when it comes to the best interests test in child care proceedings, your judgement, and that of your department, will be important, but your judgement about the best interests of the child should be based on an analysis of the evidence, not your opinion.

The following sources of evidence may be used.

Sources of evidence

TABLE A Child development dimensions

Description of harm	Examples of evidence
Indications of poor health for which there is no organic explanation	Paediatric assessment
Delayed speech and language	Speech and language therapy assessment
Physical injuries	Paediatric assessment
Behavioural problems	Systematic social work observations, including attachment styles
	Psychiatric assessment
Sexual abuse	ABE interview disclosure
	Paediatric assessment
Emotional harm	Social work interviews with child
	Systematic social work observations, including attachment styles
	Psychiatric assessment
Poor educational development	School reports
	Educational psychology assessments

TABLE B Parenting capacity dimensions

Parenting omissions and commissions	Evidence
Neglect	Assessment of parenting activities
Alcohol/drug misuse	Assessment of what, where, when, and how of alcohol or drug use, plus the effect on the parenting
	Psychiatric assessment
Parental mental health	Psychiatric assessment
	Social work assessment
Domestic violence	Assessment of what, where, when, and how of domestic violence, plus the effect on the parenting
Learning disabilities	Assessment of impact of learning abilities on parenting
	Educational psychology assessment

TABLE C Family and environmental dimensions

Description of harm	Examples of evidence
Family history and functioning	Psycho-social history
	Assessment of adult attachment styles
	Assessment of relationship quality
Wider family and support	Assessment of who is available to help with practical and emotional support
Income, housing, community services	Social work assessment of the likely impact of wider society

Cross-examination

Cross-examination is the means by which your credibility and your evidence is tested in court. It is an important stage in the adversarial legal system, which depends upon evidence and cross-examination to establish truth. As well as challenging the evidence you gave in direct examination, cross-examination may raise issues which you have not covered. The point of doing so is to suggest that what you have omitted to say suggests that another conclusion can be reached on the evidence before the court.

Advocates are able to ask *leading* questions in cross-examination. Leading questions are questions which suggest an answer. So, an advocate in cross-examination can ask 'Isn't it true that you told Mrs X that she did not need to worry about her husband's behaviour?' Such a question would not be allowed in direct examination. Here the advocate would be limited to asking you, 'What did you say to Mrs X?'

There are a number of questions regularly asked by people who are facing cross-examination. Below we suggest some answers:

- What is the best way to respond to cross-examination?
  - We would suggest that you provide short, polite answers to the question that has been asked—don't expand upon your answer, be direct and to the point, and above all do not be defensive.
- What if the advocate interrupts me during my answer?
  - If the advocate interrupts it suggests that either you have given him what he wanted or that he is clear he is not going to get out of you what he wanted. Either way we would suggest that you simply stop giving the answer you were giving and answer the new question. Cross-examination is not a good time to point out to someone that you are still answering the first question or to try to strategize, at least not until you are experienced.
- What if my mind goes blank or I just can't speak?
  - The court is likely to be sympathetic—giving evidence is stressful. On the other hand, you are required to answer questions asked. We would suggest you take a deep breath and focus on the question asked. Ask for a pause, or a glass of water—these will give you a chance to think.

- What if something I say comes out wrong?
  - Say just that—ask the court if you can rephrase your answer so that it more accurately reflects what happened.
- I am newly qualified, and these are my first court proceedings. Will this be held against me?
  - The lawyer cross-examining you may make something of your lack of experience. Don't let this throw you. If you are confident that you have made the right decisions based on an accurate understanding of the facts, then your lack of experience is irrelevant.
- Can the advocate ask me personal questions?
  - This is a tricky one. The advocate is entitled to ask questions which expose any bias you may have and anything that might suggest that your judgement is flawed. On the other hand, he or she is not entitled to bully you. The judge has a duty to ensure that cross-examination is not oppressive. Keep an eye on your own lawyer. They will raise objections to questions they consider unfair.
- What if I am asked for a 'yes or no' answer?
  - If you think the answer is more complex, then say so and stick to your guns.
- What if the advocate keeps asking me what seems like the same question in different ways?
  - Keep providing the answer that you have already given. Be polite and consciously curb any anger you might feel as a result of the repeated question.
- What if I'm asked a stupid question?
  - It's not for you to make that judgement call. Answer the question you are asked and let the judge decide its relevance and/or value.
- Can I be asked about other people's evidence?
  - You are very likely to be asked to explain why your version of events differs from the other side's version. The advocate may well ask you if you are accusing them of lying. If you are, just say so, or if you think they have got confused, or have misremembered, then say that. Don't be rattled.
- What if I realize that I know one of the magistrates?
  - Tell your lawyer and he or she will deal with the issue.

Evidence FAQ

Can anyone help me with my evidence?

The simple answer is 'No'. Once in the witness box, you are on your own. Preparation of your evidence gives some assistance, as long as it is still your own evidence, and it is truthful. There is nothing to prevent you discussing what you will say (so long as no one coaches you).

Can I refuse to answer questions?

No, unless the answer would incriminate you—that is, leave you personally vulnerable to criminal charges. Since s. 98 of the Children Act, you are unlikely to see a witness being allowed to refuse to answer a question on this ground, for the rule of self-incrimination no longer applies in a case involving children.

Can I refer to notes?

You may refresh your memory from notes, if you made these notes when the events were fresh in your mind. Before being allowed to refresh your memory, you will be asked a few questions about when you made the note.

The cross-examining lawyer is entitled to look at the note and if it is, as is normal, in a file, the whole file becomes open to inspection. Suddenly you may get a totally unexpected question: ('But it says here that . . . ').

There are two safe options. One is to rely on memory only. This is advisable only if your memory is clear, for it will be fully tested under cross-examination. The other (recommended) option is to use the whole file. You should, as a matter of course, have prepared every entry in the knowledge that it may be the subject matter of skilled cross-examination. Every opinion must then be justifiable, every fact accurately recorded, with the name of the person making the note (and the time and place) also recorded. Your legal department should already, as a matter of course, have informed any other parties of material within the files which is helpful to them.

Can I refer to other people's notes?

If something is recorded on the file which is of particular importance but of which you cannot give first-hand evidence, then calling the witness, using a summons if necessary, should be considered.

Otherwise, as we saw when discussing hearsay, file notes and other records compiled by others are admissible, and will help you, in your own evidence, to give the court a full picture. You must make it clear, in oral testimony or in your statement, what part of any evidence is not derived from your own observations. You must explain the source, and the date, and circumstances in which any file record was created, or other information supplied. The more careful the record keeping, the more likely the hearsay content is to be useful as evidence.

Can I withhold information from my file?

Even if you do not choose to bring your file to court, as you will see in chapter 5, a person called a children's guardian can inspect your file, take copies, and produce the contents in court, whether you like it or not. There is, as we discussed in chapter 4, no concept of privilege for what social workers put in their files, and if potentially relevant, a court will not allow it to be withheld.

What if my opinion is different from that of my employer?

As an employee of your agency, you must abide by directions given to you by your managers. If you are told to instruct your lawyers to commence care proceedings, you do so. Of course, as a professional, you make it plain that in your view this is not the best course. If you testify in the case, you answer all questions truthfully, giving your opinion professionally and honestly, regardless of what your colleagues and managers say: the alternative is perjury.

Am I allowed into court when I am not giving evidence?

If a local authority social services department is party to the case, it is represented through the social worker in charge of the case, who must be allowed to remain in court even if also called as a witness. But this is subject to the court's overall discretion to allow witnesses and non-parties to be present and also to exclude people, even the social worker who personifies the agency.

If you are a witness in a criminal trial, you will certainly have to remain outside court until you have given your evidence.

Mental capacity and mental health

It is not always easy to know when the provisions of the Mental Capacity Act 2005, apply including the DoLS or when the Mental Health Act 1983 is more applicable. The Mental Health Act 1983 Code of Practice provides a useful flowchart to help with decision making (Department of Health, *The Mental Health Act 1983 Code of Practice* (TSO, 2015), www.gov. uk/government/publications/code-of-practice-mental-health-act-1983). Neither the flowchart nor the accompanying guidance should be used alone without careful consideration of the merits of each case by social workers and other professionals. The flowchart (see **Figure B**) and guidance is replicated here for ease of reference.

Guidance notes

The first question in the flowchart is to ask whether the individual in question is suffering from a mental disorder for which they require assessment or treatment in a hospital. If the answer is 'no', then detention under the Act is not an available option.

If the answer is 'yes', then the decision maker should consider a second question. The second question is, 'Does the individual in question lack the mental capacity to consent to being accommodated in the hospital for the purpose of being given the proposed care or treatment?' If the answer is 'no', then the Mental Capacity Act and the DoLS are not an available option.

However, if the answer is 'yes', (in other words the individual in question is suffering from a mental disorder for which they require assessment and treatment in hospital *and* they lack the capacity to consent to being accommodated in the hospital for the proposed care or treatment), then the next question to be asked is, 'Could the care plan result, or be likely to result, in a deprivation of liberty?'

If the answer is 'no', then the individual could be admitted to the hospital on an informal basis (i.e. not detained under the Act) or treated under the provisions of the Mental Capacity Act (without the need to use the DoLS).

If the answer is 'yes' (there is, or is likely to be, a deprivation of liberty), then the next question is whether the care and/or treatment plan could be amended to reduce any restraints or restrictions in place—thereby preventing a deprivation of liberty from arising. If the answer is 'yes', the care and treatment plan should be amended so that there is no deprivation of liberty.

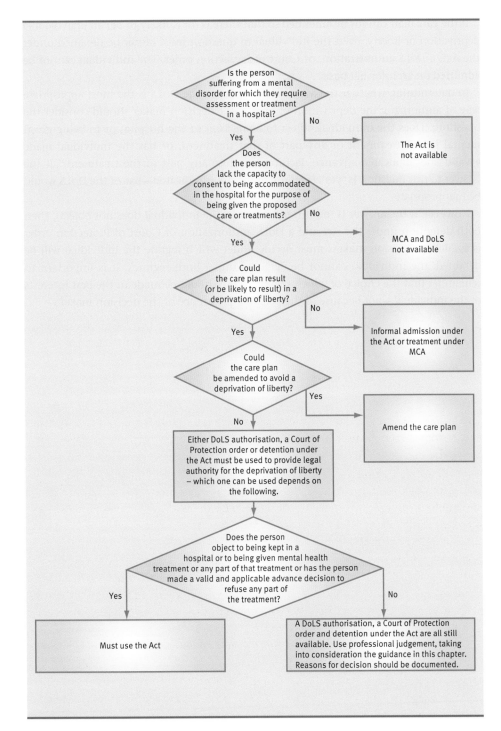

FIGURE B   Deciding whether the Mental Capacity Act or the Mental Health Act will be available to use

Source: Department of Health (2015), The Mental Health Act 1983 Code of Practice (London: TSO).

If the care plan cannot be amended so that there is (or is likely to be) an unavoidable deprivation of liberty, then the individual in question must either be detained under the Act, a DoLS authorization, or Court of Protection order. The individual cannot be admitted on an informal basis.

In determining whether the Mental Health Act or the DoLS is the most appropriate way of authorizing the deprivation of liberty, the decision maker should consider the question, 'Does the individual object to being kept in the hospital or to being given mental health treatment or any part of that treatment, or has the individual made a valid and applicable advance decision to refuse any part of the treatment?' If the answer to this question is 'yes', then use of the Act is indicated—use of the DoLS would be inappropriate.

However, if the answer is 'no' (in other words, the individual does not object), then both detention under the Act and a DoLS authorization or Court of Protection order is available. Decision makers must decide under which regime the individual will be detained; the individual cannot be detained under both regimes. It is important to remember that the choice of which regime to use should be made in the best interests of the individual—not because of the personal preference of the decision maker.